MEDIEVAL WESTMINSTER

Westminster from the north bank of the Thames. View westwards from the riverside near the Strand. Drawing, c.1730.

Medieval Westminster
1200–1540

Gervase Rosser

CLARENDON PRESS · OXFORD
1989

Oxford University Press, Walton Street, Oxford OX2 6DP
Oxford New York Toronto
Delhi Bombay Calcutta Madras Karachi
Petaling Jaya Singapore Hong Kong Tokyo
Nairobi Dar es Salaam Cape Town
Melbourne Auckland
and associated companies in
Berlin Ibadan

Oxford is a trade mark of Oxford University Press

Published in the United States
by Oxford University Press, New York

British Library Cataloguing in Publication Data
Rosser, Gervase
Medieval Westminster: 1200–1540.
1. London. Westminster: (London Borough).
Westminster. History
I. Title.
942.1'32
ISBN 0–19–820156–7

Library of Congress Cataloging in Publication Data
Rosser, Gervase.
Medieval Westminster 1200–1540/Gervase Rosser.
p.   cm.
Bibliography: p.   Includes index.
1. Westminster (London, England)—History. 2. Cities and towns,
Medieval—England—London—History. 3. London (England)—History—
To 1500. 4. England—Civilization—Medieval period. 1066–1485.
I. Title.
DA685.W5R67 1989   942.1'32—dc20   89–9399   CIP
ISBN 0–19–820156–7

Typeset by Cotswold Typesetting Ltd, Gloucester
Printed and bound in
Great Britain by Biddles Ltd,
Guildford and King's Lynn

For My Mother
and in Memory of My Father

ACKNOWLEDGEMENTS

It is a pleasure to thank those whose encouragement and advice have helped the writing of this book. Caroline Barron, who first suggested its subject, has been both a generous thesis supervisor and a loyal friend. Barbara Harvey has given repeatedly of her unrivalled knowledge of the Westminster muniments and of the social world of a medieval Benedictine monastery. Derek Keene provided an inspiring example, and many specific insights. For much creative discussion I am especially grateful to Jane Garnett, Bill Kellaway, and Susan Reynolds; also to my colleagues in the Department of Medieval History at Birmingham University, in particular Chris Dyer. John Clark of the Museum of London and Robert Cowie of the Inner London Archaeological Unit kindly answered archaeological questions.

The muniments of Westminster Abbey are housed in a gallery of the south transept. I am grateful to the late Nicholas MacMichael, formerly Keeper of the Muniments, and to the Dean and Chapter of the Abbey, for the privilege of working in those evocative surroundings over a long period. In addition, the late Howard Nixon, formerly Librarian, and Mrs Enid Nixon, now Acting Librarian, were constantly welcoming. I have also appreciated the help of librarians and archivists in the Bodleian Library, Oxford, the British Library, the Corporation of London Library, Eton College, the Guildhall Library, the Institute of Historical Research, London, the Public Record Office, The Queen's College, Oxford, Trinity College, Cambridge, and the Westminister Public Libraries.

Research was helped by the Rector and Fellows of Lincoln College, Oxford, who elected me to a Junior Research Fellowship, held in 1983–4; and by Birmingham University, which granted a term's study leave in 1987. Finally I thank Robert Faber, my editor at Oxford University Press.

CONTENTS

LIST OF ILLUSTRATIONS

LIST OF FIGURES

LIST OF TABLES

ABBREVIATIONS

Assumption guild accts	Accounts of the guild of the Virgin's Assumption, Westminster (Westminster Abbey Muniment Room)
BL	British Library
Cal Ch R	*Calendar of Charter Rolls* (HMSO, 1903–)
Cal Cl R	*Calendar of Close Rolls* (HMSO, 1892–)
Cal F R	*Calendar of Fine Rolls* (HMSO, 1911–)
Cal Inq p m	*Calendar of Inquisitions post mortem* (HMSO, 1904–)
Cal Letter-Bk	*Calendar of Letter-Books Preserved Among the Archives of the Corporation of the City of London, 1275–1498*, ed. R. R. Sharpe, 11 vols. (London, 1899–1912)
Cal Lib R	*Calendar of Liberate Rolls* (HMSO, 1916–)
Cal Pap Reg	*Calendar of Entries in the Papal Registers relating to Great Britain and Ireland. Papal Letters* (HMSO, 1893–)
Cal Pat R	*Calendar of Patent Rolls* (HMSO, 1901–)
Cal Plea & Mem R	*Calendar of Plea and Memoranda Rolls preserved among the archives of the Corporation of the City of London*, 6 vols., ed. A. H. Thomas (i–iv) and P. E. Jones (v–vi) (Cambridge, 1926–61)
CLRO	Corporation of London Record Office
Customary	*Customary of the Benedictine Monasteries of Saint Augustine, Canterbury, and Saint Peter, Westminister*, ed. E. Maunde Thompson, 2 vols., Henry Bradshaw Society, xxiii, xxviii (1902, 1904)
CWA	Churchwardens' accounts of St Margaret's, Westminster (Westminster Public Libraries, Archives Department)
Econ Hist Rev	*Economic History Review*
ECR	Eton College Records
Harvey, *Estates*	B. F. Harvey, *Westminster Abbey and its Estates in the Middle Ages* (Oxford, 1977)

King's Works	*The History of the King's Works*, ed. H. M. Colvin, 6 vols. (HMSO, London, 1963–82)
LN	Liber Niger Quaternus (a cartulary, now WAM Bk. no. 1)
LP	*Calendar of Letters and Papers, Foreign and Domestic, Henry VIII*, ed. J. S. Brewer, J. Gairdner, and R. H. Brodie (HMSO, 1864–1932)
Matt Par Chron Maj	*Matthaei Parisiensis Chronica Majora*, ed. H. R. Luard, 7 vols., Rolls Series (1872–83)
PCW	Peculiar Court of Westminster, Will Registers (named volumes in Westminster Public Libraries, Archives Department)
Pearce, *Monks*	E. H. Pearce, *The Monks of Westminster* (Cambridge, 1916)
PRO	Public Record Office
Reg Bk	WAM Register Book
Rot Parl	*Rotuli Parliamentorum; ut et petitiones et placita in parliamento, 1278–1504*, 6 vols. (Record Commission, 1832)
Rounceval guild accts	Accounts of the guild of St Mary Rounceval, Westminster (Westminster Abbey Muniment Room)
TLMAS	*Transactions of the London and Middlesex Archaeological Society*
WAM	Westminster Abbey Muniment(s)
WD	Westminster Domesday (a cartulary, now WAM Bk. no. 11)

... Finally the journey leads to the city of Tamara. You penetrate it along streets thick with signboards jutting from the walls. The eye does not see things but images of things that mean other things: pincers point out the tooth-drawer's house; a tankard, the tavern; halberds, the barracks; scales, the grocer's . . . From the doors of the temples the gods' statues are seen, each portrayed with his attributes—the cornucopia, the hourglass, the medusa—so that the worshipper can recognise them and address his prayers correctly . . . Your gaze scans the streets as if they were written pages: the city says everything you must think, makes you repeat her discourse, and while you believe you are visiting Tamara you are only recording the names with which she defines herself and all her parts.

Italo Calvino, *Invisible Cities*, tr. W. Weaver (1979), 15.

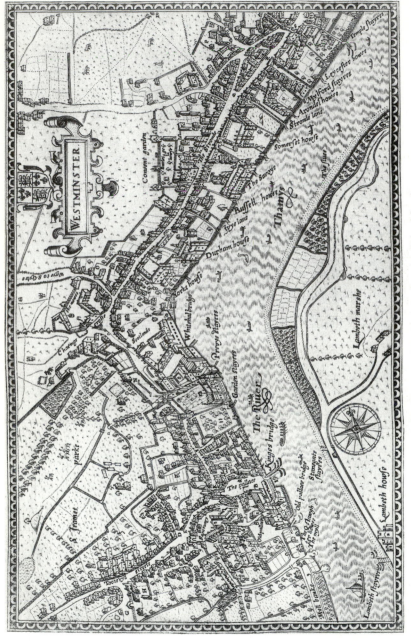

ILLUS. 1. Westminster. Bird's eye view by John Norden, 1593.

Introduction

Themes

The subject of this book is the small town which grew up, largely between the thirteenth and the sixteenth centuries, around the royal abbey and palace of Westminster. Two of the largest buildings in medieval England, Westminster Hall and the great church of Westminster Abbey, embodied the twin focus of the town, their sheer size expressing something of their wider importance. In this book, however, these national institutions play a role which, although essential, is secondary to the object of main concern: the secular society of resident townspeople.

The central argument of the book is an attempt to define that society. In order to do this, it is necessary to come to terms with a number of problems. The first of these is the frequent failure of legal structures accurately to embody the true character of particular societies in the past. Overshadowed by the legal preoccupations of those who, in the late nineteenth century, first studied the medieval history of English towns, urban historians have continued to concentrate their attention upon those places classified in the documents as chartered boroughs or cities. Yet Westminster—notwithstanding its untypicality in certain other respects—was characteristic of a large and neglected class of towns whose legal status and institutions were identical with those of agrarian villages, but whose economic and social life was thoroughly urban.[1] That is the first problem. The second is the continuous variation in the size of the local population. Demographic fluctuations and geographical mobility—both phenomena increasingly well documented in late medieval England, although research into these matters has only just begun—are challenges to

---

[1] Exceptions to this neglect are the recent studies by Rodney Hilton of the category of, for the most part, very small market towns. The society and economy of such a place as Westminster, however, were more complex than those of simple market towns. See R. H. Hilton, 'The Small Town and Urbanisation—Evesham in the Middle Ages', repr. in id., *Class Conflict and the Crisis of Feudalism* (London, 1985), 187–93; and further below, chs. 5, 7.

the historian, to whom a single town may begin to appear insufficiently stable and coherent to justify individual study. This is indeed a good argument for future work along regional, rather than more narrowly local, lines. But to abandon the locality altogether as a focus of study would be to avoid a crucial question which there is every reason for historians to face squarely, since contemporaries were themselves compelled to do so. How, given dramatic fluctuations in population size, could a tolerable degree of continuity be maintained? Westminster's population before the mid-sixteenth century varied widely, rising to a peak of over three thousand; nor was the pattern one of consistent growth, but rather of unpredictable vagaries.[2] The question is sharpened by a third problem which besets the urban historian: the bewildering diversity in the composition of the town society. To the severe contrast between rich and poor was added a complex intervening hierarchy of social distinctions, determined by occupation, nationality, and sex. A cosmopolitan centre such as Westminster attracted a significant population of immigrant foreigners, in addition to English migrants; and like other towns, it drew to itself also a marginal class of beggars, vagrants, and criminals.[3] This sounds like a recipe for chaos; yet the society of Westminster did, nevertheless, cohere sufficiently to survive as a town.

How was that sufficient coherence achieved? That anarchy or social struggles were largely contained is in part attributable to the influence of a relatively small élite of wealthy individuals, who exploited the respect their material substance commanded; in public life and through the local court, which they directed, they imposed upon others standards of social behaviour which secured and reinforced their own position. In the absence, however, of more directly effective means of domination, such as a police or military force or even, in the case of Westminster, a system of craft regulation, the available mechanisms of control would appear to have been inadequate, alone, to contain the conflicts within the highly complex urban population. Of course, those conflicts were *not* always contained; Westminster like other towns experienced violent manifestations of tension. But to the critical extent that these pressures were kept within tolerable bounds, it is argued in this book that the principal explanation is to be found in strategies

---

[2] See ch. 6, sect. 1.
[3] See ch. 6.

of collective behaviour adopted by the population. The urban community which was given tangible form at moments of collective action—whether over a practical public issue such as water supply, or in the less pragmatically useful, yet equally expressive, rebuilding of the parish church, or again in public processions on festival days—was fragile and impermanent; for the rest of the time other loyalties, to neighbours, kin, or self, prevailed over allegiance to the wider body of the town. But the periodic re-creation of the urban community, through a variety of practical and ritual forms of association, was the best, and arguably the only, guarantee of the town's continuance.

   The first two chapters of the book summarize the development of Westminster as the administrative capital of a kingdom, and the implications this had for local society. Chapters 3 to 6 describe that society, giving emphasis to changes which occurred in its composition and in its economic life during the long period between 1200 and 1540. This section concludes at the end of Chapter 6 with a review of the complexity and inequality of the urban population. Chapters 7 to 10 then consider four different contexts in which associative responses to the particular needs of town society helped to prevent the escalation of conflict beyond bearable limits: the manorial administration; the parish; fraternities; and finally charitable organizations.

Sources

The available historical sources are rich, by the standards of small medieval towns; but it is important to be aware of their limitations as well as of their strengths. Archaeological evidence is tantalizingly exiguous. The rich material retrieved, in difficult circumstances, from the Treasury site in Whitehall shows what a wealth of potential information once existed underground. But the excavation, during the past century, of subterranean basements and tunnels has largely destroyed the archaeological record of Westminster. In most cases not even notes were kept, as the layers were cut away.[4]

   Documentary materials, on the other hand, have survived in relatively lavish quantities. The most important of these are

---

[4] The archaeological evidence for Westminster's early history is reviewed in ch. 1.

preserved where they have always been stored, in the Muniment Room of Westminster Abbey; for, as principal landlords of the town, the monks created voluminous records concerning the management of their urban property. The most useful of these records fall into two major categories: deeds and accounts. Some two thousand deeds and leases relating to the abbey's estate in Westminster are extant from between the late twelfth and the mid-sixteenth centuries. These survive either as original documents or as more or less contemporary copies in the monastic cartularies (the early fourteenth-century Westminster Domesday and the later Liber Niger Quaternus) and (from the late fifteenth century onwards) in leasebooks. The estate was divided among the various monastic obedientiaries, as part of their respective endowments.[5] Six of the obedientiaries together held the greater part of the Westminster property, which itself amounted to about two-thirds of the total urban area. These were the sacrist, almoner, cellarer, and domestic treasurer, and the wardens of the Lady chapel and of the 'new work'. The annual accounts of the obedientiaries complement the evidence of the deeds. Where the latter give laconic yet valuable descriptions of the properties in question, the obedientiary accounts contain yearly rentals listing all property held by the abbey, with the names of occupants and the level of their rent. In addition, the account rolls record expenditure by the monks on the renovation or development of their urban estate. The 'upkeep of houses' section of the accounts is especially informative in the late fourteenth century, when the monks were pursuing a general policy of new investment in the town. A scatter of accounts survives from as early as *c*.1300; but the rate of preservation in all series improves markedly from the third quarter of the fourteenth century. From this point until the Dissolution the proportion of extant annual accounts in all relevant cases is as good as two-thirds. The value of the obedientiary rolls is enormous. It should be noted, however, that parts of Westminster—amounting to perhaps a third

[5] From the late eleventh century onwards there evolved in the abbey of Westminster an 'obedientiary system' of conventual administration, whereby separate accounting departments were created for the various monastic officers entrusted with duties in the running of the abbey. To each department a portion of the monastery's resources was allocated, sufficient (in theory) to finance the requisite tasks. As the total endowment of the house was built up, the separate holdings of each obedientiary might eventually comprise a small miscellany of land, rents, ecclesiastical pensions, and other dues.

of the district in total—not under monastic control are largely unrecorded, and are blank areas in any reconstruction of the town. The topographical information contained in this kind of material can be very valuable for urban history, as is most clearly demonstrated by Derek Keene's study of medieval Winchester.[6] While the evidence does not quite suffice for a plot-by-plot reconstruction of the entire area of Westminster, such as Dr Keene was able to present for the much larger town of Winchester, the analysis of property-holding in Chapter 3 owes much to the example of the Winchester survey. In Chapter 3 the topographical evidence is used to provide a rough index of demographic change over the period, and also to establish the physical context for the succeeding discussion of other aspects of the town.

The sources which come into play in the ensuing chapters are very miscellaneous, and no purpose would be served by listing them all here.[7] But it should be recognized that the scattered nature of the evidence is itself symptomatic of Westminster's anomalous legal status. Lacking a centralized urban government, the town generated a diversity of written records, many of which remain in different corners of the abbey archive. Local government in Westminster is partially recorded in a series of court rolls of the manorial court, which runs from 1364 to 1514; records of the abbot's bailiff from the years 1288 to 1336 supplement the information in the court rolls. But, apart from a clutch of accounts of the great fair of Westminster around 1300, economic developments must be pieced together from various sources, including some among the central government records in the Public Record Office. These have been supplemented by printed and some manuscript records of the medieval London government. Parochial records survive only from 1460 onwards; nevertheless Westminster is in fact unusually fortunate to possess churchwardens' accounts from so early a date. Without these, there would exist a fine surviving parish church of *c*.1500, but virtually no evidence as to who paid for its construction. The wills of Westminster inhabitants, which also bear upon this and related subjects, and of which some

[6] D. J. Keene, *Survey of Medieval Winchester*, 2 vols., Winchester Studies, ii (Oxford, 1985). The major earlier work of this kind was done by Salter and Urry. See H. E. Salter, *Survey of Oxford*, 2 vols., Oxford Historical Society, new ser., xiv, xx (1960–9); W. Urry, *Canterbury Under the Angevin Kings* (London, 1967).

[7] A list of the principal manuscript sources is given in the Bibliog.

two hundred survive from the period 1504 to 1540 (when such wills were registered in a newly created peculiar court of the liberty of Westminster), are almost entirely lacking from before this time. The records of two guilds from the late fifteenth and early sixteenth centuries complement the other materials in the evidence they contain concerning the organization of local society. From these indications, the weighting of some of the most important non-topographical evidence towards the end of the period under study is apparent.

Well over a century has passed since the appearance of the last, and indeed the only existing, study of the historical development of Westminster. Mackenzie Walcott, the author of an engaging work of antiquarianism, first published in 1849, stands alone.[8] Walcott described his then popular subject, close as it was to the heart of Victorian parliamentary piety, as 'the classic ground of England'.[9] In the century which has succeeded Walcott's, a slightly less idealized view of English representative institutions has prevailed; yet studies of the growth of national government have been legion, and it is perhaps surprising that since the mid-nineteenth century, with the exception of a stimulating short essay by Tout, the closely related development of the district immediately adjacent to Westminster Palace, as a small town intensely characterized by its dependence upon that governmental expansion, has been almost entirely ignored.[10] Canon Westlake was the first to draw significantly upon the resources of the Westminster Abbey Muniment Room to illustrate the history of the convent itself; he also used the churchwardens' accounts in a book on St Margaret's parish

[8] M. E. C. Walcott, *Westminister; Memorials of the City, Saint Peter's College, the Parish Churches, Palaces, Streets, and Worthies* (Westminster, 1849); a second edition, with the title *The Memorials of Westminster*, was published in 1851. The fine book by J. T. Smith, *The Antiquities of Westminster, &c.*, 2 vols. (London, 1807; 2nd edn., 1837), contains valuable materials which, however, relate chiefly to Westminster Palace and to St Stephen's Chapel therein.

[9] Walcott, *Westminster*, p. v.

[10] T. F. Tout, 'The Beginnings of a Modern Capital: London and Westminster in the Fourteenth Century', *Proceedings of the British Academy*, x (1921–3), 487–511. Further, very brief, studies are H. F. Westlake, *Westminster; A Historical Sketch* (London, 1919); and L. E. Tanner, 'Westminster Topography', *TLMAS* 2nd ser., x (1948–51), 234–43; xi (1952–4), 10–15. The work of Laurence Tanner (formerly Keeper of the Muniments of Westminster Abbey), of which an account is given in his delightful *Recollections of a Westminster Antiquary* (London, 1969), will always be an inspiration to students of this subject, even though he did not treat it at length in his published writings.

church.[11] Barbara Harvey has recently made very much more intensive use of the abbey muniments in an analysis of the management by the monks of their estates in general.[12] Yet the town of Westminster has been neglected. The time has come for a fresh investigation, in the light both of sources hitherto ignored and, even more necessary, of a new set of questions.

[11] Westlake, *Westminster Abbey. The Church, Convent, Cathedral and College of St. Peter, Westminster*, 2 vols. (London, 1923); id., *St. Margaret's Westminster. The Church of the House of Commons* (London, 1914).
[12] Harvey, *Estates*.

ILLUS. 2. Westminster. Panorama, from the abbey and palace (left) to Charing Cross (right). Detail of the 'long view' of Westminster and London by Anthony van den Wyngaerde, c.1550.

I

The Making of a Royal Capital, to 1300

I. BEFORE 1200

The year 1200 is taken as an appropriate starting-point for this study of medieval Westminster, not only on account of the first appearance of documentary evidence from around this date, but also because the establishment of the chief base of royal government at Westminster under Henry II and his successors marked a watershed in the history of the locality. Nevertheless the date is to a degree arbitrary. The context for developments after the late twelfth century is provided by archaeological evidence of a history of continuous settlement in the area since at least *c*.800. This, like all later evidence, must be perceived in relation to the physical setting. The geology of Westminster is simple (Fig. 1). The clay of the Thames estuary covers most of the area, which was regularly flooded even so recently as the seventeenth century.[1] A wide ditch, carrying branches of the Tyburn stream, enclosed the tiny island of gravel on which the abbey and the palace were built. The marshiness of the ground immediately surrounding this island was always a constraint upon building in Westminster before the construction of Victoria Embankment.

The Saxon finds, made in the early 1960s, from the Treasury site in Whitehall have been variously interpreted[2] (Fig. 2). It is at least

[1] *Matt Par Chron Maj*, iii. 339; iv. 230; I. M. Cooper, 'Westminster Hall', *Journal of the British Archaeological Association*, 3rd ser., i (1937), 192–3; P. S. Mills, *et al.*, 'Excavations at Broad Sanctuary, Westminster', *TLMAS* 2nd ser., xxxiii (1982), 350.

[2] H. M. Green, 'Evidence of Roman, Saxon and Medieval Westminster Revealed During the Current Rebuilding of the Treasury and Downing Street', *Illustrated London News*, ccxlii (1963), 1004–7; Green, R. Huggins, *et al.*, 'Excavations of the Treasury Site, Whitehall, 1961–1963', *TLMAS*, forthcoming (1989). Some of the conclusions published in these reports are controversial. The information shown in Fig. 2 is derived from R. Cowie, 'Saxon period sites in the Strand survey area', Sites and Monuments Record Document (Department of Greater London Archaeology, Museum of London, May 1988).

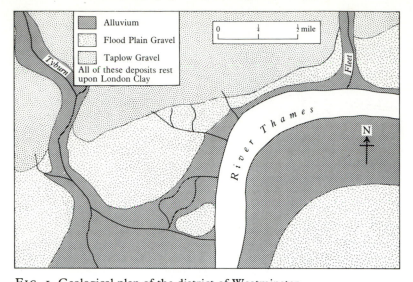

FIG. I. Geological plan of the district of Westminster

Source: Geological Survey London Sheet NV S.W. (1936) (slightly simplified).

clear, however, that this site, then located on an inlet of the Thames, was occupied from the ninth century onwards. More tentatively, the recovered implements of cloth making and pieces of imported pottery may be related to trading activity in the mid-Saxon period. This possibility is greatly strengthened by the evidence supporting the hypothesis, first advanced in 1984, that *Lundenwic*, the trading centre of mid-Saxon London, was located not within the perimeter of the Roman and later medieval city, but in a western suburb, extending along the Thames foreshore beside the Strand.[3] Since this suggestion was first made, on the basis of the distribution of previous random finds, subsequent excavations, notably at Jubilee Hall in Covent Garden and as far west as the National Gallery in Trafalgar Square, have substantiated the picture of a large extramural area, straddling the Strand, intensively settled between

[3] A. Vince, 'The Aldwych: Mid-Saxon London Discovered?', *Current Archaeology*, xciii (Aug. 1984), 310–12; M. Biddle, 'London on the Strand', *Popular Archaeology*, vi (July 1984), 23–7; B. Hobley, *Roman and Saxon London: A Reappraisal*, 1st Annual Museum of London Archaeology Lecture (Museum of London, 1986).

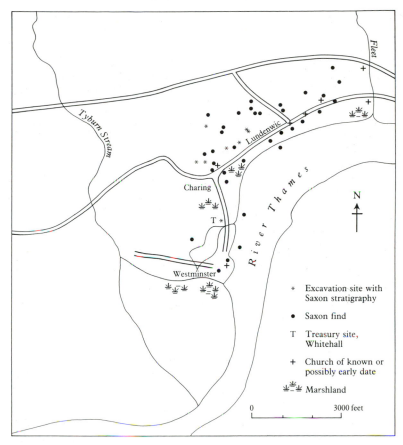

FIG. 2. Westminster and *Lundenwic* in the Saxon period

the seventh and ninth centuries, and busily engaged during that
period in commerce with northern France, the Low Countries, and
the Rhineland.[4] The mid-Saxon finds from Whitehall, which
appeared, to say the least, remarkable when they were partially
published in 1963, now fit comfortably into the newly identified
setting of a major pre-Viking market and international port. The
arrival of the Vikings in the late ninth century led to the virtual
abandonment of *Lundenwic*, as King Alfred (in all probability)

[4] R. Cowie, '*Lundenwic*. "Unravelling the Strand"', *Archaeology Today* (June
1987), 30–4.

consolidated the defences of the old city of London, and laid out new streets there to reaccommodate the population within the walls.[5]

It seems a priori likely that the district of Westminster itself suffered disruption during the first Viking incursions. Nevertheless the Treasury site yielded pottery from all periods between the ninth and twelfth centuries; and the abbey quarter, also, shows signs of continuous occupation since the tenth century at the latest.[6] Although the first fully-fledged monastery, of the kind recognized as authentic by the Benedictine reformers of the tenth century, was not established at Westminster until St Dunstan's foundation of c.960, it is possible, and perhaps likely, that this was preceded by a minster church. The late eleventh-century historian of the abbey, a monk of the house named Sulcard, claimed for it a first foundation in the time of King Aethelbert of Kent and, more credibly, a refoundation by King Offa, who is probably to be identified not as Offa the Great but as the Offa who was king of the East Saxons in the early eighth century.[7] Middlesex would at this date have belonged to Offa's kingdom, and with it the royal palace at Aldermanbury within the walled area of London. The pattern of a Saxon king who founded a minster church on his estate, at a little distance from his palace or manorial residence, was a common one; such minster creations were often located on sites apparently chosen for their potential as regional commercial centres.[8] In view of what is now known of the commercial life of the Strand and Whitehall area in the eighth and ninth centuries, the foundation of a minster here at some time after 700 would not be extraordinary. Often, too, minster sites were selected for their historical associations, which might lend legitimacy to the founders.[9] However, although the number of Roman finds from Westminster is now sufficiently substantial to indicate an important Roman site in the vicinity, no more than this

[5] T. Tatton-Brown, 'The Topography of Anglo-Saxon London', *Antiquity*, lx (1986), 24–6.

[6] Excavation by Peter Mills in the undercroft of Westminster Abbey: 'Medieval Britain and Ireland in 1986', *Medieval Archaeology*, xxxi (1987), 133–4.

[7] Harvey, *Estates*, 20–1.

[8] J. Blair, 'Minster Churches in the Landscape', in D. Hooke (ed.), *Anglo-Saxon Settlements* (Oxford, 1988), 35–58. Cf. also E. Ewig, 'Résidence et capitale pendant le haut Moyen Age', *Revue Historique*, ccxxx (1963), 25–72.

[9] Blair, 'Minster Churches'.

can at present be vouchsafed.[10] The eleventh-century and later accounts of a Roman temple of Apollo which allegedly stood here are, in the present state of knowledge, best prized simply as a rival story to that which sets St Paul's in London on the site of a sanctuary of Diana.[11]

When Dunstan, at the height of the monastic reform in c.960, founded the abbey of St Peter at Westminster, the land was made available by King Edgar.[12] His programme of ecclesiastical reform aside, the timing and location of Dunstan's monastic foundations appear to be closely related to the political drive of the Wessex monarchy. During the first twenty or thirty years of the reform, these foundations had been concentrated in the West Country, and it was only from the 960s that they spread into the territories by this date subsumed within Mercia. Seen in this light, the new religious establishment at Westminster may have represented the assertion of King Edgar's hegemony over the London region.[13] Edgar himself had evidently appropriated the land—either from the secular lord or from a minster community if such existed—before granting it to Dunstan. Westminster's dual importance as a centre both of royal power and of a religious cult therefore dates from its earliest securely recorded history. These two elements would give the later medieval town its peculiar character.

King Edgar's grant to the monks of their estate at Westminster was confirmed (although not so often as Osbert of Clare, the abbey's

[10] W. H. Black, 'Observations on the Recently Discovered Roman Sepulchre at Westminster Abbey', *TLMAS* iv (1871), 60–9; Royal Commission on Historical Monuments, *London*, ii (London, 1925), 173–4, 208, 215 ff.; G. Black, *et al.*, 'Excavations in the Sub-vault of the Misericorde of Westminster Abbey, February to May, 1975', *TLMAS* 2nd ser., xxvii (1976), 142; Green, Huggins, *et al.*, 'Excavations of the Treasury Site', section: 'Roman'.

[11] A paper by John Clark of the Museum of London, on the Diana legend, read to the Medieval London Seminar at the Institute of Historical Research, London, May 1981. For the Westminster story see J. A. Robinson (ed.), *The History of Westminster Abbey by John Flete* (Cambridge, 1909), 2–11, 34–5.

[12] P. H. Sawyer, *Anglo-Saxon Charters: An Annotated List and Bibliography*, Royal Historical Society (London, 1968), no. 670. There accepted as a Saxon copy of a more or less genuine original. The impossible date it bears, 951, is usually corrected to 959, within Edgar's reign, on the ground that Dunstan was bishop of London in 959–60. Cf. Harvey, *Estates*, 23. But Dunstan is in fact referred to in the charter as archbishop, so a date of 960 or later might be preferable. See C. A. Ralegh Radford, *Westminster Abbey Before King Edward the Confessor*, Westminster Abbey Occasional Papers, xv (1965), 5.

[13] N. Banton, 'Monastic Reform and the Unification of Tenth-century England', *Studies in Church History*, xviii (1982), 71–85, esp. p. 77 n.

major twelfth-century forger, would have had it believed) by later
kings, and the land remained a part of the monastery's lordship
throughout the Middle Ages.[14] It included a large area, stretching
from the abbey almost as far as the walls of London (Fig. 3). This
study is concerned, however, not with the whole of the Westminster
estate but with its heart, the vicinity of the abbey and palace,
extending northwards to Charing. The latter district coincided
after the mid-thirteenth century with the parish of St Margaret,
with what was usually called *villa Westmonasterii* in Latin
documents, and equally with the area identified by late medieval
inhabitants, in vernacular records, as 'the town of Westminster'.[15]

When the contributions of Edgar and perhaps of Offa, and of the
mid-Saxon residents of *Lundenwic*, have been duly acknowledged,
the urban development of Westminster in the later medieval period
remains substantially the posthumous achievement of King
Edward the Confessor. The double identity which Westminster
inherited from Dunstan and Edgar received in the following
century the blessing of one both saint and king. Edward, evidently
disenchanted with his London base at Aldermanbury, in the mid-
eleventh century removed to Westminster.[16] His construction here
of a royal palace and his refoundation of the abbey and election to be
buried within it prepared for the growth of this complex into the
political, and in some sense the religious, capital of the realm.[17] The
two qualities are inseparable, for although St Edward has never
enjoyed a large popular cult, it was his appeal to later kings which
led to the choice of Westminster Abbey as the coronation and burial
church of the English monarchy and to the increasingly regular
resort to the neighbouring palace of the agents of royal government.

[14] Osbert's forgeries are discussed by P. Chaplais in 'The Original Charters of
Herbert and Gervase, Abbots of Westminster (1121–57)' in P. M. Barnes and C. F.
Slade (eds.), *A Medieval Miscellany for D. M. Stenton*, Pipe Roll Society, new ser.,
xxxvi (1962), 89–110.

[15] See ch. 7, sect. 2.

[16] A paper by Tony Dyson of the Museum of London on Aldermanbury, read to
the Medieval London Seminar at the Institute of Historical Research, London, May
1981; see J. Schofield, A. Dyson, *et al.*, *Archaeology of the City of London. Recent
Discoveries by the Department of Urban Archaeology, Museum of London* (City of
London Archaeological Trust, 1980), 42–3.

[17] F. Barlow, *Edward the Confessor* (London, 1970), 229 ff.; R. D. H. Gem, 'The
Romanesque Rebuilding of Westminster Abbey', in R. A. Brown (ed.), *Proceedings
of the Battle Conference of Anglo-Norman Studies III, 1980* (Woodbridge, 1981),
33–60.

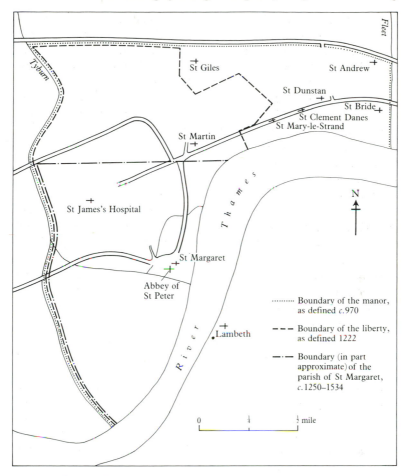

FIG. 3. The manor, liberty, and parish of Westminster

In turn, abbey and palace together were to be the catalyst of urban growth, offering employment to officers, traders, and craftsmen upon whom the royal household and the monastic community themselves depended for their survival.

The Confessor's abbey, now housing eighty monks where Dunstan's foundation had provided only for twelve, and the new palace complex adjacent, with its concomitant officialdom, may well have attracted new residents to the neighbourhood.[18] Yet the relics of the Confessor did not make the fortune of Westminster overnight. The Domesday survey of the entire manor of Westminster in 1086 recorded nineteen villeins and forty-two cottars, both groups apparently holding small plots for rents, in addition to twenty-five houses inhabited by the knights and other men of the abbot.[19] This suggests that extensive parcelling out of the land had not yet taken place. A little more than a century later, however, deeds preserved in the abbey testify to the existence of a busy property market in the core area of Westminster, which was by 1200 designated as 'the vill'. Although earlier material of this nature has certainly been lost, the impression of increased activity from the late twelfth century is no doubt accurate. For it was precisely in the reign of Henry II that the incipient specialization of the departments of the king's household and the settlement of certain among them at Westminster began to necessitate, for a number of royal officers, the purchase of *pieds-à-terre* in the neighbourhood.

2. THE THIRTEENTH CENTURY

When the documentary sources begin to clear the mists from the early settlement in the marshes of Westminster, in the second half of the twelfth century, two features are prominent in the social landscape. One is the preponderance, among the already established landholders of the district, of laymen whose official or semi-official titles link them with the abbey. The other is the arrival, at this very moment, of a new colony of settlers whose affiliations were with the Angevin rulers and their administration. It was from the former group that a number of the latter would acquire their convenient footholds in Westminster. The moving force behind this colonization was the concurrent translation of the centre of gravity of the royal court, away from the old Wessex capital at Winchester and towards Westminster and London. Edward the Confessor had been a prophet of this removal, but it was given

---

[18] For the numbers of the religious, see D. Knowles, *The Monastic Order in England, 940–1216* (2nd edn., Cambridge, 1963), 49 n., 714: app. XVII. For the possibility that the parish church of St Margaret was first built in the late eleventh century—which, if true, might be in part related to a growth of population—see ch. 8, sect. 1.

[19] *Domesday Book*, 2 vols. (Record Commission, London, 1783), i. fo. 128ᵛ.

decisive practical direction by the governmental reforms of Henry II. Although the royal household continued to be peripatetic, Henry II's justice Ranulph Glanvill could describe the court at Westminster, for the first time, as 'the chief court' of the monarchy.[20]

The prominence of officials among the major holders of property in Westminster in the twelfth and thirteenth centuries deserves emphasis. The names of substantial landlords recorded around 1200—such as Edward the reeve, Walkelin, sergeant of the almonry, William the abbot's usher, and Simon of the gaol—show that in the preceding period the monks had partially broken up their Westminster estate in order to provide accommodation for their principal lay servants.[21] The 'other men of the abbot', noted alongside the abbey knights of Domesday Book, doubtless included officers of this kind;[22] the evidence of c.1200 suggests that the endowment of lesser monastic servants had been extended in the intervening period.[23] Whether any of these lay property holders occupied their land in Westminster in fee remains doubtful; the monks were certainly careful to control the fragmentation of so important an estate, and may not, even in the cases of the Domesday knights, have relinquished their baronial authority over the land.[24] Nevertheless the class of abbey servants was well established by the late twelfth century, and was soon to be joined by a complementary body of servants of the crown. In their particular composition, these two officialdoms were distinctive to Westminster. However, other towns before 1300 show a comparably prominent body of ministerial property holders.[25] Their presence underlines the importance, in the early development of towns, of the role of lords and their retainers.

[20] W. L. Warren, *Henry II* (London, 1973), 331–2.
[21] Simon of the gaol: WAM 17323. The remainder: see below.
[22] See above.
[23] Cf. the similar sequence at Peterborough. E. King, *Peterborough Abbey 1086–1310. A Study in the Land Market* (Cambridge, 1973), 58–61.
[24] B. F. Harvey, 'Abbot Gervase de Blois and the Fee-farms of Westminster Abbey', *Bulletin of the Institute of Historical Research*, xl (1967), 127–42. In S. Harvey, 'The Knight and the Knight's Fee in England', *Past and Present*, xlix (1970), 10, it is assumed that the knights of Domesday Book held parts of Westminster, in return for their service, in fee. They may have done so, but the case is unprovable.
[25] e.g. P. R. Coss (ed.), *The Early Records of Medieval Coventry*, Records of Social and Economic History, new ser., ix (1986), pp. xxxviii ff.

At the same time, the expansion of Westminster in the late twelfth and thirteenth centuries occurred during a period of continuing demographic and economic growth, which gave rise to an increase in the number and size of towns. Apart from its administrative and political significance, therefore, Westminster in the thirteenth century should be seen in the context of a quickening of commercial life and concomitant urban vitality. Lords themselves were well aware of the economic potential of these developments, and engaged actively in the promotion of urban centres on their estates. The Westminster monks were no exception.[26]

The topographical and social development of Westminster during the thirteenth century is documented in contemporary deeds. As in many other towns, property deeds are the principal documentary source to survive from before 1300. The information they provide is inevitably fragmentary; moreover precise dating is often impossible, since the deeds themselves are rarely dated. The clearest way to present the evidence of the early Westminster deeds will be by a perambulation of part of the area, in which particular attention will be given to signs of social change in the thirteenth century. The two districts of the palace and of Tothill reflect clearly the transformation of Westminster which was effected by the arrival of the court.

It is possible to plot the residences in Westminster of some of the first royal officers to submit to the pull of the king's 'chief court' (Fig. 4). An early swallow of the migration was a 'king's minister' named Gerin, who shortly before 1158 bought land beside the Thames at Enedehithe in Westminster from Walkelin, a servant of the abbey almonry.[27] The *terra de Anedeheða* (the name meant 'wharf frequented by ducks')[28] lay close to the area of mid-Saxon

---

[26] All of these processes, of course, had their origins well before the twelfth century. For the twelfth and thirteenth centuries in particular, however, see E. Miller, 'England in the Twelfth and Thirteenth Centuries: An Economic Contrast', *Econ Hist Rev*, 2nd ser., xxiv (1971), 1–14; M. Beresford, *New Towns of the Middle Ages* (London, 1967); S. Reynolds, *An Introduction to the History of English Medieval Towns* (Oxford, 1977), 46–65.

[27] WAM 17311. Dated to the abbacy of Gervase (1138–c.1157). Gerin was probably keeper of Westminster Palace; cf. F. Barlow (ed.), *Vita Aedwardi Regis* (London, 1962), 126–7. Walkelin, the almoner's servant, held property at the end of the century in Long Ditch. WD, fo. 509ᵛ: witnessed by Odo the goldsmith (for whom see app. 1).

[28] J. E. B. Gover, A. Mawer, and F. M. Stenton, *The Place-Names of Middlesex*, English Place-Name Society, xviii (1942), 168.

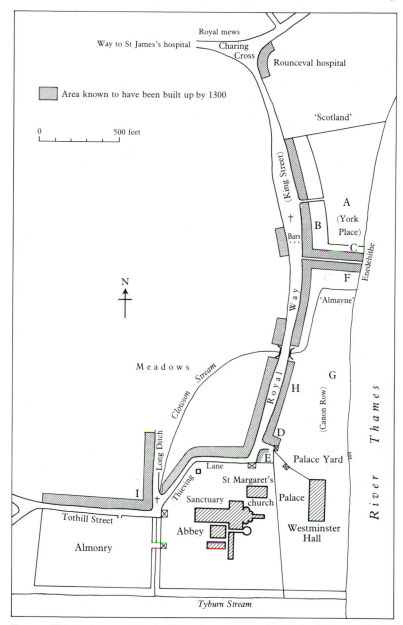

Way to St James's hospital

Royal mews

Charing Cross

Rounceval hospital

Area known to have been built up by 1300

0   500 feet

'Scotland'

(King Street)

N

A
(York Place)

B

Bars

C

F

Enedehithe

'Almayne'

Way

M e a d o w s

Clowson Stream

Royal

G

H

(Canon Row)

R i v e r   T h a m e s

D

E

Long Ditch

Lane

Palace Yard

Thieving

St Margaret's
church

I

Tothill Street

Sanctuary

Palace

Abbey

Westminster
Hall

Almonry

Tyburn Stream

FIG. 4. Westminster. Area built up by 1300, and principal late medieval
   features

occupation identified at the Treasury site in Whitehall.[29] Gerin's grant may have included buildings on the site, associated with the commercial function of the wharf. In the next generation Richard FitzNigel, a great-nephew of Roger of Salisbury and treasurer to Henry II, owned 'houses' in 'the vill of Westminster' which lay to the north of the wharf at Enedehithe[30] (Fig. 4: A). Indeed it was probably in his riverside house at Enedehithe that FitzNigel describes himself, in 1176–7, 'sitting at a turret window overlooking the Thames', when he was drawn into the discussion which he published in the form now known as the *Dialogue of the Exchequer*, 'the earliest treatise upon the working of a government "department" in England'.[31] The arrival of the royal treasurer heralded the advent of the king's permanent treasury, which continued to be kept at Winchester so late as the 1170s but which by 1200 was divided between Westminster and the Tower of London.[32] The exchequer, FitzNigel's charge and the subject of his study, was the first sector of royal government to detach itself from the king's personal entourage and to form a distinct establishment at Westminster.

Later occupants consolidated the semi-official residence at Enedehithe. In 1195–6 Richard FitzNigel's kinsman, William of Ely, succeeded to this accommodation, at about the same time as the latter's own promotion to the treasurership.[33] William of Ely made further purchases here including, in 1201, a messuage 'within his close' which he bought from Roger Enganet, lately the abbot's reeve of the vill of Westminster.[34] William of Ely flourished under King

[29] See above.

[30] WAM 17313; WD, fo. 341ᵛ. See also *Survey of London* (London County Council, 1900–63; Greater London Council, 1966–83; Royal Commission on Historical Monuments, 1985–), xiii. 51–2.

[31] *Dialogus de Scaccario*, ed. C. Johnson, with corrections by F. E. L. Carter and D. E. Greenway (Oxford, 1983), 5; S. B. Chrimes, *An Introduction to the Administrative History of Medieval England* (Oxford, 1952), 51–2.

[32] R. A. Brown, ' "The Treasury" of the Late Twelfth Century', in J. Conway Davies (ed.), *Studies Presented to Sir Hilary Jenkinson* (London, 1957), 35–49. Whether the exchequer at Westminster was actually located, at this date, within FitzNigel's house or within the royal palace is not known.

[33] WAM 17313; WD, fo. 341ᵛ; and see H. G. Richardson, 'William of Ely, the King's Treasurer (?1195–1215)', *Transactions of the Royal Historical Society*, 4th ser., xv (1932), 45–90.

[34] PRO, CP25(1)/282/4/23; *The Great Roll of the Pipe for the Third year of the Reign of King John*, ed. D. M. Stenton, Pipe Roll Society, new ser., xiv (1936), 263. For Enganet, see app. 1. From Marwanna, daughter of William, the treasurer bought her neighbouring messuage at *Anedeheia*, on the understanding that Marwanna's son and daughter-in-law might live there during her pleasure. WD, fo. 342ᵛ.

John, but failed to ride the storm of his patron's later years. He may, therefore, have had less need of his houses, which, between 1218 and 1221, he granted away to Westminster Abbey; the monks undertaking in return to pray for the souls of King Henry II, King Richard, and King John, of Richard FitzNigel and of William of Ely himself.[35] The complex was now purchased by another high-ranking royal official, the ambitious justiciar Hubert de Burgh. Having himself risen to prominence under King John, between 1222 and 1224 Hubert de Burgh paid the monks 140 marks for William of Ely's former property at Westminster.[36] The 'houses and court, with free chapel to celebrate and hear divine service for himself and his household, together with a stable adjoining the same court but not part of it', were evidently a substantial residence, perhaps not altogether unworthy of the epithet, *nobile palatium*, accorded to it by Matthew Paris.[37] For about ten years, until his own dramatic fall in 1232, the justiciar could direct from this Westminster base his policy of strong and centralized royal administration. But after the abrupt termination of his political career, between 1234 and 1240–1 Hubert de Burgh transferred all his holdings in Westminster 'to God', in redemption of an unfulfilled vow to go to the Holy Land.[38] The mortal trustees sold the property to Walter de Gray, archbishop of York, the deed being confirmed by de Burgh in 1240–1. In 1245 Walter de Gray gave the 'palace' to the see of York in perpetuity; and until the fall of Cardinal Wolsey, 'York Place' remained the London residence of the medieval archbishops.[39]

In the local orbit of this influential base of operations, lesser officers and clerks of the crown fixed their Westminster courses. A

[35] WD, fo. 342ᵛ; Richardson, 'William of Ely', 89.
[36] WD, fo. 347ʳ⁻ᵛ: Ralph de Nevill, bishop-elect of Chichester, 1 Nov. 1222–21 Apr. 1224, witnessed the grant. Hubert also, before he became earl of Kent in 1227, made three additional purchases of property in or close to his capital messuage at Westminster. PRO, C52/34/2–6. For Hubert de Burgh's career see F. M. Powicke, *The Thirteenth Century* (Oxford, 1953), 23 ff.
[37] *Matt Par Chron Maj*, iv. 243–4.
[38] WD, fo. 347ᵛ. The earl's right to hold the houses had been confirmed in 1234. *Cal Cl R 1231–4*, p. 443.
[39] *The Register, or Rolls, of Walter Gray, Lord Archbishop of York*, ed. J. Raine, Surtees Society, lvi (1870), 199–201; *Cal Ch R 1226–57*, p. 284. In 1246 Walter de Gray granted to Taylifer de Kinahesil and Matthew de Lawic two houses in Westminster next to *La Charing*, reserving hospitality to the archbishop when required. *Register of Walter Gray*, 257. At the end of the thirteenth century York Place was occupied for a time by the royal family. *King's Works*, i. 505. See also C. L. Kingsford, 'Historical Notes on Mediaeval London Houses: York Place', *London Topographical Record*, xii (1920), 62–5.

row of houses is recorded, from the second quarter of the century, as lying to the west, between the palace of the treasurer, justiciar or archbishop and 'the royal way of Westminster' (i.e. King Street) (Fig. 4: B). A messuage here, 'between the royal street and the wall of the archbishop of York', was in *c.*1257 granted by the monks to a king's clerk called John of Langtoft. The royal concession made in connection with this grant, that John of Langtoft should not be subject to billeting of the king's men without his assent, refers to 'the said land and all houses built or to be built thereon, and the owners of them', suggesting a relatively large plot still in process of development.[40] Protection from royal purveyance of lodgings was an insurance obtained for a number of houses newly built in Westminster in the middle decades of the thirteenth century, and was a reflection of the major pressure, generated by the crown, upon accommodation.[41]

Immediately to the south of York Place, in the angle between the lane of Enedehithe (later Endive Lane) and the river, more houses are documented, by the end of the century, in the occupation of successive keepers of the king's wardrobe (Fig. 4: C). The 'greedy and self-seeking' Walter of Langton, who held this office during the years 1290–5, kept 'his houses with his whole *mansio*' here by 1293; and two years later added to his holding the adjacent tenement to the west, which he acquired from the sacrist of Westminster Abbey.[42] John of Droxford, Langton's successor as keeper of the wardrobe (1295–1307), was in 1297 likewise in possession of houses at Enedehithe. The presumption that Droxford had inherited Langton's houses together with his office is confirmed by an account of building works at York Place in 1298–9, which refers to the raising of a wall between the archbishop's court and the houses of 'Drokensford'.[43] The presence in Westminster of these promi-

---

[40] The immediately previous occupants were Richard Gulafre and his wife, Rose of St Denis. WAM 17337, 17349; PRO, CP25(1)/147/19/363; *Cal Ch R 1226–57*, p. 469. Further messuages here: WD, fos. 535ᵛ–536ʳ, 542ᵛ, 551ʳ⁻ᵛ; WAM 17500.

[41] e.g. *Cal Ch R 1226–57*, p.190; *Cal Pat R 1247–58*, pp. 181, 463, 607 (with WAM 17356); ibid. *1247–58*, p. 632; ibid. *1272–81*, p. 435; ibid. *1292–1301*, pp. 62, 228; ibid. *1307–13*, pp. 147–8. Cf. also the recorded presence in Westminster of Roger *le herbegeour* or purveyor of lodgings. WD, fo. 522ʳ: *temp.* Henry III.

[42] *Cal Pat R 1292–1301*, p. 62; WD, fo. 385ʳ⁻ᵛ; Tout, *Chapters in the Administrative History of Medieval England*, 6 vols. (Manchester, 1920–33), ii. 16; vi. 26.

[43] *Cal Pat R 1292–1301*, p. 228; PRO, C47/3/31; *Survey of London*, xiii. 5–6. For Langton and Droxford see also Tout, *Chapters*, ii. 15–17; and Powicke, *King Henry III and the Lord Edward* (Oxford, 1947), 696–7.

nent wardrobe officials speaks eloquently of the growth in importance of the royal wardrobe under Edward I. As 'the office which gavé unity of policy and direction to all the departments of state', the wardrobe, despite travelling with the household, was at this period coming to need a fixed base in the capital as much as did the exchequer and the chancery. For a time under Edward I this base—the Great Wardrobe—was established at Westminster, and specifically, it appears, at Enedehithe. In the next reign it was transferred to London, where it settled finally, in the 1360s, close to the Blackfriars at Baynard Castle.[44]

To the south of Enedehithe lane lay the precinct of the royal palace. Among those who gravitated to this quarter in the course of the thirteenth century, the king's own family and servants were naturally prominent. An early focus of domestic and commercial buildings was the palace gateway leading from the southern end of King Street, where a huddle of houses probably stood already by 1200[45] (Fig. 4: D). Throughout the thirteenth century, property around the palace gate remained largely in the control of two families, the Levelonds and the Marshals. It was characteristic of the locality that one, and almost certainly both, of these families held offices in the palace. Shortly before 1200 Nathaniel de Levelond, the hereditary keeper of the king's palace at Westminster, gave to his daughter, Juliana, on the occasion of her marriage, a messuage at the palace gate.[46] In the next generation John de Upton, marshal (also known as John Marshal), who was probably a sergeant of the crown, received royal licence to build here, outside the king's gate, and in 1240 was confirmed in possession of his completed messuage.[47] He had evidently built, adjacent to his own residence,

[44] Tout, *Chapters*, ii. 48–9; iv. 397–406; M. Prestwich, *War, Politics and Finance under Edward I* (London, 1972), 151 ff.

[45] The great outer gate of Westminster Palace was not built until 1287–9; but (*pace King's Works*, i. 547–8) the abbey deeds imply the earlier existence of a gate of some kind leading from the highway, e.g. a deed concerning Juliana de Levelond's former messuage by the gate (see below) is endorsed *strata regia*. WAM 17509. See also *King's Works*, i. 493 and n. 8.

[46] WAM 17375. The keepership of Westminster Palace was held by the Kentish family of Levelond from the mid-twelfth century (perhaps earlier) until the end of the Middle Ages. Nathaniel died in 1200–1; his son and heir in 1216–17. C. T. Clay, 'The Keepership of the Old Palace of Westminster', *English Historical Review*, lix (1944), 1–21.

[47] *Cal Ch R 1227–56*, p. 251. A John Marshal of Westminster, king's sergeant, is recorded as having lost his sight in the royal service in 1254, received thereafter a pension of 6*d.* a day at the exchequer, and died in 1267. *Cal Lib R 1251–60*, p. 206; *Cal Cl R 1256–9*, pp. 26, 179, 220; ibid. *1264–8*, pp. 13, 281, 346.

some less substantial houses in addition. In *c.*1250 he made of one of these houses a wedding present for his daughter, Joan, who married a provision merchant to the king's building works named Richard of the cellar. There was also a shop near the door of the house, apparently an early encroachment upon the highway, held of John Marshal by the wife of William the cobbler.[48] Two additional small houses flanked that of John Marshal's dowry.[49] Development in the thirteenth century around the palace gate was evidently intensive. Commercial and residential pressure on this site caused the substantial residence of John the marshal to be, in effect, set back from the street frontage, behind a fringe of smaller houses and a shop.

More houses clustered to the south of the palace entry, between the king's gate and that of the abbey precinct (Fig. 4: E). In *c.*1250 the plot here adjacent to the royal gateway was described as 'vacant'.[50] But by 1343 at the latest the site had been developed as *le Holetaverne* or *le Holewetaverne* (1374), i.e. the Holy Way tavern, which was perhaps a resort of pilgrims.[51] Outside the cemetery gate of the abbey, on the east side of the entry, two tenements were acquired towards the end of the thirteenth century by Ralph Vineter; the high recorded purchase prices indicate that these were built up with houses or shops.[52] The presumed connection of the Vineter family with the wine trade gave it a natural interest in premises close to the royal household. Of the various investments of the Vineters in this area two further tenements, whose exact position is unknown, were held initially of Richard Woolward.[53]

---

[48] WAM 17365. The house measured 14 feet by 20 feet in plan. It was almost certainly this property which, in the third quarter of the century, Joan granted to Ralph, the son of William Vineter, when it was described as a house with a shop on the north side of the entrance way of the king's gate. WAM 17382. See also WAM 17473, 17492, 17498, 17559. For Richard of the cellar see H. M. Colvin (ed.), *Building Accounts of King Henry III* (Oxford, 1971), 228 (1253), 382 (1259), etc.

[49] WAM 17549A, 17470.

[50] WAM 17369: witnessed by Edward Clericus, who was the son of Odo the goldsmith of Westminster, and by Richer de Cruce (for Odo and Richer see app. I).

[51] PRO, CP40/335/2, m.1; BL MS Cart. Harl. 46 E.26.

[52] For one, Ralph paid Hugh de Mohant 90 marks (£60); the other, adjacent, was secured from the grandson and heir of Thomas le Cofrer in exchange for a cancelled debt of £20. WAM 17377, 17513, 17426, 17479–80. A reserved rent of 13s. 4d. p.a. was collected in 1343, by William de Walden, from the tenement of Joan la Vineter, formerly of Ralph le Vineter, next to the north gate of the abbey, on the east side. PRO, CP40/335/2, m.1.

[53] WAM 17547; see also WAM 17475.

This individual was a great-grandson of Nathaniel de Levelond, and himself inherited the keepership of the royal palace after 1286.[54]

In addition to the king's own immediate retainers, housed in Westminster Palace, the households of subsidiary members of the royal family also demanded accommodation within the town. The north part of the palace precinct originally extended to the lane at Enedehithe; within this northern section there evolved in the mid-thirteenth century the great house (*mansio*) of 'Almayne' (Fig. 4: F). The name recalled its builder and first occupant, Richard, earl of Cornwall. Earl Richard was king of the Germans from 1257 until his death in 1272, during which time he dallied ineffectively with aspirations to the imperial throne. As the brother of Henry III, the earl had evidently been provided for his accommodation with an appanage of the crown's Westminster estate. Richard's career was one of continual vacillation, and his loyalty to the English throne was at best unreliable; Henry no doubt hoped by this provision to keep his younger brother under his eye. The initial grant of the site must have shortly preceded a gift from the king in 1234 of thirty oaks from the royal forest for the construction of Earl Richard's houses at Westminster.[55] It was here, in 1243, that Richard's marriage to Sanchia of Provence was celebrated with a feast, according to Matthew Paris, of thirty thousand dishes.[56] Unfortunately, however, Richard's unusually committed support for the king in the conflict of 1263–4 provoked a London mob to plunder and vandalize his houses at Westminster. It may well have been at this point that the king of Germany abandoned the residence to his eldest son, Henry, who in turn granted it in 1270 to Westminster Abbey.[57] The valuable property thus became detached from the palace and passed from royal into monastic hands.

To the south of this site, in the second quarter of the century,

[54] See WAM 17509, 17375. The seal legends on WAM 17509 show that Richard Woolward was the son of Alice Woolward; the latter was the daughter of Juliana de Levelond, daughter of Nathaniel. The name Woolward appears to derive from Juliana's husband, Wilfward the carter. For Richard Woolward's tenure of office see B. F. and C. R. Byerly (eds.), *Records of the Wardrobe and Household, 1285–1286* (HMSO, London, 1977), no. 1693. Richard's predecessor, Stephen de Levelond, died in 1286. Clay, 'The Keepership', 11.

[55] *Cal Cl R 1231–4*, p. 409.   [56] *Matt Par Chron Maj*, iv. 263.

[57] 'Mansionem eiusdem regis (sc. Ricardi), quae in suburbio Londoniae prope Westmonasterium sita fuerat, solo tenus diruebant, non reliquentes lapidem super lapidem quem sibi necessarium decrevissent, eradicantes virgulta, lateres seu tegulas, et lapides universos qui prodesse poterant turribus abducentes'. Chronicon

stood the houses of Odo, the king's goldsmith (Fig. 4: G). These, which began as a large complex, were rapidly broken up into smaller units by the mounting pressure upon accommodation in the neighbourhood. Odo was brought to prominence by the patronage of Henry III, whose favourite goldsmith and clerk of works he became. His local standing is reflected in his appointment, before 1217, as reeve of Westminster; and his name appears with great frequency among the witness lists on deeds of local property.[58] He was involved at the highest level in all the king's building projects, and especially at Westminster, from *c.*1219 until *c.*1239, after which date his son, Edward of Westminster, became clerk of works in his turn and enjoyed even greater responsibility and fame.[59] Odo was living at his chief court 'near the sluice' (i.e. the 'close bridge', where the Clowson stream passed beneath King Street) by 1236–7, when he granted to the monks of Westminster an annual rent of 4*s.* in return for the right to keep his free chapel there. He also acquired the privilege of a chantry in the chapel, upon condition that his estate and houses remain within his family. Clearly, Odo lived on a grand scale.[60] In the time of his grandchildren, however, at least part of the property passed from the family's possession, as more royal agents jostled for quarters near the palace. In March 1265, Peter de Montfort, head of the English family of that resonant name, was confirmed in his tenure of an inn in the houses late of Odo's son, Edward of Westminster.[61] De Montfort's tenancy was curtailed by his death at the battle of Evesham in August of the same year, whereupon the king regranted the houses to Roger Leyburn, a former rebel who ironically had saved Henry's life at Evesham; this was one of many rewards picked up by that adventurer in the aftermath of the civil war.[62] Odo, a son of Edward of Westminster

Thome Wykes, in *Annales Monastici*, ed. H. R. Luard, Rolls Series, 4 vols. (1864–9), iv. 141. The house was evidently stone-built, unless Wykes's *lapides* were rhetorical. For the damage they did here and at Isleworth, the citizens of London were made to pay Richard 1,000 marks. N. Denholm-Young, *Richard of Cornwall* (Oxford, 1947), 132. Henry of Almayne's grant is WAM 17360; see also *Cal Ch R 1257–1300*, p. 146.

[58] See app. 1.
[59] R. Kent Lancaster, 'Artisans, Suppliers and Clerks: The Human Factors in the Art Patronage of King Henry III', *Journal of the Warburg and Courtauld Institutes*, xxxv (1972), 81–107.
[60] WAM 17454, 17333.   [61] *Cal Pat R 1258–66*, p. 413.
[62] *Cal Ch R 1257–1300*, p 55. See also A. Lewis, 'Roger Leyburn and the Pacification of England, 1265–1267', *English Historical Review*, liv (1939), 193–214.

and grandson of the goldsmith, gave to Leyburn what must have
been a confirmatory grant of this house.[63] At the same time Odo also
parted with a messuage and land next to the messuage formerly of
John Marshal.[64] In 1272, the family yielded to further pressure
from incomers, as yet another king's minister acquired from them a
base here, in convenient proximity to the palace.[65] This was Robert
Burnell, the confidential friend of the new king, who was about to
embark on his important career in the chancery.[66] Once again, the
installation of a crown servant carried the process of fragmentation
a step further.

To the west of Odo the goldsmith's houses, and facing on to the
highway, a string of tenements existed by the mid-thirteenth
century, generally occupied by more royal officials, both small and
great (Fig. 4: H). In *c.*1260 Joan, widow of Richard the crier,
granted to Hamo the usher a messuage here; it is probable that
Richard and Hamo were both employed in the palace.[67] By about
twenty years later, when Hamo's son, Walter, made another grant
of this property, a new neighbour had moved in on its northern side.
The arrival was William de Huntingfield, who was cook to
Edmund, earl of Cornwall, Edward I's brother.[68] A royal grant to
the earl's cook of 1281 states that the cook's house stood close to that
of Otho de Grandison. This great personage may in fact have been
living here by *c.*1274, when he appears as 'one of the king's
household and the king's secretary'.[69] Sir Otho's was no doubt a
more substantial house than most of its neighbours; in 1292 it was

---

[63] PRO, E40/2508. Roger Leyburn's house was inherited by his son, William; for
a certain messuage fronting on the highway was said to abut at the back, first, on the
tenement of Master Edward the clerk of Westminster and later, on that of Master
William de Leyburn. WAM 17441, 17555. For William Leyburn see Lewis, 'Roger
Leyburn', 208.

[64] PRO, E40/2508. Since John Marshal's former messuage (as has been seen)
adjoined the north side of the abbey gate, it appears that Odo the goldsmith's
property had extended from 'Almayne' to the north as far as the courtyard of the
palace (later known as New Palace Yard) to the south. Odo of Westminster, who is
presumably to be identified with the grandson of the famous goldsmith, was a melter
of the exchequer 1263–85 and a remembrancer of that department 1273–90; he died
in 1290–1. See D. Crook, 'The Early Remembrancers of the Exchequer', *Bulletin of
the Institute of Historical Research*, liii (1980), 15–16, 22.

[65] *Cal Cl R 1268–72*, p. 566.

[66] Burnell was chancellor to the Lord Edward by *c.*1272, and was the king's
chancellor, 1274–92. Tout, *Chapters*, ii. 11; vi. 6, 116.

[67] WAM 17441.

[68] WAM 17555.

[69] *Cal Pat R 1271–81*, pp. 389, 435.

the venue of a royal council.[70] It was later occupied by Edmund of Woodstock, Edward I's youngest son. In 1321, in which year he became earl of Kent, Edmund received from his royal brother, Edward II, certain houses (formerly belonging to a king's clerk named John de Okham) 'at Clousebrigge' in Westminster; these must from the description have lain near the messuage of Otho de Grandison, which the earl also held at this death.[71] After the regency government of Queen Isabella and her paramour, Mortimer, had cynically sentenced Earl Edmund to execution in 1329, the earl's Westminster houses escheated to the crown, and were promptly appropriated by Isabella herself.[72] About twenty years after this, King Edward III consolidated the royal hold on this part of Westminster, allocating a site here (as Canon Row) to the staff of his newly created college of St Stephen's Chapel.[73] The bitter jurisdictional dispute which ensued, between St Stephen's and the monks of Westminster Abbey, reflects the increasing premium set on the control of land close to the royal palace.[74]

While the Thames waterfront was increasingly built up in the course of the thirteenth century, development was also in progress to the west of the abbey, in the area of Tothill. Here the vanguard around 1200 was led by the Mauduit family, who were hereditary chamberlains to the crown. Like the arrival of the Ely family, the coming of the Mauduits to Westminster was symptomatic of the

[70] The council was held 'in domo Ottonis de Grandison extra palacium domini regis apud Wetmonasterium'. *Rot Parl*, i. 76. See also C. L. Kingsford, 'Sir Otho de Grandison, 1238?–1328', *Transactions of the Royal Historical Society*, 3rd ser., iii (1909), 125–95, esp. p. 130.
[71] *Cal Pat R 1317–21*, p. 568; *Cal Inq p m* vii, p. 222. The location of the earl's property is confirmed by a quitclaim of 1325 of a messuage which stretched from the royal way to the king's palace ditch, abutting on one side the court of Edmund of Woodstock, earl of Kent. PRO, CP40/261A/1, m.5.
[72] *Cal Pat R 1327–30*, p. 506; *Dictionary of National Biography*, s.n. Edmund of Woodstock.
[73] *The Victoria County History of London*, vol. i (London, 1909), 566–70; *King's Works*, i. 510–27.
[74] LN, fos. 118 *et seq.*; BL MS Cott. Faust, A.iii, fos. 293ʳ *et seq.* (another copy). See also J. T. Smith, *The Antiquities of Westminster* (2nd edn., London, 1837), 101–6 and plan opposite p. 124. The canons' site stretched from the palace courtyard (later New Palace Yard) to the south as far as 'Almayne' to the north, and from the Thames to the east as far as a boundary wall to the west, newly built, separating it from various houses fronting on to King Street. These latter properties were probably given by the king at this date to St Stephen's canons, in whose hands they are recorded as being in *c.*1508. WAM 18599. For the Wool Staple, also constructed here in the mid-fourteenth century, and for the enclosure of the palace yard, see *King's Works*, i. 547 n., 552.

contemporaneous shift of royal government. The Mauduits, who were lords of Hanslope in Buckinghamshire and Northampton-shire, had since before the Conquest found it convenient to own property in and near Winchester. But in the last quarter of the twelfth century William Mauduit (1157/8–94) bought property in Westminster, and his son Robert (1194–1222) proceeded to make systematic purchases of contiguous plots to accumulate a substantial base in the new capital.[75] Between 1194 and 1200, Robert Mauduit was confirmed by the abbot in possession of his 'houses' in Westminster, at Long Ditch; they appear to have stood on, or close to, the corner of Tothill Street (Fig. 4: I). These houses were said to have been previously given to the monastery by William, the usher of Abbot Walter (1175–90), which provides a *terminus post quem* for the appearance of the Mauduits of *c.*1175.[76] To the established ministerial class of the monastery, represented by the abbot's usher, succeeded the new officialdom of the Westminster-based monarchy.

Like the royal family itself, although on a lesser scale, the Mauduits, with their household and servants, created a highly localized society within the wider body of the growing town. The former property of William the usher became the core of the Mauduits' Westminster estate. In the 1190s it was granted to the family that they might maintain a chapel here, provided they did not infringe upon the rights of the parish church of St Margaret.[77] Meanwhile the small domain was progressively extended. In 1182 × 1186, by the earliest approximately datable transaction of

[75] Meanwhile, and as part of the same process, similar large residences in Winchester were at this period falling into decay. M. Biddle (ed.), *Winchester in the Early Middle Ages*, Winchester Studies, vol. i (Oxford, 1976), 389–92.

[76] WAM 17614; BL MS Add. 28024, fo. 46ᵛ (copy). The latter MS has been edited as *The Beauchamp Cartulary Charters, 1100–1268*, by E. Mason, Pipe Roll Society, new ser., xliii (1980). For the family estates, see Biddle (ed.), *Winchester in the Early Middle Ages*, 41–3; and *Beauchamp Cartulary Charters*, pp. xxvi ff. William Mauduit died 2 Oct. 1194; see *Annales Monastici*, ed. Luard, Rolls Series, ii. 249–50.

[77] Churchings of women were to be made in the chapel only in the presence of the parish priest, who was to receive all the offerings; no weddings were to take place there of any parishioners of St Margaret's; and, should any member of the Mauduit household be mortally sick, he was to receive the last rites from St Margaret's church, making due payment to the same. In the absence from Westminster of Robert Mauduit and his wife, the remainder of the household were to attend mass in the parish church, and to render their appropriate contributions there. WD, fo. 352ʳ⁻ᵛ. For St Margaret's church see ch. 8.

the series, William Mauduit bought a messuage at Long Ditch from Adam of Westminster. The latter, as a nephew of Richard of Ilchester, one of the justices of the exchequer, was himself in all likelihood an exchequer official.[78] At the time of the Mauduits' arrival, however, much of the land on the north side of 'the great way of Tothill' (as the potential Tothill Street was then described) belonged to the family of Edward, the abbot's reeve of Westminster (d. *c*.1199): another monastic servant whose estate was now acquired by officers of the king. A quitrent was due from the houses once of William the usher to John, son of Edward the reeve; and the land to the west of these houses, which Robert Mauduit purchased between 1194 and 1197 from the sons of Ralph of Tothill, had previously been held of Edward the reeve himself.[79] A string of houses fronting southwards on to the highway was likewise held from Edward the reeve; in one of these, in *c*.1196, Robert Mauduit's secretary, William of the Temple, was installed.[80] It would appear that the antecedents of Edward the reeve, being in possession of the land adjacent to 'the way of Tothill', had initiated development by the construction of houses at the road's beginning.[81] Yet again, local property had been taken up by ministers of the crown,[82] and the secular officialdom of the abbey was able to profit from its stake in the expanding town of the late twelfth century.[83]

[78] At the same period William Mauduit bought neighbouring land from Alexander, son of William the priest of St Martin's. BL MS Add. 28024, fos. 47ᵛ–48ʳ; *Beauchamp Cartulary Charters*, 107–8 (for dating); *Dictionary of National Biography*, s.n. Richard of Ilchester. In 1203 × 1213, Robert Mauduit acquired from the widow of William the priest two messuages and a meadow at Long Ditch. BL MS Add. 28024, fos. 45ʳ–46ʳ; *Beauchamp Cartulary Charters*, 112–14.

[79] BL MS Add. 28024, fos. 46ᵛ, 47ʳ (*ter*); *Beauchamp Cartulary Charters*, 114–15.

[80] BL MS Cart. Harl. 49 G.30; WD, fo. 556ʳ; Richardson, 'William of Ely', 84–6. For the earlier descent of William of the Temple's portion: BL Cart. Harl. 50 A.10; BL Cart. Harl. 50 A.32; BL Cart. Harl. 51 C.47.

[81] See also WD, fos. 520ʳ–521ʳ; WAM 17393: Edward the reeve died *ante* 1200 (see app. 1), while Adam, the bishop's nephew, a witness to this grant, was ill in Oct. 1212 (see *Beauchamp Cartulary Charters*, no. 186 n.); BL MS Add. 28024, fos. 44ᵛ, 47ʳ: Richard de Dol, abbot's seneschal, a witness to both grants, was seneschal to Abbot Ralph Arundel (1200–14), and also held office as reeve in the 1190s (see app. 1, and *Beauchamp Cartulary Charters*, no. 191 n.).

[82] In 1268 the Tothill estate passed from the Mauduits to the Beauchamp family, which in 1344 sold it back to Westminster Abbey. WAM 17635–7; *Cal Pat R 1343–5*, p. 246; and see *Cal Inq p m* v, p. 397.

[83] On 'Mauduitsgarden', which from the fifteenth century was known as 'Petty Calais', see also below ch. 3, sect. 2.

More government officials swam in the wake of the Mauduits. Among those who came to live at Tothill about the middle of the thirteenth century were an usher of the exchequer named Peter, and John Giffard (whose house opposite the almonry became known as 'Giffard's Hall'), a teller in that department.[84] A near neighbour of Giffard was John of Wallingford, one of the king's messengers; the house between the two was later acquired by John de Alfreton, who was a saucer (*salsarius*) in the household of King Edward I.[85] William le Rus, also a local property holder, was water-bearer (*aquarius*) to Henry III;[86] another was King Henry's cook, Geoffrey of Bath.[87]

The household of one royal servant living at Westminster in the second quarter of the thirteenth century can be envisaged in some detail, as a result of an unfortunate incident which took place there. In the early hours of Monday, 14 May 1235, 'Henry Clement, envoy of the justiciar of Ireland, was murdered at Westminster in the house of Master David the surgeon'. Henry Clement appears to have been a minor agent in a much greater political scandal; his own foolish boast of being involved led to his elimination. The examination of witnesses in the case has preserved an account of the house and its occupants at the time of the murder.[88] Master David was surgeon to King Henry III, and his accommodation at Westminster lay conveniently hard by the palace gate; the house fronted on to the palace entry. The lady called Alice who was described as the *hospita* of Master David was evidently the mistress of the house, with whom the surgeon lodged. He appears subsequently to have married his landlady, for his widow was named in 1248 as Alice, and David and his wife, Alice, were later said to have jointly held their tenement in Westminster from the king.[89] But though Alice had children in 1235, they were

---

[84] Peter of the exchequer: WAM 17422. (For Peter and his wife, Matilda, and their son, Robert Capellanus, see also WAM 17520, 17545.) John Giffard, *narrator*: WAM 17467. For the succession of Giffard's house to 1325 see WAM 17552, 17530, 17493, 17561, 17585.

[85] WAM 17467. For John of Wallingford see M. C. Hill, *The King's Messengers, 1199–1377* (London, 1961), 66, 106; *Cal Cl R 1272–9*, p. 13.

[86] WAM 17408–9.   [87] WD, fos. 512ᵛ, 516ʳ.

[88] *Curia Regis Rolls*, xv. 372–4. See *Matt Par Chron Maj*, iii. 327; iv. 193–6; F. W. Maitland, 'The murder of Henry Clement', *English Historical Review*, x (1895), 294–7; and Powicke, *Henry III and the Lord Edward*, app. B.

[89] *Cal Cl R 1247–51*, p. 24; *Cal Pat R, 1266–72*, p. 262. See also *Cal Cl R 1237–42*, p. 422.

presumably by a previous marriage. On the night of the crime, Alice lay in her own room (*in quadam camera in domo sua*), together with her young children—one a daughter old enough to give evidence—and a maid. Master David, meanwhile, slept in a separate solar, which on this occasion he appears to have shared with Clement, the visiting envoy. The hall of the house was reached directly by a door opening from the street; from the hall a stairway mounted to Master David's solar. Hearing his would-be attackers, the victim tried to escape by the window in this solar, but seeing further assailants waiting in the street below, drew back. The murderers found him in the room by the light of a burning torch, which they extinguished as they crossed the threshold. Afterwards they fled into the neighbouring sanctuary of Westminster Abbey. The killers appear the more bold in view of the large number of people staying in the house at the time. In addition to those already mentioned, there was a king's messenger called William Perdriz; where he slept is unknown, but his servant 'lay in the hall'. This lad was the first to see the intruders when they broke down the front door, but was too scared to do anything but hide his head under a leather sheet. Henry Clement's boy, on the other hand, was billeted with other youths in a stable in the courtyard (*in quodam stabulo in curia*); when the assassins were heard breaking into the hall, Alice opened a window in her room on to the yard and called out, in a vain attempt to wake these boys in the stable. 'An outhouse in a stable' had moreover been assigned to a second messenger from the justiciar of Ireland. A corner was also found, somewhere in these crowded lodgings, for the servant of one Thomas le Messager, whose name suggests yet another ambassador. The house of Mistress Alice, at the gate of Westminster Palace, was clearly not only the permanent base of the king's surgeon but also a favoured short-term resting-place for the many messengers passing to and from the royal capital. The *ad hoc* sleeping arrangements, in this single case, show something of the demand for temporary accommodation in Westminster at this date. The pressure upon housing in the royal capital is further demonstrated by the fact that two of those interviewed by the murder inquest, Roger of Norwich and Godfrey the cobbler, were living, outside the palace gate, in tents (*in tentoriis ante portam domini regis*).

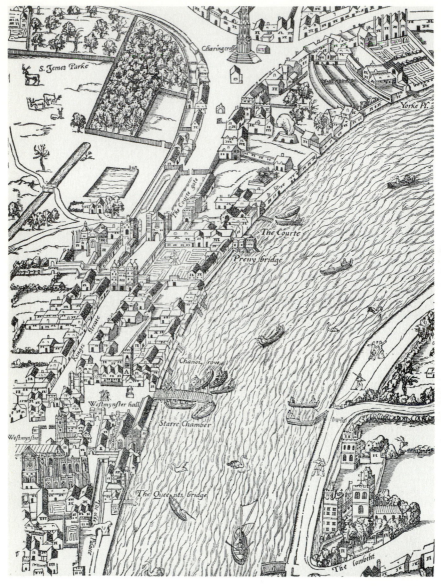

ILLUS. 3. Westminster in the mid-sixteenth century, after the construction of Whitehall Palace. Detail from the contemporary 'Agas' woodcut map of London.

2

The King's Capital, 1300–1540

By 1300 the main lines of Westminster's character during the later medieval period had been delineated. Nevertheless the fortunes of the town in these centuries were by no means predetermined. In 1300 the idea of a political capital remained only partially realized.

The character of a political-cum-religious cult centre which Westminster Abbey was given in the thirteenth century would never have sufficed, alone, to sustain an attendant urban community. The offerings of pilgrims at the shrine of St Edward the Confessor may be expected to have been at a peak in the mid-thirteenth century; those recorded by the abbey sacrist after 1300 reflect an important cult, but not one of overwhelming popularity.[1] The cash donations were not altogether negligible sums; moreover, they may have been supplemented by other, unrecorded presents, in particular by the rings commonly bought by pilgrims for this purpose. Nevertheless, it seems probable that the Confessor, whose regal character and associations may have seemed somewhat exclusive, never enjoyed a massive popular following.[2] He suffered from the usual shifts of loyalty of medieval pilgrims. Pilgrimage continued to be a widespread form of devotion in the later Middle Ages, but the fashions moved on, leaving some saints outmoded and neglected.[3] It was only at a relatively low level that popular

---

[1] WAM 19650–807. Some detailed notes of the shrine-keeper's receipts are preserved from the early sixteenth century: WAM 33293. The annual cash receipts of the keeper were about £26 in 1317–18, £17 in 1346–7, and £30 in 1354–5. The third quarter of the fourteenth century appears to be marked by a widespread vogue for St Edward, whose yearly offerings, in eight documented years between 1358 and 1380, fluctuated between £74 and (in 1372–3) £103. The amounts fell after the 1380s (as the records also become fuller). The late-fourteenth-century average was about £40 p.a., dropping to £20 and then to £10 or something less in the early and mid-fifteenth century; at this reduced level it remained at the beginning of the sixteenth century.

[2] See also Barlow, *Edward the Confessor*, 256 ff.; Harvey, *Estates*, 43–5.

[3] J. Sumption, *Pilgrimage. An Image of Medieval Religion* (London, 1975), 268–9; R. C. Finucane, *Miracles and Pilgrims. Popular Beliefs in Medieval England* (London, 1977), 191–202; B. Spencer, 'King Henry of Windsor and the London

veneration for St Edward, still manifest in Chaucer's Westminster, outlived the author of the *Canterbury Tales.*

Meanwhile, although the foundations of the royal administrative capital had been laid by the end of Henry III's reign, Westminster's subsequent realization of that political role was not achieved by a smooth continuous process. The Welsh and Scottish wars of Edward I and II came close to destroying the still nascent administration at Westminster, by the creation of a new base of monarchy in the north, at York.[4] Abandoned in the mid-fourteenth century, the possibility of a northern capital was seriously considered again in Richard II's reign.[5] The inhabitants of Westminster who in the 1330s presented a petition against the removal of the royal courts were right to stress the vital importance to the local economy of the return of the king's government.[6] The outbreak of war with France in 1338, and the consequent reversion of the royal administration to a southern axis, was crucial to Westminster's survival. In 1339 the exchequer and the common bench (the court of common pleas) returned to Westminster for good. From the mid-1360s (in response to a petition from the commons) the king's bench, too, took up permanent residence in Westminster Hall, and at the same period the chancery virtually ceased to perambulate with the monarch, but settled with the other courts in William Rufus's great chamber.[7] Great as that was, it had not been designed to accommodate so much activity as this, and it was doubtless to ease the resultant congestion that the brilliant carpenter Hugh Herland was commissioned, in 1393, to dispense with the dividing arcades by reroofing the hall in a single, vast span.[8]

Pilgrim', in J. Bird, H. Chapman, and J. Clark (eds.), *Collectanea Londinensia. Studies in London Archaeology and History Presented to Ralph Merrifield*, London and Middlesex Archaeological Society Special Paper No. 2 (1978), 235–64.

[4] The royal courts were absent from Westminster, on account of campaigns in Scotland, from May 1298–Christmas 1304; Sept. 1319–Feb. 1320; Apr. 1322–July 1323; Oct.–Dec. 1327; and May 1333–Sept. 1338. D. M. Browne, 'Exchequer Migrations to York in the Thirteenth and Fourteenth Centuries', in A. G. Little and Powicke (eds.), *Essays in Medieval History Presented to T. F. Tout* (Manchester, 1925), 291–300.

[5] J. H. Harvey, 'Richard II and York', in F. R. H. du Boulay and C. M. Barron (eds.), *The Reign of Richard II* (London, 1971), 202–17; and see also Barron, 'The Quarrel of Richard II with London, 1392–7', ibid. 181–2, 193.

[6] For the petition see ch. 5, sect. 1.

[7] Tout, 'The Beginnings of a Modern Capital'. For the disposition of the various courts within Westminster Hall, see *King's Works*, i. 543–5.

[8] *King's Works*, i. 527–33.

This was only the latest of a series of extensions and improvements whereby the palace of Westminster was transformed, under Edward III and Richard II, into a permanent headquarters of central government.[9] It was, moreover, in the mid-fourteenth century that Westminster became the usual venue for the deliberative assemblies of the English parliament. The crown's need to pay for the Hundred Years War necessitated the issue of regular invitations to the members of parliament, who from 1339 (in contrast to their previous wanderings) met almost invariably at Westminster.

These institutions of government were not monolithic, but continued to evolve; and the fluctuations in their fortunes were inevitably felt by the local population. The courts of common pleas and king's bench reached a peak of activity in the late fourteenth and early fifteenth centuries. From about 1415, both benches began to lose business, and this trend persisted thereafter.[10] However, although this development was accompanied by what may have been a growing preference for the settlement of disputes out of court, through informal means of negotiation and arbitration,[11] the decline of the older established courts in Westminster Hall was, from the second half of the fifteenth century, more than offset by the growth of chancery as a court of equity. In the later Middle Ages, therefore, the central organs of royal justice were, collectively, busier than ever, serving an intensively litigious public. Some three thousand new suits were opened in the king's courts at Westminster every year (not to mention those not brought to any officially recorded conclusion).[12] This 'law-mindedness' was the basis of the careers, not only of the four hundred or so common lawyers engaged at Westminster (for, as the saying ran, 'angels work wonders in Westminster Hall'), but also of a large class of local tradespeople.[13] Whether the petitioner fared well or ill in his case, the hucksters and shopkeepers of the district awaited his custom

[9] Ibid. i. 504–46.
[10] M. Hastings, *The Court of Common Pleas in Fifteenth-Century England; A Study of Legal and Administrative Procedure* (Ithaca, 1947), 190; M. Blatcher, *The Court of King's Bench. A Study in Self-Help* (London, 1978), 15–28.
[11] E. Powell, 'Arbitration and the Law in England in the Late Middle Ages', *Transactions of the Royal Historical Society*, 5th ser., xxxiii (1983), 49–67.
[12] E. W. Ives, *The Common Lawyers of Pre-Reformation England* (Cambridge, 1983), 7 and *passim*.
[13] Id., 'The Common Lawyers in Pre-Reformation England', *Transactions of the Royal Historical Society*, 5th ser., xviii (1968), 146–7, 161.

with confidence. When Langland's cowardly character of False-
ness, for fear of just judgement, balked at entering Westminster
Hall and turned away into the streets of the town, then naturally

> marchantz mette with hym and made hym abide,
> And bishetten hym in here shope to shewen here ware,
> And apparailled hym as a prentice the people to serue.[14]

The institution of parliament also suffered vicissitudes in the
later Middle Ages. Indeed, so far from 'slowly broadening down,
from precedent to precedent', parliament in the fifteenth century
came close to extinction. Its meetings occurred far less often after
1400 than during the sixty preceding years. From 1339 until 1399, a
parliament was summoned to Westminster (in accordance with a
half-recognized principle) almost every year. Between 1400 and
1509, however, this rate was cut by a half; and only seven
parliaments convened between 1510 and 1540.[15] Although the late
medieval assemblies tended to be of longer duration than their
predecessors, the readiness of the crown to dispense with their
services altogether was at times, notably in the reign of Henry VII,
only too evident.[16] Nevertheless, the fifteenth century saw significant developments in the organization and activities of parliament,
and with these the birth of a principle that not only private
petitions, but also public matters of wide importance, ought by
right to be discussed in its sessions.[17] When the MPs—up to 270
members of the commons, and nominally 100 or so of the lords—

[14] William Langland, *The Vision Concerning Piers Plowman*, Passus II, ll. 212–14,
cited from the edition of J. A. W. Bennett, *Piers Plowman. The Prologue and Passus
I–VII of the B Text* (Oxford, 1972), 19–20. *bishetten hym*: shut him (up). See also
ch. 5.

[15] List of parliaments in Powicke and E. B. Fryde (eds.), *Handbook of British
Chronology* (2nd edn., Royal Historical Society, London, 1961), 499–535. See also
J. C. Wedgwood and A. D. Holt, *History of Parliament, 1439–1509* (London, 1936),
pp. vi–vii.

[16] Richardson and G. O. Sayles, *The English Parliament in the Middle Ages*
(London, 1981), ch. 26, p. 40; J. S. Roskell, 'Perspectives in English Parliamentary
History', repr. in Fryde and Miller (eds.), *Historical Studies of the English
Parliament*, 2 vols. (Cambridge, 1970), ii. 296–323; G. R. Elton, ' "The Body of the
Whole Realm": Parliament and Representation in Medieval and Tudor England',
repr. in id., *Studies in Tudor and Stuart Politics and Government*, vol. ii (Cambridge,
1974), 19–61.

[17] For these correctives to the extreme revisionist view, see A. R. Myers,
'Parliament, 1422–1509', in R. G. Davies and J. H. Denton (eds.), *The English
Parliament in the Middle Ages* (Manchester, 1981), 141–84; and G. L. Harriss (ed.),
Henry V: The Practice of Kingship (Oxford, 1985), 137–9.

did foregather at Westminster, therefore, they may have brought with them after the late fourteenth century an increased sense of responsibility, or at least of self-importance. For a few busy, sociable, and extravagant weeks the body of the parliament men would have been a conspicuous sight in the neighbourhood. Their presence was welcome to local retailers, such as those (among them William Caxton) for whom new stalls were specially erected between the abbey and Westminster Palace in 1488–9, and leased 'during the time of parliament'.[18] The rowdiness of the commons may, on the other hand, have aroused different feelings in the monks who were forced to accommodate them.[19] Removed from the abbey's chapter house in *c*.1380 (probably on account of their recorded maltreatment of the room), the MPs continued thereafter to cause damage both to other parts of the convent, including the refectory, their new meeting-place, and to their lodgings, which the monks, as landlords, had to repair.[20] No amount of respect for the achievements of late medieval parliaments should be allowed to obscure the boorishness of some of their members, satirized in a hostile account of 1399–1400:

> Some members are there like a nought in arithmetic, that marks a place but has no value in itself. Some had supped with simony the previous evening, so that the shire they represented lost all value from their presence . . . Some members slumbered and slept and said very little . . . Some were so pompous and dull-witted that they got hopelessly muddled before they reached the close of their speeches.[21]

Yet the presence even of these was as grist to the mill of the bakers and brewers of the town.

But what made Westminster, by the end of the Middle Ages, more than the hive of civil servants and the occasional resort of parliamentarians and legal counsellors which it remains today was the presence of the royal household. While the exchequer, the

---

[18] WAM 19736 *et seq.*

[19] I. M. Cooper, 'The Meeting-places of Parliament in the Ancient Palace of Westminster', *Journal of the British Archaeological Association*, 3rd ser., iii (1938), 118–20.

[20] Mats in the chapter house destroyed by the parliament men in 1377–8 and 1379–80: WAM 19637, 19639. A table in the refectory broken in the time of parliament in 1383–4: WAM 19870. Damage done to the cloister by the MPs in 1448–9: WAM 19057. Repairs to several houses 'broken during parliament' in 1403–4: WAM 19009.

[21] *English Historical Documents*, vol. iv, ed. Myers (London, 1969), 453–4.

chancery, and the crown lawyers had progressively 'gone out of court' to fix their abode at Westminster, the household had naturally continued to follow the monarch. But the king, too, came to reside more and moré frequently at his palace of Westminster. One result of this was that the royal council, whose competence and activity grew enormously at this period, and especially under the early Tudors, met at Westminster with ever-increasing regularity.[22] In addition, officers of the royal household—squires of the king's body, yeomen of his kitchen, ushers of his bedchamber, sergeants of his ewery—became increasingly familiar figures about the town. The size of the royal household fluctuated: in the later part of Edward III's reign the number involved was between 350 and 450; under Henry V it was closer to 200; and under Edward IV, around 400.[23] An exaggerated description from the late fourteenth century evokes more vividly than do these bare figures the bustle of the court, crowded with an excess of officers, servants, and hangers-on:

> Truly I herd Robert Ireleffe saye,
> Clerke of the grenecloth, that to the houshold
> Came every daye for moost partie alwaye,
> Ten thousand folke by his messis tould,
> That folowed the hous aye as thei would,
> And in the kechin three hundred servitours,
> And in eche office many occupiours;
>
> And ladies faire with their gentilwomen,
> Chamberers also and lavenders,
> Three hundred of theim were occupied then.[24]

The fifteenth century saw a marked increase in the proportion of royal household servants among the recorded resident population of Westminster; a change which cannot be quantified but which is reflected, for instance, in the appointments to local office in the

---

[22] J. R. Lander, 'The Yorkist Council and Administration, 1461 to 1485', *English Historical Review*, lxxii (1958), 27–56; id., 'Council, Administration and Councillors, 1461 to 1485', *Bulletin of the Institute of Historical Research*, xxxii (1959), 138–80; Elton, *The Tudor Constitution* (2nd edn., Cambridge, 1982), 88–94, 102.

[23] C. J. Given-Wilson, 'The Court and Household of Edward III, 1360–1377', Ph.D. thesis, Univ. of St Andrews (1976), 172–5, cited in V. J. Scattergood and J. W. Sherborne (eds.), *English Court Culture in the Later Middle Ages* (London, 1983), 4; J. Catto, 'The King's Servants', in Harriss (ed.), *Henry V*, 84; Myers (ed.), *The Household of Edward IV. The Black Book and the Ordinance of 1478* (Manchester, 1959), 14 n., 87–8. Note also the presence of separate households of other members of the royal family. Ibid. 93 ff.

[24] *The Chronicle of John Hardyng*, ed. H. Ellis (London, 1812), 346–7.

town.[25] The Elizabethan and later concept of 'the court' as a seasonal social event, for which all who could afford it travelled regularly to Westminster, in quest of perquisites, high living, and gossip, was born at this period.[26] The potential was recognized, and given further encouragement, by Henry VIII's spectacular rebuilding of Whitehall Palace after 1530.[27] There the new breed of courtier found such irresistible social amenities as tennis courts, the tilt-yard, the cock-pit, and (one which has survived) the exotic birds in St James's Park.[28]

The private inhabitants of medieval Westminster therefore lived often in the king's presence, always in the shadow of his palace and of his royal abbey. But whatever the wider significance of the central institutions of the monarchy, to the resident population they represented primarily a source of livelihood. From those institutions it is now the moment to turn, to leave the convent cloister and the king's hall, and to approach the houses, the shops, and the market-stalls of the town.

> The mynstralce, the service at the feeste,
> The grete yiftes to the moste and leeste,
> The riche array of Theseus paleys,
> Ne who sat first ne last upon the deys,
> What ladyes fairest been or best daunsynge,
> Or which of hem kan chanten best and synge,
> Ne who moost felyngly speketh of love;
> What haukes sitten on the perche above,
> What houndes liggen on the floor adoun,—
> Of al this make I now no mencioun.[29]

[25] See app. VIII; and also ch. 6, sect. 4.
[26] For some of the later developments see L. Stone, 'The Residential Development of the West End of London in the Seventeenth Century', in B. C. Malament (ed.), *After the Reformation* (Manchester, 1980), 167–212.
[27] See *King's Works*, iv. 300 ff.
[28] *London Topographical Record*, xix (1947), 113: bread and bran purchased from Henry VIII's Whitehall account in order to feed 'the king's fowls within the park'.
[29] Chaucer, *The Canterbury Tales*, ll. 2197–206, in F. N. Robinson (ed.), *The Works of Geoffrey Chaucer* (2nd edn., London, 1957), 38 (printing 'moste' for 'meeste' in l. 2198). In l. 2202, 'chanten' replaces the probably erroneous 'dauncen' of the manuscripts. See ibid., 679, 890.

ILLUS. 4. Late medieval and early modern houses in Long Ditch and Thieving Lane, Westminster. Drawing by J. T. Smith, 1808.

3

Landlords, Tenants, and Houses

I. INTRODUCTION

Not one of the domestic buildings which housed the population of
medieval Westminster stands today. There survives, indeed, barely
a nail or splinter of their physical presence. Even the simple
medieval street plan, although still essentially preserved in the
modern configuration, is obscured by the pretentious, impersonal
scale of the office blocks now imposed upon it. 'Ag. and Fish',
Admiralty, Ministry of Defence, Treasury, Home Office—these
absurdly and misleadingly named piles have not merely buried the
levels of earlier occupation but, boring deep underground through a
labyrinth of radiation-proof cellars and tunnels, have utterly
obliterated almost all archaeological trace of the former town.[1] To
reconstruct, in the mind's eye, the physical appearance of medieval
Westminster therefore requires a considerable effort of the
imagination. Surviving documentary evidence, however, makes the
task, to a limited degree, possible.

By far the greater part of the documentary evidence in question
relates to the urban estate of Westminster Abbey. Since that estate
by the fourteenth century comprised about two-thirds of the urban
area of Westminster, the abbey records' coverage of the town is
remarkably good. It is not, however, complete; and the existence of
a scatter of other landlords, for some of whom fragmentary
documentation is also available, should not be forgotten. The
present chapter, nevertheless, is largely based upon the records of
Westminster Abbey, which by virtue of their sheer volume make it
possible to build up a general picture of the topographical evolution
of the town, of both institutional and, to a lesser extent, private
policies of exploitation, and of significant changes in the market for
property. These materials present an unusual opportunity for the

---

[1] For discussion of such limited archaeological investigations as have been feasible
see ch. I, sect. I.

study at close quarters of the evolution of a late medieval small town.

Neither the royal grant to the monks of the manor of Westminster in *c.*960, nor the Domesday record of 1086, defines the precise relationship, at those dates, between the monastic lords and the land comprised within the later town.[2] By 1200, however, as the result of grants made by the abbot during the previous two centuries, a considerable part of the area had passed into the hands of lay landholders. These grants had not been made indiscriminately,[3] and it is unlikely that land so close to the abbey would ever have been subjected to wholesale alienation. Nevertheless when, with increasing rapidity in the course of the thirteenth century, the fee came to be built up as never before, the monks were at first largely prevented by the earlier grants from realizing the cash value of their endowment.[4] It was evidently this heightened activity in the property market, combined with a growing need of funds in coin, which stimulated the religious, at the turn of the twelfth and thirteenth centuries, to embark upon a policy of establishment of control. The management of the vill of Westminster by the monks in the thirteenth century formed part of a wider policy applied to their manors in general. As a result of this policy, the religious landlords improved their returns, not only in produce from demesne farms but also, perhaps more significantly, in rents from tenant-lands.[5]

By a combination of solicited gifts and, more particularly, hard purchase, the monks began to extend their portfolio of rents in the neighbourhood of Westminster. At first these were exclusively quitrents, or rents of assize, fixed annual payments (like modern ground-rents) which were alterable only with great difficulty, if at all, with the changing value of property. But in a second stage of the process, which was largely concentrated between the late thirteenth century and the late fourteenth, a broadly successful attempt was made by the monks, generally by money purchase, to secure the direct management of many of the same properties. The result was that these holdings, which ultimately comprised two-thirds of the built-up area of the late medieval town, could now be let by the

[2] See ch. 1, sect. 1.
[3] B. F. Harvey, 'Abbot Gervase de Blois'.
[4] On the early grants see ch. 1, sect. 2.
[5] Cf. Harvey, *Estates*, 65–6.

abbey on leases for fixed terms of years, at economic rents adjustable on renewal. The earliest such leases date from around 1300. *Pari passu* with these two stages of recovery, the land thus acquired for St Peter was allocated to the several monk-obedientiaries within the abbey, to form in each case a part of the endowment.[6]

The summary picture which emerges from the evidence of property holding, and which will be described in fuller detail below, is as follows. The thirteenth century was a period of growth in the vill of Westminster: property changed hands rapidly, plots were subdivided and developed with new buildings. Whether this expansion continued after 1300, however, is uncertain. The first half of the fourteenth century, an enigmatic period in Westminster's history, may have seen the end of the phase of expansion; it is even possible that a reverse trend set in before 1350. But the half-century after 1360 was marked by much development in the town as—plague epidemics notwithstanding—tenants once more abounded. Much of the recorded building in this period was undertaken by the monastic landlords, who profited greatly by their policy. Investment in new building abruptly ceased to be profitable, however, in the decade 1410–20.. During the fifty years which ensued, falling rents and empty houses give clear signals of a demographic recession. In the third quarter of the fifteenth century there occur the first references to a fresh phase of house building, which thereafter gathered momentum until the mid-sixteenth century and beyond. In this period the active builders of property were not the monks, but lay tenants who clearly anticipated large returns on their investment. Evidently the population had again begun to grow after the mid-fifteenth-century slump.

2. THE ABBEY ESTATE

The Thirteenth Century Accumulation

Between *c.*1200 and *c.*1300 the monastery greatly extended its estate in Westminster. This policy coincided with a period of furious activity, and consequently rising values, in the market for land in

---

[6] See introd., n. 5. For a map which distinguishes the parts of Westminster assigned respectively to the various obedientiaries see A. G. Rosser, 'Medieval Westminster: The Vill and the Urban Community, 1200–1540', Ph.D. thesis, Univ. of London (1984), Fig. 8.

the neighbourhood.[7] It is clear that the monks were leading participants in a boom of investment in local property, and that their immediate motive was profit. To vendors, the monks' growing interest in local property offered the chance of a cash sale which might be particularly opportune. In *c.*1250 Thomas, son of Andrew of the king's exchequer, parted with Westminster rents totalling 2*s.* p.a. in return for 18*s.* paid him by the sacrist in order 'to expedite his business in London'.[8] When Matilda Brand died in *c.*1235, she had directed in her will that her houses in Westminster should be sold in order to settle her debts in Jewry and elsewhere. Once again, a ready buyer was found by her executors in the monk-warden of the abbey Lady chapel, who not only paid 11 marks (£7. 6*s.* 8*d.*) down to acquit the debts, but also provided for a priest to pray for the soul of the testatrix for two years.[9] The long catalogue of Westminster rents which the monastery was receiving by the end of the thirteenth century was drawn up in the great *Domesday* cartulary of soon after 1300.[10]

The reward for a grant made to a religious house in the Middle Ages was never solely financial. Indeed, the monks of Westminster encouraged the laity to make outright gifts of their property to the abbey, on the understanding that the spiritual benefit of intercessory masses offered in the monastery would redound upon the donors. So in *c.*1230 the widow Wluena, daughter of Nicholas Cok, granted to the abbey almonry her messuage, which had belonged to her brother, in Long Ditch, 'in soul-alms for herself, her husband Henry FitzGeoffrey, her parents and ancestors'.[11] Benefactors were assured of prayers for themselves and their families, or of a commemorative candle to burn for them at the altar of St Edward,

[7] See also ch. 1, sect. 2.

[8] WD, fo. 357ᵛ (the sacrist in question, William de Bedford, held office in 1247, see Pearce, *Monks*, 196).

[9] WD, fo. 545ʳ⁻ᵛ: among the executors was the chaplain of Hubert de Burgh, not here styled earl of Kent; this gives a date after de Burgh's fall in 1232, and probably before his removal from Westminster in 1241 (see ch. 1, sect. 2).

[10] A mid-century sacrist, paying ten-and-a-half years' purchase to obtain a rent in Westminster of 4*s.* p.a., finalized his possession by receipt of 'all muniments which the grantor had touching the said messuage'. This usual procedure explains the abbey's ownership of deeds concerning properties from periods before they came into the monks' hands. WD, fos. 359ʳ–60ʳ (for the sacrist, William de Bedford, see above, n. 8).

[11] WD, fo. 458ᵛ: witnessed by Edward, son of Odo the goldsmith and by Richer de Cruce (for whose dates see app. 1).

the high altar or the Trinity altar in the nave of the abbey church.[12] In such cases of grants made 'in soul-alms', 'in free alms', or 'in frankalmoin', the likelihood often remains that an unspecified financial inducement was additionally held out to the giver. Nevertheless there is no reason to doubt that the spiritual authority and power of the monks weighed heavily with some of those making grants, especially in the decades around 1200. After 1250, grants declared to be made in free alms virtually ceased; a fact which adds to the probability that the language of pious donation had previously not been altogether devoid of meaning. The change in the form of grants after *c.*1250 may be symptomatic of a shift of loyalty on the part of local benefactors, away from the monastery which appears previously to have been the focus of enthusiastic interest and support.[13]

Of the various departments of the abbey responsible for the acquisition of property in the thirteenth century, that of the Lady chapel was especially prominent. Its history at this period shows well how the ownership and development of property in the town was intimately bound up with the life of the major religious institution in its midst. The earliest record of a warden of St Mary's altar at Westminster Abbey, in the late twelfth century, occurred in a time of increasing popular devotion to the Virgin, with which the appearance of this officer may reasonably be connected. The growing celebration of the Virgin's cult ultimately necessitated in most large religious houses the provision of a separate Lady chapel. At Westminster, the new chapel of St Mary was begun, at the east end of the Romanesque church, in 1220.[14] But during the thirty years before this date, a groundswell of pious enthusiasm for the Virgin Mary had already found expression in a flood of grants to her altar in the abbey church; cash payments by the monks had provided an added stimulus.[15] The mid-thirteenth-century

---

[12] WD, fos. 357^v, 357^r, 350^r (and WAM 17319).

[13] Two extremely rare later grants made in the form of free alms are WAM 17358: dated 1261; and WD, fo. 537^r: *temp.* Abbot Walter de Wenlok (1283–1307). Both were grants to the Lady chapel. See also ch. 8, sect. 2.

[14] *Matt Par Chron Maj*, iii. 59.

[15] The particular local importance of the Lady chapel may explain how the chapel warden, alone of all the monastic obedientiaries, came to preside over a quarterly court for his Westminster tenants. In the mid-thirteenth century a grant to the chapel of a rent in the vill was made 'in the presence of the tenants of the altar and other *virum legalium*'. WAM 17442. Tenants of the chapel owed suit four times each year at St Mary's court. No reference to the court, however, survives from later than 1315. See WD, fos. 521^v–522^r, 515^r; WAM 23179, 17565.

Customary of the abbey records that the first to acquire rents for the Virgin's altar was Prior Robert de Molesham (*c.*1189–97), whose anniversary was subsequently kept at her expense.[16] Prior Robert is recorded in five deeds of purchase whereby he secured quitrents to the annual value of 12s. 2d. and two plots of land, one of which was afterwards leased at 2s. p.a.; the total cost to the convent was about £12.[17] Robert de Molesham's example was energetically followed by Ralph de Gloucester, who was 'warden of the work of the Virgin Mary' around 1240, when the new chapel was being brought to completion. At this period Ralph de Gloucester disbursed a total of £21. 16s. on six transactions by which the abbey acquired 'a plat with a garden' in Tothill Street, a messuage in what would later be called King Street, opposite Enedehithe,[18] further houses in Westminster, a 'plat' in the adjacent manor of Eye, and quitrents worth 3s. $3\frac{1}{2}d$. p.a.[19] Ralph de Gloucester may also have been behind the construction at about this date of a row known as 'the new rent of the Blessed Virgin Mary' on Tothill: a development clearly designed to generate revenue for the Lady chapel.[20]

Meanwhile, active lay interest in the Virgin's cult, in the period prior to the commencement of the Gothic Lady chapel, was revealed in a grant of Abbot Ralph de Arundel (1200–14). 'At the petition of Robert Mauduit, the king's chamberlain, and of Isabel, his wife, and other good men', the abbot decreed that the names of all who conferred gifts on the altar should be inscribed in the monastery's bede-roll (*in martyrologio nostro*), and that they should share in the benefits of the good works of the church, as prayers, fasts, vigils, masses, and disciplines and all other alms.[21] Robert Mauduit, chamberlain to King John, was currently setting up in

[16] *Customary*, 92; Pearce, *Monks*, 195. In the 1220s the procurator of the altar was the subprior, Henry of Colchester. WD, fos. 510ᵛ, 521ʳ: both witnessed by Robert de Crokesle, reeve, and by Odo the goldsmith (for each of whom see app. 1). The fact that the office in this active period *c.*1200 was held by the prior or subprior, and not yet a separate officer, strongly suggests that the accounting department of the Lady chapel was at this very time in process of formation.

[17] WD, fos. 509ʳ⁻ᵛ, 520ᵛ–521ʳ; WAM 17414, 17417, 17329, 17323.

[18] On this site, see a forthcoming art. by S. Thurley and G. Rosser.

[19] WD, fos. 516ʳ, 545ʳ⁻ᵛ, 550ʳ, 564ʳ; WAM 17148A, 17379. Yet further acquisitions by Ralph de Gloucester, in Knightsbridge and elsewhere: WAM 16196, 4771. Ralph de Gloucester is otherwise recorded as warden of the Lady chapel in 1240–7 (see Pearce, *Monks*, 195).

[20] See ch. 5, sect. 7.

[21] WD, fos. 507ᵛ–508ʳ.

grand style in a house at the abbey end of Tothill Street; as a Westminster notable, it was appropriate that he should patronize devotional movements in the town.[22] Abbot Ralph's successor, William de Humez (1214–22), by a grant which made definite reference to the 'new work' of the Virgin's chapel, begun in 1220, extended the rewards accruing to donors to include participation in the spiritual offices of all the churches bound by close fraternity to Westminster, namely: Malmesbury, Malvern, and Fécamp in Normandy, with their cells, the church of Hurley and Sudbury Priory. Moreover, the abbot of Westminster had obtained for contributors to the work a portion of all the blessings thereafter to be enjoyed in the entire Cistercian Order; a notable instance of co-operation between the old Order and the new, in the service of the patroness of Cîteaux and all her daughters. A special indulgence of twenty-one days was attached to the work, in addition to the hundred days already awarded to benefactors of the abbey. At Westminster, thirteen masses were to be celebrated for sponsors each week during their lifetimes, and twenty after their decease.[23] The laity were thus invited to make material contributions to the ministry of the altar in return for spiritual privileges; a bargain commonly employed in the Middle Ages to finance specific building schemes.[24]

Apart from these considerable incentives, the wording of individual grants reveals additional, personal motives which guided benefactors to the altar. In *c.*1210 John, son of Edward the reeve of Westminster, acted on the instructions of his mother, Cecily, when he gave a rent of 4*s.* ' for the sake of his father and mother and all his ancestors, in soul-alms to St Mary's altar in Westminster, to support the lamps there'.[25] Alan of Eye contributed a rent of 2*s.* in

---

[22] See ch. 1, sect. 2.

[23] WAM LVIII; WD, fo. 507[v] (a copy). the passage relating to Cîteaux runs: 'Nos etiam a venerabili patre Abbate Cystercii participationem omnium bonorum que in ordine Cysterciensi fient inperpetuum benefactoribus ipsius operis impetravimus.' There appears to be no record of this grant in the Cistercian statutes printed in *Statuta Capitulorum Generalium Ordinis Cisterciensis*, ed. J. M. Canivez, vol. i (1116–1220), vol. ii (1221–61) (Louvain, 1933–5).

[24] C. R. Cheney, 'Church-building in the Middle Ages', repr. in id., *Medieval Texts and Studies* (Oxford, 1973), 346–63.

[25] WAM 17393: Adam the bishop's nephew, a witness, is recorded in 1212 (*Beauchamp Cartulary Charters*, no. 186 n.); Edward the reeve died *c.*1199 (see app. 1). Many grants were made simply to support lights before the altar; five examples from the first half of the century are WAM 17330, 17375, 17413, 17418, 17438: all witnessed by Odo the goldsmith (for whom see app. 1).

the nearby vill of Eye, 'to refresh the poor on the day of St Mary's Purification [2 Feb.]'.[26] Edric of the garden—probably a servant in the monastery garden—explained in *c.*1220 'that he, having no lawful heirs by his wife, has made the Virgin Mary heiress of all his lands'.[27] Towards 1200 one Ernulf, formerly a baker at the house in King Street of Richard FitzNigel, bishop of London, was buried within the abbey at the (old) altar of St Mary. Later, possibly in the 1230s, Ernulf's widow, Emma, granted to that altar all the land which she and her husband had acquired from Walter, lately Bishop Richard's chamberlain.[28] This reference to the burial within the abbey of a mere baker, albeit of a distinguished household, suggests that there existed close ties of friendship and patronage between the monks and the townspeople in this early period. Numerous other grants made to the abbey in the early thirteenth century leave the same impression.[29]

These urban rents, together with the remaining income, were deployed by the monks to support themselves in their life of religion.[30] The running costs of a great monastery were high. The main fabric of the church required from the sacrist an expenditure of £25 in most years, but at a busy period, as in the 1470s and 1480s, his bill might regularly be double this amount. The major building project of the late Middle Ages, the replacement of the nave of the abbey church, entailed the creation of a separate accounting department, that of the 'new work'. Between 1376 and 1534 the enormous sum of £21,000 was spent on the nave.[31] Within the church, regular expenses were headed by candles: the sacrist and the Lady chapel warden between them invested some £30 every year in this way. Reliquaries and liturgical ornaments were also in

[26] WD, fo. 562ᵛ (1230s): witnessed by Richer de Cruce, not yet styled reeve (see app. I).
[27] WD, fo. 515ᵛ: witnessed by Odo the goldsmith, reeve (for whom see app. I).
[28] WAM 17428: witnessed by Odo the goldsmith and Robert de Crokesle (see app. I); see also WAM 27815 and WD, fo. 547ʳ (a copy). Richard FitzNigel died in 1198; but his Westminster house had passed to William of Ely in 1195–6 (see ch. I, sect. 2). Emma, widow of Ernulf the baker, however, was alive in 1230, when she confirmed a grant of all the land which she and her husband had held in Westminster to Joan, the daughter of Thomas Belet. *Curia Regis Rolls*, xiv. 69. For Emma to make her gift to the abbey, Joan must, presumably, have returned the property to her at a date after 1230.
[29] On relations between the monks and the townspeople see also ch. 8, sect. 2.
[30] The value of their Westminster holdings to the chief of the monastic accounting departments to which they were allocated is summarized in app. IV.
[31] See below, n. 69.

the sacrist's care; pictures for the high altar and the repair of books were for him typical supplementary expenses. [32] All this is to say nothing of the domestic provisions required to sustain the body of fifty or sixty religious.[33] The monks' investment in houses and shops outside their gates was, therefore, primarily a business arrangement, intended above all to ensure the survival of the religious community and its cloistered life of prayer. Yet although the Benedictine discipline of Westminster Abbey was maintained in isolation from the secular world round about, the monastery impinged in many ways upon the lives of its neighbours in the town. While the monks' activities as landlords were to have a major impact on the physical development of Westminster, they also (as later chapters will show) played other parts in the lay community: as employers, patrons, relatives, and friends—and at times as the objects of adverse criticism. Monks and townspeople led separate lives, and were not as a rule on terms of close intimacy. But from observation at close quarters, and from daily interaction, they knew each other well.

The Fourteenth Century: Exploitation

The Turn to Urban Rents

It was not until the fourteenth century that the monks began systematically to let those properties in their direct control at economic rents, on leases for fixed terms of years. Before 1300 they were not yet convinced of the importance of distinguishing between fixed or assized rents and adjustable, economic rents, and between perpetual or lifetime leases and leases for fixed terms of years. Profit, however, dictated the need for these distinctions, which in the abbey were first thoroughly drawn after 1300. Although the monastic economy was in practice subdivided among various administrative departments, half a dozen of which ultimately managed substantial rentals in the town of Westminster,[34] there were no essential differences in the policies pursued throughout the

---

[32] e.g. an entry for 1339–40: 'Item in canevacio pro zonis et pro tabula cum magestate dipicta empto. 3s. 1½d.. Item in cole et coloribus emptis pro dicta tabula renovanda una cum stipendia 2 pictorum. 3s. 4d.' WAM 19621. In 1354–5 the sacrist had a missal made for the high altar at a cost of £11. 3s. WAM 19623.

[33] On the internal life of the monastery see the forthcoming book by Barbara Harvey.

[34] See introd.

Middle Ages by the different monastic obedientiaries.[35] The policy
of the Lady chapel wardens in the thirteenth and fourteenth
centuries with respect to Westminster rents may therefore be taken
as typical of the obedientiaries in general. In the 1260s the rents of
the chapel were valued in total at £24 p.a.; in 1299–1300, the actual
income from rents (almost exclusively in Westminster) amounted
to about £20.[36] Of this latter sum by far the larger part (£17. 8s. 4d.)
was represented by 'rents of assize', whereas 'rents at farm' or
economic rents amounted to relatively little (£2. 7s.). Assized rents
were always extremely difficult to alter, for each successive tenant
could dispose of his holding as he wished and it was rare for the
landlord to obtain vacant possession. In addition the wardens of the
altar, together with the other obedientiaries, were slow to appreciate
the drawbacks to the perpetual lease, prolonging its survival in
many of their own grants of properties bequeathed to them during
the thirteenth century.[37] The variant form of grant for the duration
of a tenant's life, though probably introduced in the thirteenth
century as a deliberately restricted alternative to the perpetual lease,
was in practice of little or no additional benefit to the grantor.[38] The
monks were still making life grants of property in Westminster
around 1300.[39] Their hold on land in the neighbourhood was
therefore at this date still uncertain.

But in the course of the fourteenth century, and most particularly
in the decades after 1360, the monks engaged in thorough
exploitation of their potential as the major landlords of the town of
Westminster. In the case of the warden of the Lady chapel, the next
time after 1300 at which his total annual rents can be compared is in
1363, by which date his assized rents had fallen (to £8. 5s. 8d.) and
had been overtaken by economic rents (now £9 15s. 4d.).[40] Thereafter the gap widened, assized rents remaining more or less stable

[35] Such differences as pertained were the incidental results either of discrepancies
in the precise endowment of the various departments, or of the personal qualities and
interests of individual office-holders.
[36] *Customary*, 93; WAM 23179B.
[37] See WD, *passim*.
[38] A. W. B. Simpson, *A History of the Land Law* (2nd edn., Oxford, 1986), 70–4.
[39] e.g. WAM 17494: dated 1304, a Westminster grant for life from the Lady
chapel; WAM 17501: dated 1306, a similar grant from the sacristy. By 1290 God's
House in Southampton had likewise adopted a policy of making grants for terms of
lives in preference to grants in perpetuity. J. M. Kaye (ed.), *The Cartulary of God's
House Southampton*, Southampton Records Series, xix (1976), vol. i, p. lxiv.
[40] WAM 23183.

while the value of properties at farm increased throughout the late fourteenth century and rose again, after an intervening period of uncertainty, in the second half of the fifteenth century. This pattern is observable also in the accounts of the other obedientiaries holding Westminster properties (see app. IV). Westminster Abbey's new commitment to the exploitation of town rents in the fourteenth century, and especially from 1350 onwards, finds parallels in the management of urban estates by other ecclesiastical institutions in this period. The trend exemplified in Westminster was evidently widespread.[41]

Leases

Coupled with the resolution to establish direct control over property on their fee was a new treatment of leases by the monks. After *c.*1350 grants in perpetuity and leases for terms of lives were altogether abandoned in favour of shorter-term arrangements. Indeed the period *c.*1350–1420 was marked by an overwhelming preference, on the part of the monastic landlords, for lettings at will by the year. This policy, which allowed rent levels to be frequently adjusted upwards, was clearly a reflection of high pressure of market demand for property in this period. From *c.*1410 a slump in demand was in turn indicated by the general adoption by the monastic obedientiaries of leases for terms of twenty or forty years or even longer. [42] This more cautious method of letting guaranteed a safe if unimprovable return over a relatively extended period, and relieved landlords of responsibility for unremunerative repairs, which fell instead upon tenants. This changing pattern of the abbey's urban leases between the mid-fourteenth and the mid-fifteenth centuries followed a course very similar to that of both monastic and private landlords in the city of Winchester during the same period.[43] The Westminster pattern appears therefore to be of more than local significance.

It might be anticipated that the stabilization and even reduction of rent levels which occurred in the fifteenth century would be offset by the introduction and subsequent increase of entry fines. In

---

[41] e.g. the estate of St John's Hospital, Winchester: Keene, *Medieval Winchester*, i. 203–4, 243–8; the estate of the vicars choral of York Minster: *The Victoria History of Yorkshire: The City of York* (London, 1961), 85; and for the latter also S. Rees-Jones, Ph.D. thesis, Univ. of York, forthcoming.
[42] See below in this section.　　　　[43] Keene, *Medieval Winchester*, i. 192.

not a single instance before the mid-sixteenth century, however, is
there clear evidence that an entry fine was levied upon the recipient
of an abbey lease in Westminster. The same observation has been
made of leases in Winchester before *c*.1550.[44] Rent, therefore, was
the Westminster monks' sole source of income from their town
properties before the Dissolution. It is notable, however, that long
leases continued largely to be preferred by the religious landlords
throughout the period *c*.1410–1540, notwithstanding other signs
that the local property market began to recover from *c*.1470.[45] After
the latter date, the abbey's tenants were subletting at a handsome
profit, and institutional rents are therefore in this case an unreliable
index of the market value of urban property during the seventy
years before the Dissolution. In the late fourteenth and early
fifteenth centuries, on the other hand, the initial development by
the abbey of 'new rents' and the overall increase of rent charges, and
the subsequent reductions which accompanied the general blight of
vacancies after *c*.1410, were short-term adjustments of a kind which
clearly does provide an accurate measure of the level of demand for
property.

Signs of Decay, c.1300–c.1350

A poverty of documentation in the first half of the fourteenth
century makes it difficult to gauge the extent to which the monks
had begun to assert their role as landlords before 1350. Such rentals
as survive from the decades before the mid-century, however,
suggest that the local property market was then less active than it
had been in the thirteenth century, and therefore that the incentive
for landlords to adopt a vigorous policy was concomitantly reduced.
By the early fourteenth century the assized rents in Westminster
owned by the abbey almoners were worth in theory about 25*s*. p.a.
But the extant almoners' accounts for 1317, 1319–20, 1321–2,
1340–1, and the plague year of 1349 all record numerous 'rents
lacking' in the town.[46] In a few cases the default is explained in the
documents by reference to the disappearance of 'tenements' or
buildings.[47] In 1317, for example, Richard de Nottele's former

[44] Ibid. i. 197, 237.   [45] See below, sect. 4.
[46] WAM 18964, 18965*, 18966, 18977, 18980.
[47] The term *tenementum*, although possibly ambiguous in thirteenth-century
contexts, after *c*.1300 seems to have been used in Westminster, as elsewhere, almost
exclusively to denote a built-up site. Cf. Keene, *Medieval Winchester*, i. 137–8.

tenementum in Long Ditch had become a *vacua placea*; the same fate was reported in 1340–1 of the sometime *tenementum* of Martin de Laleham, and of four or five more former tenements in Westminster.[48] The Westminster rental of the monastic sacrist was similarly shot through with gaps at this period. The earliest sacrist's rental, of February–Michaelmas 1340, lists a small handful of Westminster properties, whose notional annual value was at this time just £3.[49] But in 1340 the sacrist was experiencing difficulty in finding tenants for these properties. A shop at Enedehithe was rented, for the three quarters recorded in the account, for 1s. 6d., but 'the rest of the cottages there' yielded nothing, for they stood unlet and empty. Matilda Godhyve paid for her house next to the Clowson bridge, for two quarters, 2s., but no more because the house was decayed (*in decasu*).[50] These fragmentary references show that, at least in certain parts of the town, by the second quarter of the fourteenth century the demand for property had declined from a putative level at which nearly all rents were occupied. In the absence of earlier rentals, the date at which these gaps began to appear in the occupied area of the town cannot be fixed precisely. In view, however, of the intensive property exchanges and development recorded during much or all of the thirteenth century,[51] the change must have occurred towards or shortly after 1300.[52]

The Consolidation of Control

By 1400, however, the six obedientiaries with substantial Westminster holdings were together enjoying from this source an annual revenue in the region of £250.[53] This dramatic realization of the increased value of urban rents had been effected—chiefly, if not entirely, during the period after 1350—by a threefold policy. First, the monks seized opportunities to press their claims over properties previously held from them at uneconomic assized rents; second, they purchased outright extensive properties in the town over which they had no effective previous claim; and third, they built

---

[48] WAM 18964, 18977.
[49] WAM 19621.
[50] Ibid.
[51] See above in this sect., and ch. 1, sect. 2.
[52] See further ch. 6, sect. 1.
[53] In app. IV, nb that in all cases the years around 1400 marked a peak within the period 1375–1425. For the domestic treasurer, see WAM 18532: rental of 1399–1400.

new houses and shops as speculative developments. The incentive behind this policy of new investment must lie in a demographic recovery at the local level since the losses indicated in the early part of the fourteenth century, and despite the depredations of the plague.

The acquisition by the abbey of a site at Enedehithe provides an example of the first of these procedures, and illustrates at the same time the attendant difficulties which could arise. The site in question, on the north side of the lane (later Endive Lane) which ran between King Street and the Thames, was large, measuring some 220 feet wide along King Street by 300 feet in length to the river bank.[54] The *terra de Anedeheða* had been granted away from the abbey by Abbot Gervase in the mid-twelfth century.[55] By the thirteenth century an assized rent of 10*d*. here, at 'Enedehuthe', had been assigned to the cellarer.[56] In *c.*1355 Sir Robert de la Warde died seised of 'certain tenements at Henedehuthe in the vill of Westminster', consisting of a messuage and garden held of the abbey at an assized rent of 5*s*. 2*d*. p.a.[57] Sir Robert left only female heiresses (a widow and two daughters), and the monks' prompt demand that his house should revert to themselves was upheld in the royal courts in 1357.[58] The case, however, did not rest there. The widow, Ida, took a second husband, Hugh de Nevyle; and although Ida herself died in 1361, ten years later one Margaret de Nevyle was described as 'kinswoman and one of the heirs of Sir Robert de la Warde'.[59] The Nevyles evidently claimed the house in Westminster as the putative heirs of the de la Warde estate; for not until 1361 were the monks able to secure, by issue of a writ *cessavit*, the property now described as 'two plats at Enedehuth, formerly of Sir John de Nevyle'.[60] At last, in *c.*1371, the cellarer, to whom the holding was allotted (no doubt on account of the assized rent here to which he had been entitled since the thirteenth century or earlier), was able to grant to Adam le Vynour a forty-year lease, at 10*s*. p.a., on this 'tenement at Hendeth'.[61]

---

[54] The site is defined by WAM 17964, 17889; Reg Bk, i, fos. 117^v–118^v.
[55] WAM 17311. See also ch. 1, sect. 2.
[56] WD, fo. 347^r.
[57] PRO, C133/126/9.
[58] LN, fo. 117^r.
[59] *Cal Inq p m* xi, p. 145; ibid. xiii, p. 70.
[60] WAM 18844–5.
[61] WAM 18856–84.

New Purchases of Urban Property

The problems attendant upon the recovery of the land at Enedehithe explain why the extension of the monks' possessions on their fee of Westminster in the fourteenth century was more commonly effected by cash purchase.[62] The readiness of the monks to invest heavily in fresh acquisitions of property at this period is evinced above all in the endowment of the two administrative departments which were newly created within the abbey in the middle and late fourteenth century, respectively: those of the 'new work' and of the domestic treasurer. The former, first established in c.1335, was responsible from 1376 for the major work of rebuilding the abbey nave, an undertaking which remained incomplete at the Dissolution; the latter was founded to administer a group of chantries within the abbey. The major endowment of the new work was acquired in 1365.[63] In that year the treasurer of the monastery purchased from the widow of Robert Longdon a collection of lands and tenements in the vill of Westminster. The widow received a dower payment of 100 marks ($£66. 13s. 4d.$).[64] In addition, the convent contracted to pay her an annuity during her life of $£10$.[65] This pension was still being paid in 1378, by which time the bill for the Westminster property had amounted to about $£200$.[66] In 1375 the treasurer parted with the further sum of $£36. 13s. 4d.$, together with one of the Longdon rents, to acquire another tenement in the town.[67] From c.1379 these Westminster rents[68] annually swelled the

---

[62] The restrictions of the Statute of Mortmain of 1279 meant that it was best for religious, if they made purchases, to buy property belonging to their own fee; for here secular interests were least likely to be offended. See S. Raban, *Mortmain Legislation and the English Church, 1279–1500* (Cambridge, 1982).

[63] See R. B. Rackham, 'The Nave of Westminster', *Proceedings of the British Academy*, iv (1909), 36.

[64] WAM 19860; LN, fo. 145 (copy of the relevant extract from the treasurer's account).

[65] WAM 22937.

[66] From 1374 the pension was in fact paid not to Longdon's widow but to Master John Doly, who was presumably her trustee. WAM 19634–5, 19637.

[67] LN, fo. 145^r (extract from treasurer's account).

[68] The properties were allocated initially to the sacrist, in whose extant account rolls they appear between 1372 and 1378. Their absence from the sacrist's account for 1379–80, however, suggests that they had been transferred in that or the previous year to the new work, where they are found recorded in 1387, when the *novum opus* rolls resume their sequence after a long gap of twenty-two years. WAM 19633–9; 23460.

revenue of the new work by between £25 and £30; this was usually about a quarter of the total income. Between 1376 and 1534 approximately one-fifth of the total bill for the new nave of £21,000 was raised from the urban rents in Westminster allocated to the work.[69]

The endowment of the domestic treasury with Westminster rents was occasioned by one of the more dramatic episodes in the long history of uneasy relations between the monks of Westminster and their royal patrons and neighbours. King Edward III's love of magnificent display necessitated the provision of more storage room at his private palace in Westminster for the plate and jewels in use there. But being already cramped for space, and loth to sacrifice his garden, the king directed his master mason, Henry Yevele, to erect a tower for the purpose at the south-west corner of the palace, where its site encroached upon part of the adjacent precinct of the abbey. The construction of the Jewel Tower and its surrounding moat, which was completed in the years 1365–6, was observed by the monks with understandable indignation. Their sense of outrage is recorded in a gleeful account in the fifteenth-century compendium known as the *Liber Niger* of how the then keeper of the privy palace, William Usshebourne, who had added insult to injury by making a fish tank in the tower moat, invited some neighbours to dinner, but himself greedily devouring a large pike from this moat, promptly choked and, falling into a delirium, died without the last rites.[70] About ten years after this incursion, Abbot Litlington rebuilt the broken stretch of the precinct wall, 40 feet to the west of its former alignment; good fences make good neighbours.[71] Meanwhile, the monks demanded compensation for the loss of their land. In 1372,

[69] See app. IV; and Rackham, 'The Nave of Westminster', 89.

[70] 'Quasi in amentia versus cepit clamare sic dicens: Ecce venit ecce venit ille qui me vult suffocare. Et sic miserrime sepius exclamans miserabile expiravit.' LN, fo. 80ᵛ. On the Jewel tower see *King's Works*, i. 535–6; A. J. Taylor, *The Jewel Tower, Westminster* (2nd edn., HMSO, London, 1965).

[71] See Green, *et al.*, 'Excavations of the Palace Defences and Abbey Precinct Wall at Abingdon Street, Westminster, 1963', *Journal of the British Archaeological Association*, cxxix (1976), 59–76. The evidence of this report suggests that a dividing wall already existed in Henry III's reign. This qualifies an older view that 'a definite division was not made until the fourteenth century'. For the latter see M. B. Honeybourne, 'The Sanctuary Boundaries and Environs of Westminster Abbey and the College of St. Martin-le-Grand', *Journal of the British Archaeological Association*, xxxviii (1932–3), 316–17 and refs. A fence of some kind certainly stood by 1356, when palace servants broke through a postern gate into the monastic infirmary garden. Westlake, *Westminster Abbey*, 335–6.

six years after the tower was finished, this was granted in the form of a licence to purchase, notwithstanding the Statute of Mortmain (but of course at the abbey's own cost), property to the annual value of £40.[72] Yet it was not until 3 August 1392 that this licence was used in large part to acquire eleven messuages, two tofts, twelve shops, six acres of land, and one acre of meadow in Westminster; three messuages, thirteen shops, and ten acres of land in Eye, Knightsbridge, and Westminster; and certain, relatively less-substantial property elsewhere in Middlesex, Kent, Hertfordshire, and Surrey.[73] The lands, buildings, and rents in Westminster thus amortized to the prior and convent were known collectively as 'the rents of the new purchase'. The department set up to manage these properties was the domestic treasury.

The grantors of the Westminster property to the abbey in 1392 were themselves agents of the monks: Saer Bunde, chaplain, Thomas Aston, and John Thurstan. These individuals, with another named John Kymbell, had in fact been holding the lands and tenements in question, on the abbey's behalf, for varying periods of up to sixteen years before the date of amortization.[74] The employment of secular feoffees was common practice by religious houses in this period, being a simple circumvention of the 1279 Statute of Mortmain.[75] Their position of trust required that such nominees be closely connected with the abbey: Thomas Aston was an official of the cellar, and Saer Bunde an abbey sergeant, while John Thurstan appears as another valet of the monastery, who was later to be seneschal to the abbot.[76] John Kymbell, meanwhile, was a tailor whose wife, Alice, made copes and other things for the monks' vestry.[77] All of the purchases made by Aston, Thurstan, Kymbell, and Bunde can be specified and dated, and it is noticeable that the grantors in most of these transactions had themselves only recently been enfeoffed of the properties concerned. A tenement on the west side of King Street acquired in 1380 by Aston, Thurstan, and

[72] *Cal Pat R 1370–4*, p. 193.

[73] Ibid., p. 133; LN, fo. 87ᵛ. This same licence had been used in part in 1380 to acquire lands, valued at £5 p.a., in Battersea, Wandsworth, and Heyford. *Cal Pat R 1377–81*, pp. 534–5.

[74] The annual accounts which they drew up in the period 1381–91 are WAM 24263–5; 18519–24.

[75] The employment of this strategy by the Westminster monks has been discussed in Harvey, *Estates*, 183 ff. See also Raban, *Mortmain Legislation*, 114 ff.

[76] Harvey, *Estates*, 184; WAM 19876–925.

[77] See app. VIII, s.n.

Bunde from John Kymbell himself and William Kempston, chaplain, had recently been in the occupation of Richard Rooke, senior.[78] A similar history of ownership is recorded of a row of tenements under the sanctuary wall at the bottom of Long Ditch, held in 1369 by Richard Rooke, senior, which subsequently passed through various hands before coming to Kempston and Kymbell. The latter in turn granted them in 1390 to Thomas Aston, Simon Barton, chaplain, John Thurstan, and Richard Gatyn.[79] The same Richard Rooke had been seised in 1359 of a croft on the west side of King Street which Ralph Archer, stainer of Westminster, granted to Aston, Thurstan, and Bunde in 1381.[80] Richard Rooke, junior, apparently a younger brother of the first, in 1351 held another tenement which was eventually, in 1387, secured by Aston, Thurstan, Kymbell, Kempston, and Barton.[81] The Rookes, indeed, were ubiquitous; and they frequently acted as nominal purchasers, both in Westminster and beyond, for the abbey.[82] The property market in Westminster was clearly very active in this period, and provided scope for a few buyers to amass sizeable holdings. Prominent among these investors, thinly disguised under the cloak of nominees, were the Westminster monks.

The complete portfolio of Westminster property accumulated by the abbey's domestic treasurer was extensive. The bulk of the total was comprised in the purchases amortized in 1392.[83] Among the

[78] LN, fo. 132[r–v].

[79] LN, fos. 132[v]–133[r].

[80] LN, fos. 115[v]–116[r].

[81] LN, fos. 111[v]–112[r].

[82] See app. VIII, s.n. Other parties named in these transactions may also have been acting in collaboration with the abbey. William Kempston, chaplain, noted above, was in 1370–90 the parish priest of St Margaret's church in Westminster, the rectory of which was vested in the abbey (see app. II). Alexander Wynkebourne, who had held two tenements in Westminster acquired for the domestic treasury, acted as bailiff and in other offices on the abbey's Worcestershire estates. WAM 18519, 21043–5, 21059–60, 21084–5, 21291.

[83] The list of these was as follows: Steynour's Toft, bought from Ralph Archer, stainer of Westminster, in 1376: LN, fo. 116[r–v]; Steynour's Croft, bought from the same in 1381: LN, fos. 115[v]–116[r]; 'Richard Rooke's tenement', bought in 1380: LN, fo. 132[r–v]; 'Prattestenements' in King Street, bought from Thomas Holte of London in 1381: LN, fos. 112[v]–115[v]; John Weston's King Street inn afterwards known as the Boar's Head, bought in 1384: LN, fos. 130[v]–131[r]; two tenements bought from Alexander Wynkebourne, one adjacent to 'Prattestenements', the other at the east end of Tothill Street, on the north side, prior to 1385: see WAM 18519; extensive premises at the Clowson bridge, on the east side of King Street, which Thomas Gynes sold in 1385: PRO, CP25(1)/151/78/78; two adjacent tenements on the west side of King Street, one of which was later called the Wool Sack bakery, acquired in

remainder, a King Street tenement which subsequently became the Swan inn was, like the first group, acquired in 1386 by the abbey's buyers.[84] But in June 1391 the latter passed it, not directly to the convent, but to King Richard.[85] Whether or not this was a device to avoid the inclusion of the property in the tally of permitted purchases, the king was thereby enabled to make a practical donation to his beloved abbey, for in the following month he gave this tenement to the monastery.[86] The monks continued to extend their holdings in Westminster into the fifteenth century, when all new acquisitions were allocated to the domestic treasury. The Bell inn, situated in Tothill Street outside the abbey's western gate, was bought by the abbey in 1416–17.[87] The purchase of two tenements next to the Swan inn in *c.*1421 was, however, one of the latest recorded instances of this amassing of urban property.[88] This catalogue reveals that the monks had begun as early as the middle of

1387 from John Orewell: LN, fos. 111ᵛ–112ʳ; and a small row of tenements at the south end of Long Ditch, formerly of William Kempston, purchased in 1390: LN, fos. 132ᵛ–133ᵛ. The amortization of all of these in 1392 was precipitated by the tightening up of legislation on mortmain in that year. Raban, *Mortmain Legislation*, 127–9.

[84] WAM 17710. For the earlier descent of this property from 1306, see WAM 17499, 17602–3, 17609, 17670, 17707–8.
[85] WAM 17713. See *Cal Pat R 1388–92*, p. 459.
[86] *Cal Ch R 1341–1417*, p. 326. The endowment of the domestic treasury was further supplemented by the rents and produce of an estate in Westminster called Mauduitsgarden, which had been repossessed by the monks in 1344. For the name of this garden, see ch. 1, sect. 2.
[87] See the conventual treasurer's account for 1416–17: 'Sol' Roberto Axey et Ade Barbour pro 1 tenemento in Totehullestret nuper Johanne (*sic*) Walden perquisito ad usum ecclesie. £8. 6s. 8d.' WAM 19910. The Bell was described on its first appearance in the domestic treasurer's rental in 1418–19 as 'newly acquired'. WAM 18562. It was then said to have belonged to John Walden; the abbey employed a bailiff of this name at Pyrford, Surrey, 1406–7. WAM 27435.
[88] The legal expenses recorded in the account for 1421–2 relate to this purchase, for which see further below; the tenements first occur in the rental in 1423–4. WAM 18566, 18568. WAM 17729, 17732 are deeds of 1416 and 1417 respecting the same tenements, which had belonged to Reginald Denyas (for whom see app. VIII, s.n.). One other small estate in Westminter, which came under the aegis of the domestic treasurer from the 1430s, was a row of tenements built before 1419 within the monastic precinct, the revenues from which supported the anniversary in the abbey of John de Waltham (d. 1395), late bishop of Salisbury and Richard II's treasurer. The tenements were presumably paid for out of the endowment of the anniversary, founded in 1412, which included a cash sum of £333. 6s. 8d. WAM 5262A; Harvey, *Estates*, 380 and n., 397 (no. 57) and n. The annual accounts of the wardens of these tenements (which were known as the 'Sarum rents') 1419–44 are WAM 24622–49; after 1444 the accounts were sewn together with those of the domestic treasurer.

the fourteenth century to build up a major holding in the town, and that they continued to pursue this policy into the third decade of the fifteenth century, when a halt was called.[89]

It is not easy to put a precise figure on the financial investment by the abbey represented by these purchases. The ramifications of the transactions, however, underline the value set upon them by the monks. The licensing process under the Statute of Mortmain carried incidental costs, notably the sum of £5. 13s. 8d. spent by the conventual treasurers when the newly acquired Westminster properties were amortized in 1392, in order to gain the sympathy of the king's escheator and a bevy of attendant clerks.[90] Such gratuities doubtless helped to keep valuations within the limits set by the licence. The records of actual sums paid for property are consequently, in their turn, liable to be misleading. The figure named in a fine as the official price is indeed usually too well rounded to be credible.[91] A probable example of this is the £20 supposedly given in November 1387 to John Orewell, sergeant-at-arms to the king, and his wife by the abbey's representatives for two messuages on the west side of King Street in Westminster.[92] But even if roughly accurate so far as it goes, the official sum is never a full tally of the expense incurred. In this case, the feoffees' accounts record miscellaneous fees totalling 9s. 4d. paid to the clerks and other officials of the court of common pleas when the fine was levied.[93] Nor, in the Middle Ages, did a business transaction terminate at the door of Westminster Hall. The occasion was marked in more jovial fashion, first by drinks all round, which cost 9d., and then by a dinner for Orewell and his wife, the bill for which came to 9s. 3d.[94] Similarly, wine, beer, and nuts were served to celebrate the transfer of seisin of William Kempston's tenements in Long Ditch in 1390.[95] In that instance, however, expenses did not stop at refreshments. Kempston's former servant, not content with

[89] For the domestic treasurer's management of his accumulated holdings see the annual accounts: WAM 24263–5; 18519–93; 23074–178.

[90] WAM 19876; and see Harvey, *Estates*, 179.

[91] Cf. *Calendar of Kent Feet of Fines to the end of Henry III's reign*, Kent Archaeological Society, Records Branch (1956), introd. (by F. W. Jessup), p. lxxxvii.

[92] PRO, CP25(1)/151/78/90; LN, fos. 111ᵛ–112ʳ. For Orewell see *Cal Pat R 1381–5, apud indicem.*

[93] WAM 18521.

[94] The totals are enrolled on WAM 18521; the meal bill itself is still attached.

[95] WAM 18523.

the concession that he should retain his house in the row for three years after his master's death, on the expiry of the term in 1392, grumbled sufficiently about his eviction to win an extra £4 in satisfaction.[96] Compensation also took the form of the provision of free alternative accommodation for the vendor. In 1384 a local barber named John Weston sold to the abbey's trustees a hostelry in King Street (later known as the Boar's Head) which he had acquired eight years before.[97] By 1391 at the latest, Weston and his wife had been comfortably rehoused in a tenement on the corner of King Street towards the palace gate. Until Weston's death in 1403 and for six years thereafter, the high annual rent of £4 for this tenement was paid to the landlord (who happened to be the abbey's warden of the new work) by the domestic treasurer on the occupants' behalf.[98] A similar allowance was granted to Thomas Gynes of Westminster and his wife, Matilda, who in 1385 sold to the same concern a large property between King Street and the Thames, at the Clowson bridge.[99] Thomas Gynes was already linked with the abbey, for he was heir to a sergeanty in the kitchen there.[100] After the sale, the couple were assigned two cottages of their former premises, rent-free, for their lifetimes, during which they were also, as corrodians, provided with firewood every winter to the value of 10s. 8d. In addition, they received robes each year between 1387 and 1411 as valets of the monastery. The monks looked after Gynes in his last sickness, and saw to his burial in 1412. His widow survived him by only a few months, having moved to another cottage provided for her by the domestic treasurer. Moreover, one Alice Cookes, who lived with the other two and held a hereditary claim to their property, was accommodated at no charge in a nearby shop, and received until her death in 1392 an annual pension of 26s. 8d.[101]

Despite such precautions as these, there always remained the danger that disgruntled parties might take their grievances to law. Like the expenses already noted, contentious litigation, which

[96] WAM 18524–5.
[97] LN, fo. 131^{r-v}; PRO, CP25(1)/151/77/72. According to the fine, the consideration was £20.
[98] WAM 18525–44.
[99] PRO, CP25(1)/151/78/78. The notional price was 100 marks.
[100] WD, fo. 94^{r-v}; WAM 5886*, 5906, 19875–900. A Thomas Gynes was employed by the domestic treasurer in 1397–8 and in 1399–1400 on repairs to the roofs and walling of certain houses in Westminster. WAM 18530, 18532.
[101] WAM 19875–900, 18519–50.

could be costly and could erupt long after the initial transaction, must be reckoned as a regular part of the cost of investment in urban property. In 1381 the abbey's commissioners acquired from Thomas Holte of London various premises in King Street known collectively as 'Prattestenements'.[102] Yet legal wrangles with Holte and his wife in connection with this property extended over the next dozen years.[103] The domestic treasurer had also to contend with fraudulent claimants to property. Such a one was William Tamond, a London girdler with a variety of criminal tendencies, who in 1401 fabricated deeds purporting to demonstrate his right to the King Street tenement which King Richard II had given to the abbey just ten years earlier. The Swan inn, with its royal associations, was surely a bad choice of target for such trickery; in any case the monks, with their more than adequate legal resources, made short work of Tamond's amateur forgeries.[104] But deceits of this nature may have been encouraged by the busy, and at times no doubt confused, state of the market in this period. The legal costs of the domestic treasury soared in the early fifteenth century, when the abbey's right to add to, and indeed to retain, its Westminster rents was repeatedly challenged. The monks are not known to have held a licence to purchase in mortmain the Bell inn in Tothill Street and two tenements beside the Swan in King Street, acquired *c.*1417 and *c.*1421, respectively. The frequent entertainments provided for the Middlesex escheator in connection with these properties in the 1420s and 1430s suggest that it was becoming increasingly hard for the monastery to invest in this way.[105] Expenses in court in 1421–2

---

[102] PRO, CP25(1)/151/76/36. The stated payment was 100 marks. See also LN, fos. 112ᵛ–115ᵛ, 87ᵛ.

[103] WAM 24264, 18527.

[104] WAM 17724–5; *Cal Cl R 1399–1402*, pp. 343, 539–40. Tamond at the same time submitted an equally spurious claim to freehold land in Westminster near the inn of the archbishops of York. WAM 17625 is a confected deed of his concerning this land, which has been endorsed by the monks with an indignant list of proofs of its falsehood. These include patent contradictions in the measurements and abutments, as well as the *mala et incongrua orthographia*; all the criticisms are demonstrably just. See WAM 17727–8. In Oct. 1402 'William Tamond de London, girdler', was said to have insulted a panel of Westminster jurors (including William Sudbury and Thomas Perne, for whom see app. VIII, s.n.) in Westminster Hall, saying 'quod omnes juratores sic impanellati sunt falsi et maledicti latrones'. PRO, KB9/178/43. In the same year, Tamond found himself in Maidstone gaol, following an assult on a traveller on the Rochester to Gravesend Road. In the summer of 1403, in London, he was bound over for threatening behaviour. *Cal Cl R 1402–5*, pp. 26–7, 181.

[105] WAM 18573–80.

concerning the tenements at the Swan amounted to over £28.[106] In 1435–6 the Bell was actually forfeited for a time into the hands of the king's escheator, and the price of its recovery was almost £15.[107] The worst blow, however, fell in the following year, 1437. The escheator then seized in the king's name most of the properties which had been bought in the 1380s and 1390s, on the suspicion that they had been acquired without licence. The abbot, by his representative in chancery, John Bate, was able to vindicate the monastery's rights, but not without cost; in the years 1436–8 the domestic treasurer recorded disbursements in retainers, 'recreations', and *douceurs* paid to lawyers and their clerks totalling £59. 2s. 8½d.[108] The scarcity of licences has sometimes been interpreted to mean that controls on alienations in mortmain were light in this period; but this was not the experience of the monks of Westminster.[109]

All things considered, the abbey's investment in urban property in the late fourteenth and into the early fifteenth centuries was a laborious and expensive process. By the 1430s, at the end of the period of expansion, the accumulated Westminster rental of the domestic treasurer was worth about £40 gross p.a.[110] This was a respectable, if not a spectacular, sum to set against so high a cost of endowment. The justification for the policy of investment was the intense pressure of a growing population upon housing, in the period *c*.1360 to *c*.1410.

New Building Developments

Their rights to properties in Westminster once established, the monks were free to exploit their holdings as creative landlords, actively developing the urban landscape. The period in which they did this most effectively was that of the late fourteenth and very early fifteenth centuries. At this time the abbey enjoyed a degree of overall prosperity greater than at any other time after *c*.1270. Much of the standing remains of the abbey complex itself bears witness to the wealth of the monks in these decades. Abbots Simon Langham

---

[106] WAM 18566.
[107] WAM 18585.
[108] WAM 18586–8; see WAM 17729*. The hearing of the case is recorded in PRO, C44 (pleas in chancery)/27/20.
[109] Raban, *Mortmain Legislation*, 180–1.
[110] WAM 18584. The total in 1381–2, the year of the first extant full annual account, was about £10. WAM 24263.

(1349–62) and Nicholas Litlington (1362–86) presided over a prodigious amount of building work within the abbey. In 1376 the rebuilding of the monastery church was resumed after a prolonged interruption.[111] Shortly before this date the great free-standing belfry in the north part of the sanctuary had been reconstructed,[112] while between 1366 and 1377 the gate leading from the sanctuary into Tothill Street had also been rebuilt.[113] In 1382–3 new offices were erected for the monastic sacrist,[114] and the 1380s in addition saw the erection of a new cellarer's range, at a cost of almost £500.[115] By 1394 an even larger sum of almost £800 had been spent over ten years on a new malthouse brewery.[116] This extensive building programme within the convent proceeded alongside equally impressive construction work in the neighbouring town.

Each department within the monastery with Westminster holdings pursued the same broad policy of development in this period. Not all the obedientiaries, however, commanded equivalent financial resources to fund development. Therefore to enable a small department, such as that of the Lady chapel, to profit from the work, support might be provided from elsewhere within the convent. In 1395 the sacrist, Peter Coumbe, took from the warden of the Lady chapel a twenty-four-year lease on a piece of empty ground near Charing Cross, between St Catherine's hermitage and the hospital of St Mary Rounceval. The site, which measured about

[111] WAM 23452 *et seq.*; Rackham, 'The Nave of Westminster'.
[112] WAM 19626–8. Its predecessor had been completed in 1253. See *Cal Cl R 1247–51*, p. 409; ibid. *1251–3*, p. 280. The late-fourteenth-century belfry was pulled down in 1750, at which date the antiquary William Stukeley drew it and confusingly mis-identified it as 'the sanctuary'. W. Stukeley, 'The Sanctuary at Westminster', *Archaeologia*, i (1770), 39–44 (Stukeley's original sketch is in the Archive Department of the Westminster Public Libraries: Plans and Drawings, box 50, no. 22). The massive timber foundations were excavated when the Middlesex Guildhall was built early in the present century. See P. Norman, 'Recent Discoveries of Medieval Remains in London', *Archaeologia*, 2nd ser., xvii (1916), 14–18. The Queen Elizabeth II Conference Centre now stands on the site.
[113] At a cost of over £320. WAM 18850–60; and see LN, fo. 79ᵛ. The relevant accounts (those of the cellarer) for 1368–70 are lost. The gatehouse incorporated the abbot's prison in the upper storey. This was broken into by rioters who freed the prisoners in June 1381.
[114] WAM 19640. The cost was nearly £70.
[115] WAM 19875; LN, fos. 145ᵛ–146ʳ. This part of the monastic buildings remains partially intact, incorporated within Westminster School, on the east side of Dean's Yard. Royal Commission on Historical Monuments, *London*, vol. i (London, 1924), 89–90 and pl. 174.
[116] WAM 19876–9.

fifty yards long beside the street, had been let in 1388 as 'one toft' at 4*s.* p.a., and in 1392, at the impoverished rate of 12*d.* p.a., as 'a vacant corner plot'.[117] The sacrist's yearly rent was 2*s.* In the first year he built there a row of ten shops, which he leased, some at 4*s.*, others at 6*s.* 8*d.* p.a.[118] The sacrist's rolls do not record the costs of construction, but it may be guessed that by 1416, when, shortly before the termination of the lease, the shops were relinquished to the chapel warden, the sacrist had been able to recoup his expenses. The warden proceeded to let eight of the shops at 5*s.* each, and the remaining two at 6*s.* 8*d.* each p.a.[119] As a finishing touch, the warden himself paid a few shillings in 1417 for the addition to each shop of a pentice; this must have been in effect a permanent, continuous awning along the street frontage.[120]

The most remarkable feature of this programme of domestic building by the monastic landlords was its penetration of the very sanctuary of the convent itself. Although periodic trading is likely to have preceded the holding of St Edward's fair within the abbey precinct,[121] permanent secular buildings are not known to have existed there before the late thirteenth century. St Margaret's church, possibly first built in the late eleventh century, stood until this time in isolation, as it does today. But with the advent of the annual fair of St Edward there began the commercial development of the monastic precinct which, in the following centuries, was to populate the sacred ground with bakers and butchers, bureaucrats and tavern-keepers, to the great profit of the religious. Most of the northern part of the sanctuary was under the aegis of the sacrist, whose office stood in the angle between the north transept and the

[117] WAM 23188 *et seq.* Reg Bk, ii, fo. 151[r–v], a later lease, gives the measurement.
[118] WAM 19659–60. The new row appears to have been ultimately paid for by the gift of one of the monks. At an unspecified date, Brother John Feryng gave to Brother Peter Coumbe 10 marks, with which to maintain a lamp at the tomb of Abbot Simon Langham. 'With this money (Coumbe) had the new rent opposite Charing Cross made, which is worth 50*s.*', LN, fo. 92[v].
[119] WAM 23210 *et seq.*
[120] WAM 23211. For new rows of shops built by wardens of the Lady chapel, respectively at Charing in 1388–9 and at Tothill in 1392–3, see WAM 23188, 23192–3. Unfortunately, four of the shops at Charing were occupied in the 1390s by servants of the duke of Lancaster, who afterwards decamped without paying the rent, taking the keys with them. WAM 23190. In the 1350s and 1360s, Lancaster had similarly appropriated three tenements in the Strand, opposite his inn of the Savoy, to the abbey cellarer's loss of 9*s.* 8*d.* p.a. WAM 18840–5. Among those who burned the Savoy on 13 June 1381 were perhaps evicted neighbours.
[121] See ch. 4.

first five bays west of the crossing of the abbey church.[122] It was the sacrist, therefore, who reaped the bulk of profits from the development of this area. The first recorded secular encroachments were 'fair houses' put up in the late thirteenth century to accommodate traders at the international fair.[123] But it was not until the late fourteenth century, after the decline of the October fair, that the sanctuary became almost entirely built up with permanent domestic housing and premises for local trade.[124] By 1400 the houses in the sanctuary, both 'large' and 'small' (but otherwise undifferentiated in the rental), were worth upwards of £80 a year in rents.[125]

Because the rentals of the sacristy do not begin to give a detailed breakdown of individual properties in the sanctuary before the 1420s, and because leases giving descriptions of these same properties are rare before *c.*1450, it is not possible to document with precision the entire progress of building in the second half of the fourteenth century. Nevertheless, the available indications are suggestive. The earliest references occur under the year 1354–5: 'The full cost of making the house next to St Margaret's church: £20.'; and in the same year a shop was erected at the King Street gate of the precinct.[126] A damaged account of slightly later date records one payment to carpenters 'for making six shops in the north part of the cemetery of the church', adding by way of justification that the shops had been let for the coming year for £6.[127] Shops were constructed by the northern gate of the precinct in 1364–5, in 1371 and in 1374–5; and four more shops appeared 'in the cemetery' in 1377–8.[128] In 1392–3, when Peter Coumbe was sacrist, 'new buildings', both inside and outside the sanctuary,

---

[122] Westlake, *Westminster Abbey*, 314; *King's Works*, i. 144.

[123] See ch. 4, sect. 1. It was probably in connection with the 'fair houses' that the abbot and convent were, in 1293–4, charged with having made unlicensed purprestures upon public ground within the sanctuary. PRO, JUST 1/544, m.65.

[124] See also ch. 5, sect. 8.

[125] WAM 19659 (1399–1400). The figure in 1407–8 was *c.*£98. WAM 19660.

[126] WAM 19623. The former entry was actually disallowed by the auditors of the account, *quia sine consenu conventus*. The criticism was, however, probably levelled at the sacrist's method of accounting rather than at his investment in building work.

[127] WAM 19628* (fragment). That this is a sacrist's roll is clear from the expenditure upon houses within the precinct and at 'Almayne' in King Street, where the sacrist also owned property. At 'Almayne', this account records the making of four new shops out of one in ruins at a cost of 26*s.* 8*d.*; a distinct row of four shops was also put up at 'Almayne' in 1385–6. WAM 19643 (and *dors*).

[128] WAM 19630 (and *dors*), 19631–2, 19635, 19637 (and *dors*).

pushed the *custos domorum* account up to £78. 2s. 6d.[129] Not all of the new construction undertaken at this time was the work of the monks.[130] But the weight of the evidence strongly suggests that the leading role in the new development of the period was taken by the religious.[131]

Meanwhile the almoners of the monastery had also realized that their greatest potential asset lay literally at their feet, in the almonry site itself, at the western end of the abbey complex (Fig. 5). During the second half of the fourteenth century, successive almoners erected rows of shops along the north side of the almonry, until by 1400 the entire Tothill Street frontage, hitherto undeveloped, was built up. 'The march of laths and plaster', as it must have appeared to contemporaries, progressed chiefly westwards from the abbey. First to appear were three shops outside the sanctuary west gate, let in 1359–60 for 21s. p.a. in all. They had not been there in 1357, and must therefore have been built in 1358—the account for which year is lost—when Walter de Warfeld (1355–61) was almoner.[132] Standing partially over the water of Long Ditch, they shared the site with a common privy, the proximity of which facility was a mixed blessing. In the years 1364–6 it was almost impossible to let the smallest of these shops, 'on account of the stench of the public latrine'.[133] A thorough cleansing operation was required before permanent tenants could be found.[134] Despite this planning error, Brother Walter, evidently encouraged by the success of the first venture, in 1361 put up five more shops, adjoining the first, at a cost

[129] WAM 19651. Peter Coumbe was sacrist in the years 1385–99 and 1411–13 (Pearce, *Monks*, 197).

[130] e.g. 'a void plot in the sacrist's garden' in the sanctuary, leased in 1355 to a merchant of London named Adam Canon, within a dozen years had become, presumably due to Canon's own efforts, 'his house', WAM 17659; 19629.

[131] It was again characteristic of this expansive period that, when the Tothill Street gate of the abbey sanctuary was rebuilt (above, n. 113), the cellarer, who was responsible for the site, at the same time modernized two shops, one just within and one just outside the gateway, which were then leased to tenants for the first time, as also was a room within the new gate itself. WAM 18853, 18871: the tenement outside the gate 'rebuilt' in 1370–1 for £3. 2s.; and a stall and pentice installed here in 1388–9. WAM 18881; Reg Bk, ii, fo. 215^{r–v}: £5. 10s. spent in 1398–9 on the 'enlargement' of the shop within the gate (which in 1525 measured 39 feet by 22 feet in plan) and on the installation there of two brick chimneys. Unfortunately, in the following year the new shop was commandeered by servants of the king, who paid no rent. WAM 18882.

[132] WAM 18984, 18986.

[133] WAM 18991–2.

[134] WAM 18993.

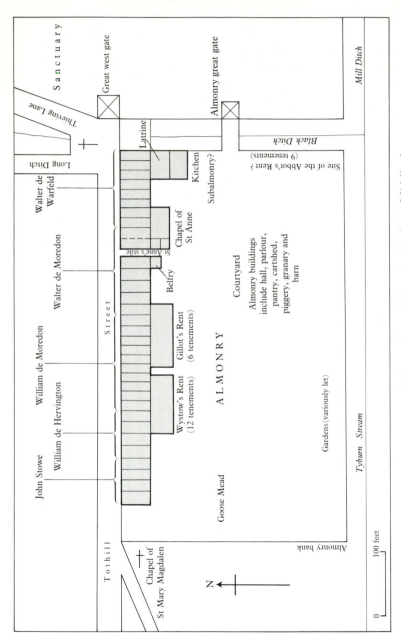

FIG. 5. The almonry of Westminster Abbey in the later Middle Ages. Diagrammatic plan to show the development of the site

of £31. 1s. 1d.[135] These were let at the higher rate of 11s. p.a. each. A slight but significant drawback to this development was a structural problem characteristic of building anywhere in Westminster off the gravel island whose bounds were marked by the main abbey complex (excluding the almonry) and the palace: subsidence. Within ten years it was necessary to raise the first shop in the row upon a new platform of clay.[136] The evident ease of this operation must reflect the simplicity of construction of the buildings. There is no clue as to the appearance of Walter de Warfeld's shops before the later fifteenth century, when, however, despite certain modern improvements, they probably remained basically unchanged. All seem to have been on two floors, probably with the kitchen upstairs, thus maximizing the commercial area below.[137] The construction of an *asiamentum* in one of the tenements in 1473 suggests that they had not originally been furnished with private lavatories.[138] In the course of renovation in the 1460s, at least two brick chimneys were built—a common modernization in this period—and the replastered walls were decorated with 'red ochre'.[139] Another feature of the later period was the addition of stalls and pentices, for the greater convenience of both shopkeepers and shoppers.[140] The original tenants of these properties were modest tradesmen; in 1370–1 three of the row of five shops were occupied by William the butcher, William the baker, and Walter the smith (doubtless an occasional maker of candlesticks).[141]

The new shopping street was extended by Walter de Warfeld's

---

[135] WAM 18988. In the following year five doors were purchased to complete the work. WAM 18989.

[136] WAM 18994. In the fifteenth century it became more usual for the 'underpinning' to be renewed with stone or, later still, brick. Thus in 1463–4 the first three of the shops built under Walter de Warfeld were hoisted, with the help of the neighbours, upon inserted brick foundations. WAM 19070: 2s. 4d. spent on beer and victuals for the *adiuvantes et vicinos*. Stone was employed to bolster houses in Tothill Street in 1408–9 and in 1424–5. WAM 19013, 19030.

[137] See repairs to the stairs leading to the (?) kitchen in J. Swan's tenement, the third of the row of five, in 1472–3; and to the stairs in Henry Grene's, one of the three by the latrine, in 1510–11. WAM 19079, 19116. Houses built within the sanctuary in the fifteenth century also had upstairs kitchens. See below, sect. 4. The upstairs kitchen, over the shop, was common in London housing by 1400. Schofield, *The Building of London From the Conquest to the Great Fire* (London, 1984), 91.

[138] WAM 19079.

[139] WAM 19070.

[140] e.g. WAM 19115.

[141] WAM 18994.

successor, Walter de Moredon (1361–3), who in his last year of office erected seven more shops, investing in them over £38, equal to three-quarters of that year's income.[142] Two, abutting on the north side of the almonry chapel of St Anne, had solars above; they were let for a time as one, at 24s. p.a., and later, from 1393, at 40s. p.a. They measured between 30 and 40 feet along each of their four sides, and were described in 1488 as 'two tenements or mansions, with a parlour and shops and with solars built above'.[143] The remaining five, single-storeyed, stood to the west of the small almonry gate into Tothill Street known as 'St Anne's stile', and were let at 6s. 8d. p.a. each. The almoner's manor of Claygate in Surrey supplied most of the wood for building, although some was purchased from the warden of the Lady chapel. Laths were acquired at Kensington, and other materials pillaged from a demolished house at the nearby Rosamund's Manor.[144]

Next in the line of speculating almoners was William de Hervington (1363–9/70). In 1367–8 he put up two houses in Tothill Street opposite the messuage on the north side of that street afterwards known as the Cock inn.[145] They cost £20 to build, and were let in the same year, to a carpenter and a bell-maker, for 40s. p.a. together. By 1370–1 William de Hervington had built two more houses there, leased to Thomas Carter and his brother at 13s. 4d. p.a. each.[146] Only one of these four houses was explicitly said to have a solar; this was further described in 1465 as 'a tenement or manse with shop and solar built thereon, and with a garden adjacent'.[147] The almoner William de Moredon (1382–7) excelled all his predecessors in this enterprise. During his term, the gap left between Walter de Moredon's buildings and William de Hervington's was filled with a row of no less than ten shops. The

[142] WAM 18989.

[143] WAM 17885; Reg Bk, ii, fo. 290[r–v].

[144] The fragility of these buildings is again suggested by the fact that the five smaller shops had to be rebuilt within eighty years. WAM 19051, 19053.

[145] WAM 18993. The houses were 'ex opposito Roberti Hakeborne'. The extant lease to Hakebourne of 'Lawestenement', the later Cock inn, is dated 1371 (WAM 17686); but he was probably in occupation before. In any case the position of the other almonry buildings dictates that William de Hervington's houses must have lain more or less across from the Cock.

[146] WAM 18994; WAM 18995 confirms that William de Hervington was the builder.

[147] WAM 17790. The extensive repair clauses of this lease suggest that no major alterations had been made since the time of construction.

cost this time was £50.[148] Two of these shops were stated in 1493 to include solars and, together, to measure 25 feet long by 36 feet wide; a standard width of 18 feet may be inferred.[149] The initial rent for each was 10s. p.a., although after the early fifteenth century they tended to be let in groups of two or three.

The apparently easy profits to be made from this game must by now have seemed irresistible. To the west of William de Herv-ington's row lay a garden of the almonry which since 1373 had been let for 3s. a year. But in 1389–90 there was no rent from the garden, the reason being given that three new shops had been built there by the then almoner, John Stowe (1387–1411).[150] Later leases of one of these shops give its width along the street as 14 feet, its length as far as, but not including, the garden as 46 feet.[151] In 1387–8 Stowe had also built a large house on Tothill Street, apparently very close to this slightly later development, at the great expense of £15. 14s. 6d.[152] But it appears that the tenant market was not inexhaustible, for John Stowe's new premises proved much harder to let than recent experience would have suggested. The three shops were offered first at 13s. 4d. p.a. each, but, finding few takers, were reduced in 1396–7 to 10s. p.a., and in 1406–7, still neglected, to 8s. p.a. The big house, likewise, was knocked down from 26s. 8d. to 20s., to 16s. and finally, in 1420–1, to 13s. 4d. p.a.[153] The lack of interest might be explained by faults in the particular properties, were it not that the other obedientiaries were experiencing the same problem at just this time. The monks were finding to their discomfort that, for the time being, the demand for property had reached its limit.[154]

The character of the buildings erected by the monks in such large numbers between c.1360 and c.1410 was remarkably consistent. The overwhelming preponderance was of small-scale housing and retail premises. These quantities of newly built cottages and shops,

[148] WAM 18962: a fragment of a roll, on which, faintly legible, is an account 'for ten new shops next to the almonry'. The roll for 1387–8 first records 'ten shops built by W. Moredon'. WAM 18999. WAM 19005 establishes that this was *William* de Moredon.

[149] WAM 17903.

[150] WAM 19000. The section of this roll containing the details of construction is lost. See also WAM 18996 *et seq.*

[151] e.g. WAM 17870 (1483).

[152] WAM 18999.

[153] WAM 50773, 19001–25.

[154] See below.

let (for the most part by the quarter or the year) at relatively modest rates, were intended to accommodate a large, and evidently increasing, population of small craftsmen and shopkeepers. The increasing local population which these building developments reflect must be attributed in large part to immigration during these decades.[155] In so far as they were migrants and not Westminster-born, the tradesmen and women who took tenancies in the new rents of the town brought with them a modest but solid prosperity attained in their previous communities, and demonstrated by their migration a determination to improve upon this success. To such people the move to Westminster represented a step upwards, into a world of greater opportunity than had been afforded by their places of origin.

The Fifteenth Century: Contraction

The Down-turn in Demand

Early in the fifteenth century the picture changed dramatically. The period 1400–20 saw the cessation of investment by the monastic landlords in the 'new rents' which had characterized the previous half-century. The profits from the abbey's Westminster rentals stopped increasing, and in some cases even suffered a reduction (see app. IV). The histories of numerous individual properties show clearly that the change in investment policy at this time was counselled by a sharp down-turn in the demand for local property. Westminster's population had ceased to grow, and had even begun to decline.

The fate of the chantry houses of Walter Cook was typical. In *c*.1404 a row of tenements was built at the western end of the Westminster sanctuary at the costs of Walter Cook, a wealthy canon of Lincoln. In 1401–2 Cook had obtained papal permission to found a chantry chapel at Knowle in his native Warwickshire.[156] Since the manor of Knowle belonged to Westminster Abbey, it was necessary to secure the abbot's blessing on the project. Consequently, Cook in 1404 came to an arrangement with the abbot whereby, in return for the sum of 300 marks (£200) and the patronage of the chapel, the

---

[155] See further ch. 6, sect. 2.
[156] WAM 619. The chapel still stands; see *The Victoria History of Warwickshire*, vol. iv (London, 1947), 98; N. Pevsner, *The Buildings of England: Warwickshire* (London, 1966), 329.

abbey undertook to provide in perpetuity a salary of 10 marks yearly to maintain a chaplain in the chantry.[157] A portion of the 300 marks was evidently allocated to the erection within the abbey precinct at Westminster of five 'Knowle chantry houses of Walter Cook'. The houses, however, were never more than a qualified success as an endowment. Their rent value reached its peak, at £8. 13s. 4d., in the years 1427–9, but tailed off thereafter, plunging sharply in the 1440s. Between 1450 and the mid-1480s, indeed, the houses for the most part stood untenanted: *nihil quia vacua* is the telling refrain of the rentals. Only from the latter date is a recovery observable, most of the houses subsequently finding occupants until records cease in 1534; the rent value in this last phase was between £3 and £4.[158] It is to the credit of the monks that, notwithstanding these vicissitudes in the endowment, the salary of the chaplain at Knowle continued faithfully to be paid at the rate of £6. 13s. 4d. each year.[159] But the case shows how the construction of domestic housing, which had proved so profitable in the late fourteenth century, met in the second quarter of the fifteenth century with disillusioning failure.

The monk-warden of the Lady chapel suffered a similar blow at the same period. Towards 1400 there remained a gap in the buildings along the west side of King Street, opposite the entrance to Endive Lane. The site was a large garden belonging to the Lady

---

[157] See W. B. Bickley (ed.), *The Register of the Guild of Knowle* (Walsall, 1894), p. xiii. The register contains a list of the members of a guild founded by Walter Cook within his chapel. John Islip, treasurer and later abbot of Westminster Abbey, was a brother of this guild in 1486–93. Ibid., pp. 93, 108.

[158] WAM 23809–969. The annual rent values for the years 1443–53 were as follows: 1443–4: £6; 1444–5: £5. 5s.; 1445–6: £4. 6s. 8d.; 1446–7: £3. 6s. 8d.; 1447–8:£2; 1448–51:£1. 6s. 8d.; 1451–2: 15s.; 1452–3: *nil*. (NB notes at the feet of the accounts for 1447–9.) The round sums of £4. 16s. 8d. or £4. 16s. entered each year in the rental between 1457 and 1469 are almost certainly derived from a different source; see the foot of the account for 1456–7 (WAM 23834), where this figure first appears, evidently as a supplementary grant from central funds to compensate the warden for his loss of rents.

[159] In 1404–7 the Knowle chaplain received his salary from the convent treasurer. By 1422, however, his pay was being drawn on the account of the sacrist, in whose sanctuary rental of this year (after a gap in the sacrist's records) the chantry tenements first appear. Later, in 1442, the tenements and the responsibility for the chaplain were transferred to the monk-warden of a group of manors assigned to the anniversary of Queen Eleanor of Castile, of which Knowle was one; the warden contracted to pay the sacrist 26s. 8d. p.a. in compensation for the tenements. WAM 19890–4; 19663–85; 23805 *apud pedem* (and see WAM 23802–3). WAM 30565 is an acquittance, dated 4 Oct. 1524, from Sir John Johnson, priest, warden of Knowle, for his annual salary of £6. 13s. 4d. received from Westminster Abbey.

chapel, occupied since 1355 by a gardener, John Penehalowe, who paid 3s. 4d. p.a. for it and lived in the adjacent house.[160] On the expiry of Penehalowe's lease in 1394, the garden was taken in hand for development as commercial premises. In 1397–8 the then warden, Peter Coumbe (whose building activities have already been noticed),[161] accounted for the erection of three shops there, at a cost of £22. 7s. 4d.[162] They were offered for let in 1398–9 at 20s. p.a. each, but without success. The reduction of the rate to 16s. in 1400–1 brought little improvement; and the shops at last found tenants only in 1411–12, at a mere 13s. 4d. p.a. apiece.[163] In 1401 Peter Coumbe again commissioned a new building for the chapel, this time a single tenement in Long Ditch, to replace two old cottages there. When completed, the edifice (which later became known as the White Horse inn) cost no less than £58. 11s. 9d.[164] The rent started at £2. p.a., but in the early 1420s the property was standing empty, and in c.1426 the rent was dropped to 26s. 8d. p.a. It remained at this level (apart from a brief interlude in the 1430s at 33s. 4d.. p.a.) in five successive leases, until 1520.[165]

A parallel history is recorded of a property of the cellarer at Charing Cross, to the south of the graveyard of the church of St Martin-in-the Fields. This site, already partially built upon with three shops, was recovered by the convent from secular possession in 1383–4.[166] In the following year the cellarer invested the substantial sum of £56 in the construction of nine additional shops beside the existing three, along a street frontage which measured 170 feet in total.[167] Unfortunately for the monks, no sooner had the new development been completed than, at Easter 1387, their tenure

[160] WAM 17657; 23187 *et seq.*

[161] Above, n. 129.

[162] WAM 23195.

[163] WAM 23196–204.

[164] WAM 23201.

[165] The account for 1420–1 is WAM 23213 + 23221. For the rent in 1426–1520 see WAM 23214–96; Reg Bk, i, fo. 105ʳ. By 1520 a fresh rebuilding had become necessary. But now the inn was cautiously leased to a bricklayer, Robert Guy, who undertook the reconstruction himself. The rent from 1520 until at least 1549 was 33s. 4d. p.a. WAM 18001; 23296–311; Reg Bk, iii, fo. 148ᵛ.

[166] WAM 18865: 'Et in diversis custibus et expensis factis circa recuperacionem ten' et shop' apud Charyng quondam Andr' Broun per diversis vices. 58s. 2d.' In the same account, William Yppegrave and Henry Baker are named, in addition to Andrew Broun, as former holders of the property. Their quitrent had been due to the warden of the abbey Lady chapel. See WAM 23187 *et seq.*

[167] WAM 18866–8. For dimensions, see a lease of 1502: Reg Bk i, fos. 145ᵛ–146ʳ.

of the site was successfully challenged by one Thomas de la Hay. The convent consequently enjoyed no rent in return for its investment for nine years, until in *c.*1396 the property was once more recovered into the monks' possession.[168] The nine new shops were then let by the cellarer for 9*s.* p.a. apiece to tenants at will, and the three old shops at 5*s.* p.a. each. The only named occupants of this row are Thomas Haket, a baker, and his wife, Alice, who lived here in 1432.[169] Fully occupied with such small tradespeople, the shops would have repaid the cost of the new building in twelve years. The extant rentals of the early fifteenth century, however, show that the shops increasingly stood vacant for lack of tenants. The three old shops may have been in need of repair which, however, they did not receive, for they disappear from the rentals after 1417. The dearth of tenants in the new row, meanwhile, can only reflect a decline in demand for such property.[170]

The Abandonment of Direct Control

The rent reductions and the introduction of long leases in the early fifteenth century, made in the context of increasingly numerous properties standing altogether vacant, are genuine indicators of a slump in the market. After the mid-fifteenth century, however, by which time the new policy had been fully effected, the monastery's rentals cease to be a clear index of the level of demand. This becomes obvious when it is realized that, while the monks never made a committed return to short leases, increased rents, and fresh investment in urban property before the Dissolution,[171] new and highly profitable building ventures were being undertaken with increasing momentum, from the third quarter of the fifteenth

---

[168] WAM 18878 *et seq.*

[169] WAM 18890.

[170] Throughout the fifteenth century, the cellarer's recorded yearly receipts from this site never rose above 78*s.*, and in 1501 they fell so low as 33*s.* 4*d.* WAM 18878–908. From 1502 the cellarer took the simpler option and let the entire surviving row of 'nine cottages' on a forty-year lease, at 53*s.* 4*d.* p.a., to John Smyth, a gentleman of the king's chapel. The lessee's own profits are unknown; but it may well be that the cellarer had mistimed his decision, while Smyth was able to capitalize on an improving market. See below. The lease: Reg Bk, i, fos. 145ᵛ–146ʳ; WAM 18911 *et seq.* Smyth: *LP* i, nos. 20 (p. 18), 82 (p. 41); PCW Wyks, 115–16.

[171] Entry fines, as a means of improving revenue from property alternative to raising the rent, seem never to have been employed by the abbey's administrators of their urban estate before the Dissolution. See also above, n. 44.

century onwards, by lay tenants on the abbey's land.[172] The latter were in some cases collaborators with the monks, whose properties they renovated at no cost to the abbey, in return for low rents and the chance to share in the profits of redevelopment. In other instances the lay builders of this period may have acted entirely for private interest. In either eventuality their activities reflect a recovery of population which was evidently, to judge from these speculative ventures, in full swing by 1480.[173]

Two reasons may account for the monks' reluctance to involve themselves directly in property development in this potentially advantageous period. One concerns the internal condition of the abbey's economy, which was thrown seriously off balance between 1440 and 1470 by a disastrous succession of two incompetent abbots, who left large debts and a severely weakened house behind them.[174] The resources available to prime new investment were consequently restricted during the second half of the fifteenth century.

The further explanation for the monks' abandonment of an active role as urban landlords concerns the nature of the growing demand for housing, as recorded in sources other than the abbey rentals, from the late fifteenth century onwards. The expanding population of Tudor Westminster was increasingly polarized. As the royal court finally made Westminster its permanent home, courtiers in increasing numbers chose to live nearby.[175] Meanwhile lists of subdivided and overcrowded dwellings show that many of those seeking a roof over their heads in sixteenth century Westminster were poor.[176] Homes for the prosperous middling class of royal

---

[172] Unrecorded subleasing is a hazard which in general attends the use of institutional rentals as indicators of economic life in the late Middle Ages, as Eleanora Carus-Wilson pointed out in relation to rural manors in Gloucestershire. E. M. Carus-Wilson, 'Evidences of Industrial Growth on Some Fifteenth-century Manors', *Econ Hist Rev*, 2nd ser., xii (1959–60), 196–7.

[173] See below, sect. 4.

[174] The disastrous abbots were Edmund Kyrton (1440–62) and George Norwich (1463–9). The latter was forced to retire, but not before damage had been done. Part of the problem was that the abbey's economy was overstrained by continuing expenditure on the new nave. V. H. Galbraith, 'A Visitation of Westminster in 1444', *English Historical Review*, xxxvii (1922), 83–8; Harvey, *Estates*, 67. Similarly at Durham Priory in the 1440s, strict economies were called for after a series of almost ruinous building expenses. R. B. Dobson, *Durham Priory, 1400–1450* (Cambridge, 1973), 235.

[175] See ch. 6, sect. 4.

[176] See ch. 6, sect. 1.

servants required heavy and possibly uneconomic investment. This was proved by the monk-warden of the new work, in an extremely rare instance of monastic investment in urban building after the mid-fifteenth century. A substantial house beside the palace gate called the Saracen's Head had, like so many other Westminster properties, fallen in rent value at the turn of the century. Around 1400 it had been leased at £8 p.a.; but by 1409 the rent was reduced to £5. 6s. 8d., and until the end of the century did not rise thereafter above £6 p.a. In 1486–7 the house, together with four adjacent smaller houses which were separately leased, was rebuilt at the expense of the monastery's department of the new work, as the owner of the property. The total cost was £230. This very nearly ruined the department, and in 1498 the deficit had simply to be written off. The result was a fine principal dwelling in the new Saracen's Head, with an upper hall and 'great inner parlour', sufficiently comfortable to attract an officer of the royal court such as William Tebbe, gentleman sergeant of King Henry VIII's vestry, to live here in the years 1496–1511. But the rent for the house nevertheless reached a ceiling of only £6. 13s. 4d. p.a. before the Dissolution. The investment was quite out of proportion to the return on such a property.[177]

On the other hand, the partitioning and rack-renting of tenements housing poor and often very short-term lodgers was a business which required constant vigilance and which, again, may have seemed to the monks an uneconomic proposition. The modestly prosperous, petty commercial class of small traders, which provided the principal demand for the many rows of shops and cottages erected by the monks in the years before and just after 1400, was (though still present) proportionately less prominent in the growing population of the Tudor period than it had been in that of the late fourteenth century. Rows of cottages of the late-fourteenth-century type continued to be built—generally by lay investors—from the late fifteenth century onwards, but in many cases the profitable way to let both these and older tenements was in

---

[177] WAM 23470–593; the building accounts of 1486–7 are contained in WAM 23560. WAM 33280 is a daily wages book covering a part of the period of operations. Useful lease description of the Saracen's Head are given in WAM 17909 (William Tebbe's lease of 1496) and Reg Bk, iii, fos. 170ᵛ–171ʳ (1550). For Tebbe see also app. VIII, s.n.

small units of a room or two apiece. Thus although leaseholders found no difficulty in filling their properties with numerous subtenants, it is noticeable that 'vacancies' among the Westminster houses of, for example, the sacrist, were running at around 18 per cent in the 1520s; a proportion significantly above the normal.[178] The implication would seem to be that many would-be tenants could not afford even the relatively low rents offered for entire tenements by the abbey. Much of the demand was not for comfortably sized, self-contained properties but for quarters in a section, perhaps even just a room, within a subdivided tenement. Wealthier private leaseholders who, unlike the monks, had both the resources and flexibility to rent a house as one unit and sublet it as half a dozen could find poor immigrants to the town unable to fare any better. The character of the market may, therefore, at least in part, explain the monks' preference for delegating to secular leaseholders the direct exploitation of Westminster rents in the early Tudor period.

3. THE REDUCED DENSITY OF SETTLEMENT IN THE MID-FIFTEENTH CENTURY

The topographical evidence which records a contraction of settlement in Westminster after *c.*1400 can be compared with some recent studies of other English towns. A slump in rent levels, following upon a late-fourteenth-century increase, occurred more or less simultaneously on urban estates in Canterbury, York, and Winchester, and in the central part of the City of London.[179] Vacations of tenements and a growing preference among landlords for the security of long leases were, as at Westminster, additional symptoms in these other towns of a down-turn of demand. Derek Keene's study of Winchester, in particular, has shown how a falling population created open spaces within the formerly built-up area of

[178] WAM 19779–807: rentals and separate lists of 'vacations of tenements', 1520–30. The previously prevailing rate of vacancies was closer to 10%.

[179] A. F. Butcher, 'Rent and the Urban Economy: Oxford and Canterbury in the Later Middle Ages', *Southern History*, i (1979), 37–42; Rees-Jones, Ph.D. thesis on late medieval York, Univ. of York, forthcoming; Keene, *Medieval Winchester*, i. 237–48; id. and V. Harding, *Cheapside and the Development of London Before the Great Fire* (forthcoming).

the town.[180] The reduction in the density of settlement in Westminster was evidently part of a more widespread recession. Future studies may show how far this trend extended throughout English towns in the fifteenth century.

In Westminster, as will be shown, signs of a fresh increase in settlement begin to occur from soon after the mid-century, and gather in intensity from the 1470s onwards. The duration of the reduced level of population in Westminster was thus between thirty and fifty years. Again, future work on other places is required before general conclusions can be drawn. It is already clear, however, that Westminster's recovery, as shown in rent levels and building work, was precocious when compared with that of the Cheapside district of central London, where these indicators do not record new growth until the very end of the sixteenth century.[181]

Different urban centres may prove more closely comparable with Westminster in their respective chronologies,[182] but it should also be noted that the composition of a growing population is as important as its volume. Other evidence suggests that much of the population increase in early Tudor Westminster was represented by the immigrant poor.[183] Drawn to the metropolis by the possibility either of employment or of charitable assistance, the poor would gravitate not to the costly commercial centre of the city of London, but to the urban fringes, where rents were lower and where, in addition, they were constrained by fewer jurisdictional controls.

4. MONASTIC AND PRIVATE ENTERPRISE IN THE LATE MEDIEVAL EXPANSION

During the expansive phase of the late fourteenth and early fifteenth centuries, it is not surprising to find private developers

---

[180] Keene, *Medieval Winchester*, vol. i, ch. 6 and vol. ii, *passim*. Gloucester also provides evidence of urban buildings going out of use in the first half of the fifteenth century. R. A. Holt, 'Gloucester: An English Provincial Town during the Later Middle Ages', Ph.D. thesis, Univ. of Birmingham (1987), 31–3; id., 'Gloucester in the Century after the Black Death', *Transactions of the Bristol and Gloucestershire Archaeological Society*, ciii (1985), 158.

[181] See ch. 6, n. 36.

[182] The currently available evidence is in some cases negative, such as the absence of any sign of demographic increase in York, Bristol, or Norwich before the very end of the fifteenth century. Dobson, 'Urban Decline in Late Medieval England', *Transactions of the Royal Historical Society*, 5th ser., xxvii (1977), 20–1.

[183] See ch. 6, sect. 1.

ILLUS. 5. Late medieval houses in King Street, Westminster. Drawing, c.1790.

investing in urban property alongside the monks of the abbey, even though the latter have prominence in the surviving documentation.[184] After 1450, however, secular builders took the lead in development. By grants of building leases the monks, from the early fifteenth century onwards, kept their own expenses down by encouraging tenants to undertake renovations on their own part. The delegation of responsibility for structural improvements increasingly deprived the monks of much of the economic value of their property as, from the third quarter of the fifteenth century, others came forward to profit from urban building in their stead. In the decades after 1450, a class of lay investors gradually gained prominence, signalling by their activities a revival in the urban property market following upon the slump which had lasted from *c*.1410–20 until *c*.1450–70.

Among these speculative builders was John Millyng, a yeoman of London who in 1466 took a lease from the domestic treasurer on a 'vacant piece of land' by the white cross in King Street once known as Steynour's Croft. This was a marshy site, where willows grew.[185] Millyng's rent was 5s. p.a., and he undertook to build on the ground within sixteen years.[186] By the time of his death in 1490 he had put up seven cottages and a barn. Successive tenants, however, continued to render only 5s. annually to the domestic treasurer, despite regular renewal of the lease, for a property which was worth far more.[187] An unusually detailed rental of 1530 reveals that the sum rent value of the property, to the holder of the head lease, was then no less than £8. 1s. 4d. p.a.[188] Recent lease-holders had naturally been prosperous individuals: John James, an abbey official who held much other property from the monastery,[189] and Dr Duck, the dean of Cardinal Wolsey's chapel in York Place across the road.[190]

---

[184] For secular developers in this period see above, n. 130 and Rosser, 'Medieval Westminster: The Vill and the Urban Community, 1200–1540', 175–7.

[185] The sale of osier rods gathered in Steynour's Croft had been worth several shillings a year; see WAM 18519–22.

[186] WAM 17792.   [187] WAM 23115 *et seq.*   [188] WAM 18049A.

[189] WAM 17924, 17965. For James see app. VIII, s.n.

[190] WAM 18038; *LP* iv, nos. 2073, 3216. Nearer to Charing Cross on the same side of King Street, a 'vacant plot' opposite St Catherine's chapel was let in 1474 to William Skelton for fifty years at 2s. p.a. By 1524, when this lease had expired, 'divers cottages' had been built on the site. WAM 23249; 23300; 17193. For the further, extremely profitable, development of this site after 1524 by William Salcote, a carpenter, see ch. 5, sect. 7.

A garden beside the royal Mews on the north side of Charing
Cross was similarly built up during this period. It was leased out in
1417 for a term of fifty years at 2*s*. p.a., rising to 3*s*. 4*d*. p.a. after
forty years. In 1459 the lessee initiated development by erecting a
house in the garden; eight years later a renewal of the lease was
granted to John Noreys, who was then said to have 'rebuilt' the
property as a messuage or inn called the Rose, with two adjoining
cottages.[191] Noreys, who was elsewhere described as a 'yeoman of
Eybury' and who held office in the local court of Westminster,
received a further lease in 1493, at 13*s*. 4*d*. p.a., on the terms that he
would, within two years, build and furnish a brewery on the site.
Noreys's contract with the carpenters, Richard Waryn and
Nicholas Halywode, was drawn up in the same year. The carpenters
undertook to construct within four months a brewhouse 31 feet
long, and a 'crosshouse' between the (existing) stable and bake-
house, 27 feet long, adjoining the new brewhouse on the south.
Materials were to be supplied by the workmen, whose total fee was
£8. 13*s*. 4*d*.[192] Large as it was, Noreys's investment may have been
no greater, at this period, than the annual rent value to himself of the
extended Rose inn.[193]

Apart from filling in gaps in the street frontages in this way, the
attention of developers from the late fifteenth century also
penetrated deeper within the monastic sanctuary than even the
monks themselves had done by their developments of *c*.1400.
Principally affected was the precinct of the almonry where, the
street frontage towards the town having earlier been entirely faced
with shops, new building necessarily extended further into the
confines of the abbey (Fig. 5). In *c*.1459 a new row of a dozen
tenements was erected here, backing on to the shops in Tothill
Street, by Thomas More, a prosperous haberdasher of Westminster. More's rent was a mere 13*s*. 4*d*. p.a.; but when in 1511 the

[191] WAM 23230, 23243; and see refs. cited in the following note.
[192] WAM 17178A–B. WAM 17178B is the building contract, which is printed in
full in L. F. Salzman, *Building in England Down to 1540* (Oxford, 1952), 552–3. For
Noreys see app. VIII, s.n. The site of the Rose is now occupied by the eastern end of
the National Gallery.
[193] For comparison, the Boar's Head in King Street was occupied by the subtenant
in 1479 for a rent of £10. 3*s*. 4*d*.; the annual due owing to the chief landlord in this
case was £7. 6*s*. 8*d*. p.a. WAM 6645 *apud pedem*; 23081–105. Nevertheless the abbey
lease issued to Noreys's widow of the entire property at Charing Cross was still
granted at the annual rent of only 13*s*. 4*d*., with, as usual, no recorded hint of an entry
fine. WAM 23285–312; Reg Bk, ii, fos. 167ᵛ–168ʳ.

almoner finally took the property in hand it was leased piecemeal by the quarter or the year for £7 or £8 annually. The row was known as 'Wystow's rent', after the last lessee.[194] Hard by Wystow's rent stood 'Gillot's rent'. In 1471 Richard Burton, 'husbandman' of Fulham, rented an old barn on this site. His lease of fifty-one years was granted on the understanding that within four years he would redevelop the plot, which measured 62 feet by 27 feet, as five tenements with brick chimneys; the new tenements were not to obstruct the light of neighbouring buildings.[195] Within a year, Burton had put up not five but six shops, on which his profit, over the building costs and the trifling rent to the almoner of 6s. 8d., was doubtless highly satisfactory.[196] Only in 1524, on the expiry of the lease of one John Gillot, did the almoner choose to keep these tenements in hand, and to let them individually by the year at 13s. 4d. each.[197]

As Gillot's rent had been a barn, so 'Woodman's rent', the exact position of which within the almonry is uncertain, had been a stable; the pressure of people was driving out animals and their fodder from the precinct. The stable in question was granted to Peter Curteys, an officer of the king's household, in c.1462; by 1471, when the almoner employed a plasterer there, it was described as a 'tenement' in which one Robert Thomsyn lived.[198] Further transformation was to come, however, for William Smith, who took it in 1473 as 'one tenement and garden', bequeathed it to Robert Woodman thirty years later as 'divers tenements'.[199] The property

[194] WAM 19066, 19116 *et seq.* WAM 17970, a lease of a pair of William de Moredon's shops (above, n. 148), establishes that Wystow's rent lay behind these. For More, who at his death in 1467–8 was buried in the Trinity chapel of St Margaret's church, see PRO, E40/10226; CWA i. 71.

[195] WAM 17806.

[196] WAM 19076; see 19082. The rent increased during the final three years of the lease to 26s. 8d. p.a.; but the rent reverted with each new lease to 6s. 8d. p.a. See WAM 17858; Reg Bk, i, fos. 100ᵛ–101ʳ.

[197] In the event, however, there was difficulty in finding tenants, partly because of the already decayed state of the properties, which had perhaps been crudely built by the speculator; one was described in 1534 as 'ruinous'. WAM 19136–52.

[198] WAM 19069, 19074–8. For Curteys, who was later keeper of Westminster Palace and of the king's wardrobe under Henry VI and Edward IV, who sheltered in Westminster sanctuary during Richard III's reign, and who received a pardon and new offices from Henry VII, see *Cal Pat R 1467–77*, p. 295; ibid. *1476–85*, pp. 198, 222, 438, 513; ibid. *1485–94*, p. 26; and Kingsford, *English Historical Literature in the Fifteenth Century* (Oxford, 1913), 181–2 n.

[199] WAM 19080, 19114–15.

was first let piecemeal by the almoner in 1514, as ten rooms or tenements, at rents of between 3s. 4d. and 13s. 4d. p.a., with the exception of one room which Joan Woodman, Robert's widow, occupied until 1528 rent-free, 'out of the alms' of the landlords.[200] Finally, at the western end of the almonry lay a meadow called Goose Mead. In 1476 John Pacche, esquire, leased 'one mansion, with a barn, garden, banks and vacant pieces of ground' within this meadow.[201] Ten years later, when Thomas Hunt, gentleman and seneschal of Westminster Abbey, succeeded to Pacche's ground, the single mansion had been multiplied to three houses. Moreover, Hunt and his wife undertook to build a fourth house there, to measure 36 by 12 feet, of good oak timber.[202] In 1534, the lessee then being Thomas Kempe, gentleman, the tenements were described collectively as the Red Lion hostelry.[203] In the displacement of grazing geese by bibbing citizens is summarized the transformation of the almonry from monastic sanctuary to social townscape.[204]

The outstanding case of the individual property developer in late medieval Westminster was a chandler named Robert Powle. Powle collaborated closely and repeatedly with the abbey authorities, and should perhaps be regarded as semi-officially engaged by the monks to renovate their urban properties. However, the main financial profits were the developer's, not the monastic landlords'. Powle's enterprise was ubiquitous, and his activity reflects very clearly the gathering momentum of demand in particular for cheap accommodation in the town from c.1470 onwards. In 1475 Powle took a lease from the sacrist on 'a row of eight old tenements in the sanctuary', on the east side of the belfry, on the agreement that, within four years, he would have built in their stead seven new tenements, each

---

[200] WAM 19119 *et seq.*

[201] WAM 17831.   [202] WAM 17878.

[203] WAM 19149; see 18037.

[204] Similarly the cellarer's vineyard within the sanctuary, first let to farm before 1431, by 1481 had been partially built up with houses, to which the tenant in that year undertook to add another. The nearby hostelry garden, to the south of the Mill Ditch, which belonged to the hosteller of the monastery, was said in 1497 to have been 'lately new built up' by John Freeman, a carpenter, with 'houses and four cottages'. WAM 18890 *et seq.*, 17852; Reg Bk, i, fos. 98ʳ–99ʳ. (Freeman was employed on the 'new work' of the abbey in the 1480s: WAM 23556–61.) One other such row, untypically of the period, was built in the almonry by the monks themselves, with the specific purpose of maintaining the anniversary of Abbot Richard Harweden (1420–40). The construction accounts do not survive, but 'the abbot's rent', comprising nine dwellings, was first put on the market in 1472. WAM 19080, 19105.

of two storeys and with a brick chimney.[205] Six years later Powle returned the lease, having squeezed ten rather than seven new tenements on to the site (which measured 112 feet by 28 feet 7 inches), demonstrating a speculator's eye for space. Subsequent leases provide descriptions of three of these dwellings. Each had a cellar, a ground or 'shop' floor, and a kitchen above. The ground floor measured 10 or 11 feet by 20, the kitchen rather less.[206] Five of the tenements Powle retained on a fresh lease at 48*s*. p.a., presumably subletting them at a profit.[207] Of the rest, four can be traced in the sacrist's records, two being let as a pair at 26*s*. 8*d*. p.a., the third at 13*s*. 4*d*. p.a., and the fourth at 10*s*. p.a.[208] By way of further improving his property, at no cost to himself, the sacrist attached additional maintenance clauses to later leases: that the tenant should have made a fireplace with a grate in the kitchen (which suggests that Powle had skimped on the construction), and that a lead pipe should be fitted to connect the kitchen, through the sanctuary wall, with the ditch in Thieving Lane.[209]

A year or two earlier, in 1472–3, Robert Powle had leased an adjacent pair of gardens at Charing Cross, on the north side of the Strand, respectively from the conventual Lady chapel and sacristy.[210] His total annual rent was 10*s*. By 1495–6, three tenements stood in the chapel warden's garden, and four more 'newly built' tenements had appeared in the garden of the sacrist; Powle's responsibility need not be doubted. Subsequent tenants held the two properties simultaneously, which shows that Powle had developed them as a single block.[211] In yet another instance, shortly before 1481 Powle replaced an old tenement belonging to

[205] WAM 17819.
[206] WAM 17861; Reg Bk, i, fos. 50ᵛ–51ʳ. On upstairs kitchens see above, n. 137.
[207] WAM 17873.
[208] WAM 19728 *et seq*. The fifth tenement mysteriously disappears.
[209] WAM 17876; Reg Bk, i, fos. 50ᵛ–51ʳ.
[210] The dimensions of the Lady chapel warden's garden were approximately 85 feet by 40 feet. WAM 23247; Reg Bk, i, fos. 79ʳ, 89ᵛ–90ʳ. The sacrist's property had been described in the 1450s as 'three cottages at Charing Cross', of which, however, only one was then occupied; by the 1460s they were 'ruinous'. Powle leased the site in 1473 as 'a garden plot with a vacant plat'. WAM 19705*–20; 17803; 17173. This site measured approximately 85 feet by 50 feet. Reg Bk, i, fos. 79ʳ, 89ᵛ–90ʳ.
[211] The abbey, in four successive leases of the two properties before the Dissolution, persisted in asking no more than Powle's original low rents, of 3*s*. 4*d*. p.a. and 6*s*. 8*d*. p.a., respectively. For Hugh Moreland, gentleman, and the other lessees, this was unquestionably a bargain. Reg Bk, i, fos. 79ʳ, 86ʳ⁻ᵛ, 89ᵛ–90ʳ, 130ᵛ–132ʳ; Reg Bk, ii, fos. 28ᵛ–29ᵛ, 190ʳ⁻ᵛ.

the abbey hosteller in Long Ditch, called the Vine, with a row of six new tenements.[212] Like most of the other developments of the period which have been noted, Powle's buildings were of a consistent type: rows of small, even very small, cottages or shops. There was clearly a concentration of demand at this modest end of the market for housing. One of Powle's rents, however, was ultimately adapted to suit a different class of tenant, equally characteristic of late medieval Westminster, though less numerous than the other. The Bell inn in Tothill Street, outside the sanctuary gate, was described as 'decayed' in 1469, when it was leased at a reduced rate to Robert Powle. Within a few years Powle had converted the inn into a row of five tenements. The domestic treasurer, as the principal landlord, first let these new tenements individually in 1498–9, respectively to a tallow-chandler, a barber, two tailors, and a glazier, who paid various rents of 26s. 8d. and 33s. 4d. p.a.[213] The following years, however, saw these tenements standing empty with increasing frequency. It appears that the small craftsmen for whom Powle's row had evidently been designed were in this case either too few in number, or else insufficiently wealthy, to pay the rents demanded.[214] In 1511 the five tenements were instead leased collectively to another well-to-do chandler, Thomas Clement, *alias* Jackson, who readapted the premises as his single residence; he paid £4. 6s. 8d. p.a. to live there. Clement, who also rented a small tenement nearby in Long Ditch from the abbey sacrist, who held local office in the town, and who asked in his will for an inscription to be made on his tomb in St Margaret's church, naturally preferred to live on a more gracious scale than the domestic treasurer and Powle, between them, had thought most profitable to provide for.[215]

---

[212] The hosteller proceeded to let the new row at the low rate of 10s. p.a. LN, fos. 83ᵛ–84ʳ; WAM 17855. In 1470 Powle had also leased a cottage in Long Ditch, this time from the sacrist, at a reduced rent of 2s. 6d. p.a., agreeing to rebuild it within seven years. This, however, he appears not to have done, for in 1497 Robert Ederich, a carpenter, took a lease of the same property on the condition that he would build there a new tenement with four solars, each containing a brick chimney, within three years. Ederich fulfilled his contract. WAM 19716 *et seq.*; 17803; Reg Bk, i, fo. 92ʳ⁻ᵛ; and see Reg Bk, ii, fos 85ᵛ–86ʳ. (The repetition of a building clause on a lease of 1501 is a scribal error: WAM 17925.)

[213] WAM 23082 *et seq.*; 23126.   [214] See WAM 23127–40.

[215] WAM 17966; 23142–78. Clement's lease was renewed in 1535, and at his death in 1538 he left 'his dwelling house' outside the west gate of the abbey sanctuary in Tothill Street to his second wife. Reg Bk, ii, fo. 312ʳ; PCW Bracy, fos. 64ᵛ–65ʳ. See also app. VIII, s.n. Clement.

The sheer quantity of new building in these years indicates a decisive recovery of demand since 1450. The extent of that recovery, however, is seen more clearly in the full levels of rent which leaseholders were now extracting from subtenants. While the monks, as chief landlords, benefited from the building and repairing leases which they granted, whereby their housing stock was maintained at others' expense, the abbey failed to realize more than a part of the improved value of its urban rents in this period. A small estate of the monastic cellarer at Endive Lane shows this well (see Fig. 6). In *c*.1425 a row of eleven cottages had been built here, between King Street and the Thames, out of the endowment of a

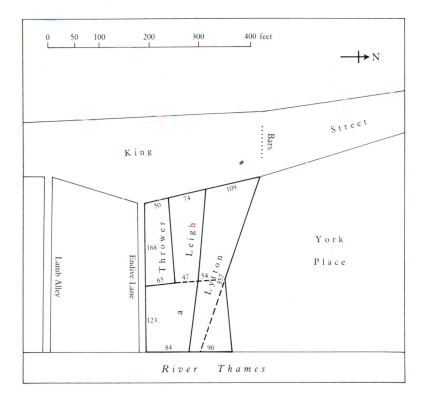

FIG. 6. Property of the abbey cellarer at Endive Lane

chantry founded in the abbey.[216] In the second quarter of the
century the cellarer had let these cottages, with a room over a gate
leading into the lane, separately to tenants at will, who paid rents of
a few shillings p.a. each.[217] At this relatively low social level, the
names of these tenants—John Tynker, William Carpenter, John
Carter, John Glover, William Mason, John Boteman—probably
still, at this date, indicate their occupations. They suggest, in any
case, humble labourers and small craftsmen. The local demand for
such artisan dwellings may not, however, have remained buoyant
throughout the mid-fifteenth century. As in other similar cases at
this period, this is the most plausible explanation for the cellarer's
decision, around the mid-century, to divide the cottages into three
blocks, and to grant these on leases for terms of forty or fifty years.[218]

By 1500 the appearance of the site had been transformed. This
alteration, however, owed nothing to the direct involvement of the
monks. One of the three holdings at Endive Lane (on which since
the development of *c.*1425 six cottages had stood) had become 'one
great gate with a chamber and six tenements, with a garden adjacent
and'—in addition—'four cottages towards the lane called "le
Endif" '.[219] The perpetrator is unknown, but there is no suggestion
that the cellarer was more than indirectly responsible. Again,
Thomas a Leigh, esquire, who renewed his lease on this property in
1500, undertook to have the same six tenements rebuilt within ten
years, of good oak, and with a brick chimney in each, reaching to a

---

[216] The founder of the chantry was Henry Merston, clerk of the king's works,
prebendary of St Stephen's Chapel, Westminster and simultaneously holder of
many other ecclesiastical preferments. In 1432, after a gap in the relevant accounts
since 1417, eleven new cottages 'at Endive', with a gate leading into the lane there,
make their first appearance in the cellarer's rental, when they are specifically stated to
have been built to finance Merston's obit 'after his death'; his anniversary was kept in
the abbey from 1440. In July 1425 Abbot Richard and Brother William Sonewelle
his fellow-monk (and cellarer) of Westminster Abbey were charged in the king's
bench with having caused an obstruction by erecting six posts in the royal way of
King Street *apud Endethe*; perhaps here were the new cottages under construction,
WAM 18890; 18891 *et seq.*; 5255*; 5264A; PRO, KB9/221/1/21. For Merston see
Cal Pat R 1401–5, p. 58; *Cal Pap Reg*, vi. 194; ibid. vii. 312; *King's Works*, ii. 1045;
WAM 17734; and *Cal Pat R, passim*.
[217] WAM 18891: Feb. to Michaelmas 1440. The cellarer's accounts are much less
well preserved from this period than are those of the other obedientiaries. Between
1407 and 1463, only the years 1416–17, 1431–2, 1440, 1446–7, and 1448–9 are
represented. WAM 18888–95.
[218] WAM 18892 *et seq.*
[219] WAM 18893; Reg Bk, i, fos. 117ᵛ–118ᵛ.

height of four feet above the roofs, and furthermore to remake the wooden embankment against the Thames.[220] Thomas a Leigh had no doubt calculated on making a profit, after the fulfilment of these obligations, over his annual rent to the cellarer of 33*s.* 4*d.*; he certainly anticipated no shortage of tenants at this date. By a fortunate chance, it is possible in this case to ascertain the value of the property to the lessee, and the names of some of the subtenants who actually lived on the premises. A list is extant of *c.*1508, evidently drawn up by the monks, of 'the names of the tenants with the lords of the soil, that is to say in King Street on the east side'.[221] Against Thomas a Leigh's name is entered 'the broad gate with other small tenantries within the same gate', and in addition four named subtenants, with their occupations: a brewer, a butcher, a tiler, and a waterman. A similar, fragmentary list of *c.*1516 records the rents paid by Leigh's subtenants in the gatehouse and the six tenements fronting on to King Street (though not those in the four cottages in Endive Lane).[222] These rents amounted to no less than £5. 6*s.* yearly, and thus represented a striking annual profit to Leigh (even omitting the unknown rate for the four cottages) of 220 per cent on his rent to the cellarer. Similar evidence can be adduced from the same sources for the remainder of the cottages at Enedehithe. One portion, comprising in 1449 two cottages and a piece of garden, had by 1463 already been multiplied to five cottages, again no doubt thanks to the attentions of a speculating lessee.[223] From 1485 until 1531 these 'five tenements and gardens' were leased by the distinguished family of Lytton (among them Robert Lytton, under-treasurer of England around 1500), at a rate of £2. 10*s.* 8*d.* p.a.[224] The list of *c.*1508 shows that these tenements, then held by Richard Lytton, were in fact occupied by at least nine subtenants, whose trades were given as mason, baker, weaver, tailor, pin-maker, spurrier, and (in three cases) cobbler.[225] A few years later William Lytton was receiving annual rents from ten subtenants here totalling as much as £10. 4*s.* 8*d.*; more than three and a half times the sum rendered to the cellarer, leaving a profit of

[220] Reg Bk, i, fos. 117[v]–118[v].
[221] WAM 18599.
[222] WAM 18049C.
[223] WAM 18893, 18895.
[224] Reg Bk, i, fo. 69[r–v]; WAM 17694, 18901–46.
[225] WAM 18599.

over 260 per cent.[226] The third and last part of the cellarer's land at Enedehithe was let in 1516 to Joan Thrower, a carpenter's widow of Westminster, as 'three tenements with gardens', for a rent of £2 p.a.[227] Yet the more detailed rental of about the same date lists four distinct tenements on this site beside King Street, in addition to a stable in Endive Lane, none of these being ocupied by Mistress Thrower herself. That lady collected in rents from the actual occupants a yearly sum of £9. 5s., an income more than four and a half times the payment due to the landlord, yielding to the widow an annual profit of more than 350 per cent.[228] In sum, the cellarer's holding at Enedehithe in the early sixteenth century was worth £6. 4s. p.a. to the monastery, but £24. 15s. 8d. to the lay leaseholders.[229] Urban property was potentially a far more valuable investment at this period than the monastic rentals alone would suggest.

5. MOTIVES FOR URBAN PROPERTY HOLDING

The need for private accommodation and, perhaps, for a workplace was the sole motive for holding urban property which weighed with the vast majority of Westminster residents. Those institutions and individuals, however, who held large or small urban estates beyond personal requirements call for separate comment. It is possible briefly to consider the wider importance of urban property holding in relation, on the one hand, to the ecclesiastical corporation of Westminster Abbey and, on the other, to individual laymen.

During the late fourteenth and early fifteenth centuries there can be no doubt of the proportionately and absolutely increased value to the Westminster monks of their rents in the town. It is striking that the obedientiaries' busy commitment to local secular building at this period coincided with the introduction of another new policy, whereby very many of the abbey's more remote estates were granted out on leases. The reorientation away from direct management of agricultural manors is first observed on the

[226] WAM 18049C.
[227] WAM 17979; 18925 *et seq.* See WAM 17971, 18921–3; PCW Wyks, 238–40.
[228] WAM 18049C.
[229] A similar observation can be made of a row of properties standing on land belonging to the sacrist to the south of Endive Lane; see app. v.

Westminster Abbey estates, as on certain other great seigneurial holdings, around the mid-fourteenth century; it gained rapidly in momentum everywhere after 1400.[230] The trend is most reasonably explained as the result of a combination of increased labour costs with falling prices, both the consequences of a declining population in the wake of the epidemics. In these circumstances the turn to urban rents in Westminster proved, for a time, highly profitable; until *c.*1420 the local urban population remained remarkably buoyant, despite the plague.[231] As a great institution, moreover, the abbey could command resources sufficient to weather the mid-fourteenth century crisis and subsequently to make the heavy investment in urban building which has been described.[232] This new enterprise in the town of Westminster contributed substantially to the healthy state of the abbey's economy in the late fourteenth century.[233]

The setback of falling rent-values in the first half of the fifteenth century, however, naturally discouraged the religious from further development of this kind. When the market began to move again after the mid-century, they preferred to delegate maintenance and development work to private tenants. But although the abbey was no longer extracting the maximum rents from its Westminster houses, it continued until the Dissolution to derive from them a substantial proportion of its total income. The manor of Westminster had in 1086 represented about 2 per cent of the convent's resources. In the later Middle Ages Westminster Abbey was the

---

[230] Harvey, *Estates*, 148 ff.; ead., 'The Leasing of the Abbot of Westminster's Demesnes in the Later Middle Ages', *Econ Hist Rev*, 2nd ser., xxii (1969), 17–27. Cf. R. A. L. Smith, 'The Central Financial System of Christ Church, Canterbury, 1186–1512', repr. in id., *Collected Papers*, ed. Knowles (London, 1947), 23–41, esp. pp. 39–40; Dobson, *Durham Priory*, 272; E. Searle, *Lordship and Community: Battle Abbey and its Banlieu, 1066–1538* (Toronto, 1974), 452, app. III; Du Boulay, 'A Rentier Economy in the Later Middle Ages: The Archbishopric of Canterbury', *Econ Hist Rev*, 2nd ser., xvi (1963–4), 427–38; G. A. Holmes, *The Estates of the Higher Nobility in Fourteenth-Century England* (Cambridge, 1957), 119–20.

[231] Cf. ch. 6, sect. 1.

[232] For the resilience shown by other great lay and ecclesiastical lords at this period, see Holmes, *Estates of the Higher Nobility*, 114–15; *The Cambridge Economic History of Europe*, vol. i, 2nd edn., ed. M. M. Postan (Cambridge, 1966), 588–9 (the estates of the bishopric of Winchester); R. A. L. Smith, *Canterbury Cathedral Priory* (Cambridge, 1943), 194; and further, J. L. Bolton, *The Medieval English Economy, 1150–1500* (London, 1980), 220 ff.

[233] See Harvey, *Estates*, 66: 'The actual income of the Abbey rose by as much as 47 per cent between the beginning and the end of the fourteenth century.'

second wealthiest religious house in the country, with lands in a score of counties. Yet in 1530 no less than 13 per cent of the abbey's annual income was derived from rent collected in the tiny urban estate of Westminster.[234]

The lay investors who are unevenly recorded throughout the period, and who gain prominence in the sources during the late fifteenth and early sixteenth centuries, in some cases enjoyed considerable profits on their outlay. Given that it was possible in the early sixteenth century to collect an income of almost £14 a year (less maintenance costs) on an investment in rent of £3. 6s. 8d. p.a.,[235] there was obviously considerable incentive to acquire urban rents as a potential source of wealth. The chandler Robert Powle, who repeatedly contracted with the abbey to redevelop sites in Westminster in the 1470s, served his own as well as the monks' financial interests.[236] The case is an extreme illustration of the value of property as an investment at this period, and the example was not wasted on private speculators. Doubtless some of the individuals recorded as holding more than a single property used the additional premises for their work, or to house their servants or apprentices.[237] Thus John Pomfrett, brewer at the Lamb brewhouse in King Street from 1511 until 1531, from 1526 held in addition the White Lion brewhouse at Charing Cross, which surely reflects a simple expansion of Pomfrett's business.[238] Similarly the chandler William Russell described a tenement which he held in the Wool Staple by King Street as his 'wax house and working house'.[239] Others, however, held considerably more properties at one time than are likely to have been useful to their work, and the probability is that these were treated as a source of revenue. Even the chandler William Russell held, in addition to his 'wax house', a row of nine

---

[234] £374: £2,827. See Harvey, *Estates*, 332, 354–5. The 1530 figure for the town of Westminster is the sum given in the Valor Ecclesiasticus of 1535, supplemented by £33, being the value of the chief Westminster Abbey properties purchased by the king in 1531 for incorporation of their sites in the new palace of Whitehall. These properties had belonged to the sacrist (£20: see WAM 19804, 19807), the domestic treasurer (£7. 1s.: see WAM 23169, 23171) and the cellarer (£6. 4s.: see WAM 18944, 18946). For the record of the purchase, see *LP* v, no. 404.

[235] See app. V.

[236] For Powle see above, sect. 4.

[237] Such cases are also known in fourteenth-century Winchester. Keene, *Medieval Winchester*, i. 218–30.

[238] App. VIII, s.n. Pomfrett.

[239] App. VIII, s.n. Russell.

cottages next to his dwelling house at the Bell, beside the bars in
King Street. Russell paid the abbey £2. 5s. p.a. for the Bell and the
cottages together; by subletting all of the latter to various tenants he
supplemented his income by £6. 15s. p.a.[240] Thomas Brightman,
'yeoman', had evidently no personal use for the property which he
rented at Endive Lane and sublet to others as wharfage, stabling,
and Cardinal Wolsey's laundry; from the total of his lettings here he
received £10. 13s. p.a. over the rent he paid to the abbey.[241] The
same must be observed of a number of other 'yeomen', 'gentlemen',
and crown and abbey officers in Westminster who, between the
mid-fifteenth and the mid-sixteenth centuries, held collections of
tenements probably superfluous to private needs.[242] Private landlords may have been less concerned than were big institutional
landowners with the long-term security of rent income; but on the
other hand, provided they were living locally, they could keep a
closer eye on their tenants than could the officers of an unwieldy
corporation, even one so conveniently placed as Westminster
Abbey.[243]

It has been suggested that urban property is unlikely to have
provided a major source of capital in the medieval economy.[244]
There is indeed no evidence that rent was the principal source of
revenue of those private individuals in Westminster who collected
it. Nevertheless it is clear that some private landlords supplemented
their income substantially in this way. How they invested their
gains, however, is less easy to perceive. Economically creative
investment of the dividends may not, in fact, have been a common
priority. Most of the 'gentlemen' and 'yeomen' concerned may have
valued their Westminster rentals primarily, not as a source of
income, but as security for loans.[245] Possession of urban rents was a
mark of financial respectability. Moreover, they could, as a rule, be
sold quickly at need to realize liquid cash, as some of the vendors of

[240] WAM 18012, 18026, 18049A.
[241] App. v.
[242] e.g. app. VIII, s.n. Attewell, Bradding, Forster, Lorde, Marble.
[243] Cf. Keene, *Medieval Winchester*, i. 233–4.
[244] Hilton, 'Some Problems of Urban Real Property in the Middle Ages', in C. H.
Feinstein (ed.), *Socialism, Capitalism and Economic Growth* (Cambridge, 1967),
326–37; id., *The English Peasantry in the Later Middle Ages* (Oxford, 1975), 214;
Butcher, 'Rent and the Urban Economy: Oxford and Canterbury', 12–18.
[245] Cf. Keene, *Medieval Winchester*, i. 230; R. A. Holt, 'Gloucester in the Century
After the Black Death', 155.

local property to the abbey in the thirteenth century appreciated.[246] Urban property might also be used to ensure the provision of accommodation in old age, as it was by those who made such provision a condition of their sale of houses in Westminster to the abbey in the late fourteenth century.[247] And by others such property was assigned to endow chantries, providing an insurance for eternity.[248]

[246] See above, sect. 2.
[247] See above, nn. 97, 101.
[248] e.g. above, nn. 12, 157–8, 216, and ch. 9, n. 54.

4

Fairs and Markets

I. THE GREAT FAIR OF ST EDWARD

Trading was carried on in Westminster from the early Middle Ages onwards; but it changed dramatically in character between the ninth and the sixteenth centuries. In the mid-Saxon period Westminster appears to have taken part in the international commerce focused upon *Lundenwic*; in the thirteenth century a great cosmopolitan fair gathered here each year. In the later Middle Ages, however, this international role was lost; after the early fourteenth century Westminster's enduring importance was as a centre of purely local marketing.

The archaeological evidence indicative of trading activity in Westminster in Saxon times[1] strongly suggests that the fair which Henry III promoted here had its origins at a much earlier date. Both the royal court from the eleventh century onwards, and the religious community from a previous period, may have encouraged such commerce.[2] Nevertheless, the mid-thirteenth century seems to reflect a significant extension of the importance and prestige of the Westminster fair. It was in 1245 that the monks of Westminster received from King Henry their first charter to hold *two* annual fairs, each of three days, respectively about the deposition (5 January) and the translation (13 October) of St Edward the Confessor.[3] In 1248 the period of the latter fair was extended to a fortnight. In addition, the business of all other fairs held throughout England at this time of the year was suspended; and all the shops of London were closed for the duration of the fair by royal command.[4] The chronicler Matthew Paris makes clear that the

---

[1] See ch. 1, sect. 1.
[2] For early markets, especially in such contexts as this, see Sawyer, 'Fairs and Markets in Medieval England', in N. Skyum-Nielsen and N. Lund (eds.), *Danish Medieval History: New Currents* (Copenhagen, 1981), 153–68.
[3] *Cal Ch R 1226–57*, p. 286.
[4] *Matt Par Chron Maj*, v. 28–9; *Liber de Antiquis Legibus*, s.a. 1248, in H. T. Riley (ed.), *Chronicles of Old London* (London, 1863), 15–16.

king's dual intent by these grants was both to provide additional financial aid to the great work of rebuilding Westminster Abbey, which was taken over by the crown at this very date, and at the same time effectively to tax his recalcitrant subjects, the citizens of London.[5] The extravagant gifts of money and of 'a highly precious vase', which the Londoners were prepared to offer to the king for the remission of the fair, are the first indications of its significance.[6] All remonstrance, however, was in vain: 'whether they would or no', in October the traders of London must make their way to Westminster for the fair of St Edward.[7]

It is apparent from the vivid account of Matthew Paris that little thought had been given to the practicalities of officially establishing Westminster as one of the great annual fairs of western Europe. The site, the abbey churchyard, was far too small for the attending crowds, and did not even provide covered stalls, an inconvenience aggravated by torrential rain. The keeping of a major fair so late in the year may be explained in part by the need to avoid infringement of the privileges of existing fairs, in part by the inordinate devotion of the monarch to his adopted patron saint, reckless of the inclement season of that saint's feast. Crushed, drenched, and muddied, the unhappy merchants wished themselves at home by their hearths, among their families.[8] After three years of such discomfort, it was decreed that the fair should be removed from the churchyard to Tothill.[9] Ecclesiastical censure of the desecration of holy ground may also have affected this decision; in 1285 Edward I would legislate (ineffectually) against the keeping of fairs in churchyards.[10] But in fact at Westminster there is no evidence that the transfer was ever made; indeed, the marshy fields of Tothill (a 'hill' in little but

---

[5] *Matt Par Chron Maj*, v. 127–8. Cf. King John's foundation of Stourbridge fair to support the lepers of St Mary Magdalen. *The Victoria History of Cambridgeshire and the Isle of Ely*, vol. ii (London, 1948), 308.

[6] *Matt Par Chron Maj*, v. 485.

[7] Ibid. v. 333. Unlike some other fairs, to which ref. will be made, Westminster fair has not hitherto been studied.

[8] *Matt Par Chron Maj*, v. 28–9, 334. The chronicler does not mention the additional turmoil of the abbey building site, which can only have exacerbated the situation.

[9] *Cal Pat R 1247–58*, p. 76.

[10] *Statutes of the Realm*, 11 vols. (London, 1810–24), i. 98. The holding of markets in churchyards had been forbidden by the third Lateran Council in 1178; the decree was clarified and expanded in 1215 and 1248. See also E. Lipson, *The Economic History of England*, vol. i (12th edn., London, 1959), 232; Salzman, *English Trade in the Middle Ages* (Oxford, 1931), 124–5.

name) must have appeared an even less suitable venue for an international mart than the cramped, but at least better drained, gravel soil of the churchyard. Here, then, the October fair remained. In 1298 the fair in early January (even more hopeful of the climate in its conception than the other, albeit equally pious) was discontinued, the autumn event being prolonged to a total of thirty-two days.[11] The latter had become established as a fixed point in a cycle of fairs, to which merchants travelled in turn: from St Ives (Easter), through Boston (June), Winchester (August), and Westminster (October) to Northampton (November).[12]

Some idea of the nature and size of the Westminster fair in its early years may be obtained from the records of purchases made there by the king. From these it would appear that the main traffic was in furs and cloth. Roger, the king's tailor, in the fair of 1250 spent the large sum of £300.[13] But other wares were also sold. Moreover, the names of recorded traders suggest a wide range of geographical origins. To promote the fair, it was publicized throughout England, and even on the Continent, that no royal prises would be taken there; this was a notable and a unique attraction.[14] In 1250 a skinner named Bydan Sauvet supplied from the fair £59. 10s. worth of rabbit skins.[15] In the following year southern wine was retailed by William de Orn' of Montpellier, while the Flemish- or Teutonic-sounding Rumbald de Sosac' and Conrad de Sosac' cried their wax.[16] 'Grey work'—calaber, grey squirrel fur—could be had in that year of Frend, son of Baldwin and Peter, son of Legard.[17] Another northerner, Folkard de Ordenburg, stood among the chandlers in 1252.[18] In 1253 the drapers included in their number Michael Clincard, James de Boninbrok (both from

[11] Original charter in Westminster Public Libraries, Archives Department, MS E. Deeds No. 2. See also WAM 1576, 25268A–B; *Cal Ch R 1257–1300*, p. 471.
[12] For evidence of merchants attending these fairs in succession, see *Cal Pat R 1232–47*, p. 239.
[13] *Cal Lib R 1245–51*, p. 307; see also ibid., pp. 257, 337.
[14] WAM 1578; *Cal Pat R 1247–58*, pp. 73, 104; *Cal Ch R 1226–57*, p. 334; ibid. *1257–300*, p. 479. Cf. E. W. Moore, *The Fairs of Medieval England. An Introductory Study*, Pontifical Institute of Mediaeval Studies, Studies and Texts, lxxii (Toronto, 1985), 20, 127–31.
[15] *Cal Lib R 1245–51*, p. 310. *Sauvet*: of Savoy?
[16] *Cal Lib R 1251–60*, pp. 83, 88.
[17] Ibid., p. 108.
[18] Ibid.

Douai in Flanders), Baudettus de Waseris and John Saer.[19] The catalogue of names alone faintly evokes the cosmopolitan cacophony and excitement of the fair at this period.

Since the sole records of transactions in the fair at this time concern purchases made by the king, it is uncertain what goods were taken away from it by the Flemings and other foreigners who traded there. Part of the answer is surely English wool, then so much, and increasingly, in demand for the cloth manufacturing industry of the Low Countries. This suggestion, which can reasonably be made for the foreign buyers in the June fair at Boston,[20] might seem less plausible at Westminster in October, remote from the flocks and distant in time from the shearing. Nevertheless in the early 1300s up to 550 sacks of wool were being sold at Westminster fair,[21] and this therefore appears certain to have been an attraction to the foreigners who came in the mid-thirteenth century. At the same time it may be of equal significance that the location of the Westminster fair, in particular, guaranteed good sales made to the king's buyers for all who brought their goods there to trade, whether in exchange for wool or for cash.

During several decades no more than temporary provision was made for the accommodation of merchants staying at the fairs.[22] Shortly before 1280, however, Abbot Richard de Ware built within the churchyard a 'long house' by the sanctuary wall, between the north gate and the free-standing belfry, primarily for fair-time occupation. The profits from this house were dedicated to the maintenance of lights at the high altar in the abbey church and at St Edward's shrine.[23] By 1288 an annual rent of £4 was being collected from the houses assigned to the skinners at St Edward's fairs; and reference was made in that year to 'the abbot's houses already or

---

[19] Ibid., p. 152. See also ibid., pp. 321, 253; ibid. *1267–72*, pp. 207, 259. Michael Clincard was a Douai merchant who also traded at St Ives fair. Moore, *Fairs of Medieval England*, 71, Table 10A. Boinebroke was the name of a prominent bourgeois family of drapers at Douai in this period. See G. Espinas, 'Jehan Boine Broke, bourgeois et drapier Douaisien (?–1310 environ)', *Vierteljahrschrift für Social- und Wirtschaftsgeschichte*, vol. ii (1904), 34–121, 219–53, 382–412.

[20] S. H. Rigby, 'Boston and Grimsby in the Middle Ages', Ph.D. thesis, Univ. of London (1982), 174–5.

[21] See Table 1 for receipts from the tronage of wool; PRO, SC6/1109/4 records (s.a. 1308) that the rate was 4*d.* per sack.

[22] The precinct to the north of the abbey was empty of buildings, apart from St Margaret's church, before the second half of the thirteenth century. See also ch. 3 n. 123.

[23] WAM 17458; *Cal Pat R 1272–81*, p. 418.

hereafter to be erected for the said fairs'.[24] In 1289 Abbot Walter de Wenlock made a purchase, for the sum of 53 marks, of three houses outside the north gate of the sanctuary, which were also allocated to merchants in the fairs.[25] The revenues from these houses Abbot Wenlok donated to the convent, to be managed on its behalf by the sacrist.[26]

A picture of the October fair in the early fourteenth century is provided by three extant rentals of the houses and stalls let to traders in the years 1311, 1313, and 1314, together with briefer royal ministers' accounts from two abbatial vacancies in 1308–9 and 1315–16[27] (see Fig. 7 and Table 1). The most expensive premises were four houses (*domus*) immediately outside and immediately within the sanctuary gate towards King Street; these clearly included the three bought in 1289. The combined rent for these houses, including a solar (*totum solarium*), a pentice (*penticium cum altis luminibus*), and a cellar (which in 1314 contained three shops), which were separately let, was about £75 for the month of the fair alone. A dozen stalls (*rengae*) were arranged in rows near the belfry. These varied between 12 and 60 feet in length, the maximum size being charged at a rate of £6 or £7 for the month. A tiny booth (*selda*), on the other hand, could be had for 2s. About twelve dealers rented places (*placeae*) 'beneath the cemetery wall'. The standard fee here was 1s. for a stretch of 3 feet, and plots taken varied between lengths of 9 and 48 feet. The houses or selds (*domus, seldae*) of the skinners, four in number, stood within the sanctuary, adjacent to one of the houses by the gate.[28] Four additional rows were allocated

[24] The skinners' houses may be identical with the 'long house' of 1280; see further below. In 1288 the sum of £4 due from the skinners was assigned by the abbot in perpetuity to the sacrist, to buy spices for the monks on the morrow of St Barbara (5 Dec.), and to spend the cash remaining on a conventual pittance. But within a year the abbot reclaimed the skinners' rent, although he partially honoured his promise by providing spices for the brethren at his own cost. WD, fo. 87r; *Documents Illustrating the Rule of Walter de Wenlok, Abbot of Westminster, 1283–1307*, ed. B. F. Harvey, Camden, 4th ser., ii (1965), 20, 98 and n., 169.

[25] WD, fos. 86v–87r; WAM 28044**, 28842.

[26] *The History of Westminster Abbey by John Flete*, 116; *Documents . . . of Walter de Wenlok*, 239. See also *Cal Cl R 1343–6*, p. 499.

[27] WAM 50684A–B, 50787–9; PRO, SC6/1109/4–5. The enrolled total receipts in 1306–7 are derived from the abbot's receiver's accounts: WAM 24257, 24260.

[28] 'Selds' recorded at Winchester fair and in Cheapside in the city of London were long structures within which there were numerous *fenestre* let out to individual traders. The principal meaning of the term thus seems to have been a substantial structure of this kind, containing separate places for trading. Sometimes, however, 'seld' was interchangeable with 'shop'. Keene, *Medieval Winchester*, i. 138; Keene and Harding, *Cheapside and the Development of London*.

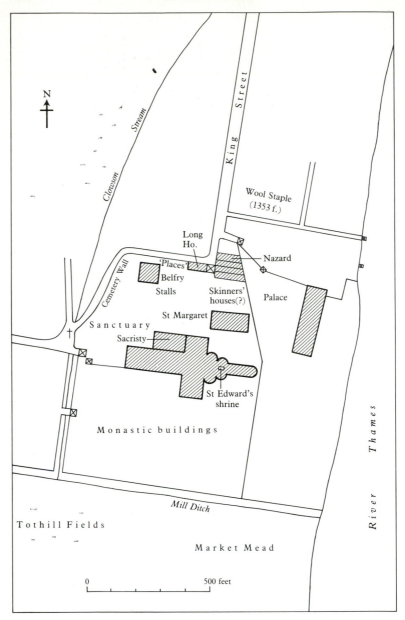

FIG. 7. The site of the October fair of St Edward at Westminster

TABLE 1. *Receipts from Westminster fair, 1306–1316*

Year	Total			Rents			'Fines'			Court			Tolls			Tronage			Source
	£	s.	d.	£	s.	d.	£	s.	d.	£	s.	d.	£	s.	d.	£	s.	d.	
1306	92	4	4							1	3	0							WAM 24257
1307	94	0	1																WAM 24260
1308	130	12	7¾	107	11	0	6	16	8	4	14	6	2	18	7¾	8	11	10	PRO, SC6/1109/4
1309	130	19	8¼	106	2	10	11	9	0	3	1	1	2	4	6¼	8	2	2	PRO, SC6/1109/4
1311	125	11	8	101	4	4	7	0	0	6	8	0	2	10	4	8	18	1	WAM 50684A, B
1313	121	4	5½	104	18	10	6	6	4	1	6	6	2	9	1½	6	3	8	WAM 50687–8
1314	117	2	10½	102	4	6	4	1	2	2	0	6	3	1	0½	5	15	8	WAM 50689
1315	112	15	7	95	19	4	5	0	0	3	8	0	2	11	3	5	17	0	PRO, SC6/1109/5
1316	98	18	4	89	5	8	2	13	4	1	14	8	1	16	8	3	7	6	PRO, SC6/1109/5

to the skinners, presumably adjacent to their selds. The sum of the skinners' rents in these years was about £3 p.a.; the sum of rents for the fair stalls was around £100 p.a. Finally, the rentals note the fines, which rose so high as £11. 9s. in 1309, charged on resident tenants of houses outside the sanctuary gate, whose normal business must have benefited greatly from the fair-time conflux.[29]

All business of the fair was under the authority of the abbot of Westminster. Henry III endowed St Edward's fair with all the customs and privileges enjoyed by the August fair of St Giles at Winchester.[30] The Winchester customs are known from the confirmatory charter of Edward III, a copy of which was made by the careful Westminster monks.[31] The administration of the fair was entrusted jointly to the abbot's bailiff and to a temporary marshal, whose first task was the proclamation in London demanding the closure of all shops within a radius of ten miles of the fair.[32] In the fourteenth century the sacrist of the monastery paid for the announcement in London of the fair, and also of indulgences attached to the abbey's relics, an additional draw at the time of St Edward's feast.[33] Toll stations were set up at all approaches to the fair—at Tothill, Rosamund's Manor in the fields towards Eye, Charing, and 'Westminster Gate', the riverside wharf at the palace (later 'Westminster Stairs')—where a scale of dues was charged on goods brought for sale. In 1308–16 the annual receipts from the toll were about £2 or £3.[34] Further taxes were levied on the weighing

[29] There was not unnaturally competition to secure the best places in the fair, which the abbot's steward granted for an additional fee. *Documents . . . of Walter de Wenlok*, 159.

[30] WAM 9315*. See also WD, fo. 68ʳ; *Cal Ch R 1257–1300*, p. 239 (another copy).

[31] G. W. Kitchin (ed.), *A Charter of Edward III, Confirming and Enlarging the Privileges of St. Giles Fair, Winchester, A.D. 1349*, Winchester Cathedral Records, vol. ii (London and Winchester, 1886); a copy in LN, fos. 93ᵛ–96ᵛ. See an entry in the Westminster sacrist's roll under 1363: 'Et dat' uni clerico in cancellaria domini regis pro copia statuti ferie Wynton' habenda et aliis diversis brevibus. 14s. 4d.' WAM 19629.

[32] *Septem leucas*. The *leuca* was usually about 1½ miles, but sometimes two or more. The marshal, or warden, of the fair was retained for six weeks, for a fee of about £6 or £7.

[33] WAM 19623, 19630, 19634–5. In 1318 the sacrist rewarded the monks who guarded the relics during the fair. WAM 19619.

[34] See Table 1. In 1313–14 seven toll-collectors were paid totals of 16s. 11d. and 16s. 8d. The rental accounts noted above, in combination with the Winchester customs, are the chief sources of the information contained in this paragraph. WAM 29181 is an acquittance of 1305 from William de Grafton for a mixed green shirt and

and sale of commodities in the fair: for example, 4*d*. each on the sale of a cask of wine or cider, a bear (should there be one), or a ferret. The office of 'tronage', the weighing of wool, in St Edward's fair was granted in 1312 to Richard de Chiriton for life; although invited to dine with the abbot during the fair, he was not to retain any of the fees which he charged.[35] In the recorded years between 1308 and 1316, the tronage was worth from £5. 15*s*. 8*d*. to £8. 18*s*. 1*d*.

The immediate supervision of the business of the fair was the responsibility of the marshal, who was also to control the lighting of fires and, at sunset, to ride through the fair and declare it closed until the morrow.[36] Legal cases arising from fair-time transactions were heard in the abbot's court of the fairs. The extant records of this body for the years 1313, 1328–9, and 1334 are typical of such courts at this period.[37] The chief matters dealt with were debts, broken contracts, and the use of false measures in the fair, in addition to the assizes of bread and ale.[38] An important case in 1302, which was transferred to the court of king's council in parliament, concerned the abbot's right to distrain upon the goods of merchants who broke the laws of the fair. Certain drapers had rented premises in the precinct of the king's palace which had not been allocated for fair-time trading, and the abbot's seizure of their very valuable cloths was ruled to be legitimate retribution for their transgression.[39] The abbot's profits of pleas in his court of the fair fluctuated in recorded years between £1. 3*s*. in 1306 and £6. 8*s*. in 1311.[40]

a blue overtunic, received as wages for collecting the toll of St Edward's fair. The house of John de Benstede, where a few pence only were collected in toll, was that called Rosamund's. See *Cal Pat R 1307–13*, p. 58.

[35] WAM 50685. A new weigh-beam (*trona*) was bought for 9*s*. in 1307. *Documents . . . of Walter de Wenlok*, 211. See also *Cal Plea & Mem R 1298–1307*, 8.
[36] Customs of the Winchester fair, loc. cit. [37] WAM 50686, 50694–6.
[38] Cf. the proceedings of the fair court of St Ives between 1270 and 1317. C. Gross (ed.), *Select Cases Concerning the Law Merchant*, vol. i, Selden Society, xxiii (1928), 1–107. On the St Ives fair see also Moore, 'Medieval English Fairs: Evidence from Winchester and St Ives', in J. A. Raftis (ed.), *Pathways to Medieval Peasants*, Pontifical Institute of Mediaeval Studies, Papers in Medieval Studies, ii (Toronto, 1981), 283–99; and ead., *Fairs of Medieval England*.
[39] *Rot Parl*, i. 150–2; WAM 50754.
[40] See Table 1. In eight subsequent recorded years, between 1317 and 1335 inclusive, the profits of the fair court, as noted in the general account rolls of the abbot's bailiff, did not exceed £3. 4*s*. 11*d*. in any year. WAM 24698, 24701, 24708–10, 24714–15.

All told, the profits of the abbot of Westminster from his fair varied in the decade 1306–16 between £92 and £130.[41] These were large sums, indicative of the continuing importance of St Edward's fair at the beginning of the fourteenth century. They may be compared with somewhat earlier data for other English fairs. The bishop of Winchester's annual takings from his fair reached a peak in 1250 of almost £160, and subsequently fluctuated around £110 until the 1290s.[42] The profits of St Ives fair were £101 in 1207, in 1211 £180.[43] St Botolph's fair in 1280 was worth £290 in rents, tolls, and profits of jurisdiction.[44] The indications in all of these cases, however, are that a decline had become apparent by the 1270s at the latest.[45] The Westminster fair may, therefore, have been even more lucrative in the thirteenth century than at the beginning of the fourteenth.

The main trade at the fair continued in this period to be in furs and cloth. The abbot's steward could purchase here all the materials necessary to make up the caps, robes, and furs issued to the servants and valets of the convent. In 1311–14 his shopping-list included striped and single-dyed cloths for gowns, lambskins, both domestic and imported (the latter were called *budget*), and Baltic squirrel skins in various forms, as *popel* (skins of early summer), *grosvair* (the whole skins), and *minever* (furs made of bellies only, white with a little grey surrounding them). He also bought rabbit skins and squirrel caps for the abbot's sisters and nephews.[46] Other trades represented were evidently of secondary importance. An apothecary is named in the rentals, and a spicer; also a poulterer and a butcher, and a cook 'under the belfry'; in 1314 the latter paid no rent, being poor. As necessary to the conduct of business as the cook was the scribe (*scriptor*), who paid just 6d. for his place behind the gate.[47]

[41] See Table 1.
[42] Keene, *Medieval Winchester*, ii. 1124.
[43] Gross (ed.), *Select Cases Concerning the Law Merchant*, i., p. xxxii; see also Moore, *Fairs of Medieval England*, 208.
[44] Rigby, 'Boston and Grimsby' (1982), 177; and see ibid., 177–225, *passim*.
[45] See refs. cited in preceding notes, and further below.
[46] WAM 50684, 50687–9. These items are debited against the abbot's income from the fairs, which had evidently ceased to be devoted to the rebuilding of the abbey as Henry III had intended. See also *Documents . . . of Walter de Wenlok*, 131. On the nomenclature of pelts see E. M. Veale, *The English Fur Trade in the Later Middle Ages* (Oxford, 1966).
[47] Two probable dyers are noted below.

But if the goods remained the same, the merchants who sold them were a significantly different group from those of the mid-thirteenth century. Of the identifiable traders in the earlier period only two, Stephen Bukerel and John de Northampton, represented the mercantile interest of the city of London.[48] As has been seen, many more of the recorded names suggest origins farther distant than London. The evidence of the late thirteenth and early fourteenth centuries, however, reflects the disappearance from St Edward's fair of this distinctive cosmopolitanism, and its replacement by an overwhelming preponderance of Londoners. The vendor of the houses by the sanctuary gate bought by the abbot in 1289 was a harbinger of the change. This was Stephen de Cornhill, a sheriff of London in the 1280s, who had made his fortune by trade in cloth and jewels. Cornhill's temporary investment in a base at Westminster in the last quarter of the century was a natural move, once the fair had become established.[49] The three early fourteenth-century rentals provide many more names of Londoners. Foremost among these was Henry Nazard. Nazard was a foreigner perhaps hailing originally from Arras, but became an alderman of London in 1318 and was 'the most important city draper in the early fourteenth century'.[50] In 1311–14 Nazard rented one of the houses outside the sanctuary gate, at the enormous cost of £14. 13s. 4d. on each occasion.[51] The great solar above these houses was shared in 1311 by Simon de Abyndon and Simon de Swanlond, both members of powerful aldermanic and clothier dynasties recently settled in the city of London.[52] John Simeon and Thomas Cok, who traded in another house there, and Edmund de Chiltren, who rented the pentice along the front of the same houses, can also be identified as

---

[48] *Cal Lib R 1251–60*, p. 153. For these important aldermen, see G. A. Williams, *Medieval London: From Commune to Capital* (London, 1963), *apud indicem*.

[49] WD, fos. 86ᵛ–87ʳ; 28044**, 28842. See also *Cal Letter-Bk A*, 161, 203, 213; and W. R. Powell, 'English Administrative Families in the Twelfth and Thirteenth Centuries, with Special Reference to the Cornhill Family', B.Litt. thesis, Univ. of Oxford (1952), 155 and *passim* for the Cornhill family in general.

[50] A. B. Beaven, *The Aldermen of the City of London*, 2 vols. (London, 1908–13), i. 70, 381; Williams, *Medieval London*, 129–30, 151; S. L. Thrupp, *The Merchant Class of Medieval London* (Ann Arbor, 1948), 357.

[51] WAM 50684, 50687–9. All the names in the remainder of this paragraph are derived initially from these sources. Years later, the great house by the gate was known as 'Nazardhouse', e.g. WAM 19622 (1347).

[52] Beaven, *Aldermen*, i. 70, 80, 197, 264, 381, 384; Thrupp, *Merchant Class*, 321, 368; Williams, *Medieval London*, 128, 131–2. Their rent for the solar was £13. 6s. 8d.

London drapers.[53] Most of the stall-holdings by the belfry were also
taken by cloth-sellers from London. The first and largest of these
stalls, let at the rate of £7, was shared by John Mire, Roger Harold,
Richard Costentyn, and Richard de Ansty. The first three, and
probably the fourth also, of these individuals appear in contemporary London records as drapers and, in one case, as an alderman.[54]
Others who kept stalls in the same block in the years 1311–14 were
William de Wyndsor, called 'the hosier', and James le Hosier.
William de Wyndsor, 'draper', is found in London at about this
period, and was in 1310 one of the London wardens of the fair of St
Botolph in Lincolnshire; James le Hosyer, called 'le Frensshe',
made his will in London in 1349.[55] William de Welles and John de
Welleford, also stall-holders here, are likewise described in London
documents as 'chaucers', or hosiers, of that city.[56] In 1306 the sons
of John de Armentiers bought cloth at St Edward's fair on behalf of
their father, who, despite his foreign appellation, was a member of
the Drapers' Company of London, in addition to being an alderman
of the city.[57] Most of the skinners also demonstrably came from
London.[58] It is significant that the fraternity of that craft was at this

[53] *Cal Letter-Bk D*, 111; ibid. *E*, 14, 116. Edmund de Chiltren was associated in
1316 with Simon de Abyndon. Ibid. *E*, 70.

[54] John Mire: *Cal Letter-Bk B*, 23, 39, etc.; ibid *C*, 100, 217–18; ibid. *D*, 119, etc.
Roger Harold: ibid. *B*, 226. Richard Costentyn, alderman 1336–43: ibid. *C*, 205;
ibid. *E*, *vide apud indicem*; Beaven, *Aldermen* i. 16, 128. Richard Anesty was
associated with one Mark le Draper as pledge for another man in the London mayor's
court in Sept. 1303. *Calendar of Early Mayor's Court Rolls . . . 1298–1307*, ed. A. H.
Thomas (London, 1924), 147.

[55] *Cal Letter-Bk B*, 154, 156, 163; ibid. *D*, 233; *Calendar of Wills Proved and
Enrolled in the Court of Husting, London, A.D. 1258–A.D. 1668*, ed. R. R. Sharpe, 2
vols. (London, 1889–90), i. 601.

[56] *Cal Letter-Bk D*, 142, 160; ibid. *E*, 27. See *Middle English Dictionary*, s.v.
'chaucer': 'a maker of coverings for legs and feet'. A Richard de Welleford, draper,
was a sheriff of London in 1311–12. *Cal Letter-Bk D*, 20. He, or another of this name,
was a warden of Winchester fair in 1329. *Cal Plea & Mem R 1323–64*, 89; see also
ibid., 71, 192. Roger le Lunge de Wynton, on the other hand, who also occupied a
patch near the belfry, was a draper of Winchester and mayor of that city, which he
also represented as an MP. Keene, *Medieval Winchester*, ii. 1286, s.n. Roger (le)
Long.

[57] *Cal of Early Mayor's Court Rolls . . . 1298–1307*, 250; A. H. Johnson, *The
History of the Worshipful Company of the Drapers of London*, vol. i (Oxford, 1914),
184; Beaven, *Aldermen*, i. 166.

[58] The skinners who came from London to the Westminster fair were: John de
Thorp (Simon de Thorp also appears in the rentals): *Cal Letter-Bk B*, 24; Richard
Gentilcors: ibid. *B*, 47, 212, etc.; Nicholas de Stamford: ibid. *D*, 94; Henry de Bury
(Ralph de Bury is also named): ibid. *E*, 233, 286; and Laurence de Hanyngton: ibid.
E, 17–19. A prominent contemporary London skinner named William de Hanington

very time emerging as an active corporate body within the city.[59]

In marked contrast to the mid-thirteenth century, not a single name among those listed in the early fourteenth-century rentals speaks of an authentic continental derivation. The point should not be overstressed; foreign merchants did continue to attend the fair. Yet a rare instance in which they are recorded only confirms the reality of the change. In 1319 certain unnamed merchants of Brabant present at St Edward's fair were sued for debt by an influential London woolmonger named John Priour. Although the final outcome of the case is unknown, Priour's continued harassment of the Brabanters over several years, and his arrogant and illegal seizure and concealment in a house in Westminster of a load of cloths belonging to them, testify to the domineering self-confidence of the Londoner in a market no longer open.[60] Two citizens not yet named who rented stalls near the belfry in 1311–14 were Robert and William de Upton. In 1296 Robert de Upton, with his brother Stephen, had been charged in the London court of aldermen among certain 'drapers and other merchants of London staying at Westminster fair . . . to the prejudice of the liberty of the city aforesaid'.[61] But if the aldermanic court continued to frown upon the fair of St Edward as a royal insult to the city's franchise, individual members of that court, and other wealthy London merchants, by the early fourteenth century had so far overcome their hostility as to secure a virtual monopoly on trade at the fair. The challenge to the mercantile independence of London had thus been turned to the city's advantage.

At this same time, however, the fair's very existence was in jeopardy. Indeed, it was on the brink of collapse. In its decline in the

is described in Veale, *Fur Trade*, 43–4. Two probable dyers present at the fair may also have been visitors from London. Robert le Woder, presumably a woad merchant, could have been a relative of the individual of the same name who made his will in London in *c*.1301, *Cal Wills . . . in the Court of Husting*, i. 162. John de Watfeld may have been the John de Watford, 'teynturer', named in London in 1320. *Cal Letter-Bk E*, 117.

[59] Veale, *Fur Trade*, 39–52.
[60] WAM 50692. For Priour, who was an alderman in 1322–35, see Thrupp, *Merchant Class*, 361. Cf. the haughty claim of John de Abyndon, cited before the Westminster fair court in 1313, that a burgess of London could not be made to plead outside that city. He was adjudged to be wrong—for this exemption did not apply to courts merchant—but evidently continued recalcitrant. WAM 50686.
[61] *Cal Letter-Bk C*, 22. A draper called Ralph de Upton was an alderman in 1333–42. Thrupp, *Merchant Class*, 371.

fourteenth century Westminster fair shared in the misfortunes suffered by international fairs in general at this period. It is worth looking closely, however, at the chronology of decline; for in some respects Westminster's experience was both unique and significant. The first point to observe is that the figures of receipts from the Westminster fair in the decade 1306–16, though they may reflect a gradual contraction of business, do not suggest that the fair-time trade had yet failed.[62] Later still, in 1334, the citizens of Northampton could petition parliament for the right to a new fair, on the grounds that their present fair was held in early November, 'De quoi nul avantage ne cret a nule, par reson de la Feire de Westmenstre'.[63]

By the middle of the fourteenth century, however, the scale of St Edward's fair was drastically reduced. In 1347 Abbot Simon de Bircheston re-dedicated all his emoluments from the fair to the projected completion of the interrupted rebuilding of the abbey church.[64] This was no more than justice to the memory of King Henry III, who a century before had created the fair for this very purpose. But the later gift was less valuable than the first. It was in fact the sacrist, whose original endowment included most of the ground within the sanctuary, and who already controlled the three houses by the gate presented earlier by Abbot Wenlok, who assumed the administration of the fair.[65] During the 1350s the warden of the new work, the accounting department created in c.1335 to supervise the rebuilding, acknowledged receipts from the sacrist of proceeds from the fairs; but the lump sums are not easy to interpret.[66] A more explicit source is a rental of 1353 of 'the fair houses late belonging to the abbot's portion'.[67] Five houses are

---

[62] See Table 1. However, the reduced rent income in 1315–16 was indeed in part due to the lack of tenants in most of the skinners' row of houses in those years; and in part to the decayed stated of some of the other fair houses. PRO, SC6/1109/5.

[63] *Rot Parl*, ii. 85–6. That the complaint was delivered at this date and not before, however, indicates that Northampton's problem in the 1330s was a more general *malaise*.

[64] Abbot Bircheston made the gift in return for the monks' promise to keep his anniversary. WD, fo. 63ʳ; *The History of Westminster Abbey by John Flete*, 129.

[65] See above, n. 26.

[66] The credited amounts varied from £5. 6s. 'pro duobus domibus in Nundinis' in 1350 to £40, not explained but presumably not from exactly the same source, in 1355. WAM 23454–5. These payments appear to have ceased after 1357.

[67] WAM 50698. Under expenses, this account records the distribution of 2s. to each monks for the anniversary of Abbot Bircheston, as he had requested.

listed, all in or near the sanctuary. One was actually new-built in this year; the remainder presumably correspond, more or less exactly, with the fair houses of the earlier lists. But although they retained the name, the fair was no longer their primary *raison d'être*. The tenants of 1353 paid rents for a quarter, six months, or a year, without reference to the October fair. Moreover, the rental makes no mention of the temporary stalls with which the sanctuary had used to be crowded during that month. There would, in any case, have been less room for these than formerly, for in this period, and progressively throughout the later Middle Ages, the sanctuary was being built up with permanent lodgings unconnected with the fair.[68] The rents collected from the 'fair houses', their cellars and solars, in 1353 amounted to £31. 8s. The sacrist continued until the end of the century to account for the 'fair house rents' as a distinct group; the enrolled sums of these averaged about £22 each year between 1371 and 1400.[69] The account for the year 1399–1400, which provides more detail than the others, lists seven 'fair houses' and one 'seld', the rents from which totalled £21. 6s. 8d. As two of these houses were additionally offered to let 'extra tempus nundinarum' among the sacrist's other properties, it appears that at least some of the 'fair houses' still fulfilled their original purpose.[70] But because of the uncertainty regarding the lengths of the tenancies accounted for, the late-fourteenth-century figures probably cannot be simply compared with the rentals of 1311–14, which related to the period of the fair alone. Even were the comparison just, however, the fall from a sum of £100 to one of less than £25 would be eloquent of a dramatic fall in business.

St Edward's fair survived into the fifteenth century, but so diminished as hardly to deserve the once great name. In 1400 the sacrist conceded to the warden of the new work direct control of two of the 'fair houses', namely those which stood immediately without the northern sanctuary gate. The rentals of the latter officer in the early fifteenth century again record the collection of two separate annual rents from each of these houses, for the period 'outside fair-time' and for the fair's duration. The rates for eleven months of the year were 26s. 8d. and 30s., respectively, while occupation during

---

[68] See ch. 3 n. 124.
[69] WAM 19634–49.
[70] WAM 19659. See also WAM 19660 (1407).

the fair was charged at between one and two marks in each case.[71] Compared with the figure of £14. 13s. 4d. which Henry Nazard had paid for one of these houses in each of the fairs of 1311–14, these were paltry sums. It is moreover apparent from the irregularity of the fair-time rents, and from the repeated vacancies recorded in these years, that the warden of the new work had come too late into his inheritance. After 1419 there were no further fair-time lettings of these houses.[72] The sacrist, meanwhile, had hoped to raise money by levying a fee on his sanctuary tenants for licences to sublet their houses during the fairs. The single extant reference to this arrangement, however, which relates to the fair of 1407, records that not one resident considered it worthwhile to take up the offer.[73] The last references to the renting of houses in the fairs date from the 1420s, when the sacrist collected about £4 on each St Martin's day (11 November) from three or four of the 'fair houses' in the sanctuary.[74] One of the few traders present at this approximately terminal date was John Gedney, who was well known to contemporaries as a wealthy London clothier, and who was an alderman and mayor of the city between 1415 and 1449.[75] Gedney's presence suggests that while the scale of the fair had changed over the preceding century, its domination by London merchants had not.[76] Indeed, even at this late date the London company of drapers continued to exercise its right of search at 'Westminster fair', although by this time the search can have been little more than a jealously maintained tradition and an excuse for an annual excursion to the suburb.[77]

There are further symptoms of the fair's fading vitality. The abbot's fair court ceased by the later fourteenth century to be concerned entirely, or even primarily, with business arising from

---

[71] WAM 23470 et seq.

[72] WAM 23488 et seq.

[73] WAM 19660.

[74] WAM 19663–72. Salisbury cloth was sold in the fair in 1421. A. R. Bridbury, *Economic Growth: England in the Later Middle Ages* (London, 1962), 51.

[75] Beaven, *Aldermen*, ii. 4; see also app. VIII, s.n.

[76] In 1375 William Draper and John Draper, both of London, were charged in the abbot's 'court with pleas of the fair' with having used false measures in the fair; each was fined 3d. WAM 50706.

[77] Johnson, *Drapers of London*, i. 101–2, 116–19, 286, 301, 313, 318, 320. While, however, a few shillings were collected each year from fines levied by the company at the fair of St Bartholemew, no such fines are recorded in the fifteenth century at Westminster.

the fairs. This was a development noticed and resented by contemporaries in other places besides Westminster.[78] The clearest indicator of all is the list of amounts collected by the sacrist from the tolls of the fair. In contrast to the sums of about £2 or £3 received in the years 1308–16, the annual total after 1372, when the extant sacrist's rolls begin to record it, was never more than a few shillings.[79] Finally, in 1487 the levy of toll at the fair ceased altogether. There is no reference to the holding of St Edward's fair after this date, and it may be assumed to have been discontinued.[80]

The failure of the Westminster fair needs to be seen in the context of the general crisis of the international fairs in the thirteenth and fourteenth centuries.[81] In 1363 it was said that the fair of St Ives had not been held for over twenty years, 'owing to the absence of foreign merchants'.[82] Similarly, at Boston in 1335, 'foreigners did not come to the fair as they used to do'.[83] A more precise chronology is available for Winchester, where, peaks of prosperity having been achieved in the late twelfth and in the mid-thirteenth centuries, income from the fair fell off thereafter. An accentuated slump in the 1290s, the result of the Gascon wars which disrupted the wool trade, was followed by a slight recovery, but this was inadequate to halt the general trend of decline.[84] The great fairs of continental Europe, in Flanders and Champagne, had also been contracting from around 1260.[85] This general phenomenon was evidently the

---

[78] e.g. WAM 50706, 50708 (1375–6), etc. The heading on the later rolls of the autumn court is usually 'curia *cum* placitis nundinarum'; but few if any cases recorded therein appear to relate to the fair. In *c.*1480 the court was still known as the abbot's 'temporal court of piepowder'; but the matter then in question had nothing to do with the fair, PRO, C1/66/262. It may be that this piepowder court had extended to become a general judicature for local trade; but too few records survive to admit of certainty on this point. Cf. Lipson, *Economic History of England*, 240 and n.; and see also ch. 7, sect. 2.

[79] Table 1; WAM 19633 *et seq.*

[80] In this year, 1487, the Londoners actually forbade their traders to attend any fair or market outside the city. Although this measure was almost immediately annulled by parliament, it may have been the final death blow to the Westminster fair. *Cal Letter-Bk L*, 240, 242, 245; 3 Hen. VII c. 9. Cf. also Lipson, *Economic History of England*, 240 and n.

[81] Summarized in Moore, *Fairs of Medieval England*, 204–22, 289–90.

[82] Gross (ed.), *Select Cases Concerning the Law Merchant*, i., p. xxx.

[83] *Cal Inq p m* vii. 426; cf. Rigby, 'Boston and Grimsby' (1982), 177 ff.

[84] Keene, *Medieval Winchester*, ii. 1091–132, esp. 1119 ff.

[85] O. Verlinden, 'Markets and Fairs', in *The Cambridge Economic History of Europe*, vol. iii, ed. Postan, E. E. Rich, and Miller (Cambridge, 1963), 119–53, esp. 137.

consequence of a fundamental shift in the pattern of trade. Urban
development, the provision in the larger towns of year-round
trading facilities, made redundant the seasonal commerce of the
international fairs.[86] The monks of Durham, for example, changed
their purchasing policy: whereas in 1298 they had spent £148 in
Boston fair, by 1330 they were making most of their purchases in
the vicinity of Durham itself.[87] Equally significant, meanwhile, was
the growth of London. Until the difficulties of the 1290s,
Winchester fair had regularly welcomed numerous merchants from
London. After 1300, however, the Londoners ceased to attend. The
change highlights a more gradual shift in the kingdom's centre of
gravity, whereby Winchester was progressively abandoned in
favour of the concentration of both political and economic business
in London and Westminster.[88] A close parallel is found in France,
where the consolidation of the royal capital drew the trade in luxury
goods away from the fairs of Champagne, to be concentrated
instead in Paris, where the court was now based.[89] The presence of
the English royal court in Westminster explains both the active
interest of London merchants in St Edward's fair long after they
had snubbed the fair at Winchester, and the continued buoyancy of
Westminster fair into the second decade of the fourteenth century,
by which date most other fairs were conspicuously ailing. The
respective fortunes of the fairs of Winchester and Westminster
around 1300 thus provide a coda to the story, begun in the mid-
eleventh century, of the removal of the king's political capital from
the former to the latter place.

Like the rest, however, albeit on a slightly later time-scale than
most, Westminster fair was doomed. A late foundation as an
officially promoted enterprise, its fate was already sealed in the late
thirteenth century by the growth of the city of London. By 1350,
and probably before, the cloth and furs which had been the main
staples of the Westminster fair could be purchased much more
readily in the shops of London. Even the royal family transferred its

[86] Cf. the characterization of fairs as 'an indication of a pioneer rather than of a
mature economy' by N. J. G. Pounds, *An Economic History of Medieval Europe*
(London, 1974), 357–61.
[87] Moore, *Fairs of Medieval England*, 204–6.
[88] Keene, *Medieval Winchester*, ii. 1121; and above, chs. 1, 2.
[89] R.-H. Bautier, 'Les Foires de Champagne. Recherches sur une évolution
historique', *Recueils de la Société Jean Bodin*, vol. v (Brussels, 1953), 97–145, esp.
p. 144.

custom to the city.[90] After their exploitation of the fair of St Edward in the early fourteenth century, the merchants of London could later afford to ignore it.

2. THE LITTLE FAIR OF ST PETER

In the later Middle Ages not only the majority of the great fairs, but also many of the local fairs and markets, founded in the thirteenth century and before, disappeared. In the sixteenth century, however, a new trend can be discerned, in which markets and little fairs began once again to proliferate; doubtless many of these new ventures had existed for some time before receiving their charters.[91] One such new local event, created in the fifteenth century, was the Westminster fair of St Peter. St Peter's fair is first recorded in 1422; and from 1487 onwards the small toll collected before that date at St Edward's fair was levied instead at fairs on both of the two feasts of St Peter (St Peter and St Paul, 29 June, and St Peter in Chains, 1 August).[92] In *c.*1527, the sacrist of the monastery collected the modest sum of 11*s*. 10*d*. from the lease of 'the standing for booths on the two feasts of St Peter'.[93] Thirty years after this, the June fair of St Peter was attended by the diarist Henry Machyn, whose brief description evokes a parochial scene, far removed from the great concourses of the thirteenth century.

The xxix day of June, was sent Peters day, was a smalle fare keft [*i.e.* kept] in sant Margatt cherchyerde, as wolle and odur smalle thynges, as tornars [*i.e.* turners' wares] and odur: and the sam day was a godly prossessyon, the

[90] Veale, *Fur Trade*, 52–3; Williams, *Medieval London*, 107–8. See also Moore, *Fairs of Medieval England*, 216; Carus-Wilson, *Medieval Merchant Venturers* (2nd edn., London, 1967), 242–3 n. For the establishment of royal wardrobes in the city of London in the second half of the fourteenth century see also above, p. 23 and n.

[91] A. Everitt, 'The Marketing of Agricultural Produce', in J. Thirsk (ed.), *The Agrarian History of England and Wales*, vol. iv (Cambridge, 1967), 466–592, esp. 476. Where one of the former great international fairs survived until the sixteenth century, it is found to have performed very different, more local, functions from those of earlier times. Rigby, 'Boston and Grimsby' (1982), 379–80.

[92] WAM 19663 *et seq.*; 19735 *et seq.* In 1525 it was found by royal inquisition that the abbot of Westminster had for many years been used to hold at Westminster, within the monastic precincts, a fair each year on the feast of St Peter and St Paul and another on the feast of St Peter in Chains; but by what right or title this was done could not be established. WAM 50779. St Peter was, of course, joint patron with St Edward of Westminster Abbey.

[93] WAM 19810.

wyche my lord abbott whent with ys myter and ys crosse and a grett nomber of copes of cloth of gold, and the wergers, and many worshephull gentyllmen and women at Westmynster, went a prossessyon.[94]

3. THE MONDAY MARKET

Meanwhile, probably of far greater value to the local population throughout the period was a weekly Monday market for the neighbourhood, held (unlike the others) on Tothill. The right to hold a market here each Monday had been given official sanction in 1256.[95] The probable site was a field to the south of the monastery near the Thames, known in the later Middle Ages as 'Market Mead'.[96] The third quarter of the thirteenth century was a peak period for the promotion of such local markets.[97] On the other hand, the Westminster charter of 1256 is unlikely to have effected a wholly original creation. Small markets are doubtless ancient; and they survived into modern times, despite the growth of towns. No further evidence sheds detailed light on Westminster's Monday market. The 'alien' brewers, bakers, and others regularly listed in the court rolls of Westminster must, however, have set up their stalls here.[98] The weekly market was an event of greater significance to the local people whom it continued to serve than was the grandiose, but transient, great fair of the Blessed St Edward.

[94] *The Diary of Henry Machyn, Citizen and Merchant-Taylor of London, 1550–1563*, ed. J. G. Nichols, Camden Society, original ser., xlii (1848), 140–1. The fair of a week kept at the former hospital of St James, also visited by Machyn, had been granted by Edward I; it was evidently, at any rate in the sixteenth century and probably throughout the intervening period, another very localized event. Ibid., 240–1; *Rot Parl*, i. 57; *Placita de Quo Warranto* (Record Commission, London, 1818), 477.

[95] Original charter in Westminster Public Libraries, Archives Department, MS E. Deeds No. 1; see *Cal Ch R 1226–57*, 452.

[96] Reg Bk, i, fo. 11[r].

[97] The escalation of grants in this period appears to be due not solely to increased royal activity but, at least in part, to the appearance of genuinely new fairs. R. H. Britnell, 'The Proliferation of Markets in England, 1200–1349', *Econ Hist Rev*, 2nd ser., xxxiv (1981), 209–21.

[98] WAM 50752 *et seq.*

ILLUS. 6. Palace Yard, Westminster. View westwards, showing (from left to right) Westminster Hall, Westminster Abbey roof, the fountain, the King Street gate, and the clock tower. Drawing by Wenceslaus Hollar, 1647.

5

Occupations

I. INTRODUCTION

No town is an island. Medieval pictures of cities sometimes show a dense patchwork of brightly coloured houses fringed by a perimeter wall, beyond which extends an undifferentiated and alien country-side. But economic reality sewed town and hinterland together, threading the gates in the city wall with a continuous movement of humans and goods. These ties of interdependence require that the medieval town be viewed not as a free agent but as an integral part of the economy as a whole.[1] Within that global economy the medieval town's most distinctive role was as a market-place for the retail of commodities, broadly defined. Production, of course, there was also. In some areas of late medieval England, such as the cloth towns of the Cotswolds and Pennines, or the mining centres of Cornwall, industrial output was relatively intense;[2] meanwhile in the big cities a high degree of specialization of craft skills could be found.[3] Yet in most of the small towns and some even of the larger, the division of labour in industrial production remained minimal, and the scale of operation small.[4] The nature of available evidence has led research to be concentrated on the production rather than the distribution side of the medieval economy.[5] But, in view of the low level of production by most individual businesses, the primary concern of

[1] Hilton, 'Towns in Societies—Medieval England', *Urban History Yearbook* (1982), 7–13.
[2] Carus-Wilson, 'Evidences of Industrial Growth'; J. Hatcher, *English Tin Production and Trade Before 1550* (Oxford, 1973).
[3] Veale, 'Craftsmen and the Economy of London in the Fourteenth Century', in A. E. J. Hollaender and W. Kellaway (eds.), *Studies in London History Presented to P. E. Jones* (London, 1969), 133–51.
[4] Keene, 'Some Concluding Reflections', in D. W. Crossley (ed.), *Medieval Industry*, Council for British Archaeology, Research Reports, xl (1981), 151–3.
[5] On patterns of consumption, however, see the forthcoming book on medieval standards of living by Christopher Dyer.

many medieval townsmen was rather with the retail of goods direct to the consumer.

These two characteristics—the participation in a wider economy, and the preponderance of small-scale crafts—were present to an extreme degree in medieval Westminster. The consumer market to which the local economy catered comprised an unusually large proportion of transients. The continuous ebb and flow of courtiers and parliament-men, suitors at law, and pilgrims to St Edward's shrine, was as the movement of the life-blood of the small town to which they came. The economic life of Westminster remained in consequence exclusively geared to the production, on a small scale, of goods ready for immediate sale to the consumer. As many as four-score different crafts and occupations are recorded in Westminster in the late Middle Ages.[6] From this list, however, the primary industrial processes in the clothing, leather, pottery, and metal trades are almost completely absent; finishing and retail trades are overwhelmingly preponderant. An account of the medieval economy of Westminster must be largely concerned with small-scale craftsmen and with the shoppers upon whom they depended.

There can be no statistical breakdown of the trades and occupations practised in medieval Westminster (such as is partially facilitated in York, for example, by the registers of freeman admissions), yet there are sufficient fragmentary indications to make feasible a *pointilliste* depiction of the local economy. The natural first dab of the brush is a statement made in 1337 by the inhabitants themselves. Faced with a demand for royal taxation, they pleaded inability to pay, blaming their economic difficulties upon Edward III's removal of the royal courts to York, where they had remained since 1333. The petitioners' vision was limited; their reasoning did not fully explain their problems. Nevertheless they drew attention to an important truth. The core of this manifesto, notionally at least the communal expression of 'les liges gentz de la ville de Weymonster', ran as follows:

Come la dite ville ne est citee, burgh, (ne ville) marchande, et lour principal gayn et sustenance soleit estre del commun Bank et del Escheker et des

---

[6] This is a smaller figure than that of 180 recorded in fourteenth-century London. Veale, 'Craftsmen', 139. Yet it is considerably greater than the range of occupations in most of the small towns discussed by Hilton, 'The Small Town as Part of Peasant Society', in id., *The English Peasantry in the Later Middle Ages*, 76–94, esp. p. 80.

altres places lorsque ils furent a Westmonstre . . . il soient del tut anyentiz et enpoveriz puis le departir de la court de iloek.[7]

The substance of their claim, that the town possessed not two carucates of land, that its wealth consisted in rents, and that its tradesmen depended heavily upon the advent of visitors to the royal courts, was moreover entirely vindicated by the subsequent royal inquiry.[8]

One hundred and seventy-five years later, Abbot John Islip of Westminster (1500–30) had occasion to comment upon the economic activities of his local tenantry. In a petition to parliament of *c*.1511 the abbot referred to the 'great resort' which was had to Westminster during sessions of parliament and the four law terms of the year. At these times especially, 'somyche vitayle is utterid [*i.e.* sold] to a grett multitude of the kyngs soietts' that 'it is ryght . . . and behovefull to have the assize of brede, ale and all other vitaylis duely obervyd and kept'. The abbot went on to complain that the twelve chief pledges or 'headboroughs' of his manor court had made themselves self-electing, to the derogation of his own authority, and moreover that the officers in question were particularly unsuited to administer the crucial assizes of victuals because 'the seid hedbor-owis soo by and among themselff chosen be oft tymes for the most parte the grettest vitaylers themselff of and in the seid towne'.[9] The list of chief pledges between 1364 and 1514 confirms, so far as occupations can be established, that at any date in this period about half of the jury of local notables was made up of victuallers; and this proportion doubtless continued unchanged between 1514 and 1540, for although names of chief pledges at this time are lacking, many of those known to have been churchwardens or officers of the prestigious Assumption guild, themselves commonly victuallers, will certainly, as before, have served in the court.[10] The townsmen in 1337, and the abbot in *c*.1511, had each put their finger upon the distinctive character of Westminster's economy. As this chapter will show, the town derived its living throughout the later Middle Ages primarily from a captive market generated by the alluring presence of the abbey and the palace.

[7] PRO, SC8/78/3889.
[8] PRO, C145/132/7; *Cal Cl R 1337–9*, pp. 552–3, 563.
[9] WAM 6576. See app. VII for the full text of this document.
[10] See app. VIII, *passim*.

The local economy was characterized additionally by Westminster's status as a liberty. It was a feature of London's suburbs attractive to many that they lay outside the realm of effective control by the city authorities. The vitality of commerce in Westminster was the greater for being unconstrained by civic or craft regulations. The wide range of service trades which flourished in the liberal environment of Westminster is illustrated in Fig. 8, which shows the occupations represented within the southern half of King Street in the early sixteenth century.

2. ALEHOUSES, TAVERNS, AND INNS

In response to the growth of the consumer market, the residents of Westminster offered in return an appropriate range of services. These, as will be seen, were of all kinds, yet the most characteristic at all times was the drinking-house. Although hostelries existed in Westminster before 1350, the records reveal only a few; the sudden appearance, in the decades around 1400, of numbers of named taverns may be due not merely to an increase of evidence but to a real proliferation at this time of such relatively grand establishments, identified by permanent signs. By the early sixteenth century it would be easy to list two score lining King Street alone; and in Edward VI's reign fifty-eight taverns were enumerated between Tothill Street and Charing Cross. In 1585 the Westminster court of burgesses attempted to limit the number of 'common alehouses' in St Margaret's parish to sixty.[11] Already in c.1400 Thomas Hoccleve, a clerk who lodged 'at Chester's Inn right fast by the Strand' and who travelled daily to the privy seal office in Westminster Palace, passed on his way so many taverns, distinguished by their inviting signs, that it was quite impossible to avoid them.

> The outward signe of Bachus and his lure
> That at his dore hangith day by day
> Exciteth folk to taaste of his moisture
> So often that man can nat wel seyn nay.[12]

[11] J. C. Jeaffreson (ed.), *Middlesex County Records*, vol. i (London, 1886), 11; W. H. Manchée, *The Westminster City Fathers* (London, 1924), 215.
[12] Thomas Hoccleve, *La Male Regle de T. Hoccleve*, ll. 121–4; and see id., *The Regiment of Princes*, l. 5; printed in *Selections from Hoccleve*, ed. M. C. Seymour (Oxford, 1981), 15, 31. For Hoccleve see also ch. 6, sect. 4.

There were different kinds of hostelry, offering a variety of refreshment.[13] For Bacchus, of course, Hoccleve would have turned in to a wine tavern such as the Bell at the southern end of King Street, kept in his day by Thomas Nightingale.[14] Visitors to the royal courts complained that Nightingale's prices were excessive— 8*d*. instead of the statutory 6*d*. a gallon (*lagena*) for ordinary red and white (Gascon) wine, 16*d*. instead of 12*d*. for sweet Malmsey and 'Romeneye'[15]—but others found that the same was true at John Clynk's Saracen's Head beside the palace gate, and at the nearby taverns of John Wigmore, John Haxay, and Reginald Shepeye.[16] Such exorbitance was characteristic of medieval Westminster, as modern tourists will appreciate.

At the time of Hoccleve, at least some of these taverners were supplied by London vintners, who thereby evaded scrutiny by the city authorities. William Bromley, tavernkeeper of Westminster, and Hugh Short, vintner of London, in 1394 conspired to sell (naturally at an inflated price) bad La Rochelle wine which they had sweetened with honey.[17] But by the late Middle Ages Westminster's large retail trade had attracted leading vintners to base themselves here. An early instance was Ralph le Vineter, a prominent inhabitant of Westminster around 1300.[18] Among the more numerous later local wine-merchants was David Selly. Of foreign extraction, Selly, who sailed his own ships to and from Bordeaux, was a great merchant and a 'gentleman'. He became, as a juror of the Westminster court and a master of the Assumption guild, a distinguished figure in the town.[19]

[13] Distinctions between the humble alehouse, the wine-tavern, and the more substantial inn are drawn by P. Clark, *The English Alehouse. A Social History 1200–1830* (London, 1983), 5–15. As will appear below, however, and as indeed Professor Clark would agree, the functions of these various establishments, especially in the medieval period, overlapped extensively.

[14] WAM 23467–504. To its occupant in 1508 this was 'the tenement wine tavern in the which I dwell called the Bell'. PCW Wyks, 84–92; WAM 23587.

[15] This was a superior kind of Malmsey.

[16] PRO, KB9/183/6; see also M. K. James, *Studies in the Medieval Wine Trade* (Oxford, 1971), 193–4. For Nightingale, Clynk, and Wigmore, see app. VIII, s.n.

[17] PRO, KB9/172/1/23; and see James, *Wine Trade*, 163. Cf. also PRO, KB9/187/42: the supply to a Westminster consumer in 1401 of two pipes of (corrupt) red wine, by Richard Walworth, vintner of London. Earlier, in 1312, Ralph de Billingsgate, citizen and vintner of London, had supplied wine on credit to Roger de Presthoft, taverner of Westminster (probably Roger de Presthope, for whom see app. I). WAM 9274.

[18] See ch. I, sect. 2.

[19] See app. VIII, s.n. For another example see ch. 6 n. 88.

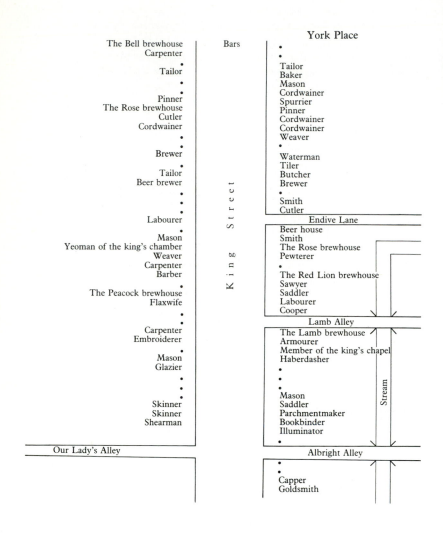

FIG. 8. King Street (south of the bars) in *c*.1508. Diagrammatic plan to show distribution of occupations

Source: WAM 18599 (with some complementary leases and rentals).

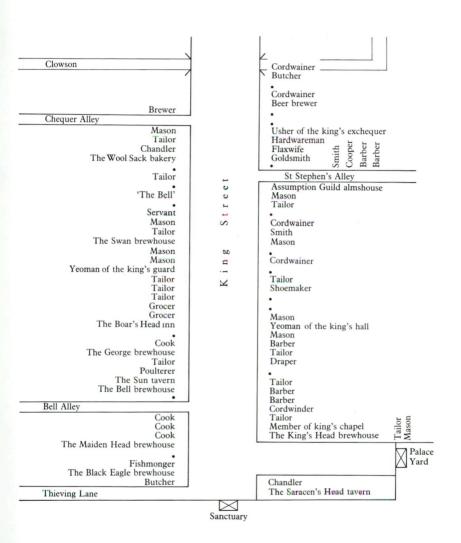

Clowson

Brewer

Chequer Alley

Mason
Tailor
Chandler
The Wool Sack bakery

Tailor

'The Bell'

Servant
Mason
Tailor
The Swan brewhouse
Mason
Mason
Yeoman of the king's guard
Tailor
Tailor
Tailor
Grocer
Grocer
The Boar's Head inn

Cook
The George brewhouse
Tailor
Poulterer
The Sun tavern
The Bell brewhouse

Bell Alley

Cook
Cook
Cook
The Maiden Head brewhouse

Fishmonger
The Black Eagle brewhouse
Butcher

Thieving Lane

King Street

Cordwainer
Butcher

Cordwainer
Beer brewer

Usher of the king's exchequer
Hardwareman
Flaxwife
Goldsmith

Smith Cooper Barber Barber

St Stephen's Alley

Assumption Guild almshouse
Mason
Tailor

Cordwainer
Smith
Mason

Cordwainer

Tailor
Shoemaker

Mason
Yeoman of the king's hall
Mason
Barber
Tailor
Draper

Tailor
Barber
Barber
Cordwinder
Tailor
Member of king's chapel
The King's Head brewhouse

Tailor
Mason

Palace
Yard

Chandler
The Saracen's Head tavern

Sanctuary

In Edward I's reign, ale for the king's household at Westminster was bought in large quantities direct from brewers in the city of London;[20] a century later the London governors expressed concern that ale, like wine, was being exported from the city for resale by hucksters in Westminster.[21] In the fifteenth century the Westminster court rolls confirm the presence each year of a dozen or more 'foreign' brewers, whose 'fines', levied by the court, may rather have been licensing fees for the right to trade in the liberty. In 1445 these included 'William atte the Cock in Dowgate', 'Thomas atte the stewes syde' (in Southwark), 'John Chaterich atte the rose in Flete Strete' and 'William atte the purse in Holbourne'.[22] But there can never have been a shortage of locally brewed ale, for perhaps the majority of private households produced and sold it, as the court rolls again make clear. Those presented in 1493 included, in addition to ten 'brewers', eight 'inn-holders' and one 'tavern-keeper', no fewer than 127 'tipplers' (*tipulatores*: petty retailers, rather than imbibers, of the liquor), operating within the area of St Margaret's parish.[23] Specialists in other crafts, like William Jarden, tailor, or Richard Russell, carpenter, very commonly ran an alehouse as a subsidiary concern; their fines in the court confirm their active involvement in the brewing premises which they rented.[24] But in such cases it may be assumed that the brewing was done by the men's wives.[25] The trade was indeed substantially in the hands of women,[26] to whom it offered not only an independent economic status but also a highly sociable activity, vividly evoked in John Skelton's tale of Elynour Rummyng of Leatherhead, who

---

[20] PRO, E101/368/23 (1305–6).

[21] *Cal Letter-Bk H*, 215.

[22] WAM 50752.

[23] WAM 50766.

[24] For Jarden, see app. VIII, s.n. Russell leased the Bell inn at the King Street bars from 1512, in which year he was presented in the court as a 'hosteller'. Reg Bk, ii, fo. 38^{r-v}; WAM 50775; PCW Wyks, 249–51.

[25] In late-fourteenth-century Exeter, women accounted for only 9.3% of brewing fines, yet they were involved in no less than 39% of all debts concerning drink in the Exeter courts between 1378 and 1388. M. Kowaleski, 'Local Markets and Merchants in Late Fourteenth Century Exeter', Ph.D. thesis, Univ. of Toronto (1982), 205–6.

[26] E. Power, *Medieval Women* (ed. Postan, Cambridge, 1975), 67; Clark, *English Alehouse*, 21; P. J. P. Goldberg, 'Women in Fifteenth-century Town Life', in J. A. F. Thomson (ed.), *Towns and Townspeople in the Fifteenth Century* (Gloucester, 1988), 107–28. See also the qualifying remarks of Hilton, *Class Conflict and the Crisis of Feudalism*, 214–15.

> breweth noppy ale,
> And maketh thereof port-sale
> To travellars, to tynkers,
> To sweters, to swynkers,
> And all good ale drynkers.[27]

Female hucksters, however, who merely sold ale brewed by others, were much less well-established figures than Elynour Rummyng; the leaden vessels used in ale-brewing were expensive. The Westminster court rolls list many hucksters who simply dispensed ale from (often unmeasured) cups. Their relatively lowly status, close to the margin of society, is typified by Petronella, the daughter of the vicar of St Martin-in-the Fields church, recorded in 1368. By this date it was unrespectable to be a priest's child, and it is no surprise to find Petronella accused of trading in ale with unlicensed measures.[28] Beer-brewing, which is referred to not at all before 1400 and relatively rarely thereafter, was a more complex process, and was associated in at least some cases with the Flemings who settled in Westminster in considerable numbers during the fifteenth century.[29]

The greatest of the Westminster brewers were influential men. James Atkynson, who in the 1490s owned leases on two brew-houses, the Cock and Tabard in Tothill Street and the Fleur-de-Lys in the Strand, held office as one of the constables of the liberty and was on gift-giving terms with the abbey.[30] John Pomfrett, 'gentleman', was a very 'baron' of the Westminster brewing trade. One of the half-dozen richest men in the town in the 1520s and at various times churchwarden of St Margaret's and warden of the Assumption guild, Pomfrett also managed two establishments, the White Lion at Charing Cross and the Lamb in King Street; but in Pomfrett the lion ruled over the lamb. He was a ruthless competitor, who did not shirk to use open violence in an attempt to drive his neighbour in King Street, John Henbury of the Red Lion, out of

---

[27] John Skelton, *The Tunnyng of Elynour Rummyng* (date of composition *c*.1520), printed in *John Skelton. The Complete English Poems*, ed. J. Scattergood (Harmondsworth, 1983), 214–30. *noppy*: strong

[28] WAM 50705.

[29] *Cal Cl R 1454–61*, p. 279; and see Salzman, *English Industries of the Middle Ages* (London, 1913), 193. For the Flemings, see below, ch. 6, sect. 2.

[30] New York University Law School, Frederick Brown Collection (no nos.), will of James Atkynson, brewer, dated 22 Apr. 1496. (I owe this ref. to Dr C. M. Barron.) See also WAM 23260–9; Reg Bk, i, fos. 7ᵛ–8ᵛ; 50761.

business, by forcibly seizing Henbury's valuable Thames-side wharf. Yet Henbury, himself a master of the Westminster fraternity of St Cornelius, and later a warden of the Rounceval guild, was not without resources; having secured Thomas Cromwell as his attorney, in the end he survived the menaces of his rival. The fight on the waterfront between the respective servants of these two is symptomatic of the deadly seriousness with which powerful men vied with one another to control this particularly lucrative local industry.[31]

Taverners commonly sold ale in addition to wine, blurring their distinction from alehouse keepers; and both could be expected to provide their customers with food. The cookshop was notionally different from the drinking-house; and in 1585 the Westminster court of burgesses stipulated that 'no person or persons that now keepeth or that hereafter shall keep any cook's shop shall also keep a common alehouse (except every such person as shall be lawfully licensed thereunto)', and *vice versa*.[32] Yet this very proclamation, and even more its revealing proviso, imply that the two forms of hostelry were commonly amalgamated; and indeed it was characteristic that while John Wigmore, in 1398, purveyed wine and ale, food was served, presumably in the same parlour, by his wife, Agnes.[33] Cooking, like ale-brewing, was a largely non-specialized industry, in which many, like Walter Thomas, skinner, and his wife in 1405, engaged on a part-time basis; rather as country-dwellers today offer teas in season.[34] John Gybbs, on the other hand, who described himself in 1516 primarily as a 'cook', presumably presided at the Rose (which he held of St Stephen's Chapel and which was therefore probably close to Canon Row) over a veritable restaurant.[35] A more specialized establishment was the pie-shop outside the palace gate, kept for thirty years of the late fifteenth century by Thomas Watts, pie-baker.[36] Watts enjoyed a prime location; those unable to obtain premises so close to the courts crowded the thoroughfares instead with temporary stalls. The

---

[31] PRO, C1/517/57. For Pomfrett see app. VIII, s.n. For Henbury see WAM 19765–807; CWA ii, s.a. 1521–2, 1522–3, 1525–6. For other brewers see e.g. app. VIII, s.n. Nyk, Smallwood, Taillour, Valentyne.
[32] Manchée, *Westminster City Fathers*, 214 ff.
[33] PRO, KB9/183/6.
[34] PRO, KB9/201/1/12.
[35] PCW Wyks, 258–9.
[36] WAM 17781; 23516–63.

disconsolate protagonist of the fifteenth-century *London Lickpenny* was hailed by these vendors as he came away from Westminster Hall:

> Then to Westminster gate I went
> When the sun was at high prime:
> Cooks to me they took good intent,
> Called me near for to dine,
> And proffered me good bread, ale and wine:
> A fair cloth they began to spread,
> Ribs of beef both fat and fine;
> But for want of money I might not speed.[37]

In 1422 that succulent beef might have been grilled on the spot at the 'roasting-hearth' which William Cros had set up in the middle of the street; although a poor suitor might well look to his purse, for in about that year the Westminster cooks were charging a full 1*d.* over the just price of $2\frac{1}{2}d.$ for a rib (*costa*).[38] These cooks' stalls were evidently an early form of 'take-away stand'; and they were an interminable nuisance to traffic. Others, equally obstructive, were outdoor extensions of cook-houses: 'pavement cafés'. John Pokerych, 'potcook', who rented a tenement on the west side of King Street in the 1390s, was among a number charged at that period with having arranged chairs, stools, and benches in King Street, for which his customers, if not passers-by, were doubtless grateful.[39] From the time of Walter Sampson, who placed a table outside his window in 1376, to that of John Sampson, victualler at the Maiden Head in King Street in the 1520s, when he was presented 'for setting of tubs annoying the king's high way', the Westminster taverns spilled perpetually, importunately, out into the street.[40]

The grandest hostelries were the inns,[41] which offered guest bedrooms and stabling for horses.[42] One such was the Boar's Head

---

[37] *London Lickpenny*, in E. P. Hammond (ed.), *English Verse from Chaucer to Surrey* (Durham, NC, 1927), 238.

[38] WAM 50745; PRO, KB9/224/300. For similar 'hearths' and a cook's 'furnace' in the street see WAM 50718 (1386), 50734 (1396).

[39] WAM 19659; 50720, 50727, 50732.

[40] WAM 50707; 50772–6; Assumption guild accts (rentals), s.a. 1515–21.

[41] For comparison, and for the distinction between the inn which was a large private house and that which was designed for the commercial accommodation of guests, see Keene, *Medieval Winchester*, i. 167–9.

[42] Even the Westminster monks, when travelling, hired horses from the local inns. Thus, in 1444–5, Brother John Flete, visiting manors of the abbey in Middlesex, hired three horses from the Saracen's Head in Tothill Street; the charge for seven

inn on the west side of King Street, which was acquired for the domestic treasury of Westminster Abbey at the end of the fourteenth century. The main hall of the inn lay, as was usual in large houses, at right angles to the street, and was raised on a stone vault over a cellar at 'lower ground' level. This cellar or undercroft, which in 1392–3 was let separately from the rest of the premises, was reached by stone steps which probably led directly from the street; a pair of windows in the cellar is also likely to have looked on to the street.[43] The domestic treasurer enlarged the inn by the construction of stables with rooms above, presumably at the rear of the house. In 1396–7 he spent £41 on a new stable block incorporating three brick chimneys and roofed with 18,000 tiles, evidently designed for human as well as equine comfort; and five years later a further £30 on four more stables, with four rooms over.[44] The upper part of the main block of the inn was rebuilt on a lavish scale in the years 1417–20, at a total cost to the abbey of more than £160. Two-thirds of this sum was represented by the bill of the carpenter, Robert Couper; a number of stone-dressed brick chimneys was installed; and a well was made (or remade), probably in the newly paved yard to the rear of the hall block. Beyond this yard stood the old separate kitchen range and great latrine. The street elevation of the new edifice featured a 'great window over the door', doubtless in the end of the hall.[45] For interior decoration done at the Boar's Head in 1430–1 8s. 4d.-worth of red lead was used, in addition to size, 'painter's oil', varnish, and 'powdered dust', and four dozen *motyffs*, which cost 16d. and were possibly 'motifs', or stencils, used to make patterns.[46] The application of this large quantity of red paint appears in an inventory of the Boar's Head of 1479, which names two 'red rooms' and a third 'crimson room'; the curtains and bed hangings in these rooms were of the

days was 7s. altogether. In the same year four horses were hired at the same inn for the abbot, who travelled with them to 'the western parts'—doubtless the monastic estates in Gloucestershire and Worcestershire—and back; the total rate for three days and four nights was 6s. 10d. WAM 24271.

[43] WAM 18526. The abbey's master mason, John Thirsk, was paid £5 for mending the vault of the hospice in 1443–4. WAM 18593. The cellar steps were repaired with stones in 1400–1. WAM 18533. Ironwork was supplied for two windows there in 1407–8. WAM 18542. The dimensions of the inn are not recorded.
[44] WAM 18528, 18535. The latter was a case of replacing an older building which was dismantled, the materials being conserved for reuse.
[45] WAM 18561–4. For the great latrine next to the kitchen see WAM 23077.
[46] WAM 18579.

same colour.[47] The same inventory (which is incomplete) lists, apart from the hall, the adjacent parlour and the kitchen, sixteen bedchambers containing a total of about twenty-seven beds. The larger rooms included 'St Mary's room', 'St John's room', and 'the falcon chamber'; no doubt the rate was less for a bed in the room next the coal-house or the oathouse chamber. The sparseness of furnishings in all the rooms was typical of the period. Apart from the paintwork already referred to, illustrated wall-hangings (not, unfortunately, detailed in the inventory), and some decorated testers over the beds, the only recorded embellishment was a single alabaster head of John the Baptist. Nevertheless, this was clearly a grand establishment. After 1489–90 the eye of the traveller approaching down King Street would have been drawn to the painted signboard suspended from a high beam that projected from a post fixed before the inn, braced with an iron stay-bar at its foot and another hooked to the interior of an upper room. In addition to the board, a carved wooden boar's head hung from the beam.[48] One might have been put up in relative comfort at such an inn as this, though doubtless at greater expense than two Oxford dons who at a succession of provincial inns in 1331 paid altogether 2*d.* on each occasion for their beds.[49]

Not all visitors, however, stayed at inns.[50] Local residents grumbled that when the royal household settled upon Westminster purveyance was taken unreasonably, not only at taverns but in private houses, to the extent upon occasion that occupants were driven from their homes;[51] and the monks, who bore their share of

---

[47] WAM 6645.

[48] WAM 23114. Henry Swift, joiner, received 3*s.* 4*d.* for carving 'le Borishede'.

[49] J. E. Thorold Rogers, *A History of Agriculture and Prices in England*, 7 vols. (Oxford, 1866–1902), i. 135; ii. 635–42; G. H. Martin, 'Road Travel in the Middle Ages: Some Journeys by the Warden and Fellows of Merton College, Oxford, 1315–1470', *Journal of Transport History*, new ser., iii (1975–6), 159–78.

[50] In Southwark in the mid-sixteenth century, the authorities of the Guildable Manor insisted that, since accommodation, especially at the lower end of the market, was in short supply, all alehouse keepers should undertake hosting obligations, and that all 'tipplers' who had 'a house and cellar' should keep two beds for travellers. M. Carlin, 'The Urban Development of Southwark, *c.*1200 to 1550', Ph.D. thesis, Univ. of Toronto (1983), 558.

[51] e.g. *Cal Pat R 1330–4*, p. 219. Cf. arrangements made for the reception of Catherine of Aragon in Oct. 1501: 'Item that my lord chamberlain send certain of the ushers of the king's chamber to take up Heron's house within the sanctuary, and to search all the lodgings that be within the abbey and Canon Row, and cause the owners of them to dress and furnish them with convenient stuff.' *Letters and Papers Illustrative of the Reigns of Richard III and Henry VII*, ed. J. Gairdner, Rolls Series, i (1861), 405–6.

the royal impositions, had similar complaints.[52] Yet the temptation
to ordinary householders to turn a penny by taking in paying guests
during peak times, such as the legal terms, must have been great,
and this was no doubt common practice.[53] When John de Whalley, a
monk of the Cistercian abbey of that name in Lancashire, came to
Westminster in Lent, 1404 to prosecute certain cases in the courts
(*ad diversa negocia et sectas faciendum et prosequendum*), he stayed in
the house (*hospitabatur in domo*) of Alice Hull. The night was an
eventful one for Brother John, who (by a ruse, according to his
account) was found naked in bed with Alice by her friend and
pretended husband, Thomas Worsop. Crying 'False monk and
traitor!' Worsop dragged the hapless visitor by his legs out into the
street, where he spent three cold hours before a payment of 5s. 8d.
was accepted for his readmittance. As John de Whalley, once
gratefully returned to his monastery, might have put it to his prior
when accounting for his costs, lodgings in the capital could be
fearfully expensive.[54]

   Tavern life was thus of the essence of medieval Westminster. It
could be dangerous for the unwary. As Simon Helgey, vicar of
Turvey in Bedfordshire, made his way along Tothill Street on a
February day in 1397, he was accosted at her door by Alice atte
Hethe, proprietress of the Cock inn. Taking him by the breast of his
clothing (*per pectus*), she enticed him in for a drink, whereupon the
ostler and another appeared, daggers drawn, and relieved the vicar
of his outer garments, his ring, and his purse. Helgey was fortunate

----

[52] Of the monks, the most vulnerable was the almoner. When the king rested at
Westminster, his horses were housed in the almonry stables, and there was a frequent
battle to prevent the royal grooms from feeding them out of the almonry barns. For
example, in 1317 the keepers of the king's great horses helped themselves to most of
the almoner's store of hay, paying nothing for it; it is not clear whether it was before
or after this robbery that they were tipped 2s. 'lest they should break the doors of the
barn to take the oats'. WAM 18964. Not only the horses but some of the officials of
the royal household were wont to accommodate themselves in the almonry, where
their behaviour was not always as sober as might have seemed appropriate. In
1318–19 the ministers of the queen staying in the almonry were paid protection
money on several occasions 'lest they should make destruction'; in that year three
locks broken by them had to be repaired. WAM 18965. The next year, still more
embarrassing, there was fighting in the almonry between adherents of the court party
and of the barons; 250 laths were needed in consequence for repairs. WAM 18965*.
During the reign of Henry IV there was frequent trouble of this sort. WAM 19009*,
19013, 19016–17.
   [53] Cf. the crowded conditions at the palace gate in the thirteenth century: ch. 1,
sect. 2.
   [54] PRO, KB9/193/9.

that the bailiff, when summoned, was able to recover his possessions from the premises.[55] The provincial gull was regarded as fair game by the tavernkeepers of Westminster. But for most the many hostelries must have been a valued asset. A regular visitor, such as John Paston, could receive messages forwarded to him in the country by a maid at one of the Westminster inns where he was a familiar figure.[56] Thomas Hoccleve, clerk of the privy seal, was proud to be thought a worthy customer by the hostellers of the town:

> Wher was a gretter maister eek than Y,
> Or bet aqweyntid at Westminster Gate?
> Among the taverners namely
> And cookęs whan I cam eerly or late.
> I pynchid nat at hem in myn acate
> But paied hem as that they axe wolde;
> Wherfore I was the welcomere algate
> And for a verray gentil man yholde.[57]

3. VICTUALLING

All medieval towns retained some of the sights and smells of the countryside, in particular those of agricultural activity.[58] At times when the pressure on inner-city housing was relatively low, increased space could be found for gardens and orchards in the middle of a town.[59] But it was the suburbs and agricultural hinterland whose economy was more lastingly affected by the concentration of demand in the city.[60] London's suburbs had an ambivalent identity. On the one hand, they formed part of the total

[55] PRO, KB9/175/3, 8, 9.
[56] *Paston Letters and Papers of the Fifteenth Century*, ed. N. Davis (Oxford, 1971–), i. 430.
[57] Hoccleve, *Male Regle*, ll. 177–84; ed. Seymour, *Selections from Hoccleve*, 16. ('Gate' substituted for 'Yate'.) *pynchid*: complained *acate*: bill
[58] A classical account of this theme, in relation to Cambridge, is contained in Maitland, *Township and Borough* (Cambridge, 1898). Cf. Hilton, *A Medieval Society* (London, 1966; 2nd edn., Cambridge, 1983), 185; Keene, *Medieval Winchester*, i. 151–5.
[59] Keene, *Medieval Winchester*, i. 153 and Figs. 153–5.
[60] For the hinterland see E. A. Wrigley, 'A Simple Model of London's Importance in Changing English Society and Economy, 1650–1750', *Past and Present*, xxxvii (1967), 44–70.

urban mass, which operated collectively as a stimulus to supply and suffered together in times of shortage. Thus the Westminster Chronicler observed of a dearth in the region in 1391:

If people outside [*extrinseci*] had not lent their aid, the whole London area and its neighbouring districts [*tota plaga Londoniensis cum suis adjacentibus*], deprived of their food supply, would have wasted away from the deadly effects of hunger and starvation.[61]

On the other hand, Westminster, in common with other districts on the fringes of London, engaged (so far as local demand permitted) in the profitable business of supplying the city with agricultural produce.[62] In this pursuit Westminster enjoyed the advantage of well-watered meadows and gardens (difficult or impossible to build on) between Tyburn and Thames.

In the late sixteenth and the seventeenth centuries, Westminster was famed for its nurseries, representative of a general growth of market gardening, at that period, in the environs of the expanding and hungry metropolis.[63] But there was nothing new about this production apart from its scale. Specialist nurserymen were already known in medieval Westminster, where, for example, Thomas le fruter is recorded in 1236, and Thomas Maysent and Thomas Haye, also both fruiterers, in the mid-fifteenth century rented gardens, respectively, in Steynour's Croft to the west of King Street and at 'Frerepyes' (once of the 'pied friars') in the Strand.[64] A later tenant of 'Frerepyes', John Papard, gardener, who died in 1510, had prospered sufficiently to seek his tomb inside St Margaret's church, 'as nigh the holy water stoop as ye may'.[65] In 1345 the professional gardeners to 'earls, barons, and bishops' were among those who claimed a traditional right to retail their surpluses near St Paul's in London; no doubt some of their 'cherries and vegetables' were

---

[61] *The Westminster Chronicle 1381–1394*, trans. and ed. L. C. Hector and B. F. Harvey (Oxford, 1982), 474–5.

[62] Further refs. cited in Rosser, 'London and Westminster: the Suburb in the Urban Economy in the Late Middle Ages', in Thomson (ed.), *Towns and Townspeople*.

[63] F. J. Fisher, 'The Development of the London Food Market, 1540–1640', *Econ Hist Rev*, v (1935), 46–64; J. H. Harvey, *Early Nurserymen* (London and Chichester, 1974), 39 ff.

[64] PRO, CP25(1)/282/6/68; WAM 18576–93; 23074–77; 19698–710.

[65] WAM 19767–91; PCW Wyks, 125–8. At least two more gardeners, William Mownton and Thomas Ellyott, were buried within the parish church in the 1530s. PCW Bracy, fos. 17ʳ, 59ʳ⁻ᵛ; CWA iii, s.a. 1537–8, wk. 18.

nurtured in the gardens of magnates in Westminster, such as the great ecclesiastics who lived along the Strand.[66] The royal palace likewise gave employment to gardeners, who naturally combined their duties with private retail businesses. Royal expenses show that a horticultural trade existed locally by the second half of the thirteenth century.[67] John de Standerwyk, keeper of the king's gardens at Westminster, in 1335 was robbed of crops and timber growing at his houses in the town; and between 1355 and 1401 John Penehalowe, king's gardener, rented a messuage with two nearby gardens on the west side of King Street.[68] Research by the gardeners of the hospital of St Mary Rounceval at Charing in the later Middle Ages produced the Rounceval pea, a new and popular strain of that vegetable.[69]

The monks of Westminster Abbey in the thirteenth and fourteenth centuries also grew locally produce in excess of their needs, which they sold; but after 1400 they largely forsook gardening and left fruit-growing to tenants. Whereas in the late fifteenth and early sixteenth centuries the cellarer retailed super-fluous stores of food and drink for £20 or £30 in most years (but sometimes very much less), in the last three decades of the fourteenth century this figure had been £60 annually. Furthermore it may be surmised (although it is harder to demonstrate) that a hundred years earlier still, at the apogee of the great age of high farming, the marketing of produce had been an even more important sector of the cellarer's and of the abbey's economy.

---

[66] Riley (ed.), *Memorials of London and London Life in the XIIIth, XIVth, and XVth Centuries* (London, 1868), 228–9; J. H. Harvey, *Mediaeval Gardens* (London, 1981), 61. John of Gaunt, appointing a gardener for his manor of the Savoy in the Strand in 1373, allowed him the profits of all produce surplus to the needs of the duke's household. *John of Gaunt's Register*, ed. S. Armitage-Smith, 2 vols., Camden, 3rd ser., xx–xxi (1911), ii. 61 (no. 999).

[67] Harvey, *Early Nurserymen*, 40, and cf. 32–3. The 42 cottars recorded in Domesday Book as holding gardens in Westminster in 1086 may already have been provisioning the royal household with their produce. See above, ch. 1 n. 19; and C. Dyer, 'Towns and Cottages in Eleventh–Century England', in H. Mayr-Harting and R. I. Moore (eds.), *Studies in Medieval History presented to R. H. C. Davis* (London, 1985), 91–106, esp. pp. 96, 101.

[68] *Cal Pat R 1334–8*, p. 217; ibid. *1343–5*, p. 448; *Cal Cl R 1364–8*, p. 167; ibid. *1401–5*, p. 502; WAM 17657; 23187–98.

[69] Harvey, *Early Gardening Catalogues* (London and Chichester, 1972), 71; id., *Early Nurserymen*, 39; id., *Mediaeval Gardens*, 121. 'The first historical London nursery' was established in Tothill Street, Westminster, by the Banbury family in the late sixteenth century, id., *Early Nurserymen*, 40–1.

Indeed it appears from the cellarer's early accounts that until *c.*1340 this was almost his sole source of income. The regular sale of unused grain, of draff (the dregs of malt left after brewing) and of verjuice (a drink made of crushed grapes) persisted throughout most of the medieval period. In addition, the cellarer in the fourteenth century disposed of the produce of the great convent garden north of the Strand, which has more recently provided the venue of a famous fruit and vegetable market. In the thirteenth century a distinct obedientiary, the gardener, rendered account for the area now known as 'Covent Garden'. In the later fourteenth century, however, this office was combined with that of the cellarer, who no doubt continued to supply the brethren with their customary apples on St James's day (15 July), and cherries, plums, large pears, nuts, and medlars in season.[70] The remaining fruits of the garden, meanwhile, were sold for about £5 annually.[71] But from a date between 1407 and 1416 the garden was granted out on a lease to lay tenants. The rate, £5 p.a., more or less, approximated to the value of the produce; but the change was symptomatic of a broader contemporary shift of interest on the part of the monks, away from direct farming and gardening, in favour of a less-energetic and less-enterprising policy of leasing.[72] After 1448 the apples, cherries, and nuts, or the profits from their sale, were enjoyed by the family of Sir John Fortescue, chief justice of the king's bench (d. 1476), who were succeeded as lessees in 1516 by Thomas Docwra, prior of the hospital of St John of Jerusalem in England, of which the main house stood not far off, at Clerkenwell.[73] The extent of the Westminster monks' reliance upon the market for basic provisions in the late Middle Ages is apparent from the bills of the abbey kitchener. In the late fifteenth and early sixteenth centuries, eggs and cheeses were purchased in the Westminster Monday market, at St James's fair, or in London; oats, corn, and bran were regularly bought in (in part from London suppliers); and the kitchener's creditors also included poulterers, butchers, fishmongers, and bakers both in Westminster and in the city of London.[74] An idea of

[70] *Customary*, 89–91; Westlake, *Westminster Abbey*, 371–2. See WAM 18843 *et seq.*

[71] WAM 18873 (1389–90).

[72] WAM 18889 *et seq.* See also ch. 3 n. 230.

[73] WAM 18893 *et seq.*; 18925 *et seq.* The abbey kitcheners continued to employ a single gardener in the abbey garden in the early sixteenth century. WAM 33322–3.

[74] WAM 33317, 33331.

the scale of consumption represented by a religious institution of the size of Westminster Abbey is provided by an unusually full account of the cellarer for the year 1402–3. During these twelve months, 40,000 loaves were consumed in the monastery (at a rate of about 110 each day), and more than 80,000 gallons of ale.[75]

While many tenants in the town enjoyed the use of gardens adjacent to their houses, some rented additional 'allotments' farther off, in the fields to the west of King Street or within the monastic precinct, where part of the almonry was divided up for this purpose.[76] Keeping up their separate gardens in the almonry in the late fifteenth century were such amateur horticulturalists as a brewer, a butcher, a skinner, a barber-surgeon, and King Edward IV's secretary.[77] A private garden in Tothill Street in 1437 contained (until depleted by thieves) apples, pears, nuts, and other fruits.[78] In view of the obvious local need, it seems probable that many medieval residents tended their kitchen gardens with an eye on the market as well as on domestic consumption. Even so, demand exceeded local sources of supply, which were supplemented by victuallers from the surrounding countryside. Robert White of Kensington and Juliana Combe of Hammersmith were two such 'common victuallers, retailers of beans, peas, oats, cheese, and butter'. Upon occasion in 1410, as they plied to London from these outlying villages with their produce, they were intercepted by a forestaller, Margaret Neuport, who bought out their stock in order to sell it again in Westminster; for demand there was such that she could mark up her prices by a half.[79]

As this incident suggests, Westminster's ability to produce a

---

[75] WAM 18887. *Lagena* is taken to be a gallon, following R. E. Zupko, *A Dictionary of Weights and Measures for the British Isles. The Middle Ages to the Twentieth Century* (Philadelphia, 1985), 220–1. On the 'heroic' consumption of ale by medieval monks see Knowles, *Monastic Order*, 717: app. xx.

[76] See Fig. 5.

[77] WAM 17846, 17910.

[78] PRO, KB9/229/3/11. It also contained sixteen hens. Around 1400 a goldsmith grew pears, apples, figs, and walnuts in his close at Charing. E. Rickert (ed.), *Chaucer's World* (London, 1948), 70.

[79] PRO, KB9/198/23. In the early 1400s John Cuttyng, William Hampton, and Isabel Capon, all cooks, were accused in the Westminster court of forestalling pullets, butter, cheese, fish, and other victuals as they were brought to Westminster, for resale in the town at higher rates; in Cuttyng's case his regrating in particular of capons, faggots, and coal led to a charge in king's bench. WAM 50738 (1407); PRO, KB9/185/2/54 (1401).

regular surplus for export to the city should not be exaggerated. There is much evidence of trade in the opposite direction. In addition to the drink and grain trades which have been noticed, other basic commodities such as oil, wax, and vinegar were regularly supplied to Westminster by London factors.[80] Nevertheless, the value of Westminster's fields as a source of food for the city, which must have been apparent from an early date, was greatly enhanced by a general increase of the urban population in the sixteenth century. Queen Elizabeth's reign was to see controversy and violent protest over moves by enterprising Londoners to enclose former common lands around Hyde Park, where Westminster butchers pastured their stock, in order to produce corn for the city market.[81]

A distinctive feature of the Westminster victualling trade was the prominence of local butchers. Prosperity came to butchers everywhere in the late fourteenth and the fifteenth centuries, when personal living standards rose in proportion to losses in population,[82] and the Westminster trade in particular was promoted by the London ordinance, passed in 1361, which (although without complete success) banished slaughter-houses from the city.[83] Even without the London end of the urban market, the provision of royal banquets at Westminster Palace and of the daily fare of the monks of the abbey would have sufficed to populate the meadows of Westminster with cattle, sheep, and pigs in droves. In the early sixteenth century the royal household consumed approximately

---

[80] WAM 33317, fo. 10^v; 17767; Reg Bk, i, fos. 72^v–73^r; 33331. Such regular imports explain the abbey kitchener's possession of a boat. WAM 33317, fo. 11^r.

[81] BL MS Lansdowne lxxi, fos. 34^r–38^r, 42^r–43^r.

[82] The evidence for this statement is suggestive, though not clear-cut. See C. C. Dyer, 'English Diet in the Later Middle Ages', in T. H. Aston, Coss, Dyer, and Thirsk (eds.), *Social Relations and Ideas* (Cambridge, 1983), 214 ('the age of "carniverous Europe" had begun'); G. G. Astill, 'Economic Change in Later Medieval England; An Archaeological Review', ibid., 243–4; Keene, *Medieval Winchester*, i. 240, 256, 259.

[83] E. L. Sabine, 'Butchering in Medieval London', *Speculum*, viii (1933), 335–53; *Cal Cl R 1377–81*, pp. 363–4; ibid. *1389–92*, pp. 409–10, 521, 567; Barron, 'The Quarrel of Richard II with London', 175–6; P. E. Jones, *The Butchers of London* (London, 1976), 78–80. An increase in suburban butchering is also documented in the areas to the east and north of the city in the later Middle Ages. K. G. T. McDonnell, *Medieval London Suburbs* (London and Chichester, 1978), 60–1; D. Moss, 'The Economic Development of a Middlesex Village', *Agricultural History Review*, xxviii (1980), 110–14; M. K. McIntosh, *Autonomy and Community: The Royal Manor of Havering, 1200–1500* (Cambridge, 1986), 153–4, 227–8, 230–1.

1,500 head of cattle and 7,500 sheep every year,[84] while the Benedictine monks, observing a papal constitution on diet of 1336, abstained from meat on Wednesdays, Fridays, and Saturdays but ate beef and other animals regularly (if less copiously than the courtiers) on the other four days of the week.[85] Yet John Waryn, who in the mid-1380s bought fifty-seven oxen from the cellarer of Westminster Abbey, who leased a flock of three hundred sheep belonging to the monks, and who was unsurprisingly summonsed for overcrowding the common pasture on Tothill with his animals, did have a trading connection with London.[86] Furthermore, a Westminster butcher with a regular surplus of tallow could contract to export this to chandlers in London, where the supply of lighting for the city's houses was always at a premium.[87]

In the late fourteenth century the monastic cellarer was himself prominent in the butchering trade. In an extraordinary year, 1400–1, the cellarer sold ninety-three cows for £115. 8s. 2d. and sixty pigs for £11.[88] Among consumers with whom he traded directly, his neighbour, the king of England, was the most notable, though not the most reliable in the payment of his bills.[89] But soon after 1400 the cellarer 'went out of' cattle and swine for the market, even as he ceased to engage in fruiting, and retained only such limited stock as supplied part of the needs of the convent.[90] This

[84] *LP* iv, no. 3084. Earlier English royal household accounts are insufficiently detailed for analysis in this respect; but an idea of the scale of consumption in the late fourteenth century is given by an informed Parisian of the period, who noted that the households of the French king and queen consumed jointly two hundred sheep, twenty-eight oxen, twenty-eight calves, and twenty-four pigs each week, *The Goodman of Paris*, tr. and ed. Power (London, 1928), 222.

[85] WAM 33322–3 (kitchener's accounts, early sixteenth century). Meals including meat were taken not in the main refectory but in the misericorde.

[86] WAM 18866–7, 18869; 5984; 50718; *Cal Plea & Mem R 1364–81*, 270. In 1359 John Lorymer of Knightsbridge similarly leased from Westminster Abbey two bulls, forty-three kine, and three heifers, together with two geese, three drakes, two cocks, twelve hens, twenty-four capons, two peacocks, two peahens, and three peachicks, all being within the manor of La Hyde (later Hyde Park). WAM 4878.

[87] PRO, C1/338/26 (1504 × 1515); cf. *Munimenta Gildhallae Londoniensis*, ed. H. T. Riley, 3 vols., Rolls Series (1859–62), i. 279.

[88] Further sales of produce brought this element of the cellarer's income in that year to £190. WAM 18884.

[89] Fourteen head of cattle were delivered to the king's household in 1384–5; but in 1400–1 the cellarer was allowed £24 credit against his account by the auditors in respect of twenty beasts sold to the late King Richard but evidently never paid for. WAM 18866, 18884.

[90] WAM 18889 *et seq.*

change was part of the general reorientation of the monastic economy.[91] Lay entrepreneurs, however, came forward to engage in this profitable trade which could absorb substantial capital investment. The trading links of a prosperous butcher stretched out from his base of operations, along drovers' roads across the country. So John Meryden, who traded as a butcher in Westminster, where he became a prominent local figure, between *c*.1450 and his death in 1489, nevertheless described himself as being of Wing; and indeed his will makes clear that he maintained lands and extensive contacts, doubtless including other graziers, in the Buckinghamshire area.[92] An undoubted attraction of Westminster was that, if the Common Council of London experienced difficulties in enforcing controls upon city butchers, the Westminster manor court imposed many fewer restrictions. Out of bounds of civic or guild constraints, John Henbury, ale-brewer at the Red Lion in King Street in the 1520s, could simultaneously go into business as a butcher and keep 'slaughter houses' in the very middle of Westminster, at the corner of King Street and Thieving Lane, causing the maximum possible public offence.[93]

Meanwhile the court rolls reveal that a remarkable number of local residents, whatever their primary occupations, invested in the meat market by keeping pigs, in quantities surely beyond the capacity of domestic consumption, and frequently beyond the endurance of their neighbours. Twenty-seven individuals were charged in 1408 with owning stray pigs; in the previous year Simon Bellringer was said to keep no fewer than twenty of these animals, and two sheep besides.[94] It was when John Twynyng, carpenter, bought a boar, two sows, and eight piglets, at Pentecost in 1398, that his neighbourly relations with Richard Hardegray, mason, began to deteriorate. Twynyng did not trouble to feed his new charges, but left them permanently in the street to rootle for themselves. By Midsummer they had wrought havoc with the road surface and then, in hope of better fare, had broken into Hardegray's house, breaking crockery as they arrived.[95] Popular alarm was fed by still

[91] See ch. 3 n. 230.   [92] See app. VIII, s.n.
[93] WAM 50778, fo. 7ᵛ; 18059. For Henbury's activity as a brewer see above, n. 31.
[94] WAM 50737-8.
[95] PRO, KB9/183/1. For Twynyng's profession see WAM 19652, 19660; for Hardegray's see Harvey, 'The Masons of Westminster Abbey', *Archaeological Journal*, cxiii (1957), 97. The scene of the pigs' crimes was probably Long Ditch, where both men are known to have rented gardens. WAM 23187, 23204-6.

greater terrors when John Missenden's sow was caught in September 1404 with Thomas Angwyn's infant son, Robert, in its mouth, 'intending to devour him'.[96] A fatal precedent of 1293–4 shows that the hazard was both genuine and perennial.[97] Thomas More's *mot* about English sheep eating men might have been applied to the ubiquitous swine of Westminster.[98]

Even the families of butchers, however, had to vary their diet on Fridays and the vigils of religious feasts. The Westminster fishmongers congregated within the north gate of the sanctuary, as though claiming a reflected holiness from their fast-day trade. Here, presumably, was kept the fish market to which oysters, mussels, and other fresh fish were brought from the Thames stairs at the Wool Staple in 1495.[99] The river at Westminster was fished by local amateurs; William Baynard, brewer, in 1511 bequeathed his 'great boat and fishing net' to the Westminster brotherhood of Our Lady's Assumption.[100] But the bulk of supply appears to have been channelled through London. John Maxey (or Maxfelde), a fishmonger who moved from the city to Westminster in *c.*1475, continued to buy large quantities of stockfish, salt fish, fresh fish, and herrings from William Ramsey and Henry Shitford of London.[101] The sanctuary fishmongers around 1500 also included John Freston, 'late of London', and Thomas Kneseworth, who was at the same period an alderman and (in 1505) mayor of the city.[102] Westminster evidently offered an attractive outlet to London suppliers. Many of their catches fetched up on the refectory table in the abbey. The monks traditionally claimed by right the tithe of all salmon caught in the Thames between Staines and a point below Gravesend, according to a grant supposedly made by St Peter

---

[96] PRO, KB9/193/9.

[97] PRO, JUST1/544, m. 64 *dors.*

[98] Complaints about pigs persist throughout the court rolls of the fifteenth and sixteenth centuries. Pig-keeping was also a prominent feature of late-medieval Southwark. Carlin, 'Urban Development of Southwark', 587–8, 594. Repeated bans on pigs within the city jurisdiction, even if only partially successful, encouraged suburban dwellers to keep them for the urban market. See *Munimenta Gildhallae Londoniensis*, i. 270, 335, 590–1.

[99] WAM 50768.

[100] PCW Wyks, 133–5; see app. VIII, s.n. Baynard.

[101] PRO, C1/157/25–6. See also *Cal Cl R 1468–76*, p. 97; CWA i. 140. A Thomas Maxfelde, fishmonger, rented a tenement outside the north sanctuary gate in 1496–8. WAM 23573–5.

[102] Freston: WAM 17876; 19730–2; *Cal Plea & Mem R 1458–82*, 98. Kneseworth: WAM 17936; 19759–70; Beaven, *Aldermen*, ii. 20.

himself, when a fisherman ferried the saint across the river at the time of the abbey's consecration. This notion was kept alive by two men who carried salmon in the monks' annual procession on their patronal feast of St Peter; however, the offering of the tithe fishes, recorded in the late fourteenth century, was then said to be falling into desuetude.[103] In any case, the religious also purchased more conventionally a wide range of both marine and freshwater fish. Throughout the later Middle Ages they placed bulk orders with fishmongers in and around Thames Street and Fish Street in the city of London;[104] though they would also buy direct from the fishermen on their boats as they anchored in the Thames.[105] The twenty-one species of fish of which bones were found on the site of the Westminster Abbey misericorde include not only eels, haddock, cod, and whiting but also such delicacies as sole, John Dory, and sturgeon.[106] This was the wealthy end of the market. Humbler Lenten repasts could be bought from such as Thomas Pytfyn, who kept a stall of preserved stockfish in the north part of the sanctuary in the early sixteenth century.[107]

The greater part of the inhabitants of Westminster was involved in victualling, on a large or small scale, professionally or on a part-time basis. Of them all, there were always a certain few victuallers who carried themselves with particular dignity through the streets of the neighbourhood. Such, for example, were the respective masters of the monastic brewery and bakery, who wore the robes of servants of the convent.[108] Others, like William a Lynne, baker at the Wool Sack bakery in King Street, who supplied the household of Lord Henry Stafford during his stay at Westminster in 1469, earned distinction as purveyors to the aristocracy.[109] The composition of the manor court (as the abbot remarked with annoyance) reflected the status of the local victuallers. In a typical year the jury of twelve included three brewers, a butcher, a baker, and a

[103] e.g. WAM 19621 for the procession. See also *The History of Westminster Abbey by John Flete*, 39, 64–7; Westlake, *Westminster Abbey*, 296–7.
[104] WAM 5784 (1321); 33317 (1482–3).
[105] e.g. in 1482–3: '100 [1 cwt.?] of Scarborough fish bought of a Scarborough man in the ship, price 48s. 4d.', WAM 33317 (abbey kitchener's account), fo. 3ʳ.
[106] A. G. Jones, 'The Fish Bones', in G. Black, *et al.*, 'Excavations in the Sub-vault of the Misericorde of Westminster Abbey, February to May 1975', *TLMAS* 2nd ser., xxvii (1976), 170–6.
[107] WAM 19743, 19760, 19764; Reg Bk, i, fo. 64ʳ.
[108] See below, sect. 9.
[109] WAM 12184; app. VIII, s.n. A Lynne.

fishmonger.[110] In contrast to other towns, in which the leading economic sector produced goods for markets often some distance removed, the key to Westminster's survival was hospitality, a business which depended upon the physical presence, hunger, and thirst of its patrons. To those who could afford its prices, therefore, Westminster presented itself as a giant cornucopia of food and drink. Unhappily, the bread and ale which one local victualler generously thought to distribute to poor people at his funeral[111] only serves as a reminder of the penniless suitor leaving the law-courts:

for want of money I might not speed.

4. PROSTITUTION

Like victualling, prostitution was a trade which afforded returns to operators at a variety of levels. In some cases the resort of helpless poverty, in others it was the basis of a fair material prosperity. The famous stews at Southwark were subject to elaborate controls, one of which prohibited trade while parliament was meeting at Westminster.[112] But MPs in town for the session were not thereby saved from temptation, for the virtually unregulated whores of Charing, already celebrated in the mid-thirteenth century, were to be found throughout the later Middle Ages in the Westminster taverns and brothels.[113] Prostitution was a major business for some, like William Chamber, clerk, reputed in 1407 to let his houses at Charing exclusively to whores, and John Norton, clerk of London, who later in the century managed suburban brothels at Westminster, Shoreditch, and elsewhere in Middlesex.[114] There were also female entrepreneurs, such as Katherine Rasen of the parish of St Olave Jewry in London, a spinster accused with others in 1504 of keeping a chain of brothels in houses at Westminster and other

---

[110] PRO, SC2/191/66 (1510); app. VIII, s.n. Bate, Baynard, Hogan, Kyng, Waller, Wrygger. For the abbot's comment see above, n. 9.
[111] PCW Bracy, fos. 62ᵛ–63ʳ: will of John Hall, victualler of Westminster, dated 13 Feb. 1538.
[112] J. Post, 'A Fifteenth-century Customary of the Southwark Stews', *Journal of the Society of Archivists*, v (1974–7), 418–28. Prostitution was officially outlawed within the city of London. *Cal Letter-Bk A*, 218 (1276–8); Riley, *Memorials*, 535 (1393); CLRO, City Journal 1, fo. 18ᵛ (1416).
[113] *English Historical Documents*, iii, ed. H. Rothwell (London, 1975), 881.
[114] WAM 50738; PRO, C244/161/69.

places near London.[115] Here was another sector of Westminster's economy in which the relative absence of restrictive regulation enabled even small-scale investors to generate regular cash profits. Exploiting the labour-value of the women they employed, the pimps and brothel-keepers of London's medieval fringes were archetypal early capitalists.[116]

Others, such as Elizabeth, wife of John Waryn, skinner, and Stephen Essex's wife, who together kept a 'bordelhouse for monks, priests, and others' in 1409, evidently ran a more modest domestic sideline.[117] It was a trade to which foreigners (like Simonetta de Francia in the 1390s) and widows (like Margaret, widow of Thomas Cambridge of Knightsbridge, 'bawd *alias* housewife', in the 1420s) occasionally turned.[118] Jane Apryce, who ran a brothel in lodgings within the precinct of Westminster Palace in Henry VIII's reign, had adopted this profession after leaving her second husband (a lawyer, who in consequence lost his wits) when her first, presumed dead, shocked everyone by reappearing. Unlike Martin Guerre, however, this man had taken another wife, leaving Jane to an allegedly scandalous independent career.[119] Some brothels were family concerns, like those of Matilda Tydyman and Sarah Phybard and their respective daughters around 1410.[120] The last two were the notorious haunts of thieves and vagabonds; such establishments certainly generated at times a mood of criminality and latent violence. But for the mass of clerks and suitors (the vast majority of them male) who thronged the streets of Westminster, it was simply a more-or-less interesting fact that many of the local ale-wives were also prostitutes. It was both inevitable and appropriate that, in the early sixteenth century, one on the very point of entering Westminster Hall, past the curiously named chambers nearby, would have been provocatively invited to pause at the ale-stand of Jane Paradise, of the wife of Purgatory, or of Margaret of Hell.[121]

[115] PRO, KB27/876, rex roll, m. 6.
[116] Cf. Marx, *Theories of Surplus Value*, Pt. 1, tr. E. Burns (Moscow, n.d.), 160–4.
[117] PRO, KB9/198/27.
[118] WAM 50734; PRO, KB9/224/239.
[119] PRO, STAC2/10/130–1; 10/133; 25/176; 27/6. Cf. N. Z. Davis, *The Return of Martin Guerre* (Cambridge, Mass., 1983).
[120] PRO, KB9/198/21; KB9/199/2.
[121] All three, *persone male gubernate corporum suorum*. WAM 50773. 'Paradise', 'Purgatory', and 'Hell' were the names of three houses or chambers adjacent to Westminster Hall. See *Cal Pat R 1494–1509*, p. 314.

5. CLOTHING AND LEATHER TRADES

Clothing

It was characteristic of the primacy of retailing in Westminster's economy that the cloth trade was represented chiefly by tailors.[122] Isolated fullers, weavers, and dyers are recorded, but none is known to have attained the distinction of local office as juror, churchwarden, or functionary of the Assumption guild, as tailors regularly did in the late Middle Ages.[123] That the craft already enjoyed local prominence in the thirteenth century is shown by the regular appearance of tailors and parmenters (who may variously have been tailors, robemakers, or furriers) among the distinguished inhabitants who at that period witnessed property deeds in the abbot's court.[124] In choosing their own premises tailors may have particularly concentrated on the major thoroughfares. John le Taylor of Charing was well placed, at that busy junction, to notify an endless passing trade of his business, whose natural emblem, a pair of tailor's scissors, may have hung outside John's shop as it was engraved on his personal seal.[125]

The tailors of medieval Westminster doubtless owed their elevated status in large part to court patronage. It was in the orbit of the fourteenth century kings that fashion in dress became paramount, and tailoring an art. In consequence, according to the author of *Richard le Redeless*, a tailor in that circle might charge twenty times the cost of his material.[126] The fashionable excesses of court *couture* were one of the sights of late medieval Westminster, and the common butt of satirists. Thomas Hoccleve, as a poor clerk

---

[122] The Wool Staple, is omitted as being of no more than incidental relevance to Westminster. The Staple, established in 1353 for the control of wool exports, was from its inception an exclusive preserve of Londoners. See Rich, 'List of Officials of the Staple of Westminster', *Cambridge Historical Journal*, iv (1932–3), 192–3. In any case, the monopoly of the Staple lasted barely six years. See Power, *The Wool Trade in English Medieval History* (Oxford, 1941), 97–8; T. H. Lloyd, *The English Wool Trade in the Middle Ages* (Cambridge, 1977), 207–14.

[123] See app. VIII.

[124] WAM Westminster deeds, *passim*.

[125] Impression of seal attached to WAM 17460 (third quarter of the thirteenth century).

[126] G. Mathew, *The Court of Richard II* (London, 1968), 25–7; see also Sherborne, 'Aspects of English Court Culture in the Later Fourteenth Century', in Scattergood and Sherborne (eds.), *English Court Culture*, 15–16.

wanting promotion in a government office, joined his embittered voice to the criticism of aristocratic display in Westminster, where wasteful consumption by the rich was at its most conspicuous:

> But this me thinketh an abusioun,
> To see one walk in gownes of scarlet,
> Twelve yerdes wyd, with pendant sleves downe
> On the grounde, and the furrour ther-in set
> Amounting unto twenty pound or bet;
> And if he for it payde have, he no good
> Hath lefte him where-wit for to bye an hood.[127]

Official robes, ecclesiastical vestments, and ceremonial hangings were also among the commissions which supported the Westminster tailors in their high degree. With William Jarden, who made robes for the masons working at the abbey, the monks in 1464 had run up a bill of £20.[128] Tailors and their wives sometimes worked as partners in the business, as did Robert Nevill, 'browderer' or 'vestmentmaker', and his wife, Christiana. These two, who rented a house in King Street between 1484 and 1508, worked for the vestries both of the abbey and of the parish church, for which in 1475 Robert Nevill made an altar covering of cloth of gold. Husband and wife were both buried in St Margaret's at their deaths.[129] For the coronation of Queen Margaret in 1445, an altar frontal embroidered with Lancastrian swans was supplied to the abbey by Thomas Setter, a tailor living in the sanctuary; in the following year Setter was asked for a stained cloth for the high altar, to which he presumably put the finishing touches, decorated with representations of the Apostles.[130]

London drapers and tailors were drawn to open 'branches', and even to take up residence in this fashionable district.[131] An example is Robert Morley, a draper. Morley came to London from Guisborough in North Yorkshire in 1482 to be apprenticed to a draper, and subsequently took up the freedom of the city as a

---

[127] Thomas Hoccleve, *The Regiment of Princes*, ll. 421–7; in *Hoccleve's Works*, vol. iii, ed. F. J. Furnivall, Early English Text Society, extra ser., lxxii (1897), 16.

[128] App. VIII, s.n.

[129] WAM 23105–36; 19717, 19757; CWA i. 115, 161, 485, 540, 551; CWA ii, s.a. 1522–3, wk. 2; PCW Wyks, 94–5. William Letot, 'tapisser', and his wife, similarly collaborated at St Margaret's in 1467–8, CWA i. 85–6. See also app. VIII, s.n. Kymbell.

[130] WAM 19684–708, esp. 19694–5.

[131] See further below, sect. 8.

member of the Drapers' Company in 1495. He first appears in Westminster records three years later, in 1498. For a decade, until his death, Morley lived at Westminster, in a wine-tavern at the south end of King Street called the Bell. While his will confirms that the Bell was his dwelling-house, Morley rented additional premises, possibly for the retail of cloth, within the Westminster sanctuary. Morley became so far a Westminster figure as to hold local office, serving a three-year term as a warden of the Westminster Assumption guild from 1502, and subsequently as one of the abbot's twelve jurors in the court of the vill. It was symbolic of Morley's connections in life that after his death, chantries were maintained for him both by the Assumption guild at Westminster and by the Drapers' Company in the City of London.[132]

Leather

The Westminster butchering industry was linked to a range of subsidiary trades but, again, the intermediary stages between grazing beast and finished leather article are relatively thinly represented. A skinner was occasionally elected to the manor court; but it was a very rare tanner who, in 1422, fouled the Clowson stream with rotting skins.[133] Perhaps hides were dispatched across the river to Southwark, where tanning was a major industry, to be then returned to Westminster for finishing as saddles, purses, gloves, or shoes.[134] In the thirteenth century the making and mending of shoes was performed by a hierarchy of cordwainers, corvesers, and cobblers, all of which trades were represented in Westminster.[135] Later the terms 'shoemaker' and 'cobbler' were used less discriminately. In Westminster the craft came to be strongly associated with the foreigners who, numerically at least,

[132] London, Drapers' Hall, Drapers' Company MS +403, fos. 25ʳ, 60ʳ, 76ᵛ, 80ᵛ; PCW Wyks, 84–92; CWA i. 548; WAM 50770–1; 23576–87; 19760–4. For the comparable instance of James Fytt, see ch. 9, sect. 2.
[133] App. VIII, s.n. Clerk, Middleton; WAM 50745.
[134] See D. J. Johnson, *Southwark and the City* (Oxford, 1969), 79. The King Street house of a saddler in 1476 was occupied in 1479 by a cobbler. WAM 17828, 17843. Another King Street property, held in 1520–2 by a 'leather-seller, *alias* pouch-maker', passed in 1523 to a 'leather-seller, *alias* glover'. WAM 17995; 18017; 23158–78.
[135] e.g. WAM 17343: *cordwanarius*; WD, fo. 357ᵛ: *corveyser*; WD, fo. 536ᵛ: *sutor* (all mid-thirteenth century). Cf. Biddle (ed.), *Winchester in the Early Middle Ages*, 434–5.

appear to have dominated the local trade in the late Middle Ages.[136] Not for nothing was the Dutch cobbler a stock figure in Elizabethan London.[137] Some of the footwear designed and repaired by the Westminster shoemakers was, naturally, the most stylish of the moment. The contents of an early Tudor cobbler's workshop, found in the fill of a pit on the west side of King Street, illustrate the change in fashion in men's shoes from the pointed toe popular in the fifteenth century to the rounded style which replaced it. The new look—which in a courtly extreme became very wide indeed, permitting the leather in the toe to be slashed and a contrasting material stuffed between—was a trend set by King Henry VIII.[138]

6. METALWORKING

The material fortunes which could be made out of the élite consumer market concentrated at Westminster are encapsulated in the nickname of a goldsmith living close by the abbey and palace in the 1490s: Henry Hundredpound.[139] His was another craft in which Flemings and Germans were prominent. The north-western area of continental Europe was traditionally celebrated for its metal-workers, and the art of goldsmiths (who also worked silver) from this region met with appreciation in the extravagant environment of Westminster.[140] A goldsmith's shop on the west side of King Street can be traced throughout most of the fifteenth century in the almost continuous occupation of German or Flemish craftsmen.[141] John Mone, goldsmith, lived here with his wife, Marion, from 1423 until 1444, when they were succeeded by Hans Mone, goldsmith, presumably their son. As Hans had been born in 'Swavene [*i.e.* Swabia] in Almain', the family must have come to England from Germany around 1420. John and Hans were successively employed

---

[136] See refs. cited in Table 3; and cf. Keene, *Medieval Winchester*, i. 289.

[137] e.g. Thomas Dekker, *The Shoemaker's Holiday* (1599). See also ch. 6, sect. 2.

[138] Together with shoes and leather offcuts were found cobblers' tools. Green, Huggins, *et al.*, 'Excavations of the Treasury Site', sub J. E. Thornton, 'Tudor leather' and I. H. Goodall, 'Leather making tools'. Leather scraps and iron tools found on the site of the sanctuary imply the practice of leather-working here, also, at the end of the Middle Ages. Mills, *et al.*, 'Excavations at Broad Sanctuary, Westminster', 350.   [139] WAM 19745–7.

[140] Three alien goldsmiths of Westminster joined the city of London company of this trade in 1497, T. F. Reddaway and L. E. M. Walker, *The Early History of the Goldsmiths' Company, 1327–1509* (London, 1975), 173–4.

[141] WAM 19666–757; and refs. cited in the following notes.

by the sacrist of Westminster Abbey to gild and repair crosses, censers, and other plate; in 1453–4 Hans, by then employing two foreign servants, earned £10 from this source alone.[142] On the latter's disappearance in 1458 the business passed to an obvious co-national called Symkyn Peterson, who in his turn worked regularly for the monks (for whom he mended, for example, 'an angel' in 1462–3) and for the parochial churchwardens (whose best cross was delivered to him in preparation for the patronal feast in 1467). A gold cross made by Peterson for a servant of the monk-bailiff of the abbey was doubtless a typical private commission for the Westminster market. Even in times of recession such as this in Westminster, the demand for luxury goods may remain buoyant among the more fortunate. At any rate, Peterson himself expansively left the sum of £10 to the new work of the abbey at his death in 1476.[143] Peterson's widow, Katherine, subsequently married the son of a yeoman of the king's kitchen; a match which reflects the high social standing of a goldsmith in medieval Westminster.[144] When this second husband died in 1497, the shop was once again inherited by a foreign goldsmith, Dederic van Riswyk, under whose management it remained almost until the turn of the century.[145]

Workers in baser metal also catered primarily to the individual consumer, concentrating their production for the most part on small-scale objects. Whereas the noisy and pollutant industry of bell-founding was among the antisocial crafts which characterized London's eastern suburb around Aldgate, Westminster was typified by the trio of the spoonmaker, the wiredrawer, and the goldsmith who in the 1490s rented adjacent shops within the sanctuary.[146] Pinmakers and a spurrier were at work on either side of

---

[142] WAM 17765; *Cal Pat R 1429–36*, p. 551; PRO, E179/141/69; WAM 19663, 19684, 19704.

[143] WAM 19711, 19714–20; CWA i. 14, 85; PRO, C1/66/262; WAM 23545. When the obit of 'Simon Goldsmith'—as he is usually called in the records cited here—was kept by the Assumption guild, it appeared that he had appointed Garlow Rust, a Dutch cobbler, as his executor. Assumption guild accts, s.a. 1476–7.

[144] In 1476 Katherine Peterson, widow of Symkyn, married Richard Gurney, son of John Gurney, 'master cook of the royal mouth', and of Isabel, John's wife. WAM 19724–7; 17804; Reg Bk, i, fos. 74ᵛ–75ʳ; *Cal Pat R 1452–61*, p. 508; app. VIII, s.n. Gurney. [145] CWA i. 155; WAM 19728 *et seq.*; PRO, E179/141/94.

[146] WAM 19713; cf. Schofield, Dyson, *et al.*, *Archaeology of the City of London*, 47. Heavier industry was represented, exceptionally, by a small number of armourers, e.g. Nicholas Long, brigandine-maker, recorded in the 1460s; and John Bene, armourer (d. 1507), who held a tenement in King Street. Long: CWA i. 30–2, 68–9; *Cal Cl R 1461–8*, p. 326. Bene: WAM 23119–21; PRO, C1/287/20; PCW Wyks, 77–8.

King Street, south of the bars, in the early sixteenth century; archaeological evidence of the former craft has been found nearby.[147] The pilgrim traffic at Westminster encouraged industry at both ends of the scale of metals. While gold was worked into rings for wealthy visitors to donate to St Edward's shrine, poorer pilgrims patronized the vendors of leaden badges which, cast with the saint's image, were kept as souvenirs of the journey accomplished.[148] Well placed to catch the casual buyer was William Pemberton, a London pewterer who around 1470 rented a tenement by the north door of Westminster Abbey; characteristically, Pemberton was also described as a 'chapman', or seller of petty wares.[149] Income from the sale of goods could be supplemented in various ways. William Borowe, a pewterer in King Street, in 1521–2 mended a branched candlestick which stood before the image of St Margaret in the parish church, and hired out a service of pewter vessels to be used at the annual feast of the guild of St Mary Rounceval.[150] But the retail trade was doubtless preferred; and probably all the metal craftsmen of Westminster advertised their skills by shop-window displays which must have resembled, albeit on a somewhat smaller scale, the eye-catching splendours of the goldsmiths' rows along Cheapside in London.[151]

7. BUILDING TRADES

Considering the size of medieval Westminster, it was extraordinary that, almost every working day, at least one part of the town resounded with the noise of the mason's chisel, the blacksmith's anvil, or the carpenter's saw; this continuous din lasted from 1200 until 1540, and beyond. Between the palace, the abbey, and the

---

[147] See Fig. 8. Cf. Green, Huggins, *et al.*, 'Excavations of the Treasury Site', sub A. R. Goodall, 'Non-ferrous Metalwork'; Huggins, 'Bone tools'; and Figs. 78–9, 82.

[148] Cf. Spencer, 'King Henry of Windsor and the London Pilgrim'.

[149] WAM 23247–55; 17817; 17937; *Cal Cl R 1468–76*, pp. 168, 282. Cf. Adam Chapman of Hungerford, who in the 1360s rented a shop outside the north sanctuary gate; and Henry Knycknack, whose shop around 1490 lay close to the almonry. WAM 17675; 19098.

[150] WAM 19762; 17987; 23157; CWA ii, s.a. 1521–2; Rounceval guild accts, s.a. 1521–2.

[151] See the copy of a contemporary picture of the coronation procession of Edward VI, showing the south side of Cheapside, reproduced in colour in Keene, *Cheapside Before the Great Fire* (Economic and Social Research Council, 1985), 10–11.

parish church, Westminster offered more work for the building
craftsman than many larger towns.[152] The builder's job tended to be
seasonal, and the worker himself therefore a continual migrant. On
the abbey site during 1253, for example, the number of workmen of
all classes fluctuated between a small nucleus in the winter months
and a peak, at Midsummer, of 435.[153] During refurbishment of
Westminster Palace in preparation for Edward II's coronation in
1308, a great horn was blown each morning to summon the vast and
scattered workforce; another blast of the horn marked the end of the
working day.[154] When a building campaign was in full swing, the
resident population was forced to accommodate this large and
partially aloof body of the labour force. The craftsmen who,
because of the generally scarce nature of their work, tended most to
be transient were the masons. In consequence, wherever they
travelled to find employment, they created their own miniature
society, focused upon the masons' lodge.[155] The chief lodge at
Westminster in the later Middle Ages was situated in the abbey
sanctuary, against the north side of the nave.[156] The respect which
was accorded to the master of the masons by his employers and by
the local population at large was no doubt inspired by a mixture of
regard for the importance of his task and suspicion of the private
army, billeted upon the town, which he commanded. Occasionally,
resentment flared into open violence, as when, in 1324, a fight broke
out between seven monks of Westminster with seven of their
servants and some of the king's masons, of whom one was killed; or
when, in 1506, three local residents were involved in affrays with
five of the royal masons and carpenters.[157] The building-site
remained a partially closed world, with its own organization and its
own social life.[158]

To the extent, however, that some craftsmen took up permanent
residence in Westminster, occasionally finding jobs on domestic

[152] *King's Works*, i. 130–57, 491–552; ibid. iii. 206–22; ibid. iv. 286–343;
Rackham, 'The Nave of Westminster'; Harvey, 'The Masons of Westminster
Abbey'. See also ch. 3 above and sect. 7 below.
[153] Salzman, *Building in England*, 35.
[154] *King's Works*, i. 506. Six horns were bought for the same purpose at the
Whitehall Palace building site in 1532. *LP* v, no. 952 (p. 446).
[155] Salzman, *Building in England*, 33–4, 39–40.
[156] Rackham, 'The Nave of Westminster', 10.
[157] Salzman, *Building in England*, 56; WAM 50771.
[158] e.g. CWA ii, s.a. 1525–6: 'Item paid for a pricksong book bought of Browne at
the request of master mason. 6s. 8d.'.

housing when work at the major sites was slack, the building trades were assimilated into the society of the town. In the thirteenth century a concentration of building craftsmen was to be found in 'the Virgin Mary's rent', a development on abbey land in Tothill Street of *c.*1230 which seems to have been intended specifically to house the workmen engaged at the abbey.[159] The row comprised some dozen messuages of approximately equal size.[160] The first occupants included William of Hertford, Alexander of Tothill, Alan of Corfe, and John Athelard, all masons, in addition to Adam Fundur (or 'founder') and Richard of the cellar, a supplier to the royal works at the abbey and elsewhere.[161] Some workmen, unlike their peripatetic fellows, even entered into life-long contracts with the abbey, in exchange for accommodation and security of work. In 1354 John Stafford, carpenter, with his wife, Petronella, received a shop in the precinct with a small garden, at a rent of 10*s.* p.a., it being agreed that John would work for the sacrist *in opere carpentarie.* John promised to perform the sacrist's commissions before all others' except the king's, receiving in return 'royal pay', that is, 3*s.* a week.[162] Walter Sely, glazier, described as 'servant' of the abbey, was granted in 1434 one of the sacrist's houses in King Street, rent-free, together with a suit of livery and a corrody each year, in return for his work as glazier to the sacrist.[163] The master of the abbey masons also received free accommodation with his appointment. Robert Stowell, the master of the masons over more than three decades from 1471 until his death in 1505, became in that period an eminent local figure, commanding public office, extensive property in the town, and, finally, a tomb in the new parish church which he himself had probably designed.[164] The jury of the manor court would not unusually include at one time, as in 1376–7, two masons, a glazier, and a carpenter.[165] Among the jurors between

---

[159] For the building work then in train see ch. 1, sect. 2; and *King's Works*, i. 130–1.

[160] The recorded widths in two cases were $7\frac{1}{4}$ ells and $8\frac{3}{4}$ ells, respectively, while the common length from the road was about 200 feet; the standard rent was 4*s.* p.a. WD, fos. 520^r–527^r.

[161] WD, fos. 520^r–527^r, *passim.* For Alan of Corfe, 'marbler', and Richard of the cellar, see also Colvin (ed.), *Building Accounts of King Henry III*, 408; 228, 248, 264, 296, etc.

[162] WAM 17656.

[163] WAM 17753; 19676–90.

[164] App. VIII, s.n.

[165] App. VIII, s.n. Grendon, Kentbury, Payable, Hull.

Occupations 153

1445 and 1453, and concurrently chief constable of the liberty
before 1450, was a noted glazier named John Prudde. Prudde, who
was sergeant-glazier to the crown from 1440 and who worked at
Eton, the Beauchamp Chapel in Warwick (where windows by him
survive), and the royal palaces of Sheen and Greenwich, rented
during the period of these commissions a large house in Westminster at the corner of King Street and Endive Lane, with a garden,
'cloister', dovecote (though the doves were the abbey kitchener's),
and stone wall towards the Thames. After his death in c.1461, his
widow retired to the nunnery of Haliwell at Shoreditch, where she
became sub-prioress; but before her departure she donated two fine
altar-cloths to St Margaret's church, in her husband's memory. In
his lifetime, John Prudde had clearly been an elder statesman of the
town.[166]

The diversity of work available to the building craftsman should
be emphasized. The royal works in various parts of Westminster
throughout the Middle Ages indubitably constituted a major focus
of endeavour; but it is making too much of this to talk of a 'court
school' of architecture. The monks of Westminster, not to mention
other employers in the city of London, were no less influential
patrons of local builders.[167] A mason such as Henry Redman could,
in the early sixteenth century, contract to work both for the
Westminster monks and for the parishioners of St Margaret's on
the rebuilding of their respective churches, in addition to undertaking projects for the crown.[168] Similarly Christopher Wodeland,
Henry VIII's master smith, was also engaged on a regular basis at
Westminster Abbey.[169] On the other hand, whereas in other towns
the Reformation spelled unemployment to building craftsmen and
in particular to masons and glaziers, in Westminster grandiose
secular designs at Whitehall Palace continued after 1540 to provide
work for a host of skilled and unskilled labourers.[170]

Among the craftsmen resident in Westminster, one category
stands out from the rest: the carpenters. Carpenters never lacked
employment in a medieval town, in which most buildings were of

[166] App. VIII, s.n.
[167] Colvin, 'The "Court Style" in Medieval English Architecture: A Review', in
Scattergood and Sherborne (eds.), *English Court Culture*, 129–39, esp. p. 133.
[168] Harvey, *English Mediaeval Architects. A Biographical Dictionary down to 1550*
(2nd edn., Gloucester, 1984), 246–9.
[169] App. VIII, s.n.
[170] Cf. D. M. Palliser, *Tudor York* (Oxford, 1979), 172.

wood, and their constructive role endowed them with a peculiar importance. Less itinerant, therefore, than masons, carpenters sometimes founded dynasties which became prominent in the locality. Examples are the early sixteenth-century families of Richard Russell, 'the leading carpenter of his day', who for his own part rented the Bell inn at the King Street bars from 1512 until his death in 1517; and of Nicholas Palle, tenant of the nearby Peacock inn between 1517 and 1520, whose son-in-law was another carpenter named Thomas Duffeld.[171] The variety of the carpenter's trade may even have exceeded that of others'. In the years around 1480, John Freeman not only worked regularly on the construction of the abbey nave, but also undertook repairs at St Margaret's parish church, made a set of wooden candelabra for St Nicholas's chapel in the abbey, and erected stands in the sanctuary for crowds attending jousts held there in 1477–8.[172] So far as domestic building is concerned, the golden age of abbey-funded projects in the town was, as has been shown, the late fourteenth century.[173] Towards the middle of the next century, it was significant that a carpenter, John Lyndsey, was among the first of the new wave of private investors to engage in speculative building on his own part. His site was a property of the domestic treasurer of the abbey at the Clowson bridge, on the east side of King Street. Between 1436 and 1473 Lyndsey replaced a single messuage skirted with five smaller cottages and shops by a neat row of seven tenements, with a standard street frontage of about 11 feet.[174] In a later instance of 1524, William Salcote, carpenter, took a long lease on 'divers cottages' at Charing Cross, which he undertook to rebuild within six years as a new messuage, 32 feet by 14 in plan, of good oak, with a brick chimney and roofed with tiles. Since his annual rent was only 3s. 4d., he was able to improve the value of the property at no cost beyond his own labour and materials, with some assistance on the chimney and roof. When, eight years later, Salcote's premises were

---

[171] For Russell, see D. R. Ransome, 'Artisan Dynasties in London and Westminster in the Sixteenth Century', *Guildhall Miscellany*, ii (1964), 236–47. In addition to the family's honours noted there, Richard Russell's elder son was a churchwarden of St Margaret's, and his younger son was an MP for Westminster in 1545. See app. VIII, s.n. Russell. For Palle see WAM 23154–78; Reg Bk, ii, fo. 113ʳ; Reg Bk, iii, fos. 49ᵛ–50ʳ; PRO, E40/12837.
[172] WAM 23552; 23556–61; 19725; CWA i, 160.
[173] See ch. 3, sect. 2.
[174] WAM 18585–6; 23090; Reg Bk, ii, fo. 112.

engulfed in the extension of Whitehall Palace, his compensation was £7. 13s. 4d.[175] The commissioned job for the private client was probably always to be had, though is almost never recorded. A rare example is described in a contract of c.1480, whereby three carpenters agreed to make for John Manfeld, a clerk of the privy seal, an extension to his house beside Charing Cross called the Swan. The new construction was to include a chamber, to extend 10 feet from the existing hall, and a gatehouse, with a high room or garret lit by a bay window over the entrance. Two of the workmen having absconded 'into strange countries', the task was left to the third, John Salcote, presumably a forebear of the William Salcote who worked nearby in the 1520s; from generation to generation, the work of the carpenter was never done.[176] It would be true to say of him, as perhaps of no other resident, that his trade was vital to the town's very existence.

8. COMMERCE IN THE SANCTUARY

The powers of the local court of Westminster to regulate trade were minimal; yet even these did not carry within the sanctuary.[177] When, for illustration, in 1489 all the fishmongers of Westminster 'remained within the precinct of the sanctuary', none was presented in the manor court, because the quality of their goods was beyond investigation by that authority.[178] The authority which did preside within that hallowed space was that of the monk-archdeacon of Westminster. In 1391 a butcher who kept his shop in the sanctuary entered into a bond with the archdeacon, whereby he submitted to the supervision of his trade by the servants of that officer.[179] But beyond such conditions the monks appear to have had few scruples about the economic development of their churchyard. By the early fifteenth century the area was crowded with the premises of shopkeepers and tradesmen of all kinds.[180] Those who resorted to

[175] WAM 17193; PRO, E40/6071.
[176] PRO, C1/63/213–15. For Manfeld, who died in 1481–2, see J. Otway-Ruthven, *The King's Secretary and the Signet Office in the Fifteenth Century* (Cambridge, 1939), 158, 183; WAM 19066–78; CWA i. 197; PRO, C1/104/9–12.
[177] For the court see ch. 7.
[178] WAM 50763.
[179] WAM 5993–4.
[180] See ch. 3, sect. 2.

this refuge included a large assembly of marginal types, destitute or criminal, or both, who were glad of this protection from the law.[181] At the same time, the sanctuary population also included a substantial minority of wealthy merchants, chiefly of London origin. To a trader desiring both complete immunity and convenient proximity to the city, nowhere offered greater safety than the sanctuary of Westminster Abbey.[182]

Among those who took advantage of this security were some who were obviously grateful to leave behind them what might be politely termed 'business difficulties'. The stormy career of John Saddler, a London vintner, reached its climax in the summer of 1421, when he was charged and sentenced to imprisonment on account of certain fraudulent transactions. These involved the pretended sale of wine, oil, pepper, and iron to various customers including the Emperor Sigismund, upon which the goods had been immediately repurchased from the buyers' representatives at lower rates, to Saddler's handsome profit. It was probably no coincidence that, within two years of this denouement, Saddler and his wife had forsaken the city for a house in the 'Sarum rents' inside the sanctuary of Westminster, where they were to remain for eighteen years.[183] One day in 1477, the wardens of the Mercers' Company of London 'marvelled greatly' to receive a letter from one of their fellow-members, John Baron, which was unconventionally delivered by the hand of his wife. Baron, as it transpired, had taken sanctuary at Westminster, and being therefore 'not at large', begged the company to act on his behalf with regard to 'divers articles grievous and great complaining [against] John Fyssher the elder'. The outcome of the dispute with Fyssher is unknown, but it may be that Baron had not expected to prevail, for on 28 August in the previous year, shortly before his disappearance from London, he had transferred all his goods to

---

[181] See ch. 6, sect. 7. Surviving registers of sanctuarymen at Durham (1464–1524) and Beverley (*c.*1478–1539) reveal a catchment similar in scope to that recorded at Westminster. *Sanctuarium Dunelmense et Sanctuarium Beverlacense*, Surtees Society, v (1837).

[182] London itself contained such religious precincts where civil legislation did not penetrate; as did other towns. M. B. Honeybourne, 'The Extent and Value of the Property in London and Southwark occupied by the Religious Houses (including the Prebends of St Paul's and St Martin's le Grand), the Parish Churches and Churchyards, and the Inns of the Abbots and Bishops, Before the Dissolution of the Monasteries', MA thesis, Univ. of London (1930). Cf. Palliser, *Tudor York*, 79–80; Keene, *Medieval Winchester*, i. 70–5.

[183] *Cal Plea & Mem R 1413–37*, 17–18, 56–8, 98–9, 100–2; WAM 24626–47.

trustees; and by 1479–80, when he reserved a pew for his wife, Alice, in St Margaret's church, he was well settled in the Westminster sanctuary. Husband and wife rented a succession of tenements here until they died, in *c*.1503. Safely ensconced, Baron could ignore the indignant cries of his creditors, and still emerge periodically from the sanctuary to travel, with royal safe-conducts, on the king's business.[184] John Baron, whatever the justice of his particular cause, exemplified a constant bugbear of certain trading interests in the commons: the debtor who 'goes to sanctuary or other places privileged', there remaining and continuing to do business undisturbed.[185] By 1535 the privilege of sanctuary had, for political reasons, attracted the grim attention of Secretary Cromwell, who was duly informed that one William Staverton, late of London, grocer, 'lyke an untrue man conveyd hym self with his sustance yn to the Sanctuary of Westminster, where he contynued duryng his lyffe, and dyed very substancyall both in lands and goods.' Staverton, who had died on 6 November 1534, had taken sanctuary, 'for debt', as early as 1509, since which date he and his wife, Katherine, had occupied a succession of houses in that protected enclosure. Little in the way of material sacrifice seems to have been necessitated by the move, for Staverton was able to contribute £10 to a loan raised by the abbot from local residents in 1522; in the following year his lands were valued at £20; and at his death, after which he was buried within St Margaret's parish church, he bequeathed apparently intact his lands and tenements in Daventry, Northamptonshire.[186]

Throughout the later Middle Ages, the sanctuary of Westminster remained an island of ungoverned commerce: to the poor huckster, a zone of free enterprise; to the city merchant, a 'tax haven'. No doubt its privileges were open to abuse, but the monks, who collected in rents from the sanctuary over £100 a year, did not

---

[184] *Acts of Court of the Mercers' Company, 1453–1527*, ed. L. Lyell and F. D. Watney (Cambridge, 1936), 98–9; *Cal Plea & Mem R 1458–82*, 173; *Cal Cl R 1476–85*, p. 25; CWA i. 157; WAM 19728–59; Reg Bk, i. fos. 91ᵛ–92ʳ; *Cal Pat R 1485–94*, pp. 2, 45, 144; *Cal Cl R 1500–9*, p. 204.
[185] *Statutes of the Realm*, ii. 513; see also *Cal Plea & Mem R 1413–37*, xx.
[186] PRO, SP1/100, pp. 127–8; SP1/70, p. 151; WAM 19765–807; Reg Bk, ii, fos. 145ᵛ–146ʳ, 183ʳ⁻ᵛ, 230ᵛ, 275ᵛ–276ʳ, 309; 12366; PRO, E179/238/98; PCW Bracy, fos. 43ʳ–44ʳ; CWA ii, s.a. 1534–5, wk. 24. In 1569, by which date the right to take sanctuary at Westminster was confined to debtors, eleven sanctuary men were listed there, who owed sums ranging between £106 and £5,427. WAM 9594.

trouble to ask questions of that sort.[187] Indeed, when, in 1566, it was
moved that sanctuaries should finally be abolished, the dean and
chapter of Westminster rested their objection on the ground that
the privilege brought tenants to the neighbourhood.[188]

9. SERVICE IN COURT AND CLOISTER

The two great households of Westminster, respectively of the royal
family and of the Benedictine community, each represented to the
inhabitants of the town a large pool of regular or casual employment. In the later Middle Ages the royal household numbered
between two and four hundred, a proportion of which total
remained at Westminster even in the absence of the monarch.[189]
The monastic community of fifty or sixty religious, meanwhile,
retained continuously an army of upwards of a hundred miscellaneous servants.[190] Almoners, butlers, cooks, door-keepers, and
many other workmen, petty office-holders and sinecurists were
maintained by one or other of these major employers.[191]

The level of secular support required to minister to the monks in
the abbey is indicated by the nicknames of lay residents recorded in
the thirteenth century: William of the brewhouse, Adam of the
cellar, and Stephen of the buttery; William of the garden, Brand of
the kitchen, and Roger of the refectory; Gregory of the parlour,
Thomas of the infirmary, and Ralph of the tailors' workroom.[192]

---

[187] See ch. 3 n. 125.

[188] R. Widmore, *Westminster Abbey* (London, 1743), 141. For the campaign
waged against sanctuaries by parliament and the crown in the sixteenth century,
which ultimately led to the final suppression of the Westminster sanctuary—one of
the last survivors—in 1623, see I. D. Thornley, 'Sanctuary in Medieval London',
Journal of the British Archaeological Association, 2nd ser., xxxviii (1932–3), 293–315;
ead., 'The Destruction of Sanctuary', in R. W. Seton-Watson (ed.), *Tudor Studies
Presented to A. F. Pollard* (London, 1924), 182–207; and Ives, 'Coroners, Sanctuary
and Royal Authority under Henry VIII', in M. S. Arnold, T. A. Green, S. A.
Swilly, and S. D. White (eds.), *On the Laws and Customs of England* (Chapel Hill,
1981), 296–320.   [189] See ch. 2 n. 23.

[190] This approximate tally was characteristic of large monastic houses. Cf. Christ
Church Priory, Canterbury, where, as in Westminster, 'it is probably true to say that
by the year 1400 there were twice as many servants as monks'. Smith, *Canterbury
Cathedral Priory*, 50.

[191] See also ch. 6, sect. 4.

[192] WD, fo. 564ʳ; WD, fo. 513ᵛ; WAM 17517; WD, fo. 351; WAM 17319; WAM
17448; WD, fo. 327ʳ⁻ᵛ; WD, fos. 525ᵛ–526ʳ; PRO, CP25(1)/148/26/33. There are
many other examples.

Certain offices in the abbey were held by particular families by right of inheritance, a form of association which could and did persist over centuries. In the mid-twelfth century, Abbot Gervase (1138–*c*.1157) confirmed the tenure of William de Wandene of offices (*ministeria*) in the abbey and tenements (the latter apparently held in sergeanty) which belonged to William's father-in-law.[193] In 1298 a later William de Wandene was still in possession of two sergeanties, with attached corrodies, respectively in the vestry and the buttery of the abbey. These titles were in that year, however, quitclaimed to the abbot, in exchange for a new arrangement whereby William de Wandene received £16 p.a. during his lifetime, and a perpetual chantry in the abbey for himself, Robert de Wandene and his wife, and John Giffard.[194] Another lay office, of uncertain duties, was that of the summoner (*ministerium summonicionis*), which in 1302 Nicholas, called 'le Fraunceys', granted to his son, together with lands in the neighbourhood of Westminster.[195]

Of the obedientiaries of the monastery, the single largest employer of local labour was the cellarer, who accounted for the annual wages of about twenty-five lay servants. In a typical year these included a master brewer and a master baker with their assistants, a swine-herd, winnower, miller, carter, stable-hand, cooper, janitor, and servant in the parlour.[196] In some later accounts the chief of these employees are noted by name, when they can often be identified as residents of the town. The convent brewery in Henry VIII's reign was in the charge of Thomas Valentyne, a Westminster brewer with a house in Long Ditch, and his kinsman, Thomas Owen.[197] A local baker named Thomas Hogan ran the monks' bakery at the same period, while John Clerk, who leased houses and lands in the neighbourhood and who kept animals which he pastured on the common field at Tothill, tended St Peter's pigs— or rather, presumably, hired the man who did so.[198] These

---

[193] WAM L; WD, fo. 87ᵛ (copy).

[194] WAM 5879*, 5783, 5785, 5787, 5903; WD, fos. 87ᵛ–88ᵛ (copies); Harvey, *Estates*, 393–4. See also WAM 28037, 19839–42. For Giffard see ch. 1 n. 84.

[195] WAM 17488. In the second quarter of the thirteenth century Thomas de Harmondsworth held a sergeantry in the abbey brewery, WAM 17406.

[196] WAM 18841 (1354–5).

[197] See app. VIII, s.n. Valentyne.

[198] Hogan: app. VIII, s.n. Clerk: WAM 18922, 18943, 18945; 18927–8; 18000, 18930–46; 19751–807; Reg Bk, i, fos. 101ᵛ–102ʳ; Reg Bk, ii, fos. 198ᵛ, 232ᵛ–233ʳ; WAM 50778.

stipendiaries were in their own right prominent figures in the
locality; Valentyne was a churchwarden of St Margaret's, while
Hogan was a chief pledge of the local court and twice master of the
guild of St Mary's Assumption. The robes which they wore as
valets of the convent represented in part a reward (in addition to
their wage) for their professional services, in part an honorific
recognition accorded by the monks to the standing of some of their
secular neighbours.[199] Less exalted employees of the abbey might
also enjoy such privileges as free accommodation in the town, like
the pair of chambers in Long Ditch, and tenements respectively in
the same alley and next to St Anne's chapel in the almonry, which
were severally allocated gratis to servants of the misericorde in the
1530s.[200]

Because the two households respectively of the convent and of the
royal court were organized in some respects along similar lines, it
was possible to make the transition between them within a single
career. Robert Penne, a singer, started out in the 1490s in the
secular choir of Westminster Abbey; by the end of Henry VII's
reign Penne had been taken on at the royal chapel, where he
continued to work until his death in 1538.[201] By the fifteenth
century, a large proportion of the multifarious officers of the royal
court was resident in and assimilated to the society of Westminster,
as elections to local offices bear witness.[202] The royal entourage was
never self-enclosed, but merged osmotically into its surroundings.
One foot in the door of promotion at court never prevented the
other being kept firmly in the world of trade. No individual proves
this more clearly than a London vintner's son of the fourteenth
century who, from beginnings as a diplomatic secretary, pursued a
successful if unspectacular career as a servant of the crown. For
Geoffrey Chaucer royal service was simply a job; it was incidental to
his chief concerns as a writer. Chaucer's literary output is not
known to have received more than the very slightest encouragement

[199] App. VIII, loc. cit.
[200] WAM 19149, 19152-3. It was in the neighbourhood of Tothill Street, Long
Ditch, and the sanctuary that lay servants of the monastery tended to be
concentrated.
[201] WAM 19472, 19991-4, 18902-5; *LP* i, no. 20 (p. 18); *LP* i, g. 1948 (65); WAM
12366; PCW Bracy, fo. 66ʳ⁻ᵛ. Penne's accommodation in the Westminster sanctuary:
WAM 23126, 19114-15, 18923-5; Reg Bk, ii, fos. 113ᵛ-114ʳ.
[202] See app. VIII, *passim*.

from the court.[203] None of his poems evinces a desire to address primarily an aristocratic audience; his patrons and readers were rather working officials of royal government and, perhaps, merchants.[204] It was with these families—his own kind—that Chaucer fraternized most easily, and not with a courtly élite whose dominance of cultural patronage is easily exaggerated. At his town house, first in and near Aldgate on the edge of London and later in the sanctuary at Westminster, Chaucer wrote poetry for the townspeople who were his neighbours.[205]

10. CONCLUSION: RETAILING IN THE URBAN ECONOMY

The Primacy of the Retailer

The economy of medieval Westminster was based primarily upon the entrapment of the consumer. The profits of local retailing were supplemented in some cases by trade with the city of London; but for almost all residents the one vital source of revenue was the visitor. This crucial figure came in many guises: as pilgrim, messenger, or lawyer, as suitor, courtier, or MP, as king of England or as outlaw seeking sanctuary. Yet whatever his status, he might be persuaded to part with cash. This susceptibility in the traveller was heightened by the excitement of unfamiliar, cosmopolitan surroundings; and at the first sign of weakness, the traders would press upon him every conceivable portable or consumable commodity. Would he be fitted for a suit of armour? Would his wife like a length of cloth for a new dress, or a gem? Would he dine? Or drink?

The character of Westminster's economy was in part conditioned by its status, within the total urban area of London, as an independent liberty.[206] All medieval towns were riddled with such

[203] See Scattergood, 'Literary Culture at the Court of Richard II', in Scattergood and Sherborne (eds.), *English Court Culture*, 30–2; and P. Strohm, 'The Social and Literary Scene in England', in P. Boitani and J. Mann (eds.), *The Cambridge Chaucer Companion* (Cambridge, 1986), 9–13.
[204] For the former group see Tout, 'Literature and Learning in the English Civil Service in the Fourteenth Century', *Speculum*, iv (1929), 365–89.
[205] Chaucer's tenement near to the Lady chapel of Westminster Abbey is described in his lease of 1399: WAM LVII. The documents relating to his life are gathered in M. M. Crow and C. C. Olson (eds.), *Chaucer Life-Records* (Oxford, 1966).
[206] Rosser, 'London and Westminster'.

franchises, pockets of independence which defied the claims of city charters to guarantee full control to town councils. Liberties typically permeated the entire urban area, but were concentrated above all on the fringes. The liberty of Westminster in the later Middle Ages offered scope for enterprising speculation by a burgeoning class of commodity producers and retailers. Some of these were substantial merchants; many more were smaller operators. The attraction of peddling at all periods has been that it is a form of trade which circumvents the official market, with its attendant restrictions. On the largely unregulated fringes of medieval London, peddlars flourished.

The conspicuous absence from Westminster of any significant concentration of heavy industry (the building industry excepted) may have been due not only to the nature of local demand but also, in part, to active hostility from the crown and those in royal government. Somewhat later industrial developments provoked the composition, in 1705, of a parliamentary bill, whose words evoke a scene which was in other respects unchanged since the Middle Ages:

> Whereas the City of Westminster hath for many ages past been the principal Residence of the Kings & Queens of this Realm, and the place for the Courts of Justice, as also where Parliaments are usually held, the Records are preserved, the Exchequer, & other Offices of the Crown are kept, which occasions a great & constant resort thither of persons of all Ranks, & many also of the Nobility and Gentry have their habitations there, for these Reasons the Air of the said City ought to be preserved as clear, wholesome and free from Annoyances as possible; And whereas several persons have presumed to erect offensive workhouses too near the said palace, thereby infecting the Air, & damaging the records,

it was urged that such factories should be closed at once.[207]

The Innovations of the Retailer

The market made captive at Westminster was eager for novelty. Tailors were not alone in promoting fashion in material possessions, and creating new, more-or-less imaginary needs among their

[207] BL MS Stowe 597, fos. 105^v–106^r: transcript of 'A Bill to Suppress & prevent Glasshouses, &c., Presented, but not passed' (1705). The concern of the courtier and bureaucrat under Queen Anne to keep Westminster safe for the royal records deserves the recognition of the modern historian.

customers. The objects of new desire came typically from abroad. Such were the Italian maiolica-ware dishes found in an early Tudor context on the west side of King Street, together with such fine native wares as a redware bowl decorated with a sgraffito bird and flowers.[208] While these objects are sufficiently clear evidence of both relatively short- and long-distance trade, it is not clear exactly where the Westminster householders purchased them; for no crockery shops are recorded. In other towns a particularly varied stock, including pottery wares, is known to have been kept by chandlers.[209] It seems likely that the chandlers of Westminster, some of whom were locally prominent men, were among the immediate sources of supply of such exotic and elegant dishes.

Not only goods, but their makers, too, were drawn to this Mecca of luxury retailers. Westminster's expensive gift trade brought here Anthony Tresylyan, clockmaker, whose craft and whose personal connections both evince Flemish or German origins. From 1513 until his death in 1532, Tresylyan kept in King Street a shop of the sort which must have invested that thoroughfare in the Middle Ages with something of the air of present-day Bond Street. At Tresylyan's death his stock included a gilded cuckoo-clock, valued at £10.[210] Also among the more rarefied technical skills thus imported were those of William Organmaker, named in a list of aliens of 1455, who had charge of instruments both at the abbey and at St Margaret's, and who was honoured at his death in 1475–6 with burial inside his adopted parish church. Organ building was developing rapidly at this time, with the spread of chromatic instruments and the addition of stops, and the new techniques appear to have been introduced into England by Flemings, such as those evidently drawn to Westminster by its importance as a

---

[208] Green, Huggins, *et al.*, 'Excavations of the Treasury site', sub R. M. Huggins, 'Pottery' and Figs. 37.1, 43, 47.

[209] Cf. A. D. Dyer, *The City of Worcester in the Sixteenth Century* (Leicester, 1973), 130–1.

[210] PCW Bracy, fos. 25ᵛ, 49ᵛ–50ʳ; WAM 23146–8; 23290–311. Tresylyan was in all likelihood 'the clockmaker of Westminster' summoned on horological business to Hampton Court in 1530. *LP* v, no. 1799 (pp. 750–1). Tresylyan's estate included 'uno horologio cuco quadrato et deaurato appreciato ad summam £10'. The supervisor of his will was John Sleke, a tailor of Westminster, whose own will records that he was born in 'Geldislond'. PCW Bracy, fo. 49ʳ⁻ᵛ. The witnesses to Tresylyan's will—Ralph Votyer, smith, William Capper and Henry Stevenson, goldsmith—also sound Dutch or German. Tresylyan and his wife were both buried in St Margaret's church, Westminster. CWA iii, s.a. 1531–2, wks. 31, 35; ibid., s.a. 1533–4, wk. 11.

musical centre.[211] English printing began here, as another import
from the continent, at the same period;[212] and Dutch spectacle-
makers, too, found some of their first English customers among the
blear-eyed clerks of Westminster.[213] The Flemings would gather in
Palace Yard like an expectant flock of starlings, waiting to swoop
chattering down upon one leaving the hall:

> Without the doors[214] were Flemings great wone,
> Upon me fast they gan to cry,
> And said, 'Master, what will ye copen or buy,
> Fine felt hats, spectacles for to read
> Of this gay gear?'—a great cause why
> For lack of money I might not speed.[215]

The Ubiquitous Retailer

Goods for sale literally pursued the potential purchaser about the
streets of Westminster. From the shops which lined the thoroughfares, temporary stalls advanced into the path of their human prey,
while some hucksters, yet more mobile, peddled their wares from
packs slung around their necks. It is appropriate to conclude this
account of Westminster's economy by looking within Westminster
Hall itself, where the capital seat of the king's justice presented a
scene which most closely resembled, not a solemn tribunal, but a
bazaar. From the moment in the mid-fourteenth century when the
royal courts took up their permanent stations in the hall, they were
surrounded by the stalls and booths of petty retailers and by
perambulating chapmen. These remained until comparatively
recent times.[216] A description of Westminster Hall in *c.*1700 may

[211] WAM 19715; CWA i. 84, 107. See H. C. Baillie, 'London Churches, their
Music and Musicians, 1485–1560', Ph.D. thesis, Univ. of Cambridge (1958), 118;
The New Grove Dictionary of Music and Musicians, ed. S. Sadie (London, 1980), xiii,
736, 747. At the abbey, 'new organs' were made for the Lady chapel in 1415–16, and a
new 'pair' of organs was bought to replace an existing instrument in 1441–2. WAM
23209, 19685. For lists of aliens see below, p. 194.
[212] See ch. 6, sect. 5.
[213] The earliest recorded spectacle-maker in England is a Dutchman active in
Southwark, across the river from Westminster, in 1458. M. Rhodes, 'A Pair of
Fifteenth-century Spectacle Frames from the City of London', *The Antiquaries
Journal*, lxii (1982), 57–73.   [214] i.e. the doors of Westminster Hall.
[215] *London Lickpenny. great wone*: in great numbers
[216] *Cal Fine R 1337–47*, 122; *Cal Cl R 1349–54*, 208. See also H. S. Cuming, 'The
Old Traders' Signs in Westminster Hall', *Journal of the British Archaeological
Association*, 1st ser., xlii (1866), 137–42; Cooper, 'Westminster Hall'.

stand for the same scene in the later Middle Ages. In the minds of constitutional historians, Westminster Hall tends to acquire the dignity of a hallowed abstraction; to local residents in the medieval period, however, its importance was less venerable, but more vital.

Barristers troop down to Westminster at Nine; cheapen Cravats and Handkerchiefs, Ogle the Semstresses, take a whet at the *Dog*, or a Slice of Roast-beef at *Heaven*,[217] fetch half a dozen Turns in the Hall, peep in at the Common-Pleas, talk over the News, and so with their Green Bags, that have as little in them as their Noddles, go home again.[218]

[217] See above, n. 121.
[218] T. Brown, *A Comical View of . . . London and Westminster*, sub 31 Oct., in *The Works of Mr Thomas Brown*, 4 vols. (London, 1707–9), i. Aa. 51. See also id., *Amusements Serious and Comical* (London, 1700), 39–40.

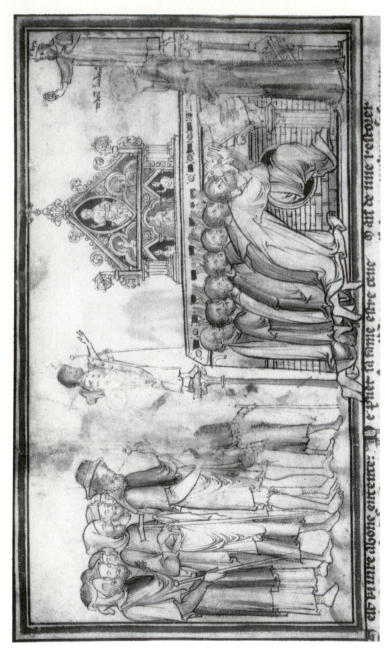

ILLUS. 7. Pilgrims at the shrine of St Edward the Confessor in Westminster Abbey. From a manuscript of the Life of St Edward, mid-thirteenth century.

6

Population and Society

How many people lived in medieval Westminster? The topographical materials discussed in Chapter 3 provide a crude measure of the fluctuations, during the course of the period, in the size of the local settlement. Now an attempt must be made to estimate absolute population figures. For any medieval town this is an extremely difficult exercise; but for Westminster the attempt can realistically be made at two points: in the early fifteenth century and in the early sixteenth. The evidence in the former case is the tally of houses in the town contained in rentals of Westminster Abbey. To this list, estimated figures must be added for the sanctuary, which is not at this period detailed in the rentals, and for the parts of Westminster in the hands of other landlords than the monks. A standard multiplier can then provide the total number of occupants of houses in Westminster. The calculations are necessarily crude and imprecise, but the end result will, nevertheless, be valid as an approximate index.

The date chosen for this assessment is 1407–8, which period happens to be well documented in the records of those monastic obedientiaries with significant holdings in the town. The abbey rentals of this date list a total of 188 inns, tenements, houses, cottages, and shops in the town of Westminster.[1] The sanctuary, which is not recorded in detail, was already built up by this date, and yielded almost £100 p.a. in rents.[2] In 1444, the first year in which such a detailed record is provided, the sanctuary contained 25 per cent of the total complement of the abbey's houses in Westminster.[3] To account for the sanctuary, the number of houses

---

[1] WAM 19660, 23203, 19012, 18542 (all 1407–8); 18888 (1406–7); 23475 (1408–9).   [2] WAM 19660.

[3] 72:287. WAM 19687, 23223*, 19053, 18593, 24649 (all 1443–4); 23509 (1442–3); 18892 (1446–7).

belonging to the abbey in the early fifteenth century should therefore be augmented to 251. The proportion of all houses represented by the fees of other landlords can be gauged in 1513, when a full survey lists all tenancies in the town, with their lords.[4] The relevant proportion is 35 per cent, which implies that the full tally of houses in 1407–8 was 386. Each of these properties, large or small, may be understood to be a separate dwelling. The number of families in a medieval town tended, however, to exceed the number of tenements by about 10 per cent.[5] Assuming this to have been the case in Westminster, there must have been 425 households in 1407–8. The size of the average medieval urban household is problematic. A factor of between four and five occupants per household seems, however, not unreasonable,[6] and this gives a figure for the population of Westminster in 1407–8 in the range of 1,700 to 2,125. Finally, this must be supplemented to take account of religious institutions. The clerical poll tax of 1381 provides the best figures for St Stephen's royal chapel (23), St James's hospital (5), and St Margaret's parish church (6),[7] while the monks and living-in servants of Westminster Abbey together numbered around 100. The total population in 1407–8 was therefore in the region of 1,834–2,259. From these calculations the king's palace has been omitted; when present at Westminster, the royal household added several hundred persons to the local population.[8] While the fluctuations caused by these and other transients are acknowledged, however, it may be stated that Westminster's resident population at the very beginning of the fifteenth century was about 2,000.[9]

[4] Out of a total of 608 residences listed, 215 belonged to lords other than the monks of Westminster. Of the latter group, seventy-four belonged to St Stephen's chapel in Westminster Palace. WAM 33308. For discussion of the document see below, n. 45.

[5] Keene, *Medieval Winchester*, i. 366, citing R. Mols, *Introduction à la démographie historique des villes d'Europe* (Louvain, 1955), 136–40.

[6] J. Krause, 'The Medieval Household: Large or Small?', *Econ Hist Rev*, 2nd ser., ix (1956–7), 420–32; P. Laslett and R. Wall (eds.), *Household and Family in Past Time* (Cambridge, 1972), 197; C. V. Phythian-Adams, *Desolation of a City: Coventry and the Urban Crisis of the Late Middle Ages* (Cambridge, 1979), 246.

[7] A. K. McHardy (ed.), *The Church in London, 1375–1392*, London Record Society, xiii (1977), nos. 391–3.   [8] See ch. 2 n. 23.

[9] It should be noted that this figure is greater by a factor of four than the largest sum (500) which could be projected from the evidence of the poll tax of 1377 for Westminster. The difference cannot be explained by a credible degree of intervening growth, and must be put down to the inadequacy of the tax return. For the poll tax see PRO, E179/141/23/9; and J. C. Russell, *British Medieval Population* (Albuquerque, 1948), 119–46. The present conclusion replaces that of Rosser, 'The Essence of Medieval Urban Communities', 95.

The figure for 1407–8 may represent a net reduction from that of *c*.1300. The intense activity in the local property market during the period 1200–1300 reflects a rapidly expanding population,[10] which may have reached its maximum density around the turn of the thirteenth and fourteenth centuries. This phase would correspond with the broad movement of the population of England as a whole.[11] A nearby analogy is provided by the central area of the city of London, where the level of population had risen by 1300 to a peak, from which it subsequently fell away throughout the later medieval period, not to attain the same density again until *c*.1600.[12]

At the local level there are indications that Westminster, during the two or three decades before the plague epidemics began in 1348, was already experiencing a contraction of population.[13] The evidence is not conclusive; the known topographical symptoms of demographic recession noted in Chapter 3,[14] though clear in themselves, are insufficient firmly to establish the overall trend. The impression of relative depopulation in this period may, however, be strengthened by the witness of the inhabitants themselves. In 1334 and the following years Westminster, with the rest of the country, was assessed for the king's lay subsidy, at a rate of one-fifteenth of its wealth. But in 1337 the townsmen protested that Westminster was now poorer than it had been, and that many people who had formerly lived there had 'departed', leaving their houses to fall to ruin. They therefore asked that their assessment for the subsidy (fixed in 1334) should be reduced.[15] The petitioners blamed their economic difficulties upon Edward III's removal of the royal courts to York, where they had remained since 1333. This reasoning was sound, so far as it went; the courts were indeed a vital element in the local economy.[16] Yet it did not entirely account for

[10] See chs. 1, 3.
[11] *The Cambridge Economic History of Europe*, i. 563–5.
[12] Keene and Harding, *Cheapside and the Development of London*.
[13] For the view that a crisis of overpopulation occurred in the early fourteenth century, causing increased mortality, the available evidence appears less strong than it did formerly. See the critique by Barbara Harvey, 'The Population Trend in England Between 1300 and 1348', *Transactions of the Royal Historical Society*, 5th ser., xvi (1966), 23–42. See also D. G. Watts, 'A Model for the Early Fourteenth Century', *Econ Hist Rev*, 2nd ser., xx (1967), 543–7. The theory of 'Malthusian crisis' is summarized in *The Cambridge Economic History of Europe*, i. 565–9; ibid. iii. 37.
[14] pp. 54–5.
[15] PRO, SC8/78/3889.
[16] See ch. 5, sect. 1.

the problem, for in 1339, a year after the return of the courts, the
men of Westminster complained that this had not brought the
anticipated relief.[17] Moreover, in 1331, and again in 1341, the
contrary grievance was voiced that the very presence of the royal
household was too burdensome, on account of the purveyance
which was exacted from both tavernkeepers and private
householders.[18] The petitions appear to be signs of a deeper crisis
than those to which they refer. The royal commissioners who
inquired into these repeated declarations of poverty (naturally
suspect in the eye of the tax-collector) were evidently impressed by
their validity, for the collective assessment for the vill of Westminster with the parishes of St Mary-le-Strand, St Martin-in-the-
Fields, and St Clement Danes was promptly cut by well over half,
from £10. 13s. 7½d. to c.£4. 12s. 6½d.[19] The evidence appears to
vindicate the inhabitants' claims to be in difficulties, yet does not
clearly identify the causes. Among possible non-demographic
explanations, apart from the temporary absence of the court, the
most relevant is likely to have been the general fall in English prices
after c.1320, which would have adversely affected retailers,
particularly in the short term.[20] Yet the evidence does also allow of
demographic interpretation; and the suggestion cautiously
advanced here is that, after the thirteenth-century expansion, the
local population of Westminster was indeed contracting by the
second quarter of the fourteenth century.

The local impact of the Black Death, in the first and subsequent
outbreaks, is unrecorded outside Westminster Abbey, where in
1349 half of the monks died.[21] In general, towns, by virtue of the
relative density of their populations, were worse affected than the

---

[17] *Cal Cl R 1339–41*, p. 184.

[18] *Cal Pat R 1330–4*, p. 219; *Cal Cl R 1341–3*, p. 89.

[19] PRO, E179/141/6–7 (1334), printed in R. E. Glasscock, *The Lay Subsidy of
1334* (London, 1975), 191; *Cal Cl R 1339–41*, p. 184 (1339); ibid. *1341–3*, p. 200
(1341); PRO, E179/141/11–12 (1345). The area continued to be levied for the
subsidy at the same rate in the fifteenth century. Having won this early reduction,
Westminster was the only part of Ossulstone Hundred in Middlesex not to be
granted an abatement on grounds of poverty in 1445. PRO, E179/141/78.

[20] See N. J. Mayhew, 'Numismatic Evidence and Falling Prices in the Fourteenth
Century', *Econ Hist Rev*, 2nd ser., xxvii (1974), 1–15; M. Mate, 'High Prices in Early
Fourteenth Century England: Causes and Consequences', *Econ Hist Rev*, 2nd ser.,
xviii (1975), 1–16.

[21] There were about twenty-five survivors; the usual complement was around
fifty. Westlake, *Westminster Abbey*, 110.

countryside by plague epidemics. Westminster's overall losses, in 1348 and in the renewed attacks of the 1360s, are likely to have been of the terrible order of 40 per cent.[22] Yet by 1370 the house-building which has been described in Chapter 3 indicates that the depredations had been checked. Further evidence of this kind testifies to a population which was actually expanding for forty years, before the collapse of the early fifteenth century.[23]

In the decade *c*.1410–20 Westminster suffered an abrupt contraction of population, which was to last for half a century. During the fifty or sixty years between *c*.1410–20 and *c*.1470, the depleted level of settlement was apparent to all in the decreased density of housing and the virtual cessation of domestic building developments. The causes of this demographic contraction are not altogether clear. It is unlikely, however, that the drying up of immigration could alone have effected so marked a change in the density of settlement. An increased level of mortality in the resident population seems to be implied. In the decades around 1500, when rough statistics are available, a high base-rate of mortality prevailed in Westminster;[24] a similar pattern may have become established during the first half of the fifteenth century. Within the monastic community of Westminster Abbey, it has been shown that the proportion of monks dying each year rose significantly between *c*.1400 and *c*.1500, from an annual rate of 25–30 per 1,000 at the beginning of the century to one of 40–50 per 1,000 between 1460 and 1510.[25] A roughly parallel increase in mortality among the lay population of the town would go far to explain the contraction after 1410. As will be seen, however, the urban demographic recovery in the last quarter of the century appears to have occurred despite death tolls of equal or heightened severity compared to those of the preceding period. An increased level of fertility after 1450 therefore seems to be implied.

It is now possible to set Westminster's mid-fifteenth-century experience of demographic recession within a wider context. A down-turn in population also became evident in other towns at the

[22] See R. S. Gottfried, *Epidemic Disease in Fifteenth Century England* (New Brunswick, 1978), 138–42.
[23] See ch. 3, sect. 2.
[24] See Fig. 9 and below, n. 61.
[25] I am grateful to Barbara Harvey for her permission to cite these as yet unpublished results of her research on mortality in the monastic community of Westminster. The death rates are calculated on a thirteen-year moving average.

beginning of the fifteenth century.[26] The reduced level of population was not, however, confined to the towns but (perhaps with local
exceptions) affected the country at large.[27] The precise chronology
of demographic decline varied with local circumstances. The
continued buoyancy of at least some urban populations throughout
the plague epidemics of the late fourteenth century, until the slump
of the early fifteenth, was probably the artificial result of increased
migration into the towns from the countryside.[28] In rural areas a
thinning of settlement may have become apparent more rapidly in
the aftermath of the Black Death attacks which, having begun in
1348, were renewed with undiminished severity in the 1360s.[29] In
towns the population losses seem generally to have begun to make a
decisive impact around 1400 or a little later.[30] Westminster,
presumably for special reasons connected with its unique importance as the royal capital, appears to have continued to attract
immigrants and to have maintained its level of population for a
decade or so longer than some other towns. By 1410–20, however,
the signs of recession were unmistakable, in Westminster as
elsewhere.[31]

[26] The main points of reference are Keene, *Medieval Winchester*, i. 94 and ch. 4,
passim; and Keene and Harding, *Cheapside and the Development of London*. Further
comparative evidence, indicative of urban demographic recession in the early
fifteenth century, is provided by J. N. Bartlett, 'The Expansion and Decline of York
in the Later Middle Ages', *Econ Hist Rev*, 2nd ser., xii (1959–60), 17–33; Dobson,
Durham Priory, 45–6; Phythian-Adams, 'Urban Decay in Late Medieval England',
in Abrams and E. A. Wrigley (eds.), *Towns in Societies* (Cambridge, 1978), 164–9;
id., *Desolation of a City*, 33–5; Butcher, 'Rent, Population and Economic Change in
Later Medieval Newcastle', *Northern History*, xiv (1978), 67–77; id., 'Rent and the
Urban Economy: Oxford and Canterbury in the Later Middle Ages', *Southern
History*, i (1979), 11–43; Rigby, '"Sore decay" and "fair dwellings": Boston and
Urban Decline in the Later Middle Ages', *Midland History*, x (1985), 56–7.
[27] Postan, 'Some Economic Evidence of Declining Population in the Later
Middle Ages', *Econ Hist Rev*, 2nd ser., ii (1950), 221–46; Hatcher, *Plague,
Population and the English Economy*; id., 'Mortality in the Fifteenth Century: Some
New Evidence', *Econ Hist Rev*, 2nd ser., xxxix (1986), 19–38.
[28] Since towns were more vulnerable to disease than rural areas, this seems a
necessary conclusion. See J. M. W. Bean, 'Plague, Population and Economic
Decline in England in the Later Middle Ages', *Econ Hist Rev*, 2nd ser., xv (1963),
435.
[29] Such relatively earlier losses on the land would not be inconsistent with the fact
that some great estates, by dint of increased efficiency, suffered reductions of profits
of less than 10 per cent between the 1340s and the 1370s, holding off the major slump
until the end of the fourteenth century. Holmes, *Estates of the Higher Nobility*,
114–15; Hatcher, *Plague, Population and the English Economy*, 32.
[30] See refs. cited above, n. 26.
[31] See pp. 74–81.

While individuals, within this context of reduced competition, in some cases enjoyed increased personal prosperity,[32] the global drop in population inevitably affected the trades upon which urban economies relied. Given the limitations of medieval technology, a reduced workforce spelled in most sectors a proportionately reduced output. Moreover, in an economy so far dependent upon the present consumer as was Westminster's, a diminished market equally brought a loss of business to many local producers. The economic difficulties of mid-fifteenth-century Westminster were not unrelieved. Population losses brought improved living standards to survivors of the epidemics; and individual traders in consumable and household luxuries (such as wine, meat, and pewter vessels) fared well in the period.[33] Expansion in trade in material luxuries may indeed explain how towns were able, within the contracted global economy, to maintain and even to increase their proportion of the total national wealth, compared with the countryside, between the early fourteenth and the early sixteenth centuries.[34] Nevertheless the losses suffered both by Westminster's resident and by its transient populations during the middle decades of the fifteenth century inevitably entailed, overall, a marked economic recession.[35]

---

[32] C. C. Dyer, 'A Redistribution of Incomes in Fifteenth-century England?', repr. in Hilton (ed.), *Peasants, Knights and Heretics: Studies in Medieval English Social History* (Cambridge, 1976), 192–215.　　　　　[33] See ch. 5.

[34] So far as it goes, and with due acknowledgement to differing views of the matter, this statement is defensible. However, it should be emphasized that the evidence of taxation upon which it is based does not admit of closer analysis of the comparative fortunes of town and country. Nor does it shed any light on the intervening period of two centuries between the tax points of the 1330s and the 1520s. For a summary of the debate on this issue, with refs. to earlier bibliog., see S. H. Rigby, 'Late Medieval Urban Prosperity: The Evidence of the Lay Subsidies', *Econ Hist Rev*, 2nd ser., xxxix (1986), 411–16; Bridbury, 'Dr Rigby's Comment: A Reply', ibid., 417–22; and J. F. Hadwin, 'From Dissonance to Harmony on the Late Medieval Town?', ibid. 423–6.

[35] This conclusion does not assume a general theory of demographic determinism. However, the small scale and simple technology of urban crafts made them relatively inflexible when hit by major demographic fluctuations. Where diversification was possible, for example in the luxury trades noted above, the population decline might work to the benefit of urban craftsmen and retailers. The suggestions made in Bridbury, *Economic Growth*, chs. 4–5, in this connection have yet to be tested. That, in the countryside, reorientation and innovation *was* possible is already clear. See R. Brenner, 'Agrarian Class Structure and Economic Development in Pre-industrial Europe', *Past and Present*, lxx (1976), 30–75; and the ensuing exchange in *Past and Present*, repr. in Aston and C. H. E. Philpin (eds.), *The Brenner Debate* (Cambridge, 1985).

Signs of a recovery in the national population may be expected to be found at various dates in diverse places; the discrepancies may prove revealing about the nature of different kinds of settlement. The findings of recent research on London and its immediate environs, for example, are indicative of a contrast in this respect between the city centre and the suburban areas. In the central, Cheapside area of the city of London, a major and decisive reduction in the density of occupation occurred shortly after 1400; here Westminster's experience is mirrored directly. This demographic down-turn at the centre, however, was not reversed for well over a century and a half, until 1580 or even later.[36] The suburbs present a divergent picture. After an equivalent contraction in the early fifteenth century, Westminster, Southwark,[37] and the suburb without Aldgate[38] each experienced a fresh phase of population growth from between the late fifteenth and the mid-sixteenth century, reflected in speculative building, in the recovery of rent-values and—at least in the case of Westminster—in evidence of actual population figures.[39] By the second half of the sixteenth century, and doubtless sooner, the difference was obvious to contemporaries;[40] and after 1600 the relative rate of suburban compared to city expansion continued to increase.[41] Two related explanations for this differential growth in city and suburb may be advanced. Notwithstanding the subsidence of pressures on inner-city housing, the high rents for erstwhile premium sites did not fall in equal proportion,[42] and when, around 1500, population growth was once again in train, the relatively lower rates for accommodation on the urban fringes were more attractive to incomers. This was the more significant because many immigrants to the capital from the late fifteenth century onwards were poor.[43] In view of the

---

[36] Keene, 'A New Study of London Before the Great Fire', *Urban History Yearbook* (1984), 18–19; id. and Harding, *Cheapside and the Development of London*.
[37] Southwark: Carlin, 'Urban Development of Southwark', 381–2, 610 and Gazetteer, nos. 86, 158, 160, 162, 164, 220.
[38] Aldgate: information from Dr Derek Keene.
[39] For Westminster's sixteenth-century population see below. For the chronology of new building see ch. 3.
[40] J. Stow, *A Survey of London*, ed. Kingsford, 2 vols. (Oxford, 1908), ii. 66, 72, 74, 367–8 and refs. cited by the editor.
[41] R. Finlay and B. Shearer, 'Population Growth and Suburban Expansion', in A. L. Beier and R. Finlay (eds.), *London 1500–1700: The Making of the Metropolis* (London, 1986), 37–59.
[42] Keene and Harding, *Cheapside and the Development of London*.
[43] See pp. 179–82.

anti-vagrant legislation which began to accumulate within the city (in tandem with the royal statute book) during the Tudor period, the decision to stay in the suburbs was determined not only by their relative cheapness but also by the relative absence there of jurisdictional controls.

The starting-point for an estimate of Westminster's population in the first half of the sixteenth century is the return of the 1548 chantry commissioners, who declared the number of 'houselings' or communicants (men and women aged fourteen and over) in St Margaret's parish in that year to be 2,500.[44] With the addition of a notional proportion of two-fifths for the children aged less than fourteen, the resultant total is 3,500. The commissioners' figure is obviously a rounded approximation, but other indications bear out its accuracy. One piece of corroborative evidence is a house-by-house 'directory', compiled in 1513, of all rentable properties in Westminster.[45] Within the area of the parish of St Margaret or vill of Westminster (otherwise defined as the district from Tothill to Charing Cross), altogether 608 distinct rent-payers or tenements are enumerated. While it cannot be asserted that every tenant or property listed represents a separate dwelling (although in many cases this fact is verified by the monastic leases) and while, on the other hand, unrecorded subtenancies would doubtless add to the total, the figure of six hundred households is probably a fair approximation to the actual tally in 1513. If the average medieval urban household is allowed to have contained between four and five occupants,[46] this gives a figure for the population of Westminster in 1513 in the range of 2,400 to 3,000.

[44] *London and Middlesex Chantry Certificate 1548*, ed. C. J. Kitching, London Record Society, xvi (1980), no. 139. The area represented was slightly reduced from that of 1377, on account of a redefinition in 1534 of the boundary at the north end of King Street between the parishes of St Margaret and St Martin-in-the-Fields. See *LP* viii, nos. 228, 1423; and below, p. 253.

[45] WAM 33308. The list, which is in book form, was evidently made for the abbey, where it is stored (and whose rents are noted within it with particular care), although it includes the properties held of other lords, such as St Stephen's Chapel and Abingdon Abbey, in addition to those held of the Westminster monks. The catalogue is divided under headings such as 'le Ambrey' (the almonry), 'Theven Lane', 'Woolstaple', etc.; and correlation with the monastic rentals of the same date confirms, wherever possible, that the list proceeds in order through the town. It begins in the abbey precinct and progresses along Tothill Street, back to Long Ditch and Thieving Lane, up King Street on the west side to the bars and back down on the east side, and finally from the King Street bars to Charing Cross. The rentals also establish that the document, dated 5 Henry VIII, was made in 1513.

[46] See above, n. 6. Meanwhile, it should be remembered that while some properties in Westminster were empty, others were overcrowded. See below, n. 65.

Further evidence, admittedly difficult to interpret, is provided by the assessments of 1524 and 1544 for the new lay subsidy. This tax, introduced in 1523, was imposed according to a graduated scale of wealth, and was by far the most sophisticated venture of its kind on the part of the English government to this date. Caution has rightly been urged with regard to the use of these asessments for demographic purposes. It has been pointed out that 'the Act makes no mention of "heads of household", and it is wrong to correlate the number of taxpayers with the number of households in the vill.' Instead, the assessments provide 'a list of most of the men [*and, be it added, a tiny proportion of the women*] over the age of fifteen in each taxation unit.'[47] As such, however, the assessments—caveats having been issued with regard to those sufficiently poor, sufficiently ordained, or otherwise sufficiently adept to avoid inclusion in the tax—do record an absolute minimum total of the male property-holders and wage-earners of a particular place. In the case of Westminster, this minimum figure for the adult male lay population (plus some half-dozen widows in each case) was 457 in 1524, and 527 in 1544.[48] A population which supported these quantities of grown men cannot have numbered in total much less than 2,000. Indeed, in other small towns, where complementary evidence is available, the difference between the number of taxpayers in the 1520s and that of the total population is expressed by a factor of six.[49] Applied to the Westminster statistics, this multiplier produces, once again, a population of about 3,000.

A population of approximately 2,000 in the early 1400s had been transformed by the beginning of the sixteenth century into one of about 3,000. The Westminster rentals, as has been seen, indicate that much of this significant increase must have been concentrated towards the end of the period. The evidence which was presented in Chapter 3 of renewed pressure on local housing in the late fifteenth and early sixteenth centuries corresponds with what must have been a phase of rapid population growth. The authors of the 1585 Act for the borough of Westminster observed how 'the people

[47] J. Sheail, 'The Regional Distribution of Wealth in England as Indicated in the 1524/5 Lay Subsidy Returns', Ph.D. thesis, Univ. of London (1968), 45–6, 128.
[48] PRO, E179/238/98; E179/141/139.
[49] J. Cornwall, 'English Country Towns in the 1520s', *Econ Hist Rev*, 2nd ser., xv (1962–3), 54–69; id., 'English Population in the Early Sixteenth Century', *Econ Hist Rev*, 2nd ser., xxiii (1970), 32–44.

thereof are greatly increased', and noted the 'erection and new building of diverse houses and . . . the parting and dividing of divers tenements' there.[50] But this observation of the 1580s is far from marking the beginning of the phase of expansion to which it refers, which indeed had commenced as long ago as a century before.

The recovery of Westminster's population after the late medieval slump followed a course which, although distinctive in detail, was broadly parallel to that of the country as a whole. A particular feature is the relatively early date of the start of that recovery in Westminster, compared with the centre of London. Future research on other places will doubtless reveal further significant variations. Once the resurgence was under way, however, there is no sign in Westminster's sixteenth-century history of a 'crisis' in its demographic evolution, such as has been identified in Coventry in the early sixteenth century and has been related to evidence of difficulties in other provincial cities.[51] The typicality of Coventry's apparently disastrous depopulation in the 1520s remains controversial; counter-examples have been adduced to show that there was no 'urban variable' within the overall demographic pattern,[52] and certainly the trend of Westminster's population seems to have been buoyant or ascending throughout the Tudor period.

The demographic recovery after *c*.1470 is probably to be explained by increases both in the birth rate and in immigration to Westminster. Fertility, which is unquantifiable at this period, is likely to have played its part in the demographic changes. Certainly, population-growth was not the result of an improvement in life expectancy, which on the contrary seems to have worsened during the 1490s and early 1500s. Data on mortality are provided by the churchwardens' accounts of St Margaret's parish church, the series of which begins in 1460 (see Fig. 9). Few sets of churchwardens' accounts survive in an almost complete sequence from so early a period as do those of St Margaret's, Westminster, and the

---

[50] 27 Eliz. c. 31.

[51] Phythian-Adams, *Desolation of a City*; see also Dobson, 'Urban Decline'.

[52] N. R. Goose, 'In Search of the Urban Variable: Towns and the English Economy, 1500–1650', *Econ Hist Rev*, 2nd ser., xxxix (1986), 165–85. In the countryside, recent studies have indicated a firm demographic increase from *c*.1520 onwards. This is somewhat later than the urban growth observed in Westminster. I. Blanchard, 'Population Change, Enclosure, and the Early Tudor Economy', *Econ Hist Rev*, 2nd ser., xxiii (1970), 427–45; L. R. Poos, 'The Rural Population of Essex in the Later Middle Ages', *Econ Hist Rev*, 2nd ser., xxxviii (1985), 515–30.

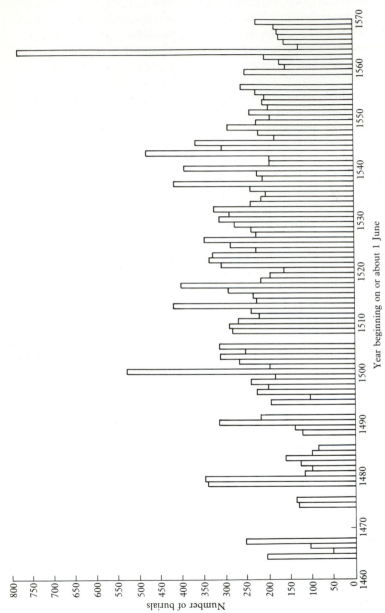

FIG. 9. Annual numbers of burials at St Margaret's church, Westminster,
1466–1570

demographic source-material these offer is therefore unusual. Indeed, the rarity of the source gives it particular importance, in the context of the wider debate on late medieval population changes. The evidence takes the form, in the period 1464–1540 (the first years' accounts are partially illegible), of listed receipts from the sale of candles at the burial of parishioners. Before the Reformation all seem to have been lighted to their graves in this way.[53] From 1539 the churchwardens' accounts are complemented by the parochial register of deaths instituted by statute in 1538.[54] In Figure 9 crude annual totals of burials at St Margaret's church are shown for the period 1464–1570.[55] The interpretation of these mortal statistics is complicated by the incidence of plague, 'sweating sickness', and other infections. The 1460s and 1470s and the early years of the sixteenth century, the 1540s, 1557–8, and 1563 are all known to have been especially deadly periods, both on a national scale and in London and Westminster in particular, and the external evidence finds corroboration in the exceptionally high totals of deaths recorded in Westminster in these periods.[56] Even when these peaks are set aside, however, the rate of mortality in Westminster in ordinary years appears to have been frighteningly high.

A high mortality rate may already have prevailed in Westminster before 1450;[57] but the years 1490–1510 show a sharp increase in the annual numbers of deaths in the town. Having climbed steeply during this period from around 100–25 a year to 225–50, the usual rate then dipped a little, steadying out at 200–25 until the mid-sixteenth century. No credible amount of growth in the local

[53] Entries for children and for people described as 'poor' confirm the inclusiveness of the list of the dead for whom candles were bought.

[54] The parish register is printed in A. M. Burke, *Memorials of St. Margaret's Church, Westminster* (London, 1914). A short overlap between the two sources provides a control of the value of the churchwardens' accounts. During the twelve-month period from 1 June 1539, 223 burials were recorded in the parish register. In the same period (with the possible variance of a day or two), the churchwardens' accounts contain 225 entries for individual sales of burial candles. This excellent correspondence strengthens the authority of the churchwardens' list as a tally of burials.

[55] The area represented by the parish of St Margaret was also that of the vill, or town, of Westminster; with the qualification that from 1514 the parish was very slightly reduced in size by the movement of its northern boundary. See ch. 8 nn. 9–10.

[56] See the list of epidemics in C. Creighton, *A History of Epidemics in Britain* (Cambridge, 1894), 231–301; and Slack, *The Impact of Plague in Tudor and Stuart England* (London, 1985), 145–51 and *passim*.   [57] See above, n. 171.

population in the period around 1500 could account for so marked a rise in the graph.[58] The explanation, therefore, must be an increase in the rate of mortality. That this was indeed the harsh experience of the local population appears the more likely in the light of corroborative evidence from within the abbey of Westminster. For the life expectancy of the monks, which had already fallen considerably between 1460 and 1480, plunged again between 1490 and 1510, the very period which stands out in the evidence from the town.[59] The cause of this increased rate of mortality in the period 1490–1510 is not yet apparent; nor are comparative statistics available to indicate how far this experience was typical of the country at large. It is clear, however, that Westminster, probably a dangerously unhealthy place already, became markedly more so in the years around 1500. The authorities on the subject have proposed an annual mortality rate for the country as a whole at this time of about 30 per 1,000.[60] But this would certainly be too low for Westminster where, unless the population were much more numerous than the 3,500 implied by the evidence considered earlier, mortality *in non-exceptional years* was running at an annual rate of 50–60 per 1,000.[61] Even allowing for the fact that these figures must have been inflated by visitors, the conclusion seems inescapable that for the resident population sixteenth-century Westminster was a 'death-trap'.

It was earlier suggested that the population losses of the mid-fifteenth century must have created hardship for many of the surviving inhabitants of Westminster. It would, however, be mistaken to imagine that the demographic expansion of the late fifteenth and sixteenth centuries brought, of itself, a general

[58] Nor do the churchwardens' accounts reveal any change at this time in the practice of buying candles at burials. I am grateful to Dr Richard Smith for his helpful comments and suggestions on these data.

[59] I must again thank Barbara Harvey for these results of her work on the monastic community.

[60] Wrigley and R. S. Schofield, *The Population History of England, 1541–1871* (London, 1981), 192, where crude death rates of 'around 28 per 1,000 in the 1540s and no more than 33 per 1,000 in the exceptionally mortal 1550s' are cautiously put forward.

[61] This is indicated by an annual death toll (as shown in Fig. 9), in non-exceptional years, of around 200 to 225. To bring the death rate down mathematically to a perhaps more credible 40 per 1,000 would require a live population of 5,000. Other demographic evidence, reviewed above, makes this very unlikely.

prosperity to the town. Many of those seeking accommodation in sixteenth-century Westminster were probably poor, and likely to remain so.[62] Rack-renters of cramped dwellings flourished,[63] while the abbey authorities noted the poverty of their tenants, as a cause of the decay of tenements.[64] The high pressure upon cheap accommodation soon led to the degradation of the housing stock. By Elizabeth's reign this process was far advanced. A survey of St Margaret's parish of 1584 found 383 short-term tenants or lodgers (described as 'inmates'), many of whom were crowded in conditions which cannot have been salubrious. It was noted, for example, that within the previous twenty years the lessee of the Saracen's Head in Tothill Street had divided this property into five cottages, where thirteen tenants were now lodged; and that, in the same street, the Catherine Wheel had similarly been partitioned into seventeen dwellings, into which the almost incredible total of fifty-three occupants had been crammed.[65] Although evidence of mid-seventeenth-century date is of no more than indirect relevance to the early sixteenth century, the impression of an increasing level of poverty in early modern Westminster is confirmed by the parliamentary surveys of 1650–1, which record dramatically contrasted extremes of comfort and deprivation. A few wealthy residences gave the district a high overall valuation; but at the same time Westminster contained very large numbers of shed-dwellings in multi-occupancy, suggestive of severe overcrowding and poverty. In 1664 almost 50 per cent of houses in Westminster were so poor as to be non-chargeable for the hearth tax.[66] These details

[62] See also pp. 79–80.

[63] A contemporary observer, in a memorandum addressed in the 1530s to Henry VIII, 'argued that landlords alone were to blame for empty houses and homeless men. By raising rents and especially entry fines, they were putting houses out of the reach of many; even those who could afford to pay had then nothing left over to attend to repairs. And when a house began to show neglect, the landlord would eject the tenant after a court action designed to make him do what his means simply barred him from attempting. In this manner, men lost their houses to join the wandering rabble on the roads.' Elton, *Reform and Renewal: Thomas Cromwell and the Common Weal* (Cambridge, 1973), 107.

[64] C. S. Knighton, 'Economics and Economies of a Royal Peculiar: Westminster Abbey, 1540–1640', in R. O'Day and F. Heal (eds.), *Princes and Paupers in the English Church, 1500–1800* (Leicester, 1981), 50.

[65] BL MS Lansdowne xxxv, fos. 101^r–106^r.

[66] M. J. Power, 'The East and West in Early-Modern London', in E. W. Ives, R. J. Knecht, and J. J. Scarisbrick (eds.), *Wealth and Power in Tudor England* (London, 1978), 167–85.

indicate that during the early modern period Westminster society was polarized. They also show that the recovery of population was not necessarily accompanied by a return to prosperity. In fact the contrary appears to have been the case. The characteristic symptoms of penniless transients living in squalid conditions are revealed already in the early sixteenth century. An official search of King Street in 1519 led to the following arrests: two men, professing to be servants respectively of Sir William FitzWilliam, Cardinal Wolsey's treasurer, and of Lewis Gryffyth, who 'lay in Lewis Gryffyth's chamber in a bed next to him and to his wife in a poor house'; in a lodging beneath this, 'two women, an old drab and a young wench, upon a sheet cast upon the ground'; Faux Vyncent, 'stranger', and Betres Lewys his bedfellow; Philip Umfrey, 'servant to the king, as he saith, taken in a house by himself in a chamber, and a woman in a chamber underneath, without shutting of doors'.[67] The scene is a salutary reminder that there is no simple correlation between demographic and economic growth.

2. THE ORIGIN OF THE POPULATION

The British Isles

Given high rates of mortality attendant upon unsanitary conditions, it is probable that all medieval towns depended heavily, for the maintenance of their levels of population, upon immigration. There may have been relatively small provincial towns in England to which this rule did not pertain,[68] but it was certainly applicable to the capital. In the thirteenth century much of the extraordinary growth of London,[69] as of many newly promoted towns, can only be explained by large-scale immigration. And when, in the seventeenth century, London's population was once again rapidly expanding, the actual scale of growth required that (assuming a relatively low rate of mortality) as many as one in six of all people born in England outside the capital, and surviving to adulthood, migrated to live there.[70] Such absolute figures cannot be advanced

[67] *LP* iii (1), no. 365 (10).
[68] Cf. Goose, 'In Search of the Urban Variable', 179.
[69] Keene and Harding, *Cheapside and the Development of London*.
[70] Abrams and Wrigley (eds.), *Towns in Societies*, 220. The figure is, naturally, approximate.

for the thirteenth-century phase of expansion, but another index is available of the degree of a town's attractiveness to immigrants. The distance which a migrant is prepared to travel to a place is a reflection of his perception of its importance. For the period before 1350, the record of personal bynames indicative of places of origin makes it possible to chart the distances covered by incomers to English towns. Comparison between towns can then provide a guide to their relative status.

The use of personal bynames as evidence of migration is not straightforward. But a methodology has been devised by Peter McClure which is adapted to meet the main problems; his system is followed here.[71] With its help it is possible to plot the distribution of places of origin of migrants to Westminster before 1350, and to tabulate these according to bands of distance measured as the crow flies. The result will show both the strength of Westminster's pull upon migrants, and the particular geographical directions in which it operated; these results may then be compared with other towns for which figures are available. In appendix VI are listed all places in the British Isles occurring in the bynames of property-holders in Westminster before 1350.[72] This arbitrary terminal date corresponds approximately to the period at which locative bynames (together with occupational bynames and nicknames) were generally replaced in written records by inherited surnames. The 286 names upon which appendix VI is based were derived from deeds datable to the period before 1350; the overwhelming majority belong to the thirteenth century, with a relatively small handful from the early fourteenth and a few from the late twelfth. The nature of the source material—property deeds—predetermines that the sample excludes poor, propertyless migrants who may (their existence is unrecorded) have drifted to Westminster for lack of employment elsewhere. The known group represents instead a

[71] P. McClure, 'Patterns of Migration in the Late Middle Ages: The Evidence of English Surnames', *Econ Hist Rev*, 2nd ser., xxxii (1979), 167–82.

[72] The sources, cited in app. VI, are almost exclusively deeds. In many cases the individuals recorded are shown by the deeds which preserve their names to have held property in Westminster. In other instances they appear as witnesses to transactions concerning such property. The role of witnesses as guarantors of the grants to which they testified required that they be themselves recognized and respectable local residents; complementary deeds frequently confirm that those who witnessed Westminster deeds did also live there. Holders of ecclesiastical positions and titled lords have been excluded from all calculations.

relatively prosperous body of incomers, who will have been among the more substantial members of their native communities. Their motive in migrating to Westminster is therefore likely to have been ambition, born of previous success, to fare even better in the capital.

A difficulty which arises in the use of these listed names is that many English place-names are common to more than one settlement. This leaves two options: either to ignore all recorded ambiguous place-names and to tabulate only those which are non-ambiguous, or else to assume, in an ambiguous case, that the place referred to is the one nearest to the migrant's goal. Despite attendant complexities, there is much in favour of the latter procedure, especially where long distances are involved, since it is likely that a traveller from a far-off village bearing the same name as one close by would be identified instead by a more distinctive place-name near to his settlement of origin. By this token, the exclusive tabulation of non-ambiguous names may result in under-representation of short-distance migration. On the other hand, progressive migration by stages, which can sometimes be documented in the Middle Ages and was doubtless almost as normal then as it was in the nineteenth century (except in so far as the Middle Ages provided fewer towns in which to break the journey), would lead to under-appreciation of the distances some migrants had, in total, covered.[73] In Table 2 the distances of these places from Westminster are shown according to the two procedures, taking respectively the 'nearest places' and the non-ambiguous names. Although the 'nearest place' tabulation shows, as expected, a slightly greater weighting of short-distance migration, the two sets of figures do not otherwise differ significantly.

The striking conclusion which emerges from Table 2 is that Westminster's gravitational pull upon migrants before 1350 extended over a very great distance indeed. This fact is underlined by comparison with available figures for early fourteenth-century London, Bristol, York, Norwich, Nottingham, and Leicester, and for thirteenth- and early fourteenth-century Winchester.[74] In the

---

[73] e.g. Butcher, 'The Origins of Romney Freemen, 1433–1523', *Econ Hist Rev*, 2nd ser., xvii (1974), 16–27. Cf. A. Redford, *Labour Migration in England, 1800–50* (Manchester, 1926), 158–60.

[74] McClure, 'Patterns of Migration', 178; S. Penn, 'The Origins of Bristol Migrants in the Early Fourteenth Century: The Surname Evidence', *Transactions of the Bristol and Gloucestershire Archaeological Society*, ci (1983), 123–30; Keene, *Medieval Winchester*, i. 371–9.

TABLE 2. *Distance of migration to Westminster in the thirteenth and early fourteenth centuries as shown by bynames*[a]

Distance in miles	Property-holders[b] in Westminster recorded before 1350			
	Nearest place		Non-ambiguous names (61%)	
	No.	%age	No.	%age
1–5	19	7 } 12 ⎫	12	7 } 10 ⎫
6–10	14	5 } ⎬ 25	6	3 } ⎬ 22
11–15	22	8 } 13 ⎭	12	7 } 12 ⎭
16–20	14	5 }	8	5 }
21–5	15	5 } 11 ⎫	9	5 } 9 ⎫
26–30	16	6 } ⎬ 20	7	4 } ⎬ 15
31–5	11	4 } 9 ⎭	5	3 } 6 ⎭
36–40	15	5 }	6	3 }
41–5	11	4 } 9 ⎫	6	3 } 8 ⎫
46–50	13	5 } ⎬ 17	8	5 } ⎬ 15
51–5	16	6 } 8 ⎭	10	6 } 7 ⎭
56–60	6	2 }	2	1 }
61–5	13	5 } 7 ⎫	9	5 } 7 ⎫
66–70	6	2 } ⎬ 11	3	2 } ⎬ 12
71–5	4	1 } 4 ⎭	3	2 } 5 ⎭
76–80	8	3 }	6	3 }
81–100	34	12	23	13
101–20	21	7	15	9
121–40	14	5	13	7
141–60	2	1	2	1
161 and over	12	4	10	6
TOTAL	286	102	175	100

[a] cf. app. VI.

[b] Including those recorded as witnesses to local deeds, who can in many cases be shown to have held property in Westminster, and may be assumed necessarily to have done so. See p. 183, n. 72.

cases of all the provincial cities, a marked tapering off in the intensity of migration reflected in bynames is apparent at distances above twenty miles. This is most marked in York, Norwich, and Leicester, where more than half of the (non-ambiguous) places from which inhabitants took their names lay within twenty miles of the town in each case. Both Winchester and Bristol evince a wider sphere of attraction; the twenty-mile band contained only 35 per cent and 32 per cent, respectively, of places of origin of migrants, while in these two towns half of the (non-ambiguous) places occurring in bynames lay upwards of forty miles or so away. As centres of attraction, Winchester and Bristol were positioned midway between York and London. London stood well out above the rest, its magnetic field extending fairly evenly over a zone sixty miles and more in radius; here the decline of attractive power with distance was least abrupt. Westminster's pattern (Table 2) is quite unlike that of any of the provincial centres, and is similar only to that of London. The similarity between Westminster and London in this respect is remarkably close: London's tallies were 21.1 per cent to twenty miles, with an additional 26.5 per cent to forty miles, 18.2 per cent to sixty miles, 7.0 per cent to eighty miles, and 11.3 per cent to one hundred miles. The most notable difference between the two is Westminster's greater proportion (23 per cent) of places upwards of one hundred miles away as compared with the London figure (16 per cent); overall the distribution of Westminster's sources of migrants was even more uniform across the range than was the case in London.

The major explanation for the readiness of migrants to travel so far to Westminster in the thirteenth and early fourteenth centuries is without doubt the presence of the royal government. A similar wide catchment of immigrants had characterized the city of Winchester in the eleventh and early twelfth centuries, when the king's administrative capital had been located there.[75] During the later twelfth and thirteenth centuries, the move to Westminster and the great expansion of the bureaucracy of government attracted its employees to the new centre from far afield.[76] Additionally, Westminster before the mid-fourteenth century should be seen as participating with London in a joint expansion of these twin

[75] Biddle (ed.), *Winchester in the Early Middle Ages*, 193–9 and Fig. 3.
[76] See ch. 1, sect. 2.

elements of the capital. This expansion evidently proceeded at a rate, reflected in the geographical extent of the catchment of migrants in both cases, which far outstripped that of other established urban centres. One difference between the tables for London and Westminster, the greater proportion of places over a hundred miles away recorded in Westminster, is probably to be explained by the fact that the London figures are derived exclusively from evidence (tax lists) of the early fourteenth century. By this date it may be that the rate and the average distance of migration to the capital was beginning to fall from a putative thirteenth-century level closer to that indicated in the Westminster table.

It is also possible to consider whether migrants to Westminster came from the same areas as did those coming to London, or to what extent Westminster's catchment was distinctive.[77] In Figure 10 all the place-names listed in appendix VI are plotted, including 'nearest places' in cases of ambiguity. Figure 10 reveals two particular points of comparison with London: a high degree of immigration to Westminster from those Home Counties lying to the north of the capital; and a further marked scatter of sources of migrants in East Anglia and the East Midlands. The prominence of the latter zone in London's catchment—which was so great as to determine, in the fourteenth century, the very character of London speech—is explicable as the product of close commercial ties based on the trade in wool and cloth.[78] In Westminster such ties were surely less common, although the fair of St Edward may have generated connections of this sort.[79] But in any case, this area supplied many fewer of Westminster's immigrants than it did of those to London. Westminster's hinterland of potential migrants was dominated more clearly, after the parts of north Middlesex, Hertfordshire, and Bedfordshire, by the middle Thames valley. The straggle of small towns along the river represents the line of a trade route which linked London with a vital source of grain. Its western location, up-river from London itself, may in part explain Westminster's large number of migrants from this quarter. This avenue of approach to Westminster can be traced back further northward and westward

---

[77] For London see E. Ekwall, *Two Early London Subsidy Rolls* (Lund, 1951); id., *Studies in the Population of Medieval London* (Lund, 1956).

[78] Id., *Two Early London Subsidy Rolls*, 70–1; id., *Studies*, pp. xliii ff.

[79] See ch. 4.

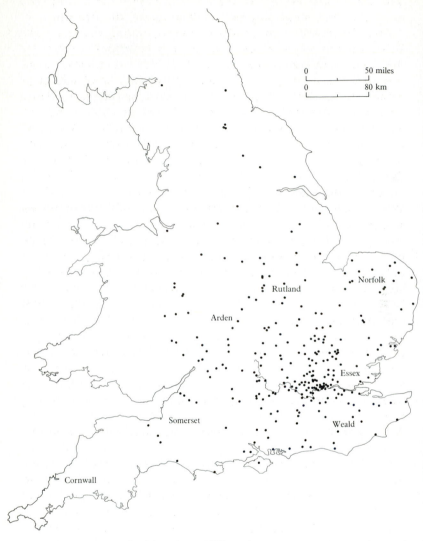

FIG. 10. Immigration to Westminster, *c*.1200–*c*.1350

into the feldon district of south Warwickshire: another grain-producing area which may have been supplying the capital.

Apart from such commercial connections, the decision to move to Westminster might have been determined by contact made through the extensive network of the estates of Westminster Abbey. Those places sending migrants which were also estates of the Westminster monks are indicated in the list of names in appendix VI. They include a number of centres in Hertfordshire and Essex which are otherwise unremarkable, but in addition one or two more remote places appear, whose occurrence may be the result of a personal recommendation transmitted by one of the abbey's bailiffs in the shires. Oakham in Rutland is one of these, and Deerhurst in Gloucestershire another. Indeed, the extensive estates held by Westminster Abbey in the south-west Midlands may partially account for the otherwise surprising groups of Westminster immigrants hailing from Worcestershire and the Welsh Borders. If the monastic connection may have inspired some of those arriving in Westminster from the country, others had no doubt been led to hope for a place at court. The itinerations of the monarch and of his justices must have sown in at least a few provincial minds the notion that Westminster, the seat of an only too powerful and demanding royal government, could be a place of opportunity. And that royal patronage did in fact reward some such hopefuls is witnessed by the building craftsmen who, being employed on the king's works, took up residence in Westminster: Corfe (close to the Purbeck limestone quarries in Dorset) and Beverley (where construction-work on the abbey was proceeding in parallel with that at the church of Westminster) each sent a son to Westminster in the thirteenth century on this account.[80]

Patronage of one kind or another doubtless lay behind much of the 'betterment migration'—the voluntary movement of those hopeful of advancement, distinguished from the forced itinerancy of the simply unemployed—which continued throughout the later Middle Ages. The slump in Westminster's population during the fifteenth century indicates that fewer settlers came then, and perhaps that those who did so usually travelled shorter distances than their predecessors. Yet movement to the town continued (though patchily) to be recorded. The lure of the king's court to

[80] See also ch. 5, sect. 7.

those attracted by the honeypot of royal patronage gained in strength over the period, as monarchs lengthened their stays in their principal palace. The general effects of the court upon migration to Westminster are illustrated in the abrupt appearance in the town, in the early Tudor decades, of unprecedented numbers of Welshmen. Some of these basked in the favour of the Welsh royal dynasty, as did David ap Rees, one of Henry VII's grooms of the chamber and a resident in Long Ditch.[81] Others doubtless followed where one had led the way,[82] to set up their humbler trades in reassuring proximity to some elevated fellow-countryman. Such was Morgan ap Howell, who from 1520 ran the Wool Sack bakery in King Street.[83] Some, however, were to be found in the poorest of lodgings, and this was also true of the Irish.[84] For every success story about the one who, by dint of hanging around at court, persuaded some official to add his name to a payroll, there were others to whom such advancement was denied.[85] Many of the poor who so uncontrollably swelled the body of migrants to Westminster in the Tudor period must have lacked the advantage of a cousin in office or a letter of recommendation. Their fate in many cases would be no better than that of Thomas a Ley, an otherwise unknown Scotsman who in 1520–1 was taken into the hostel of St Mary Rounceval to die.[86]

Aliens

The fair of St Edward in the thirteenth century and royal diplomacy throughout the medieval period lent to Westminster a cosmopolitan

[81] WAM 19756–86, 23270; *LP* i (1), no. 20 (p. 13); PCW Wyks, 179–80.

[82] Contact might be maintained by migrants with their places of origin, which were sometimes remembered by testators. Thus John Meryden, a Westminster butcher, recalled in his will of 1489 the parish church of his birthplace at Dorking, where he had been baptized. PRO, PROB 11/8, PCC 25 Milles. Similarly Thomas Swallow, a brickmaker who made his will as a Westminster resident in 1541, requested masses to be said for him in the church at Thundridge in Hertfordshire, and left money for repairs to the road there between Westmill and Ware. PRO, PROB11/28, PCC 25 Alenger. The poorer migrants, however, did not make wills; and the very poorest may have had no reason to sustain links with the places they had been compelled to leave behind.

[83] WAM 18003; 23518–61. Cf. Morgan Taillour (1532–3). WAM 19148.

[84] Cf. Margaret Iryssh, living in 1461 in 'a cellar' in Our Lady's Alley off the west side of King Street. WAM 23234. Celtic immigrants were also found in menial employment, like the 'Scots and Irishmen' engaged by the abbey sacrist on dyking and road-mending in 1428–9. WAM 19670.

[85] See further below, sect. 7.   [86] See below, p. 318.

air, which was intensified by the 'aliens' who took up permanent residence here. While their absolute numbers were never over-whelming, aliens naturally tended to form cohesive groups, and made themselves conspicuous within the communities in which they settled. Those in the London area were chiefly concentrated in the suburbs, where they evaded investigation by the monopolistic city craft guilds, from which they were generally excluded.

Those foreigners in Westminster who, in the thirteenth century, bore locative bynames from the lands of France, represented chiefly the northern coastal areas: Boulogne in the Pas-de-Calais, Falaise in Normandy, and Dol in Brittany.[87] Later the emphasis was rather on the south-west. Elias Hugon, a vintner, came to England with others of his occupation in the 1450s, as a refugee from war-torn Bordeaux; he subsequently rented a large house in the sanctuary at Westminster.[88] Among his neighbours within the sanctuary was a Gascon knight called Louis de Bretailles. De Bretailles had fought on the English side in the French wars, and afterwards served Edward IV as a diplomatic agent.[89] Less-exalted French immi-grants may also have been driven to wandering by the conflicts, ultimately to find themselves on the margins of Westminster society; a number of single French women are so recorded.[90]

More Italians were to be seen in Westminster than actually made the place their home. Those craftsmen who came may generally have remained only long enough to complete the commissioned task; by definition their rarified skills would not easily find regular employment. Such, typically, was the case of the Italian workers in marble brought from Rome to Westminster in *c.*1268 by Abbot Richard de Ware and King Henry III. Over a decade, this highly sought-after workshop produced elaborate pavements and royal tombs in the abbey (still in part extant); but its base of operations remained in Rome, to which in due course it returned.[91] Of those

---

[87] WD, fos. 355, 365; WAM 17324. It is possible that these particular bynames were acquired by Englishmen who had been to those places.

[88] *Cal Cl R 1476–85*, p. 58; WAM 17808, 19720–5; James, *Wine Trade*, 86.

[89] WAM 19720–43, 17868, 23105–15; CWA i. 280 (de Bretailles's burial at St Margaret's, Westminster, in 1491–2). See also C. L. Scofield, *The Life and Reign of Edward IV*, 2 vols. (London, 1923), i. 260; ii. 100, 271, 273. See also below, n. 197.

[90] e.g. Dionys Frenchwoman, in a cottage in Our Lady's Alley in 1465–6. WAM 23239. Further examples below, sect. 7.

[91] W. R. Lethaby, *Westminster Abbey and the King's Craftsmen: A Study of Mediaeval Building* (London, 1906), 309–28; id., *Westminster Abbey Re-examined* (London, 1925), 217–33.

Italians who came to Westminster to trade, many were probably living in London. Lodowic Gentyl of Genoa, for example, who was robbed on the quayside at Westminster in November 1376, returned immediately to London to report the incident to the mayor.[92] Another Italian, Peter Gracyan, on the other hand, in 1390 held at Westminster such extensive and valuable stock as to suggest that he was resident there.[93] Earlier in the fourteenth century Bonaventure Benintende of Florence held a row of shops in Westminster. Benintende, rejecting the enforced bachelordom of most Italian businessmen living abroad, took a wife, Wimarca— evidently, from her name, an Englishwoman—by whom he had a son.[94] After the mid-fourteenth century Italians cut less of a figure in London as bankers and cloth merchants than formerly, but they continued in the later Middle Ages to operate in the north European markets as brokers. Antonio Parisola was a Genoese merchant who was registered with the Merchant Adventurers' Company of London as a broker in 1479. Three years later he received letters of denization; by 1483 he was living in a house within the abbey almonry at Westminster, where he was on hand to importune clients at court.[95] At about the same period, between *c.*1489 and *c.*1516, an Italian poet entertained his muse at Westminster; first within the abbey precinct, and later in a house which formed part of the nearby hospital of St James. This was Pietro Carmeliano, a native of Brescia, and one of the 'busy–bees' who disseminated Italian humanism in the courts of northern Europe. Though not the only Italian to find patronage at the early Tudor court, Carmeliano may at times have felt a little isolated in Westminster. But perhaps his accommodation at St James's hospital, which was described as a 'tower house', reminded him of home.[96]

[92] *Cal Plea & Mem R 1364–81*, 21, 231.

[93] *Cal Pat R 1388–92*, p. 313.

[94] Ibid. *1334–8*, p. 229; ibid. *1343–5*, p. 546; *Cal Cl R 1339–41*, p. 21; ibid. *1343–6*, p. 613; *Cal Inq p m* viii. 576. And cf. in the mid-thirteenth century Henry Vineter, Lumbard, and Laurence Lumbard of Westminster. BL MS Add. 28024, fo. 47ᵛ; WAM 17465; WD, fo. 536ᵛ.

[95] Lyell and Watney (eds.), *Acts of Court of the Mercers' Company*, 111; *Cal Pat R 1476–85*, p. 323; WAM 19092.

[96] WAM 23114–18; ECR, MS 62/AB/1, pp. 168, 186, etc.; ECR, MS 61/RR/G/ 9–17; CWA, ii, s.a. 1516–17. On Carmeliano, whose residence in Westminster has hitherto been only assumed, see R. Weiss, *Humanism in England During the Fifteenth Century* (Oxford, 1957), 170–2. See also below, n. 207. Master Adrian de Bardi, evidently a fellow-Italian and a friend of Carmeliano, lived from 1500 until 1512 in

The bronze effigy in Westminster Abbey of King Henry VII, which was made by the Italian Pietro Torrigiani, is enclosed by a grille of Anglo-Flemish work, produced in *c.*1505 under the direction of one Thomas Ducheman.[97] In the thirteenth century, men from Flanders and from the German territories to the east were regular visitors to Westminster around the time of St Edward's fair; occasionally one is recorded as having taken up residence there.[98] It is probably not a mere trick of the evidence, however, that their numbers appear greatly increased in the later Middle Ages. Lists of foreign nationals in the town compiled for taxation purposes after 1440 (when a levy was introduced on all aliens) show a preponderance of the northern Europeans known generally as *Doche*.[99] The numbers listed in the mid-fifteenth-century tax returns indicate a total alien population in the vill of Westminster of about two hundred; a significant element in a small district whose sum of inhabitants was at this period probably little more than two thousand[100] (Table 3). Most of the immigrants are distinguished by Dutch or Germanic names and indeed, in another list of 1436 which gives the places of origin of thirty-eight foreigners in Westminster, almost all of those named hailed from the Low Countries or the Rhineland.[101]

The new settlers were inclined to congregate together, and to form a semi-distinct communion within the wider one of the town. A favoured nucleus of the *Doche* immigrants was a particular row of half a dozen small tenements on the east side of King Street, at the

the same row in the Westminster sanctuary as had been occupied by Carmeliano himself in 1489–93. De Bardi, a clerk who may, like Carmeliano, have been a canon of St Stephen's Chapel, received in 1509 a royal pardon for an unspecified offence; he died ten years later at Westminster. WAM 23127–44; *LP* i, no. 438 (1, m. 16); CWA ii, s.a. 1519–20 (bequest at death of 40s. to St Margaret's church steeple, delivered by the hand of Master Peter Carmelianus).

[97] L. Stone, *Sculpture in Britain: The Middle Ages* (Harmondsworth, 1955), 230.

[98] e.g. Robert le Flemyng. PRO, E40/1535.

[99] For discussion of the evidence see Thrupp, 'A Survey of the Alien Population of England in 1440', *Speculum*, xxxii (1957), 262–73; ead., 'Aliens in and around London in the Fifteenth Century', in Hollaender and Kellaway (eds.), *Studies in London History*, 251–72. The figures for Westminster (Table 3) do not correspond with Thrupp's general conclusion ('Aliens in and around London', 259) that the number of aliens in the London area declined between the 1430s and the 1480s.

[100] See above, sect. 1.

[101] *Cal Pat R 1429–36*, pp. 541–88. Large numbers of *Doche* were recorded in the London suburb of Southwark at the same period. Carlin, 'Urban Development of Southwark', ch. 15.

TABLE 3. *Aliens in the vill of Westminster, 1440–1483*

Year	Total (adult males)	Householders	Servants	Source PRO, E179/
1440	75	33	42	141/69
1441	81	36	45	141/68
1455	82	27	55	235/57
1457	95	31	64	235/69
1483	94	29	65	141/94

Notes:
(i) The area represented is that of the parish of St Margaret, which is distinguished in the records from adjacent parishes.
(ii) Wives, where they are named with their husbands, are excluded from the table. The figures therefore represent resident foreign males (and a few independent females) aged approximately twelve and upwards.

Source: Alien subsidy returns.

Clowson bridge. Here, in the late fifteenth and early sixteenth centuries, were concentrated the shops of Garlow (or Gerard) Rust and Dederic Harrison, 'Dutchman', both cobblers, John Assyng and Cornelius Williamson, goldsmiths, Daniel Dutchman, 'hardwareman',[102] Peter van Sconebek, and many others of their compatriots.[103] The solidarity of the alien group is also evinced in the habit of naming one another as trustees or executors. Mutual support extended to bind together the many *Doche* who were scattered throughout London and particularly around its edges. Thus Godfrey Vandermer, a Westminster tailor, in 1454 acted as a trustee for a beer-brewer in Southwark, Richard van Colen; and in 1458 a Greenwich beer-brewer, Herman Jonson, performed the same service for John Derykson, beer-brewer and hatmaker of Westminster.[104] The foundation of a guild at Westminster under the patronage of St Cornelius, first recorded around 1500, was probably inspired by the *Doche*, among whom that distinctive name

[102] Cf. Michael Dutchman, also described as 'Michael Marchand' and as 'Michael Hardwareman', who held a shop near the east end of the abbey church in 1500–6. WAM 19756–61.
[103] WAM 23090–152.　　[104] *Cal Cl R 1447–54*, p. 489; ibid. *1454–61*, p. 279.

was popular.[105] Such a guild provided a focus for social activity both reassuring to the expatriots and acceptable—for it played its part in such works as the rebuilding of the parish church—to their English neighbours.[106]

Relations between the alien and native societies were, for the most part, co-operative. If some preferred to name fellow-foreigners as trustees, others, perhaps for reasons of respectability, chose Englishmen. Garlow Rust, one of the cobblers at the Clowson bridge, thus secured two highly respectable Westminster figures in Henry Bradford, gentleman, and William Moreland, a clerk of chancery.[107] William Moreland was in addition a close personal friend of another foreigner, Quentin Poulet. Originating from Lille in Flanders, Poulet came to Westminster in *c.*1500 to become librarian to King Henry VII. As a thoroughly naturalized denizen of his adopted country, Poulet was even co-opted to serve both on the local jury of Westminster and as a warden of the major guild of the town, that of the Virgin Mary's Assumption.[108] Yet such harmony was fragile. The foreigners' proclivity for settling in concentrated pockets, in addition to their naturally distinctive manners of dress and speech,[109] made them conspicuous and by that token vulnerable. At times of economic tension, they were tragically obvious targets of persecution.[110] No major outbreak of xenophobic conflict is recorded in Westminster, in contrast to other parts of the city and suburbs of London; yet the latent tensions were revealed in

[105] Three *Doche*, Alard Deryk and John a Cleve, cobblers, and Nicholas Strete, tailor, made bequests to the fraternity or to the altar of St Cornelius in St Margaret's church in the early sixteenth century. PCW Wyks, 71–2, 174, 176–7, 102–3. Strete's *Doche* extraction is inferred from the names of his wife, Jacomyn, and of the overseers of his will, Gerard Rust and Godfrey Risyng (or Russyng). One of the wardens of the guild in 1520–1 was John Kaysar, who was evidently of similar origin. Other known masters and wardens of the guild, however, were Englishmen; the society was nationally mixed. CWA ii, s.a. 1520–5. On this guild see also ch. 9, sect. 1.

[106] Cf. the guilds of St Catherine, of the cobbler saints Crispin and Crispinian and others formed by *Doche* in the city of London. Thrupp, 'Aliens in and around London', 263–4. In Southwark in the 1550s, a *Doche* priest was employed at St Olave's parish church. Carlin, 'Urban Development of Southwark', 420–1.

[107] *Cal Cl R 1468–76*, p. 176 (1471).

[108] See app. VIII, s.n.

[109] Cf. p. 164.

[110] Cf. A. Pettegree, 'The Foreign Population of London in 1549', *Proceedings of the Huguenot Society of London*, xxiv (1984), 141–6.

a regular incidence of personal violence.[111] The potential danger of escalation was vividly presented in Westminster on 22 May 1517, when those city apprentices accused of the murders of numerous aliens living in London, during riots on 'Evil May Day', were brought into Westminster Hall. Each bore a halter around his neck and came crying for mercy.[112] The mix of nationalities in the capital was beneficial both to trade and to the development of new industries there.[113] But integration was never complete and when, as happened in the sixteenth century, social pressures increased, the scapegoat for misunderstood ills was only too conveniently at hand.

3. WOMEN

Women in the Middle Ages in Westminster, as elsewhere, were denied any political status. As a result of this subordination they are grossly under-represented in medieval documents. Yet much evidence suggests that, their political and social disabilities notwithstanding, in multifarious ways women played an active and independent part in the late medieval economy. This was true both of married women and, more particularly, of single women, of whom it has been argued that a general north-west European pattern of late marriage created a large class. The evidence is especially rich during the fourteenth and most of the fifteenth centuries, and distinctly less so in the immediately preceding and succeeding periods. The late-medieval phase of relative female independence coincides with an era of reduced pressures in the economy at large, in which a contracted population competed less hotly for both resources and employment than either in the thirteenth or in the sixteenth century. When high population levels made work and profits scarce, it has been suggested, men asserted their claimed superiority, forcing women out of the labour market and into purely domestic or otherwise marginal roles.[114] Within this

[111] e.g. Richard Bowyer's murder of Peter Fauconer, Fleming, in 1386; and the alleged attack by Garlow Rust, a Flemish cobbler, upon John Colyns, skinner of Westminster, in 1467. *Cal Pat R 1385–89*, 134–5; WAM 50758. For similar affrays, throughout the fifteenth century, between individuals with English and *Doche* names, respectively, see WAM 50738 (*bis*), 50746 (*bis*), 50749, 50761.

[112] (E. Hall), *Hall's Chronicle* (London, 1809 edn.), 591.

[113] See ch. 5, sect. 10.

[114] Goldberg, 'Women in Fifteenth Century Town Life', in Thomson (ed.), *Towns and Townspeople*.

context of increased scope for their participation during the late-medieval period, Westminster women can be shown to have engaged in a great variety of economic activities.

The late-medieval 'age of opportunity' for women must, however, be seen in proportion. By no means all women found desirable employment who wished or needed to do so. It is probable that a large element among immigrants to Westminster were single women, for whom work was a necessity; but it was not always to be found.[115] Some of these, as has been seen, resorted to prostitution. This was a recourse often adopted to supplement income when trade was slack; thus Alice Shepster, accused of prostitution in 1396, was probably a dressmaker.[116] Even those with a specialized craft skill were usually, because of the small scale of their labour, very insecure. A silk woman living in a garret in King Street might easily be driven to diversify into procuring prostitutes to eke out an existence.[117] Silk-spinning was a craft unusually dominated by women;[118] as a rule, craftswomen were dependent for their capital and raw materials upon men. When Maud Smith, who made purses at Westminster in the 1440s, assaulted the wife of a local skinner, her motive may have sprung from resented reliance upon the supplier of the leather which she worked.[119]

Greater freedom was enjoyed by women traders who, as stall-holders in the Monday market and doubtless on other days too, were less directly bound to a chain of economic dependence upon men.[120] Women operated at all periods of the Middle Ages as

[115] Statistics can almost never be discovered, but a rare exception is provided by the Worcestershire market town of Halesowen where, in the late thirteenth century, about three out of four immigrants were single women. Hilton, *Class Conflict and the Crisis of Feudalism*, 212. See also Goldberg, 'Female Labour, Service and Marriage in the Late Medieval Urban North', *Northern History*, xxii (1986), 20–1.

[116] WAM 50734. Cf. also Isabella Huxter of Charing, similarly charged in 1402. WAM 50735. Occupational bynames were probably current for longer at this humble social level than in other contexts; see Keene, *Medieval Winchester*, i. 392.

[117] 'Le silkwoman modo inhabitans super le strayres iuxta le Boreshed est communis pronuba.' WAM 50767 (1494).

[118] M. K. Dale, 'The London Silk Women of the Fifteenth Century', *Econ Hist Rev*, iv (1932–4), 324–35. Exceptionally, a silk woman might be an independent person of some consequence, as was Margaret Hurtebees of St Clement Danes parish, named in 1470 as a fellow-trustee of a Westminster 'gentleman' alongside the bishops of Durham and Exeter. *Cal Cl R 1468–76*, pp. 126–7, 181; *Cal Pat R 1467–77*, p. 325.

[119] *Cal Pat R 1441–6*, p. 265; for the skinner, John Rawlyn, see app. VIII, s.n.

[120] Cf. Hilton, 'Women Traders in Medieval England', in id., *Class Conflict and the Crisis of Feudalism*, 205–15.

retailers, in particular of food and drink. As hostellers, women engaged very widely in the selling of ale. Meanwhile market women in Westminster sold bread, milk, cheese, vegetables, and cooked meats, as well as ale.[121] At best, however, the profits of petty marketing were small. It was symptomatic of the precariousness of this trade that in 1377 Isabella Puddyngwyf—who probably, as her name suggests, sold meat puddings for a living—was fined, with her child, for stealing the tithes of corn during harvest.[122] Moreover, even in small-scale victualling, male dominance obtruded. Isabel Capon, cook, charged in the abbot's court in 1410 with having offered for sale a cut of roast beef which was bad, whereby, as she said, she 'lost her good name of a retailer of victuals', blamed her male supplier: John Curteys, butcher, who in the first place had sold her the meat for 20*d*.[123]

The collaboration of wives with their husbands was common at Westminster in both the hostelling and the tailoring trades;[124] but Anastasia Barnwell, who took in sewing work at her house in Tothill Street, was a 'singlewoman'. In 1508 the guild of the Virgin Mary's Assumption paid her 3*s*. for three dozen 'liveries'—presumably either hoods or badges with the guild emblem—to be worn at a feast.[125] The wife of Robert Harrison, a smith, similarly worked on her own account, washing and mending clothes, including the vestments in the parish church.[126] Washerwomen were concentrated in Long Ditch, where running water was readily available.[127] Like laundering, the trade of 'the great midwife' who in the early sixteenth century lived in Our Lady's Alley on the east side of King Street was, in the Middle Ages, exclusively a female occupation.[128]

---

[121] Cf. Margaret la Bredmongestere, who held a messuage in the mid-thirteenth century; and 'the Goodwife Walsh', who supplied the abbey kitchener with milk and cheese in the early sixteenth. WD fo. 384[r-v]; WAM 33331. For other examples see ch. 5, sect. 3. The usual practice of citing husbands in court for retailing offences of their wives causes a probably large underestimation of the latter as, for example, ale-sellers. Yet in 1392 some thirty female victuallers were listed in the Westminster court roll. WAM 50726.

[122] WAM 50709.   [123] PRO, KB9/197/14.

[124] See also ch. 5, sects. 3, 5. And cf. the mid-thirteenth-century Westminster duo of Richard Vannarius or le Faner (a winnower, as the image of a winnow on his seal confirms) and his wife, Margaret le Heymongestere. WAM 17364, 17367, 17506.

[125] Assumption guild accts, s.a.; WAM 23560–87.

[126] CWA ii, s.a. 1514–15, 1520–6, for both Robert Harryson and his wife.

[127] WAM 50699 (three *communes lotrices . . . prope Langedyche* in 1364); CWA i. 85 (*sol' cuidam lotrici in Langdich pro lavacione 16. towell'. 16d.* in 1467–8).

[128] Assumption guild accts (rental), s.a. 1517–18.

Servanthood, which was perhaps the commonest occupation for young, unmarried women, is particularly difficult to document. Female servants, however, are very often recorded in the households of those sufficiently prosperous to make wills.[129] Servanthood might not only entail domestic duties, but commonly involved the performance of chores and the acquisition of skills relating to the business of the master.[130] The process of a single girl's assimilation into local society through service might be marked by her adoption of her employer's family name.[131] Another largely feminine preserve was the sale of flowers and herbs. Women provided the red roses which decorated St Margaret's church at Corpus Christi.[132] They were also suppliers of rosemary used to freshen the chambers of houses: in the 1530s rosemary was bought from Mistress Stephens of St Margaret's parish for use in the king's palace of Whitehall, 'to strew in the windows of the lodgings' of the little princesses, Mary and Elizabeth.[133]

Apart from their economic activities, medieval Englishwomen enjoyed a degree of independence by virtue of their legal right to hold property. In thirteenth-century Westminster even married women possessed their own seals for use in property transactions and, especially if they were important heiresses, tended to keep their maiden names.[134] The wills of later Westminster widows show them to have managed both businesses and complex holdings of property formerly registered in their husbands' names.[135] A propertyless widow choosing to stay unmarried could lead a

---

[129] Cf. also the matter-of-fact way in which John Mane, scrivener of Westminster, entrusted his two daughters at his death to their uncle, 'for their putting forth to service'. PCW Wyks, 180–2 (1513). In Coventry in the 1530s, living-in servants comprised almost a quarter of the recorded population of the city. Phythian-Adams, *Desolation of a City*, 204.

[130] See Goldberg, 'Female Labour, Service and Marriage'.

[131] This appears to have been the case of 'Margaret Lentall', named by Henry Lentall in his will of 1530 as 'his servant'. It is possible, however, that she was a remote member of the family who had been despatched to the care of Henry Lentall (who was himself a servant of the prior of Westminster). Margaret received from him a bed and a pewter service, on the evident assumption that she would shortly marry. PCW Bracy, fo. 17ᵛ.

[132] CWA i. 11, 45, 235.

[133] *London Topographical Record*, xix (1947), p. 116. Cf. also ibid., p. 114: rosemary bought from Goodwife Reyd of Westminster.

[134] Cf. Keene, *Medieval Winchester*, ii. 1410.

[135] e.g. Alice Lord, who in 1539, six years after the death of her husband Edmund (q.v. in app. VIII), elaborately divided lands and goods among seven sons. PRO, PROB11/27, PCC 32 Dyngeley; PROB10/8.

comfortable life, as Catherine Vampage did at St James's hospital in the early sixteenth century.[136] Lay women are not known to have lived together in common at Westminster;[137] nor did they form a guild whose membership was exclusively female, as may have occurred elsewhere.[138] Yet they were able to join all non-craft guilds, and women belonged, both as wives of male members and as independent females, to all the guilds of Westminster. These societies may for some have provided a source of marriage partners.[139]

   In many ways the lives of women were too much a part of Westminster society in general to be susceptible to separate treatment, and an excess of special consideration would be misleading. In most of the other chapters of this book (that on urban government most notably excepted) they play their parts alongside the men. Yet a final point is worthy of consideration. During the later Middle Ages, women showed themselves the equals of men in many crafts and trades. At the same time, the qualities which are peculiar to women, and which have been variously valued at different periods, led them to play certain distinctive roles not common to men. Female members of the guild of Our Lady's Assumption at Westminster undertook special responsibility for a member lately dead; and in connection with this role of care and protection, it is worth remarking upon the prominence at Westminster of the patronage of female saints: chiefly St Margaret, St Mary, St Anne, and St Catherine.[140] St Margaret was regarded as the special protectress of women in pregnancy, and was commonly invoked at childbirth.[141] The parish church housed 'St Margaret's circlet', a headband which was hired out to girls at their weddings and was presumably worn as a symbol of fertility.[142] That women in

---

[136] See ch. 10 n. 80.

[137] Cf. the (very slight) evidence of such female households in Norwich, which have, interestingly though perhaps unrealistically, been compared to the *béguinages* of the Low Countries. N. P. Tanner, *The Church in Late Medieval Norwich, 1370–1532*, Pontifical Institute of Mediaeval Studies, Studies and Texts, lxvi (Toronto, 1984), 64–6.

[138] Carlin, 'Urban Development of Southwark', 416.

[139] See ch. 9.

[140] See also chs. 8, 9.

[141] J. Mirk, *Festial*, ed. T. Erbe, Early English Text Society, extra ser., xcvi (1905), 202; *Biblioteca Sanctorum* (Rome, 1970), s.n. Marina/Margherita.

[142] The circlet was hired for 16*d.* on each occasion. It had been given by the wife of one Anthony Goldsmith. CWA ii, s.a. 1510–11 (inventory); CWA iii, s.a. 1532–3.

another aspect were acknowledged in some cases to hold privileged access to spiritual power is shown by the succession of female anchorites associated with St Margaret's church.[143] Enclosed in a chamber on the south side of the chancel of the church, at the heart of the town, the anchoress, a lay woman of recognized spiritual authority, represented a direct link between the secular society and the intercessory power of the saints.[144]

4. PROFESSIONAL SERVICES: LAW, MEDICINE, AND GOVERNMENT

Chapter 5 demonstrated the primary importance, within the economy of Westminster, of service trades. Among the complex of attractions which drew visitors to the town there existed in addition, by the late Middle Ages, a variety of services of a professional kind. The emergence, from the fourteenth century onwards, of a distinct class of professional practitioners, of whom some were in minor orders but a growing proportion were laymen, has not yet been extensively studied.[145] Westminster pre-eminently offered openings in professional careers. The market for such services was generated in particular by the increasing complexities of both government and legal practice in the late medieval period; and it was natural that Westminster should be precocious in this respect. The helpless reliance of the modern lay public upon skilled counsellors in matters of local administration and law, of health,

[143] All of the recluses recorded as living in the anchorage next to St Margaret's church were female. Male hermits also existed in Westminster, but these were for the most part attached to the abbey church. Westlake, *Westminster Abbey*, 18–21.

[144] The recluse who represented solitary reflection in the middle of the busy town was a common figure. See R. M. Clay, *The Hermits and Anchorites of England* (London, 1914), 66–72. For the location of 'the anchoress's house', adjacent to St Margaret's church, see WAM 36057; also Westlake, *St. Margaret's Westminster*, 336–8. Joan Germyn, the anchoress who died in 1466–7, was buried inside St Margaret's church, the rarely rung great bell being sounded at her funeral. CWA i. 63, 83. Her successor who died in 1489–90 left the sum of £5 to St Margaret's church; in c.1508 'My Lady Ancres' held three tenements in King Street. These evidently personal possessions indicate that those who chose the restricted life of an anchoress at Westminster may typically have been women of middling means. The widowed state of Cecily Norton, the Westminster anchoress who received a royal gift in 1443, may also have been common. CWA i. 255; WAM 18599; *Cal Pat R 1441–6*, p. 177.

[145] See, however, the essays in C. H. Clough (ed.), *Profession, Vocation and Culture in Later Medieval England* (Liverpool, 1982).

and of education is not an eternal condition, but has specific historical origins in the late medieval period. Professional monopolies of these respective spheres developed only gradually. A relatively early stage in this evolution is reflected in Thomas Littleton, a doctor (*medicus*) who from 1428 until 1447 occupied a house in the 'Sarum rents' within the Westminster sanctuary. A man of many parts, Littleton could also be described in 1437 as being of Turnmill Street (Finsbury, Middx.), parchmentmaker (*parchemener*), alias of Westminster, physician (*phesico*), surgeon (*sirurgico*), scrivener (*scriptori*), or sergeant-at-law; and in 1464 he is found acting as legal attorney for the Westminster monks.[146] He illustrates the expanding spheres of practical wisdom in which the unlearned layman increasingly desired assistance, but which had not yet become the exclusive preserves of professionals.

Law

Of the growth of secular fields of specialized knowledge the rise of the legal profession was one of the manifestations which particularly affected Westminster. Remarkably few lawyers, however, chose to rent permanent quarters in Westminster itself; many more evidently preferred to reside in the legal district around Holborn and Chancery Lane.[147] A significant reason for the absence of lawyers from the Westminster rentals is that, for most, their work in the capital lasted precisely for the duration of the four legal terms of the year. For the rest of the time, those who would find employment were driven to seek it in the provinces. Richard Livermore, born of an Exeter family in the early fifteenth century, trained as a lawyer and was retained as an attorney both by the dean and chapter and by the city councillors of his native town. Their payments to him, meanwhile, show that during term-time he was based at Westminster, and indeed the monks of Westminster were also numbered among his regular clients. Livermore was one lawyer who did, for over thirty years, lease a house in the capital, at the southern end of

[146] WAM 17744; 24629–49; 23074–7; 23236; PRO, C67/38, m. 15. (The last ref. was kindly provided by Dr N. Ramsay.) Littleton is designated *medicus* in the Westminster rentals.

[147] E. Williams, *Early Holborn and the Legal Quarter of London* (London, 1927). See also N. L. Ramsay, 'The English Legal Profession, c.1340–c.1450', Ph.D. thesis, Univ. of Cambridge (1985); and Ives, *The Common Lawyers*.

King Street, opposite the great gate leading to Palace Yard and Westminster Hall. He was sufficiently a Westminster resident to belong to the guild of the Assumption of the Virgin Mary, to be elected to the manor court, and to find his grave, at his death in 1481–2, in St Margaret's parish church.[148]

Medicine

Basic medical care and remedies remained throughout the Middle Ages—the rich excepted—outside the sphere of costly professionals.[149] For the universal panacea of blood-letting, however, regular resort would be had to barbers, who were never far to seek in Westminster. Some of the Westminster barbers were prosperous men at their deaths, perhaps as a result of having provided more specialized and expensive services to ailing aristocrats on visits to Westminster.[150] There were always opportunities here for physicians and surgeons, such as the celebrated John Arderne, the most famous doctor of medieval England, who was retained at the abbey in 1378, and the succession of fourteenth-century royal doctors who resided in a house reserved for them by the palace gate.[151] Others with practices at court in this period were rewarded with the mastership of St James's hospital, an appropriate appointment although the hospital itself provided only too little work for their skill.[152] In 1486 Thomas Warde, MD, a surgeon of Westminster with connections in the court, received from the abbot the wardenship of St Mary Magdalen's chapel in Tothill Street, a small sinecure perhaps granted in lieu of a fee.[153] Edward IV's chief physician was a Dutchman named James Fries (from Friesland, whence he came). In 1462 the king presented Fries with a messuage called the Great Bell in the parish of St Botolph, Aldersgate, outside

[148] App. VIII, s.n.
[149] On hospitals, see ch. 10.
[150] Cf. the wills of two kinsmen in the trade, Richard Hall (d. 1506) and Robert Hall (d. 1539). The latter left to his two male servants the equipment in his shop: basins, ewers, shaving cloths, knives, candlesticks, and chairs. PCW Wyks, 62–4; PCW Bracy, fos. 69^r–70^r. Also the will of Thomas Stocdale (1558): PCW Bracy, fo. 142^{r-v}.
[151] Arderne: WAM 19356; and see C. H. Talbot and E. A. Hammond, *The Medical Practioners in Medieval England* (London, 1965), 111–12. Royal doctors: *Cal Pat R 1334–8*, p. 556; ibid. *1348–50*, p. 307. See also above, ch. 1 n. 89.
[152] See ch. 10, sect. 4.
[153] *Cal Cl R 1447–54*, p. 270; WAM Reg Bk, i. fo. 55.

the wall of London; but from 1478 until his death about ten years later the doctor and his wife, Elizabeth, rented accommodation in Westminister, at first in King Street and finally, from 1485–6 onwards, within the abbey almonry.[154] In return for his minist-rations to the royal body Fries enjoyed an annual salary of £20, a sum which would have commanded respect in the town.[155] Christopher Crowe, who was Cardinal Wolsey's surgeon and whose house lay conveniently in King Street, was honoured with a succession of local offices, including wardenships both of the guild of the Rounceval hospital and of the guild of St Cornelius; at his death in 1531 he was buried within St Margaret's church.[156] The distinctive attributes of Crowe's art are sketched in his will: 'all my instruments and drugs and salves, glasses and pots that [are] in my surgery house'.[157]

Government

Two great changes came over the officers of the royal household and administration after the mid-fourteenth century. They became, as has been noted above, increasingly stabilized in Westminster, and from the same period they began to include a growing proportion of laymen.[158] The consequence of these developments for the town of Westminster was that the king's servants (salaried now in cash rather than ecclesiastical benefices) rented accommodation for themselves and their families in the vicinity of their offices, and thus gradually permeated the society of the district. Certain lay figures prominent in national government had always kept residences in or near Westminster: Gerin, king's minister, at Enedehithe in *c.*1150; the Mauduits, hereditary royal chamberlains, in Tothill Street around 1200; Sir John de Benstede, controller of the wardrobe and justice of the common pleas, at Rosamund's Manor towards Eye in

[154] *Cal Pat R 1461–7*, pp. 79, 188; ibid. *1476–85*, p. 251; WAM 17841; 23255–60; 19095. Fries's obit was kept in 1487–90 by the Westminster guild of the Assumption. Assumption guild accts, s.a. See also Talbot and Hammond, *Medical Practitioners*, 96–8.　　　　　[155] PRO, E403/848, m. 8.

[156] WAM 12366; Assumption guild accts, s.a. 1505–8; Rounceval guild accts, s.a. 1520–2; CWA ii, s.a. 1524–5; CWA iii, s.a. 1531–2, wk. 7. Crowe was made a constable for King Street in 1507, and a scavenger there in 1509. WAM 50772, 50774. In 1530 he held property in London, in the parish of St Michael Paternoster. *LP* iv, no. 6490 (29).　　　　　[157] PCW Bracy, fos. 23ᵛ–24ʳ.

[158] R. L. Storey, 'Gentlemen-bureaucrats', in Clough (ed.), *Profession, Vocation and Culture*, 90–129.

the early fourteenth century; Sir John de Stonor, shortly afterwards chief justice of the same bench and chief baron of the exchequer, at the great house west of King Street called 'Stonors' or the Mote.[159] It is also true that the royal chapels of St Stephen and St Martin-le-Grand continued throughout the Middle Ages to function as residential quarters for royal clerks. Yet it was in the fifteenth century that the curial and the urban spheres first thoroughly intermingled. At an elevated level, this is observed in the appointment of royal officers as dignitaries of the town. Peter Curteys, a member of the households successively of Richard III and Henry VII, Richard Doland, Henry VII's clerk of works, and Sir Hugh Vaughan, governor of the Isle of Wight under Henry VIII, were each successively honoured as bailiff of the vill of Westminster.[160] This development anticipates the patronage which William Cecil, Lord Burghley, would exercise over appointments to local administrative offices when, in 1585, he created himself the first lord high steward of the newly chartered city of Westminster.[161] As the monarchs and their councillors spent ever-longer periods in Westminster, their concern to control local politics increased.

Other administrators were involved in local life in more personal ways which flowed from residence in the neighbourhood. Two years before his death in 1480, William Hatclyf, King Edward IV's secretary, moved with his wife, Elizabeth, to a tenement in the Westminster sanctuary. Since before 1477 Hatclyf had belonged to the local guild of the Assumption, while he was also *persona grata* at the abbey, to which on his death he bequeathed both 20s. in cash, towards the completion of the new work, and his body, for burial in the Lady chapel.[162] One of the witnesses to Hatclyf's will was a

---

[159] Gerin: ch. 1 n. 27. Mauduits: ch. 1 n. 76. Benstede: *Cal Pat R 1307–13*, p. 58. Stonor: *Cal Cl R 1333–7*, p. 339; PRO, C135/128/11; *Dictionary of National Biography*, s.n.; Kingsford, 'Historical Notes on Mediaeval London Houses: The Mote, Westminster', *London Topographical Record*, xi (1917), 48–9. See also ch. 1, *passim*. [160] See app. 1.

[161] J. Merritt, 'Office-holders of St Martin-in-the-Fields ... c.1525–1625', talk given to the London seminar at the Institute of Historical Research, London, June 1988. For the 1585 Act see chap. 7.

[162] *Cal Pat R 1461–7*, p. 476; ibid. *1476–85*, p. 208; WAM 17837; 19727; 23552; Assumption guild accts, s.a. 1477 (subscription arrears); PRO, PROB11/7, PCC 1 Logge. Further on Hatclyf, see G. E. Burtt, 'The Activities of Household Officials in the Fifteenth Century as Illustrated by the Hatclyf Family', M.A. thesis, Univ. of London (1955), esp. 153–4; and A. B. Emden, *A Biographical Register of the University of Cambridge to 1500* (Cambridge, 1963), 292.

neighbour of his in the sanctuary, a clerk of the privy seal named Edmund Gregory.[163] Forty years later another privy-seal clerk, Richard Kelk (or Kylte) was fondly remembered in the prayers of the Westminster guild of St Mary Rounceval, to which he had been a generous benefactor.[164]

At the close of the Middle Ages the organization of a centralized civil service, uniformly responsible to the crown, still lay in the future.[165] But as successive elements of the royal household had detached themselves to form separate establishments in Westminster and along the Strand, the characteristic attitude of mind of the professional bureaucrat had already begun to crystallize. From the end of the fourteenth century the regulated working hours of the clerks in the king's courts were sounded by the great bell called 'Edward of Westminster' which hung in the clock tower on the north side of Westminster Palace Yard.[166] In Henry IV's reign, one of those who quickened his pace along King Street as the bell rang was Thomas Hoccleve, a married clerk of the privy seal who, with a household to keep, commuted daily from the Strand to work at a desk job in the palace which tired the eyes and dulled the brain. The artisans who worked around him in Westminster—the tailors, goldsmiths, carpenters, and the rest—seemed blessed with a happy lot compared to his. In his verse, Hoccleve speaks for all his kind:

> Thys artificers se I day by day
> In the hootteste of al hyre bysynesse
> Talken and singe and make game and play
> And forth hyr labour passyth with gladnesse.
> But we laboure in travayllous stilnesse.
> We stowpe and stare upon the schepys skyn
> And kepe must oure song and wordys in.[167]

[163] See WAM 19728–41; Reg Bk, i, fos. 55^v–56^r; Otway-Ruthven, *The King's Secretary and the Signet Office*, 159.

[164] See ch. 10 n. 118.

[165] See Catto, 'The King's Servants', in Harriss (ed.), *Henry V*, 75–95, esp. p. 76.

[166] *King's Works*, i. 509.

[167] Hoccleve, *The Regiment of Princes*, ll. 1009–15, in Seymour (ed.), *Selections from Hoccleve*, 35. On privy-seal clerks, and on Hoccleve in particular, see A. L. Brown, 'The Privy Seal Clerks in the Early Fifteenth Century', in D. A. Bullough and Storey (eds.), *The Study of Medieval Records* (Oxford, 1971), 260–81, esp. pp. 270–2; Tout, *Chapters*, v. 75, 106–10; and S. Medcalf (ed.), *The Later Middle Ages* (London, 1981), 123–40.

5. EDUCATION AND BOOKS

Schooling

It may have been for book-learned advice on legal matters that a Bristol chandler named John Lukke, coming to Westminster in October 1393 with documents concerning his inheritance, sought out Master Henry Hum, the master of the scholars (*magister scholarum Westmonasterii*).[168] A grammar school kept in the almonry of Westminster Abbey first becomes distinguishable from the cloister school for novices in 1355, at a period when such almonry schools were becoming widespread.[169] Teaching at a lower level is likely to have been provided by the parish clergy of St Margaret's church, and perhaps of the guilds. The grammar school was attended only by a minority; yet it made a tangible contribution to education in the town. The appointment of a secular master of the scholars (who received a worldly furred gown as part of his stipend and who is in some cases known to have been married) can be traced continuously from the late fourteenth century until the Dissolution.[170] Of these schoolteachers, the evocative name of Henry Hum is the earliest known. In the first half of the fifteenth century George Mortymer, 'schoolmaster of Westminster', was assisted by a 'servant and sub-master' named Robert Goldsmyth; while Mortymer was married, the deputy (notwithstanding his robbery of his employer, with the confederacy of the latter's wife) was on his way to becoming a priest.[171] The master was usually housed in the monastic sanctuary, near the Tothill Street gate and so close to the almonry. John Newborough, 'schoolmaster', and his wife, Margaret, were allocated a rent-free tenement here from 1424

[168] The two were ambushed and robbed of these documents. PRO, KB9/185/1.
[169] The existing published refs. to Westminster School in the Middle Ages are: A. F. Leach, *The Schools of Medieval England* (London, 1915), 219–21; L. E. Tanner, *Westminster School: A History* (London, 1923), 1–2; J. D. Carleton, *Westminster School* (London, 1965), 1–2; E. Pine, *The Westminster Abbey Singers* (London, 1953), esp. p. 25. None is satisfactory. For the context, see N. Orme, *English Schools in the Middle Ages* (London, 1973), esp. pp. 243–5.
[170] WAM 18982 *et seq.* The 'master of the almonry boys' is named as the recipient of a robe or winter fagotts from the convent treasurer from the 1420s. WAM 19921 *et seq.* In 1427–8 the master's wife received a robe. WAM 19926.
[171] PRO, C1/17/263. A George Mortimer, perhaps identical with the schoolmaster, was buried in Westminster Abbey, most probably at this period. He was described as a bastard. Harvey, *Estates*, 386.

until 1434; Otwell Fuller, recorded as 'schoolmaster of Westminster' from 1474–5 onwards, also lived here with Agnes, his wife, in 1482–3; and so, too, did Arnold Lawes, 'master of the scholars', in 1484–5.[172] It reflects favourably on the educational establishment maintained by these men that Otwell Fuller combined schoolteaching with the sale of books, and may have commissioned from Caxton's press new pedagogic works for the benefit of his charges.[173]

There were twenty-eight schoolboys in 1386, but the later employment, at least on occasion, of a second master suggests that the class may have grown.[174] In the early sixteenth century, as no doubt also in the preceding period, the catchment area for the intake of pupils reached as far as London, where the subalmoner inquired after eligible boys from their parents and guardians. When young William Fynnes was admitted to the school, the subalmoner paid 3s. 4d. to assist the boy's guardian in London, 'because he had nobody to help him in his sickness', and 1s. to the child's mother, 'to have her good will'. William himself was given a uniform russet cap, such as was worn by all the schoolboys; and entertainment was provided when his mother and sister came to visit him at Westminster.[175]

The master's cash salary was small (26s. 8d. p.a. in the late fourteenth century, rising to 35s. p.a. in the late fifteenth) but will have been supplemented by his livery, probably by a corrody in the abbey and probably, too, by pupils' fees; a common rate was 8d. a quarter, though it could have been higher, and certainly 2d. a week is heard of in London.[176] Nevertheless, it may be a sign of the schoolmaster's improving status in sixteenth-century Westminster that Roger Crytoft, who held the post in the 1520s and 1530s, was dignified with the title of 'gentleman'.[177] The school was unusually fortunate to escape suppression at the Dissolution. The scheme for the new cathedral establishment drawn up in 1541 provided for the

[172] Newborough: WAM 19666–75; 50747. Fuller: WAM 23879–81; Reg Bk, i, fo. 62[r–v]; CWA i. 101. Lawes: WAM 19729*–30.
[173] See G. D. Painter, *William Caxton* (London, 1976), 93.
[174] Orme, *English Schools*, 244.
[175] WAM 33301, fos. 2[r]–3[r].
[176] Orme, *English Schools*, 117–18, 156–60; Thrupp, *Merchant Class*, 159.
[177] Crytoft lived with Clemence, his wife, in Tothill Street. WAM 18042; 23168–78; 23305–11. In 1524 his goods were assessed at £6. 13s. 4d. PRO, E179/238/98.

schoolmaster, now on a comfortable annual salary of £20, and for forty scholars.[178] Indeed, the medieval school appears to have enjoyed the rare blessing of continuous survival until the reign of Elizabeth I and beyond.[179]

Books and Reading

In 1475–6 a wise businessman of long international experience made a shrewd assessment of Westminster, when he chose it as the site of the first printing-press to be set up in England. William Caxton's decision is extremely revealing of the character of the town in which he elected to settle. He clearly anticipated finding there both wealthy patrons and a lively market, and the event entirely justified his speculation. Since the thirteenth century the royal court had rivalled the chief monastic houses as a centre of book production, although its actual output must be inferred from a bare handful of extant examples notoriously difficult to allocate.[180] The abbey, meanwhile, exerted its own pull on scriveners and illuminators; so much so, indeed, that the scribe of the Litlington Missal, a de luxe manuscript made for the abbot in 1383–4, not only received his board and total salary of £4 for the two years of his commission but, finding the environment irresistibly congenial, subsequently entered the house as a brother.[181] The productions of a later Westminster scribe and contemporary of Caxton, William Ebesham, who leased a tenement in the sanctuary in the 1470s, illustrate the range of work to be picked up in this context: a monastic cartulary (the *Liber Niger Quaternus*), the official history of the house by John Flete, an English chronicle, and a variety of pietistical and meditative writings by such authors as Richard Rolle and St Bridgit of Sweden. In addition to the monks, Ebesham's employers included Sir John Paston; and while Paston was slow to

[178] PRO, E315/24, fo. 37ʳ.
[179] The school was functioning under Philip and Mary. WAM 18961.
[180] For surveys of court patronage see R. Marks and N. Morgan, *The Golden Age of English Manuscript Painting* (London, 1981), esp. pp. 13–14, 16–17, 23–4; J. J. G. Alexander, 'Painting and Manuscript Illumination for Royal Patrons in the Later Middle Ages', in Scattergood and Sherborne (eds.), *English Court Culture*, 141–62; A. I. Doyle, 'English Books in and out of Court from Edward III to Henry VII', ibid., 163–81.
[181] M. R. James and J. A. Robinson, *The Manuscripts of Westminster Abbey* (Cambridge, 1909), 7–8. The abbey's medieval library is almost entirely lost.

pay his bills Ebesham may well have found other lordly visitors to Westminster more prompt to reward his services.[182] The efficient production of manuscript books required close co-operation between different craftsmen. The parchmentmaker, limner, and bookbinder who worked in adjacent shops in King Street in the early sixteenth century were in effect a small factory for the making of copies of books by commission.[183] It was perhaps an indirect result of the esteem in which the written word was held in Westminster that a parchmentmaker was numbered among the chief pledges of the local court.[184]

Beyond the immediate circles of the royal household and the abbey, a bookish atmosphere may have pervaded the medieval town. The library of the king's clerk, John of Norwich, who was master of St James's hospital in 1375, included a cross-section of conventional reading-matter: St Bernard's *Commentary on the Song of Songs* and Bede *super vitam residuum* (?), evidently both for spiritual sustenance; the grammatical *Derivations* of Hugutio of Pisa; a set of Decretals for legal reference; and the encyclopedia of Bartholomeus Anglicus, appraised by its owner at £5.[185] The clerks of the royal chapel of St Stephen were also, as one would expect, literate men. John Langisloo, a chantry priest there, in 1535 left his books to be distributed among his fellow clergy of the chapel, to 'each of them one book, and such a book as shall seem best to their capacities and wits, praying them to pray for me'.[186] William Moreland, a chancery clerk and prebendary of St Stephen's, who died in c.1491, combined books of statutes and writs with two works of use for preaching: the *Legenda Aurea*, and the more unusual sermons of a contemporary Flemish mystic, the Franciscan Henry Herpe.[187] Perhaps Moreland's two-volume *Legenda* can be identi-

[182] Doyle, 'The Work of a Late Fifteenth-century English Scribe, William Ebesham', *Bulletin of the John Rylands Library*, xxxix (1956–7), 298–325.

[183] WAM 18599: see Fig. 8. The limner was one Martin van Boven, evidently a German or Dutchman. Several bookbinders were of the same origin, e.g. Denis Ducheman, Derek Bookbinder, and Michael Goner, all recorded in the early years of the sixteenth century. WAM 23131–3; CWA i. 559; PCW Wyks, 19. For their *Doche* contemporaries, Wynkyn de Worde, printer, and Elias Snethe, stationer, see below, nn. 205, 208.   [184] See app. VIII, s.n. John Corby.

[185] London, Guildhall Library, MS 9171/1, fo. 32ʳ.

[186] PCW Bracy, fos. 52ᵛ–53ʳ.

[187] PRO, PROB11/9, PCC 11 Doggett; *Cal Pat R 1467–77*, pp. 245, 590; ibid. *1476–85*, p. 252; and see P. Heath, *The English Parish Clergy on the Eve of the Reformation* (London, 1969), 86. Moreland's legal clients included the abbot of Westminster. WAM 19977–87.

fied with the 'book called a legend', half of which was commissioned by the dean and canons of St Stephen's as a body, earlier in the fifteenth century, from William Dixon, scrivener, for the substantial fee of £10.[188] At prices of this order, any book was still a prestigious possession; in the same period, the vicar of St Martin-in-the-Fields was compelled to borrow his daily mass book.[189] But the Westminster market was ripe, if any was, for the revolution brought by Caxton. By the end of the century printed copies of the *Golden Legend*, in Caxton's own edition and translation, were selling locally (in the vestry of St Margaret's church) for just 5*s.* apiece.[190] Imported printed books were also available. There survives in the abbey library a printed copy of a moral treatise, the *Destructorium Viciorum* of Alexander Carpenter, produced in Paris in 1497, which bears at the end the owner's inscription:

> 1543 Jhon Kynnard Surugen dwellynge in
> Westminster in the lytyll Sayntuary.[191]

By *c.*1530 even so relatively poor a clerk of Westminster as Roger Drewe, whose few household goods were all worn and broken, could own a 'great chest full of books', roughly valued at £5, and 'sixty more books, great and small', assessed at £2. With his books, his musical instruments—virginals, viols, and lutes—and the remarkably large quantity of beer (120 kilderkins) which he ordered, shortly before his death, from a local brewer, Roger Drewe presents an attractive picture of the life of a clerk in late medieval Westminster.[192]

Caxton, though his choice of works for publication was never especially 'aristocratic', makes clear in his colophons that in the courtly environment of Westminster he was particularly well placed to enlist the sort of dedicatees who would give the best *cachet* to his productions. In 1477 the *History of Jason* was (re-)dedicated to the

---

[188] PRO, C1/17/399.

[189] PRO, C1/75/79.

[190] H. M. Nixon, 'Caxton, his Contemporaries and Successors in the Book Trade from Westminster Documents', *The Library*, 5th ser., xxxi (1976), 305–26, esp. pp. 314–17.

[191] Westminster Abbey Library, shelfmark CC.31. In 1550 John Kynnard, surgeon, and his wife, Bryde, moved to another house elsewhere in the sanctuary. Reg Bk, iii, fo. 172ᵛ. On the book which Kynnard owned see G. R. Owst, *The Destructorium Viciorum of Alexander Carpenter* (London, 1952).

[192] PRO, C1/906/1–6.

young prince of Wales, and by such tactful devices Caxton retained the favour of successive royal families.[193] His Cicero translation, *Of Old Age*, was dedicated in 1481 to King Edward IV himself,[194] and after 1485 the new dynasty was wooed with a judicious promotion of the Welsh story of St Winifred in Caxton's version of the *Golden Legend*.[195] His success was demonstrated in the presentation of *Eneydos* to Arthur, prince of Wales, in 1490.[196] The edition of one of Caxton's most popular works, the *Dictes of the Philosophers* (1477), was prompted—and 'rewarded' in advance—by its translator, the Earl Rivers, who declared that he had himself been introduced to the book, while on a sea voyage to Galicia, by Louis de Bretailles. Bretailles, a Gascon knight and diplomatic agent of Edward IV, lived near Caxton in the sanctuary at Westminster. The impression is created of an aristocratic circle of readers in the orbit of the court, bound by personal acquaintance.[197] The grandeur of those names which are carefully dropped in Caxton's prologues and epilogues should not, of course, be seen as an indication that his readership was thus circumscribed, but rather the contrary: it was a device to appeal to a far wider market.[198]

When he selected Lydgate and Chaucer among his first authors for publication in England,[199] Caxton evidently had in mind a lay, and not particularly highbrow, readership. On the other hand his production, at about the same period, of the *Sarum Ordinal*, and possibly also of the *Sarum Hours*, may reflect the draw of the monastic market.[200] The presence of the abbey was probably not

---

[193] It has been suggested that *Jason* was originally published prior to 1477, and first dedicated to the duke of Burgundy. L. Hellinga, *Caxton in Focus. The Beginning of Printing in England* (London, 1982), 95–8; see also Painter, *William Caxton*, 85–6.

[194] N. F. Blake (ed.), *Caxton's Own Prose* (London, 1973), 122–3. See also M. Kekewich, 'Edward IV, William Caxton and Literary Patronage in Yorkist England', *Modern Language Review*, lxvi (1971), 481–7.

[195] M. J. C. Lowry, 'Caxton, St Winifred and the Lady Margaret Beaufort', *The Library*, 6th ser., v (1983), 101–17.   [196] Painter, *William Caxton*, 173.

[197] Ibid., 86–90; Hellinga, *Caxton in Focus*, 77–80; and above n. 89.

[198] Cf. Blake (ed.), *Caxton's Own Prose*, 28–31. In general on the market which Caxton addressed see H. S. Bennett, *English Books and Readers 1475 to 1557* (Cambridge, 1952), 12–18; and N. J. Kerling, 'Caxton and the Trade in Printed Books', *The Book Collector*, iv (1955), 190–9.

[199] For the chronology of Caxton's early printing in England see Hellinga, *Caxton in Focus*, which makes numerous adjustments to previously accepted dates.

[200] But Caxton addressed his advertisement of the *Ordinal* to 'any man spiritual *or temporal*' (emphasis added), who he anticipated might wish to purchase it, at the sign of the red pale, in the almonry at Westminster. One of two extant copies of the advertisement is Oxford, Bodleian Library, Arch. G e.37.

crucial to Caxton's choice of Westminster as his base; yet this additional source of custom must have weighed in his decision. The house and business premises ('at the sign of the red pale') where Caxton took up residence lay within the abbey almonry. The shop which he rented in addition, strategically situated beside the path which led from the south transept of the monastery church to the palace, may stand for the place of the book trade in Westminster: surrounded by the merchant residents of the sanctuary,[201] while at the same time poised between court and cloister.[202]

Westminster offered, additionally, the kind of jobbing order which might profitably fill a pause between the stages of a large-scale production such as the *Canterbury Tales* (printed by Caxton in 1476). The prime category of such jobbing work was indulgence printing; for indulgences were printed in their tens of thousands before the Protestant attack on Purgatory removed their *raison d'être*. Caxton printed several indulgences at Westminster, the earliest of which was executed in 1476, in close collaboration with the abbot of Westminster. The commissary for this indulgence was the abbot of Abingdon, John Sant, a personal friend of Abbot Eastney of Westminster and the owner of a great house (the Mote) nearby in King Street. Sant and Eastney must have worked together to involve Caxton in the printing of Sant's indulgence, which was subsequently offered for sale in the abbey church at Westminster. The proceeds were supposed to be devoted towards a new crusade against the Turks. But the chief profits from the Westminster sales appear to have been directed instead into the building fund for the new nave of the monastery church, a work vigorously promoted by Eastney during his abbacy. Whether the recorded 'offerings at stations in the church, made at the time of the indulgence of the abbot of Abingdon', were in fact direct payments made to the abbey by purchasers of the pardon, or whether they were (more innocently) incidental oblations made by visitors drawn to the monastery primarily to buy the advertised indulgence, the substantial sum of £60 was generated from this source towards the building work.[203] The abbot had proved the valuable potential of

---

[201] See ch. 5, sect. 8.

[202] Caxton's precise accommodation in the sanctuary is located in Nixon, 'Caxton, his Contemporaries and Successors in the Book Trade'.

[203] Some of the Westminster monks themselves were among the purchasers of the indulgence. Although some money was eventually returned to the papal curia from the sale of this indulgence, suspicion attached to Abbot Sant, and a papal inquiry was

the new technology.[204] The example underlines the sometimes forgotten fact that Caxton himself (like his successors in the trade) was not a disinterested lover of good writing, but a commercial man with an eye on profit.

It is a reflection of the business sense of their publishers that the two hundred or so different works which came off the Caxton and de Worde press at Westminster during the quarter-century between 1476 and 1500 were not in themselves markedly adventurous titles; they sought to meet rather than to educate popular taste. Nevertheless, the very processes of the collation and (in Caxton's case) translation of a great number of texts to produce the printed editions were a catalyst of intellectual inquiry.[205] For this reason the early printing-houses were the constant haunts of renaissance humanists.[206] It is symptomatic of this cultural impact of the press in the immediate context of the society of Westminster that the *Sex Epistolae* (a piece of Venetian propaganda) of 1483 were stated in the colophon to have been 'printed by me William Caxton and diligently emended by Petrus Carmelianus Poet Laureate, at Westminster'. For Pietro Carmeliano, who had come from his native Lombardy to Westminster, was a poet, musician, and generally learned ornament to the courts of Henry VII and Henry

instituted into his alleged malversation of the proceeds. It was later said that the pope believed himself to have been robbed over the indulgence. See Rosser, 'A Note on the Caxton *Indulgence* of 1476', *The Library*, 6th ser., vii (1985), 256–8 (and refs. cited); and W. E. Lunt, *Financial Relations of the Papacy with England, 1327–1534* (Cambridge, Mass., 1962), 586–90.

[204] For further indulgences printed by Caxton at Westminster, including one for the hospital of St Mary Rounceval, see Painter, *William Caxton*, 105, 115, 153, 168–9; and P. Needham, *The Printer and the Pardoner. An Unrecorded Indulgence Printed by William Caxton for the Hospital of St. Mary Rounceval, Charing Cross* (Washington, 1986). See also below, ch. 10 n. 115.

[205] For de Worde's productions before his removal to Fleet Street in 1500 see E. G. Duff, *A Century of the English Book Trade* (London, 1905), 173; and H. R. Plomer, *Wynkyn de Worde and his Contemporaries* (London, 1925), esp. pp. 43–61. The one other fifteenth-century press in Westminster was that of Julian Notary, who operated from King Street between 1498 and c.1500–3. Duff, *The Printers, Stationers and Bookbinders of Westminster and London from 1476 to 1535* (London, 1906), 37–40. After 1500, printers seem temporarily to have forsaken Westminster for Fleet Street and the city of London.

[206] E. L. Eisenstein, *The Printing Press as an Agent of Change*, 2 vols. (Cambridge, 1979), i. 50 ff.

VIII.[207] A lively interchange of ideas was no doubt fostered, too, among customers in the shop kept by Elias Snethe, between 1518 and 1528, near Lamb Alley on the east side of King Street. Variously described as 'printer', 'stationer' (he was a member of the London company of stationers), and 'bookbinder', Snethe (whose name suggests a Dutchman) was undoubtedly, among other things, a seller of books.[208] As he was in 1524 one of the five wealthiest men living in Westminster (his goods being assessed at £100), his stock and turnover must have been a bibliophile's dream, comparable, perhaps, with that of his Oxford contemporary, John Dorne.[209] It would not be extravagant to claim that the printing-houses and bookshops of late medieval Westminster performed, to some degree, the role of a university.

6. AMUSEMENTS

Together with food and drink and professional advice, entertainment was another of the alluring commodities offered for sale in medieval Westminster. Professional entertainers and public games were among the universal attractions of towns, where they tended to be concentrated away from the main business areas, and especially in the suburbs. A combination of practical and moral considerations lay behind the bans issued by many an urban corporation upon leisure activities, which consequently burgeoned just beyond jurisdictional limits, on the city's edge.

Westminster was already known in the thirteenth century as a resort for those seeking amusement. In a catalogue of the

[207] Painter, *William Caxton*, 135–6; Blake (ed.), *Caxton's Own Prose*, no. 95; WAM 23114–18; ECR, MS 62/AB/1, pp. 168, 186. For Carmeliano see also above, n. 26. Caxton's *Eneydos* was similarly 'overseen and corrected' by John Skelton, another poet laureate and evident *habitué* of Caxton's shop. Painter, *William Caxton*, 176–7.

[208] Some of the facts about Snethe are collected by Nixon, 'Caxton, his Contemporaries and Successors in the Book Trade', 325–6; more are revealed by his will, PRO, PROB11/22, PCC 29 Porche. For the activities in general of London and suburban stationers see G. Pollard, 'The Company of Stationers Before 1517', *The Library*, 4th ser., xviii (1937–8), 1–38.

[209] PRO, E179/298/98; F. Madan, 'Day-book of John Dorne, bookseller in Oxford, A.D. 1520', *Collectanea*, 1st ser., Oxford Historical Society, v (1885), 73–177. Cf. also D. M. Palliser and D. G. Selwyn, 'The Stock of a York Stationer, 1538', *The Library*, 5th ser., xxvii (1972), 207–19.

distinguishing features of English places, alongside other such natural affinities as ships of Southampton and Yarmouth herring, Oxford schools and Cambridge eels, were listed 'relics of Westminster' and 'prostitutes of Charing'.[210] The pilgrimage to the Confessor's tomb at Westminster, whose merits were sometimes advertised in the city of London, provided both an uplifting and a spectacular diversion; for the shrine, which was periodically displayed to the public, was one of the sights of medieval England.[211] (Illus. 7.) Meanwhile some of those who did not reach the abbey and its relics found their desired distraction sooner, with the whores of Charing or of Westminster itself.[212] Purveyors of other forms of amusement were doubtless also present from an early date; but the multiplication of records in the fifteenth century may reflect a genuine increase at this period in the level of organization of the business of suburban entertainment. Bowling alleys began to appear at Westminster after 1460, even as they did, in records of slightly later date, in other parts of London's fringes, at Southwark and in the eastern suburb around Aldgate.[213] Archery butts were set up in the infirmary garden at Westminster Abbey, also in the 1460s;[214] and tennis, too, was played here, long before Henry VIII built his courts at Whitehall Palace.[215] Some of these sports will have been played competitively for money, as were other games of chance. The professional gambler, deluding the greenhorn with high stakes and loaded dice, was a familiar figure of fifteenth-century Westminster, even as the three-card tricksters still dupe the tourists on Piccadilly.[216] Gambling, tennis, archery, bowls, whoring: every one of these delights was officially proscribed within the city of London; Westminster offered all in exciting abundance.[217]

[210] *English Historical Documents*, iii. 881–4.
[211] J. G. O'Neilly and L. E. Tanner, 'The Shrine of St Edward the Confessor', *Archaeologia*, c (1966), 129–54.
[212] See ch. 5, sect. 4.
[213] WAM 50757 (1464: the first ref. in Westminster to *closshe banes*, or bowling alleys); Stow, *A Survey*, ii. 102. See also Carlin, 'Urban Development of Southwark', 49–50; CLRO, Portsoken Ward Presentments, 5–22 Edw. IV, 23 Hen. VII, *passim*.
[214] WAM 19443.
[215] An isolated ref. to 'le lodge pro le tenyspleyers' near Westminster Abbey occurs in 1447–8. WAM 23513.
[216] PRO, KB9/223/1/52.
[217] CLRO, City Journal 8, fo. 127ᵛ (1476); and see above, ch. 5, sect. 4. Only archery, as (naturally) a suburban pastime, was countenanced by the civic authorities. *Cal Letter-Bk G*, 194.

To the inhabitants of Westminster this suburban role of the provision of amusements offered one more way to a quick profit. Even the non-participatory entertainments, such as processions, generated by the abbey and court brought spin-off benefits to local retailers. At a royal coronation Westminster staged spectacular, crowd-pulling shows. For the coronation of Queen Margaret in 1445, as at other royal events later in the century, splendid jousts were held in the precinct of the abbey. Stands for the crowds were erected in the sanctuary, and viewing places were even created on the roof of the abbey nave. The preparations were financially worthwhile; for the monks were able to charge their tenants within the sanctuary a supplementary levy for the valuable privilege of continuing to trade there during the festivities.[218] On other occasions, as at Prince Arthur's wedding in 1501, the lists were set up before Westminster Hall. For that event raised platforms lifted royalty and the mayor of London above the proceedings, while double stages all around the perimeter of the field provided viewing terraces for the groundlings.[219] Further spectacles included public theatrical performances in Westminster Hall, such as the Twelfth Night plays for which scaffolds were erected there in the Christmas season of 1493–4 (*ut ludi sive la disguisyngs nocte Epiphanie populo exhiberentur*).[220] This courtly patronage of drama is the genuine antecedent of the aristocratic theatre companies which, ultimately, gave its distinctive character to London's West End.

7. THE MARGINS OF SOCIETY

While any medieval town depended upon the recruitment of immigrants to sustain its numbers, not all of the outsiders who presented themselves became integrated, stable members of urban society. Many, although they might stay for long periods, remained

---

[218] Jousts in the sanctuary: WAM 19694, 19698 (coronation of Margaret of Anjou); 19711 (coronation of Edward IV); 19713–15 (coronation of Elizabeth of York); 19725 (1477–8); 19713 (coronation of Henry VII); also R. Flenley (ed.), *Six Town Chronicles of England* (Oxford, 1911), 120, 172 and n. On royal pageants at Westminster see in addition S. Anglo, *Spectacle, Pageantry, and Early Tudor Policy* (Oxford, 1969), 99–103, 111–13.

[219] Anglo, *Spectacle*, 100–3.

[220] *King's Works*, iv. 286. For plays sponsored by the parishioners and guilds of Westminster see below, ch. 8 n. 114, ch. 9 n. 55.

on the margins of the various neighbourhood and civic bodies which collectively comprised the more respectable element of the town's population. Westminster in the Middle Ages attracted to itself an unusually large complement of such marginal inhabitants, both because of the presence of the royal courts, which the poor suitor having no alternative might haunt for years in vain hope of redress, and because of the relative absence of local jurisdictional interference. In contrast to more heavily policed areas such as the nearby city of London, in Westminster visitors were troubled with few questions. To one already on the wrong side of the law, Westminster was too small a place to provide the anonymity of the modern city; but it offered an even securer protection, in the form of the sanctuary. Westminster Abbey possessed one of the most highly privileged sanctuaries of medieval England, and the monastic precinct hosted a correspondingly *louche* population of social outcasts. The sanctuary oath was sufficient entrée to this distinguished company, which the oath itself created a separate society within the town.[221] The right of the monastery to give asylum to felons, first elaborated in the twelfth century, was officially extended in Richard II's reign to encompass debtors,[222] a class which became particularly numerous within the sanctuary population during the fifteenth and sixteenth centuries. In a famous diatribe incorporated within his *History of Richard III*, Thomas More expressed the resentment of those opposed to sanctuary:

What a rabble of thieves, murderers, and malicious heinous traitors, and that in two places specially: The one at the elbow of the City [Westminster], the other in the very bowels [St Martin-le-Grand] . . . Now unthrifts riot and run in debt, upon the boldness of these places; yea and rich women run thither with their husbands' plate, and say, they dare not abide with their husbands for beating. Thieves bring thither their stolen goods, and there live thereon. There devise they new robberies; nightly they steal out; they rob and reve [plunder] and kill, and come in again as though those places

[221] Three versions of the sanctuary oath: LN, fo. 139^v (fifteenth century); WAM 9595 (early sixteenth century); BL MS Lansdowne xxiv, fos. 206^r–207^r (1577?).

[222] *Rot Parl*, iii. 51. Debtors had been denied the right to claim sanctuary; Westminster was made an exception to this rule. The extension of the declared privileges of the Westminster sanctuary in Richard II's reign was made in the context of contemporary controversy over the subject. See Robinson, *Gilbert Crispin Abbot of Westminster* (Cambridge, 1911), 162–3; *The History of Westminster Abbey by John Flete*, 13–15; *The Westminster Chronicle 1381–1394*, 497. See also above, ch. 5, sect. 8.

gave them not only a safeguard for the harm they have done, but a licence also to do more.[223]

Though partisan, More's picture is, so far as it goes, entirely accurate. Both within and outside the sanctuary, the liberty of Westminster in the late Middle Ages accommodated the entire spectrum of the unsocialized.

Here was the demobilized soldier, 'Thomas Glasebrook of Westminster, that hath been in the wars in France with King Harry the Fifth', in which he suffered crippling crossbow-bolt and spear wounds, now, together with his wife, dependent for his living upon a licence to beg in the streets of Westminster.[224] Here was the professional horse-thief, William Burgh, 'an old tramp who travels the roads like a beggar', haunting the western approach routes to London to catch his prey at Knightsbridge, Tothill, and Charing.[225] Here too, in the sanctuary, was a wizard who claimed to conjure the devil by his arts, and who drove his unwilling youthful accomplice insane for fear.[226] Another beyond the pale of orthodoxy was the suspected heretic John Russell, a wool-packer who was accused with others in 1430–1 of disseminating Lollard doctrines in the suburbs of London.[227] Russell was additionally charged with having forged coin of the realm within the Westminster sanctuary; a venture also attempted at the same date by a chapman and a glover of Westminster.[228]

Many of the alleged participants in crimes of robbery and violence in Westminster were 'foreigners' of remote or unknown origin, and recent arrivals in the town.[229] The archetype was

[223] *The Complete Works of St. Thomas More*, ii, *The History of King Richard II*, ed. R. S. Sylvester (Yale, 1963), 30–1 (spelling modernized). Cf. also a royal letter of Edward (IV), addressed to the archdeacon of Westminster, urging him to punish those vicious persons within the sanctuary, whom he credited with 'many abominable vices, murders, and affrays, bawdry, lechery and other mischievous deeds'. WAM 9612 (1474).

[224] PRO, Cl/16/389.

[225] *Vacabundus senex quasi mendicus transiens per vias.* PRO, KB9/174/6.

[226] PRO, KB9/176/73.

[227] PRO, KB9/225/21–2. See also Riley (ed.), *Memorials of London*, 630–4; and M. Aston, *Lollards and Reformers* (London, 1984), 33.

[228] PRO, KB9/225/35. Cf. also Norman Dunstan, *alias* Multeplyere, *alias* Monymakere, who counterfeited groats in St Giles-in-the-Fields parish in 1400. PRO, KB9/178/45.

[229] This was also typical of criminals in fourteenth-century Paris. B. Geremek, *The Margins of Society in Late Medieval Paris*, tr. J. Birrell (Cambridge, 1987).

Thomas Stanley, who took part in an ambush and robbery at
Westminster in 1399, and who was described as a 'travelyngman'.[230]
The concentration of rich pickings in Westminster was doubtless
the making of many a thief, as it was the undoing of not a few
identified in legal records. The gang which burgled the bishop of
Durham's house near Charing Cross in 1478 typically comprised a
soldier from Southwark, a tailor from Newton Abbot in Devon, and
a chaplain described as being 'of Scotland, alias of Wales, alias of
London'.[231] A Celtic origin was not unusual among those involved
in violent incidents at Westminster;[232] and while such lawless
migrants were not made generally welcome, they might find shelter
with those inhabitants who were themselves distanced from the
politer body of resident society, as did an Irish horse-dealer at
brothels in Knightsbridge and Westminster in 1426.[233] 'Trowns-
lawe Iryshman' was the pithy alias ascribed to one of the felons
recorded in a catalogue of the Westminster sanctuarymen of
1532.[234] Here at the same date were also two Welshmen, separately
suspected of murder. A third Welshman typified a different sub-
group among those taking asylum: a poor man, John ap Howell was
in trouble for stealing hens. Like John ap Howell, a number of his
fellows were debtors, among them a point-maker and his wife,
another horse-trader and a serving-man. Two others had robbed
churches; an apprentice with the foreign name of Deger Chonter-
elle had embezzled his master's goods; and William Calverley was a
former sea-pirate.[235] The list reads like the *dramatis personae* of a
play by Thomas Dekker; but it records a reality harsher than the
sanitized view of the criminal poor usually presented in the
Elizabethan London theatre.

The victims of legal oppression and clerical neglect who swelled
the marginal population of Westminster did, however, find an
articulate representative, and that in one of their own number. It
was from a base in the Westminster sanctuary that the poet John

[230] PRO, KB9/185/1, m. 24.
[231] PRO, KB9/224/172. Cf. the Yorkshireman accused of stealing a gold casket
from the high altar of Westminster Abbey in 1439. PRO, KB9/231/1/82.
[232] Cf. Morgan Walscheman, weaver of Westminster, who was at odds with the
under-bailiff of the town in 1439. PRO, KB9/232/1/59.
[233] PRO, KB9/224/239.
[234] PRO, SP1/70, pp. 151–2. Forty-nine names are listed; but the document is
damaged, and may be incomplete.
[235] Ibid.

Skelton launched verse broadsides, in both manuscript and print, against the regime of Cardinal Wolsey.[236] While he was thoroughly unromantic about the social disorders of his day, Skelton spoke up for the privileged sanctuaries, against government threats of suppression, as the refuges of the helpless poor—and in his own case, at least, of an independent political voice. The vulnerability of the poor was perhaps nowhere more dramatically evident than in Westminster, where gross displays of wealth provided a constant foil.

> So gorgyous garmentes, and so myche wrechydnese,
> So myche portlye pride, with pursys penyles;
> So myche spente before, and so myche unpayd behynde—
> Syns Dewcalyons flodde ther can no clerkes fynde.
>
> So many vacabondes, so many beggers bolde,
> So myche decay of monasteries and relygious places;
> So hote hatered agaynste the Chyrche, and cheryte so colde;
> So myche of my lordes grace, and in hym no grace ys;
> So many holow hartes, and so dowbyll faces;
> So myche sayntuary brekyng, and prevylegidde barryd—
> Syns Dewcalyons flodde was nevyr sene nor lyerd.[237]

8. THE DISTRIBUTION OF WEALTH

It is already clear that riches were spread very unevenly through Westminster society. The single period at which it is possible to quantify this distribution is the first half of the sixteenth century. Assessments of 1524 and 1544 for royal subsidies provide the evidence upon which Tables 4 and 5 are based.[238] Table 4 shows that in 1524, more than two-fifths of the town's taxable wealth was concentrated in the hands of less than 4 per cent of the taxpayers,

---

[236] Skelton is first definitely recorded in Westminster (although he was in the vicinity earlier) in July 1511, when he dined with the prior of the monastery. By 1518 he was occupying a house within the sanctuary. He died there in 1529, and was buried before the high altar in St Margaret's church. WAM 33325, fo. 17ᵛ; Reg Bk, ii, fos. 146–7; CWA ii, s.a. 1529–30, wk. 7. See also M. Pollet, *John Skelton* (London, 1971).

[237] Skelton, *Speke Parrott*, ll. 459–62, 498–504 (date of composition: autumn 1521); printed in *John Skelton. The Complete English Poems*, ed. Scattergood, 244–6. *lyerd*: learned.

[238] The fundamental guide to the interpretation of these subsidy returns is Sheail, 'The Regional Distribution of Wealth'.

TABLE 4. *Distribution of assessed wealth in Westminster in 1524 and 1544*[a]

(a) 1524

Amount of assessment (£)[b]	Total value, assessed valuation (£)	Percentage of total vill assessed valuation	Percentage of taxed population: N=457
40–100	1,113	42.8	3.7
20–39	367	14.1	3.7
10–19	408	15.7	7.7
5–9	235	9.0	8.8
1–4	475	18.3	43.5
	2,598	99.9	67.4[c]

(b) 1544

			N=527
40–150	1,315	31.5	3.2
20–39	957	22.9	8.0
10–19	583	14.0	9.5
5–9	583	14.0	19.2
1–4	739	17.7	60.2
	4,177	100.1	100.1[d]

[a] The area represented at both dates is that of St Margaret's parish.

[b] An individual was only taxed on his *main* source of income.

[c] This is the sum percentage of those inhabitants assessed for the 1524 tax on their goods. The remaining 32.6% were assessed instead on annual wages. Almost all of those taxed on wages were assessed at the relatively low rate of between £1 and £4 p.a.

[d] In 1544 the commissioners apparently did not differentiate wages from goods.

Source: PRO, E179/238/98, E179/141/139.

and that the situation was little different in 1544. The concentration of taxpayers at the lower end of the scale of assessed wealth is slightly less marked in 1544 than at the earlier date; but the overall impression, nevertheless, is of a severe disequilibrium between the rich few and the, at best, moderately prosperous many. The tax threshold—20*s.* in goods or yearly wages—was set sufficiently low to embrace those at the level of a very modest competency indeed;

TABLE 5. *Topographical distribution of assessed wealth in 1544*

Assessed wealth[a] £	Distribution of taxpayers, by class (%)						
	King Street	Alleys off King St[b]	Tothill Street	Long Ditch and Thieving Lane	Sanctuary and Almonry	Palace[c]	Unspecified
1	5.2	30.6	14.5	26.0	23.0	0.0	0.0
2–4	27.6	50.0	49.4	56.0	50.5	44.0	0.0
5–9	32.8	8.3	24.1	10.0	16.5	24.0	0.0
10–19	17.2	8.3	6.0	4.0	3.9	20.0	0.0
20–39	16.4	2.8	6.0	4.0	5.8	12.0	6.0
40–150	0.9	0.0	0.0	0.0	0.0	0.0	94.0
	100.1	100.0	100.0	100.0	99.7	100.0	100.0
Total number of taxpayers	116	108	83	50	103	50	17

[a] No distinction is drawn between goods and wages.
[b] St Stephen's Alley, Duffeld's Alley, Sey Alley, Chequer Alley, Bell Alley, and Our Lady's Alley; and the Long and Round Wool Staples.
[c] Including the King's servants.

Source: PRO, E179/141/139.

yet the unknown figure of those even poorer than this, and therefore unrepresented in the assessments, was growing in the sixteenth century.[239] Their number, could it be added to the table, would broaden still further the wide, depressed base of the pyramid of wealth. The contemporary tax assessments of such larger provincial towns as Norwich, York, Exeter, and Worcester show distributions closely comparable to that at Westminster; the relative incidence of untaxable degrees of poverty, however, is unknown.[240] But these statistics are, in any case, of strictly limited value. They show no more than should be expected; and in themselves they reveal virtually nothing about the workings of society.[241]

The distribution of assessed wealth by area within the town (Table 5) shows a little more clearly how inequality operated. The greatest concentration of rich taxpayers lay in King Street, the one street in Westminster with some pretention to grandeur. The prominence of wealth and relative absence of poverty seen here was also a notable feature of the palace precinct. The poorer taxpayers, meanwhile, were not far away, but were crowded in the alleys behind King Street; Thieving Lane was perhaps the extreme case of this highly localized concentration of the poor at a little distance from the main thoroughfare.[242] The sanctuary, Long Ditch, and Tothill Street also contained a heavy preponderance of low assessments. This subtle degree of segregation notwithstanding, rich and poor were very close neighbours in late medieval Westminster; the contrast was immediate and inescapable.

---

[239] See above, n. 65.

[240] J. F. Pound, 'The Social and Trade Structure of Norwich, 1525–1575', *Past and Present*, xxxiv (1966), 49–69; Palliser, *Tudor York*, 134–9; W. T. MacCaffrey, *Exeter, 1540–1640. The Growth of an English Country Town* (Cambridge, Mass., 1958), 246–83; Dyer, *The City of Worcester*, 174–6.

[241] In the UK in 1970, 1% of the adult population owned almost 30% of the total personal wealth of the country, and 5% of the population owned 51.9% of the total personal wealth. Yet neither in this case nor in those of sixteenth century towns do the numbers alone provide an intelligible picture of the societies in question. For the 1970 figures, see Royal Commission on the Distribution of Incomes and Wealth, *Report No. 7* (HMSO, London, 1979), 93 (Table 4.4).

[242] This relationship was the reverse of that which had pertained, at least along parts of King Street, in the thirteenth and in the late fourteenth centuries. See ch. 1 n. 47; Rosser, 'Medieval Westminster: The Vill and the Urban Community, 1200–1540', 176.

9. CONCLUSION: A DIVERSE AND UNEQUAL SOCIETY

It needs no further emphasis that the society of medieval Westminster was highly varied, and that its precise composition changed continuously. Life in Westminster entailed constant exposure to the extremes of wealth and poverty, to the continual immigration of strangers, and to a severe degree of criminality. Couched in these general terms, the picture is broadly applicable to other town societies, medieval and modern, although diversity and inequality take different forms in each case. Recognition of heterogeneity must be, however, not the end but the beginning of inquiry. The question to which it gives rise, in medieval Westminster as elsewhere, is this: In what sense, if any, did this *hétéroclite* collection of individuals belong to a single society? It must be asked whether the tensions created by their proximity to one another led to violent denial of any shared experience. The fact that anarchy evidently did not prevail is remarkable, and calls for explanation. At least a part of the answer might be expected to lie with a dominant élite capable of containing the latent chaos. That hypothesis must be considered in the light of the available instruments of control. To anticipate one of the conclusions of the next chapter, it will be seen that the weakness of local government in Westminster denied the possibility of crude oppression. In so far as breakdown was held at bay, the explanation must largely be sought elsewhere. The alternative hypothesis advanced in the remaining chapters of this book takes as its starting-point the tensions which have been identified within urban society. But urban society concerns more than conflict, or it could not endure. If conflict could not have been suppressed by main force, the possibility must be considered that it was, on occasion, transcended by a shared awareness of the neighbourhood as a whole. The argument to be advanced in the chapters which follow is that the population of medieval Westminster, despite its diversity and frequent fluctuations both in size and in composition, did develop effective strategies for communal behaviour.

7

Urban Government

I. INTRODUCTION: WHAT IS A TOWN?

In vernacular records, Westminster in the late Middle Ages was normally described as a 'town'.[1] This was doubtless the current conversational usage and, in view of the density of Westminster's population, the range of its social composition and the variety of its economic life, it is easy to agree with the medieval inhabitants who identified the place as urban.[2] It evidently did not strike them as anomalous that, in legal terms, this 'town' was not an incorporated city or borough but a mere manorial vill: *villa Westmonasterii* was the almost invariable terminology of medieval Latin documents. The *villa* of Westminster was from its beginning, and remained until the Dissolution, a dependency of its single lord, the abbot of St Peter's monastery there. As such, its framework of seigneurial jurisdiction continued essentially unaltered before the sixteenth century. Because the town did not receive the formal recognition of a parliamentary Act until 1585, its medieval institutions of local government have neither impressed nor even attracted the interest of urban historians. The great eighteenth-century historian of London, William Maitland, accurately summarized the strictly legal case (albeit with an instinctive sinister overtone): 'Until the Reformation, *Anno* 1539, the Village, or Town of Westminster, was under the arbitrary Government of the Abbot and Monks of that name.' Maitland went on to describe the Act of 1585 which ratified a system of local administration in Westminster, and by virtue of which 'the Government thereof is lodged in the Hands of the Laity'.[3] J. E. Smith, who alone has treated this subject at any

---

[1] e.g. WAM 6576 (*c*.1511). Vernacular refs. of any kind are extremely rare before 1500.   [2] Cf. chs. 5, 6.

[3] W. Maitland, *The History and Survey of London from its Foundations to the Present Time*, 2nd edn., 2 vols. (London, 1756), ii. 1348. See 27 Eliz. c. 31: 'An Acte for the good Government of the Cyttie or Burroughe of Westmynster' (1585). The continuing assumption of the importance of this Act underlay the celebration of its anniversary, held in Westminster Abbey in 1985. See the *London Standard*, 24 July 1985.

length, followed Maitland's lead when in 1889 he described how it was not until the years after the Reformation that, 'As the priestly supremacy subsided, the laity spontaneously, though gradually, assumed direct and important functions in parochial matters.'[4] It was taken for granted not only by Maitland and Smith, but equally by the Whiggish historians who first charted the progressive accumulation of English urban liberties, that although certain towns, such as St Albans, might owe their origins to the traffic generated by religious institutions, the development of urban life properly so called was impossible under the secular control of the church. This, indeed, was a principle to which many medieval townspeople themselves subscribed. The medieval history of Bury St Edmunds supplies the *locus classicus* of a protracted struggle between monks and townsmen over the control of jurisdiction and, more fundamentally, of economic resources.[5] Yet the inference commonly made from such local conflicts, that 'by the later fifteenth century formal incorporation, recognizing the right of the community to act collectively, had become the acknowledged summit of a town's ambition', is erroneous.[6]

Historians' expectations of towns in the past have been heavily conditioned by two great legal writers of the late nineteenth century, Charles Gross and F. W. Maitland, who laid down criteria for the definition of towns which stressed above all the theme of administrative independence.[7] Fundamental legal differences were supposed to distinguish the town, or borough, from other forms of local society, in particular the village. 'Burghal status', and the features held to be associated with it—such as the existence of a civil constitution, the right to representation in parliament, and the free tenure of property—have been exhaustively analysed by

[4] [J. E. Smith], *Special and Annual Report of the Vestry of the United Parish of St Margaret and St John the Evangelist, Westminster; with Notes on Local Government in Westminster from Pre-Reformation Times to the Present Day* (Westminster, 1889), 16.

[5] M. D. Lobel, *The Borough of Bury St Edmunds* (Oxford, 1935), 59–60, 123, and ch. 3, *passim*; Gottfried, *Bury St Edmunds and the Urban Crisis: 1290–1539* (Princeton, 1982), 167–80. See further below.

[6] The quotation, which expresses a widely held view, happens to be taken from Clark and Slack, *English Towns in Transition, 1500–1700* (Oxford, 1976), 6.

[7] Gross, *The Gild Merchant* (Oxford, 1890); Maitland, *Township and Borough* (Cambridge, 1898). The emphasis upon the legal autonomy of towns has been strengthened by the prestige of the great medieval cities of Flanders, Germany, and Italy, which repeatedly exemplify the trade centre fighting or bargaining to achieve communal independence from lords. See esp. H. Pirenne, *Medieval Cities: Their Origins and the Revival of Trade* (Princeton, 1925), ch. 7.

subsequent writers, notably James Tait.[8] The resulting publica-
tions have contained much of value, but it should be recognized that
the concepts of 'burghality' and 'borough status' are the anachro-
nistic inventions of modern historians, and in consequence not the
most reliable framework for the study of the past. A safer point of
departure is the realization that 'there was no particular legal
capacity, or degree of legal capacity, which attached to boroughs as
such'; that, in fact, 'towns did not normally need any special
liberties or privileges (let alone charters) in order to function as
collective units'.[9] The point is underlined by the recognition that
any medieval town, so far from being an island of privileged
autonomy set in a feudal sea, was an integral part of medieval society
as a whole; town and country were inseparably linked.[10]

Once this clarification is made, it becomes possible to perceive,
even in places which neither attained nor yet strove for self-
governing independence, other characteristics which distinguished
the medieval town from the village. The secular inhabitants of
medieval Westminster evolved no elaborate set of institutions to
compete with those of the abbot. They lived, it may even be said,
under 'priestly supremacy' without recorded protest. Nevertheless,
the records of the abbot's local courts reveal that these assemblies
were significantly modified in the later medieval period, to admit of
a degree of self-determination by the townsmen. In response to
developing problems of a distinctly urban nature, the inhabitants of
Westminster, notwithstanding the limitations imposed upon their
powers by the abbot's authority, evolved collaborative means of
ordering their physical and social environment. The semi-official
secular government thus created was dominated by the wealthy

---

[8] J. Tait, *The Medieval English Borough* (Manchester, 1936); M. Weinbaum, *The Incorporation of Boroughs* (Manchester, 1936). The persistent preoccupation with boroughs is evinced by Beresford and H. P. R. Finberg, *English Medieval Boroughs: A Handlist* (Newton Abbot, 1973), introd. The compilers explain that they 'resisted the temptation to include a place simply because it is known to have had an urban character in the Middle Ages. 'Urban', on analysis, turns out to be an even more elusive concept than burghality' (25–6).

[9] S. Reynolds, 'Medieval Urban History and the History of Political Thought', *Urban History Yearbook* (1982), 16–17. See also ead., *Kingdoms and Communities in Western Europe, 900–1300* (Oxford, 1984), 59–64; and ead., 'Towns in Domesday Book', in J. C. Holt (ed.), *Domesday Studies* (Woodbridge, 1985), 296: 'Charters, special tenures or rules of law, walls, market squares, mints, town halls, or insignia of independence do not define towns. They are characteristics of some towns in particular circumstances'.

[10] Hilton, 'Towns in Societies—Medieval England'.

élite of the town. Such transference of social divisions into local politics is familiar enough; the ruling councils of other medieval towns (chartered and otherwise) were similar in character. But of greater interest in the present case is the creation of a political structure which could not only serve as a platform for the self-advertisement of an élite, but which at the same time represented— although in no democratic sense—the urban society as a whole. The primary loyalties of an inhabitant of medieval Westminster were doubtless to himself, his family, his household, and neighbours. But when practical problems arose which affected a large proportion of local society, the inhabitants were capable of a collective response. The possibility of co-ordinated discussion of an issue which was of vital importance to the neighbourhood as a whole was demonstrated in the petition about local economic difficulties, submitted to the crown in 1337 by 'les liges gentz de la ville de Weymonster'.[11] In providing both a forum for public debate, and a focus for the expression of private interests in the wider prosperity of the town, the court of Westminster played a crucial part.

2. THE LORDSHIP OF THE ABBOT

In order to set these late-medieval developments in their context, it will be well first to envisage the manorial system within which they took place. The manor of Westminster, which contained the evolving town, had been a royal gift to the monks in *c*.960. Its boundary at that time followed the Tyburn northwards to the old Roman 'military way' (the present Oxford Street), where it turned east as far as the church of St Andrew, Holborn, then south by the Fleet ditch to the Thames and so back, 'by land and strand', to the abbey.[12] In a decree of papal judges of 1222, however, the abbey's 'liberty' of Westminster was stated to exclude the parishes of St Mary-le-Strand and St Clement Danes, in addition to the precinct of the Savoy and such portions of the parishes of St Giles and St Andrew, Holborn, as had been included in *c*.960. The area remaining to the abbey, which then coincided with the parish of St Margaret, Westminster, was declared to be exempt from the

---

[11] See ch. 5, n. 7.
[12] M. Gelling, 'The Boundaries of the Westminster Charters', *TLMAS* 2nd ser., xi (1953), 101–4; and see above, ch. 1, sect. 1, and Fig. 3.

ecclesiastical jurisdiction of the bishop of London.[13] The abbots also acquired extensive rights of secular government within their manor of Westminster, in addition to those attaching to lordship. Edward the Confessor announced that he had conceded to the jurisdiction of Westminster all such rights as he himself possessed.[14] Henry III, in a charter of 1235, was more specific as to the privileges granted.[15] Consequently by 1293 the abbot could claim to exercise in his manor of Westminster a number of regal prerogatives: judgement of pleas of the crown, and of all pleas which the king's sheriff had in the county except appeals and outlawries; the view of frankpledge; and the assize of bread and ale.[16]

By c.1300 St Margaret's parish was reduced from its extent of 1222 by the creation of the parish of St Martin-in-the-Fields. St Margaret's was now confined to the south of a line drawn between the Tyburn and the Thames, passing through the ornamental water of the later St James's Park.[17] From this date onwards the contracted parish of St Margaret was normally identified with the *villa* or, in vernacular documents, the 'town' of Westminster. The parish or vill comprised a topographical unity, embraced by the two axes of King Street and Tothill Street. The area was distinguished in another way by the effective economic control exercised over much of the property within it by the monastic landlords, who were relatively unconcerned with rents in the farther reaches of their manor of Westminster.[18] Yet for all these defining characteristics, there was no permanent element of jurisdiction which applied specifically to the vill. Such institutions of secular government as existed pertained exclusively to the abbot, either as lord or as the recipient of royal grants of authority within his demesne; in legal principle they related to the entire manor of Westminster.

---

[13] *Acta Stephani Langton . . . 1207–1228*, ed. K. Major, Canterbury and York Society, vol. 1 (1950), 69–73; WAM 12753 (an original copy); a later copy in *The History of Westminster Abbey by John Flete*, 61 ff. See also the not entirely reliable G. Saunders, 'Results of an Enquiry Concerning the Situation and Extent of Westminster, at Various Periods', *Archaeologia*, xxvi (1836), 223–41. For the ecclesiastical purpose of defining the liberty, the *villae* of Knightsbridge, Westbourne, and Paddington, which lay outside the manor of Westminster, were said to belong to St Margaret's parish. The secular jurisdiction of these places was, however, independent of that of Westminster.
[14] Sawyer, *Anglo-Saxon Charters*, no. 1127.
[15] *Cal Ch R 1226–57*, pp. 208–9; see also ibid. *1257–1300*, pp. 238–9.
[16] *Placita de Quo Warranto* (Record Commission, London, 1818), 479.
[17] See ch. 8, sect. 1.   [18] See ch. 3.

The abbot's secular authority in his manor was represented primarily by two lay officials of his own appointment. The first of these was the seneschal (*senescallus*) of all the abbot's lands, whose title was sometimes anglicized in the later Middle Ages as 'steward'. This officer was the overall head of the abbot's judicial system; each succeeding abbot appointed his personal steward of the lands. The second was a local officer, known in the twelfth and much of the thirteenth centuries as the reeve (*prepositus*), but from *c.*1280 as the bailiff (*ballivus*) of the liberty of Westminster. The reeve or bailiff was not necessarily liable to be replaced by a new abbot. From the late fourteenth century the titular office became a sinecure, the work being done by a sub-bailiff.[19] In the absence of extant records of local courts held prior to the mid-fourteenth century, the government of the manor in the earlier period can be reconstructed only from the evidence of deeds relating to local property.[20] The regular prominence, among the listed witnesses to these deeds, of the abbot's seneschal and reeve suggests that such transactions were made public in a court of free tenants of the manor (who would be entitled to buy and sell land), presided over by these officers. Deeds were sometimes said to be witnessed, in the presence of the seneschal or reeve by 'the whole halimote (*totus halimotus*) of Westminster'.[21] Such halimotes (whose name suggests their origin as assemblies of tenants in the lord's hall) were in the twelfth and thirteenth centuries typically summoned by the lord's seneschal to an outdoor landmark, such as a particular tree—at Westminster the obvious site would perhaps have been the churchyard to the north of the abbey—to hear cases concerning tenants of the demesne. All tenants owing suit of court would probably, in this period, have been expected to attend in person; trial of cases was by judgement of the suitors. Halimotes were generally summoned at three-weekly intervals; that such was the case at Westminster is implied by a later reference, in 1434, to the abbot's three-weekly manor court.[22] Like such courts elsewhere, however, the Westminster halimote may in

[19] See app. I.

[20] The exception to the dearth of early court rolls are those of the abbot's piepowder court, for which see ch. 4 n. 37.

[21] e.g. WAM 17321, 17414: both name Odo the goldsmith, and are therefore datable to approximately the middle of the first half of the thirteenth century (see app. I).

[22] WAM 50749. The bailiff was directed to distrain upon all those 'qui debent sectam ad curiam dicti domini Abbatis de tribus septimanibus in tres'.

fact have met, in the thirteenth and later centuries, much less frequently than this. Indeed, the isolated reference of 1434, when a special effort was made (evidently as a scheme to raise money) to fine those who should, but presumably did not, attend the court, indicates that the institution was by then dormant, if not moribund.[23]

In addition to his manorial jurisdiction the abbot of Westminster claimed, as has been seen, the right to summon his tenants at intervals to the view of frankpledge: the trial of offences against the king's law. At Westminster the view of frankpledge was essentially held once in the year, on the Monday after the feast of St Barnabas (11 June).[24] The session also incorporated the business of the traditional (formerly 'three-weekly') manor court. The extant records of the June meetings thus include, in addition to the royal assizes concerning such matters as the baking of bread and the brewing of ale, numerous petty affairs which fell within the natural competence of the seigneurial administration. The June court of the abbot was therefore the principal judicial forum of late medieval Westminster.

3. THE MANOR COURT AS URBAN GOVERNMENT

The court was convened each June by the abbot's bailiff or seneschal.[25] Both free and unfree tenants of the manor would have attended the court together; but in fact no servile tenants are recorded in Westminster after 1200.[26] Although in the thirteenth

---

[23] No records have survived of any ordinary meetings of this court. The stylized account of the halimote given above is principally based upon the description of that held by the monks of St Albans, for which much better records survive than for Westminster, given in A. E. Levett, *Studies in Manorial History* (Oxford, 1938), 134–53.

[24] The right was also exercised, for a time, on a second occasion in the year, about All Saints' Day. This assize originated in the thirteenth century as court of piepowder associated with the October fair of St Edward. Described alternatively as *curia cum placitis nundinarum* and *curia generalis abbatis*, this court has left only a very few records of its proceedings from the late fourteenth and early fifteenth centuries. These are scattered among the series of the June court rolls, for which see below, n. 28.

[25] The presidency at the court of the seneschal, bailiff, or sub-bailiff is sometimes made explicit in the court rolls (cited below), and may otherwise be assumed.

[26] The absence of record is—at any rate for the thirteenth century—admittedly inconclusive. However, there are no more than one or two refs. to tenurial services in the Westminster deeds of the thirteenth century, and none in the manor court rolls of 1364–1514.

century all suitors may have been physically present, after the mid-fourteenth century this would have been unusual.[27] During the documented century and a half between 1364 and 1514 (from which period about seventy rolls of the June court are extant),[28] the representative character of the court was vested largely in the seniors of the local society: a body of twelve tenants known as the 'chief pledges' (*capitales plegii*) of the vill. These jurors probably originated, here as elsewhere, as the respective heads of the tithings, or subdivisions of the manor.[29] Prominent in the court from the 1360s onwards, these dozen elder statesmen replaced the wider participation which had no doubt been characteristic of Westminster, as it was of other manors, in the thirteenth century.[30] But if this development represented an abandonment of mass meetings in favour of 'government by committee',[31] it appears to have been associated additionally with an increasing assertiveness and administrative creativity on the part of the more substantial tenants of the manor. While this last-mentioned group affirmed by their judicial and political activity their own perceived superiority, they at the same time engaged in public issues which affected and involved the town (rather than the manor) of Westminster at large. They gave currency to the idea of the town as an entity, which could intermittently be realized in order to assist the resolution of communal problems.

The primary function of the chief pledges was to present, before the seneschal or bailiff, transgressors against the customs of the manor and, so far as had been granted, the laws of the crown. A disputed or a serious case might be referred to the bailiff or his deputy, who could summon a special inquest, consult with the abbot, or, more drastically, imprison a grave offender in the abbot's gaol.[32] This gaol was situated over the Tothill Street gate of the

[27] J. S. Beckerman, 'Customary Law in English Manorial Courts in the Thirteenth and Fourteenth Centuries', Ph.D. thesis, Univ. of London (1972), 95–100.

[28] WAM 50699–777; and a stray at PRO, SC2/191/66. A very small proportion of these documents relates to meetings held around 1 Nov., which were similar to the more important sessions of June; see above, n. 24.

[29] It is evidence of this that the first entry on every court roll comprises a list of those men and boys over the age of twelve, known to the chief pledges to have stayed for more than a year and a day within the demesne, but failing to register as they should as members of their tithings.

[30] Beckerman, 'Customary Law', 100.

[31] Ibid.

[32] e.g. WAM 50723 (inquest), 50749 (consultation), 50760 (imprisonment). A pillory stood in Tothill Street. WAM 23198.

monastic sanctuary, and was furnished with such distressing implements as a great iron bolt called 'St Peter's boots', to which were attached three iron shackles.[33] The bailiff also had at his command a cucking-stool; and, in one sombre entry in his own account roll, paid the hangman to dispose of a thief.[34] Distraint much more commonly, however, took the form of a petty fine. The financial proceeds of the courts—the tally of fines—belonged to the abbot, as lord of the manor. But while they continued, under the supervision of the bailiff, to impose and collect the amercements which were the lord's usual profits of justice, the chief pledges of the June courts began, of their own accord, to develop new means of law enforcement, and even to issue their own injunctions with regard to certain issues of general concern.

The chief pledges—or 'headboroughs', as they were sometimes called[35]—although in theory appointed by the abbot, were in actuality very far from being mere pawns in the seigneurial administration. The fact that their names begin to be fully recorded in the late fourteenth century, shortly after the series of extant court rolls commences, may indicate that their importance was growing in this period.[36] By the early sixteenth century at the latest, but probably from a very much earlier date, they had become self-electing, to the abbot's expressed indignation.[37] On the basis of 129 names of chief pledges recorded between 1364 and 1514, they may be characterized as a body of substantial local residents who were, however, neither outstandingly wealthy nor exclusively representative of any particular trade or interest group. Throughout the recorded period, royal courtiers and lawyers, innkeepers and

[33] WAM 17699 is a schedule of prison gear of 1379. While the Tothill Street gate housed the gaol for the abbot's fee, the inner abbey gate, adjoining the first to the south-east, contained a prison for clerks of the bishop of London taken within the liberty of Westminster. Stow, *A Survey*, ii. 122. See also ch. 3 n. 113.

[34] A small handful of accounts of the Westminster bailiffs is extant, principally of early-fourteenth-century date. A new cucking-stool was made in 1317–18. WAM 24698. The hangman's fee for the task mentioned (in 1319–20) was 6*d*. WAM 24701.

[35] e.g. WAM 6576. Headboroughs are found in many rural manors, principally as the heads of tithings. Cf. *Oxford English Dictionary*, s.v.

[36] On the earliest rolls of all, those of the 1360s, the names merely of two or three 'affeerors'—specially appointed auditors—appear at the foot. From the 1370s, however, the twelve chief pledges are fully listed by name at the *head* of the record. WAM 50705 *et seq*. The change reflected here, whereby the jurors as a body assumed full responsibility for the fines and other dealings of the court, was a general one in the fourteenth century. Beckerman, 'Customary Law', 97.

[37] WAM 6576; see app. VII.

bakers, carpenters, masons, chandlers, and tailors all sat together on
the court, which represented a fair cross-section of the activities
pursued in medieval Westminster.[38]

Of the known chief pledges, two groups were particularly
associated, respectively, with the abbey and with the royal palace.
The former group was represented by William Norton, one of the
chief pledges of 1377, who was also coroner of the liberty from 1379
until 1410, and who additionally served the prior of Westminster in
the probably honorary capacity of 'chief esquire'.[39] John Oliver
collected the rents in Westminster of two of the monastic
departments, and received a yearly robe as a valet of the convent, in
the years before 1434. In that year he was elected one of the chief
pledges, an honour he held until his presumed death in 1450.[40]
Royal servants became more numerous among the known chief
pledges from the mid-fifteenth century onwards, a trend which, if
correctly identified, reflects the increasing permanence of the king's
court at Westminster.[41] Those courtiers who took up residence in
the vicinity included Thomas Bough, a gentleman usher of the royal
exchequer and a prominent local figure. Bough and his wife rented
several houses in the abbey sanctuary, and another, with an
adjoining close, in Tothill Street. He was a churchwarden of St
Margaret's parish church in the years 1474–6 and, from
1476 × 1486 until his death in 1515, he was a chief pledge in the
Westminster court. Thomas Bough was buried in St Margaret's in
the chapel of St Erasmus.[42] The body of chief pledges also included
King Henry VII's librarian, Quentin Poulet, who was in addition a
clerk of the privy seal. Poulet, a Fleming who received denizen
status in 1500, was made a chief pledge of the court of Westminster
at about the same date.[43] Meanwhile, keeping company with these
two groups of abbey and palace officers, there stood no less
prominent bands of victuallers and building craftsmen. In a typical
year, some half-dozen of the former and three of the latter would
find their places on the jury of chief pledges.[44] This broad range of
representation does not tally with the predominant view of late

[38] See app. VIII, *passim*.
[39] App. VIII, s.n.
[40] App. VIII, s.n. For like instances see e.g. ibid., s.n. Forster, Kymbell.
[41] See ch. 5, sect. 9.
[42] App. VIII, s.n.
[43] App. VIII, s.n.
[44] See ch. 5 nn. 110, 165.

medieval towns in general as dominated by exclusive and ever narrowing interest groups.[45] The chief pledges of Westminster were not, of course, democratically elected. They were, by the later Middle Ages, the self-identified 'better sort' of the various trades and professions of the town, admitted to office by co-option. In Aristotle's sense of the word, they constituted an aristocracy. Yet it is an assumption of historians far more than of contemporaries that the few 'more discreet' individuals *necessarily* sacrificed communal interests in the selfish pursuit of their own. The Aristotelian ideal, after all, was that these should be the few men best suited to act on behalf of all.[46] The general character of the chief pledges of Westminster gives some support to the possibility that, at least on occasion, they could have been perceived in this way.

Under the aegis of the jury of chief pledges, in the course of the last third of the fourteenth century, a number of new local functionaries made their first appearance in Westminster. These officers were elected at the meetings of the court in June, apparently by the chief pledges themselves, the gaps in whose number were filled on the same occasions. Those newly appointed were sworn in before the seneschal.[47] From 1375 a coroner of the liberty was chosen by the court. In a sense this 'election' was merely confirmatory, for the coroner, who was responsible for important cases, such as manslaughter, touching the crown, was necessarily a royal appointee. The coroner within the franchise of Westminster named in 1375 was Richard Rooke, an extremely influential local figure who already exercised that office in the county of Middlesex by virtue of a royal grant.[48] The formal procedure of election is, however, in itself a sign of a growing sense of self-importance among the heads of the court. In the same year, 1375, there occurs the first reference to a pair of ale-tasters; and two years later there is record of the election of two such officers, as well as of two constables of the liberty.[49] These were the seeds of a prodigious multiplication of minor officers in the vill. The force of constables

---

[45] It is current orthodoxy that 'the fundamental fact of Tudor urban life was that the great majority of the population were completely excluded from all government and gilds and any kind of civic recognition'. This statement is taken from W. G. Hoskins, *The Age of Plunder, King Henry's England, 1500–1547* (London, 1976), 104. Likewise Clark and Slack, *English Towns in Transition*, 126–40; and refs. cited in Reynolds, *English Medieval Towns*, 171 n.

[46] Reynolds, 'Medieval Urban History', 20–1.

[47] See WAM 50749.   [48] App. VIII, s.n.   [49] WAM 50706, 50709.

grew from the initial two of 1377 to a strength, remarkable for so small an area yet maintained throughout the late fifteenth and early sixteenth centuries, of between twenty and thirty. Groups of these constables were allocated specific 'beats' within the liberty, which varied a little but usually included Tothill Street, Long Ditch, King Street, and Charing Cross, in addition to further districts along the Strand and towards St Giles-in-the-Fields. From the late fourteenth century, one of these officers was designated 'chief constable of the liberty'. Ale-tasters, meanwhile, continued to be appointed in pairs. In 1508 another department of local government was set up, that of the scavengers. Half a dozen of these 'city cleaning officers' were appointed annually, exclusively for the King Street and Tothill Street area.[50] This emerging system clearly reflects the influence of that which operated from a much earlier date within the administrative area of the city of London. There, the surviving wardmote returns for 1422 record an officialdom in each ward usually composed of a beadle, constables, scavengers, and aleconners; a hierarchy which was already old by the early fifteenth century.[51] The later-developing structure at Westminster remained more haphazard during the medieval period, but fulfilled some of the same funtions.[52]

The appearance and growth in importance of these various local officers was not the expression of a deep-rooted hostility between the townsmen and their lord the abbot. From the abbot's point of view, on the contrary, a moderate degree of self-government by his tenants was to be encouraged. The ideal was perhaps a co-operative balance in which the townspeople were at liberty to order their affairs so long as the ultimate authority of the lord was recognized.[53]

[50] WAM 50733 *et seq.*
[51] *Cal Plea & Mem R 1413–37*, 116 and see pp. xxx ff.; Barron, 'The Government of London', 40–8.
[52] At a date in the mid-sixteenth century, but almost certainly not before 1540, the manor of Westminster was officially divided into twelve wards, each represented by one of twelve burgesses; just as the chief pledges had, in all probability, represented the original twelve tithings of the manor. The adapted structure was referred to in the 1585 Act as being already in existence at that date. For the Act, see above, n. 3.
[53] Such a balance was not always achieved so harmoniously as appears to have been the case at Westminster. Cf. the case of the unincorporated town of Reading, where in the late fifteenth century the townspeople, complaining of bad government by the abbot's officers, unconstitutionally elected their own. N. M. Trenholme, *The English Monastic Boroughs*, University of Missouri Studies, ii (3) (Columbia, 1927), 72–3.

Such co-operation can be observed when, for example, in 1375, the two ale-tasters had to report that they had been prevented by a certain brewer from carrying out their office; naturally, some residents resented the interference of the new petty vigilants. The bailiff was consequently requested 'to go with the said tasters whenever required by them to make the assay of ale'.[54] However, such collaboration could not always be guaranteed, although there is no evidence of any fundamental conflict of interests between the bailiff, as the abbot's representative, and the elected officers of the court. The troubles of Robert Raby's term of office as sub-bailiff (1486–95) seem to have been due largely to his own high-handed behaviour. The complaints levelled at Raby by the chief pledges in the court of 1495 were nevertheless revealing of their own desire to secure and retain a large measure of control in local administration. Raby was criticized for his 'presumptuousness' in making unwarranted arrests: 'The said under-bailiff and his servants have walked many and divers nights to take their preys, *without any constable or constables with them*, contrary to the statute.'[55] He was also accused of keeping his victims in 'a common gaol' within his own house, 'contrary to the statute'.[56] This 'statute' was an ordinance made by the court in 1489 concerning the proper procedure for the delivery of prisoners to the gatehouse gaol.[57] The heads of the court in drafting the ordinance had not even troubled to refer to the bailiff, but treated only arrests made by the constables, who were always, when taking such action, to be accompanied by two of the chief pledges of the vill. Clearly, on the evidence provided, Raby had exceeded his rightful powers. Equally clearly, the leading members of the court were extending their own activities well beyond their mid-fourteenth-century sphere, and would even, perhaps, if they could, have made the abbot's man redundant.[58]

The actual business of the court was, like most justice, largely retributive: the meting out of fines to petty offenders. But in

[54] WAM 50706. In 1467 the bailiff was asked by the court to issue warnings to offenders. WAM 50758.
[55] WAM 50768 (emphasis added).
[56] Ibid. For Raby see also app. I and app. VIII, s.n.
[57] WAM 50763.
[58] A similar dispute arose in 1514, when Maurice Davy, then sub-bailiff, was charged with fining offenders involved in affrays without seeing the cases brought to the court, before the chief pledges, in the proper manner. The abbot's seneschal was prevailed upon to punish Davy with a fine. WAM 50777.

addition to this negative role, the members of the court are found, from the early fifteenth century onwards, occasionally taking positive steps to order and improve the social environment. Such initiative was demanded by the inadequacy of the manorial institutions to cope with urban problems. In some cases, it was the scale of a problem which was beyond the scope of the traditional framework; in others, the problem itself was unknown to the agrarian environment to which that framework was adapted.[59]

A vital issue to any urban society is the supply of fresh water. The scouring of drainage ditches is a pungent theme encountered in many medieval court records, but at Westminster, where the ground was low-lying and predominantly marshy, the subject was of fundamental importance. Every year's record contains a long list of blocked runnels, rivulets, and pipes, causing 'annoyance' and sometimes worse, to be cleared on pain of fine. In the absence of a regular common fund, extensive public works were normally beyond the means of the court. In the mid-fifteenth century, however, this crucial issue precipitated a significant instance of public financing, organized by the townspeople. King Henry VI in 1447 made a grant to the town of the overflow of water from his own, elaborately piped conduit which supplied the palace; his charter was addressed to 'the more worthy men'—by whom the chief pledges were probably meant—'and the community of Westminster' (*probis hominibus et Communitati Westmonasterii*).[60] Apart from the payment which would have been required for the issue of the

---

[59] On this general point see Hilton, 'The Small Town as Part of Peasant Society', 91. For the distinctively 'urban' character claimed for the issues discussed below cf. the very similar proceedings of the mayor's frankpledge court of fifteenth- and early-sixteenth-century Oxford, of which extracts are printed in Salter, *Medieval Oxford*, Oxford Historical Society, c (1936), 146–63. Close comparison can also be made with the records of the city of London wardmotes, cited below. *Per contra*, a glance at the equivalent records of a truly agricultural manor shows up the utterly different character of late medieval Westminster, e.g. the court records of the New College, Oxford, manors of Newton Longville (Bucks.) and Great Harwood (Bucks.), printed in W. O. Ault, *Open-Field Farming in Medieval England. A Study of Village By-Laws* (London, 1972), 145–54, 159–71.

[60] *Cal Pat R 1446–52*, p. 45; an original copy in Westminster Public Library, Archives Department. The text is printed in *Proceedings of the Society of Antiquaries of London*, 2nd ser., xi (1885–7), 105–6. It seems likely that the improvement to Westminster's water supply at this time was directly influenced by the work being carried out from the 1430s in the public water supply of London (which was derived from the abbey of Westminster's manor at Paddington). See Barron, 'The Government of London', 266–77.

charter, 'the men of Westminster' (*homines ville Westmonasterii*) are recorded, a few years later in 1454, investing sums of money in lead and solder for use in the construction of their own 'new conduit'.[61] The form of this town water-pipe is unknown; the royal conduit already supplied a public fountain in New Palace Yard, and it is probable that the new creation was another fountain or pump nearby, perhaps in King Street.[62] More tantalizing is the absence of information as to the means by which the necessary funds were raised in the town. The materials bought in 1454 alone cost some £14: not a massive sum, but unquestionably requiring extraordinary measures of collection, such as a levy on householders. The project shows the readiness and ability of the townspeople— and at the least, a wider group of these than the chief pledges alone—to collaborate in a perceived common interest. Awareness of this particular matter of public concern was demonstrated again when, in 1491, the positive step was taken to appoint a local commission of 'supervisors of the ditches of Westminster'.[63] And a few years later eight of the chief pledges of the vill (describing themselves as headboroughs), in collaboration with the bailiff, jointly hired a ditcher to clean the water-courses of the neighbourhood. The Lambeth man who undertook the job complained of not receiving due payment; but the significant fact here is the co-operative measure taken by the leading townsmen to maintain essential public services.[64]

Associated with water supply was the wider civic issue of sanitation. From the early fifteenth century, there begin to appear at the foot of some of the court rolls the texts of innovative ordinances drawn up and agreed by those attending. One such injunction, passed in *c.*1500, decreed that dung-heaps should be cleared from their property by individuals at the end of each month, on pain of a 20*d.* fine; a few years later, as has been noted, this campaign to

[61] PRO E364/87, m.9. The materials (4,857 lbs. lead, and 46 lbs. solder) were sold to the townsmen by the clerk of the king's works.

[62] For the king's conduit and the Palace Yard fountain, see *King's Works*, i. 550; R. Edwards, 'The Fountain in New Palace Yard, Westminster', *The London Archaeologist*, ii (3) (1973), 60–1; and B. Davison, 'A Carved Fragment of Purbeck Marble from a Late Twelfth Century Fountain in the Palace of Westminster', *Antiquaries Journal*, lv (1975), 399 and pl. lxxxiii.

[63] WAM 50764.

[64] PRO, C1/326/87: datable to the chancellorship of Archbishop Wareham (1504–15).

sweeten the environment was strengthened by the creation of teams of scavengers.[65] To the same end, the court repeatedly invoked the responsibility of property-owners (including the monks) to maintain neighbouring roadways and ditches, as in an outburst of the 1530s concerning

the hyee way goyng in to Totehyll by Saynt Armylls chapell . . . it lyeth so fowle of doung & caryen . . . & other fylthry to the great infeccyon & noyaunce of the kyngs liege people comyng or goyng . . . that waye, and also it stoppyth the comon sewer [the Tyburn stream] so that water maye nott have . . . course bothe ebbyng & flowyng.[66]

Housing regulations were also increasingly necessary as the town became more densely built up. Encroachments upon the street or upon the common pasture frequently engaged the court's attention, as likewise did dangerous premises, roofed with straw or containing a wooden chimney.[67] These topics are as prominent in the Westminster records as they are, for example, in those of the city of London wardmotes (preserved in enrolled versions for 1422–3, and in the original returns for Portsoken ward for 1465–82 and for 1507).[68] Inevitably, however, there is no evidence at Westminster of an Assize of Buildings such as was drawn up for London as early as *c*.1200.[69]

Regulation of Westminster's economic life was equally hampered by the limitations of the court's legislative authority. Moreover, private cases, concerning such matters as debt, did not fall within the competence of the June court, but were presumably heard by the abbot's (barely recorded) piepowder court in October.[70] Nevertheless, the chief pledges of the summer courts were energetic in their attempts to control trading practices. Butchers, for example, were a constant bone of contention. If comparison be

---

[65] See WAM 50773; and above, n. 50.

[66] WAM 50769: n.d., but contains a ref. to the king's park wall, part of the Whitehall extensions begun in *c*.1530. St Armil's chapel was that formerly known as St Mary Magdalen's; see M. Robbins, 'A Site in Westminster, or, Whoever was St. Ermin?', *London Topographical Record*, xxiv (1980), 113–30.

[67] e.g. WAM 50758, 50760 (*bis*), 50765.

[68] *Cal Plea & Mem R 1413–37*, 115 ff., 150 ff.; CLRO, Ward Presentments, Portsoken Ward, 5–22 Edw. IV, 23 Hen. VII.

[69] Riley (ed.), *Chronicles of Old London*, 179–87; and for the date see H. M. Chew and W. Kellaway (eds.), *London Assize of Nuisance, 1301–1431*, London Record Society, x (1973), pp. ix–xi.

[70] For the piepowder court, see above, n. 24.

made again with the London wardmote presentments, it is apparent
that butchering was a distinctive and outstanding local issue in
Westminster, as indeed has already been shown.[71] The butchering
'boom' which began in the late fourteenth century created a series of
local problems, to which, in the absence of the controls of a craft
organization, the chief pledges responded as best they could. The
earliest reference to the subject in the court rolls occurs under the
year 1378; thereafter, in every recorded year some half-dozen
butchers were presented for the sale of unwholesome or over-priced
meat.[72] Butchering was, moreover, associated with offensive
subsidiary processes and with related industries which, although
never practised extensively in Westminster, could be noxious. A
tailor was fined in 1422 for having sublet his land to butchers who
were using it as a tip for their offal.[73] The common land on Tothill
had to be protected from overstocking by butchers. In 1523 six
individuals were arraigned for having overcrowded the common
with between six and twenty-three animals; and another (whether a
grazier or arable farmer is not clear) for having enclosed ground in
St James's fields 'contrary to the custom of old'.[74] There were in
addition other, less purely economic, aspects of the trade which
troubled the court. When the bailiff and ale-tasters visited the shop
of Henry Cornwall, butcher, in 1391, his response to their enquiries
was to brandish a knife.[75] When Robert Keene, a local butcher, was
arrested by the sub-bailiff on an unknown charge in 1512, another
butcher lost his life in a violent rescue attempt.[76] Butchers, indeed,
seem to have been a particularly violent group, who possessed
potential weapons only too conveniently within reach.[77] It is not
surprising, therefore, that a number of the ordinances promulgated
by the court should have related to butchering. The careful penning
of animals was the subject of decrees issued in 1422 and twice more
in the 1480s.[78] In 1505, the times were stipulated when butchers
might dispose of offal and carcasses; this was only to be allowed
between 8 p.m. and 6 a.m. in winter, and 10 p.m. and 3 a.m. in

[71] See ch. 5, sect. 3.
[72] WAM 50712 *et seq.*
[73] WAM 50745. For the effects of tanning see ch. 5 n. 133.
[74] WAM 50778, fos. 2ᵛ, 5ʳ.
[75] WAM 50720.
[76] *LP* i, no. 1494 (11).
[77] Further examples: PRO, KB9/221/1/4 (1424); KB9/224/224 (1428).
[78] WAM 50745, 50760–1.

summer.[79] The hostelling and related trades which were particularly characteristic of medieval Westminster also received constant attention. Most of the references to innkeepers, brewers, bakers, and cooks relate merely to the imposition of penalties upon offenders, but two pieces of creative, if unoriginal, legislation were enacted in 1488 and 1494, by virtue of which bread baked in Westminster was to conform to London standards, and all victuals were to be charged at London prices.[80]

The overriding purpose to which all these regulations and penalties were directed was the maintenance of the social order. This preoccupation of the heads of the court is particularly apparent in their concern with unsociable or suspicious behaviour. For this, even if not actually illegal, was treated as potentially criminal. 'Night-walkers', 'eavesdroppers', and 'rioters all night playing at the dice and cards' all fell within this category.[81] William Falkoner was an exemplary target, contriving, in the eyes of the court, to embody all of these subversive tendencies. He was arraigned in 1407 for being 'a common night-walker and vagabond, sleeping by day and dicing by night, to the disturbance of the neighbours and the king's peace'.[82] By the same token, charges would be brought against a resident for the resort of suspicious persons to his house.[83] Gossips and scolds, to whom medieval courts sometimes seem to give undue attention, were clearly regarded as a similar threat to social harmony. At Westminster in 1380, for example, sixteen individuals were fined on this score, all of them (as was commonly the case) being women.[84] It may be that in a society which permitted no official forum for female discussion of public matters, the behaviour which men called 'gossiping' was merely the unofficial conversation about such subjects to which women were confined.

The same concern with social stability led the chief pledges of Westminster, like their equivalents in the secular jurisdiction of other towns, to extend their pronouncements to moral offences.

[79] WAM 50770. Fishmongers were to be subject to the same regulations. For regulations of butchers introduced in the city of London from the late fourteenth century see Sabine, 'Butchering in Medieval London'.
[80] WAM 50761, 50767.
[81] e.g. WAM 50745 (1422), 50774 (1509); PRO, SC2/191/66 (1510).
[82] WAM 50738.
[83] e.g. WAM 50778, fo. 8ᵛ (1523).
[84] WAM 50715.

Prostitution, it has already been observed, flourished to an unusual degree in this peculiarly male-dominated neighbourhood of royal officers, parliament-men, and clerics.[85] As it is today, a leading argument against prostitution, in the minds of the chief pledges of medieval Westminster, was that it attracted other and more overt crimes. Thus brothels were regularly described as being the haunts of robbers and other nefarious characters.[86] Since the business could not be regulated here the Westminster authorities' only resort, other than the common but evidently innocuous fine, was to expel undesirables from the vill. In a bout of reforming zeal in 1508, thirty-one people said to be 'ill-governed of their bodies' were driven out from the franchise.[87] This was in fact strong action of a sternness unprecedented of the Westminster court, and may represent an increased determination to bring this matter under control; two years previously a similar attempt had been made to close the official stews in Southwark.[88] Although such moral cases were properly the concern of the church courts, the assumption of responsibility by secular justices was widespread by the end of the Middle Ages. These were areas of moral conduct which bore directly upon the social order and which secular governors, ever preoccupied with the maintenance of stability, could therefore not afford to ignore.

4. CONCLUSION

Although it remained, in law, a seigneurial manor of the kind usually associated with agricultural villages, Westminster by the end of the Middle Ages exhibited a variety of economic life, and a range of concomitant social problems, which were the equals of those to be found in any medium-sized English town of the period, incorporated or otherwise. The response of the inhabitants to these phenomena, on the other hand, notwithstanding the apparent inadequacies of the traditional judicial framework, was both energetic and practical to a degree worthy of the most chartered of

[85] See ch. 5, sect. 4.
[86] e.g. WAM 50737 (1408).
[87] WAM 50773.
[88] Stow, *A Survey*, ii. 55. It is perhaps not surprising that neither purge was of lasting effect. But the age encouraged such attempts, as witnesses the literally trumpeted reclosure of the Bankside stews in 1546. Ibid.

borough corporations. The positive attempts of Westminster's leading residents to regulate public amenities, trades, and the social order reflect a growing sense of communal interests and purpose. As new developments changed the character of the medieval town, its members reacted by the introduction of appropriate new measures into the customary jurisdiction of the manor. The first conclusion which must be drawn regarding the government of medieval Westminster, therefore, is that the lack of a charter was a matter of no importance.

If relations with the lord were good, manorial status could be a positive advantage to an expanding town, as the contrasted fortunes of the Lincolnshire towns of Grimsby and Boston clearly demonstrate. The former was an ancient royal borough with a chest-full of civic charters; but it was the latter, a seigneurial dependency subject to no less than three separate lords, which grew during the thirteenth and fourteenth centuries to become a major port and one of the wealthiest towns in England.[89] Many late medieval towns owed their promotion to seigneurial initiative,[90] and such a major centre as Leicester became demonstrates the perceived advantages, in some cases, of continued co-operation between townsmen and their lords.[91] Conflict was certainly not inevitable.

Yet conflict did occur, and did so with particular frequency in towns subject to monasteries. The list of Bury St Edmunds, St Albans, Abingdon, Reading, and Cirencester conjures up bloody images of revolt and harsh reprisals, especially in the fourteenth century.[92] Of the series of rebellions in monastic boroughs two

---

[89] Rigby, 'Boston and Grimsby in the Middle Ages: An Administrative Contrast', *Journal of Medieval History*, x (1984), 51–66.

[90] e.g. J. Le Patourel, *The Manor and Borough of Leeds, 1066–1400*, Thoresby Society, xlv (1957); Beresford, 'The Six New Towns of the Bishops of Winchester, 1200–1255', *Medieval Archaeology*, iii (1959), 187–215; Carus-Wilson, 'The First Half-century of Stratford-upon-Avon', *Econ Hist Rev*, 2nd ser., xviii (1965), 46–63.

[91] For Leicester see *Records of the Borough of Leicester*, vol. i, ed. M. Bateson (London, 1899), pp. xxxviii–xl.

[92] Bury: Lobel, *Bury St Edmunds*. St Albans: Levett, *Studies in Manorial History*, 178–205. Abingdon: G. Lambrick, 'The Impeachment of the Abbot of Abingdon in 1368', *English Historical Review*, lxxxii (1967), 250–76. Reading: C. F. Slade, 'Reading', in M. D. Lobel (ed.), *Historic Towns*, vol. i (London, 1969), 3–4. Cirencester: Finberg (ed.), *Gloucestershire Studies* (Leicester, 1957), 74–9; *The Cartulary of Cirencester Abbey*, ed. C. D. Ross, 3 vols. (London, 1964–77), vol. i, pp. xxxvi–xl and nos. 12, 124–31, and vol. ii, no. 738. A non-Benedictine (Praemonstratensian) case, in a small town, is that of Halesowen in Worcestershire: Z. Razi, 'The Struggles Between the Abbots of Halesowen and their Tenants in the

observations may be made. In the first place they were, almost without exception, failures. Precipitated most commonly by the excessive exactions of a lord whose presence was only too immediately felt, the risings were almost inevitably suppressed by this 'resident deathless body which had the support of the crown'.[93] Although in some of these cases clashes recurred over long periods, they proved little except the reactionary force of the religious communities when under pressure. The absence of strife in other places, therefore, might seem to result from a cautious deference on the part of the townspeople. But the other notable feature of the rebellions is, not surprisingly, that they occurred where there was something to fight about: some economic advantage which, seemingly, might be enjoyed by one party without the other. In Bury and Cirencester control of the regional trade in wool, cloth, and grain represented the principal bone of contention; in Reading, Abingdon, and St Albans it was the benefit of a good situation and the opportunity to take part in the profitable London market.[94] To the wealthy merchants of each of these towns, the local monastery might seem a frustrating irrelevance. Westminster differed from these particular monastic boroughs in the very limitations of its economic life. Lacking a significant trading or manufacturing base, Westminster's was essentially a service economy; its horizons were limited.[95] After the decline of the fair of St Edward in the early fourteenth century, wealth was generated within the town almost exclusively by small-scale commerce. From the lords' standpoint, the profits of taverners and shopkeepers were most readily taxed through rents. For the townspeople rent, so long as it appeared reasonable, was a fair price to pay in order to be left, in effect, to their own devices. The absence of economic competition, such as could provide a focus for grievances, thus goes some way to account for the peaceful relations between lords and tenants in Westminster.

Beyond this, however, it must be reiterated that the society of Westminster was extremely diverse;[96] more so, in all probability, than that of any of the other monastic towns which have been

Thirteenth and Fourteenth Centuries', in Aston, *et al.* (eds.), *Social Relations and Ideas*, 151–67; and cf. Hilton, 'Small Town Society', for the urban character of the place. In general: Trenholme, *English Monastic Boroughs*; and Knowles, *The Religious Orders in England*, 3 vols. (Cambridge, 1948–59), i. 263–9.

[93] Knowles, *Religious Orders*, i. 265.   [94] See refs. cited above, n. 92.
[95] See ch. 5. Cf. also Dobson, *Durham Priory*, 44–50.   [96] See ch. 6.

mentioned. A multiplicity of different loyalties cut across one another, with the result that the potential for a clear split between abbey and town was minimized. Many inhabitants, of course, had connections with the convent itself; other attachments led out of the town altogether, as in the case of members of London craft guilds, or foreign immigrants with compatriots elsewhere in the suburbs. Again, the royal servants among Westminster's leading residents might feel the less cramped by the limitations of local political institutions in so far as the palace provided an alternative stage on which to strut. Most of the inhabitants of Westminster were pulled in at least two directions by such competing claims. Resentment of the monks' lordship might be compromised by any of numerous forms of economic relationship with them, or by kinship with a member of the convent; anger at the overweening behaviour of the abbot's sub-bailiff might be defused by association with the same individual in another context, such as the ruling council of a major local guild; and so on. A large number of conflicting loyalties, therefore, may have been conducive to the quick resolution of any particular dispute.[97]

These multifarious, cross-cutting loyalties also provide a partial explanation for the absence from the record of major or extended conflict within the society of Westminster at large. Nevertheless, the hierarchy of wealth and power was too sharply differentiated for the tensions within it to be thus easily dissolved. Moreover, even among those of similar economic status, overlapping loyalties were at best an ambivalent force for unity. Nor was the economic power of the élite a sufficient basis for the imposition of order upon the remaining mass of the urban society. Wealth alone could not have sustained the narrowly based ruling councils of medieval towns. Like their successors in Victorian cities, the urban élites of the Middle Ages were necessarily used to mobilizing other groups within society, the lower orders included. And, as in the nineteenth century so in the Middle Ages, the language and procedures of corporate activity were effective precisely because they could be perceived to be beneficial at different social levels.[98]

The evidence of local government in Westminster demonstrates

---

[97] As anthropologists have observed. Cf. M. Gluckman, *Custom and Conflict in Africa* (Oxford, 1956), ch. 1.

[98] For the continuing importance of such a communal dimension of political power in the much larger cities of Victorian England, see J. Garrard, *Leadership and Power in Victorian Industrial Towns, 1830–1880* (Manchester, 1983).

an intermittent perception of shared interests within the town, leading to active collaboration over specific issues. A principal forum for the discussion of such public matters was the manor court; the frame of reference was the town as a whole. Not continuously, therefore, but periodically, at particular crises, a significant proportion of the population of Westminster perceived itself as belonging to a single community which embraced the town in its entirety, and gave tangible form to that perception in the creation of an urban water supply, public legislation on economic activities, and the protection of the common fields.

'Community' calls for definition. Of an agricultural village, the word may perhaps be used without danger of misunderstanding; in a town of up to three thousand inhabitants greater precision is required. First, it is not a continuous state, but is realized momentarily at particular conjunctures.[99] The occasion might be some regular, ritual event which, though perhaps manifesting discord in conflicts over precedence, at the same time portrays an ideal harmony which has its own potency as a remembered image.[100] But a firmer basis for the activation of community is the occasional perception of a practical public need which unites and transcends private interests. The moment of co-operation never endures; individual, divergent preoccupations soon distract attention from the shared activity; disunity prevails again. Yet the experience may survive in the memory, maintaining the possibility of a repetition. Moreover, different frameworks may be adapted to provide a context for the periodic co-ordination of interests. In medieval Westminster, the manorial administration was not the only one of these. A separate context for the fulfilment of this potential—and one in which the practical participation of the inhabitants was much more widely based—was found in the organization of the parish.

[99] See M. Taylor, *Community, Anarchy and Liberty* (Cambridge, 1982).

[100] See Phythian-Adams, 'Ceremony and the Citizen: The Communal Year at Coventry 1450–1550', in Clark and Slack (eds.), *Crisis and Order in English Towns, 1500–1700* (London, 1972), 57–85; M. James, 'Ritual, Drama and the Social Body in the Late Medieval English Town', *Past and Present*, xcviii (1983), 3–29.

ILLUS. 8. St Margaret's church, Westminster. Interior, view to east. Nave and aisles *c.*1500, east wall modern.

8

The Religion of the Lay Community

I. THE PARISH OF ST MARGARET

Between 1200 and 1540, every inhabitant of the vill of Westminster was by the same token a parishioner of the church of St Margaret. Throughout their histories, neighbourhood and parish evolved *pari passu*. St Margaret's church is first documented in about the second quarter of the twelfth century, when Abbot Herbert of Westminster (1121–*c*.1136) assigned to the high altar and to the other needs of his monastery an annual sum of 60*s*. 'from the church of St Margaret which stands in our cemetery'.[1] There was, however, a fourteenth-century tradition at Westminster that a church on the present site, dedicated to St Margaret, had first been built by King Edward the Confessor.[2] The dedication to St Margaret of Antioch would be entirely plausible at this date, for the saint was well known and, to judge from literary evidence, popular in Anglo-Saxon England.[3]

[1] 'De ecclesia Sancte Margarete in nostro cymiterio stante.' WAM 3435; BL MS Cart. Harl. 84 F.46 (another copy).

[2] '(Sanctus Rex Edwardus) fundavit primam ecclesiam Sancte Margarete in loco quo nunc sita est, que antea in navi veteris ecclesie ex parte videlicet boriali constituta fuerat ubi et parochiani convenire debuerant et divina servicia et sacramenta ecclesiastica percipere soliti erant.' LN, fo. 76ᵛ. In the north transept of Henry III's church, in a spandrel towards the east end of the north wall arcade, there survives a thirteenth-century carving which shows St Margaret and the dragon. The relief is situated at the closest point, within the abbey, to the neighbouring parish church. Additionally, the sculpture may recall a (hypothetical) chapel of St Margaret which existed inside the earlier abbey church—that of the Confessor or even its predecessor—in the days when the parishioners were later remembered to have worshipped in the monastery, 'on the north side of the nave of the church'.

[3] In the eleventh century Exeter Cathedral possessed among its relics the head of St Margaret, apparently the gift of King Athelstan. If the cult were especially associated with Wessex, as this might suggest, it could have been brought to Westminster in the wake of the Wessex expansion eastwards, or more specifically at the time of St Dunstan's foundation of Westminster Abbey in *c*.960. In the later Middle Ages the Westminster parish church owned a finger of the saint (below, n. 105), but it is not known when this was acquired. For the cult see F. M. Mack (ed.), *Seinte Marharete þe Meiden ant Martyr*, Early English Text Society, orig. ser. cxciii (1934), pp. x–xi.

Moreover, there is positive evidence that a parish church existed in William I's reign. By the late eleventh century the tithe of the parish of Westminster had been allocated to the abbey almoner; the almoners were subsequently *ex officio* rectors of St Margaret's, and this continuity may suggest (though it does not prove) that a separate parish church was present before 1100.[4] The confused story of the foundation recounted in the fourteenth century seems to imply that the parishioners of Westminster had previously been accustomed to receive the sacraments in the abbey church itself.[5] At the time of the abbey's re-foundation by the Confessor, the monks may, like other religious communities in similar circumstances, have wished to provide a separate church in order to remove a potentially disruptive lay congregation from their midst.[6] It is, indeed, most likely that the Confessor's abbey, six times greater in numbers of religious than its predecessor, and the new palace complex adjacent, would have attracted new settlers.[7] The probable growth of the local population in this period may, therefore, have prompted the foundation (or the enlargement) of the parish church.

The supreme jurisdiction of St Margaret's parish, under the pope, was a jealously guarded prerogative of the abbot of Westminster. As in the secular sphere, however, the local inhabitants, in their *personae* as parishioners, evolved means of communal association and activity which were altogether independent of the abbot's authority. As with secular government, so with this development in parochial life, a brief outline of the administrative

    [4] See an abbatial grant of Gilbert Crispin (*c.*1085–1117/18), of 1083 or a little later, to William Baynard of 'quoddam berewicam de villa Westmonasterii nomine Totenhala . . . exceptis decimis illius terre domui elemosinarie nostre constitutis'. WD, fo. 82ʳ; printed in Robinson, *Gilbert Crispin*, 38. The date of 1083 given in the copy of the grant appears not to have been in the original; the document may date from a few years afterwards. See *The History of Westminster Abbey by John Flete*, 141 ff. 'Totenhala' was the site in part of the parish of St Giles, constituted after the royal foundation of St Giles's hospital in *c.*1117, and in part of the later medieval estate of 'Blemund's Bury' (now Bloomsbury). Previously, however, 'Totenhala' would have belonged to the parish centred on the abbey or on a dependent parish church. See E. J. Davis, 'The University Site, Bloomsbury', *London Topographical Record*, xvii (1936), 19–139.
    [5] See above, n. 2 and Harvey, *Estates*, 46.
    [6] Among several examples, cf. Battle Abbey, where the townspeople so crowded the abbey church that Abbot Ralph (1107–24) built for them the church of St Mary outside the abbey walls. One of the stipulated duties of the new parish priest in this instance was to exclude seculars from the abbey church. *The Chronicle of Battle Abbey*, ed. E. Searle (Oxford, 1980), 124 ff.
    [7] See ch. 1.

framework will provide the necessary context. A dispute between the Westminster monks and the bishop of London, concerning the jurisdiction of the parish church, was settled in 1222 by a decree of papal judges, who pronounced in the abbey's favour. St Margaret's parish was then declared to be wholly exempt from any authority, after Rome, except that of the abbot of Westminster; and so it remained throughout the later Middle Ages. The parish at that date comprised the area on the Middlesex side of the Thames bounded to the west by the Tyburn, to the north by the road now known as Oxford Street, and to the east by the parish of St Giles and the church of the Holy Innocents (subsequently St Mary-le-Strand)[8] (Fig. 3). The creation of new parishes of St Martin-in-the-Fields (by *c.*1250) and later of St Mary-le-Strand (by 1393), however, entailed the diminution of St Margaret's, which already by the mid-thirteenth century was therefore confined to the area south of Charing; the area, that is, subsequently identified with the 'vill' of Westminster.[9] At the very end of the period under consideration, in 1534–5, a further slight reduction was made in the size of the parish to accommodate the sensibilities of King Henry VIII. The king, having lately appropriated Whitehall Palace, was disturbed by the passage past his door of corpses being brought from Charing to be buried at St Margaret's. The parish boundary was therefore redrawn, along a line of latitude which passed through the palace gate in King Street.[10]

The rectory of St Margaret's church belonged from an early date, indeed almost certainly *ab origine*, to Westminster Abbey, and was vested in the abbey almoner. The assignment of the rectory, with the rectorial tithe, to the almonry, evidently as part of the original endowment of that office, was presumably made according to the

---

[8] The separate townships (*villae*) of Knightsbridge, Westbourne, and Paddington were included as outliers of the parish of St Margaret, no doubt because they formed part of the foundation endowment of the abbey, upon which they for long remained dependent. See ch. 7 n. 13.

[9] For the vill see above, ch. 7, sect. 2. For the earliest refs. to St Martin's parish, see WAM 17152, 17157: both of approximately mid-thirteenth-century date. For St Mary-le-Strand see B. Saunders, 'Results of an Enquiry Concerning the Situation and Extent of Westminster at Various Periods', *Archaeologia*, xxvi (1836), 236–9. Paddington, which included Westbourne, became a distinct rectory in the fifteenth century; Knightsbridge, however, remained in St Margaret's parish until the twentieth. Harvey, *Estates*, 408–9; Saunders, 'The Situation and Extent of Westminster', 231.

[10] *LP* vii, no. 1423; ibid. viii, no. 228.

old principle that a portion of any parochial tithe should be set aside for the poor. The value of the rectory when it included Paddington, both in 1291 and in the early fourteenth century, was £20 p.a.[11] By the fifteenth century, however, the almoner's tithe was gleaned from a more restricted area, and was correspondingly reduced. In the early fifteenth century the almoner sold his tenth share of the crops annually for a sum averaging £3. 10s.; from 1466, the collection of the tithe was permanently leased at a rate of £4 p.a.[12] The visitation of the church, meanwhile, was performed not by the almoner, but by the abbot in person.[13]

The advowson (the right to present to the living), on the other hand, was in the mid-thirteenth century in the gift of the king; a piece of patronage which Henry III might naturally have assumed to himself, but which may in fact have belonged to the crown from the church's foundation, if the Confessor were partially responsible for this.[14] But at a date between 1291 and 1317, the vicarage was appropriated to the abbey, and assigned to the conventual department of the sacristy.[15] This was a relatively late date for appropriation to a monastery, a process which was at its height in the twelfth century; but the royal interest accounts for the delay in the present case.[16] The allocation to the sacristy is explained by the fact that the ground of the entire precinct to the north of the abbey church, upon part of which St Margaret's was built, notionally belonged to the sacrist's portion.[17] The successive curates of the church, from c.1300 until 1540, were therefore appointed by the sacrists, in their capacity as vicar.[18] In the early fifteenth century the sacrist provided the parish priest or chaplain with a robe each year,

---

[11] *Taxatio ecclesiastica Anglicana et Walliae auctoritate P. Nicholai IV, c. A.D. 1291*, ed. S. Ayscough and J. Caley (Record Commission, London, 1802), 17b; LN, fo. 141ᵛ.

[12] WAM 19050–72; 19074 *et seq.* Before the fifteenth century, the tithe is not distinguished in the almoner's accounts from other crops collected by that officer. After the Dissolution the tithe continued to belong to the dean and chapter of Westminster, who farmed it at a reduced annual rate of £2. 13s. 4d. p.a. Reg Bk, iii, fos. 93ᵛ, 267ʳ.

[13] e.g. WAM 18990.

[14] See app. II n. 5. King Henry gave vestments to St Margaret's church in 1252. *Cal Lib R 1251–60*, p. 40.

[15] See above, n. 11.

[16] B. R. Kemp, 'Monastic Possession of Parish Churches in England in the Twelfth Century', *Journal of Ecclesiastical History*, xxxi (1980), 133–60.

[17] See ch. 3 n. 122.

[18] See app. II.

of the convent's livery. From *c.*1450 the sacrist's patronage took the form of refection for the curate at the principal feasts of the year.[19] The sacrist, sometimes assisted by the almoner, also provided refreshment each year on the eve and feast-day of St Margaret (20 July), when some of the monks, with the secular singers of the abbey, attended mass in the parish church.[20]

The vicarage fluctuated considerably in prosperity over the later medieval period (see appendix III). The abbey's appropriation of the church in *c.*1300 occurred at a time when parochial dues and offerings will have been increased by recent population growth.[21] The lowest sums received from the vicarage were recorded in the mid-fourteenth century, after which there followed a recovery to the preceding level. The fifteenth century, after another slump in the second quarter, was marked thereafter by a dramatic increase which reached a peak in the early sixteenth century. These figures, although crude, conform with the impression derived from other sources of the broad demographic changes in late medieval Westminster, marked by phases of expansion in the thirteenth century, in the late fourteenth century, and from the late fifteenth century onwards, with troughs between these peaks.[22]

2. RELATIONS BETWEEN MONASTERY AND PARISH

The religious community of a Benedictine monastery in the Middle Ages inevitably stood in an ambivalent relationship to the secular world. Lacking the economic self-sufficiency of such enclosed orders of later foundation as the Cistercians, the black monks depended for their maintenance upon the services of the laity. Consequently the Benedictines had to reconcile their vows of world-renunciation with reliance on their secular neighbours for material support. Historians of the Reformation occasionally evince an assumption that such contact between the spiritual and mundane worlds was necessarily corrupting to the former, and so hastened the demise of the monastic life.[23] About this assumption two

[19] e.g. WAM 19670–1 (1428–30), 19702 (1451–2) *et seq.*
[20] e.g. WAM 18992, 50733, 19687.
[21] See ch. 1.
[22] See ch. 6, sect. 1.
[23] e.g. A. G. Dickens, *The English Reformation* (Collins/Fontana edn., 1964), 81–2, 86; J. Youings, *The Dissolution of the Monasteries* (London, 1971), 14.

observations may be made. In the first place, the encounter between
religious and secular, so far from being a late and decadent
development, dated from the first foundation of the Benedictine
houses. And second, it is far from clear that the *degree* of
fraternization was, in general, greater on the eve of the Dissolution
than it had been before 1200. The monks of Westminster met with
the laity throughout the medieval period in the daily administration
of affairs, yet it would be difficult to argue that the result was a
cumulative erosion, over so long a period, of the holiness of the
conventual life. Moreover, the period of greatest intimacy between
seculars and monks in Westminster may actually have ended, not in
1540, but in the mid-thirteenth century. Lay parochial activity in
the later Middle Ages reflects a proportionately reduced involvement with the abbey, and a much greater commitment to the town
church of St Margaret.

Local lay support for Westminster Abbey as a worthy recipient of
pious grants was probably at its height in *c.* 1200. The endowment of
the monastery in this period with numerous small plots of land in
the vicinity was very largely made (whether by gift or sale) in return
for the prayers of the monks.[24] Those thus entering the spiritual
fraternity of the monastery at this time included such a relatively
obscure figure as a baker's widow of Westminster, whose husband
was himself buried within the abbey.[25] Other lay grants betrayed
particular associations with individual monks. Three grants to the
abbey almonry of rents in Westminster were made to endow
anniversaries for former religious.[26] The project to construct a Lady
chapel within the abbey in the early thirteenth century was itself
greatly encouraged by lay interest in the town.[27]

This evidence of close harmony, however, abruptly receded after
1250. In contrast to the decades around 1200, after the mid-century
grants 'in soul-alms' to the abbey were almost unheard of.[28] The

[24] See ch. 3, sect. 2.

[25] See ch. 3 n. 28.

[26] Brother Gregory Tayleboys, late almoner, Brother Robert Tayleboys, and
Brother Geoffrey de Stanes. All three grants were made in the second quarter of the
thirteenth century. WD, fos. 460ᵛ–461ʳ: witnessed by Odo the goldsmith, his son
Edward, and Richer de Cruce (for whom see app. 1). The almoner was the
appropriate recipient in these cases, being responsible for the mortuary rolls
containing the names of deceased brethren, and for the distribution of money to the
poor on the death of a monk. *Customary*, 177.

[27] See ch. 3 nn. 14 ff.

[28] See ch. 3 n. 13.

enthusiasm which had attended 'the work of the glorious Virgin Mary' at the turn of the century appears to have fallen away even before the new building was complete. This would account for the long period of upwards of fifteen years which the building ultimately required, and for the embarrassing remark of Pope Innocent IV, who referred in a bull of 1245 to 'the repairs which the monks had begun in far too sumptuous a fashion, and which they were unable properly to finish'.[29] When, in that year of 1245, Henry III initiated the new plan to rebuild the entire abbey church, it was the king himself who undertook to foot the bill. After that date, private gifts to the abbey's building fund, throughout Henry III's reconstruction of the east end, were virtually non-existent.[30]

In the late fourteenth century the replacement of the Romanesque nave was taken up again by the monks, this time substantially at their own expense. The work was to drag on for a century and a half, in part as the result of a resounding lack of outside support. Even the now established tradition of royal patronage was continually compromised in the late medieval period by competing commitments and changes of dynasty.[31] Non-royal lay benefactors of the project, who are named in the accounts of the 'new work', do represent a degree of local interest in the monastic building; but they were few in number. Some were craftsmen actually employed on the site, like John Palterton, mason, and Thomas Woffeld, his mate (*socius*), who gave 13s. 4d. to the *novum opus* around the time of its inception in c.1349, before embarking upon a journey to Rome, presumably for the mid-century indulgence.[32] In 1357–8 Palterton made a further, touching bequest of £4 for the sake of Thomas Woffeld's soul.[33] John Palterton probably worked at Westminster Palace in 1344, was subsequently employed by the abbey between c.1350 and c.1379, and was master mason there from 1361.[34] John Rogerson, a plumber on the site, left £2 to the new work when he died in 1479.[35] In 1489–90 the master of the masons, Robert

[29] WD, fo. 406. The chapel, begun in 1220, was still unroofed in 1234; but Abbot Richard de Berking was buried within it in 1246. *Matt Par Chron Maj*, iii. 59; Westlake, *Westminster Abbey*, 59.

[30] *King's Works*, i. 130, 135: 'of private benefaction there is very little evidence'.

[31] See Rackham, 'The Nave of Westminster'.

[32] WAM 23454.

[33] WAM 23455.

[34] J. H. Harvey, 'The Masons of Westminster Abbey', *Archaeological Journal*, cxiii (1957), 98.

[35] WAM 23551.

Stowell, offered £3. 6s. 8d. to the project, in return for which he and
his wife were to enjoy the benefits of fraternity with the convent.[36] A
sparse scattering of like bequests was collected from other local
residents.[37] The final impression, despite these, is that the monks
found it much harder than they had done in the early thirteenth
century to enlist popular support for their enterprise.

A number of explanations account for this change. In the first
place, the monks themselves may, in the century of the Fourth
Lateran Council, have begun to stand upon their clerical dignity,
and to cultivate an aloofness from secular fraternization. Another,
contemporary development at Westminster compounded this
general trend towards the clearer segregation of monks and
seculars. Henry III in 1245 envisaged, and subsequently realized, a
new role for Westminster Abbey, for which King Louis IX of
France and the church of St Denis near Paris had supplied the
model. In this grandiose scheme, the Gothic church at Westminster
was planned as the mausoleum of the English kings, where they
would rest under the protection of their sacred forebears, Edward
the Confessor above all.[38] The grandeur of the royal patronage, and
the distinction which henceforward attached to burial within the
abbey church, undoubtedly excluded humbler benefactors, and
may have tended to cut off the religious from the mere commons of
the town. That such a separation did occur is further suggested by
the character of the chantries founded within the abbey in the late
Middle Ages. Once the royal example had been decisively set by
Henry III, Westminster Abbey became in addition the premier
church for aristocratic burial. The recorded chantries established
there in the fourteenth and fifteenth centuries were exclusively the
creations of a courtly élite.[39] No doubt lack of information conceals

[36] WAM 23563; and see app. VIII, s.n. Stowell.
[37] e.g. Alice Kymbell left 6s. 8d. to the work in 1399; in 1480–1 William Jarden
gave £1 (he gave another £1 at his death in 1484) and Richard Livermore gave
3s. 4d.; and John Attwell bequeathed £2 in 1530. WAM 23467, 23554, 23559; PCW
Bracy, fos. 13ʳ–15ʳ. See also app. VIII under each of these names. For the 1476
indulgence, the sale of which raised money for the new work, see ch. 6 n. 203. All
told, non-royal secular contributions to the new work supplied barely 1.5% of the
total cost (calculated from the figures set out in Rackham, 'The Nave of
Westminster', 91).
[38] E. M. Hallam, 'Aspects of the Monastic Patronage of the English and French
Royal Houses, c.1130–1270', Ph.D. thesis, Univ. of London (1976), 323–6.
[39] See the list in Harvey, *Estates*, 387–99. There is a brief discussion ibid., 40; and
in Rosser, 'Medieval Westminster: The Vill and the Urban Community,
1200–1540', 165–8.

the interment in the abbey, after the early thirteenth century, of some less elevated individuals, and the existence of additional, short-term chantries. Yet the evidence of the monastic records and, in the first half of the sixteenth century, of local wills is unambiguous. The narrow society of those known to have been buried, or to have requested burial, in the abbey in the late Middle Ages was typified by Edward Beaupie (d. 1504), marshal of the king's hall; John Smith (d. 1510), gentleman of the royal chapel; and Anthony Leigh (d. 1517), chief clerk of the palace kitchen. All three were local residents during their lifetimes; the former two named their parish church of St Margaret in Westminster as an alternative place of burial.[40] The group was characteristic of the distinct class of courtier gentry which became a definite element in Westminster society at the end of the medieval period.[41]

The evident narrowing of lay patronage of the abbey is even more marked when set against the records of the parish church, which in the late Middle Ages display an increasing commitment to St Margaret's on the part of the entire range of local society. The lack of local interest in the new work of Westminster Abbey stands in extreme contrast to the mass involvement in the rebuilding of the parish church around 1500.[42] Moreover, Westminster residents sufficiently wealthy to found chantries for themselves tended to do so not in the abbey but in St Margaret's, while the poorer majority who desired commemoration achieved this through the collective chantries of guilds, which were also focused in the parish church.[43]

---

[40] In the event, both Beaupie and Smith were buried in St Margaret's, which their executors may have found easier to arrange than funerals at the abbey. Beaupie: PCW Wyks, 20–2; WAM 23126–7; CWA i. 502. Smith: PCK Wyks, 115–16; Reg Bk, i, fos. 116ᵛ–117ʳ, 145ᵛ–146ʳ; WAM 19756–65; 17928; 23128–39; 18911–17; CWA ii, s.a. 1510–11. Leigh (who wished to be buried in the abbey, in a tomb decorated with a carving of the Trinity and a Latin inscription, beside his former wife and her previous husband, Richard Stone; see below): PCW Wyks, 260–5; *LP* i, nos. 20 (p. 17), 82 (p. 39); Reg Bk, ii, fos. 34ᵛ–35ʳ, 69; WAM 19760–76; 18921–5. An extensive list of medieval burials in the abbey is provided in Harvey, *Estates*, 372–86. Those not noted there, who expressed the wish to be buried in the abbey, include, in addition to the above three: William Baynard, yeoman, d. 1513 (PCW Wyks, 186–7; WAM 23124); Henry Cotton of Westminster, d. 1513 (PCW Wyks, 191–2); Robert Davy, groom of the king's chamber, d. 1533 (PCW Bracy, fos. 28ᵛ–29ᵛ); John Griffith, treasurer of St David's, d. 1523 (PRO, PROB11/21, PCC 8 Bodfelde); Thomas Petit, gentleman of Westminster, d. 1504 (PCW Wyks, 12–13); and Richard Stone, gentleman of Westminster, d. 1504 (see app. VIII, s.n.).
[41] See ch. 5, sect. 9.
[42] See below, sect. 3.
[43] See ch. 9.

These contrasts surely reflect a preference, on the part of all but the wealthiest local inhabitants, for a relatively small, community church in which even the humblest contribution made its mark. The abbey, in its awesome grandeur, swallowed any but the most substantial contributions without visible effect.[44]

To this differentiation of scale was added a widespread trend in religious endowment during the later Middle Ages, whereby patronage was transferred away from the religious orders, to favour instead local institutions over which lay benefactors enjoyed a more direct control: parish churches, hospitals, and almshouses. In the urban environment of Norwich, for example, the great age of benefaction and building of religious houses of all orders was over by 1381; after that date the direction of lay patronage shifted emphatically to the parish churches.[45] The effects of this trend in Westminster redounded to the benefit of the parish church, as also of local guild-run charities,[46] and at the same time to the cooling of lay support for the monastery as a religious institution.

Against these changes, however, must be set the continuing links between the monastic and secular communities which existed at a personal level. A number of the monks were bound by ties of kinship to families in the town of Westminster. The most likely explanation of these relationships, in most cases, is the recruitment of monks to the abbey from within the urban society.[47] In the late fifteenth century Richard Breynt, a monk of Westminster Abbey, was associated as joint holder of property in Tothill Street with his brother, Peter Breynt, who was himself a secular valet of the convent.[48] In 1513 the widow of one 'Campion', describing herself in her will as 'Margaret Wykam of Westminster', named as the executors William Campion, a London plumber, and John Campion, an organist, and as the supervisor Dan John Campion, a

---

[44] A similar distinction has been observed in both York and Norwich, where late medieval townspeople founded their chantries in parish churches rather than in the cathedrals. Dobson, 'The Foundation of Perpetual Chantries by the Citizens of Medieval York', *Studies in Church History*, iv (1967), 22–38; Tanner, *Norwich*, 97.

[45] Alan Carter, unpub. paper read to the annual Pre-Modern Towns Meeting held at the Institute of Historical Research, London, on 5 Dec. 1981. Cf. also Tanner, *Norwich*, ch. 3; Keene, *Medieval Winchester*, i. 205.

[46] See chs. 9, 10.

[47] In general on the recruitment of monks to Westminster Abbey, see the forthcoming book by Barbara Harvey.

[48] WAM 23243–63; 19965; Pearce, *Monks*, 139. 'Piers Brente' was buried in St Margaret's church in 1491–2. CWA i. 285.

monk of Westminster.[49] Such ties of blood may explain why others were drawn to Westminster. Two fifteenth-century clothiers and mayors of London, John Gedney and Robert Drope, held property in Westminster and received corrodies at the abbey, where contemporary monks with the same surnames were almost certainly kinsmen.[50] The Thornwork family was already established in Westminster when Gervase Thornwork was admitted a monk of the abbey in *c.*1443. William Thornwork had first been engaged as a mason on the new work of the monastery in 1423, and continued in employment there until his death in *c.*1460. William's married son and daughter-in-law afterwards rented various properties in Westminster, as William himself had done. Although this son does not appear on the monastery's payroll, his wife in 1482–3 expressed by a gift of £3. 6s. 8d. the family's continuing active interest in the building work at the abbey. Gervase Thornwork, the monk, who died in 1467, was perhaps an older son of the abbey mason.[51]

The association of monks and townspeople was also evinced in the enrolment of several of the religious as members of the principal guild of Westminster, that of the Virgin Mary's Assumption.[52] Occasionally inhabitants of the town were entertained within the abbey, although these guests probably tended to be of the same wealthy class as was admitted for burial. In January 1511, for example, the prior gave a dinner for Mistress Antony Leigh (who, with her husband, was in fact later buried in the abbey) 'with other wives of the town'; and in March of the following year Mr Dyngeley, groom of the king's chamber, was supposed to have received similar hospitality.[53] The prior in addition, however, cultivated good relations with the lay servants and suppliers of the

[49] PCW Wyks, 227–9.
[50] Gedney: app. VIII, s.n. Drope: Beaven, *Aldermen*, ii. 13; *Cal Letter-Bk L*, *passim*; *Cal Plea & Mem R 1458–82, passim*; WAM 23234–60; 17795; 19966–78; and for a Westminster monk named John Drope, recorded between 1462 and 1500, Pearce, *Monks*, 159. By his will, made in 1485, Robert Drope left £20 to the new work of Westminster Abbey, and £8 to Dan John Drope. PRO, PROB11/8, PCC 4 Milles.
[51] App. VIII, s.n. Thornwork.
[52] See Assumption guild accts; and Pearce, *Monks*, s.n. Thomas Arundel, William Barnell, Thomas Brown, William Chertsey, William Chinnor, Edmund Downe, Thomas Millyng, Thomas Ruyton, Richard Tedington. Whether the monks obtained licence to attend the services and meetings of the guild does not appear.
[53] WAM 33325, fos. 5ᵛ, 45ʳ.

house, inviting in September 1511 'Mistress Cheesman and the bakers and butchers, with other strangers'.[54]

A shift of lay commitment in the late Middle Ages away from the abbey as a primary claimant of local religious loyalty; a persistent degree of familiarity at the personal level: these are observable phenomena. To what extent they determined, or were conditioned by, the reputation of the monks as holy men is difficult to determine. The townspeople never hesitated to charge the religious, in the manor court, with offences of nuisance, and occasionally a note of moral censure can perhaps be detected, as in an accusation brought in 1410 against a prostitute: 'Marion who is staying in the sacrist's rent'.[55] Such ironies of ecclesiastical property holding were probably not as a rule perceived as hypocrisy. But a few years before this particular incident, a more serious accusation had been brought against the monk-archdeacon of Westminster, Bartholemew Hayne, who was said to have blackmailed fornicators in the town, exacting fines of 20*d*. or 40*d*. from whores and their pimps, 'in order that he should conceal their sins and so dismiss them unpunished, without charge'.[56] The piquancy of this situation is heightened by the fact that, at the same period, the Westminster brothels numbered monks among their clients; but in fairness to the abbey community it must be added that these religious were not specifically stated to come from the local house.[57] Urban temptations—shops, taverns, dances, brothels—were commonly too close to Benedictine communities, as fifteenth-century visitations of the abbeys of Bardney and Peterborough make plain.[58] In the absence of normal visitation records, however, the Westminster monks must be allowed to have enjoyed, so far as is known, the largely passive respect of their secular neighbours.[59] But at the dissolution of the house in 1540 the laity of Westminster made no protest.[60] The inactivity of the townspeople at this crisis appears veritable indifference when it is compared with their vigorous

---

[54] Ibid., fo. 23ᵛ.   [55] WAM 50740.   [56] PRO, KB9/179/40.
[57] See ch. 5 n. 117.
[58] A. H. Thompson (ed.), *Visitations of Religious Houses*, 3 vols., Lincoln Record Society (1914–29), ii. 14, 23, 32; iii. 272. But for a more favourable record see Dobson, *Durham Priory*, 80.
[59] It is notable that no allegations were made against the abbey by the commissioners at the Dissolution. Westlake, *Westminster Abbey*, 206.
[60] As they did in other places, possibly because these were less directly under the eye of royal government. Cf. Youings, *Dissolution of the Monasteries*, 164–5 (Exeter); F. A. Gasquet, *Henry VIII and the English Monasteries*, 2 vols. (London, 1889), ii. 35–40 (Hexham).

defence of St Margaret's parish church as soon as that building, a few years later, came under attack.[61]

3. THE REBUILDING OF THE PARISH CHURCH, 1485–1525

The life of the parish is poorly documented before the late fifteenth century; but the great rebuilding of St Margaret's church around 1500 presents a vivid and telling contrast with the desultory secular interest in the new work of the abbey throughout its slow progress from the mid-fourteenth century onwards. The church of St Margaret which stands today was begun in c.1487 and was complete by 1523.[62] The cost was divided unequally between the parish, which initiated the work and paid for the new nave and aisles in their entirety, and the monks who, as rector, financed the completion of the choir.[63] The chronology of construction, and the distribution of the expense, indicate that the dominant partner was the parish. The way in which the venture was carried out shows how effectively the parishioners could co-operate in such a major undertaking.[64]

The first point of interest about the project is its timing. The original, probably eleventh-century, church may be presumed to have been of stone, yet simple in plan; rectangular, with a single nave. There is some ground for believing that the nave of this early church was rebuilt in c.1300, to accommodate the great increase in the local population which took place during the thirteenth century.[65] Later, when at the start of the fifteenth century the abbey

[61] See below.
[62] On the present fabric see Royal Commission on Historical Monuments, *London*, ii. 99–104 and pls. 149–52; Pevsner, *The Buildings of England: London*, vol. i (3rd edn., London, 1973), 493–5.
[63] In general on the responsibility for upkeep of the fabric of parish churches in the early sixteenth century, see R. A. Houlbrooke, *Church Courts and the People during the English Reformation, 1520–1570* (Oxford, 1979), ch. 6. See also below, n. 66.
[64] The progress of the work is recorded primarily in the biennial accounts of the churchwardens (which survive from 1460), and for the choir, in the rolls of the abbey's department of the new work. See below for refs.
[65] It was believed in the fifteenth century that the church had been rebuilt under Edward I, by 'parochiani et mercatores lanarum quamplurimi'. See LN, fo. 76ᵛ. Stow was obviously mistaken in associating these merchants with the Wool Staple, which was not set up until 1353. See Stow, *A Survey*, ii. 112; followed by Walcott, *The History of the Parish Church of St. Margaret, in Westminster* (Westminster, 1847), 10; and Westlake, *St. Margaret's Westminster*, 4, 8.

sacrist (as vicar) renovated the chancel of the parish church, the parishioners contributed the cost of glazing the new east window.[66] Otherwise, however, no major work is recorded in the history of the church between the possible rebuilding of c.1300 and the great reconstruction inaugurated in the 1480s. This massive scheme was undertaken in a period which other evidence has shown to have been marked by rapid growth in the population of Westminster.[67] Nevertheless it would be wrong to conclude from the church-building that the town was currently enjoying a degree of economic prosperity commensurate with the increase in population. On the contrary, per capita wealth is likely to have been declining.[68] The enormous investment of personal resources in the public work of building St Margaret's was not the overspill of superfluous riches. Rather, within an economy which showed hardly any sign of expansion, the reconstructed parish church represented a positive commitment which had little to do with individual economic fortunes, and much more with the collective desire to erect a major public building in the town.[69]

The church which resulted is obviously the product of a single plan. It is probable that the designer and first master mason of the work was Robert Stowell, who was until his death in 1505 the master of the abbey masons.[70] The progress of the work was supervised, meanwhile, by a (probably fluctuating) group of senior parishioners. Decisions concerning the building were said to be made, for example, 'by the assent of the worshipful of the parish', or 'by the assent of divers of the honest men of the town'.[71] The church

[66] In 1399–1400 the sacrist laid out £4. 6s. 8d. 'pro s̄cura cancelle Sancte Margarete'. WAM 19659. In 1422–3 (after a gap in the records) work was in progress on the chancel roof and on 'the great window behind the high altar'. This window was glazed, at the considerable cost of £8. 13s. 4d., by the subscription of the parishioners. WAM 19663. The widening (*elargacionem*) of the chancel was evidently completed in 1424–5; and the structure was whitewashed in 1427–8. WAM 19666, 19669. In 1426–7 the almoner paid 10s. to the churchwardens of St Margaret's 'for the new chancel made there', presumably as a reward for their share in the work. WAM 19033. This instance of the parishioners' partial responsibility for the fabric of the chancel, in addition to the nave, of their church was not particularly unusual. Such an arrangement was said in 1430 to be common in London parish churches. W. Lyndwood, *Provinciale* (Oxford, 1679), 253 gloss q.
[67] See ch. 6, sect. 1.   [68] See ch. 6 nn. 63–7.
[69] Cf. Keene, *Medieval Winchester*, i. 116–18, 126–8.
[70] There is evidence of prior co-operation in 1482 × 1484, when Stowell 'lent' two masons to the churchwardens. CWA i, s.a. (entry printed in Westlake, *St. Margaret's Westminster*, 150). Further on Stowell see app. VIII, s.n.
[71] CWA i. 487, 539.

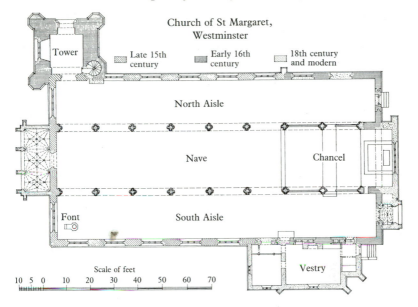

FIG. 11. St Margaret's parish church, Westminster. Plan (RCHME)

erected under their direction was broad, spacious, and light. (Illus. 8 and Fig. 11.) The first part of the new work, commenced between 1486 and 1488, was the erection of an additional aisle on the south side of the church; the existing edifice comprised only nave and a north aisle. From 1488 the churchwardens expended £20 on the roof of 'the new aisle', which was in use by Easter, 1490.[72] This lateral extension of the church indicates that, as has already been suggested, one reason for the rebuilding was a need of greater space for the accommodation of a bursting congregation. At the same time the design of the new church as a whole, which was carried forward from 1492 onwards, conforms to a general type much favoured in urban parishes in the later Middle Ages. The type

[72] The accounts for 1486–88 are lost. Only a north aisle ('St George's aisle') is mentioned in CWA before the rebuilding. CWA i. 215, 257. The works of 1489–90, moreover, included the lateral extension of the old church roof to cover the new south aisle of the Holy Trinity, which seems therefore to have been a new addition: 'paid to William Gervys for lengthening of every rafter of the old roof and returning of the same down again to the roof of the new aisle. 3s. 4d.' In that accounting year, rushes were bought 'to straw the new aisle at Easter'. CWA i. 258–9, 261, 287, 290, 292.

is distinguished by the generous simplicity of its architecture, especially in the slender piers and broad arcades of the nave and in the unfussy relationship between the different compartments of the building. All these characteristics are emphasized at St Margaret's by the architecturally unbroken unity of nave and chancel. The influence of the friars' churches is apparent, and may reflect a growth in the town parishes of an interest in preaching.[73] The choice of design by the parishioners of Westminster represented a deliberate and resounding contrast to the work simultaneously in progress at the adjacent abbey, where the nave of the monastery church was at last approaching completion according to a grandiose, essentially French design of the thirteenth century, while the eastern royal chapel of Henry VII was piling up in a *tour de force* of encrusted, fantastical high Gothic. The sober modern clarity of the town church expressed an order of piety different from both of these.

The design was carried out with expedition. In 1492 the parishioners were granted permission to demolish a building called 'the king's poultry', which stood in the way of the eastern extension of the church.[74] Two years later Henry Abingdon, the master of the king's chapel singers, gave 13s. 4d. towards the 'performing' of the choir, 'from the side door to the high altar'. At this date Richard Russell, the chief carpenter of Westminster Abbey, 'closed in' the choir between the same stated limits, doubtless in preparation for the removal of the existing eastern side chapels and the completion of the new north and south aisles.[75] Thus enclosed, the choir could meanwhile continue in use. That the remainder of the old fabric was

[73] A surviving London church of this type is that of St Giles, Cripplegate, rebuilt like St Margaret's, Westminster, by subscription of the parishioners in c.1545–50. See Pevsner, *London*, vol. i, pl. 32. None of the London friars' churches survives, but see e.g. the mid-fourteenth-century church of the Austin Friars, the nave of which survived until 1940. Royal Commission on Historical Monuments, *London*, iv (HMSO, London, 1929), 32 and pl. 51.

[74] *Cal Pat R 1485–94*, p. 389. In the preceding years, 1490–2, only relatively minor expenses on stone and craftsmen's wages are recorded. CWA i. 290–2.

[75] CWA i. 303, 310. (The accounts for 1492–4 are missing.) For Russell see Harvey, *English Mediaeval Architects*, 262–4. The earlier chancel, probably as a result of the 'widening' of c.1420–30 (see above, n. 66), opened into side chapels to north (the Lady chapel) and south (the Trinity chapel). The Trinity chapel is recorded in 1464–6, the Lady chapel in 1466–7. CWA i. 43, 84. The locations of these two fifteenth-century chapels are inferred from their respective positions after the rebuilding, and also, in the latter case, from a ref. in 1467–8 to the 'itus inter chorum et capellam beate Marie'. CWA i. 87.

dismantled, and the new erected, in sections—again with an obvious view to the continuance of services in the building—is indicated by the intermittent references to work on the new roofs, which were partially leaded in 1497–8, in 1499–1500, and in 1501.[76] The materials of the new masonry were a combination of ragstone from south-east England and the finer Caen stone from Normandy.[77] The structural walls and arcades were probably complete by 1499–1500, when Walter Martyn, the foreman of the working masons, received a reward 'for finishing of the new works'.[78] In the following year the eastern chapels (at the aisle ends) were paved, and in 1500–1 the windows of the west end and north aisle were inserted.[79] The completed roof was tiled in 1502–3.[80] It was also now possible to ceil internally the six bays of the nave, for which Richard Russell received £9. 6s. 8d. for 'the two first severies' (bays) in December 1502, and £14. 13s. 4d. for 'the two last severies next the choir door' in November 1503. Russell's carved ceiling, apparently with rosettes in the panels, so pleased the parishioners that he was voted an additional reward of £2.[81] Meanwhile, after the completion of the roof, the masons erected 'battlements' and 'pinnacles' around the crests of the outer walls of the church. Eight 'dragons' were carved in 1502, perhaps to look out from the pinnacles, and eight 'gargyns' in 1504.[82] The church was paved within in 1503–4, by which date, with the exceptions of the choir and the tower, it was essentially complete.[83]

There ensued a pause in building, which lasted for ten years.[84]

---

[76] CWA i. 345, 380, 431.

[77] The main purchases of stone were made between 1496 and 1501, and were divided as follows: Reigate stone, 78 tons and 20 loads; ragstone, 20 tons; Caen stone, 44 tons. CWA i. 339–82, *passim*. Caen stone was used to dress important features, such as 'quoins to the battlement of the church'. CWA i. 518. As a result of repeated restoration since the seventeenth century, the church is now clad in dull Portland stone.

[78] CWA i. 380.

[79] CWA i. 422, 428.

[80] CWA i. 454. The discarded materials of the old roof were sold in this year (ibid).

[81] CWA i. 455. Russell's fee for the middle two bays is not recorded. The timber was an additional cost. Russell's roof, which is no longer extant, is probably that glimpsed, at the chancel end, in the seventeenth century engraving reproduced in Westlake, *St. Margaret's Westminster*, pl. 7.

[82] CWA i. 457, 486, 489–91, 518. The cost of each set of dragons and gargoyles was 6s. 8d.

[83] CWA i. 481, 488. 8,000 paving tiles cost £9. 13s. 4d.

[84] Pews were installed in this period, and a new font. CWA i. 539; CWA ii, s.a. 1511–12.

But in 1515 the first stone of the new steeple was laid, on which occasion 'worshipful and well-disposed people of this parish' gave £6 towards its completion.[85] The first master mason of the tower, Thomas Redman, was succeeded on his death in 1516 by his son, Henry; like Robert Stowell before them, these two were also successively in charge of the abbey masons, while Henry was additionally chief mason of the crown.[86] Only the lowest stage of the present tower dates from the sixteenth century (the remainder having been rebuilt in the eighteenth); the authentic Redman plan, however, is striking above all for its scale, which is massive even in proportion to the body of the church.[87] The tower was finished in time for the consecration of the church in 1523. Meanwhile in 1517–18 the chancel was rebuilt in conformity with the overall design. The primary responsibility of the monk-rectors for the chancel was greatly reduced on this occasion by the parishioners' prior completion of the long aisles which flanked the choir to the north and south. Even so, the impatient parishioners urged the work forward with a donation of £30. The outstanding cost to the monks was a mere £160. The east wall was quickly raised, the wooden ceiling over the high altar (once more the work of Richard Russell) carved, painted, and gilded, and the great east window glazed at a cost of £15. 7s. 4d.[88] The sculptural decoration of the stonework of the new east end included the mark of the patron whose contribution had in fact been so relatively slight; the rebus of Abbot John Islip (1500–32).[89]

Despite the interruption of structural work between 1504 and 1515, the new parish church of St Margaret was completed in two impressively short bursts of activity. In contrast to the monks'

[85] CWA ii, s.a. 1515–16.

[86] CWA ii, s.a. 1515–23. Thomas Redman requested burial at his death in St Margaret's church. PCW Wyks, 218. Henry Redman died in 1528 at his house in Brentford, where he was buried in the parish church. The brass memorial to him there was recently still extant; the church is now disused. See *TLMAS* 2nd ser., xi (1954), 51–4 and pl. after p. 52.

[87] Royal Commission on Historical Monuments, *London*, ii. 101*b*.

[88] WAM 23602. The monks financed the task through their department of the new work. In 1505 the sacrist had spent a small sum on the chancel of St Margaret's, no doubt simply to make good after completion of the parishioners' work in the flanking aisles. WAM 33293, fo. 3^{r–v}.

[89] Stones carved with Islip's monogram and a foliage sprig or *slip* of a tree were found when the chancel was remodelled in 1905. Royal Commission on Historical Monuments, *London* ii, 104*a*.

expenditure on the chancel of £160, the total cost to the parishioners of their new church was in the region of £2,000.[90] This vast sum, moreover, was raised not by a few rich individuals but by the collective body of the parish. It is true that an early seventeenth-century tradition attributes the rebuilding of the south aisle to a benefaction of Lady Mary Billing. Lady Billing, whose last of three husbands had been Sir Thomas Billing, lord chief justice of England, was buried in 1499 in the new south aisle of the church, near the east end, where she erected a fine Purbeck marble monument, inlaid with brasses, to her own memory and that of her three spouses; the location and reported splendour of the tomb make her involvement with the project very probable.[91] But by far the greater part of the funds was raised by popular subscription. Whereas the ordinary annual receipts of the churchwardens, from offerings and bequests, was about £25 in this period, the most active years of the rebuilding produced dramatic increases in the parochial income. The average annual total doubled once in 1498–1502 to c.£50, and again in the following two years to £110. During the rebuilding of the tower, between 1516 and 1522, the yearly revenue fluctuated between £110 and the impressive peak of £190.[92] Virtually every parishioner was a benefactor of 'the church work', from a waterman, who gave 20*d*., to a London clothier living at Westminster, who contributed 20*s*.[93] The donors included many of the craftsmen employed on the site. The master mason of the tower, Henry Redman, each year returned his entire wage to the churchwardens, as also did the local brewer who organized the carriage of building materials.[94] John Mower, 'the lime man', and John Orgar, 'the ashlar man', each gave a shilling or two towards the steeple in 1516–17.[95] In 1497–8 Mr Cokkes, an armourer, left 'four

[90] This figure is an estimate, for which, however, reasonable accuracy can be claimed. The incompleteness of the accounts during a few busy years of the rebuilding prevents an exact addition of expenses.
[91] See CWA i. 367; J. Weever, *Ancient Funerall Monuments* (London, 1631), 493; E. Hatton, *A New View of London* (London, 1708), i. 329–30. A Purbeck marble fragment of a frieze of panels containing shields in relief, of late-fifteenth-century date and almost certainly, in view of the similar feature shown in an engraving in Weever (loc. cit.), from the Billing tomb, is still preserved at the east end of the church, attached to the south internal wall.
[92] CWA, s.a.
[93] CWA i. 308, 548 (for the clothier, Robert Morley, see app. VIII, s.n.).
[94] CWA ii, *passim*. The brewer was John Pomfrett, for whom see app. VIII, s.n.
[95] CWA ii, s.a.

pairs of brigandines' to the church; these cluttered the vestry for
some years, but were finally sold in 1502–4 for a total of 16s. 4d.[96]
One of the most humble contributions was that of 'two old boards',
given by a lay brother of the abbey in 1491–2 and sold for 8d.[97]

Fund-raising activities were organized, such as a parish lottery
and a children's 'May game'.[98] In 1497 there occurs the first
reference to the adult game of 'hocking'. 'Hock money' was exacted
on the third Monday after Easter by the men from the captured and
bound women of the parish, and on the succeeding Tuesday, when
the enslavement was reversed, by the women. This equalizing ritual
was practised in many English parishes in the Middle Ages; its first
recorded appearance at Westminster at this particular period may
have been specifically intended, leaving aside its therapeutic appeal,
to raise money for the new church.[99] The more ambitious policy
adopted by the churchwardens after 1502, to defray the cost of the
building, would now be described as an 'appeal'. In that year a
'benevolence' was introduced, to which long lists of individuals (all
honourably named in the churchwardens' accounts) were persuaded to subscribe. The 'benevolence' raised over £8 in the first
year and double that sum in the second. At the same time, separate
collections were made, from house to house throughout the parish,
which advanced the fund by a total of £50 or £60 between 1502 and
1504.[100] During the period of the rebuilding of the tower, offerings
in the ordinary parochial collection boxes, usually about £10 a year,
grew to an annual total of £15; and a fresh 'benevolence' added £5
in 1519. Meanwhile, new 'gathering boxes' placed in the church
brought in between £40 and £50 in *each* of the five years from 1516
to 1521.[101] Yet further contributions to the steeple fund, collectively
the most substantial of all, were made by various guilds maintained
by the townspeople.[102] But the most telling scene of all was
occasioned in 1522–3, by the finding of the new steeple bells. After
three bells had been cast out of the old set, and a fourth had been

---

[96] CWA i. 337, 448, 475.

[97] CWA i. 286; this was presumably the status of Bartholemew the 'lay monk'.

[98] CWA, s.a. 1502–4, 1516–17, 1518–19; and see Westlake, *St. Margaret's Westminster*, 168.

[99] Sums of £1–£3 p.a. were levied. CWA i. 335, etc.

[100] CWA i. 437, 450–1, 477, 481.

[101] CWA ii, s.a. The total contents of the special 'gathering boxes' during these five years amounted to over £230.

[102] CWA ii, *passim*. For the guilds see ch. 9.

presented by one of the parochial guilds, dedicated to the Virgin Mary's Assumption, there still lacked one to complete the peal. To provide this, the churchwardens made a collection, 'in going about the parish', of a great number of pewter pots, latten basins, and the like, which were then delivered to the founder for casting. So much potential bell-metal was accumulated that the surplus was sold for cash. When the new bells were hung at last, in 1527–8, the first peal to be rung upon them, from the gleaming white tower in the heart of the town, celebrated a genuinely communal achievement.[103]

4. IMAGES AND RITUAL

The reconstruction of St Margaret's church, the sole major public building of the town, expressed not only the religious piety, but also the civic pride, of the parishioners. The patron saint herself was a public figure, placed at the centre both of the urban church and of an elaboration of associated imagery and ritual. These, like the church-building, gave symbolic and tangible expression to the communal identity of the townspeople-parishioners.[104] The high altar, which as always belonged primarily to God the Father, naturally claimed the additional patronage of St Margaret. Here, no doubt, was kept the relic of St Margaret's finger for which a new silver case was made in 1515–16.[105] A statue of the saint also stood in the chancel, the figure bearing in her hand a cross-staff with which, surely, she smote her foe the dragon.[106] A coral rosary on a silver chain, with a pearl clasp, was given by an offerant in 1499–1500, to be hung upon the image of St Margaret each day, or each feast day, as the churchwardens thought best.[107] As often in the late Middle Ages, St Margaret was paired with St Catherine, whose own statue stood near the other in the chancel; St Catherine was distinguished

[103] CWA ii, s.a. 1522–3, 1527–8.
[104] Cf. Phythian-Adams, 'Ceremony and the Citizen'.
[105] CWA ii, s.a.; and church inventory of 1511 in CWA ii, s.a. 1510–11.
[106] CWA ii, s.a. 1515–16; the staff was painted and gilded. The dragon is not specified, but typically 'Margret ys payntyd oþur carven wher scho ys wyth a dragon undyr her fete and a cros yn her hand, schowyng how by vertu of þe cros scho gate þe victory of þe fynde'. Mirk, *Festial*, 201.
[107] CWA i. 386.

by her wheel.[108] After the completion of the rebuilding of the church, a pair of wooden 'tabernacles' was made in honour of the two saints; these were evidently large, decorated frames to contain the statues. The tabernacle of St Margaret was erected over the north side of the high altar in 1525–6, while that of St Catherine, set up in 1527–8, evidently flanked the same altar to the south. The carver, Roger Weston of St Albans, received £26. 13s. 4d. for St Margaret's tabernacle, with a further 'reward' of £3. 6s. 8d., and a like sum of £30 for the tabernacle of St Catherine. The former incorporated three 'stories' of St Margaret, carved in relief, which were painted and gilded, as were twelve additional small images on the same tabernacle. Above each tabernacle a crown (for the martyrs) was suspended.[109] Like the construction of the church itself, the making of these elaborate decorations involved the parish at large. Gifts towards the expense of St Catherine's tabernacle were made in 1527–8 by about seventy people, and came to almost £10. At this time three of the fraternities made additional contributions totally nearly £8; 'the maidens' gathering' (presumably that on May Day) added a further sum of 34s. 10d. The gilding of St Margaret's tabernacle was more than paid for by 'the benevolence of good people', who included some sixty parishioners in addition to the body of the Virgin Mary's guild.[110]

The patronal festival of St Margaret (20 July) was marked by a peak of collective parochial activity. On that day, the high altar in the church was decorated with rich Arras cloths and other hangings of silk, borrowed specially for the occasion, usually from one of the royal residences near London.[111] On the eve of the feast, a bonfire was lit before the church door, and was watched until dawn. The celebrations of the day itself began with the festive mass in the church, at which members of the abbey choir or of the king's chapel assisted, retiring afterwards with the churchwardens to the

---

[108] St Catherine's wheel was repaired in 1460–1. CWA i. 11–12. The 1511 inventory itemizes 'two curtains of blue buckram that hang before St Margaret and St Catherine'. CWA ii, s.a. 1510–11. St Catherine and St Margaret were similarly associated, for example, in the Corpus Christi procession in sixteenth-century Coventry. *Records of Early English Drama. Coventry*, ed. R. W. Ingram (Manchester, 1981), 152.

[109] CWA ii, s.a. 1523–4 *et seq.*

[110] Ibid.

[111] e.g. decorations were borrowed in 1496 from Greenwich, in 1497 from Sheen, in 1531 from York Place. CWA i. 339, 343; CWA ii, iii, s.a. In 1484 the keeper of Westminster Palace loaned cloths of gold and silk. CWA i. 235, 238.

tavern.[112] The unmarried girls of the town then made a procession through the parish, in honour of St Margaret's redoubtable chastity. The girls, attired in special costumes and no doubt preceded on their route by St Margaret's banner, were serenaded the while by a band of minstrels.[113] The highlight of the day was the performance of a play of St Margaret. The tribulations of that young lady's short career afforded material for a highly dramatic spectacle, the climax of which was the saint's encounter with a dragon. For when the monster was in the very act of devouring its victim it was caused, by the latter's declaration of her faith, to explode. Repairs to the dragon are periodically noted in the churchwarden's accounts.[114]

The main feasts of the church year were also, in Westminster as elsewhere, the occasions for parochial activity. Social priorities were observed, and indeed affirmed, by the participants. On Palm Sunday, the Passion Gospel was read by 'the principals of the parish', who also processed through the town after Easter, on Ascension Day.[115] A greater procession followed on the feast of Corpus Christi, probably led in this case by a Corpus Christi brotherhood formed by the parishioners. In 1466–7 a new canopy of cloth of gold was bought, to carry above the host in the Corpus Christi procession. On this day the parish church was decorated with garlands of red roses and other flowers, and minstrels played in the town.[116] At Christmas, the perennial decorations were brought

[112] e.g. CWA i. 163, 235.

[113] e.g. Mistress Forde provided 'the virgins' clothes' in 1523–4. CWA ii, s.a. A new banner of St Margaret was bought with the proceeds of a hock-day collection in 1509–10. CWA i. 574. In 1505 'the minstrels of London' came on St Margaret's day; in 1532 and in 1533 a minstrel named Grene performed 'before the virgins'. CWA i. 538; CWA ii, s.a.

[114] e.g. in 1491: 'For dressing of the dragon and for packthread. 4d.' CWA i. 290. For explicit ref. to 'a play' on this day see e.g. CWA ii, s.a. 1529–30. No medieval English text of a St Margaret play is known, although the saint's popularity is shown by numerous extant copies of her *Life*, and by her very frequent representation in art. There exists a sixteenth-century printed version of a French play of St Margaret, which called for a large cast of forty-four characters. *La Vie de Sainte Marguerite, Poème inédit de Wace*, ed. A. Joly (Paris, 1879), 35–46. In Italy, where the saint's body was claimed to rest, a dramatization in verse of her life ran into numerous printed editions in the second half of the sixteenth century. *La Rappresentazione di S. Margherita Vergine e Martire* (Florence, 1554, etc.).

[115] e.g. CWA ii, s.a. 1510–11.

[116] For the Corpus Christi guild see notebook accounts of the curate of St Margaret's *c.*1514: 'Item payd to corpus xp̄i brethered. 4d.' (presumably a membership fee); it seems probable that the brotherhood mentioned was based in Westminster. WAM 33300, fo. 18. For the canopy, see CWA i. 83. For the minstrels and flowers, CWA i. 11, 45, 235, etc.

in to St Margaret's; the holly bush was 'hung up' and arrayed with holm, ivy, and candles.[117] On that feast day, the children of the king's chapel choir were invited to sing in the church.[118]

In addition to these traditional festivals, the parish of St Margaret showed its responsiveness to developments in the church calendar by its adoption, in 1500, of three new Christian feast days. These were the feasts of the Visitation of the Virgin Mary (2 July), of the Transfiguration (6 August), and of the Name of Jesus (7 August).[119] The first of these, although it had been instituted by the pope in 1389, did not spread until Sixtus IV established the feast for a second time in 1475.[120] The cult of the Transfiguration was much older, but its liturgical expression was confined before the later fifteenth century to a few religious houses. It was officially promulgated as a universal feast by Callistus III in 1457, yet was not regularly incorporated in editions of the Sarum use until the 1490s, and even then was by no means everywhere accepted. It was, however, adopted by Westminster Abbey in 1487–8.[121] The Name of Jesus was a devotional cult of which a liturgical form existed in England from the mid-fourteenth century. Service-books of *c.*1500, however, 'show that the Name of Jesus was not yet at this time a generally received feast'.[122] The first observance in St Margaret's of the last-mentioned devotion antedated by a few years the erection within the abbey of a Jesus chapel.[123] The spread of this particular feast around 1500 was due in part to the patronage of Lady Margaret Beaufort; its early adoption in Westminster was therefore most natural.[124] The introduction to the parish church of all three is indicative of an awareness, on the part of some, at least, of the Westminster parishioners, of current religious trends.

[117] CWA i. 376, 429, etc.
[118] CWA i. 238.
[119] Thomas Herte was paid 40s. for 'the making, writing, noting, limning, binding and for the stuff of 3 new feasts, that is to say, the Visitation of Our Lady, *de Nomine Jhesu*, and Transfiguration of Our Lord, that is to wit in 5 antiphonaries and a legend, 4 grails, 4 mass books, and 4 processionaries'. CWA i. 383.
[120] R. W. Pfaff, *New Liturgical Feasts in Later Medieval England* (Oxford, 1970), 40–61. Caxton printed at Westminster a rare early edition of Pope Sixtus's *Officium Visitationis* in 1480. Painter, *William Caxton*, 102–3.
[121] Pfaff, *New Liturgical Feasts*, 13–39; WAM 19735.
[122] Pfaff, *New Liturgical Feasts*, 62–83. There had been earlier guilds of Jesus, such as that in the crypt of St Paul's London, probably founded shortly before 1459. *Cal Pat R 1452–61*, p. 480.
[123] See Westlake, *Westminster Abbey: The Last Days of the Monastery* (London, 1921), 108–9.   [124] Pfaff, *New Liturgical Feasts*, 83.

5. THE REFORMATION

The passage of the Reformation left remarkably few traces in the records of St Margaret's parish. The churchwardens' accounts during the 1540s contain typical entries of the period: the sale of plate to pay for the new 'high altar table'; the whitewashing of the church interior and the setting up of the Ten Commandments; the removal of the churchyard crosses.[125] Some of the changes caused regret in the hearts of at least a few parishioners. It is indeed hardly surprising that the ejection of the elaborate wooden tabernacles, which had been the proudly maintained glories of the chancel, was for some a disappointment. They were saved from destruction at this time by William Henbury, who paid 40s. for them.[126] 'Mr Sylvester', who acquired in this way 'an old screen' out of the church (presumably painted with religious images), was probably the Thomas Silvester who had been a churchwarden of St Margaret's in 1526–8 and, more recently, twice a warden of Our Lady's guild.[127] Yet, these touching acts of individual parishioners apart, the process of the Reformation appears from the surviving evidence to have caused very little disruption in the life of the parish.

The absence of recorded disturbances associated with the religious reforms is a paradox which needs to be resolved. In view of the foregoing account of parochial life in the decades before the Reformation, this phenomenon cannot be attributed to lack of interest or involvement on the part of the parishioners. Their continuing enthusiasm for the church which they had recently built was shown when in 1549 Protector Somerset attempted to pull the building down, to provide stone for the construction of Somerset House in the Strand:

The workmen had no sooner advanced their scaffolds when the parishioners gathered together in great multitudes, with bows and arrows,

[125] CWA iii, s.a. 1545–6, 1547–8, 1548–9.
[126] CWA iii, s.a. 1547–8. Mr Jenyns and Mr Ludford paid 2s. and 1s., respectively, for the mere bases of similar tabernacles which had stood in the chapels of Our Lady and of the Holy Trinity. CWA iii, s.a. 1550–1. Jenyns had been a member of the Assumption guild; Nicholas Ludford, a musician in the royal chapel, had supplied compositions to the parish church in the 1530s. See Assumption guild accts; CWA iii, s.a.
[127] CWA iii, s.a. 1550–1; see app. VIII, s.n.; and further below.

staves and clubs, and other such offensive weapons, which so terrified the workmen that they ran away in great amazement, and never could be brought again upon that employment.[128]

In fact, it is precisely their active commitment which explains the apparently surprising welcome given by the inhabitants of Westminster to the innovations of the mid-sixteenth century. The Henrician and Edwardian statutes were not necessarily regarded as militant threats by an atrophied and intransigent church, and a sullen or indifferent laity. By many in Westminster, they may have been viewed as modern features suitable for adoption in a parish which, during recent generations, had prided itself on its receptivity to new ideas. The most striking expression of this was the complete rebuilding of the parish church in a contemporary style. The forms of activity within the church were also evolving before and after 1500. Three new feasts were introduced, with their offices,[129] while the music which accompanied these and other services was equally up to date, showing off the polyphonic inventions of the composers of the nearby royal chapel.[130]

One particular feature of the Protestant reforms, the emphasis on preaching, had been anticipated in the parish. In 1482 William Jarden, a prosperous tailor of Westminster, made a grant to Queen's College, Oxford, of his Tothill Street inn called the Catherine Wheel. By one of the conditions of this bequest, the provost and masters of the college undertook to find a learned priest (he was to be a master of arts and a scholar, 'at least', in sacred theology) who would pray perpetually for the souls of William Jarden and his wife, and who also, once a year, would travel to Westminster to 'preach to the people the word of God' in St Margaret's church.[131] Although only three of the late medieval curates of the Westminster church are known to have been university graduates, nevertheless the

[128] P. Heylyn, *Ecclesia Restaurata; or, the History of the Reformation of the Church of England* (London, 1661), 72–3.
[129] See above, n. 119.
[130] The singers of St Stephen's Chapel made regular visits to the parish church. CWA, *passim*. For the originality of their compositions see Baillie, 'London Churches, their Music and Musicians', 17 and *passim*.
[131] Oxford, Bodleian Library, MS D.D. Queen's Coll. 1766. The name of Jarden's hostelry is another small sign of local fondness for St Catherine. The college held the property until 1917, when it was sold to the London Electric Railway Company for £16,600. Oxford, The Queen's College, MSS 4 N. 17, 27, 44, 109, 123. The headquarters building of London Regional Transport (no. 55, Broadway) now stands partially on the site. For Jarden see also app VIII, s.n.

visiting preacher to St Margaret's could expect a good audience.[132] When, in 1478–9, a sermon was to be given at the church by 'Dr Penkey'—who is perhaps to be identified with Thomas Penketh, a learned friar and prior provincial of the Augustinian Order in England—a pulpit was specially erected in the churchyard, which suggests that a large attendance was anticipated.[133] The very design of the new parish church begun a few years later seems to have been deliberately chosen to facilitate indoor preaching.[134] By the 1520s distinguished preachers were also being regularly invited, on the several feasts of the Virgin Mary, to the chapel of the guild hospital of St Mary Rounceval by Charing Cross.[135] The preachers here in 1520–1 included the learned vicar of St Bride's in Fleet Street, Nicholas Miles, STP;[136] and the sermon at the Virgin's Assumption (25 March) in 1522 was delivered by the vicar of Croydon, whose invitation had been booked several months in advance.[137] The latter was Rowland Phillips, 'one of the most eloquent of English preachers' and Thomas More's model for the missionary bishop in *Utopia*.[138] These visiting preachers were given a dinner for their pains; after his efforts on Lady Day in 1539, Dr Kichin was refreshed with a pike and a gallon of wine.[139] The monks of Westminster, also, made a point of providing public sermons of a high standard, some of which were presumably delivered in the abbey itself.[140]

It need, after all, come as no surprise to find such modern behaviour and attitudes in Westminster, whose proximity to the royal courts and to London exposed it to all manner of cosmopolitan influences. One of the most penetrating innovations of the period,

[132] William Ravenyng, William Balard, William Mote; see app. II.

[133] CWA i. 161. Thomas Penketh returned to England in 1479 from the university of Padua, where he had been lecturing in theology. Emden, *A Biographical Register of the University of Oxford to A.D. 1500* (Oxford, 1957–9), 1457.

[134] See above, sect. 3.

[135] Rounceval guild accts, *passim*. For the guild and hospital see ch. 10, sect. 5.

[136] Guild accts, s.a.; G. Hennessy, *Novum Repertorium Ecclesiasticum Parochiale Londinense* (London, 1898), 113. Miles was a leading London clergyman.

[137] Guild accts, s.a. 1520–2. In 1520–1 a man had been sent 'to give us warning whether the vicar of Croydon would come or no'.

[138] S. E. Brigden, *London and the Reformation* (forthcoming), chs. 1, 6, for Phillips. I am grateful to Dr Brigden for allowing me to read her book before its publication.

[139] Guild accts, s.a.

[140] B. F. Harvey, 'The Monks of Westminster and the University of Oxford', in Du Boulay and Barron (eds.), *The Reign of Richard II*, 119.

and itself a powerful contributory force in the advance of the Reformation, was the printing-press, first introduced into England by William Caxton, at Westminster, in 1475–6.[141] Parishioners of St Margaret's were among the first to own some of the new printed books, including selected lives of their favourite saints (among them Our Lady and St Catherine) in English translation.[142] After this early familiarization with the new medium, the experience of reading the Bible in printed English was probably less revolutionary than is sometimes suggested.[143]

The successes of the Reformation in Westminster cannot, in the light of these activities, plausibly be attributed to pusillanimity in the face of Thomas Cromwell's officers; though it has been claimed, perhaps not altogether convincingly, that in some places such fear was sufficient to induce the active support of parishioners in the institution of the changes.[144] Nor, in the case of Westminster at least, can the view be accepted that pre-Reformation beliefs were weakly held and therefore readily abandoned.[145] On the other hand, the suggestion has been made that a vigorous commitment to the late-medieval church was succeeded, after the Reformation, by disillusionment and 'indifference to the officially-sanctioned forms of religion'.[146] This is the argument of those historians who would see the Reformation as simply an act of state, imposed from above upon a bewildered and then disenchanted population.[147] Yet if the pre-Reformation church is carefully examined in relation to the mid-sixteenth-century changes, the religious creativity of the late-medieval laity may then appear to lead, not to an abrupt and final

[141] See ch. 6, sect. 5.

[142] See Nixon, 'Caxton, his Contemporaries and Successors', 314 ff.; and Painter, *William Caxton*, 189 and n.

[143] On the impact of printing in the early decades, before the appearance of official Protestantism, see Eisenstein, *The Printing Press as an Agent of Change*, 367–78. The first printed English Bible, in Coverdale's translation (printed initially at Cologne), was produced by the Southwark printer James Nicholson in 1535–6. J. F. Mozley, *Coverdale and his Bibles* (London, 1953), 110 ff.

[144] R. Whiting, ' "Abominable Idols": Images and Image Breaking under Henry VIII', *Journal of Ecclesiastical History*, xxxiii (1982), 30–47.

[145] Cf. R. Hutton, 'The Local Impact of the Tudor Reformation', in C. Haigh (ed.), *The English Reformation Revised* (Cambridge, 1987), 114–38, esp. p. 138: 'The English and the Welsh had a limited capacity to sustain any beliefs attacked both by leading churchmen and by the Crown.'

[146] Whiting, ' "For the Health of my Soul": Prayers for the Dead in the Tudor South-West', *Southern History*, v (1983), 68–94 (quot. on p. 89).

[147] J. J. Scarisbrick, *The Reformation and the English People* (Oxford, 1984).

apotheosis under Thomas Cromwell and Edward VI, but into more fruitful channels, at least some of which can be traced beyond the Reformation divide.[148] The doctrinal break is absolute, and not to be underestimated. But it is not easily credible that the social and intellectual vitality of the late-medieval church was killed stone dead by parliamentary statute. In the case of the Reformation in Westminster it seems preferable to see the religious changes, in part, as the continuation of late-medieval developments. All that is known of Westminster society at the end of the Middle Ages suggests that the programmes of the Reformation encountered there neither reactionary hostility nor indifference, but the reception of a sophisticated and naturally responsive audience. Among those who lived through the first phases of the English Reformation (or who indeed died in the course of events for their traditionalist beliefs) were many to whom the changes were intolerable. But the enthusiasts for the new ways were not only those who had scorned the old. One who had not was Thomas Silvester, a royal officer and a typical prosperous inhabitant of Westminster, whose recorded career began in 1523, when he held a house called the George in King Street. In the 1520s Silvester was a churchwarden of St Margaret's; in the 1530s and 1540s he was twice a warden of the major town guild of Our Lady's Assumption. When the first decrees of the Reformation were imposed, as has been seen, he appears to have bought some of the rejected imagery out of the parish church.[149] Like many others, he had participated with conviction in the life of the church as it existed before the Reformation. Yet he was fired also by the new ideas. When he came to make his will in 1554, Silvester, now a groom of the chamber to Queen Mary and King Philip, rejected the opportunity offered by the Marian reaction (and in particular by his royal patrons) to express Catholic sentiments. Instead, the verbal formulas he chose were Protestant, and sufficiently elaborate to suggest a more than half-hearted commitment: 'Considering the unsteadfastness of this world and the certainty of death, to which naturally all creatures are born', he entrusted his soul, not to the company of heaven, but

---

[148] On the fertile innovations of the pre-Reformation church see, in addition to the refs. cited in the preceding notes, C. S. L. Davies, *Peace, Print and Protestantism* (London, 1977), 143. Some continuities are brought out by Haigh, 'The Continuity of Catholicism in the English Reformation', *Past and Present*, xciii (1981), 37–69.

[149] See above, n. 127.

simply to 'God, my redeemer and saviour'.[150] Into this individual's private beliefs it is not possible to penetrate further. But a less presumptuous comment may be made on Thomas Silvester's public career. For his religious beliefs were bound up with his role as a prominent townsman and holder of successive local offices. Silvester's positive expressions of religious attachment cannot convincingly be regarded as merely opportunistic. They may be taken, rather, as a summation of the argument of this chapter: that those occasional moments when the diverse inhabitants of Westminster engaged in the collective life of their parish and its church were demonstrations, not only of religious belief, but at the same time of a sense of belonging to an urban community with a distinctive, sophisticated identity.[151]

[150] PCW Bracy, fos. 73ᵛ–74ʳ; and app. VIII, s.n.
[151] On community see also above, ch. 7, sect. 4.

9

Guilds

I. THE SOCIAL BONDS OF FRATERNITY

The most flexible of the organizations which shaped the society of Westminster was the fraternity or guild. The more recent accounts of the medieval guilds have stressed their religious dimension, rightly correcting the excessively practical and worldly picture given of them by earlier writers.[1] Yet while the importance of their religious inspiration is acknowledged, the social role of the guilds deserves closer attention than it has yet received.[2] The history of the guilds extends back before the advent of Christianity; and their occurrence in medieval Europe was related to social, as much as to religious, needs.[3] The formation of a guild very commonly gave a regular structure to an association whose existence was neither recognized nor accommodated by the alternative social frameworks of manor, parish, or borough. The diversity and mobility of medieval society created both extended and highly localized affiliations, constantly changing, to which the guilds alone were able to give a definite form.[4] The guilds had a particular relevance to a

[1] Westlake, *The Parish Gilds of Mediaeval England* (London, 1919), esp. pp. v, 84–8; Scarisbrick, *The Reformation and the English People*, ch. 2. For the older view see J. and L. Toulmin Smith (eds.), *English Gilds*, Early English Text Society, orig. ser., xl (1870), introd. by L. Brentano; and C. Walford, *Gilds: Their Origin, Constitution, Objects, and Later History* (privately printed, 1879).

[2] The different elements are sensitively integrated in Brigden, 'Religion and Social Obligation in Early Sixteenth-century London', *Past and Present*, ciii (1984), 94–102. On London guilds see also the still valuable G. Unwin, *The Gilds and Companies of London* (3rd edn., London, 1938); and Barron, 'The Parish Fraternities of Medieval London', in ead. and C. Harper-Bill (eds.), *The Church in Pre-Reformation Society* (Woodbridge, 1985), 13–37.

[3] The fundamental study on the early evolution and social importance of the medieval guilds is E. Coornaert, 'Les ghildes médiévales', *Revue Historique*, cxcix (1948), 22–55, 208–43. See also Reynolds, *Kingdoms and Communities*, ch. 3.

[4] See also G. Rosser, 'Communities of Parish and Guild in the Late Middle Ages', in S. J. Wright (ed.), *Parish, Church and People: Local Studies in Lay Religion, 1350–1750* (London, 1988), 29–55.

society—such as that of Westminster—which faltered at a stage between that of a manorial village and that of an incorporated town, and which therefore lacked constitutional means of self-definition.

Westminster, like many other populous parishes in the late Middle Ages, contained a variety of different fraternities. The majority were relatively small associations, which distinguished the bodies of their members from the wider mass of the urban population. One of the guilds, on the other hand, stood out as the premier fraternity of Westminster, and enjoyed a quasi-public status as the most prestigious and influential association in the town. The ties which united the brothers and sisters of a particular fraternity were not all-embracing. On the contrary, the guilds were exclusive clubs, defined by strict regulations. Admission charges, though commonly small, denied participation to the poorest inhabitants. These criteria were indeed fundamental to guild membership, and to the social respectability which accrued to those who belonged.[5] The smaller fraternities, therefore, comprised self-identified groups existing within the larger unit of the town. Meanwhile, the prominence of a single guild, that of the Assumption of the Virgin Mary, invested this association with the image of the town as a whole.

The chronology of guild foundations in Westminster, as elsewhere, is distorted by the weight of surviving evidence, which is concentrated at the end of the medieval period. An early Westminster guild, recorded in the mid-thirteenth century, was attached not to the parish church (as were the majority of its successors) but to the abbey, whose bells were rung by the guildsmen.[6] It is probable that lack of evidence alone conceals the existence of other such early guilds. Of those which are recorded, one was founded in the late fourteenth century, and eight more made their first known appearance before 1520. Eight of these nine fraternities were associated with St Margaret's parish church, and were dedicated, respectively, to Corpus Christi, St Christopher, St Anne, the Holy Trinity, St John, St George, St Cornelius, and, finally, the Assumption of the Virgin Mary.[7] The probable existence of a Corpus Christi guild has already been noted.[8] Those of St Christopher and St Anne, evidently small associations, made

---

[5] Ibid., 36–7.
[6] WAM 3455; WD, fo. 183ʳ; *Cal Pat R 1247–58*, p. 403; *King's Works*, i. 143.
[7] For the guild of the Rounceval hospital see ch. 10, sect. 5.
[8] See ch. 8 n. 116.

modest donations towards the church steeple in 1517–18.[9] The south-eastern chapel in the church was dedicated to the Holy Trinity, and was described by one who requested burial there as 'the Trinity guild'; occasional references to 'the Trinity priest' appear to confirm the existence of a guild of this name.[10] At the time of the rebuilding of the church the Trinity altar was 'newly made' by a Westminster priest, who may have been attached to the putative guild, named Richard Warter; Warter was buried next to this same altar in 1507.[11] The banner of the Holy Trinity, which was bought with the proceeds of the hock-day collections in 1510, was presumably kept in this chapel and carried in procession on Trinity Sunday.[12] The fraternity of St John appears to be first recorded in 1500–1, when several funerals were accompanied by 'torches of St John'.[13] The Baptist, who may have been the St John in question, was traditionally the patron of tailors. A bequest to St John's guild of 12*d*., made by a Westminster tailor in 1508, might, therefore, reflect an element of trade grouping, such as was not unusual even in non-craft guilds.[14]

The recorded name of 'St George's aisle' in the mid-fifteenth-century church of St Margaret suggests that the Westminster guild of that dedication, which is known after 1509, may have existed in the earlier period.[15] St George's standing as a national patron was consolidated in the later Middle Ages, following his association with the crown in the mid-fourteenth century.[16] In addition, his dragon-slaying prowess gave him a natural affinity with Westminster's patroness, St Margaret.[17] A reference in 1497–8 to the carrying

[9] CWA ii, s.a.

[10] PCW Wyks, 238–40: will of Robert Trower, carpenter of Westminster, dated 1516. See also Westlake, *St. Margaret's Westminster*, 43.

[11] PCW Wyks, 74–5. In 1506 Richard Wilson, who was interred here beside his wife, left two tin candlesticks to the altar. PCW Wyks, 58–9.

[12] CWA ii, s.a. 1509–10.

[13] For such torches, as for other guild lights in the church, licence had to be obtained from the churchwardens. CWA i. 392–3.

[14] A non-trade guild might evolve to become specialized upon a particular craft. See Barron, 'Parish Fraternities', 14–17. No such trade guilds, however, are known to have existed in medieval Westminster.

[15] CWA i. 162, 215, 257, 566.

[16] F. L. Cross and E. A. Livingstone, *The Oxford Dictionary of the Christian Church* (2nd edn., Oxford, 1974), 557; D. H. Farmer, *The Oxford Dictionary of Saints* (Oxford, 1978), 166–7.

[17] Cf. the case of the Norwich guild of St George, which annually performed the play of its patron, into which, by 1537, was introduced St Margaret, apparently assisting St George in his valiant deeds. E. K. Chambers, *The Medieval Stage*, 2 vols. (Oxford, 1903), i. 222–3.

of 'St George's banner' in Westminster seems to anticipate the annual celebration of St George's day (23 April) by the guild after *c.*1515.[18] This local cult had evidently been promoted by 'a piece of the head of St George, set in silver-gilt', which was preserved within the church.[19] The church also possessed a drape of special virtue called 'St George's cloth', which from 1535 was hired out for use at funerals, when it was presumably spread over the coffin. Increasing numbers of applications for the cloth were made in the following years.[20] One probable member of St George's guild, Gilbert Atkynson of Westminster, in 1511 left to a friend his 'mowlde of the crosse of Saint George', which sounds like a leaden badge of the type worn by pilgrims.[21]

Gilbert Atkynson is perhaps likely to have acquired such a badge at a greater shrine of the saint than that in Atkynson's own parish church. But the potential strength of a local cult, extending to the attraction of outsiders, is demonstrated by the Westminster guild of St Cornelius. A burial with 'St Cornelius's torches' is mentioned as early as 1498; and in 1504–5 two wardens of St Cornelius paid 16*d.* for licence to keep their candle chest within the church.[22] A chapel and altar of the saint existed there at the suppression of the chantries.[23] It has been suggested above that the cult of St Cornelius is likely to have been promoted by the substantial community of Flemings and Germans which was well established in Westminster by the mid-fifteenth century.[24] The guild of this dedication was not officially incorporated, however, until 1514, when royal permission was granted to that body to found a chantry in St Margaret's church, with one chaplain.[25] Cardinal Wolsey then granted to the guild an indulgence for all who should 'visit, give or send to it'.[26] From 1518, the brotherhood of St Cornelius kept a 'general dirge' in St Margaret's for its departed members on the patronal feast day,

---

[18] CWA i. 343; CWA ii, s.a. The entry for the guild mass always falls towards the end of the churchwardens' financial year, which came in June.

[19] CWA ii, s.a. 1510–11: church inventory.

[20] CWA iii, s.a.

[21] Or otherwise a mould for casting such badges. PCW Wyks, 143–4; app. VIII, s.n.

[22] CWA i. 353, 508.

[23] The altar was sold from St Cornelius's chapel in 1548–9. CWA iii, s.a.

[24] See ch. 6 n. 105.

[25] *LP* i, no. 5101.

[26] Oxford, Bodleian Library, Gough Gen. Top. 364, p. 661.

14 September.[27] The economic side of the guild's activities was perhaps inevitably less edifying. In *c*.1536 a petitioner to chancery claimed that he had been defrauded by the guild of St Cornelius of five messuages in Westminster. It was averred that a certain clerk, a member of the guild, had not only forged the will of a former owner of the property in question but had subsequently 'resorted much' to the widow, finally inducing her to part with the deeds, to the claimant's loss.[28] Perhaps not all gifts, even to the most popular guilds, were spontaneous. On the other hand, the guild of St Cornelius devoted a portion of its income to the maintenance of a small hospital, which was evidently for the benefit of non-guild members.[29] And in a striking testimony to the reputation of the guild, the churchwardens in 1521–2 noted the small gift of 'Joan Thriscros', of Hull, who had come as a pilgrim to St Cornelius of Westminster. Joan Thurscrosse, a pious widow who belonged to several guilds in her own town, evidently extended her interests far beyond the bounds of Hull. Her visit to Westminster provides a hint of the ties, other than the primarily economic, which brought the populations of medieval towns into contact with one another.[30]

2. THE GUILD AS SURROGATE TOWN COUNCIL

The major guild of Westminster was that of the Assumption of the Virgin Mary. This, 'the great brotherhood of Our Blessed Lady', is first documented in 1431, evidently not long after its foundation.[31] A royal licence recognizing the constitution of the guild was

---

[27] CWA ii, s.a. 1518–19 *et seq.*; cf. ibid., s.a. 1528–9. The feast of the early pope and martyr in late September coincided with a date in about the eighteenth week of the churchwardens' accounting year, the time at which the anniversary is always recorded.

[28] PRO, C1/807/41–3.

[29] See ch. 10, sect. 5.

[30] CWA ii, s.a. 1521–2. 'Joan Thriscros' is clearly to be identified with the lady whose will, made in 1523, is discussed in Heath, 'Urban Piety in the Later Middle Ages: The Evidence of Hull Wills', in Dobson (ed.), *The Church, Politics and Patronage in the Fifteenth Century* (Gloucester, 1984), 218, 222–4.

[31] WAM 18890: the ref. is to a quitrent owing from the guild to the abbey cellarer, for property in Westminster. In 1416–17, the year of the preceding extant cellarer's account, this quitrent was paid by a different party. WAM 18889. Descriptions of the Assumption guild are given in Westlake, *Parish Gilds*, 84–8; and id., *St. Margaret's Westminster*, 49–60.

obtained in 1440.[32] The motives of the founders are unrecorded, but extant accounts, of the late fifteenth and early sixteenth centuries, provide evidence of its nature and activities.[33] The price of admission to the guild was 6s. 8d. (sometimes paid in instalments) and subscription thereafter was 1s. a year.[34] The total annual sums collected of £8 or £10 indicate a body of subscribers approaching two hundred: a sizeable association in a parish of three thousand souls.[35] Its social range was limited; the membership fees were, as ever, a restricting factor. More fundamentally, as has already been observed, the limitations set upon membership upheld standards of respectability within the society which were essential to its initiates. Thus a disciplinary fine was imposed on a member 'for misbehaving him in words speaking, at a quarter day kept in the chequer chamber on St Thomas's day in Christmas, in the presence of all the masters and brethren.'[36] But within these limits, the guild officers fairly reflected the spectrum of trades practised in the town; and the guild as a whole included humbler, if not the very humblest, representatives of all these activities. Among the 118 new recruits registered in the years 1487–90, for example, were the following: barber, tailor, pointmaker, chandler, smith, mason, cart-taker, goldsmith, printer, beer-brewer, porter of the king's house, waterman, priest. The guild numbered *Doche* residents among its membership, and women, too, who tended to be excluded from the trade guilds which existed in large towns, could belong to the far greater number of non-trade guilds; their participation was natural in a guild of the Virgin Mary. Sisters of the guild watched over the body of a departed guild member; sewed liveries and prepared dishes for the triennial guild feast; or simply left money 'to be prayed for' by their fellow members.[37] Indeed, an important advantage of membership,

[32] *Cal Pat R 1436–41*, p. 448. Mounting pressure upon the guilds, as independent corporations, produced a spate of requests for confirmatory charters in c.1440.

[33] Accounts of the guild dated 1474–7, 1487–90, 1505–8, 1515–18, 1518–21, bound together with records of the guild of St Mary Rounceval, are in Westminster Abbey Muniment Room, unnumbered.

[34] Notes of arrears in 1518–21 establish the subscription rate. 1s. p.a. was common among guilds. Cf. P. Basing (ed.), *Parish Fraternity Register. Fraternity of the Holy Trinity and SS. Fabian and Sebastian in the Parish Church of St. Botolph without Aldersgate*, London Record Society, xviii (1982), p. xvii.

[35] These actual receipts are separate from sums owed by members in arrears. For the size of the population see ch. 6, sect. 1.   [36] Guild accts, s.a. 1518–21.

[37] Guild accts, *passim*; PRO, PROB11/6, PCC 16 Wattys: will of Cecily Selly, dated 1472.

for the initiates of this as of all guilds, was the benefit of intercessory masses, celebrated in the guild chapel in the parish church, for the souls of departed brethren, and the prospect of a relatively swift release from Purgatory into Heaven.[38] But affinity with the Assumption guild brought in addition benefits in this world, in the forms both of conviviality and of a less tangible yet more fundamental sense of secular community.

The political importance of the Westminster guild of St Mary's Assumption is reflected in the distinction of its rulers. The appointment of a master and two wardens took place at intervals of three years.[39] From the period between 1440 and 1545, the names of sixty different masters and wardens of the guild are recorded. These officers were invariably drawn from among the 'better sort' of local society. They were not necessarily—indeed, not usually—of outstanding wealth, but they were men of some substance, often with a relatively large stake in local property. The mastership itself was never reached except via preceding stages of public life, which commonly included a term as warden. Moreover, almost every known master or warden was a member of the jury of chief pledges in the court of Westminster. For example, Thomas Bough, a gentleman usher in the king's exchequer whose service in the Westminster court from before 1486 has already been noticed, was a churchwarden of St Margaret's in 1474–6 and held office as warden of the guild of the Assumption in 1484–7 before his election to the mastership in 1496. He was subsequently appointed to serve a second term as master in 1502. Bough must have been 'full of years' by the time of his death in 1516.[40] The personal links which connected the body of guild officers are illustrated by the fact that in

[38] The guild employed no less than three permanent chantry priests (one being a morrow mass priest), each on a salary of £6. 13s. 4d. p.a., who served at three altars in the guild chapel. See guild accts; and PCW Wyks, 220–2: a bequest to the guild, in 1516, of 20s. to provide lights for its three altars. The guild owned a great breviary, with a gilded opening initial, which John Swann, sometime a priest of St Margaret's church, had presented for the use of the morrow mass priest, who was to say an early mass for the brothers and sisters of the guild whenever they should require it. See guild accts, s.a. 1509: inventory. Some of these priests were recruited in London, where the guild beadle put up bills to advertise for one in 1515–18. Guild accts, s.a.
[39] Probably 'the old masters chose the new'. Cf. Basing (ed.), *Parish Fraternity Register*, 3 (no. 15). The inventory of the guild treasury of 1508 includes the entry: 'a great gilt cup to choose the chief master', of the gift of David Selly. Guild accts, s.a.; for Selly, see app. VIII, s.n.
[40] See ch. 7 n. 42; app. VIII, s.n.

1488 Thomas Bough had stood executor to an earlier master of the
guild, Richard Humfrey, and by the terms of his own will founded
an obit in Humfrey's memory. Humfrey, who described himself as a
'gentleman of Westminster', and who rented a large King Street
establishment called the Hart's Horn, had in his time been a warden
of the guild in 1471–4, but became master only at the end of his life,
in 1484; by that date he was also a member of the court.[41] The
master in 1499–1502 was Robert Stowell, a celebrated mason who
had been master of the works at Westminster Abbey since 1471, and
who was almost certainly responsible for the design of the new
parish church of St Margaret, then in process of building. In
addition to a term as warden of St Mary's guild in 1490–3, Stowell's
credentials included his membership of the local court since 1488
and experience as chief constable of Westminster in 1489–90. He
had also invested extensively in local property, and himself
apparently resided in a large house within the abbey sanctuary
called 'St Albans'. The guild mastership, conferred shortly before
Stowell's death in 1505, was the climax of a distinguished public
career in the town.[42] The mutual ties binding the group of such men
are again demonstrated by the marriage of Robert Stowell's
daughter, Anne, to the son of another master of the Virgin's guild,
Thomas Burgeys. The elder Thomas Burgeys, a vintner by trade,
had been head constable of Westminster in 1466–7, warden of the
Assumption guild in 1471–4, a chief pledge of the local jury from
1487, and, finally, master of the guild in 1487–90.[43] Another typical
case was George Lorde, the master in 1521–4; an usher of the royal
exchequer and a purveyor of the king's works. Lorde's property at
this period was valued at £40. He had been a local constable for
King Street in 1509, and was subsequently a chief pledge of the
court from 1513. Thereafter, he was prominent not only in the great
guild of Our Lady but also in the Westminster guild of St Mary of
Rounceval, of which he was warden in 1520–2. He survived until
1533, when he was buried in the guild chapel of the Virgin's
Assumption in the parish church, 'before my pew there'.[44] These
instances could readily be multiplied.[45] Their common pattern
shows that the mastership of the guild represented the peak of
advancement in the secular society of the town.

[41] App VIII, s.n.   [43] Ibid., s.n.
[42] Ibid., s.n.   [44] Ibid., s.n.
[45] Ibid., *passim*.

The standing of the Assumption guild in the neighbourhood may be compared with that of such prominent urban guilds of the period as those of the Holy Trinity at Coventry and of St George at Norwich.[46] Indeed, in the sphere of local politics, a proportionately greater importance attached to the Westminster fraternity in the absence of a sophisticated system of local government such as existed in those other towns. Closer parallels with Westminster are to be found in such unincorporated places as Stratford-upon-Avon, where the guild of the Holy Cross acted as 'shadow government' behind the manorial administration belonging to the bishop of Worcester; or Lichfield, where, the episcopal jurisdiction notwith-standing, urban government was even more explicitly vested in a town guild.[47] Similarly at Boston, a town in secular seigneurial possession, it has been suggested that the guild of Our Lady may have acted as an 'outlet for corporate organization'.[48] Like their counterparts in these other places, the leading officers of the Assumption guild of Westminster were precisely those individuals and families who, in an independent borough, would have occupied the chief posts in the ruling council. The path to self-government through guild formation was not always smooth, as the townsmen of Cirencester found when, frustrated in an abortive attempt to gain independence from the abbot's jurisdiction in 1343, they created an alternative forum for the expression of communal feeling in the new guild of the Holy Trinity.[49] The backlash of lordly authority which followed at Cirencester, however, was not the experience of the guild movements at Stratford, Lichfield, or Boston, nor yet of that at Westminster. Each instance may be expected to show local variations. But the guild as surrogate town council begins to appear a phenomenon of widespread significance.[50]

[46] Phythian-Adams, *Desolation of a City*, 120; M. Grace (ed.), *Records of the Gild of St. George in Norwich, 1389–1547*, Norfolk Record Society, ix (1937), esp. pp. 12–13.

[47] Hilton, *The English Peasantry in the Later Middle Ages*, 93–4; Rosser, 'The Town and Guild of Lichfield in the Later Middle Ages', *Transactions of the South Staffordshire Archaeological and Historical Society*, xxvii (1987 for 1985–6), 39–47.

[48] Rigby, 'Boston and Grimsby in the Middle Ages' (1984), 61–2.

[49] Ross (ed.), *The Cartulary of Cirencester Abbey*, vol. i, pp. xxxvi–xl; and E. A. Fuller, 'Cirencester: the Manor and the Town', *Transactions of the Bristol and Gloucestershire Archaeological Society*, ix (1884–5), 298–344, esp. p. 329.

[50] Much evidence cited in Charles Gross's magnificent work, *The Gild Merchant*, points in the same direction; but this book is made difficult to use by the author's determination to draw the contrary conclusion to that which the material seems to warrant.

The degree of practical authority vested in the rulers of such leading urban guilds must have varied according to circumstances. For some of these prominent figures, guild office may have been valued as much for its public demonstration of the occupant's social status as for any concomitant duties of local government. To this extent, the guilds provided an arena for the playing of politics by townsmen who were constitutionally debarred from such activities.[51] As the administrative capital of the realm, Westminster was itself hardly a political backwater, and the royal officers and lawyers who were so prominent in the neighbourhood were not such men as would be indifferent to the recognition of their status and the enhancement of their local influence. The guild of the Virgin Mary's Assumption, to judge from the composition of its leadership, functioned as an outlet for such aspirations.

At the same time the guild wielded considerable material influence. It is uncertain how far its claim to arbitrate in disputes involving guild members drew litigation out of the purview of the manor court; but the governors certainly upheld this principle to the extent of fining those who omitted to observe the rule.[52] The substantial economic resources of the guild were a direct reflection of the commitment of its subscribers. From 1474, the year of the earliest surviving account, its annual income amounted to some £80. Half of this sum was composed of revenues from lands and about ten tenements in Westminster; the remainder was made up of membership fees and gifts.[53] By the bestowal of endowments, the personal associations maintained between guild members during their lives could be perpetuated after their deaths. Richard

---

[51] Cf. the analysis of the relationship between the Scuole Grandi of Venice and the closed government of that city by Brian Pullan in his *Rich and Poor in Renaissance Venice. The Social Institutions of a Catholic State, to 1620* (Oxford, 1971), 99–131.

[52] For two cases see guild accts, s.a. 1518–21. The rule that disputes should be settled within the society was common in the guilds: e.g. Rosser, 'Town and Guild of Lichfield', 45–6.

[53] The foundation licence of 1440 granted the guild permission to acquire in mortmain lands to the annual value of 10 marks. In 1474 authority was given for this figure to be doubled; and a third allowance of 10 marks was secured in 1502, bringing the total to £20. *Cal Pat R 1436–41*, p. 448; ibid. *1467–77*, p. 460; ibid. *1494–1509*, p. 280. The actual income from property from 1474 onwards was in fact always nearly double the latter sum. The unspecified transgression for which the fraternity received a royal pardon in 1484 may have been an unlicensed acquisition of property. BL MS Harl. Ch. 51 H.15. For some of the endowments see *Cal Pat R 1452–61*, pp. 362–3; *Cal Cl R 1476–85*, p. 271.

Humfrey, the former master of the guild who died in 1488, left to the fraternity his tenements in King Street and the Wool Staple on the understanding that his name and that of his wife, Marion, would be entered in the 'bede table' or list of those commemorated daily, by name, by the priests of the brotherhood in their masses, 'so to be praid for daily like Mr John Stopington, David Selly and Cecily his wife, and others'. Mindful also of the living, Humfrey invited to dinner at his month's mind the officers of the guild, all the priests and clerks of St Margaret's church, and the twelve headboroughs or chief pledges of the town.[54]

The guild as a whole, in addition to the commemoration of the dead, participated in regular social events, the details of which go far to explain the guild's popularity. The chief of these occurred just once in every three years, on the anniversary of the Virgin's Assumption (15 August), when all members of the society assembled at the great house in King Street of the archbishop of York, which was graciously made available for the occasion, for a spectacular 'general feast'. The hall was hung with decorations, and servants were dressed in liveries of Our Lady, bearing her lily. Members of the guild were provided with gilt badges of the fraternity to wear, and with garlands made of crimson velvet, lined with blue silk. Music was supplied by a band of minstrels, and actors performed 'a play'. The food and drink so far surpassed description as any successful medieval banquet should: from prawns to turbot, from herons to swans, from conies to sides of beef, all spiced between with saffron, cinnamon, cloves, ginger, pepper, and mace, and simultaneously sweetened with honey, grapes, and prunes, not forgetting the good ale and wine, nothing appropriate was lacking.[55]

The complementary motives for involvement with the guild of pious observance, fraternal solidarity, and the demonstration of one's status in the community are all exemplified at the individual level in James Fytt. Fytt, a citizen and tailor of London, where he was admitted to the Tailors' Company in 1459, was yet sufficiently a Westminster figure to serve as a churchwarden of St Margaret's in

---

[54] PRO, PROB11/8, PCC 9 Milles; guild accts, s.a. For Humfrey see also above, n. 41.

[55] Westlake, *St. Margaret's Westminster*, 54–7, prints in part the expenses of the feast of 1490 (*sic*).

1458–60 and as a constable of the liberty in 1464.[56] He buried his
father, a wife, and an apprentice in the parish church of
Westminster, where he chose to seek his own grave in 1500–1.[57] In
an act of patronage which expressed his elevated standing in the
town, Fytt paid for one of the new glass windows set in St
Margaret's in 1498–9.[58] Earlier, in 1477, Fytt had granted to the
wardens of the Assumption guild his houses in the London parish of
St Mary Aldermary. In return, the guild undertook to provide
Fytt's funeral at St Margaret's church and also to keep an obit for
him, for 'his wives and friends', and for the souls of Thomas Cosyn
and Margaret, his wife, on or about 6 November 'every year for ever
to endure'. At this service, the officiating priests were to say the
Psalm *De Profundis* over James Fytt's grave. The guild wardens
were also bound, a little nearer Christmas each year, to distribute
thirteen quarter-hundredweights of charcoals to poor people of St
Margaret's parish. The parochial churchwardens were to ensure
that these observances were duly carried out. A copy of James Fytt's
grant of 1477 was carefully transcribed into a manuscript volume
which appears to have belonged to someone associated with the
Assumption guild.[59] The principal contents of this book are, first,
three *Lives* from the *Gilte Legend*, the English version of a classic
collection of lives of the saints: those of the Virgin Mary, of St
Catherine, and of St James the Apostle; and second, a copy of the
English *Brut Chronicle* of England. The latter is illustrated by a
single page of pictures, which relate in seven scenes the life of St
Edward the Confessor.[60] The volume, which is written in several
fifteenth-century hands, was bound together before the indenture
of 1477 was copied on to two blank folios at the end. The neatness of
this copy shows that its inclusion was not accidental. Moreover, in
the light of this, certain features of the main contents of the volume
are suggestive of specific connections with Westminster, namely the
interest in the distinctive trio of the Virgin Mary, St Catherine, and

[56] CWA i. 8; WAM 50757; and see refs. cited below, and in app. VIII, s.n. That
Fytt was still active in London in the 1480s is shown by *Cal Letter-Bk L*, 211, 268.
[57] CWA i. 20, 76, 132, 394.
[58] CWA i. 376. At his death Fytt bequeathed £4 to the church. CWA i. 407.
[59] Cambridge, Trinity College, MS O.9.1, fos. 230ʳ–231ʳ; see also M. R. James,
The Western Manuscripts in the Library of Trinity College, Cambridge, vol. iii
(Cambridge, 1902), 439–41.
[60] Cambridge, Trin. Coll. MS O.9.1., fo. 120ᵛ.

St Edward.[61] It is even an attractive possibility that this interesting volume was commissioned and owned by James Fytt himself, who ordered to be copied into it the record of his transaction with the guild of Our Lady. The attribution has the advantage that it accounts for the presence of the third saint selected from the *Gilte Legend*: St James, Fytt's own patron. In any event, the combination in the book of matters concerned with the spirit, with local history, and with the urban community is a fair image of the various attitudes united in such a guild as that of the Virgin Mary's Assumption.

The fraternities, therefore, played a vital part in the spiritual, the social, the economic, and even the political life of late-medieval Westminster. Yet this was not all; for the guilds did not confine their benefits and good works to their own members. The efforts which the guilds made towards the alleviation of social problems, efforts which were impressive in their intentions, if limited in their effect, will be reviewed in the final chapter.

---

[61] The omission of St Margaret admittedly makes the selection less distinctive than it might have been. But for St Catherine's particular popularity in Westminster see ch. 8 n. 108. The text of the three *Lives* from the *Gilte Legend* (i.e. the *Golden Legend*) included in the Cambridge volume is closely related to that of another MS, which contains a colophon indicating a London provenance. See R. Hamer, *Three Lives from the Gilte Legende* (Heidelberg, 1978), 28, 33. Copies of Caxton's edition of Lydgate's *Birth of Our Lady* and of Wynkyn de Worde's edition of the *Life of St Katherine* were given to the guild of the Assumption by William Caxton's executors in c.1492. Two copies of each remained in the guild's possession in 1508. Nixon, 'Caxton, his Contemporaries and Successors', 317; Painter, *William Caxton*, 189 and n.

10

Charitable Institutions

I. INTRODUCTION

In the age (while it lasts) of the social contract, and welfare for all, the state owns a practical monopoly on the treatment of poverty and ill-health. Medieval social theorists, by contrast, recognizing that the rich, no less than the poor, are always with us, founded their ideal upon the mutual dependence of the two. In exchange for the material support which the wealthy were able to dispense to beggars and sick people, the latter offered both a means to earn salvation by charitable deeds, and a spiritual lesson in humility. The rich, therefore, as Langland put it, should patronize not frivolous entertainers but 'God's minstrels', the poor:

> For-thi I rede yow riche, reveles whan ye maketh
> For to solace youre soules, suche ministrales to have;
> The pore, for a fol sage, syttynge at the heygh table,
>
> .   .   .   .
>
> And a blynd man for a bourdeoure, or a bedrede womman,
> To crie a largesse byfor oure lorde, youre gode loos to schewe![1]

The initial motivation to charity was thus the donor's selfish expectation of spiritual reward. This attitude was not conducive to the efficient systematization of social care and indeed, compared with the modern welfare state, medieval charitable assistance was at best limited and usually haphazard. Nevertheless, in the large towns of medieval Europe sophisticated relief programmes, financed in some cases out of public funds, are recorded from the early thirteenth century onwards.[2] A relatively small and unincor-

---

[1] William Langland, *The Vision of William Concerning Piers the Plowman*, B-Text, ed. W. W. Skeat, Early English Text Society, orig. ser., xxxviii (1869), passus xiii, ll. 442–9. *rede*: teach *for a fol sage*: instead of a clever fool *bourdeoure*: jester *loos*: praise

[2] Instances on the continent have been described in a spate of recent studies. A good example is the publicly funded institution of the 'Charity' at Narbonne, first

porated town, such as Westminster, could not command the urban taxes or the wealth of mercantile guilds from which such assistance was provided in the cities. During the thirteenth and fourteenth centuries, indeed, the only formal aid in Westminster was supplied by institutions which, although situated locally, stood in this respect outside the community of the townspeople. Yet notwithstanding the absence of a corporate government and civic funds, there appeared at Westminster towards the close of the Middle Ages, under the collective patronage of the inhabitants, a number of small hospices for the relief of the poor and the infirm. This modest development in charitable care reflects an emergent sense of corporate responsibility for the dependants of local society, and is therefore a landmark in the evolution of the community itself.

2. THE ROYAL HOUSEHOLD

In the thirteenth century and before, the most prodigious dispensary of charitable assistance in Westminster was the household of the king. If Langland's exhortation was addressed to all lords, it behoved kings above all to listen well and respond. An archetype of royal generosity was the story of Edward the Confessor's gift to a poor pilgrim at Westminster of a precious ring.[3] In the Confessor's time the royal hall at Westminster was daily filled with 'many of the poor and the sick in body', who received there the necessities of life.[4] When, in the early twelfth century, the king of Scots visited his sister Queen Matilda of England at her house, presumably at Westminster, he found her surrounded by lepers, whom she tended.[5] Among improvements to Westminster Palace made in the following century by Henry III was the

---

documented in 1201. See J. Caille, *Hôpitaux et charité publique à Narbonne au moyen age* (Toulouse, 1978), 40–1, 46, 89–90. For similar cases, including 'poor tables' in thirteenth-century urban parishes, see M. Mollat, *Les Pauvres au Moyen Age* (n.p., 1978), 165–91, esp. 170–2. The situation in the city of London is surveyed by C. Rawcliffe, 'The Hospitals of Later Medieval London', *Medical History*, xxviii (1984), 1–21. For a summary of medieval theoretical writings on charity see M. Rubin, *Charity and Community in Medieval Cambridge* (Cambridge, 1987), 54 ff.

[3] Ailred of Rievaulx, *Vita Sancti Edwardi*, in Migne (ed.), *Patrologia Latina*, cxcv, col. 769.
[4] *Vita Aedwardi Regis*, ed. Barlow (London, 1962), 41.
[5] *Matt Par Chron Maj*, ii. 130.

construction of a royal almshouse, under the supervision of the king's almoner.[6] Even after the erection of this almshouse, however, large numbers of recipients of the royal charity continued to be admitted on special occasions within the apartments of the palace. On 1 January 1243, 6,000 poor were fed here: the old and the sick in the great and lesser halls, the middle-aged and less afflicted in the king's chamber (otherwise known as 'the painted chamber'), the children in the chamber of the queen.[7] At the same period the royal maundy at Easter included the issue of about 150 pairs of shoes, in a ceremony which took place either at Westminster or, less frequently than of old, at Winchester.[8] The royal presence also drew to Westminster a thin stream of pilgrims who suffered from the tubercular infection called scrofula, a symptom of which was swellings in the glands of the neck. Henry III was the first English king to claim to cure this affliction by virtue of the miraculous 'royal touch' (imitating in this, as in so much else, his admired contemporary King Louis IX of France). A religious ceremony developed around the royal healing, in which the king blessed the sick, and issued a silver penny to each. Edward I, II, and III each touched several hundred individuals for 'the king's evil' annually, and in a peak year the figure exceeded two thousand; the greatest numbers were recorded at times when the king resided at Westminster.[9] The influx of these bands of scrofulous petitioners can have brought but little joy, however, to the healthy residents of Westminster; and it may also be suggested that the hordes of poor people fed at intervals at the royal board were, in all probability,

---

[6] *Cal Cl R 1231–34*, p. 114. This royal almonry is not mentioned in *King's Works*, i. 491–552; but an account for repairs at the palace in 1307–11, printed ibid., 1042, refers to 'the king's and the queen's almonries' there.

[7] *Cal Cl R 1242–7*, p. 150. See also p. 164, etc. The 'painted chamber' was the king's bed-chamber, yet it was a public room. As the ref. cited shows, it was used in the mid-thirteenth century for charitable distributions. The room was decorated with texts and images which referred explicitly to the importance of charity. These included a representation of King Edward's gift to the pilgrim. P. Binski, *The Painted Chamber at Westminster*, Society of Antiquaries of London, Occasional Papers, new ser., ix (1986), 35, 40.

[8] *Cal Lib R 1267–72*, pp. 34, 59, etc.

[9] M. Bloch, *Les Rois thaumaturges* (Strasburg, 1924), 41–9, 93–9; corrected by Barlow, 'The King's Evil', *English Historical Review*, xcv (1980), 3–27; and by Prestwich, 'The Piety of Edward I', in W. M. Ormrod (ed.), *England in the Thirteenth Century*, *Proceedings of the 1984 Harlaxton Symposium* (Harlaxton College, Grantham, 1985), 124–6.

drawn for the most part from beyond the confines of the town.[10] Local conditions may well have been worsened, rather than improved, by the king's generosity.

Edward I appears to have made even more lavish distributions than his father; yet, as ever, the guiding motivation was religious and not noticeably relevant to specific distress, which even £700 worth of random $1\frac{1}{2}d$. hand-outs per annum can have done little to alleviate.[11] The later Middle Ages were marked by less-spectacular occasions of royal almsgiving than the preceding period, and instead by more regular, even mechanical, distributions on a smaller scale. In Henry VII's day 37s. 11d. was dispensed weekly from the royal purse to the attendant poor, at Westminster or elsewhere; and Henry VIII similarly issued £10 per month to his almoner for the vicarious donation of 'private alms'.[12] It seems likely that many of those in regular receipt of such royal pittances were themselves former officers or hangers-on at court. The terms of the foundation of Henry VII's almshouses, built within the precinct of Westminster Abbey in c.1504, illustrate this important function of royal almsgiving, as a means of pensioning off retired servants. The thirteen 'almsmen of King Henry VII' (one being a priest) were to be chosen in the first instance by the king himself, and subsequently by the abbot of Westminster, 'preference being given to such as have been menial servants to the present king'.[13] Henry's Savoy hospital, although remarkable for its Italianate design, was equally irrelevant to local needs.[14] Royal charity, therefore, although at occasional feasts in the thirteenth century it

---

[10] For the potential violence of these congregations of vagabonds in the thirteenth century—'if one leper strike another with a knife . . .'—see *The Red Book of the Exchequer*, ed. H. Hall, 3 vols., Rolls Series (1869), ii. 759. In Henry VIII's reign, such charitable conventions were still said to cause 'great confusion, annoyance, infection, trouble, and dishonour'. *LP* iv, no. 1939.

[11] H. Johnstone, 'Poor-relief in the Royal Households of Thirteenth-century England', *Speculum*, iv (1929), 149–67; J. F. Willard and W. A. Morris (eds.), *The English Government at Work, 1327–1336*, Vol. i (Cambridge, Mass., 1940), 218; Prestwich, 'Piety of Edward I', 122–3.

[12] BL MS Add. 21480; N. H. Nicolas, *The Privy Purse Expenses of King Henry the Eighth* (London, 1827), 9, 19, 32, etc. See also H. Farquhar, 'Royal Charities', *British Numismatic Journal*, xii (1916), 39–135.

[13] *Cal Cl R 1500–9*, pp. 146–7, 151–4. See also *King's Works*, iii. 206–10. The Lancastrian kings had similarly retained pensioner bedemen, who prayed for the royal souls in Westminster Abbey. *Issues of the Exchequer . . . from King Henry III to King Henry VI*, ed. F. Devon (London, 1837), 410.

[14] *King's Works*, iii. 196–206.

must have attracted to the palace at Westminster crowds from far and near, was never deliberately directed to benefit the most needy among the population of the neighbouring town.

3. WESTMINSTER ABBEY

The monks of St Peter's abbey were more appropriately organized than the royal household to deal with local hardship. The duties of the monastic almoner, as set out in the *Customary* of 1266, included the reception of all who sought alms, distributions to the poor on the death of a monk, and presents of cloth at Christmas time and of left-overs from the refectory throughout the year. The subalmoner meanwhile made regular visits to the homes of the sick in the nearby streets, bringing solace (*blande consoletur egrum*) and suitable sustenance.[15] On the other hand the account rolls of the almoners, the series of which begins at the turn of the thirteenth and fourteenth centuries, evince a less active and personal involvement in the lives of the local laity than is evoked in the earlier *Customary*.[16] To be sure, during the later Middle Ages a formal hand-out was made to the poor annually, during Lent, of some 60 lb. of peas and beans, and of between £2 and £4 in cash (out of the almoner's total yearly expenditure of from £50 to £70) at Rogationtide and other times of the year; while the cellarer issued six gallons (*lagenae*) of beer every Saturday and on the eve of each principal feast.[17] Occasionally, the unimaginative repetition of these distributions was punctuated by an individual gesture or response. Thus around 1370 the almoner paid 15*d.* for the burial of two poor people, bestowed 5*s.* on two poor scholars setting off for Oxford (certainly a kind act, this), and allowed $\frac{1}{2}$ lb. of wheat to Agnes Moode, a poor parishioner of the town.[18] Abnormal circumstances, such as the political crisis of 1461, could create exceptional

---

[15] *Customary*, 176–81.

[16] WAM 18962–9145, *passim*.

[17] WAM 18887; and 18962–9145. The monastic refectory contained a *tabula pro pauperibus* in 1458. WAM 19558.

[18] WAM 18993–4. The largest cash distributions to the poor, of over £5 p.a., were recorded in the late fourteenth century. In 1394–5 the almoner doubled the year's allowance of £5. 4*s.*, because the king was in Scotland. Evidently the absence of the royal household would otherwise have meant deprivation for those normally seeking aid in Westminster. WAM 19001.

demands, not necessarily from the meek and deserving. After the bloody battle of St Albans in February of that year, soldiers and shipmen for the victorious Lancastrian cause, denied admission to London by the cautious city governors, ran amok in Westminster. In an evident attempt at pacification, the importuned brethren of the monastery invariably directed them towards the almonry—to the almoner's expressed chagrin.[19] A more continuous and local need is reflected in the monks' practice of sometimes letting their cottages in the town gratis to the poor, *propter elemosinam*. The few recorded instances of this policy date from the late fifteenth and early sixteenth centuries, in which period other indications suggest that the pressure on housing in Westminster was on the increase.[20] In addition, the monks always maintained within the almonry between half a dozen and thirteen resident 'brothers (and, occasionally, sisters) of St Edward', also described as the saint's 'poor brothers' or his 'knights'.[21] Perhaps these were similar to the oblates who contracted with other monasteries for accommodation and support in their retirement or permanent sickness.[22] But by the end of the Middle Ages, when social needs may have begun to grow with a rise in local population, the monks' energies were no longer directed towards easing the pressures to the extent that the *Customary* suggests they were in the thirteenth century and before. As has been noted in other respects, the monks in the later Middle Ages became introverted, and less concerned than previously with

[19] 'Et in denariis distributis pauperibus in diebus rogacionum aceciam lez shipmen & sowdiers quando spoliebant villam, quia fratres semper mittebant [eos] ad elemosinariam pro elemosinam: £4. hoc anno.' WAM 19067. Cf. Kingsford (ed.), *Chronicles of London* (Oxford, 1905), 173: 'And in this season [towards Easter 1461, after the second battle of St Albans] the prykkers or fore-riders of the Northern men came unto London, and would have comen in; but the mair and the comons wold not suffyr theym, and many of theym went to Westmynster and disported there.' See also id., *Prejudice and Promise in Fifteenth-century England* (Oxford, 1925), 53.
[20] e.g. a cottage in the sanctuary, granted to a blind woman in 1509–10: WAM 19765; a tenement inside the almonry to Joan Woodman, *paupera*, in 1514 *et seq.*; WAM 19119 *et seq.*; a tenement within the great sanctuary gate, to 'a little poor woman' (*paupercula*), at the reduced rate of 6s. 8d. p.a., in 1470–1: WAM 19717. For the growth in the local population see ch. 6, sect. 1.
[21] e.g. WAM 19012, 19060. The brothers of St Edward were distinct from the lay brethren of the monastery. The latter are a shadowy group, but presumably performed domestic and general chores within the convent.
[22] The wealthier class of living-in corrodians, to whom the epithet 'poor' would be ill-applied, was also increasingly in evidence at Westminster Abbey in the later Middle Ages. See Reg Bk, i, ii, *passim*, for grants of corrodies.

the needs of the broader community.[23] It seems unlikely that the monks of Westminster from the fourteenth century onwards were esteemed for their labours among the poor and sick of the town.[24]

4. THE HOSPITAL OF ST JAMES

About the turn of the twelfth and thirteenth centuries, a change has been observed in the pattern of charitable endowments in western Europe. The laity, instead of making grants to the old monastic houses to enable them to perform works of mercy, began to show a preference in their benefactions for more practical and specialized institutions, in the foundation and administration of which laymen themselves took an active part.[25] The leper hospital of St James at Westminster, beside Charing, was a product of this movement.[26] Its probably twelfth-century founders appear to have been primarily citizens of London.[27] Yet by the mid-thirteenth century the masters of St James's could dispose of extensive properties in Westminster, some of which had been granted by the hospital's neighbours in the vill.[28] At least one Westminster man, before 1200, gave his nearby meadow to the house at the time of his admission as a brother there.[29] St James's was one of a number of asylums for lepers sited in the outskirts of the capital, most of which later came under the

[23] See also above, ch. 8, sect. 2. Few religious houses were so charitably active in proportion to their wealth as was Durham Priory, which supported two small hospitals and two almshouses in Durham. Yet even here, priority was given to former servants of the convent. Dobson, *Durham Priory*, 167–9. Similarly, the 'susterhouse' or almshouse maintained in the almonry of Croyland Abbey was reserved for 'relatives of the monks and the servants of the monastery who have been reduced to old age or infirmity'. And where the principle was not enshrined in a rule, it was nevertheless sometimes observed in practice, as at Ramsey Abbey in the 1430s. Thompson (ed.), *Visitations of Religious Houses*, ii. 59, iii. 309.

[24] It has been estimated that on the eve of the Reformation a maximum of only 5% of monastic revenues in general was spent on alms and hospitality. R. H. Snape, *English Monastic Finances in the Later Middle Ages* (Cambridge, 1926), 110–18.

[25] See J. H. Mundy, 'Charity and Social Work in Toulouse, 1100–1250', *Traditio*, xxii (1966), 203–87; Mollat, *Les Pauvres*, 187–91.

[26] An account of St James's hospital was published by M. Reddan in *The Victoria County History of London*, vol. i (London, 1909), 542–6.

[27] A master of the hospital is named in *c*.1189 × 1199. WAM 13847; and see Reddan, *Victoria County History of London*, i. 545b n.

[28] See W. J. Hardy and W. Page, *A Calendar to the Feet of Fines for London and Middlesex*, vol. i (London, 1892), 27, 30, 35, 38, 40, 42, 45, 55.

[29] WD, fos. 520ᵛ–521ʳ (Hugh, son of Robert Smith).

supervision of the city governors.[30] But as it stood within the liberty of the abbots of Westminster, the hospital of St James was not subject to control from London.[31] Consequently, the house suffered from a conflict of jurisdiction between the two local powers within Westminster, the palace and the abbey. When abuses crept into the hospital community, as unfortunately they did from an early date, matters were only made worse by this rivalry.

In the mid-thirteenth century, the abbots of Westminster exercised their rights of visitation at St James's unimpeded, as a collection of their injunctions testifies. The basic constitution of the house was comprised in statutes of Cardinal Ottobon and Abbot Richard de Ware, issued *c.*1267, and further expounded and modified in visitation ordinances of the abbot or his delegates of 1277 and proximate dates.[32] The sick of the hospital were exclusively female: 'leprous girls or virgins and no others' were received there at this period, to a maximum total of fourteen or sixteen, one of whom was appointed prioress by the abbot.[33] The house was served by a complement of up to eight brothers, who observed the so-called rule of St Augustine; this was to be read aloud four times a year in English (*ydiomitate, in lingua communi*), so that all could understand. 'Because so many masses are required', sufficient of the brethren were to be priests in order that they should be said. These services included memorials for benefactors, such as Richard of Wendover, who gave 30 marks to endow a chantry for himself in 1250, and Philip Godchep, a citizen of London, who provided 100 marks for similar observances in 1273.[34] Brothers and sisters were to say daily sixty *Aves* and sixty *Pater Nosters* (unless prevented by business), to confess weekly and to communicate four times a year. All were to wear clothes of a single colour, russet or black. The master (elected by the brothers and sisters and inducted by the abbot) was responsible for the goods of the house and for the welfare of its inmates, whom he was to gather every Sunday in

---

[30] Honeybourne, 'The Leper Hospitals of the London Area', *TLMAS* 2nd ser., xxi (1963–7), 3–61.

[31] The liberty was defined in 1222; see ch. 7, sect. 2.

[32] BL MS Cott. Faust. A.iii, fos. 314^v–322^v.

[33] The foundation charter had provided for thirteen inmates, an apostolic figure extremely common in medieval hospitals. See WAM 17117.

[34] R. Newcourt, *Repertorium Ecclesiasticum Parochiale Londinense*, vol. i (London, 1708), 662; BL MS Cott. Faust. A.iii, fos. 347^r–348^r. For Godchep, who made further bequests to other hospitals see *Cal Wills . . . in the Court of Husting*, i. 12–13.

chapter. The charitable work of the hospital was not confined to its members, for it included the distribution of a portion (one-tenth) of all the bread and meat of the house to leprous pilgrims and beggars, and of any left-overs similarly to these or to other poor people. The laity in general were especially encouraged to visit about the feast of St James (25 July), when from 1290 onwards a fair of a week's duration was held at the hospital.[35] The hospital's connection with Westminster Abbey was maintained in these early days by the participation of the clergy of the house in four annual processions of the monks, on the feasts of St Peter and St Edward the Confessor; the hospital chapel contained an altar dedicated jointly to the Confessor and to St John the Evangelist, in obvious deference to the abbey.[36]

The visitation ordinances of the 1270s already sounded a warning note for the future, in bans on the fraternizing of the brothers with the sisters, and on excessive *clamor*, whether of discord or jollification. When the abbot visited again in 1317, he found that the master, William, together with the prior, John de Atteueston, had ordered the hospital's affairs to their own comfort but to the distress of the other inmates.[37] To the charges that he had sequestered a lamp from the sisters' hall and food from their table, and brewed special beer (*cervisiam delicatam*) for his private consumption, Master William offered none but the feeblest excuses. Prior John, meanwhile, had evidently conspired with the master to appropriate the oblations collected on the feasts of St James and St Dunstan, and refused to render due account for the hospital's goods. He was said to be a drunkard and had alienated the others by his rudeness; Brother John de Sydenham he referred to as a 'mangehound'. In 1319 the numbers had fallen to only three brothers and six sisters, and conditions were deteriorating.[38] Some of the sisters, feigning ignorance of the law, had alienated the hospital's property in their wills. The abbot also had to issue a reminder that married persons could not remain in a convent against the wishes of their spouses, which suggests that the invitation of the foundation charter to

[35] See ch. 4 n. 94.
[36] For the altar see the record of the Godchep chantry, cited above.
[37] WAM 17117. The abbatial inquiries of this and the following years may have been prompted by the Bull *Quia Contigit* (1311), which drew visitors' attention to abuses in hospitals. See B. Tierney, *Medieval Poor Law* (California, 1959), 86.
[38] WAM 17118.

leprous maidens had been broadened. A secular tenor was invading the house, as services were neglected (holy communion was not celebrated even four times a year) and the brothers and sisters dined in common at all hours. The situation was exacerbated by the continuing rivalry of John de Sydenham and John de Attueston, who became master in 1320. Among the seven brothers and four or five sisters named as present in that year, rumour was rife about a former sister of the house, Margery Flynthard, who had evidently left in disgrace.[39] Both Attueston and Sydenham were cleared of charges in this connection (scandal left no shortage of alternative candidates), but each blamed the other for the chaos which had overtaken the administration of the hospital. Fields were uncultivated, houses in the town were derelict so that the tenants had left, the very roof of the chapel had fallen in. Meanwhile the master's name was coupled with that of a certain *mulier* named Alice of Paris, and John de Sydenham spent the hospital's resources on French novels (*libros gallici gestus*). The sisters—angry, as Sister Laurencia declared, at their lack of proper maintenance by the master, and indignant at the poor delivery of the divine office by Prior Richard de Swynford (who explained that he unhappily suffered from a speech impediment: *dicit quod linguam habet impeditam qua nimis festinanter quandoque pronunciat*)—were in revolt. They entertained seculars in their rooms, and gallivanted out to houses in the town. Margery Flynthard and her mother, Isabel, who had also been a sister of the house, were said to have sold a cup without licence to William Edmund, a citizen of London. These activities tend to suggest that leprosy, for the relief of which the hospital had been founded, was no longer a feature of life there. And with the suffering, it seems, holiness too had departed.

By 1331 John de Sydenham had finally succeeded his rival in the mastership, and his accounts as master for the years 1331–6 show that he attempted to restore order in the ailing house.[40] The fabric of the hospital buildings was extensively renovated in these years; the amendment of its previously dilapidated state perhaps justified the introduction at the same time of occasional domestic luxuries. Thus the brothers' hall was refitted with a fireplace, a new dining-table and a reading desk (*pulputtum*), while partitions were inserted in

[39] WAM 17119–20.
[40] WAM 17122.

their dormitory to make separate bedrooms.[41] The brothers'
kitchen (*que fuit totaliter ruinosa*) and bakery were completely
rebuilt, and repairs were carried out on two solars between the
kitchen and the hall, and on a parlour next to the vineyard. The
sisters' house and kitchen also received attention (including the
erection of two crosses on the roof), as did the adjacent infirmary.
All of these buildings, together with the chapel, may be envisaged as
surrounding the *curia*, or courtyard, of the hospital. A mill which
had burned down was rebuilt, a fallen dovecote set up again, the
gardens, meadows, and vineyard were tended, and bees filled hives
with honey for the profit of the house. John de Sydenham also
recovered the hospital's rents in Westminster and London, the
collection of which had completely lapsed.[42] The income of the
house consequently rose in 1334–5 from c.£30 p.a. to a figure on
parchment of c.£70 p.a.; however, the latter sum was in fact greatly
reduced by the necessary repayment to other lords of a proportion
of the rents received (c.£10), and the actual non-payment of others
(*decasus redditum*: c.£20).

Despite these signs of economic reorganization, the original
charitable function of the hospital continued to recede from view.
The number of sisters maintained in the 1330s had slumped to two
or three; and the record of a visitation of 1334 is no more edifying
than those of fifteen years earlier.[43] The master was reported to be
consorting with one Joan la Peynteresce, while one of the sisters,
Juliana, had been seduced by Brother John de Hoton. Remarkably
enough, in 1337 this John de Hoton became master in his own turn,
and his unattractive character found scope to develop.[44] Within two
years he was arrested and confined to the gatehouse gaol in
Westminster on suspicion of having murdered a woman. But even
his forcible escape in 1345 did not prevent his free pardon and
reinstitution as master of the hospital in the same year.[45]

It appears to have been John de Hoton's depressing career which
brought to a head a fundamental conflict in the administration of the
hospital, which had been building up for almost a century, and

[41] *Pro cameris factis in dormitorio pro lectis fratrum. 12*s. Ibid.

[42] The expenditure of £18 on legal costs in 1331 may have been connected with
these rents. Loc. cit.

[43] WAM 17121 *dors.*

[44] *Cal Cl R 1337–9*, p. 107.

[45] *Cal Pat R 1343–5*, p. 544; *Cal Cl R 1343–6*, p. 655; PRO, C260/61/36. The
master in 1339, 1341, and 1344 was Henry de Purle. *Cal Cl R 1339–41*, p. 658; WAM
17123; and refs. cited below, n. 48.

which all this time had undermined moves for reform. This conflict centred upon the appointment of the master. Like many others of the private foundations which proliferated before 1200, it was only in the legalistic thirteenth century that the hospital of St James was brought under the control of the abbot of Westminster.[46] The abbots rested their claim to visit St James's upon their unqualified ecclesiastical power within the liberty of Westminster.[47] In the inquiry which blew up in 1339–40, however, it transpired that in 1252 the then master had gone to the king's treasurer, Philip Lovell, to request him to oversee the welfare of the hospital as its chief guardian. This was the origin of the royal opinion, expressed categorically in 1339, that St James's belonged to the king's patronage, and was even of royal foundation.[48] Neither case was infallible (the abbot was forced to pretend that the London citizen founders of the hospital had been tenants of his), but the abbot's plea was certainly based upon a closer historical connection with the house than that of the crown; the first royal appointment to the mastership was apparently made in 1312.[49] Thereafter, the abbots' endeavours to assert their authority were inevitably compromised by the king's installation of masters of his own choosing. The result of the investigation of 1340 was a verdict in favour of the crown. The case was reopened two years later, when the jury reversed the judgement, and found for the abbot.[50] But in the event this dispute broke the authority of the abbots over St James's, and confirmed the hospital as a de facto possession of the king. St James's was not the only medieval hospital to suffer from such quarrels over patronage.[51] Yet its decline was not inevitable, but resulted in large part from its anomalous jurisdictional position.[52]

[46] Cf. Mundy, 'Charity and Social Work'.

[47] See the decree of 1222; ch. 7 n. 13.

[48] *Cal Cl R 1339–41*, pp. 657–8; *Year Books of . . . Edward III, Years 13 & 14*, ed. L. O. Pike, Rolls Series (1886), 284–6, 359–64.

[49] *Cal Pat R 1307–13*, p. 414. The kings had, it must be allowed, made occasional grants to the hospital, such as the gift of 1,000 herrings in February 1260 (perhaps intended for distribution to the transient sick), and the more valuable charter to hold a fair in 1290. *Cal Cl R 1259–61*, p. 239; *Cal Ch R 1257–1300*, p. 353; *Rot Parl*, i. 57. See also *Cal Ch R 1226–57*, p. 269; *Cal Cl R 1272–9*, p. 262; ibid. *1307–13*, p. 483; *Cal Pat R 1301–7*, pp. 484–5.

[50] *Cal Pat R 1340–3*, pp. 456–7; LN, fos. 137^r–138^r.

[51] See R. M. Clay, *The Medieval Hospitals of England* (London, 1909), 216–17.

[52] The other leper hospitals in the suburbs of London, which came under the efficient and undisputed management of the city authorities, appear to have enjoyed healthier histories than St James's. See Honeybourne, 'The Leper Hospitals of the London Area'.

In 1348 the king was driven to order away the lepers who continued to haunt the roads between London and Westminster.[53] Later in the century, the local manor court of Westminster arraigned several inhabitants for sheltering lepers in their homes, or who were themselves leprous.[54] Nevertheless, it seems probable that the incidence of leprosy was actually declining in the fourteenth century.[55] Ironically, the history of St James's as a leper hospital was probably brought to its final close by the depredations of the plague, which in 1348 killed all of the brothers and sisters, but one. The survivor, Walter de Weston, made master in that year of the empty house, was removed two years later following charges of waste.[56] Weston had evidently incurred the enmity of another cleric named Ralph de Wyvelyngham, who with accomplices twice broke into the hospital in 1350 to raid both goods and legal records.[57] In 1353 the house was deserted.[58]

In 1354 an inquiry was ordered into the hospital's loss of property by the alienations of recent masters, and some material restoration may have been made.[59] But the king's clerks who successively held St James's during the century after the Black Death were royal place-men, who had no interest in the house as a charitable institution.[60] A sign of the way things were going is the notice of 1379 that the then master, Thomas Orgrave, king's clerk, had been erecting fashionable crenellations on a tower in the house, which he

---

[53] *Cal Cl R 1346–9*, p. 509. King Richard II in his will showed a continuing royal concern with the *leprosi* of Westminster; but the term should perhaps be taken here to refer to the generic recipients of royal charity, regardless of the specific need. J. Nichols (ed.), *Royal Wills*, 197–8; *Rot Parl*, iii. 421*a*.

[54] WAM 50700 (1364: three *communes hospites lazarorum*), 50707 (1376), 50738 (1407). As late as 1472, the governors of London reiterated the ban on lepers within the city. *Cal Letter-Bk L*, 102–3.

[55] Clay, *Medieval Hospitals*, 43. The symptoms to which the word was applied were doubtless not always those of leprosy, but are likely to have related in other cases to different skin infections.

[56] PRO, E368/123, m.49. (This ref. was noted by Gasquet, *The Black Death of 1348 and 1349* (2nd edn., London, 1908), 112.) See also *Cal Pat R 1348–50*, p. 348.

[57] PRO, KB9/66/44, 49.

[58] Refs. cited above, n. 56.

[59] *Cal Cl R 1354–60*, p. 49.

[60] John of Norwich, master from 1354 until his death in 1375, was buried in the chapel of his hospital, and left 13*s*. 4*d*. to each of the three 'sisters of St James', with 6*s*. 8*d*. for the hospital chaplain. As subdeacon of Lincoln Cathedral, however, he must often have been taken away from Westminster by affairs, as indeed his other bequests confirm. *Cal Pat R 1354–8*, p. 74; London, Guildhall Library, MS 9171/1, fo. 32[r].

tactfully if unconvincingly justified as being 'for the security of the hospital's ornaments'.[61] Seven years later Orgrave, who evidently had little occasion to stay in St James's himself, granted virtually the entire premises to Elizabeth, Lady Despenser. For a rent of 10 marks a year, Lady Despenser occupied the main hall, the upper and lower chambers at each end of the hall, the kitchen, bakery, and all the remaining buildings and gardens assigned to the master— with the sole exception of a cellar which Thomas Orgrave had recently made for the storage of his wine.[62] The lease appears to make a mockery of the papal indulgence which was extracted in 1393; the master in that year being Richard Clifford, at the start of his great career as an ecclesiastical pluralist and politician. To pilgrims and benefactors to the hospital at the chief feasts, who should assist the poor and sick supposedly gathered there (*pauperum et infirmorum ad hospitalem predictum confluencium*), seven years and seven *quadragene* (of forty days) of penance were remitted.[63] Perhaps the proceeds of the indulgence were honestly invested, for by 1431 St James's enjoyed a sufficient reputation for sanctity to attract a London mercer to choose to be buried in the chapel there.[64] But the modest recovery of the hospital in its last medieval phase was to be achieved under new management.

In 1449 St James's hospital was added to the long list of royal endowments bestowed upon King Henry VI's beloved new foundation of Eton College.[65] The subsequent influence upon St

---

[61] *Cal Pat R 1377–81*, p. 325; see also C. Coulson, 'Hierarchism in Conventual Crenellation: An Essay in the Sociology and Metaphysics of Medieval Fortification', *Medieval Archaeology*, xxvi (1982), 83. When put to the proof, the battlements did not deter thieves who in 1404 stole from the hospital a missal, a chalice, and vestments. (These goods belonged to 'Lodowic Fisissian', whose professional skills were presumably not, however, employed within the hospital at this period.) PRO, KB27/574, rex roll, m.4 *dors*. Thomas Orgrave in 1381 kept an ecclesiastical staff of four celebrant clerks. McHardy (ed.), *The Church in London, 1375–1392*, no. 392.

[62] *Cal Pat R 1385–9*, p. 215.

[63] WAM 17124; *Cal Pap Reg*, iv. 466. That a copy of the indulgence found its way to Westminster Abbey suggests that the links between St James's and the monastery had not been completely severed at this period. For Clifford's office as master see *Cal Pat R 1385–9*, p. 376; ibid. *1399–1401*, p. 3; and for his career in general, *Dictionary of National Biography*, s.n.

[64] PRO, PROB11/3, PCC 16 Luffenham (will of Thomas Denton, proved 1432).

[65] *Cal Pat R 1446–52*, p. 296. See N. Blakiston, 'The London and Middlesex Estates of Eton College', *TLMAS* 2nd ser., xx (1959–61), 51–5. The college had been founded in 1440. H. C. Maxwell-Lyte, *A History of Eton College* (4th edn., London, 1911), 4, 51–2. A member of the royal commission for the foundation was William Alnwick, bishop of Lincoln and sometime master of St James's hospital;

James's of 'the lady mother and mistress of all . . . grammar schools' appears to have been beneficial.[66] The grant was made in reversion, upon the retirement of Thomas Kemp, who had been master of the hospital since 1443; but evidently Kemp, who had become bishop of London in 1448, politely resigned the mastership, for the college bailiffs promptly began to return accounts for the hospital.[67] Their extant accounts for 1450–1 record the receipt of no less than £90 in rents, from the hospital's scattered holdings in Westminster (chiefly meadows), in London and its western suburb, in Hampstead, and in Hendon (Middx.).[68] A further sign of health was the collection of some £13 in oblations at Easter and the feast of St James. Out of these revenues, the large sum of £61 was expended in this year on repairs to the hospital buildings. Those who benefited most from this improved management were the four alms-sisters now living in the hospital. They were maintained at a weekly cost of 12*d*. each, in addition to their clothing and a barrel of the best ale on St James's day (a reward for their entertainment of pilgrims). Masses were said for them by two chaplains, each on a salary of 10 marks p.a.[69] On the feast of St James, the sisters were honoured by a visit from the provost of Eton with thirty of his young scholars. The provost in fact used St James's as his London town house.[70] Meanwhile, accommodation continued, as in the late fourteenth century, to be leased to secular tenants. In 1450–1 the 'principal hospice with the tower' was nominally let to the late master, Bishop Thomas Kemp; but Kemp allowed his collegue, Henry Beaufort, bishop of Winchester, who chose for some reason not to stay at his

perhaps Alnwick himself suggested that the hospital be added to the estates of alien priories allocated to the college. W. Dugdale, *Monasticon Anglicanum*, ed. Caley, Ellis, and B. Bandinel, 6 vols. (London, 1817–30), vi. 1434; and see *Cal Pat R 1422–9*, pp. 14, 17. The monks of Westminster Abbey may have protested, but in vain, against the royal grant; see the legal expenses of the monastic treasurer concerning St James's in 1449–50. WAM 19955.

[66] The quotation is from Henry VI's charter of 1446, printed in *English Historical Documents*, iv. 918.

[67] See *Cal Pat R 1441–6*, p. 162.

[68] ECR, MS 61/RR/A/66. Ref. is made herein to a previous account, now lost, for 1449–50.

[69] The abbot of Westminster kept alive the old connection by celebrating mass at the hospital at Rogationtide.

[70] Maxwell-Lyte, *Eton College*, 82 n. In 1504 Provost Henry Bost bequeathed to his successors his furniture in St James's hospital. Ibid., 92.

palace in Southwark in that year, to make St James's his own *pied-à-terre* in Westminster.[71]

After the Yorkist *coup* in 1460–1, Eton College forfeited St James's, with many others of its possessions, and the house fell once more to a king's clerk, Roger Malmesbury.[72] But a regrant was secured by the college in 1467, and probably became effective on Malmesbury's death and burial at the hospital in 1474.[73] By the end of the century, an even tenor characterized the college's administration of the hospital.[74] The choice of burial here by one or two Westminster residents indicates the local standing of the house in Henry VII's reign.[75] The 'tower or chief mansion', however, continued to be leased out as before, at a rate of £5. 6s. 8d. p.a. That Pietro Carmeliano, the lauded protégé of four successive English kings, should consider St James's hospital a convenient and suitable residence reflects well on the domestic comforts of the house, which Henry VIII too appears to have noticed with interest.[76]

The hospital had benefited little, on balance, from royal favour in the past. Now, even before the Dissolution, royal greed destroyed it. Having seized Wolsey's White Hall in 1530, and begun a vast scheme of enlargement of that palace, King Henry acquired for this purpose not only a large part of the town of Westminster, but also the house of St James on its northern fringe.[77] In the meadows of the late hospital, he erected courts for 'the tennis plays and cockfight'; he 'walled the park with a sumptuous wall'; and he rebuilt 'St James in the Fields, a magnificent and goodly house'.[78]

[71] ECR, MS 61/RR/A/66.

[72] Malmesbury is named as master in 1463 and 1466. WAM 17782; ECR, MS 47/99. That he was a royal clerk appears at *Cal Pat R 1461–7*, p. 129.

[73] ECR, MS 39/129; *Cal Pat R 1467–77*, pp. 62–3. Malmesbury's will is PRO, PROB11/6, PCC 17 Wattys. He there listed his not inconsiderable staff of four servants.

[74] Accounts for the years 1498–1501 resemble that of 1450–1, with the omission of building expenses. ECR, MS 61/VR/E/1.

[75] London, Guildhall Library, MS 9171/7, fo. 128ʳ (will of John Gunnace, esquire, d. 1487, who also left a mass book to St James's); PRO, PROB11/9, PCC 5 Dogett (will of Edmund Gregory, gentleman, d. 1492, late of the sanctuary at Westminster; see WAM 19743–7; Reg Bk, i, fos. 55ᵛ–56ʳ; *Cal Cl R 1476–85*, pp. 122, 130).

[76] ECR, MS 62/AB/1, pp. 168, 186, etc.; 61/RR/G/9–17. On Carmeliano see ch. 6 n. 96.

[77] PRO, E41/216; E41/238; *LP* v, no. 406. Terriers of the estates of St James's in the mid-sixteenth century are at PRO, SC12/11/42 and SC6/Edw.VI/298.

[78] *LP* x, no. 1231: notes of 1536 by Cromwell on 'things done by the King's highness sythyn I came to his service'.

The four almswomen of St James were permitted to remain until 1536, when they were turned out, each receiving entitlement to an annuity of £6. 13s. 4d.[79] One of the four named at this terminal date, Catherine Vampage, can be identified as a wealthy widow of Westminster. At her death two years later, Dame Catherine bequeathed numerous personal possessions, and asked that her body be buried inside the parish church of St Margaret, before the image of her patroness St Catherine in the chancel there.[80] Neither poor, nor sick, nor a maiden, Catherine Vampage illustrates the transformation of St James's hospital from the terms of its foundation in the twelfth century. By the early sixteenth century, the house had become a comfortable retirement home for the relatively well-to-do.

5. GUILD CHARITIES: THE HOSPITAL OF ST MARY ROUNCEVAL AND OTHERS

Not far from St James's, on the bank of the Thames at the bend in the river beside Charing, stood another medieval 'hospital', known as 'St Mary Rounceval'.[81] This began life as the chief dependency in England of a famous Augustinian priory in the pass of Roncevalles, in Navarre, which served as a hospice for pilgrims *en route* to Compostela.[82] The foundation at Westminster dated from *c*.1230, when William Marshal (d. 1231), fourth earl of Pembroke, granted to the Spanish priory his house at Charing, together with certain rents in Southampton, Netherwinter, and Ashenden.[83] The activities of the Westminster cell are largely unknown, but by analogy

[79] *LP* x, no. 775 (1–4).
[80] PCW Bracy, fos. 61ᵛ–62ʳ.
[81] Earlier accounts in J. Galloway, *The Hospital and Chapel of Saint Mary Roncevall at Charing Cross* (London, 1913); id., *Historical Sketches of Old Charing* (London, 1914); Reddan, 'The Hospital of St Mary Rounceval', in *The Victoria County History of London*, i. 584–5; *Survey of London*, xviii. 1–4 and pl. 1; Honeybourne, 'Charing Cross Riverside', *London Topographical Record*, xxi (1958), 44–78; Needham, *The Printer and the Pardoner*.
[82] For the mother house, and bibliography thereon, see Jacques de Vitry, *Historia Occidentalis*, ed. J. F. Hinnebusch, Spicilegium Friburgense, xvii (Fribourg, 1972), 150 and n., 280.
[83] See *Cal Pat R 1225–32*, p. 265; *Cal Ch R 1226–57*, pp. 167–8. In 1236 the heir of William Marshall dated a charter 'in the house of the hospital of Runchivalle' at Westminster. *Cal Pap Reg*, i. 164. The hospital's connection with the earldom of Pembroke was not to be forgotten; see below.

with the function of the parent house, it is likely that they included the shelter of pilgrims coming to the shrine of Edward the Confessor. If the charitable works of the Westminster hospital are unrecorded, its chief method of fund-raising made it a medieval byword. In 1283, one Brother Lupus was active in England on behalf of St Mary Rounceval, gathering money by the sale of indulgences; if he belied his name, Brother Lupus was the first recorded 'gentil pardoner of Rouncival'. The remittance of penance to benefactors was a financial expedient widely employed by religious houses, but the activities of the Charing hospital in this field earned it immortality in the creation of Chaucer's archetypal pardoner.[84]

In the fourteenth century the difficulty of controlling, from a centre in the Pyrenees, an offshoot house at Charing Cross became increasingly apparent. In 1293 the hospital was forced to justify its claim to a toft in the vill of Westminster disputed by one Adam, son of Walter Scot.[85] In 1321 the newly appointed proctor of the house was busy recovering English properties which had been filched since the death of his predecessor, news of which had been slow in reaching Roncevalles.[86] But in 1335 the hospital was said to have 'abandoned' its ten-acre holding at Kensington called 'Ronsceval-croft'; and by 1340 both this property and 'a tenement on the corner by the stone cross of Charing' had been seized by the royal escheator.[87] It must have been at about this juncture that the prior of Roncevalles addressed to the English king an undated petition for the return of 'une place devant la crux de Charryng ovesque autres petites rentes et trois acres de terre', all of which had escheated to the crown.[88] Despite a struggle, however, the authority of the Spanish convent over its base at Westminster was effectively lost for ever in Richard II's reign. In 1377, 'enemy aliens' were directed to leave the country for the duration of the foreign wars, their English

---

[84] *Cal Pat R 1281–92*, p. 75; Chaucer, *Prologue to the Canterbury Tales*, ll. 669 ff., in Robinson (ed.), *The Works of Geoffrey Chaucer*, 23.

[85] PRO, JUST 1/544, m.21. It is possible that Walter Scot himself had owned, and given his name to, the site adjacent to the hospital later called 'Scotland', and later still, 'Scotland Yard'.

[86] *Cal Pat R 1321–4*, p. 23.

[87] *Cal Cl R 1333–7*, p. 423; PRO, E372/186, m.16 *dors*. The 'tenement' beside Charing Cross was apparently a meadow, where the *herbagium*, or pasturage, was worth 8s. 2d. in 1340–1.

[88] PRO, SC8/193/9635.

properties being temporarily forfeit to the crown.[89] The private grievance which led, during the London riots of summer 1381, to the invasion and robbery of the house at Charing may have had xenophobic overtones.[90] By 1382 the king had assumed control and a royal clerk, Nicholas Slake, was ensconced as warden.[91] The Spanish prior fought energetically to save his endowment; in 1383 a verdict was returned in his favour, and in 1389 one Garcias, canon of Roncevalles, was confirmed in the wardenship.[92] In spite of this, however, only three months afterwards the office was again bestowed on a king's clerk, John Hadham, who was succeeded during the 1390s by three others of his kind.[93] In 1409 the Spaniards reiterated their complaints, and extracted 100 marks in satisfaction from the English incumbent.[94] But their hopes were finally quashed by the 1414 Act suppressing the non-conventual alien priories (which conveniently obviated the need to return the possessions of foreigners, impounded since 1377, at the conclusion of peace).[95] Royal appointees continued thereafter to rule undisturbed at Charing Cross.[96] It was conceded in 1432, however, that 10 marks yearly should be returned from the English hospital to the priory in Navarre, for the maintenance of the poor there; with this the mother house was obliged to be satisfied.[97]

During all this time almost nothing is known of the life of the Rounceval hospital at Charing. Such indications as there are, however, suggest that all was not well. In 1346 the representatives of the house received protection throughout England while gathering alms.[98] But in 1382 the master, Nicholas Slake, launched proceedings against fraudulent proctors who, under cover of the royal safe conduct, had been gathering 'alms' in the name of the

[89] *Rot Parl*, iii. 22–3.
[90] PRO, KB145/3/5/1. (Ref. kindly supplied by Dr A. Prescott; MS not seen because undergoing repair.)
[91] *Cal Pat R 1381–5*, p. 117.
[92] PRO, C145/224/10; PRO, C44/11/8; PRO, KB27/490, m.21 (printed in Dugdale, *Monasticon*, vi. 677); *Cal Pat R 1388–92*, p. 152. The grant of 1389 was prompted by the intervention of Charles III of Navarre.
[93] *Cal Pat R 1388–92*, p. 205; ibid. *1391–9*, p. 311; ibid. *1396–9*, p. 30; ibid. *1399–1401*, p. 25.
[94] *Cal Cl R 1405–9*, pp. 446, 450; PRO, C260/129/6; *Cal Pat R 1408–13*, p. 292.
[95] *Rot Parl*, iv. 247.
[96] *Cal Pat R 1416–22*, p. 128.
[97] Ibid. *1429–36*, p. 247.
[98] Ibid. *1345–8*, p. 196.

Rounceval hospital for their own profit.[99] The fragment of an act of confession made in 1372–3 by one Brother Lawrence 'of Ronsevale near Westminster', relating 'his crime of incontinence with Anne . . .', reflects no less unhappily on conditions within the house.[100] Morale, and morals too, may have been weakened by financial hardship. In 1389 the bishop of Lincoln issued an indulgence of fifty days to all who should respond to the appeal of the Rounceval proctors while they stayed in that diocese, because the hospital was unable to care properly for the 'multitude of weak, poor, and disabled people' said to flock thither.[101] In view of the similar and demonstrably unreliable phrasing of the indulgence granted to St James's hospital in 1393, this reference to the poor and the sick at St Mary Rounceval must be taken with a pinch of salt.[102] Nevertheless it does imply that, at the least, a small almshouse was maintained there, or had been when funds were available. In the early fifteenth century the lack of revenues evidently became acute, for in 1423 the master and brothers of the Rounceval hospital were convicted of having forged a collection of papal letters, with intent to deprive the vicar of St Martin-in-the-Fields of his parochial dues.[103] Politely overlooking the deceit, Pope Martin at the same time granted a new indulgence to raise support for the hospital, 'whose buildings are in need of no small repair'.[104]

The transfer of patronage under Richard II, which added St Mary Rounceval to the list of undemanding perquisites of king's clerks, although in theory it might have been expected to replace an impractical administration by one more efficient, was not a happy omen for the future of the house. The continuing troubles of the late fourteenth and early fifteenth centuries parallel the prolonged decay of St James's hospital while likewise under royal management. But at this very moment the situation was transformed. The decline of St Mary Rounceval was to be reversed by an interest which hitherto, so far as is known, had played no formal part in the

[99] Ibid. *1381–5*, p. 195.
[100] WAM 5974. The confession was made to the monk-archdeacon of Westminster.
[101] Lincoln, Lincolnshire Archives Office, Register Buckingham, XII, fo. 355^v. (Ref. kindly supplied by Dr C. Rawcliffe.)
[102] See above, n. 63.
[103] *Cal Pap Reg*, vii. 238, 282–3. Papal clerks disowned the forgeries, 'whose tenor, form and style differ from those common to the papal chancery'.
[104] Ibid. vii. 251.

provision for the poor and sick of Westminster: the community of local inhabitants.

On Saturday, 8 September, 1385, at the vill of Westminster . . . was inaugurated the fraternity of the glorious Virgin Mary, mother of Our Lord Jesus Christ, with the chief intention of celebrating mass on the feast of the most blessed Virgin Mary's nativity [8 September] in the chapel of Rounceval at Charing beside Westminster.

The guild which returned this account of its foundation to Richard II's inquiry of 1389 was conventional in its constitution.[105] Provisions included the annual election of four masters, and the attendance of all the brothers and sisters for services on the Virgin's feasts and at the funerals of deceased members, when each was to provide a candle. No more practical ambitions were declared at this time. But the immediately striking fact is the adoption of the erstwhile Spanish priory, just as the debilitating dispute over patronage brought the house to the nadir of its fortunes, by a group of piously intentioned residents of the neighbourhood.

A reorganization of the hospital which took place in the late fifteenth century was partly due to Jasper Tudor, the uncle of King Henry VII, to whom Henry VI granted the house in 1453. Duke Jasper (d. 1495) was afterwards remembered in the prayers of the Rounceval guild, together with William Marshall, earl of Pembroke (d. 1231), as the hospital's second founder.[106] The guild of Our Lady may have received direct encouragement from Earl (later

---

[105] PRO, C47/42/212. The general writ of inquiry is at *Cal Cl R 1385–9*, p. 624. See also Westlake, *Parish Gilds*, 92–103; id., *St. Margaret's Westminster*, 44–9.

[106] Jasper received the hospital with the earldom of Pembroke. For the earldom see *The Complete Peerage*, ed. V. Gibbs, *et al.*, 12 vols. (London, 1910–59), x. 397. For a dispute, after the earl's death, about the inclusion of the Rounceval hospital as a 'parcel' of the honour and county of Pembroke, see *Year Books, Henry VII*, ed. R. Tottel (London, 1555–67), sub termino Easter, 10 Henry VII (nos. 5, 11). It appears that the notion had persisted, since the hospital's first foundation by the earl of Pembroke in the thirteenth century, that it pertained to that earldom. The guild accounts (for which see below) for 1539–40 record, under the heading, 'founders' obit': 'low mass and dirge for the earl of Pembroke (sc. William Marshall) and the duke of Bedford (sc. Jasper Tudor). 13*d*.' The account of the guild made for the king's Augmentations Office in *c*.1544 notes more explicitly 'the obit of Duke Jasper, late duke of Bedford. 3*s*. 4*d*.'. PRO, E315/418, pp. 30–1. Earl Jasper had been made duke of Bedford by his royal nephew in 1485. *Complete Peerage*, ii. 73. As in 1453, the earldom of Pembroke had been in the possession of the crown in the years 1389–1414 (ibid. x. 396–7). But the royal clerks, noted above, who were masters of the hospital shortly before and after this period, were evidently instituted without reference to the historical claims of the earls of Pembroke.

Duke) Jasper's wardenship, for in 1475 the fraternity acquired a royal charter of incorporation.[107] An extension of this grant of three years later entitled the guild to purchase rents sufficient to maintain no fewer than three chantry priests and to relieve 'the poor people flocking to the hospital'.[108] By the 1520s and 1530s, from which period accounts of the society are extant, the brothers and sisters had assumed the entire administration.[109] Nominal masters of the hospital (as distinct from the officers of the guild) continued to be appointed from outside, but their role seems to have been minimal and characteristically opportunistic: an action was brought against the fraternity in 1523–4 for a lapse in payment of a pension to the executors of a royally appointed master who had recently died.[110] The guild's own officialdom now comprised a master and two wardens, elected biennially, who grandly styled themselves the 'head councillors' or 'stablishers' of the fraternity. The annual quarterage receipts in these decades of about £10 indicate (if the subscription fee was the common one of 1s. a year)[111] a total membership of some two hundred. The accounts of the guild demonstrate the important place now occupied by the Rounceval hospital in the local community.[112]

The guild of Our Lady of Rounceval commanded a yearly income, in the early sixteenth century, of approximately £45. Membership fees apart, this considerable revenue was derived from a variety of sources. The fraternity appointed proctors to solicit alms throughout the land, from York to Penzance and from

[107] *Cal Pat R 1467–77*, p. 542.
[108] Ibid. *1476–85*, p. 114.
[109] Accounts of the Rounceval guild for the years 1520–2, 1522–4, 1538–40 are now in the Westminster Abbey Muniment Room, unnumbered (see ch. 9 n. 33). The Rounceval guild accounts are the major source for the statements which follow.
[110] The master in question was Richard Bromfield. His successor was not installed until 1526. *LP* iv (1), no. 2002 (27). On Duke Jasper's death in 1495, all his honours became extinct, and the earldom of Pembroke continued in abeyance until 1551; this explains King Henry's freedom to make his own appointments to the mastership of the hospital. *Complete Peerage*, ii. 73; x. 397–407. Whether the masters continued to collect the rents of William Marshall's endowment in Southampton and elsewhere is not known.
[111] Cf. above, ch. 9 n. 34.
[112] The fraternity seal used in the fifteenth century bore the image of the Assumption of the Virgin Mary, a detail which might hint at a link with the great Westminster guild of the Assumption; but in surviving records the two societies otherwise appear unrelated, except in so far as their memberships overlapped. An impression of the seal: BL Seals, lxviii. 57; reproduced in Needham, *The Printer and the Pardoner*, Fig. 12.

Norwich to Llandaff. The proctors appear to have compounded for the sums they rendered, which amounted to almost £20 a year. Their work of publicizing the society was helped by the support of local ecclesiastical authorities. Thus in the 1480s Bishop Milling of Hereford (a former abbot of Westminster) granted an indulgence, to be enjoyed by contributors to the hospital, to its proctor in his diocese.[113] Contributions were raised, as of old, by the sale of pardons at the various feasts of the Virgin Mary.[114] The relaxation of penance available to benefactors was advertised before the same feasts by preachers at Paul's Cross in London and, in 1523–4, by the curates of St Sepulchre-without-Newgate and St Andrew (perhaps St Andrew, Holborn); the latter two each received 2*d*. for their pains. Modern methods were also employed by the guild in this publicity campaign. Local printers, Wynkyn de Worde ('Mr Wylkins') and Robert Copeland, were commissioned to print thousands of notices ('breves') advertising the Rounceval indulgence, which were posted 'on church doors'. In anticipation of large sales, the indulgences themselves were ordered to be printed.[115] Other oblations collected in the 'stock boxes' within the chapel totalled as much as £7. 12*s*. 6*d*. in a single year (1522–3), over and above the similar offerings made on the feast days of St Mary and additionally of St Crispin (25 October).

These gifts were supplemented by personal bequests, which show the range of support which the hospital received from the townspeople of Westminster. Among these were: Roger Gerard (d. 1505), tallow-chandler, late of Tothill Street (who left a towel for an altar cloth to the Rounceval hospital); John Bene (d. 1507), armourer, formerly of King Street (20*d*.); Godfrey Russyng (d. 1514), goldsmith of Westminster (20*d*.); Richard Russell (d. 1517), carpenter and near neighbour of the hospital at the Bell inn, next to the bars in King Street (1*s*.); Elias Snethe (d. 1528), bookbinder and stationer, one of the wealthiest men dwelling in King Street (10*s*. towards repairs); Thomas Pecock (d. 1531), bricklayer, who had also lived close by, at Charing Cross (1*s*.); and

---

[113] *Registrum Thome Myllyng Episcopi Herefordensis*, ed. A. T. Bannister, Canterbury and York Society, xxvi (1920), 96, 109, 206.

[114] These pardons sold for about 4*d*. each. Thus in 1523–4 'a gentlewoman' bought six for 2*s*.; four were sold at the Virgin's Assumption (25 Aug.) for 1*s*. 4*d*.; etc.

[115] Caxton printed an indulgence for the hospital and fraternity in *c*.1480. Needham, *The Printer and the Pardoner*.

two fishmongers of the town, Thomas Pytfyn (d. 1533: a 'wrytyn portys', i.e. a manuscript breviary) and John Wyott (d. *c*.1538: 4*d*.).[116] Nor were the announcements in the city of London wasted. In 1520–1 Anthony Borough of London, draper, gave 6*s*. 8*d*.; and in the following year an alderman named John Wylkynson and a haberdasher, Edmund Smythener, both of the same city, gave 20*s*. and 3*s*. 4*d*., respectively, while John Foster of London provided 1*s*. 'to take in a poor man lying sick'.[117] The guild also derived rents totalling about £9 from the lease of two or three tenements next to the hospital, and from endowments in Essex and in Deptford, Kent. The last-mentioned property was the gift of yet another local patron of the Rounceval hospital, one Richard Kelk (d. 1517), a former clerk of the privy seal who had lived in a house in the abbey sanctuary at Westminster. Kelk's annual obit was kept by the grateful fraternity.[118]

The 'hospital' which was maintained out of these revenues was similar to a modern urban refuge or hostel, and—unlike the almshouse at St James's hospital in this period—was resorted to only by the destitute. Perhaps none but they would have been glad of the shelter they found there, which was of the most basic. The Rounceval almshouse measured 80 feet (from east to west) by 23 feet, and contained nine or ten beds, probably ranged along opposite walls.[119] Bedding was chiefly of straw (regularly renewed); but Katherine Phillips, a barber's widow and a close neighbour of the hospital by the white cross in King Street, who hoped to be buried in the chapel of St Mary Rounceval beside her first husband, at her death in 1504 bequeathed to the inmates a feather bed, together with a bolster, a pair of sheets, a pair of blankets, and a

[116] Gerard: PCW Wyks, 46–7; see also WAM 23126–32. Bene: PCW Wyks, 77–8; see also WAM 23119–21. Russyng: PCW Wyks, 199–202; see also CWA i. 472, 570, 574. Russell: PCW Wyks, 249–51; see also above, ch. 5 n. 171. Snethe: PRO, PROB11/22, PCC 9 Porche; see also above, ch. 6 n. 208. Pecock: PCW Bracy, fo. 20ᵛ; see also WAM 17986, 23289–98. Pytfyn: PCW Bracy, fo. 32ʳ; see also above, ch. 5 n. 107. Wyott: PCW Bracy, fo. 64ʳ.

[117] Guild accts. For Alderman Wylkynson (d. 1521) see Beaven, *Aldermen*, ii. 24.

[118] Guild accts. The guild was involved in a dispute over Kelk's lands with the abbot of Bermondsey in 1523–4. Guild accts, s.a. See also ch. 6, n. 164 for Kelk.

[119] For the dimensions see a post-Dissolution lease. *Cal Pat R 1549–51*, pp. 111–12; *Survey of London*, xviii. 130, app. A. In 1523–4 nine tapestry-work covers were bought for 'the alms beds', and Lettice Ingledewe and Ellen Riden, sisters of the guild—Mistress Ingledewe also made garlands for the guild feast in 1524—made linings for them. At the Dissolution, in 1539–40, ten pairs of sheets were sold and given away in alms from the hospital. Guild accts, s.a.

coverlet.[120] Another pair of sheets was left by Dame Joan Moreland of Westminster in 1511; and seven more pairs ten years later by Mistress Constance Russell (whose husband Richard's bequest to the hospital was noted above).[121] Anthony Leigh, a gentleman of the king's household and sometime resident of Westminster, left £3. 6s. 8d. to the hospital at his death in 1518 for the purchase of sheets, blankets, and shirts.[122] 'Bucking' and 'rinsing' tubs were used (they were constantly being repaired) to wash these shirts and bedclothes; the hygienic facilities also extended to a 'pissing tub' and a pump in the yard. The invariable rate of maintenance for all inmates was 1d. a day.

The numbers of those taken into the hospital in the years recorded were small: a total of ten, for example, in the whole year 1521–2. Moreover, it seems that only men were admitted. On the other hand, there is no sign of that preoccupation with the moral worthiness or sinful state of those assisted which would characterize charitable assistance after the mid-sixteenth century. Medieval people seem to have been more reluctant to draw moral distinctions, with regard to the recipients of charity, than were Protestants of the Reformation period and later. A large proportion of those entering this small Westminster hospital were already at death's door when they came, and after a few days were duly buried in the churchyard of the Rounceval chapel. One Thomas Lewes, after a first admission for four days in 1523–4, returned later in the same year, to die six days afterwards. Others recovered their strength in the hospital, notwithstanding the absence of any but the most stark medical provision. Such were 'a lad that went on his knees', who left after ten days in 1520–1, and 'John Foster that lay in the street' in 1521–2, who had to be carried into the almshouse where he lay sick for two days.[123] Several of those received at St Mary's were among the poor immigrants whose presence in large numbers was a feature of the sixteenth-century capital. They included a Scotsman, Thomas a Ley, who died in the hospital in 1520–1, and perhaps a Welshman (William Morgan), who stayed briefly in 1522–3; an

---

[120] PCW Wyks, 24–5.

[121] PCW Wyks, 141–2; guild accts. In 1522–4 'my lady Rest of London' gave 400 ells of canvas with which to make sheets for the almspeople; but it was presumably winding sheets she had in mind. Guild accts, s.a.

[122] PCW Wyks, 260–5; and see app. VIII, s.n.

[123] Perhaps this was the John Foster of London who in the same year gave 1s. to the hospital to help a poor man who was sick. See above, n. 117.

anonymous *Docheman* sheltered in 1521–2, and his probable co-national John Flemmyng, who spent his last days here in the following year. Another element in the drifting population of sixteenth-century London was represented by the unnamed soldier buried in the churchyard in 1520–2. The hospital also bore its tiny share of clerical poverty. In 1521–2 the guild put up a priest called Sir Harry for four days and another, named Sir James Wylson, who was ill, for over three weeks. It is clear that few, if any, of those assisted were themselves members of the Rounceval guild which, unlike many other such associations, did not restrict its benefits to its own subscribers.

Members of the fraternity assembled for the biennial feast, which followed the election of the master and wardens about the time of the Virgin Mary's nativity (8 September). All members assembled in 'Our Lady's chamber' within the hospital, to partake of white bread, Suffolk cheeses, 'spiced bones', biscuits, pears, and Malmsey wine, to the accompaniment of minstrels. Towards the end of the fourteenth century, the hospital of St Mary Rounceval had been spontaneously taken over from outside ownership by the inhabitants of Westminster, by whom it continued to be voluntarily and generously maintained. In its limited provision for the poor of the town in the early sixteenth century, this small guild hospital is in some ways even more impressive than the larger establishments supported elsewhere by official or private endowments.[124] St Mary Rounceval was re-founded and managed, on behalf of the community, by members of the same community acting together.

The guild was dissolved, with others like it, by Henry VIII; the deed of surrender is dated 11 November 1544.[125] But the end had been anticipated before this. After the king had appropriated White Hall in 1530, his works department, engaged on the realization of the grandiose royal design for the palace, required new offices for the site. Within a year, the poor inmates of the neighbouring hospital had been evicted, and their erstwhile almshouse became a payhouse for the king's workmen.[126] A few years later, in 1542, the tenements beside the hospital (formerly leased out by the guild) and

---

[124] Contrast e.g. the Whittington almshouse in London, the collaborative foundation of a rich individual and the Company of Mercers. J. Imray, *The Charity of Richard Whittington* (London, 1968).

[125] *LP* xix (2), no. 590.

[126] *LP* v, p. 447; and see *King's Works*, iii. 22–4.

the Thames-side wharf there were similarly swallowed up by the expanding monster-palace.[127] In view of these developments, in addition to the alarming royal inquiries into chantries during the 1530s, it is not surprising that the annual receipts of quarterage for membership of the guild fell from the figure in the 1520s of £10 to £3. 7s. 6d. and £2. 15s. 9d. in the years 1538–40, and to only £2 at the time of the Dissolution four years later.[128] A visitor to the site in 1550 would have found Thomas Carwarden, knight, one of the gentlemen of the king's privy chamber, making himself comfortable in the former premises of the Rounceval hospital.[129]

Further provision for the poor in late medieval Westminster was made by other guilds formed by the inhabitants. The Westminster guild of St Cornelius maintained, in Cardinal Wolsey's time, 'a hospital for the relief of them that have the falling sickness', i.e. epilepsy.[130] The churchwardens' accounts of the same period twice record the burial of former inmates of St Cornelius's hospital at the parish church.[131] A third type of relief institution was represented by a small row of almshouses owned by the 'great guild of Our Lady's Assumption', the largest of the Westminster guilds.[132] These almshouses stood in a lane opening off the east side of King Street known as Our Lady's Alley. This alley belonged to the guild from 1431, the date of the society's earliest recorded existence.[133] By 1474, and thereafter until the Dissolution, four cottages there were reserved for poor people of the parish, who were not usually members of the guild.[134] Although the 'tenements' (so they are described in the accounts) were no doubt small, the almsmen and women who had their individual lodgings here were more respectable than the rootless 'down-and-outs' who found their way to the Rounceval hospital. Residents, whether male or female,

---

[127] *LP* xvii, no. 283 (54). The fraternity was given in compensation a messuage and a field in the parish of St Clement Danes.

[128] Guild accts; PRO, E315/418, pp. 30–1.

[129] *Cal Pat R 1549–51*, pp. 111–12.

[130] Oxford, Bodleian Library, Gough Gen. Top. 364, p. 661. See also above, ch. 9 nn. 22–30.

[131] The churchwardens recorded the interment in 1526 of 'Joan of St Cornelius's house', and in 1531 of 'Philip at St Cornelius's hospital'. CWA ii, iii, s.a.

[132] For the guild in general see ch. 9.

[133] WAM 18890 (the name is not given at this date). This alley is to be distinguished from another of the same name on the opposite (west) side of King Street, which belonged to the Lady chapel in Westminster Abbey.

[134] Guild accts; PRO, E301/88.

received, in addition to their accommodation, a maintenance allowance of 6*s*. 8*d*. each quarter from guild funds. Among bequests to the fraternity was that made in 1511 by Gilbert Alynson, one of the guildwardens, who left the sum of 8*d*. 'unto each of Our Lady's bede-folk'.[135] Most 'bede-folk' stayed for several years, and the regular notices, in due course, of their deaths suggest that the cottages were chiefly occupied by those who had retired from working life. Nevertheless, these were not such comfortably prosperous pensioners as found quarters for their old age in St James's hospital at this period. The 'alms brothers and sisters' of the guild of St Mary's Assumption were poor. In 1505 the fraternity beadle sold the belongings of Joan Margery, late an 'almesse woman of our Lady', for 7*s*.; and in 1515–18 Margaret Rogers and Mother Laurence, 'bedewomen', left sums of 12*s*. 2½*d*. and 43*s*. 4*d*., respectively.[136] In view of these charitable functions carried out by three of the Westminster guilds, it is likely that some of the remaining six fraternities known to have existed in the late-medieval town performed similar services for the poor of the district.[137]

6. CONCLUSION: THE TRANSFORMATION OF MEDIEVAL CHARITY

The methods of relief of the poor in Westminster underwent two major transformations in the course of the Middle Ages. The earliest form of provision, which continued to be of importance throughout the thirteenth century (as it had probably been before), was the hand-outs of clothing, food, and money issued more or less regularly by, on the one hand, the lay household of the royal palace of Westminster and, on the other, the almonry of the great Benedictine abbey. In the fourteenth century, both of these centres declined relatively and absolutely as sources of aid. Probably late in the twelfth century and early in the thirteenth, there appeared in Westminster two relief institutions of a new kind, which at this period was multiplying throughout western Europe. The hospitals

[135] PCW Wyks, 143–4. Alynson was warden in 1510, and therefore probably for the three-year term 1508–11. CWA i. 576.
[136] Guild accts.
[137] See ch. 9.

of St James and of St Mary Rounceval, unlike monastic foundations of the earlier Middle Ages, were established by their lay creators with specific charitable purposes; in one case, the care of lepers, in the other—in all likelihood—the shelter of pilgrims to the shrine of Westminster. Whatever their unrecorded initial success, however, the good intentions of both of these hospitals were vitiated by disputes over patronage which arose from the peculiar circumstances of each. Consequently faults were not rectified, and a decline set in which during the fourteenth century was all but fatal. Order was restored to St James's by its patrons from 1449, the first schoolmasters of Eton College, who presided at the end of the Middle Ages over a polite retreat for ageing gentlefolk. But far more notable was the renaissance of the Rounceval hospital after its adoption by the local townspeople as the focus of a guild. This event represents the second transformation of medieval methods of welfare. The relief provided by the Rounceval and other guilds to those in genuine need in late-medieval Westminster was inevitably limited. Yet, in the absence of a governing corporation in command of public funds, their work is the more impressive in being generated by the collective concern of the community itself.

Charity is sometimes considered by historians to be a form of 'social control', a means employed by the rich to impose order upon the potentially unruly poor. This was no doubt one intended function of the eighteenth-century workhouses. The evidence of charitable motives in the late Middle Ages, however, does not on the whole lend support to the hypothesis. In the light of the foregoing account, it would be true to say of Westminster, as of other English towns in the sixteenth century, that 'poor relief was largely confined to social groups [in Westminster: the extremely poor, the elderly, the sick] who would not anyway have been threats to public order'.[138]

Indications considered in earlier chapters suggest that Westminster's population, after a contraction in the early fifteenth century, began noticeably to increase in the late fifteenth and early sixteenth centuries; and that with this increase the level of poverty also rose.[139] Although lack of evidence may conceal charitable

---

[138] Slack, 'Social Problems and Social Policies', in *English Urban History, 1500–1780*, Open University Course A.322, Unit 11 (Milton Keynes, 1977), 77–101, esp. p. 100.
[139] See ch. 6, sect. 1.

projects of earlier periods, it seems likely that the hospices maintained by the members of local guilds between the late fifteenth century and the Dissolution represent a communal response to a growing problem of poverty in the town. It was this urban destitution, indeed, and not a changed attitude towards charity brought about by the Protestant Reformation, which created the pressing context for the extension of poor legislation and relief in the sixteenth century.[140] During that century, the level of personal philanthropy appears neither to have increased nor declined.[141] The significant changes lay rather in the forms of charitable organization.[142] The responses of the guilds, emanating from within the parish, to late-medieval social problems make understandable the Tudor government's election of the parish as the basic unit for the administration of poor relief. Intermittent attempts, during the century after the Reformation, to institute centrally organized charities, either at municipal or national level, repeatedly foundered on the refusal of support in the neighbourhood.[143] The guild charities as they existed at the beginning of the sixteenth century were small in scale, and were rapidly outdistanced by the escalation of urban poverty. Yet the possibility of their further adaptation to meet the need was denied. The dissolution of the chantries, and with them of the charitable work of the guilds, ended one vigorous and promising line of development for communally organized relief. The administration of the parochial poor rate in Elizabethan Westminster underlined the daunting size of the problem.[144] This period saw the private

[140] See J. A. F. Thomson, 'Piety and Charity in Late Medieval London', *Journal of Ecclesiastical History*, xvi (1965), 178–95; and Brigden, 'The Early Reformation in London, 1520–1547; the Conflict in the Parishes', Ph.D. thesis, Univ. of Cambridge (1978), 354–63. And cf. N. Z. Davis, 'Poor Relief, Humanism and Heresy', in ead., *Society and Culture in Early Modern France* (London, 1975), 17–64.

[141] W. G. Bittle and R. T. Lane, 'Inflation and Philanthropy in England: a re-assessment of W. K. Jordan's data', *Econ Hist Rev*, 2nd ser., xxix (1976), 203–10.

[142] On these questions in general, in the context of Elizabethan London, see I. W. Archer, 'Governors and Governed in Late Sixteenth-Century London, c.1560–1603: Studies in the Achievement of Stability', D.Phil. thesis, Univ. of Oxford (1988).

[143] Slack, 'Projects and Institutions for the Poor: English Towns 1540–1640', paper given at a conference on 'Charity and the Poor in Pre-Industrial Europe, c.1300–c.1600: England and Italy Compared', held at Somerville College, Oxford, 20 Sept. 1986.

[144] In the 1570s, as much money was being collected and distributed to poor people in St Margaret's parish as in all the neighbouring parishes of St Martin-in-the-Fields, St Mary-le-Strand, and St Clement Danes put together. BL MS

foundation of several almshouses by worthy individual parishioners of the town.[145] But for a systematic and realistic, locally organized approach to urban poverty, Westminster had to wait until *c.*1700, when the officials of the parish vestry presided over the parochial workhouse: the embodiment of a response far removed from that of the guilds.[146]

Lansdowne xvi, fos. 166ʳ–168ʳ. In Nov. 1595 almost 150 individuals in the area of the Westminster sanctuary and Tothill Street alone were deemed by the chief burgess of the city to be 'poor'. WAM 9353. The parochial poor rate was inadequate to the need.

[145] Lady Anne Dacre (d. 1595) founded an almshouse in Tothill Street for twenty poor persons, with a school for twenty people. Nearby, Cornelius van Dun of Brabant, a yeoman of the royal guard, who also died in Elizabeth's reign, built twenty houses for poor women to dwell in, rent free. Stow, *A Survey*, ii. 123, 180. For a later, similar instance see R. Weinstein, 'A Westminster Charity', *TLMAS* 2nd ser., xxxiii (1982), 376–8.

[146] T. V. Hitchcock, 'The English Workhouse: A Study in Institutional Poor Relief in Selected Counties, 1696–1750', D.Phil. thesis, Univ. of Oxford (1985), esp. 138–9, 157–8, 178, 182, 188.

Conclusion

There is a pathological aspect to the current vogue for urban studies. Newspaper writers and sociologists analyse the tensions of life in modern towns, anthropologists compare the sickening cities of the 'developed' world with other, remote, societies; and historians, tracing the case-histories of these same cities, give a chronological dimension to the diagnosis of present decay. The recent intensive examination of cities of the past has sometimes been given a particular focus by the prevalent morbid view of the contemporary urban scene; a tendency to lay stress upon evidence of 'decline' in the towns of late medieval England is perhaps symptomatic of this.[1] There is no simple sense in which Westminster either 'declined' or 'prospered' in the later Middle Ages, and in general such blanket terms are best avoided by historians. On the other hand, we are warned against an inclination to compensate for twentieth-century 'alienation' by romanticizing the past. It has been suggested that in a rootless, unstable world a myth has evolved of a former society which is fondly supposed to have enjoyed a coherence, a sense of community, which has since been lost.[2] It is right, therefore, to question whether such a feeling of common identity really existed at particular times or places in human history which have been described in those terms. Such questioning is salutary, a stimulus to precision. Yet it need not lead to the bleakness of positivism.

Despite all the attention which towns have recently received, the heart of the matter, the experience of human life in the city, continues to elude definition. Yet at least two perennial features can be identified. The first of these is the concentration within relatively narrow bounds of a large population, whose diversity is accentuated by a continuous influx of immigrants. The second outstanding feature is a variety of economic activity. A legally independent administration has also been taken by many historians to be an

---

[1] See the comment of Susan Reynolds in *Urban History Yearbook* (1980), 76.
[2] A. Macfarlane, *Reconstructing Historical Communities* (Cambridge, 1977).

essential criterion of urban identity; but the unincorporated town of Westminster shows that this aspect is of secondary importance. Westminster in the late Middle Ages exemplified unmistakably the distinctive phenomena of the concentration of population and of the diversification of economic life. These developments in Westminster, moreover, can be seen to have given rise to certain problems which are themselves eternally characteristic of the urban experience: problems associated with antisocial industries, public sanitation, overcrowded dwellings, poverty and latent threats to social order, disease, and, above all else, a frighteningly high incidence of mortality. How, it may be asked, are town dwellers ever able to tolerate such pressures? It might be expected that the strains imposed would only be exacerbated by social differences, such as Westminster contained in extremes: differences between professional lawyer and artisan craftsman, Dutch and English, cleric and layman, courtier and huckster. And yet the society of Westminster showed itself able, on occasion, to transcend these distinctions, in a common cause to relieve the tensions of life in the town and to realize in the process a common identity.

The population of medieval Westminster lived within a small compass. For all their diversity, its members experienced a degree of mutual intimacy born of physical proximity and, more particularly, of a shared interest in local issues. Apart from the more or less formal mechanisms which gave periodic expression to that common involvement, the daily encounters of the street and the exchange of gossip affirmed that the town was a small world. News-mongers broadcast the actions of their neighbours, and common report brought private lives into the public domain of the town. The currency of rumour still operated in this way in Stuart Westminster, whose population was more numerous even than the three thousand of the early Tudor period. In one of his plays Ben Jonson, who knew Westminster well, portrayed the gossips of the town. These scorn the fantastical stories of distant affairs marketed from a newly established 'staple of news':

MIRTH. But how like you the news? . . .
CENSURE. O, they are monstrous! scurvy and stale, and too exotic!

   .   .   .   .

TATTLE. . . . I have better news from the bake-house, by ten thousand parts, in a morning; or the conduits in Westminster: all the news of Tuttle-

Street, and both the Alm'ries, the two Sanctuaries, long and round
Wool-staple, with King's-street, and Canon-row to boot.

MIRTH. Ay, my gossip Tattle knew what fine slips grew in Gardener's-lane;
who kist the butcher's wife with the cow's breath; what matches were
made in the Bowling-alley, and what bets were won and lost; how much
grist went to the mill, and what besides.[3]

Active co-operation between the diverse inhabitants of Westminster in the Middle Ages was never more than intermittent. The
sense of a shared identity was not ever-present, but was realized in
response to specific practical problems affecting the neighbourhood, and on certain ritual occasions. The communal activities of
the jurors and numerous petty officers of the manor court, of the
collective body of the parishioners, and of the various guilds of the
town did not eliminate social inequalities, nor yet injustice and
hardship. But their evident vitality may begin to explain how it was
that, in the Middle Ages, civic life could be regarded, not as a barely
supportable ill, but as a good end in itself.

[3] Ben Jonson, *The Staple of News* (1631), III. ii.

APPENDIX I

Reeves, Bailiffs, and Sub-bailiffs of Westminster, c.1150–c.1540

The reeve or bailiff of Westminster and his deputy represented the abbot's secular authority within the liberty, as it was defined in 1222.[1] The area of the liberty included that of the vill but was greater than the latter; yet there was no administrative distinction between the two.[2] The replacement of the name reeve by that of bailiff also occurred in other towns in the late thirteenth century.[3]

Reeves (Prepositi)

1138 × c.1157	Richard (1)
1190-ante 1197	Edward (2)
c.1189 × c.1197	Richard de Dol (3)
1197/8	Roger Enganet (4)
1197 × 1217	{ Henry Sumer (5)
	{ Richard Testard (6)
ante 1217–	Odo the goldsmith (7)
1225–30–	Robert de Crokesle (8)
–1241–1244–	Richer de Cruce (9)
mid-13c.	Richer de Fonte (10)
,,	Richard de Solario (11)

---

[1] See ch. 7.

[2] A contrast may be drawn with Bury, where there *was* a distinction between the *banleuca* of the immediate vicinity of St Edmund's shrine and a much wider surrounding liberty of 8½ hundreds. M. D. Lobel, 'The Ecclesiastical *banleuca* in England', in F. M. Powicke (ed.), *Oxford Essays in Medieval History* (Oxford, 1934), 122–40, esp. p. 135.

[3] Cf. J. Campbell, 'Norwich', in M. D. Lobel (ed.), *The Atlas of Historic Towns*, ii (London, 1975), 12; and Lobel, *The Borough of Bury St Edmunds* (Oxford, 1935), 60–1 and n., where further examples are cited. See also W. Urry, *Canterbury under the Angevin Kings* (London, 1967), 85.

Bailiffs (Ballivi)

		Sub-bailiffs (Subballivi)
*c.*1280	Nicholas (12)	
1287–93	Philip de Worstede (13)	
1289	William de Wakerle (14)	
1301–4	Richard de Bough (15)	
1304–11	Robert de Merston (16)	
1315–16	Thomas Seman (17)	
1317–18, 1322	Roger de Presthope (18)	
1319–21	John de Swaneseye (19)	
1323–4	?John le Brewer (20)	
1328–36	Thomas Sprot (21)	
1340–1	Geoffrey Aston (22)	*Sub-bailiffs (Subballivi)*
1367	Robert Gy (23)	
1375	Richard Hayton (24)	
1391–1402		Thomas Rydyng (25)
1397	Richard Long (26)	
1404–5		John Howe (27)
1406–7	Robert Haxey (28)	Thomas Kentbury (29)
1407		Thomas Neuport (30)
1408	John Howe (31)	
1410		Richard Knappe (32)
*c.*1428–32		William Wytton (33)
1434–40		John Rawlyn (34)
1455	Richard Howe (35)	
1456–7		William ate Hethe (36)
1458–9		Stephen Reuley (37)
1462–71		T. Saunder (38)
1435–64	John Savage (39)	
1468	John Colyns (40)	
1480 × 1482–4	John Kendale (41)	
1486–95		Robert Raby (42)
1495–8	Peter Curteys (43)	
1499–1500	Richard Doland (44)	
1501–33	Hugh Vaughan (45)	
1512–20/1		Maurice Davy (46)
1530–3		William Holmes (47)
1535/6		John Carter (48)

(1) WAM 17311 (dated to the abbacy of Gervase).

(2) In office in 1190; but called himself 'formerly reeve' in 1197. Pipe Roll Society, NS, i. 157; BL MS Cart. Harl. 49 G.30. See also *Transactions of the*

Royal Historical Society, 4th ser., xv (1932), 84–5. Edward the reeve and his wife Cecily, and son John, held considerable property in Westminster, particularly in the street of Tothill; see ch. 1. Edward died *ante* 1200. *Curia Regis Rolls*, i. 234. His anniversary was kept in Westminster Abbey about this time. WAM 17323 (dated to the priorate of Robert de Molesham, for whom see Pearce, *Monks*, 46); and see *Customary*, 101.

(3) WAM 17323 (for dating see no. 2). Richard de Dol was also seneschal to two abbots of Westminster, first probably to Ralph de Arundel (1200–14) and subsequently to Richard de Berking (1222–46). WAM 17327 (which names Bishop Herbert the Poor of Salisbury, 1194–1217); WD, fo. 101^r.

(4) WAM 17080; WD, fo. 473^r (dated). See also WAM 17320 (witnessed by Adam, the bishop's nephew, for whom see ch. 1 n. 8). Roger, whose name suggests that he may have been an 'engineer', had a 'stone house' at Westminster, a sign of distinction. WD, fo. 550^v. His heir was named Walter Brun. WD, fos. 550^v–551^r.

(5) WD, fo. 342^r: a deed witnessed by both Sumer and Testard, *prepositi* (the deed concerns William of Ely, king's treasurer, who held office 1197–1217). The family of Sumer held land of the abbey at Charing and at Wandsworth. The identification of Henry Sumer as reeve of Westminster confirms Barbara Harvey's guess that he was, 'in all likelihood, an important lay official of the monastery'. Harvey, *Estates*, 116.

(6) See no. 5. For the descent of Testard's family, see *Curia Regis Rolls*, xiv. 217, 239. For property in the high street of Westminster held by the Testard family by grant of Richard de Dol (see no. 3), see WAM 17597, 17429, 17334.

(7) WAM 17443 (William of Ely, king's treasurer, 1197–1217, is named); WD, fo. 357^r (witnessed by Robert de Crokesle, for whom see no. 8). Odo the goldsmith was a servant of Henry III from at least 1219 to 1239, performing some of the functions of a clerk of works. See ch. 1 for this and for Odo's houses at Westminster.

(8) LN, fos. 2^r–3^r (dated 1225); WD, fo. 512^r (dated 1230). See also WD, fo. 351^r (a deed involving William de Bedford, sacrist; this officer is known in 1247, Pearce, *Monks*, 196). Perhaps a relative of Richard de Crokesle, abbot of Westminster (1246–58).

(9) WAM 17376 (datable before 1240/1, when Hubert de Burgh confirmed the sale of his Westminster houses, *Cal Ch R 1226–57*, p. 284); WAM 17333 (dated 1241); WAM 17371 and PRO, CP25(1)/147/13/218 (dated 1244); WAM 17367 (datable to 1244/5, see WAM 17334). Richer de Cruce, who until 1265 held a corrody in the abbey kitchen, bequeathed a rent in Westminster for the performance, after his death, of his anniversary in the abbey. WD, fos. 443^v–444^r.

(10) WAM 17539 (*temp.* Odo the goldsmith and his son, Edward; see no. 7).

(11) WD, fo. 79^v (Edward, son of Odo the goldsmith, a witness; Edward died in 1265, *Cal Pat R 1258–66*, p. 440).

(12) WD, fo. 345^v (John Sutton, then sacrist, held office in 1266 and in 1282–7, Pearce, *Monks*, 196).

(13) WAM 24694, 28938.

(14) *Cal Letter-Bk A*, 118.

(15) WAM 29101, 17490, 19839–40; WD, fos. 103^v–104^r.

(16) WAM 17530 (see 17493), 19841–3.

(17) PRO, SC6/1109/5: Thomas Seman, bailiff of Westminster, received 14d. per week, i.e. £3. 6s. 8d. p.a. wage.

(18) WAM 24698; PRO, C145/94/27. Presthope's earlier connection with the abbey is apparent from the fact that he was arrested, together with many of the brethren and lay officers, following the burglary of the royal treasury in 1303. *Cal Pat R 1301–7*, p. 195. He was one of the abbot's bailiffs (for Middlesex?) throughout the period 1316–26. WAM 32321–6. With his wife, Joan, he quitclaimed a tenement in Tothill St. in 1315. WAM 17564 (see 17573). He was alive in 1336. WAM 17163. Admitted a citizen of London 1310–11. *Cal Letter-Bk D*, 63.

(19) WAM 24701, 50693.

(20) WAM 24702. It is not always clear for which district a particular 'bailiff of the abbot of Westminster's liberty' was responsible. It can be hard, as in the present case, to distinguish a bailiff of the abbot in Westminster from the abbot's bailiff in the county of Middlesex.

(21) WAM 24708–15; BL MS Cart. Harl. 45 D.10.

(22) As the abbot's bailiff, Aston collected certain rents in Westminster, attached to the hospital of St Mary Rounceval but at this date forfeit to the crown. PRO, E372/186, m.16d.

(23) *Cal Cl R 1364–8*, p. 398. Robert Guy 'of Uxbridge' held houses and lands in Westminster and Eye in the 1360s and 1370s. LN, fos. 113^{r-v}, 115^r; *Cal Cl R 1364–8*, p. 81; WAM 4785, 4833.

(24) WAM 50706; LN, fo. 114^{r-v} (1380: 'Richard Hayton, bailiff of Westminster'). In 1383/4 Hayton was bailiff in Middlesex. WAM 24742.

(25) WAM 50720, 50726 (described in 1392 as 'keeper of the peace'); PRO, KB9/175/29 (1397); KB9/178/47 (1402). Thomas Rydyng was a royal commissioner for Henry IV in Nov. 1399. *Cal Pat R 1399–1401*, p. 163. In 1405 he was under-marshal of the marshalsea of the king's bench. *Cal Pat R 1405–8*, p. 63.

(26) PRO, KB9/175/8 (Feb. 1397).

(27) PRO, KB9/198/24; KB27/574, rex roll, m.8d.

(28) 'Supervisor of the liberty' in the vill, in receipt of a wage of 3d. a day. WAM 50736. Also held the office of janitor of Westminster Abbey, with the keepership of the gaol, from 1398. LN, fo. 84^{r-v}; WAM 18885*. Rented several properties in the sanctuary of Westminster; and apparently occupied the large house called 'Delaberes' there 1420–32. WAM

17718–19, 19663–73, 18890. Was appointed to a commission to raise a royal loan in Middx. 1420. *Cal F R 1413–22*, p. 316.

(29) WAM 50736. Named there as 'bailiff' in the vill, but on a smaller salary (26s. 8d. p.a.) than Haxey (no. 28), who is therefore assumed to have held the more elevated post. For Kentbury, who was a mason, see also app. VIII, s.n.

(30) PRO, KB9/198/24 (Aug. 1407).

(31) WAM 50737.

(32) PRO, KB9/197/4. A tailor. See app. VIII, s.n.

(33) PRO, KB9/224/35; KB9/226/111.

(34) WAM 50749; PRO, KB9/228/2/341 (1436); KB9/232/2/73 (1440). See also app. VIII, s.n.

(35) PRO, E179/141/89.

(36) WAM 19963.

(37) WAM 19965.

(38) WAM 19970–6.

(39) PRO, KB9/227/1/89 (1435); Oxford, Bodleian Library, MS D.D. Queen's College 1759; *Cal Cl R 1468–78*, no. 281; PRO, E40/2287. Described as a 'gentleman', Savage held both the Boar's Head and the Antelope hostelries in King St. in the second half of the century. He also leased, with John Barrow, the farm of Paddington manor, from c.1450. WAM 17771, 23078–80, 50756, 23516. In 1461 he was rewarded by the abbey treasurer for legal counsel given by him. WAM 19966. In 1478–9 a John Savage, possibly the same man, was door-keeper of Star Chamber in Westminster Palace. PRO, E403/848, m.9.

(40) PRO, E40/1522. The son of Robert Colyns, tiler of Westminster, and of his wife, Alice. John succeeded his parents after 1475, and until 1478 × 1480, in the tenancy of two tenements in King St. WAM 23229–53, 17773, 17789. John also rented six gardens near King St. 1467–70. WAM 23243–4.

(41) PRO, KB9/361/68; C1/61/563; WAM 19978. 'Notary public of Westminster'. *Cal Cl R 1467–85*, p. 213. Kendale wrote the churchwardens' accounts of St Margaret's church, Westminster, 1475/6; his signature, 'Kendale notarius', appears here and on a quitclaim of Westminster property, also written by him, of 1473. CWA i. 120, 122; WAM 17813. In 1478–9 × 1481 John Kendale rented a 'long house' in the sanctuary of Westminster. WAM 19727. This John Kendale should probably be distinguished from at least three more prominent contemporaries of the same name, one of whom was secretary to King Richard III. See A. F. Sutton, 'John Kendale: A Search for Richard III's Secretary', in J. Petre (ed.), *Richard III; Crown and People* (Richard III Society, London, 1985), 224–38. The wife of John Kendale (?not the notary) was buried in Westminster Abbey in 1501–2. WAM 19757.

(42) *Cal Pat R 1485–94*, pp. 151–2; WAM 50767–8. In the abbey treasurer's accounts the name is entered as John Raby, presumably in error. WAM 19979–90. For Raby's turbulent period in office as bailiff, see ch. 7; see also app. VIII, s.n.

(43) WAM 19993–4. Peter Curteys 'of the king's household' rented a stable in the abbey almonry, which he apparently converted into a 'tenement', in the 1460s. WAM 19069, 19074–5. Made keeper of Westminster Palace in 1472, from 1478 he was employed in the royal wardrobe, of which he also became keeper in 1480. *Cal Pat R 1467–77*, p. 295; ibid. *1476–85*, pp. 198, 222; PRO, E403/848, m.7. He lost these offices in Sept. 1483, and during the reign of Richard III took sanctuary at Westminster. But in 1486 Henry VII restored his former titles, and made him in addition a gentleman and usher of the king's chamber. *Cal Pat R 1485–94*, p. 26; *Materials for a History of the Reign of Henry VII*, ed. W. Campbell, 2 vols., Rolls Series (1873–7), i. 27, 49, 324, 582; ii. 517–18. Between 1467 and 1495 he was regularly MP for Appleby or the borough of Leicester. J. C. Wedgwood and A. D. Holt, *History of Parliament 1438–1509* (London, 1936), 244–5. He died in 1505. His will is PRO, PROB11/14, PCC 29 Holgrave.

(44) WAM 19996. See Reg Bk, i, fo. 78ʳ: grant, dated 6 Aug. 1495, of 'the office of bailiff of Westminster . . . in the counties of Middlesex, Surrey, and Buckinghamshire, as well as in Westminster and Brentford . . . to hold in person or by deputy', when it should next fall vacant. Doland had recently retired from the office of clerk of the king's works in England, which he had held since 1485. *Cal Pat R 1485–94*, pp. 11, 65; *King's Works*, iii. 5–6, 406. He held a tenement in the sanctuary of Westminster 1497–1500. Reg Bk, i, fo. 95ʳ⁻ᵛ; WAM 19751–4. Dining with the abbot in Mar. 1493, Doland regaled the company with a somewhat sensational story of wayside murder. WAM 33290, fos. 3–4. He died in 1500, and was buried at St Margaret's church. CWA i. 395.

(45) WAM 19998–9, 23001–4 (1501–8); 50777 (1514); PRO, C1/828/1 (dated by internal evidence to *c.*1533). Sir Hugh Vaughan was probably the most distinguished of all the known medieval bailiffs of Westminster. From 1522–33 he was captain of the island of Jersey, in succession to his presumed father of the same name. Until 1527 he also held the shrievalty of Carnarvon, north Wales, with which his family name suggests he may have been associated by birth. In 1494, then an esquire of the king's body, he had taken a lease on the great messuage near Long Ditch in Westminster called 'Caleys'. He was knighted in 1504, and moved at about that date to a large tenement in the abbey precinct (one of the 'Sarum rents'). He appears to have retired to Westminster, for after 1533 he rented further tenements within the northern sanctuary gate. His will, made in 1533, was proved in 1536. By it, he requested burial in Westminster Abbey, in the chapel of St

Michael, or else in 'Lyttleton'. *LP* i, no. 2535 (17), iii, nos. 2653, 2676–7, iv, no. 3747 (3), vi, no. 1195 (17); W. A. Shaw, *The Knights of England* (London, 1906), ii. 34; Reg Bk, i, fo. 73ʳ⁻ᵛ; WAM 23130–2, 18031, 23132–78; Reg Bk, ii, fos. 293ᵛ–294ʳ; PRO, PROB11/25, PCC 40 Hogan.

(46) Pardoned by the king in 1512 for the death of one attempting to prevent Davy from making an arrest in Westminster. *LP* i, no. 1494 (11). Reproved by the court and seneschal of Westminster in 1514 for excessive zeal shown in the execution of his office. WAM 50777. In 1515 he leased a part of Mauduitsgarden or Petty Calais in Westminster as 'Maurice Davy of the town of Westminster, underbailiff of the said town and one of the yeomen of the crown'. WAM 36400. Still in office in 1520/1. Rounceval guild accts, s.a. Died 1522; was buried in St Margaret's church. CWA ii, s.a. 1521–2, wk. 42.

(47) PRO, C1/828/1 (see no. 45). Holmes was described as a yeoman of the king's guard. In 1529 he held the Antelope inn in King St. Reg Bk, ii, fo. 255ᵛ.

(48) This officer paid for his pew in St Margaret's church in this year. CWA iii, s.a.

APPENDIX II

Curates of St Margaret's Parish Church, Westminster, c.1200–1556

The sacrist of Westminster Abbey, as vicar of St Margaret's church from c.1300 until the Dissolution, was responsible during that period for the appointment and maintenance of the incumbents.[1] The present list is largely based upon the series of account rolls of the sacrists.[2]

c.1200	Simon (1)
c.1220 × 1240	Robert (2)
c.1240	John (3)
–1268	Walter (4)
1268–	Geoffrey Norman (5)
1316	Thomas de Cherlecote (6)
1339	John de Gloucester (7)
1366	Ralph (8)
1366	William Parish (9)
1370–90	William Kempstone (10)
1390–9	Walter Donewell (11)
1399–1408	Peter (12)
1416	John Latener (13)
1422–4	Nicholas More (14)
1424–8	John (15)
1428 × 1440?	John Swan (16)
1440–77	Richard Saxilby (17)
1477–8	Thomas Norfolk (18)
1478–9	Richard Davis (19)
1479–92	Thomas Draper (20)
1492–3	John Shrewsbury (21)
1493–5	John Lightfote (22)
1495–1500	Roger Blethir (23)

[1] See ch. 8, sect. 1.
[2] Lists of the medieval clergy of St Margaret's have previously been published by M. E. C. Walcott, *The History of the Parish Church of St. Margaret, in Westminster* (Westminster, 1847), 83; G. Hennessy, *Novum Repertorium Ecclesiasticum Parochiale Londinense* (London, 1898), 438–9; and H. F. Westlake, *St. Margaret's, Westminster: The Church of the House of Commons* (London, 1914), 231–3.

1500–6	John Conyas (24)
1506/7–12	John Synes (25)
1512–14	William Ravenyng (26)
1514–15	William Balard (27)
1515–16	Robert Dandy (28)
1516–17	William (29)
1517–23	James Hall (30)
1523–5	Robert Dandy (31)
1525–30/1	William Mote (32)
1530/1–32	William Tenant (33)
1532–56	Henry Mote (34)

(1) *Capellanus* of the church. WAM 17428 (witnessed by Odo the goldsmith and Robert de Crokesle, for whom see app. 1).

(2) *Capellanus* of the church. WD, fo. 349^{r-v} (also witnessed by Odo the goldsmith, reeve; see app. 1); WAM 17445 (also witnessed by Robert de Crokesle, reeve, and by Odo the goldsmith; see app. 1). The last-mentioned is a grant of property made by another Robert Capellanus, son of Richard Capellanus.

(3) Priest of the church; executor of the will of a local inhabitant. WD, fo. 545^{r-v} (datable *ante* 1240/1, when Hubert de Burgh confirmed the sale of his Westminster houses, *Cal Ch R 1226–57*, p. 284; two immediately subsequent quitclaims of the deceased person's property are addressed to Ralph de Glovernia, monk-warden of St Mary's altar in the abbey, who held this office in 1240–7, Pearce, *Monks*, 50; WD, fo. 545^{r-v}).

(4) See no. 5.

(5) Royal chaplain, appointed by the king to 'celebrate divine service in St Margaret's church, Westminster . . . taking yearly for such celebration £3 at the exchequer for his wages, as Walter, late the king's chaplain, deceased, used to take'. *Cal Pat R 1266–72*, p. 261. The curacy was therefore at this date in the gift of the king; see ch. 8, sect. 1.

(6) *Capellanus* of the church; made a grant of his messuage and curtilage, with all his movable goods, in Tothill St., in 1316. WAM 17568–9. Described as 'chaplain' in 1321; and as 'chaplain', quitclaimed his right to lands in Westminster and Eye in 1324. But by 21 May 1323 he was 'vicar of St Nicholas's church, Paddington next Kilburn'. WAM 17584; LN, fo. 128^{r-v}.

(7) Rented 'le Presthawe' (i.e. the priest's house) next to St Margaret's church, paying 5s. p.a. to the sacrist. WAM 19621. A John de Gloucester, priest, was presented to Herdyngton (Harlington, Middx.) on 9 July 1330. *Registrum . . . Episcoporum Londoniensium, 1304–1338*, ed. R. C. Fowler, Canterbury and York Society, vii (1910–11), 293.

(8) *Capellanus* of the church. On 11 Sept. 1366 (following an abbatial

directive dated 21 July 1366), Ralph proclaimed the convention of a court before the abbot to try a case of murder in Westminster. WAM 17682.

(9) *Capellanus* of the church. WAM 17682.

(10) *Capellanus* of the church. Held the farm of the church in 1370. WAM 30030. Was said in 1373 to be of Lincoln diocese. Was in that year evidently acting as a trustee of Westminster Abbey in the acquisition of local property. WAM 17688; and see above, ch. 3 n. 82. Was named as 'William, parochial chaplain', in the poll-tax return of 1381. A. K. McHardy, *The Church in London 1375–1392*, London Record Society, xiii (1977), no. 391. Received instructions from the archdeacon in 1388 to excommunicate a debtor. WAM 5979. As '*capellanus* of the vill of Westminster', made a quitclaim of local property on 9 Mar. 1390. WAM 17711.

(11) Parish priest from 1 May 1390. For the year 1390–1, Donewell received £5 as a stipend, £5 4s. for his *mensa*, and 10s. for his *vestura*. From 1391 he held a twelve-year lease on the farm of the church, paying to the sacrist £13. 6s. 4d. p.a. WAM 19647–57.

(12) Held an eight-year lease on the farm of the church @ £13. 6s. 8d. p.a. WAM 19659–60.

(13) Took a twenty-year lease on St Margaret's vicarage in this year @ £13. 6s. 8d. p.a. Undertook to celebrate divine service in person unless prevented by illness, when he was to find a substitute. WAM 17730.

(14) In 1422–3, received £10 p.a., 'tam pro salario quam pro mensa', from the sacrist. In the following year, leased the farm of the church @ £13. 6s. 8d. p.a.; but died on 9 May 1424. WAM 19663–5.

(15) Received £10 p.a., for his salary and keep, from the sacrist. WAM 19666–9.

(16) Chaplain of the church at some date in the fifteenth century. His obit was kept there in *c*.1465. CWA i. 27. A great breviary, with a great gilded 'D' at the beginning, was given by him to the fraternity of the Virgin's Assumption in the church, for the use of the morrow mass priest. Assumption guild accts, inventory, s.a. 1508.

(17) Leased the farm of the church (for his lifetime) @ £10. 13s. 4d. p.a. WAM 19684–724. Provided a gradual for the church in 1467/8, for which the churchwardens paid him 10s. CWA i. 87. In 1467/8, gave to the church 'a choir cope of red silk with flowers, and the orphrey thereof green'. CWA i. 121. Died 1477; his obit kept in the church in 1478/9. CWA i. 130. Rented a garden in Long Ditch 1445–77. WAM 17763, 23224–51. Bequeathed (his lease on?) a tenement and garden in Long Ditch, and 20s., to the fraternity of the Virgin's Assumption. This fraternity kept Saxilby's obit in 1487–9, with seven priests and two clerks. Assumption guild accts, s.a. From 1471–6, Saxilby contributed £2 p.a. to the rebuilding of the abbey nave; in 1477, he left £6. 13s. 4d. to the same by his will. WAM 23537–47.

(18) Leased the farm of the church @ £24 p.a. WAM 19725. Thomas was the son of William Norfolk, alias Benyngton, who bequeathed 6s. 8d. to St Margaret's church in 1474 × 1476. CWA i. 112, 121. Thomas Norfolk left (*recessit*) the curacy during 1478–9. WAM 19727.

(19) Served briefly at the church, following the departure of Thomas Norfolk. WAM 19727.

(20) Leased the farm of the church @ £24 p.a.; which rate was reduced to £20 after 1488, in compensation for building work then in progress on the church. WAM 19727–41.

(21) Rendered £31. 17s. 8½d. for the farm of the church. WAM 19743.

(22) Rendered £32. 15s. 9½d. for the farm of the church in 1493–4; and £37 . . . (rest of figure lost in stain) in 1494–5. WAM 19745–6.

(23) Rendered between £30 and £40 p.a. for the farm of the church. WAM 19747–55.

(24) Rendered between £30 and £40 p.a. for the farm of the church. WAM 19756–61.

(25) Leased the farm of the church @ £30 p.a. WAM 19762/3–8. Before 1513 Synes occupied a tenement, called 'Bysett tavern', and garden in the sanctuary of Westminster, between Henry VII's new chapel and the anchoress's house on the south side of the chancel of St Margaret's. See Reg Bk, ii, fos. 48ᵛ–49ʳ. Joined the fraternity of the Virgin's Assumption in the church in 1505 × 1508. Assumption guild accts, s.a.

(26) Leased the farm of the church @ £30 p.a. WAM 19770–1. Probably king's scholar at Eton College 1496–1500; scholar and fellow of King's College, Cambridge, 1500–5/6; BA 1505/6; ordained subdeacon of Lincoln diocese 1504. A. B. Emden, *A Biographical Register of the University of Cambridge to 1504* (Cambridge, 1963), 473. Apparently autograph notes of William Ravenyng's expenses as curate of St Margaret's in 1513–14 include a reference to a visit to Cambridge in April ?1513. Trips to 'Nete' (i.e. 'La Nete', the abbot's house at Eyebury near Westminster), also mentioned, suggest friendly contact with Abbot Islip of Westminster. WAM 33300. Died 22 Apr. 1514; was buried in the chancel of St Margaret's. Bequeathed his great bed, with coverlet and tester, and two best kerchiefs, to 'my lady Ancress'. PCW Wyks, 194–5. His mother, Elizabeth Ravenyng of Westminster, who survived him by a year, was probably buried next to him. Her will refers to another son, Richard, and to two daughters, Agnes and Isabel. PCW Wyks, 213–14.

(27) 'Mr William Balard, doctor, and curate of St Margaret's', witnessed the will of a parishioner on 14 Oct. 1514; and of another on 1 Jan. 1515. PCW Wyks, 199–202, 210–11. 'Mr William, curate', leased the farm of the church in 1514–15. WAM 19773. In 1515–18, Sir William Balard was a chaplain of the fraternity of the Virgin's Assumption in the church, receiving a salary of £6. 13s. 4d. p.a. He gave various vestments and

decorated cloths, items of plate, and a mass book to the same fraternity. Assumption guild accts. On 13 Aug. 1518 the treasurer of Westminster Abbey noted the receipt of certain goods of 'Mr Balard, clerk'. These goods included vestments, plate, a gilded image of St Christopher, and a pair of spectacles with a case. WAM 6651.

It is uncertain whether the curate is to be identified with a Mr William Balard, doctor of physic, who was buried within St Margaret's church in July 1519, a memorial stone being set in the wall. CWA ii, s.a. This William Balard (or Ballard) had, since 1508, rented two successive tenements in the sanctuary. CWA i. 555, 566; CWA ii, rentals of the tenements late of Henry Abingdon; WAM 23933–41. Balard the physician bequeathed 40s. towards the gilding of the Virgin's tabernacle in the chapel of the Assumption guild. Guild accts, s.a. 1518–21.

(28) Held the farm of St Margaret's in 1515–16, and again in 1523–5. In the first period he rendered £30 p.a.; in the second, between £20 and £25 p.a. WAM 19775, 19791–2. Dandy's own notes of offerings made to him as curate in 1524–5 are extant. WAM 31886, 31894.

(29) Leased the farm of the church @ £30 p.a. WAM 19775*.

(30) Leased the farm of the church @ £30 p.a. WAM 19776–90.

(31) See no. 28.

(32) Rendered between £20 and £25 p.a. for the farm of the church. WAM 19793–804. On 18 Dec. 1529 William Mote, S.T.B., became vicar of St Bride's, Fleet St., which office, however, he resigned in the following year. He also held at various dates the rectory of St Gabriel, Fenchurch St., London, and three different livings in Essex. G. Hennessy, *Novum Repertorium Ecclesiasticum Parochiale Londinense* (London, 1898), 113 and n.

(33) 'Curate of the church.' In 1531–2 Tenant rendered £22. 13s. 10d. for the farm of the church. WAM 19807. Died in Aug. 1532; was buried at St Margaret's. CWA iii, s.a.

(34) 'Sir Henry Mote, curate of St Margaret's', witnessed the will of a parishioner on 2 Aug. 1532; and wrote that of another in June 1537. (In 1530, before becoming curate, he wrote the churchwardens' accounts of St Margaret's.) Another parishioner bequeathed to him a pair of sheets in Apr. 1538. PCW Bracy, fos. 28ᵛ–29ᵛ, 55ʳ, 61ᵛ–62ʳ; CWA iii, s.a. 1530. In 1552, again described as curate of the church, he borrowed 13s. 4d. from the convent receiver, against his wages. WAM 37383. In 1554 'Henry Mote, clerk, curate of St Margaret's parish church', received from the dean and chapter of Westminster a tenement formerly called 'the Anker house', abutting on the south side of the chancel of the church, in which tenement Mote then dwelt, subject to his performance of the cure of souls and the payment of £13. 6s. 8d. p.a. rent. Reg Bk, iii, fo. 246ʳ⁻ᵛ. Accounts, mostly autograph, of Mote's receipts of offerings, etc., are extant for the years

1546–9 and 1551–4. WAM 33190, 37160–1, 37251–2, 33214, 33185, fo. x, 37549–50. Henry Mote died in 1556. The will of 'Sir Henry Mote, curate of St Margaret's parish church', was made on 27 Aug. and proved on 20 Oct. 1556. PCW Bracy, fos. 179^v–181^r. He was buried in St Margaret's church, near the high altar. CWA iv, s.a.

APPENDIX III

The Financial Value of St Margaret's Vicarage, 1291–1549

Period	Annual value of vicarage	Source
1291	£8 0s. 0d.	*Taxatio . . . P. Nicholai* (Record Commission, 1802), 17b
Early 14c.	£8 13s. 4d.	LN, fo. 141ʳ
1317–18	£10 6s. 8d.	WAM 19618
1346–7	£6 13s. 4d.	WAM 19622
1362–3	£6 13s. 4d.	WAM 19629
1364–5	£5 0s. 0d.	WAM 19630
1372–89	£6 0s. 0d.	WAM 19633–46
1391–1428	£13 6s. 8d.	WAM 19650–60, 17730, 19665
1428–32	£12 0s. 0d.	WAM 19670–2
1432–9	£8 13s. 4d.	WAM 19673–80
1440–77	£10 13s. 4d.	WAM 19684–724
1477–88	£24 0s. 0d.	WAM 19725–35
1488–92	£20 0s. 0d.	WAM 19736–41
1492–1523	£30–£40	WAM 19743–90
1523–32	£20–£25	WAM 19791–807
1542–3	c.£18	PRO, SC6/Hen.VIII/2414, fos. 20ᵛ–21ʳ
1548–9	c.£21	WAM 37251A–D; 37252

Notes:

(i) These sums represent in some cases (a) the surplus revenues of the living remaining to the sacrist after the payment of the curate's stipend (the latter remaining, at such times, constant from 1391 onwards at £10 p.a.), and in others (b) the fixed annual farm or rent paid by the curate for his tenancy (which rent should presumably have been adjusted so as to leave the curate £10 p.a., more or less, out of the remaining profits of the living). The two forms of valuation are thus approximately, though not exactly, equivalent.

(ii) Although three sacrist's accounts survive from the period between 1347 and 1362, they record no income at all from the church: WAM 19623 (1354–5), 19626 (1358–9), 19628 (1361–2).

(iii) The reduction of the annual rate by £4 in the years 1488–92 was made explicitly on account of the rebuilding of the nave of the church, then in progress. This work may well have drawn off parishioners' contributions away from the curate and chancel.

(iv) After 1540, the advowson passed to the newly created bishopric of Westminster and in turn, after 1550, to the bishopric of London.

APPENDIX IV

Revenues of the Obedientiaries of Westminster Abbey Holding Rents in the Town of Westminster, 1350–1530[1]

(A) REVENUES OF THE SACRIST

Period	Years recorded	Net income (£ p.a.)[2]	Westminster rents 'at farm' (£ p.a.)	Westminster rents 'at farm' (% of total)
1350–75	5	225	?	
1375–1400	17	229	109	48
1400–25	4	220	108	49
1425–50	17	178	97	54
1450–75	18	188	123	65
1475–1500	22	209	121	58
1500–30	28	209	135	65

Source: WAM 19626–804

(B) REVENUES OF THE ALMONER

Period	Years recorded	Net income (£ p.a.)[2]	Westminster rents 'at farm' (£ p.a.)	Westminster rents 'at farm' (% of total)
1350–75	10	50	7	14
1375–1400	8	75	17	22
1400–25	19	63	18	29
1425–50	20	52	25	48
1450–75	14	60	35	58
1475–1500	21	65	43	66
1500–30	21	88	50	57

Source: WAM 18986–19144

(C) REVENUES OF THE CELLARER

Period	Years recorded	Net income (£ p.a.)[2]	Westminster rents 'at farm'	
			(£ p.a.)	(% of total)
1350–75	15	80	—	—
1375–1400	17	103	6	6
1400–25	3	147	8	5
1425–50	2	81	13	16
1450–75	2	68	13	19
1475–1500	8	77	13	17
1500–30	22	81	13	16

Source: WAM 18843–944

(D) REVENUES OF THE WARDEN OF THE LADY CHAPEL[3]

Period	Years recorded	Westminster rents 'at farm' (£ p.a.)
1350–75	4	10
1375–1400	7	17
1400–25	10	22
1425–50	9	21
1450–75	14	40
1475–1500	14	43
1500–30	23	42

Source: WAM 23183–310

[1] Of the six obedientiaries holding significant portfolios of Westminster rents, the domestic treasurer is omitted here, because the number of his properties continued to change over a long period.

[2] Net income is that remaining after the subtraction of any credit balance carried over from the previous annual account. No adjustment has been made to iron out the effects of extraordinary income in exceptional years. Such extraordinary income, however, does not seriously affect the pattern of receipts over twenty-five-year periods, as shown here.

[3] Westminster rents accounted for the bulk of the revenues of the Lady chapel.

(E) REVENUES OF THE WARDEN OF THE 'NEW WORK'[4]

Period	Years recorded	Westminster rents 'at farm' (£ p.a.)
1375–1400	8	25
1400–25	17	26
1425–50	14	24
1450–75	15	25
1475–1500	22	27
1500–30	28	31

Source: WAM 23460–619

[4] The total annual income of the 'new work' fluctuated greatly over short periods, but was usually around £100.

APPENDIX V

Tenants and Subtenants of Six Properties in King Street, c.1530

This appendix illustrates a theme developed in Chapter 3, where it is argued that in the late fifteenth and early sixteenth centuries, the monastic landlords were failing to collect from their Westminster tenants rents which justly reflected the actual demand for accommodation in the town.[1] This becomes particularly clear in rare instances, such as that cited here, in which the various names and rents of both tenants and subtenants are known. The considerable disparities which appear vitiate the value of the convent rentals as an index of the pressure of population during this period. Rental A is in fact an extract from the (much longer) total Westminster rental of the abbey sacrist of c.1530. It comprises a list of rents due to the convent from the leaseholders of six properties of the sacrist in King Street, between Endive Lane and Lamb Alley (see Fig. 12). Rental B is a contemporary valuation of the same six properties, which tabulates instead the rents paid to the same leaseholders by their respective subtenants. Rental B (although now preserved in the abbey) was presumably compiled for the use of the king, who in September 1531 bought out the leaseholders of all of these properties as part of the preparations for the extension of Whitehall Palace.[2] Simple comparison between the two rentals shows that, e.g., whereas Thomas Brightman paid £3. 6s. 8d. to the abbey for his 'Beer House', he collected in rents from the same property no less than £13. 19s. 8d. p.a.; and so on.

A. SACRIST'S RENTAL[3]

(1) Thomas Brightman, yeoman, for 'the Beer House at Endyf'   £3 6s. 8d.[4]

---

[1] See esp. ch. 3, sect. 4.
[2] PRO, SP1/67, pp. 82–8 (= *LP* v, no. 408).
[3] WAM 19810 (undated, but see 19804, 1529–30).
[4] See WAM 18004 (Brightman's lease of 1520). For Brightman see also PCW Bracy, fos. 86–7.

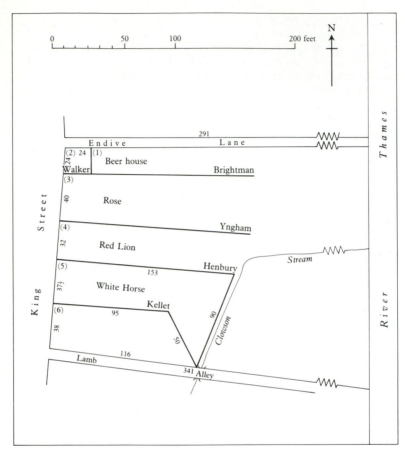

FIG. 12. Six properties in King Street, *c.*1530

(2) Richard Walker, for 'a tenement with a chamber built
above'   £1   6s. 8d.[5]
(3) Edward Yngham, gentleman and yeoman of the king's
guard, for the Rose with 'a shop and two tenements'   £4 16s. 8d.[6]
(4) John Henbury, brewer, for the Red Lion   £1   3s. 4d.[7]
(5) John Kellett, yeoman, for the White Horse   £1   6s. 8d.[8]
(6) Richard Hampkyn, buckler-maker, for three
tenements   £2 13s. 4d.[9]

B. DETAILED VALUATION[10]

Endive Lane

1. Tenements let to Thomas Brightman

A tenement and the wharf in the holding of William Perkyns	p.a.	£4 13s. 4d.
A tenement lately let to my lord Cardinal for a laundry	p.a.	£2 0s. 0d.
A great stable in the holding of Mr William Chamberlain, he bearing all manner of reparation	p.a.	£0 19s. 0d.
Three tenements above and beneath in the holding of Fyssher		£2 14s. 0d.
A tenement in the holding of Mary Onley	p.a.	£1 0s. 0d.
A tenement in the holding of John Barbur	p.a.	£1 13s. 4d.
A tenement in the holding . . . [*blank*] Sayer	p.a.	£1 0s. 0d.
Total		£13 19s. 8d.

2. Tenements let to Richard Walker by lease

A tenement with a shop in the holding of Richard Walker of Hampstead	p.a.	£3 6s. 8d.
Total		£3 6s. 8d.

---

[5] See WAM 18018 (Walker's lease of 1524).
[6] See WAM 18041 (Yngham's lease of 1528). See also WAM 12366; *LP* i, no. 1982(1); ibid. vi, no. 1195(10); PCW Bracy, fo. 46ᵛ.
[7] See Reg Bk, i, fos. 74ᵛ–75ʳ (an earlier lease of 1495); PRO, E40/1553, 1559.
[8] See WAM 18039 (Kellett's lease of 1528).
[9] See WAM 18033 (an earlier lease of 1527); PRO, E40/1536.
[10] WAM 18048 (undated, but see 19804, 19810).

King Street

3. These tenements let to Edward Yngham by lease

A tenement called the Rose in the holding of Edward Yngham	p.a.	£4	0s. 0d.
A tenement next in the holding of John Apowell	p.a.	£1	10s. 4d.
A tenement next in the holding of Walter Apowell	p.a.	£0	13s. 4d.
Total		£6	6s. 8d.

4.

A tenement called the Red Lion in the holding of John Henbury	p.a.	£9	0s. 0d.
A tenement next in the holding of Margaret Reynolds	p.a.	£1	0s. 0d.
Total		£10	0s. 0d.

5. Tenements let to Kellet by lease

A tenement in the holding of William Porter	p.a.	£3	0s. 0d.
Another tenement in the holding of John Seuell [?]	p.a.	£3	0s. 0d.
A stable in the holding of M. Tonsley	p.a.	£1	6s. 8d.
Another stable in the holding of Dr Stubbs	p.a.	£1	6s. 8d.
Another stable in the holding of Mr Donyngton	p.a.	£1	6s. 8d.
Total		£10	0s. 0d.

6. Tenements let to Hampkyn by lease

A tenement in the holding of Richard Hampkyn	p.a.	£2	0s. 0d.
A tenement next in the holding of the same Hampkyn		£2	0s. 0d.
A tenement in the holding of Harry Hays	p.a.	£2	0s. 0d.
Total		£6	0s. 0d.

APPENDIX VI[1]

Places in the British Isles Occurring in the Names of Property Holders in Westminster Before 1350

Name-form recorded	Modern place[2]	Distance (miles) from Westminster	Source[3]
Abyndon	Abingdon, Berks.	52	WAM 17641
Acton	*Acton, Middx.	5	WAM 17497
Aldebyre	*Albury, Herts.	30	WD, fo. 508v
Aldenham	†Aldenham, Herts.	16	WD, fo. 383r
Arderne	*Arden, War.	90	WAM 17593
Arundel	Arundel, Sussex	50	WD, fo. 364r–v
Asshewell	†*Ashwell, Herts.	38	WD, fo. 383r
Aston	*Aston, Herts.	27	WAM 17585
Astwyk	*Astwick, Beds.	36	WAM 17581

[1] For discussion, see ch. 6, sect. 2.
[2] Observing county boundaries as before 1974.
[3] The sources are almost exclusively deeds concerning property in Westminster. See also n. b to Table 2.

Name-form recorded	Modern place[2]	Distance (miles) from Westminster	Source[3]
Atleburgh	*Attleborough, Norfolk	88	PRO, E40/1535
Aulton	*Alton, Hants	45	WAM 17392A
Aylestone	Aylestone, Leics.	88	*Cal Cl R 1323–27*, p. 229
Badewe	N. or S. Baddow, Essex	31	WD, fo. 538ʳ
Bampton	Bampton, Oxon.	63	WAM 17576
Barra	Temple Bar, London[4]		WD, fo. 510ʳ
Bassingburn	Bassingbourn, Cambs.	40	WAM 17328
Bathonia	Bath, Somerset	98	WAM 17399
Bedewynd	Bedwyn, Wilts.	65	*Cal Inq p m* vii. 300
Begedene	Begendon, Glos.	83	WD, fo. 345ʳ
Belegrave	Belgrave, Leics.	91	WAM 17440
Bemflete	†N. or S. Benfleet, Essex	30	WAM 17585
Benestede	Banstead, Surrey	13	WAM 17610
Berking	*Barking, Essex	12	WAM 17324
Beverle	Beverley, E. Yorks.	162	WD, fo. 525ᵛ
Blockele	Blockley, Glos.	80	WAM 17449
Bocland	*Buckland, Surrey	19	BL Add. MS 28024, fo. 46ʳ
Boreham	*Boreham Wood, Herts.	12	WAM 17364
Bouleye	Beaulieu, Hants	75	WAM 17543
Brackleye	*Brackley, Northants	58	WAM 17692
Bradele	*Bradley, Berks.	52	WD, fo. 346ʳ
Bray	Bray, Berks.	25	WAM 17628

Name-form recorded	Modern place[2]	Distance (miles) from Westminster	Source[3]
Chorleton	*Charlton, Middx.	15	*Cal Pat R 1308*, p. 84
Cisestre	Chichester, Sussex	55	WAM 17441
Claygate	†*Claygate, Surrey	35	WD, fo. 357^v
Clebury	Cleobury, Salop	118	WAM 17608
Clopton	*Clopton, Northants	66	WAM 17634
Colchestre	Colchester, Essex	52	WD, fos. 562^v–563^r
Coleham	*Colham, Middx.	15	WAM 17380
Coleville	*Colwell, I.o.W.	83	WAM 17412
Condicote	Condicote, Glos.	78	WAM 17469
Corf	Corfe Castle, Dorset	105	WD, fos. 522^v–524^r
Cornewayle	Cornwall	185	WAM 17524
Cornherd	Carnard, Suffolk	52	WAM 17373
Cosham	Cosham, Hants	62	WAM 17547
Coveham	Coveham, Lincs.	135	WAM 17567
Covyntry	Coventry, War.	87	WAM 17587
Cranebroke	Cranbrook, Kent	41	WAM 17338
Crokesle	Croxley, Herts.	17	WAM 17325
Curland	Curland, Somerset	132	WAM 17311
Denham	†Denham, Bucks.	16	WAM 4785
Depden	Depden, Suffolk	61	WAM 17642
Derby	*Derby, Derby.	113	PRO, CP40/335/2, m.1
Derteford	Dartford, Kent	17	WD, fo. 529^{r-v}

Ditton	*Thames Ditton, Surrey	12	WAM 17562
Dodecote	Didcot, Berks.	50	WAM 17651
Dodeworth	Dodworth, W. Yorks.	154	WAM 17577
Dodyngton	*Doddington, Kent	42	*Cal Pat R 1326*, p. 281
Drokensford	Droxford, Hants	58	*Cal Pat R 1292–1301*, p. 228
Dureme	Durham	235	WD, fo. 513^{r}
Dyrherst	†Deerhurst, Glos.	95	BL Add. MS 28024, fo. 47^{v}
Eboraco	York	175	WD, fo. 365^{v}
Edelminton	Edmonton, Middx.	11	WAM 17338
Eie	†*Eye, Middx.	1	WAM 17614
Eltham	Eltham, Kent	13	WAM 17353
Ely	Ely, Cambs.	65	WAM 17526
Eschepe	East Cheap, London[4]		WD, fo. 359^{r}
Esseby	*Easby near Richmond, N. Yorks.	215	PRO, CP25(1)/148/25/15
Essex	Essex	10	WD, fo. 334^{r}
Farenham	*Farnham, Essex	31	WD, fo. 517^{r}
Farthingestone	Farthingstone, Northants	64	WD, fo. 350^{v}
Felmesham	Felmersham, Beds.	52	BL MS Harl. Ch. 45 H.39
Feringes	†*Feering, Essex	44	WAM 17324
Foxele	*Foxley, Northants	61	WAM 17692
Framton	*Frampton, Glos.	90	WAM 17399
Frewelesworth	Frowlesworth, Leics.	85	WAM 17448
Frostindene	Frostenden, Suffolk	99	WAM 17424
Fuleham	†Fulham, Middx.	3	WAM 17547
Fyleby	Filby, Norfolk	111	WAM 17552
Gamelegaie	Gamlingay, Cambs.	46	WAM 17401

Name-form recorded	Modern place[2]	Distance (miles) from Westminster	Source[3]
Gateslee	*Gateley, Norfolk	101	PRO, C52/34/4
Gillinge	Gilling, N. Yorks.	215	WD, fo. 529^v
Glovernia	Gloucester	95	PRO, CP25(1)/147/20/379
Guldeford	Guildford, Surrey	27	WAM 17648
Hakebourn	E. or W. Hagbourne, Berks.	50	WAM 17687
Hameslape	Hanslope, Bucks.	51	WD, fo. 520^r
Hammes	†*Ham, Essex	6	WAM 17627
Haneworth	*Hanworth, Middx.	10	WD, fo. 524^r
Hannington	*Hannington, Hants	50	WAM 17382
Hanvill	†*Hanwell, Middx.	8	WAM 17526
Harege	Harwich, Essex	68	WAM 17399
Haringey	Haringey, Middx.	7	WD, fo. 547^v; WAM 17815
Harleston	*Harlesden, Middx.	4	WAM 17641
Harlton	Harlton, Cambs.	49	WAM 17576
Harpedene	†*Harpenden, Herts.	24	WAM 17397
Hatfeld	*Hatfield, Herts.	19	WAM 17343
Hedicote	Hidcote, Glos.	82	WAM 17572
Heiton	Heighton, Sussex	49	BL MS Harl. Ch. 51 A. 12
Hendon	†*Hendon, Middx.	7	WAM 17641
Henleya	*Henley, Surrey	28	WAM 17443
Herdwyk	*Hardwick, Bucks.	38	BL. Add. MS 28024, Fo. 47^r
Hereford	Hereford	118	WAM 17378

Heriet	Herriard, Hants	43	BL, Add. MS 28024, fo. 47^r
Hermodeswith	Harmondsworth, Middx.	14	WAM 17406
Hertford	*Hertford, Herts.	20	WD, fo. 383^{r-v}
Heyford	*Upper or Lower Heyford, Oxon.	58	WD, fo. 365^r
Hillindon	*Hillingdon, Middx.	15	WAM 17427
Hobrug	Hoe Bridge, Middx.	17	WAM 17324
Hoby	Hoby, Leics.	95	WAM 17515
Hovedon	*Hoveton, Norfolk	105	PRO, CP25(1)/147/24/483
Huntingdon	*Huntingdon, Hunts.	58	WAM 17595
Huntingfeud	Huntingfield, Suffolk	88	WAM 17555
Huppinor	Upnor, Kent	29	WAM 17436
Hurle	*Hurley, Berks.	28	WD, fo. 556^r
Hyde	†*Hyde, Middx.	1	WAM 17496
Hynkele	Hinckley, Leics.	88	WAM 17541
Idelstre	Elstree, Herts.	12	WAM 17596
Ikenham	Ickenham, Middx.	14	WD, fos. 529^v–530^r
Illinge	Ealing, Middx.	7	WAM 17423
Irlande	Ireland	275	WAM 17515
Isendene	Islington, Middx.	3	WD, fo. 359^v
Itringham	Itteringham, Norfolk	109	WAM 17378
Karliolo	Carlisle	265	WAM 17329A
Kersebroke	Carisbrooke, I.o.W.	76	WD, fo. 383^v–384^r
Keynesham	*Keynsham, Somerset	104	WD, fo. 383^r
Knyghtebrugge	†Knightsbridge, Middx.	1	WAM 17562
Kyrketon	*Cheriton, Kent	62	WD, fo. 351^r
Lalham	†Laleham, Middx.	17	WAM 17485

Name-form recorded	Modern place[2]	Distance (miles) from Westminster	Source[3]
Lamhee	Lambeth, Surrey	1	WD, fo. 552^{r-v}
Langele	*Langley, Herts	27	WAM 17581
Langetoft	*Langtoft, Lincs.	83	*Cal Ch R 1226–57* p. 469
Langeton	†*Launton, Oxon.	51	WD, fo. 385^{r-v}
Lausele	Loseley, Surrey	30	WAM 17562
Lentone	*Lenton, Lincs.	96	WD, fo. 515^r
Levelande	Leaveland, Kent	47	WAM 17509
Levesham	Lewisham, Kent	10	WAM 17411
Lewes	Lewes, Sussex	45	WAM 17466
Leycester	Leicester	90	WAM 17576
Lincoln	Lincoln	122	WD, fo. 535^r
London	London	2	WAM 17459
Longedon	†*Longdon, Worcs.	98	WAM 17644
Longeford	*Longford, Middx.	14	WAM 17640
Longevyle	Longville, Salop	128	WAM 17567
Ludelawe	Ludlow, Salop	127	WAM 17366
Luton	Luton, Beds.	28	WD, fo. 330^r
Lynns	Lynn, Norfolk	91	WD, fos. 513^v–515^r
Lynton	*Linton, Kent	34	WAM 17641
Madele	*Madley, Glos.	95	WAM 17560
Malling	*Malling, Kent	27	WAM 17380
Malvern	Malvern, Worcs.	105	PRO, CP25(1)/148/28/99

Marham	Marham, Norfolk	86	Oxford, Bodl. MS DD Queen's Coll. 1745–6
Marleberge	Marlborough, Wilts.	70	WAM 17494
Massingeham	Great or Little Massingham, Norfolk	95	PRO, CP25(1)/146/9/112
Medburne	*Medbourne, Wilts.	70	PRO, CP25(1)/146/9/111
Medmeham	Medmenham, Bucks.	35	WAM 17325
Melcheburne	Melchbourne, Beds.	56	WAM 17486
Melkestrete	Milk Street, London[4]		WD, fo. 526^v
Mersshton	*Merston, Kent	24	WAM 17530
Miggeham	Midgeham, Berks.	47	WAM 17438
Morlee	*Morley St Peter, Norfolk	91	WAM 17628
Morton	*Moreton, Essex	22	WAM 17559
Neutone	*Newton, Herts.	27	WAM 17503
Norfolk	Norfolk	72	PRO, CP25(1)/148/25/20
Northampton	*Northampton, Northants	61	PRO, CP25(1)/148/25/15
Northbrok	*Northbrook near Blackheath, Surrey	7	WAM 17547
Norwico	Norwich	101	WAM 17363
Notelee	*Nutley, Sussex	36	WAM 17507
Notyngham	Nottingham	110	WAM 17558
Novo Castro	*Newcastle under Lyme, Staffs.	135	WAM 17610
Oare	*Oare, Berks.	50	LN, fo. 127^v
Odiham	Odiham, Hants	40	BL, Add. MS 28024, fo. 47^v
Offinton	*Offington, Sussex	48	WD, fo. 545^r
Okham	†Oakham, Rutland	86	*Cal Pat R 1317–21*, p. 568
Okherst	*Oakhurst, Herts.	13	WAM 17641

[4] Place-names in the city of London have been omitted from calculation of distances travelled.

Name-form recorded	Modern place[2]	Distance (miles) from Westminster	Source[3]
Orpinton	Orpington, Kent	13	WD, fo. 521^v
Oxenford	Oxford	52	WAM 17618
Padyngton	†Paddington, Middx.	1	WAM 17566
Pateshill	Patishall, Northants	62	WAM 17614
Pelham	*Pelham, Herts.	32	BL MS Harl. Ch. 51 A. 12
Perham	†*Parham, Sussex	43	WAM 17596
Peri	*Perry Green, Herts.	25	PRO, C52/34/4
Pille	Pill, Somerset	111	WAM 17345
Plumtree	Plumtree, Notts.	105	LN, fos. 131^v–132^r
Presthope	Prestope, Salop	129	WAM 17600
Pureford	†Pyrford, Surrey	21	WAM 17650
Purley	*Purley, Surrey	12	WAM 17486
Rammeseye	*Ramsey, Essex	66	WD, fo. 359^r
Redynge	Reading, Berks.	37	WAM 17581
Reseby	*Risby, Suffolk	63	BL Add. MS 28024, fo. 47^v
Richemund	Richmond, N. Yorks.	215	PRO, CP25(1)/147/21/401
Risebergh	Monks or Princes Risborough, Bucks.	35	WAM 17583
Risselep	Ruislip, Middx.	14	WAM 17530
Riston	*Riston, Norfolk	78	WAM 17400
Rocheford	*Rochford, Essex	36	BL MS Harl. Ch. 49 G. 30
Rokyngham	Rockingham, Northants	75	WD, fo. 355^r
Ros	*Ross-on-Wye, Hereford	111	WAM 17465
Rouceby	Rauceby, Lincs.	116	WAM 17580

Rowell	Rowell, Glos.	78	PRO, CP25(1)/147/24/500
Rudlond	Rutland	85	*Cal Pat R 1348–50*, p. 307
Russheton	*Rushton, Northants	72	WAM 17476
Sabrihtesworthe	Sawbridgeworth, Herts.	25	WAM 17466
St Alban	St Albans, Herts.	20	WAM 17522
St Botolph	Boston, Lincs.	103	LN, fo. 132ᵛ
St Eyse	*St Ives, Hunts.	57	WD, fo. 521ʳ
St Paul	St Paul's, London[4]		WAM 17317
Salopesbire	Shrewsbury	140	WD, fo. 365ʳ
Sandford	*Dry Sandford, Berks.	55	WAM 17491
Sandwyco	Sandwich, Kent	66	WAM 17605
Saundon	*Sandon, Herts.	34	*Cal Pat R 1266–72*, p. 262
Scardeburge	Scarborough, N. Yorks.	193	WD, fo. 355ʳ
Schoresdich	Shoreditch, Middx.	3	WD, fo. 545ʳ
Schuldham	Shouldham, Norfolk	85	PRO, CP25(1)/147/19/355
Seccheford	Sedgeford, Norfolk	102	WAM 17647
Segrave	Seagrave, Leics.	95	PRO, CP25(1)/146/6/35
Shawe	*Shaw, Berks.	52	WAM 17619
Siwelle	*Sewell, Beds.	32	WD, fo. 365ʳ
Sneleslinthe	Snelland, Lincs.	127	BL MS Harl. Ch. 45 H. 39
Somerset	Somerset	92	PRO, CP25(1)/148/26/42
Standon	*Standon, Herts.	27	WAM 17504
Stanes	†Staines, Middx.	17	WAM 17530
Stanford	*Stanford, Beds.	38	WAM 17778
Stanmere	*Stanmore, Middx.	9	PRO, CP25(1)/147/16/280
Stansted	*Stanstead, Herts.	22	WAM 17464
Stebenhithe	Stepney, Middx.	4	WAM 17311

Name-form recorded	Modern place[2]	Distance (miles) from Westminster	Source[3]
Stereford	Bishop's Stortford, Herts.	28	WAM 17326
Stockewelle	*Stockwell, Surrey	2	WD, fo. 542^r
Stowe	*Long Stow, Cambs.	46	WD, fo. 512^v
Strand	Strand, Middx.	1	WD, fo. 545^r
Stratton	*Stratton, Beds.	40	PRO, E40/1569
Sudbury	*Sudbury, Middx.	8	WAM 17605
Sunnebyre	Sunbury, Middx.	14	WAM 17399
Suthcote	*Southcott near Colnbrook, Middx.	22	WAM 17530
Sutton	*Sutton, Middx.	6	WAM 17575
Thedinworthe	Theddingworth, Leics.	78	WD, fo. 525^{r-v}
Thele	Theale, Berks.	42	WAM 17577
Theydon	Theydon Bois, Essex	15	PRO, CP25(1)/147/17/309
Thorneburwe	†*Thornborough, Bucks.	47	WAM 17337
Thorpe	*Thorpe, Surrey	18	Cal Pat R 1343–45, p. 238; WAM 17669
Titlehurst	Tilehurst, Berks.	38	WAM 17595
Toneton	Taunton, Somerset	137	WAM 17427
Trenge	Tring, Herts.	32	WAM 17602
Twyverd	*Twyford, Middx.	6	WAM 17343
Upton	*Upton, Berks.	20	Cal Ch R 1227–56, p. 251
Walden	*Walden, Essex	40	WAM 17647
Walingeford	Wallingford, Berks.	44	WAM 17409

Waltham	*Waltham Holy Cross, Essex	WAM 17647
Wandene	Wavendon, Bucks.	WD, fo. 383^r
Warewyk	Warwick	WAM 17403
Watford	*Watford, Herts.	WAM 17440
Wathamsted	†Wheathampstead, Herts.	WAM 17148A
Weld	Weald, Kent	WAM 17363
Wendlebyre	Wendlebury, Oxon.	WAM 17531
Wendlesworth	†Wandsworth, Surrey	WD, fo. 346^r
Westbourne	*Westbourne, Middx.	WAM 17512
Wike in Bray parish	Bray Wick, Berks.	WD, fo. 347^r
Wilton	*Wilton, Wilts.	WD, fo. 512^{r-v}
Windlesour	Windsor, Berks.	WAM 17614
Woxebrugge	Uxbridge, Middx.	WAM 4785
Wrotham	Wrotham, Kent	WD, fo. 365^v
Wycombe	High Wycombe, Bucks.	WAM 17545
Wymundham	*Wymondham, Norfolk	WAM 17545
Wynton	Winchester, Hants	WAM 17650
Wytcherche	*Whitchurch, Bucks.	WAM 17360
Wyteby	*Whitby, Cheshire	PRO, CP25(1)/147/19/360
Yerdelee	*Yardley, Herts.	WAM 17578

Total number ('nearest place') 286
Non-ambiguous names 175 (61%)

* signifies ambiguous place-names.
† signifies estate belonging to Westminster Abbey in 1535 (cf. Harvey, *Estates*, 47–3).

APPENDIX VII

An Account by the Abbot of the Government of Westminster, c.1511 (WAM 6576)

The text reproduced below is that of a petition, addressed to the king in parliament by the abbot of Westminster, on the subject of local government in the vill. While its primary theme is the control of the sale of victuals, the petition is incidentally revealing about the actual practice of local administration in general, which was in theory subject to the seigneurial jurisdiction of the abbot. The petition survives, incomplete, in a rough manuscript draft. The text is written on a paper roll which is badly damaged and which now lacks a portion at the beginning. The composition is undated, but the handwriting is of the sixteenth century; and a reference to Abbot John as author of the text places it within the abbacy of John Islip (1500–32). No other version of this petition has been located. Both its subject-matter and its expression, however, relate it very closely to a parliamentary Act passed in 1511, 'concerning the assising & setting of Prices of Victualls' (*Statutes of the Realm*, iii (London, 1817), 30). Since the language of this Act, in its references to victuallers in towns, exactly repeats the sense of the abbot of Westminster's petition, it seems probable that the petition (assuming it to have been delivered) formed part of the campaign which led, in 1511, to the making of the Act.

> . . . whyche that where at all tymes whenne the kyngs highnes [&] moste dred soveryn lord lyeth at his paleys of Westm' . . . and also in the tyme of the parlement holdyn at Westm' . . . as over that the iv. termys of the yeer[1] . . . holdyn & kept at Westm' aforsed / The grett resort of all the lords spirituell & temporell with the comens . . . of Englond / for the tyme beyng is within the towne of Westm' for whiche cause it is ryghte . . . & behovefull to have the assise of brede and ale & all other vitaylis duely observyd & kept within the same towne of Westm' and thoffenders contrary to the same streyghtly to be punyshed acordyng to the demeryt in that behalf / Soo it is that the reverent father in god John abbot of the monastery of Westm' forseid whiche hathe the lete & vyeu of francplegge kept but oonys a yeer as without tyme of myend it hathe been usid within the seid towne hath noon other power ner auteryte for the reformacion &

---

[1] A mutilated ref. to the four annual terms kept by the law courts.

punyshment of them that doo offende within the seid town contrary to the seid assise of brede ale & sellyng of other vitailes but only by vertu & procure of the seid lete / By autoryte wherof his officers in that behalf can putt noo maner of persoon offendyng the assise of brede & ale to the punyshement of the pyllary tumbrell or other jues[2] tyll thoffendour in that behalf be thrise at iij. severall letes there holdyn iij. severall yeers presentid & amercyed of & for the same offence and also tyll the forthe offence be foundyn in hym soo offendyng at the lete in the ivth yeer to be holdyn after his seid fyrst offence and thenne he to have his punyshement by jues / & not before whiche is to long a tract of punyshement of & for suche offenders within the seid towne where somyche[3] vitayle is utterid[4] to a grett multitude of the kyngs soietts and that as touchyng the seid amercyments they be ofte tymes by favoure of the asserours beyng hedborowis of the seid lete sett & are asserid at soo lytell a summe of mony that the seid offendours regard or fere noo thyng the losse of the seid amercyments ner by means therof doo lytell or noo thyng leve ther seid offences / and where also the hedborowis of the seid lete contrary to the ordyr of the comen lawe & the comen usage in all other letes within the seid realm make pretence of unlawfull prescripcion and sey / that they have used without tyme of myend whenne soever eny of them the seid hedborowis dyeth or wyll no lenger occupie the rome / that thenne the other hedborowis remaynyng shall at ther libertie & plesure chose such persons as they wyll to make up ther full number of xij. hedborowis whiche persons soo chosyn / the styward of the same lete for the tyme beyng shall swere ther[5] to be hedborowis & noon other at his denominacion ner otherwise / and where also that the seid hedborowis soo by & among themselff chosen by oft tymes & for the most parte the grettest vitaylers themselff of & in the seid towne and not mete to have the oversyte by ther presentement to & for the reformacion of vitaylers offendyng within the same towne / Be it therfore by the kyng oure soveryn lord and also by the lords spirituell and temporell & the comens in this present parlement assemblyd & by autoryte of the same ordeyned establyshed & enactid / That the seid abbott of Westm' for the tyme beyng his styward of the same lete also for the tyme beyng and the bayly of his franches & libertie within the precyncts of the seid lete or eyther of the seid abott or styward with ij. of the hedborowis of the same lete also for the tyme beyng such as the seid abott or his seid styward wyll therunto appoynt / Or in the absens bothe of the seid abott & his seid styward & bayly or in the absens of ij. of them / that the deputie of the seid styward & the deputie of the seid bayly in that behalff appoynted with iiij. of the seid hedborowis by the seid abott or his seid styward

---

[2] Instrument of punishment. [3] 'So much'.
[4] i.e. sold. [5] *Recte* 'them'.

thereunto appoynted as oft as it shal be thought necessary by the seid
abott & styward / shall have full poure & autoryte from tyme to tyme to
entre & goo into the howsis of the seid vitaylers & every of them & ther in
ther seid howsis or at ther shopwyndowis or in the markett & opyn strete
or ellis where within the seid precyncts of the aboveseid lete to weye
brede trie & mete all mesurs wherby ale bere wyne or other vytaile is to be
sold and also cesse the prise of all maner vitaile to be sold within the seid
precyncts in such odir maner & fourme as the maire shereffs & other
officers in London or the kyngs clerke of the markett in eny place within
the realme of England have autorite to doo / and over that to have full
powre & autoryte aftir & upon eny defaute fowndyn in eny of the seid
vitaylers within the seid precyncts touchyng vitaile corrupt not holsome
or not beyng acordyng to the seid assise or offrid to be sold at an
excessyve price or faylyng weyte or mesure / the same vitaile in almes or
other wyse to dispose at ther pleasure as thyngs forfett to the seid abbott
for the tyme beyng / and also to breke brenne or otherwyse by ther
discrecion to consume all fals vessalys weyts & mesurs not kepyng the
assise within the seid precyncts by weye of byeng & sellyng occupied and
also that aftir iiij. defauts in eny baker brewer or other vitayler by weyte
mesure or other examynacion as is aboveseid to be had made &
approvid / That thenne the seid baylyff or his deputie for the tyme
beying by the precept of the seid styward to hym made with thavyse of
the seit abott shall doo lyke punyshement of pyllary tumbrell or other
jues unto the seid vitailer soo offendyng as though his seid iiij. defauts &
offences had been at iiij. severall letes in due forme by the hedborowis of
the seid lete within the same lete presentid / and that the cunstables &
every other person resyant within the seid precyncts be aydyng &
assysstyng to the same bayly in that behalf upon peyne of forfayture to
the seid abott at every tyme 3s. 4d. and over that / that the styward of the
seid lete with thavice of the seid abott for the tyme beyng shall every yeer
whenne to hym it shall seme expedient chaunge elect & swere suche
hedborowis as to hym shalbe thought most expedient for the assise of
vitaile & good rule within the seid precynct to be had & kept and that
every hedborowe soo chosyn for an hedborowe of the seid lete take his
othe to hym gyven by the seid styward and be obedyent & doo as an
hedborowe shall doo upon peyne & forfaiture to the seid abott for every
tyme soo disobeyeng v.lī. and over that for asmyche as the seid abott
hathe to hym & his successours of the graunte & confirmacion by letters
patent of dyvers of oure sovereyn lord the kyngs progenytours among
other thyngs all fynes & amercyments growyn had or made before the
kyngs clerke of the markett as wele of all his tenaunts & resiaunts within
the seid precynct of the seid lete as of all other his tenaunts or resiaunts
within eny of the letes belongyng to his seid monastery as by the seid

letters patent more pleynly it maye appere And where also yf the seid clerke of the markett by his autoryte severally by hym self and the seid abott & his successours with the seid styward & other his officers & hedborowis shuld exercyse ther severall autorite by them selff to & for the conservacion of the seid assise of brede ale wyne & other vitayle within the precynct of the seid lete to be kept / The seid clerke of the markett exercysyng otherwyse thanne as officer to the seid abott for the seid tyme beyng shuld be a lett of the execucion of thautoryte gevyn by this seid act and hynderans of the reformacion of the seid vitailers & kepyng of good ordre & assise touchyng all maner vitayle within the seid precynct Be it therfore fyrther establyshed ordeyned & enactid by the kyng oure sovereyn lord and also by the lords spirituell & temporell & the comens in this present parlement assemblyd and by autorite of the same that the seid clerke of the markett ner eny other of the clerks of the markett that be or shalbe unto oure seid sovereyn lord or his heirs or successours from hensforth in nowyse exercyse his seid office or medle touchyng the same within the seid precynct upon peyne of x.li̅. to be forfet to the seid abot or his successours for every tyme soo exercysyng or medlyng / and this act to endure tyll the next parlement eny autoryte of the seid clerke of the markett or eny custome or prescripcion by the seid hedborowis or eny other thyng had made or used before this tyme to the contrary not withstondyng.

Office-holders in Westminster, c.1350–1540

The following list provides a profile of the group of men who held the most prominent public offices in the vill of Westminster in the later Middle Ages.[1] The catalogue contains all the known names falling into each of three categories:

(i) the jury of twelve chief pledges of the manor court (usually appointed for life, and partially recorded between 1364 and 1514 inclusive: 129 names);

(ii) the two churchwardens of the parish church of St Margaret (appointed biennially, and almost fully recorded between 1458 and 1540 inclusive: 77 names); and

(iii) the master and two wardens of the parochial fraternity of the Assumption of the Virgin Mary, maintained within St Margaret's church (appointed triennially, and partially recorded between 1440 and 1540 inclusive: 60 names).[2]

The total number of distinct entries in the list is 199. Within each biographical entry, the name and (where known) the style ('gentleman', etc.) and occupation of the individual are followed by details of his tenure of any offices comprised in the above three classes. There follow notes of any similar appointments, for example as dignitary of one of the other guilds of Westminster. Longer entries then include evidence of trade or business activities, of property held, of kin, and miscellaneous references. The chief source drawn upon has been the Westminster Abbey Muniments. These have been supplemented with the churchwardens' accounts of St Margaret's, Westminster, 1460–1540, and with the wills registered in the Peculiar Court of Westminster, 1504–40. The Calendars of Patent, Close and Fine Rolls, and the Calendars of Letter-Books of the City of London, have also been searched. Other sources are acknowledged where appropriate. The amount of information gathered on each individual varies widely; but the shortest entries have been retained for the sake of completeness.

---

[1] For the offices of the bailiffdom of the vill and of the curacy of the parish church, each different in character from the offices considered here, see apps. I and II.

[2] For full accounts of these offices, and of the nature of the records concerning them, see chs. 7, 8, and 9.

Because of the uneven survival of evidence, the catalogue has no statistical use. Its significance is to be found in a random perusal of the details recorded of these men: their occupations, the houses they rented, and above all their mutual association, not only in the official capacities which are their passport of entry to the list but also in many more personal ways, as neighbours, as witnesses to local deeds of property, as executors of each other's wills. Probably the most striking feature of the list, throughout the period *c.*1350–1540, is the variety of the kinds of men thus brought together. Very few, so far as is known, were outstandingly wealthy; they were for the most part men of the middle rank. Within this social grouping, however, the residents of Westminster considered worthy to hold local office were drawn from a remarkably wide range of callings, which indeed reflected the full spectrum of trades and occupations pursued by the inhabitants at large. The office-holders were not an 'oligarchy', nor an 'élite', in the sense in which those terms are commonly used of a hierarchy of wealth, trade, or blood. They were men of some substance, certainly, but not by any means an exclusive caste. This appears, moreover, to have been as true in 1540 as in the later fourteenth century.

Abbreviations[3]

Assmptn guild	guild of the Virgin Mary's Assumption in St Margaret's church, Westminster
b.	buried
bro.	brother
chwdn	churchwarden of St Margaret's church, Westminster
const.	constable of the vill of Westminster
cott.	cottage
c.p.	chief pledge of the manor court of Westminster
d.	died
dau.	daughter
gdn	garden
m.	married
mes.	messuage
r.	rented
s.	son
scty	the sanctuary of Westminster
St Mgt	the parish church of St Margaret, Westminster
ten.	tenement
w.	wife
wdn	warden
West.	Westminster

[3] Supplementary to the list on pp. xvi–xvii.

A LYNNE (ALEYN, *alias* BURLEY), William. Baker. Chwdn 1472–4. CWA i.
119. R. The Wool Sack bakery on W. side King St. –1489–97. W. Elen
named 1495 *et seq*. WAM 23114–24; see also Reg Bk, i, fos. 81ᵛ–82ʳ. (The
Wool Sack had been held successively by William & Thomas Burley,
alias Aleyn, 1439–*c*.1450; Thomas Burley's widow named, 1451. WAM
18591–3; 23074–7; 50756. From 1498 to 1519 the bakery was held by
Henry Aleyn. WAM 17917; 23126–57.) 'William Lynn' reserved a pew
in St Mgt for his w. 1460 × 1462. CWA i. 8. In 1459 'W. Lynne' supplied
bread to the household of Lord Henry Stafford, then resident at West.
WAM 12184, fos. 27ʳ–33ʳ. William a Lynne d. 1497; was b. in St Mgt.
CWA i. 326. He bequeathed 200 lbs lead to the church work of St Mgt.
CWA i. 337. Eleyn Lynne was b. at St Mgt 1498/9. CWA i. 358, 370.

ALYNSON, Gilbert. C.p. 1507–9; chief const. 1508. WAM 50772–4. Wdn
Assmptn guild 1508–11. CWA i. 576 (1510). R. the Maiden Head inn in
King St. 1506–8. Assmptn guild accts, s.a. Will made 9 Dec. 1511,
proved 14 Jan. 1512. PCW Wyks, 143–4. Requested burial in St Mary's
chapel in St Mgt. His widow, Joan, executrix. Richard PITTER an
overseer. Bequests to 'Mr Otwell', *sc*. John ATWELL ('all my swanys in
the Temys'), & to Walter GARDINER ('my wodknyf'). Alynson also left a
'mowlde of the crosse of Saint George' to James Dale, and 'a molde of the
armes of England and Spayn' to John Losshe.

A MERE, Thurstan. Baker. Chwdn 1538–40. CWA iii, s.a. Reserved his pew
in St Mgt 1524/5. CWA ii, s.a. His goods were valued in 1524 at £2.
PRO, E179/238/98. R. a ten. called the Ram, on E. side King St.,
–*c*.1525–. PRO, E40/1560.

ANGEWYN, John. C.p. 1434 × 1445–1450 × 1453. WAM 50752–3. R. a shop
near the almonry in Tothill St. from 1429, which in 1443–4 he rebuilt.
WAM 19035 *et seq*. D. *ante* 1460, when his widow kept his obit in St Mgt.
CWA i. 2.

ATKYNS, William. Chwdn 1510–12. CWA i. 576; CWA ii, s.a. In 1528
Atkyns signed the chwdns' accts as auditor. CWA ii, s.a.

ATTE DOUNE. See DOUNE.

ATTE SELAR, ——. C.p. 1379. WAM 50713.

ATTEWATER, Robert. ?Waxchandler. C.p. 1396 × 1402–*ante* 1407. WAM
50735, 50738. Robert atte Watere, waxchandler, received 13s. 4d. p.a.
wages from the West. Abbey sacrist in 1407–8. WAM 19660.

ATTWELL, John. Gentleman; chandler. C.p. 1495 × 1505–1514–. WAM
50770–7. Wdn (1505–8) and master (1512–15) Assmptn guild. Guild
accts. Receiver of the abbot of West. in diverse counties 1491–1525.
WAM 26220–30; 24284–92; 30618; 32858. Valet of West. Abbey
1483–98; stipendiary of the abbey cellar 1514–15; recipient from 1523 of
a corrody of 10 convent loaves a week, issued by the cellarer, 'for his good
service past and to come'. WAM 19978–94; 18922; Reg Bk, ii, fo. 199ᵛ.

R. 2 shops on N. side Tothill St. 1495–1500. WAM 23572–7. Thereafter, r. numerous tens within the abbey precinct, in the scty and almonry. WAM 17981; 17956; 19115–26; 23128–68; 19763–5; 19767–82. In 1514 Attwell bought 9 mess in the Round Wool Staple. Guildhall Library, MSS 12982–3. In 1523 he held a ten., probably close to the Wool Staple, of St Stephen's Chapel. WAM 50778, fo. 4ʳ. He also leased from the abbey almonry the parsonage of St Mgt, 1511–30. WAM 17697; 18040; 19119 *et seq.*

John Attwell d. 1530. CWA ii, s.a. 1529–30, wk. 55. Will made 11 May, proved 3 June 1530. PCW Bracy, fos. 12ᵛ–15ʳ. He requested burial in West. Abbey, beside his w. 'there new buried'. (This was probably his w. Ellen; see PCW Wyks, 28.) Attwell was survived by a second w., Elizabeth. His bequests included one of 12*d.* 'to every gentleman in my lord's [*sc.* the abbot of Westminster's?] house', and 6*d.* to every groom. The property in the Round Wool Staple was left to William Middleton, gentleman of West.; all other leases held of West. Abbey and of Cardinal College, Oxford, to Attwell's widow.

BAKER, Thomas. Waxchandler. Chwdn 1494–6; 1500–2. CWA i. 295, 389. Supplied candles to St Mgt 1498/9. CWA i. 375. R. a cott. in scty by the 'church' or 'cemetery stile', 1498–9. WAM 19754. D. 1503–4; b. in St Mgt. CWA i. 469.

BAROWE, Thomas. King's master cook. Chief const. 1494; c.p. 1494–5 × 1505. WAM 50767–8. 'Thomas Barowe, master cook of the king's house', joined Assmptn guild 1487 × 1490. Guild accts, s.a. Held leases on 4 tens and 2 shops in scty between 1488 and 1509/10; some of these by right of his w., who was the widow of Arthur Tourefort (and mother of Louis TOUREFORT). WAM 19728–65; Reg Bk, i, fos. 118ᵛ–119ʳ. Attended Henry VII's funeral in May 1509. *LP* i, no. 20 (p. 17). D. 1509–10; b. in choir of St Mgt. CWA i. 558. Was survived by his widow, Margaret.

BATE, John (the elder). Yeoman; butcher and 'inn-holder'. Const. for King St. 1509–14. WAM 50774–7. Chwdn 1516–18. CWA ii, s.a. Wdn Rounceval guild 1520–2. Guild accts. 'Mr Bate' (probably the same) was wdn Assmptn guild 1527. WAM 18035. John was the s. of William BATE, brewer. John Bate hired carts to West. Abbey 1501–2, 1514–15. WAM 18909, 19773. 'John Bate, butcher', received livery of bread and ale in West. Abbey 1516. WAM 5473. He supplied meat to Assmptn guild feast 1518. Guild accts. John Bate, 'butcher', r. the Boar's Head inn in King St. (formerly held by William BATE) 1517–29. WAM 17985; 18028; 23154–68. He held a ten. by the almonry chapel 1513–14. WAM 19117*. D. 1529; his widow, Joan, d. 1530. Both were b. in St Mgt. CWA ii, s.a. 1528–9, wk. 46; 1529–30, wk. 42. Will of 'John Bate the elder, inn-holder of Westminster', made 14 Apr., proved 30 Apr. 1529. PCW

Bracy, fos. 8ʳ–9ʳ. George LORDE, overseer. The will names John's mother, Agnes Bate; his bros, William and John Bate; his sisters, Margaret (m. to John Loove and living in Tunbridge, Kent), and Joan Nedeham; his cousin, John Bate; his w., Joan; and his children, John, Katherine, and Joan.

BATE, William (the elder). Brewer. Const. for the Wool Staple 1489–91. WAM 50763–4. Chwdn 1502–4. CWA i. 437. C.p. 1495 × 1505–1514–. WAM 50770–7. Wdn Assmptn guild 1505–8; 1515–18. Guild accts. The goods of 'William Bate the elder' were valued in 1524 at £40. PRO, E179/238/98. A William Bate kept an inn in Tothill St. 1491. From 1509, 'William Bate, senior, brewer of Westminster', r. a brewing ten. called the Catherine Wheel, a mes. called the Dragon and 9 cotts., all lying together in Petty France in Tothill St. WAM 50764; Oxford, Queen's Coll. MS 4 N.2. From 1495, William Bate r. the Boar's Head inn in King St.; from 1506 this was sublet, until in 1517 John BATE (the elder; butcher) took a fresh lease. WAM 23122–54. In 1519 'William Bate, brewer', took over from 'William Bate, stainer', extensive meadows between Tothill and the Thames. WAM Reg Bk, i, fo. 150ᵛ; Reg Bk, ii, fo. 136ʳ. The brewer d. 1525; was b. in St Mgt. CWA ii, s.a. 1524–5, wk. 52. He was succeeded in one of his leases by his widow, Agnes; and she, in turn, in 1532, by William Bate (the younger). Reg Bk, ii, fos. 214ᵛ–215ʳ; WAM 18045; 18937–54. The eldest s. of William Bate, senior, was evidently John BATE (the elder; butcher), whose mother's name was Agnes, and whose bros. were called William and John. PCW Bracy, fos. 8ʳ–9ʳ.

BAYNARD, William. Yeoman and brewer. Const. 1490. WAM 50764. Chwdn 1494–6. CWA i. 295. Wdn Assmptn guild 1502–5. Guild accts, s.a. C.p. 1495 × 1505–1510. WAM 50770–4; PRO, SC2/191/66. Valet of West. Abbey 1486–1510. WAM 19979–99; 23001–5. R. a small ten. near the almonry in Tothill St. 1484–1511. WAM 17870; 19093–116. Also r. 11 acres towards Eye 1505–8; and a gdn at Charing 1506–11. Assmptn guild accts, s.a. 1505–8; WAM 23257*–81. With William Taunt, husbandman, Baynard (described as 'brewer') farmed the parsonage and tithe of St Mgt 1502–11. Reg Bk, i, fo. 141ʳ⁻ᵛ; WAM 19114–17. Baynard d. 1511. CWA ii, s.a. 1511, wk. 25. Will made 5 Apr., proved 5 July 1511. PCW Wyks, 133–5. Requested burial in the 'new work' (*sc.* the nave) of West. Abbey, 'ageynst wher as I made the glasse window within the seyd New Werk'. Desired prayers to be said at 'Scala Coeli' in Rome for the souls of his parents, William and Alice, and for 'all his wives' souls'. Another priest was to go to Compostela, to pray for Baynard there. His 'grete bote and fyshing nete' he left to the Assmptn guild; his convent leases to his widow, Katherine. She d. and was b. in St Mgt 1528. PCW Bracy, fo. 2ʳ⁻ᵛ; CWA ii, s.a. 1528–9, wk. 28.

BAYNEBRIDGE, William. Brewer. Chwdn 1476–8. CWA i. 120. C.p. 1467 × 1486–95; chief const. –1485. WAM 50760–8. R. a brewing ten. opposite the pillory in Tothill St. 1466–*c.*1500. WAM 23241–69. Was presented in court as a beer-brewer 1467, 1486. WAM 50758, 50760. D. 1499/1500; b. in St Mgt. His widow, Agnes, was also b. there 1500/1. Their joint obit subsequently kept by Assmptn guild. CWA i. 367, 400; CWA ii, s.a. 1526–7, wk. 52; guild accts, s.a. 1521.

BEFFORD, John. C.p. 1380–92 (d.). WAM 50715–16, 50718, 50726–7. R. a cott. in Long Ditch 1387–1390–. WAM 18999–19000.

BEREWE, John. Royal officer. C.p. 1445 × 1450–1453 × 1464. WAM 50733, 50755. Wdn Assmptn guild 1455. WAM 17774. Yeoman of the crown 1449–60; porter of Wallingford 1435–54. Wedgwood and Holt, *History of Parliament 1439–1509*, 134–5.

BLAKENALE, William. Butcher. Twice wdn Assmptn guild 1480–3, 1493–6. PRO, C1/66/320 (1482); E40/13407 (1494). C.p. 1488–1495–; chief const. 1492. WAM 50761–8. Described as 'butcher' when owing quarterage to Assmptn guild 1477; fined under meat assize 1492. Guild accts; WAM 50765. R. a ten. near the palace gate in King St. –1487–1490–. Assmptn guild accts.

BOCHER, Peter. C.p. 1368–95. WAM 50704–34.

BOUGH, Thomas. Gentleman; royal officer. Chwdn 1474–6. CWA i. 91. Wdn (1484–7) and twice master (1496–9; 1502–5) Assmptn guild. Guild accts. C.p. 1467 × 1486–1514. WAM 50760–77. 'Jenet Bough, mother of Thomas Bough', was living at West. 1475/6. CWA i. 111. Bough's mother-in-law, Margaret Harreys, *alias* Harryson, was also of West. CWA i. 212, 327. With his w., Elizabeth, Thomas Bough r. a house and outbuildings in Tothill St. 1495–1506. WAM Reg Bk, i, fos. 83ʳ–84ʳ; 23121–33. Also r. various tens in West. scty, including a row of seven held jointly with Thomas Reginald, haberdasher of London. WAM 19749–804; 17911; Reg Bk, ii, fo. 141ʳ⁻ᵛ. The will of 'Thomas Bough of Westminster, gentleman usher of the king's exchequer', was made 23 Jan., proved 29 Jan. 1515. PCW Wyks, 220–2. Bough was b. in St Erasmus's chapel in St Mgt. CWA ii, s.a. 1515–16, wk. 35. He was three times m.: ws Elizabeth and Margaret, both d. *ante* 1512; the widow unnamed in the will. CWA ii, s.a. 1512–13, wk. 5. His s. Thomas, an executor, inherited all property in Middx. A dau., Agnes Blakewich, also named in the will; holdings in Essex were left to John Blakewich. Bough endowed an obit for Richard HUMFREY.

BRADDING, John. Yeoman. Const. –1450. WAM 50753. C.p. 1453–67 × 1474. WAM 50755–8. Held numerous properties in the area of Tothill St. from *c.*1450, including a ten. beyond the bars in that street, 3 shops near the almonry and various gdns, one of which he built upon. WAM 23227; 19070–9; 18892; 17652 *dors.* D. *c.*1474. Was succeeded in his properties by his widow, Joan, and subsequently by Richard Bradding. WAM 23091 *et seq.* John Bradding left 6*s.* 8*d.* to the 'new work' of West. Abbey. WAM 23549. Assmptn guild owned a chased standing cup and cover weighing 22 oz. and a mass book used at St Nicholas's altar in St Mgt, of John Bradding's gift. Guild accts, inventory s.a. 1508.

BRANDESBY, Thomas. Const. for Charing 1377; c.p. 1380–*ante* 1384. WAM 50710, 50715–16. In 1375, Thomas de Brandesby granted to Kilburne nunnery 2 shops in St Nicholas' Shambles parish, London. *Cal Pat R 1374–7*, p. 452. In 1377 he held a mes. and 4 shops in the parishes of St Clement Danes and St Mary-le-Strand without Temple Bar. His w., Alice, d. in this year. *Cal Cl R 1377–81*, pp. 87, 89. In 1380, together with William Beverley and John de Pontfreit, clerks, he held a house and gdn in the parish of St Martin-in-the-Fields. Ibid., p. 475.

BREKYNDON, Reginald. C.p. 1379. WAM 50713. In 1372, Roger SUDBURY and William HULL stood surety for the good behaviour of Reynold Brikeden towards Adam de Chestrefeld, canon of St Stephen's Chapel. *Cal Cl R 1369–74*, p. 452. *Ante* 1390, Reynold Brikendoun and his w., Katherine, acquired a mes. in King St.; in 1390 this mes. was held by John Brikendoun of Kympton, butcher. *Cal Cl R 1389–92*, p. 147.

BRENGE, William. C.p. 1364–80. WAM 50699–715. As a regular witness to Middx., Berks., and Essex deeds, Brenge was associated with Peter BOCHER, Thomas CHESE, Peter FYSSHER, William GRENDON, Robert HAKEBOURNE, William HULL, Robert KENTBURY, Richard ROOKE, Roger SUDBURY, Andrew TETTESWORTH, and John WESTON. *Cal Cl R 1369–74*, pp. 318, 597; ibid. *1374–7*, pp. 64, 78, 84, 256, 362; ibid. *1377–81*, pp. 108, 252, 512.

BROKE, John. ?Chancery clerk. Chwdn 1466–8. CWA i. 59. Valet of West. Abbey sacristy 1458–60. WAM 19709–10. R. the Boar's Head inn in King St. 1443–9; another ten. nearby in King St. 1448–*c.*1474; and a third ten. adjacent to the second 1467–*c.*1474. Also r. 'Steynour's Croft', which lay behind all these tens to W. of King St., 1449 × 1461–3. His w. Isabel named from 1463 × 1467. WAM 18593; 23074–90. D. 1474; his obit kept at St Mgt in that year and by Assmptn guild 1474–7. CWA i. 93; guild accts. This was possibly the 'John Broke, clerk of chancery', recorded 1457, 1459. *Cal Cl R 1454–61*, pp. 220, 377.

BROMFELD, John. Royal officer. Wdn Assmptn guild 1536–9. Guildhall Library, MS 12993 (1538). The lands and fees of John Bromfeld of West., 'king's servant', were assessed in 1544 at £30. PRO, E179/141/139.

BROWNE, Thomas. Esquire. C.p. 1494–5 × 1505; chief const. 1495. WAM 50767–8. With w. Edith, r. a ten. and shop in King St., outside N. scty gate, 1490–1510. WAM 17895; 23568–93. Will made 22 Mar. 1504, proved 10 Mar. 1511. Requested burial in St Mgt. PCW Wyks, 130.

BURGEYS, Thomas. Vintner. Const. 1466–7; c.p. 1467 × 1486–94; supervisor ditches of West. 1491. WAM 50758–67. Wdn Assmptn guild 1471–4; 1487–90. Guild accts, s.a. As 'vintner', witness to local deed 1482; presented in court for wine sales. PRO, E40/1461; WAM 50757 *et seq.* R. 2 tens in King St., on W. side opposite Endive Lane, 1473–*c.*1494; and another ten. nearby to S. 1461–3, 1487–94. Also r. 2 tens, a cott. and extensive gdns and meadows in and near W. end Tothill St. and Rosamund's Manor *c.*1470–*c.*1494. WAM 17815; 23078–80, 23105–19; 23248–64; 18902; Assmptn guild accts, s.a. 1487–90. D. 1494/5; b. in St Mgt. CWA i. 300. Burgeys's first w. lay beneath an inscribed marble slab in St George's chapel in St Mgt. CWA i. 61, 63. He was survived by a second w., Joan, who inherited the West. leases. WAM 23270 *et seq.*; Reg Bk, i, fos. 124^v–126^r.

Another Thomas Burgeys, bro. of William Burgeys, r. tens in West. scty from 1505, and d. 1509. These were probably ss of the vintner. WAM 19760–4; PCW Wyks, 105–6. The later Thomas Burgeys m. a dau. of Robert STOWELL.

BURGHAM, William. Yeoman; 'maltman'. Chwdn 1482–4. CWA i. 195. 'William Burgham, maltman', reserved a pew for his w. in St Mgt 1466 × 1468. CWA i. 80. 'William Burgham, *alias* Maltman', with w. Elizabeth, r. a ten. and shop and solar on S. side Tothill St. 1464–95; and in addition 3 shops close by 1473–1501. WAM 17814; 17790; 19071–112. Burgham d. 1501/2; was b. in St Mgt. CWA i. 391.

BURLEY. See A LYNNE.

CHAMBERLYN, Simon. C.p. 1374–*ante* 1376. WAM 50705–7.

CHARLES, Richard. C.p. 1508–10 × 1512; chief const. 1509. WAM 50773–4; PRO, SC2/191/66.

CHESE, Thomas. Royal officer. C.p. 1376–86. WAM 50707–18. Received daily fee at the royal exchequer 1368, 1378. *Cal Pat R 1367–70*, p. 100; ibid. *1377–81*, p. 144.

CLEMENT, (*alias* JACKSON), Thomas, Tallowchandler. Scavenger for Tothill St. 1512–14. WAM 50775–7. Chwdn 1520–2. CWA ii, s.a. Joined Assmptn guild 1505 × 1508. Guild accts, s.a. Supplied candles to St Mgt. CWA ii, s.a. 1520–2. His goods were assessed in 1524 at £20. PRO, E179/238/98. R. several tens at the corner of Thieving Lane and Long Ditch 1511–38. His w. Agnes named 1511; his w. Margery, and her dau. Alice Shale, named 1535. WAM 17966; Reg Bk, i. fo. 312^r; 19785/90–807; 23133–78. Thomas Clement ('*alias* Jackson') d. 1538. CWA iii, s.a. 1538–9, wk. 17. Will made 18 Sept., proved 10 Oct. 1538. PCW Bracy, fos. 64^v–65^v. Requested burial in St Mgt (which his body received) beside his first w.; his present w., Margery, to 'provide for me such a stone as lieth upon my first wife's grave, with a scripture of my name with the day and year of my burial'. The will again names Margery's dau., Alice. Clement bequeathed to Margery the West. Abbey leases of his dwelling house in Tothill St. outside the W. gate of the scty, and of his ten. in Long Ditch. William RUSSELL an overseer.

CLERK, John. Skinner. Const. for King St. 1422–34; c.p. 1428–34 × 1445. WAM 50745, 50748–9. John Clerk, 'skinner', held 2 tens in Long Ditch 1430 × 1432–77; 1 ten. by the Clowson bridge in King St. 1432–50 × 1454; and certain cotts in the scty called 'Rotten Row' 1467 × 1470–7. WAM 23217/9–51; 19717–24. The skinner's properties were inherited by John Clerk, 'notary'. WAM 23227 *et seq.*; 23253 *et seq.*

John Clerk, 'gentleman of Westminster', granted his property to trustees 1453. *Cal Cl R 1447–54*, p. 417.

CLOWDESLEY. See KNOWESLEY.

CLYNK, John. Taverner, and ?royal officer. C.p. 1402 × 1407–10 × 1422. WAM 50738–40. Was charged as a taverner of West. 1398/9. PRO, KB9/183/6. R. the Boar's Head inn in King St. 1392–4. WAM 18526–7. R. the Saracen's Head inn by the palace gate in King St. 1398–*c.*1436. WAM 23467–508. Was associated with Thomas TOTTESHAM as a witness to Middx. deeds.

Alice Clynk was presented as a victualler 1392; Isabel Clynk as a cook 1402, 1407–8. WAM 50726, 50735–8.

A John Clynk received in 1405 a life grant of the office of park-keeper at Petworth, Sussex; and was a royal commissioner for shipping and sergeant-at-arms 1412, 1423, 1429. *Cal Pat R 1405–8*, p. 69; ibid. *1408–13*, pp. 432, 433, 476; ibid. *1422–9*, pp. 192, 403, 552. This John Clynk d. 1432 × 1435. Ibid. *1429–36*, pp. 220, 456.

COKERYCH, John. Tallowchandler. Chwdn 1472–4. CWA i. 119. Wdn Assmptn guild 1477 (–80). Cambridge, Trinity Coll. MS O.9.1, fos. 230ʳ–231ʳ. C.p. 1467 × 1486–91; chief const. 1486. WAM 50760–3. Supplied candles to St Mgt. e.g. CWA i. 43, 288. Was presented for an encroachment on King St. near the scty gate 1467. WAM 50758. R. a shop in King St. opposite Endive Lane 1472–7; a ten. on the corner of King St. near the palace gate 1477–87; and another ten. by the palace gate 1482–95. WAM 23248–51; 23549–60; 18900–2. D. 1494/5; b. in St Mgt. CWA i. 297.

COMBES, William. Chwdn 1538–40. CWA iii, s.a. Wdn St Cornelius's guild in St Mgt 1524/5. CWA ii, s.a.

CORBY, John. Parchment-maker. C.p. 1402 × 1407–10 × 1422. WAM 50738, 50740. John Corby of Charing, 'parchemynmaker', was a mainpernor 1404, 1411–12. *Cal Cl R 1402–5*, p. 321; ibid. *1405–9*, p. 314; ibid. *1409–13*, p. 281.

CORNYSHE, Thomas. Wdn Assmptn guild 1480–3. PRO, E40/1461; C1/66/320; *Cal Cl R 1476–85*, p. 271 (all 1482). D. 1494; b. at St Mgt. CWA i. 296.

Thomas Cornyshe may have been related to the William Cornyshes, father and s., musicians of the chapel royal under Henry VII and Henry

VIII. For the latter, see H. Baillie, 'Some Biographical Notes on English Church Musicians, Chiefly Working in London (1485–1569)', *Royal Musical Association Research Chronicle*, ii (1962), 18–57.

COTMAN, William. Baker. Const. –1450. WAM 50753. C.p. 1453 × 1464–67 × 1486. WAM 50757-8. Supplied wheat to West. Abbey; valet of the convent 1453–71. WAM 19959–76. His properties included the Swan in Tothill St. and a parcel of Mauduitsgarden nearby; also tens in Knightsbridge and (held jointly with John NYK and William Broke) lands in Bucks. *Cal Cl R 1468–76*, pp. 72, 275–6; WAM 17788.

CRANE, Thomas. Chwdn 1482–4. CWA i. 195.

CROWDER, Richard. Baker. Const. for Tothill St. 1513–14. WAM 50776-7. Chwdn 1526–8. CWA ii, s.a. Presented for ale sold by him in Tothill St. 1512, 1523; and for failing to control his cows 1513, and keeping an excess of animals on the common 1523. WAM 50775-6, 50778. R. the Cock inn in Tothill St. 1535(–7). Reg Bk, ii, fo. 308ʳ. Held 2 closes at Knightsbridge 1520–7. Reg Bk, ii, fos. 154ᵛ–155ʳ, 238ᵛ. Crowder's goods were assessed in 1524 at £13. 6s. 8d. PRO, E179/238/98. D. 1537. CWA iii, s.a. 1537–8, wk. 20. Will made 2 Oct., proved 17 Oct. 1537. PCW Bracy, fos. 56ᵛ–58ʳ. Requested burial in St Mgt (which he received) beside his w. there lately b. Bequeathed the leases of his house and of his closes at Knightsbridge to Robert WEDDISBOROWE. Bequests also to his neighbour in Tothill St., Roger Crytoft (perhaps a relative of William CRYTOFT, baker); and to Crowder's goddaughter, Agnes Knowesley (perhaps a relative of Thomas KNOWESLEY, baker, who was a witness to Crowder's will).

CRYTOFT, William. Baker. Chwdn 1536–8. CWA iii, s.a. Valet of West. Abbey 1530–5. WAM 23027-9. His goods were valued in 1524 at £2; in 1544 at £20. PRO, E179/238/98; E179/141/139. R. 3 shops near St Anne's stile leading into the almonry from Tothill St. 1527–1536–. WAM 19142–52. R. the Wool Sack bakery on the W. side of King St. 1543 *et seq.* Reg Bk, iii, fos. 38ᵛ–40ʳ.

DAUNTSEY, John. Ale-taster –1396; c.p. 1396 × 1402–*ante* 1407. WAM 50734-5, 50738.

DEDDE, John. Chwdn 1508–10. CWA i. 547. Joined Assmptn guild 1487 × 1490. Guild accts. D. 1518; b. in St Mgt. CWA ii, s.a. 1517–18, wk. 52.

DENEFORD, John. ?Royal officer. C.p. 1386–*ante* 1392. WAM 50718, 50726. In 1369 John de Deneford received a grant for life of 5 marks p.a. at the exchequer; this was renewed in 1378. *Cal Pat R 1367–70*, p. 242; ibid. *1377–81*, p. 236.

DENYAS, Reginald. Ale-taster 1380; c.p. 1393 × 1396–*ante* 1402. WAM 50734-5. Was fined for an encroachment upon King St. 1377. WAM 50709.

In 1416–17 Richard Denyas, s. and heir of the late Reginald Denyas, granted away a ten. and shop in King St. (on the W. side, next to the Swan inn) called 'the Wool House'. WAM 17729, 17732.

DENYS, John. Chwdn 1492–4; 1496–8. CWA i. 293–319. D. 1498/9; b. in St Mgt. CWA i. 355.

DEWE, Richard. Gentleman; royal officer. C.p. 1435 × 1445–50 × 1453. WAM 50752–3. Richard Dewe, 'gentleman of the town of Westminster', was an usher of the king's exchequer 1433. *Cal F R 1430–7*, pp. 111, 177. He was a witness (with Robert HOUGH, John FANNE and David 'Selby', ?*recte* SELLY) to a Berks. deed 1438. *Cal Cl R 1435–41*, p. 180. R. land in Mauduitsgarden in West. 1433–63. WAM 18584–93; 23074–80. D. *c*.1465; his obit kept in St Mgt by John BRADDING. CWA i. 26.

DIXON, John. Chwdn 1536–8. CWA iii, s.a. Wdn St Cornelius's guild in St Mgt 1533 × 1536. PRO, C1/807/41. Assessed in 1524 on land valued at £6. 13s. 4d. PRO, E179/238/98. R. a ten. in the 'Sarum rents' in the precinct of West. Abbey 1523–9. WAM 23161–8.

DONYNG, Geoffrey. C.p. 1385. WAM 50718.

DOUNE (*alias* ATTE DOUNE), Henry. Royal officer. C.p. 1376–92. WAM 50707–16, 50726. Henry (de) Doune was a purveyor to the royal household 1385, 1388. *Cal Pat R 1385–9*, pp. 5, 491.

DOWNE, Robert. C.p. 1434 × 1445–50 × 1453. WAM 50752–3.

DUFFELD, John. Dyer. Chwdn 1508–10. CWA i. 547. Joined Assmptn guild 1505 × 1508. Guild accts. R. the Hart's Horn inn on the W. side of King St. 1504–10. WAM 17938; 23132–40. D. 1510; b. in St Mgt. CWA ii, s.a. 1510–11, wk. 26. Will made 16 Nov., proved 28 Nov. 1510. John DEDDE and John MAYBOURNE, overseers. Duffeld was survived by his widow, Joan, and 2 ss, William and Thomas. Joan d. within a month of her husband. CWA ii, s.a. 1510–11, wk. 30.

Two carpenters named, respectively, William and Thomas Duffeld are probably to be identified with the ss of John Duffeld, dyer. William was apprenticed to a London carpenter 1502, was himself a master in 1508 and was a member of the Carpenters' Company until the 1520s. Bower Marsh (ed.), *Records of the Worshipful Company of Carpenters*, vol. ii (Oxford, 1914), 140, 182, 203, 221–2, 234, 245. Thomas Duffeld, carpenter, m. *ante* 1531 a dau. of Nicholas Palle, carpenter of West.; from Palle's widow Thomas inherited in 1543 the Peacock inn in King St. *LP* v, no. 408; PRO, E40/12837; Reg Bk, iii, fos. 49ᵛ–50ᵛ. Thomas Duffeld was a chwdn in 1550–2. CWA iv, s.a.

EDWARD, John. Chwdn 1474–6. CWA i, s.a.

ESGAR, Walter. Const. for Tothill St. 1427; c.p. 1434–. WAM 50747, 50749.

ETON, Thomas. C.p. –1505–1513. WAM 50770–6.

EWDALL, John. ?Royal officer. Chwdn 1504–6. CWA i. 497. John Uvedale was a yeoman cart-taker to the crown 1509–12. *LP* i, nos. 20 (p. 18), 1123 (38), 3324 (38).

FANNE (*alias* FAWNE), John (1). ?Barber. C.p. 1434 × 1445–1453–; const. 1438–9, 1450; chief const. 1435. WAM 50752–5; PRO, KB9/229/2/7; KB9/230/4/47. 'John Fawne of Westminster, barber', was a trustee of a local mason 1449. *Cal Cl R 1447–54*, p. 129. John Fanne was described in 1451/2, in the petition of a *Doche* cobbler against whom Fanne and another had brought an action, as 'the greatest juror haunting Westminster'. PRO, C1/24/70. Fanne r. a ten. on the W. side of King St. 1423–49 × 1461. WAM 18568–93; 23074–7. *Ante* 1462, John Fawne, senior, his w. Katherine, and William Norton granted to John Fawne, junior, citizen, and vintner of London, *et al.*, a ten. outside Newgate, London. *Cal Cl R 1461–8*, p. 137. John Fanne (1) d. *c.*1460. CWA i. 8 (1460 × 1462). His widow, Katherine, kept in St Mgt the obit of her late husband and son *c.*1465. Ibid. 63. Katherine Fawne was b. in St George's chapel in St Mgt, beside her husband, in 1467–8. Ibid. 75. John FANNE (2) was perhaps the 'John Fawne, junior', named above.

FANNE, John (2). Yeoman. Chwdn 1492–4; 1496–8. CWA i. 293, 319. Valet of West. Abbey 1467–98. WAM 19975–94. Represented St Mgt in a legal case in the exchequer 1497/8. CWA i. 345. Kept his parents' obit in St Mgt 1467/8. CWA i. 75. Was possibly a descendant of John FANNE (1). R. 3 tens in King St. near the N. scty gate 1474–84. WAM 17816; 23549–59. R. 3 tens 'in one' in Tothill St. 1504–5/6; and 3 additional tens adjacent to these 1506–9. WAM 17953; 19114–15. Was succeeded here by his widow, Elizabeth, 1509–17. WAM 19117*–22. D. 1509; b. in St Mgt. CWA i. 559. Will made 21 Sept., proved 14 Nov. 1509. PCW Wyks, 108. Widow Elizabeth, executrix; William HEYDON, overseer.

FAWNE. See FANNE.

FOLTON, William. Wdn Assmptn guild 1457. *Cal Pat R 1452–61*, pp. 362–3.

FORD, John. Royal officer. Chwdn 1514–16. CWA ii, s.a. Wdn Assmptn guild 1515–18. Guild accts. Usher of the royal receipt 1522. WAM 12366. Evidently as an officer of the bailiff of West., John Ford drew up 'the book of the court kept at the gatehouse' of West. in 1523. WAM 50778. D. 1539; b. in St Mgt. CWA iii, s.a. 1538–9, wk. 28.

FORSTER, Robert. Abbey officer. C.p. 1428–49. WAM 50748–53. One of the four re-founders of the Assmptn guild 1440. *Cal Pat R 1436–41*, p. 448. Janitor and custodian of the gaol of West. Abbey –1445–. WAM 17762. Valet of the abbey sacristy 1440–. WAM 19941. With w. Margaret, occupied a large mes. in the scty called 'Delaberes' 1442–. WAM 17777. Held property outside the palace gate; in 1486 9 mess and 5 gdns here were found to have belonged to a later Robert Forster, who had d. 1485. WAM 23517, 23520; PRO, C142/138. Robert Forster, the janitor, d. 14 Nov. 1449. WAM 33289, fo. 38ᵛ. His obit was kept in St Mgt by Henry MARBLE 1460. CWA i. 4. Forster's w. was the dau. of William

NORTON (2). After Forster's death she m. Richard Walsh, seneschal of the abbot of West. See WAM 23517, 23520, 19955–72.

FORSTER, Walter. Royal servant. C.p. 1512–1514–; chief const. 1512–13. WAM 50775–7. Wdn Assmptn guild 1512–15. Guild accts, s.a. Underclerk of the king's works –1492–1503–; comptroller of the king's works 1509–19. *King's Works*, iii (1), 406–7. R. a ten. on W. side King St. 1511–19; also nearby cotts in Thieving Lane 1505–19. WAM 19761–77. D. 1519; b. in St Mgt. CWA ii, s.a. 1518–19, wk. 39. Was survived by his widow, Joan. WAM 19785/90–19800.

FOULER. See HULL.

FRAMPTON, Thomas. Chwdn 1464–6. CWA i. 19. In 1458 Frampton made over his property in West. and elsewhere to his s., Richard Frampton, *et al. Cal Cl R 1454–61*, p. 264. His w. was b. at St Mgt 1474/5; and his own obit was kept there in the same year. CWA i. 95–6.

FROST, Richard. Chwdn 1490–2. CWA i. 267. D. 1494/5; b. at St Mgt. CWA i. 296. Chwdns 'paid to Frost's wife for a quire of paper for a book of parcels. 3*d.*' in 1488/9. CWA i. 256.

FYSSHER, Peter. C.p. 1374–93 × 1396. WAM 50705–27.

FYTTE, James. Citizen and tailor of London. Chwdn –1460. CWA i. 8. Const. 1464. WAM 50757. Wdn Assmptn guild 1474–7. Guild accts. Was admitted to the Tailors' Company of London 1459. London, Guildhall Library, Wardens' Accounts of the Merchant Tailors' Company, vol. 2, fo. 152^r (microfilm; original at Merchant Tailors' Hall). His father b. at St Mgt 1464; also his apprentice 1467/8; and his w. (probably named Joan) 1478/9. CWA i. 20, 76, 132, 174. Paid for a glass window in St Mgt 1498/9. CWA i. 376. Granted tens in the parish of St Mary Aldermary, London, to Assmptn guild 1477, in return for an obit for himself, Thomas Cosyn and Cosyn's w., Margaret. The record of this grant is copied into a contemporary book containing a chronicle, saints' lives, etc., which may have belonged to Fytte. Cambridge, Trinity Coll. MS O.9.1., fos. 230^r–231^r; and see above, ch. 9 n. 56. Active in London 1480s. *Cal Letter-Bk L*, 211, 268. D. 1500/1; b. in St Mgt. CWA i. 394.

GARDINER, Walter. Yeoman. Chwdn 1498–1500. CWA i. 351. C.p. 1509–12 × 1514 (evidently retired from office). WAM 50774–5; PRO, SC2/191/66. Master Assmptn guild 1518–21. Guild accts. A generous benefactor of St Mgt; his gifts towards a new rood loft in 1517–18 amounted to £82. CWA ii, s.a. Will made 23 Dec. 1521, proved 5 May 1523. PRO, PROB11/21, PCC 7 Bodfelde. John MAYBOURNE and John FORD, overseers. Gardiner was b. in St Mgt. CWA ii, s.a. 1522–3, wk. 47. He was survived by his widow, Margaret.

GEDNEY, John. Draper, alderman, and mayor of London. C.p. 1402 × 1407–27; const. for King St. 1406; chief const. 1422–7. WAM 50738–47. Alderman and mayor of London 1415–49 (d.). Beaven,

Aldermen, ii. 4. Supplied suits of livery to West. Abbey 1416–18. WAM 24268–9. Corrodian of West. Abbey 1423–8. WAM 18568–74. Between 1432–5 the abbey treasurer repaid to Gedney a debt of over £60. WAM 19930–3. Held the Boar's Head inn in King St. with 1–2 tens adjacent 1396–1423. W. Margaret named 1408 *et seq*. WAM 18528–67. Held a ten. near the palace gate in King St., rent-free, 1423–9. WAM 18568–76. D. 1449 (see above).

Two monks named Gedney are recorded in West. Abbey at this period. Walter Gedney celebrated his first mass there 1396/7. Thomas Gedney celebrated his first mass 1416/17; d. 1432/3. Pearce, *Monks*, 125, 132–3.

GERARD, John. Cook. Chwdn 1488–90. CWA i. 243. John Gerard, 'cook', reserved his pew in St Mgt 1485/6. CWA i. 233. In 1491, 'John Garrerd coke made a fray apon Sir William Stanes prist & no blode shed'. WAM 40764. Presented for sale of bad food 1486, 1488; his w. fined for poultry sold by her. WAM 50760–1. John Gerard r. a ten. on W. side King St., near S. end, 1467 × 1470–95; and another in Long Ditch 1479 × 1481–7. WAM 19717–46.

GERARD, William. Yeoman; ?royal officer. Chwdn 1480–2. CWA i. 171. Wdn Assmptn guild 1484–7. Guild accts. C.p. 1467 × 1486–95–; chief const. 1488. WAM 50760–8. William Gerard r. a timber yard at the W. end of Tothill St. 1479–*c*.1497. WAM 17845; 23255–67. In 1483/4 he negotiated for the monks of West. with royal officers concerning the requisitioning of hay in Hyde and Knightsbridge. WAM 23559. D. 1497/8; b. in St Mgt. CWA i. 329.

Possibly to be identified with 'William Gerard, king's servitor', who in 1477 received a life grant of the office of keeper of the garden at Windsor Castle. *Cal Pat R 1476–85*, p. 56.

GOODWYN, William. Scrivener. Chwdn 1512–14. CWA ii, s.a. Wdn Rounceval guild 1510. *LP* i, no. 381 (96). Wrote and signed chwdns' accts 1510. CWA i. 576. As 'scrivener of the court letter of London', Goodwyn r. a ten. outside the N scty gate at West. from 1504, with an additional adjacent ten. from 1509, until 1520. WAM 17960; 23584–606. R. a store house and gdn in Thieving Lane 1506–10. WAM 19762–5. In 1518 he bought a lease on the Hart's Horn in King St., which he sublet. PRO, C1/550/49–50; WAM 23142 *et seq*. In 1513/14 he gave to St Mgt a grail 'for the organs above' (i.e. in the rood loft). CWA ii, s.a.

GRAUNT, Robert. Baker. Chwdn 1522–4; auditor of chwdns' accts 1528; deputy chwdn 1546–8. CWA ii, iii, s.a. Wdn Assmptn guild 1536–9. Guildhall Library, MS 12993 (1538); see also 12994. Supplied bran to feed the royal fowl in St James' Park *c*.1530. *London Topographical Record*, xix (1947), 113. Will made 31 May, proved 29 Aug. 1558. PCW Bracy, fos. 119ᵛ–120ᵛ. Graunt bequeathed the mes. in which he lived in

Long Ditch, called 'the bakehouse', to his grandson, Robert Graunt (s. of John Graunt, the late s. of the testator). A lease of houses and a gdn was left to the testator's sister, Mary Graunt. Residue to testator's daughter-in-law, Margaret Graunt.

GREGORY, Thomas. Chwdn 1484–6. CWA i. 221. D. 1499/1500; bequeathed 5s. to St Mgt. CWA i. 370.

GRENDON, William. Mason. C.p. 1376–1402 × 1407; const. 1377–93. WAM 50707–35. Employed on the 'new work' of West. Abbey 1390–1402. *Archaeological Jnl*, cxiii (1957), 97. Another mason of the same name had worked at the abbey 1355–65. Ibid.

GRENE, John. Royal officer. C.p. 1394 × 1396–1410 × 1422. WAM 50734–40. Const. 1396–1403. WAM 50734; *Cal Pat R 1401–5*, p. 328. Returned royal indictments for Middx. to king's bench in West. 1398/9. PRO, KB9/179/10. Yeoman of the crown 1400; yeoman of the king's chamber 1402; coroner of the royal household 1409; clerk of the king's foreign estreats in the exchequer 1411; coroner of the household to Henry V 1413; yeoman 'of the wardrobe of the king's beds' 1415. *Cal Pat R 1399–1401*, p. 20; ibid. *1401–5*, p. 167; ibid. *1408–13*, pp. 58, 278–9; ibid. *1413–16*, pp. 1, 386.

GURNEY, John. Gentleman and royal servant. C.p. 1450 × 1453–1467–. WAM 50755–7. A royal sergeant, described at various dates as 'yeoman of the king's kitchen' and as 'master-cook for the royal mouth', Gurney received in 1440 a royal grant of the ground called 'Scotland' in King St. *Cal Pat R 1436–41*, p. 434; ibid. *1452–61*, p. 508. R. the nearby Lion inn at Endive Lane from 1441, and 5 cotts in Endive Lane c.1463. Also r. a 'long house' on W. side King St., at the S. end, with a gdn in Thieving Lane, from 1441; and an adjacent 'corner house' from 1453. WAM 19685–723; 18895. With w. Isabel and s. Richard, r. in addition a ten. in the scty c.1470. WAM 17804. Henry V granted to John Gurney and Nicholas Browne a ten. called the Great Bell by the Barbican in St Botolph Aldersgate parish, in the suburb of London. *Cal Pat R 1461–7*, p. 188. D. and was b. at St Mgt 1475/6. CWA i. 110.

HACHET, William. Brewer. Chwdn 1480–2. CWA i. 171. C.p. 1488–1495–; chief const. 1491. WAM 50761–8. Wdn Assmptn guild 1493–6. PRO E40/13407 (1494). This was doubtless the 'William Hachet, brewer of Westminster', who was a feoffee of the Hammersmith man 1480. *Cal Cl R 1476–85*, p. 203. William Hachet b. a wife at St Mgt 1474, and children 1475/6 and 1484/5. CWA i. 94, 103, 222.

HAKEBOURNE, Robert. C.p. 1364–79. WAM 50699–713. With his w., Sarah, r. a mes. in Tothill St. called 'Lawestenement' (the later Cock inn) 1371–*ante* 1385. WAM 17686, 17704.

HARDEGRAY, Richard. Mason. C.p. 1392–1410 × 1421. WAM 50726–40. Was employed on the 'new work' of West. Abbey 1393–1407/8.

Archaeological Jnl, cxiii (1957), 97. R. a gdn in Long Ditch 1387, and 2 acres land in Charing Field 1391–1415. WAM 23187; 18525–56.

HAREYS. See VALENTYNE.

HASSOK, Robert. Yeoman. Const. for Wool Staple 1467, 1486–8. WAM 50758–61. Chwdn 1494. CWA i. 295. As 'yeoman of West.', stood surety in 1471 for another West. yeoman. *Year Books of Edward IV*, ed. N. Neilson, Selden Soc., xlvii (1931), 142–3. R. a vacant plot at Charing Cross and a cott. in Long Ditch 1480–94. WAM 19728–45. In 1493 Hassok held 5 tens in Long Ditch. WAM 50766. D. 1494; b. in St Mgt. CWA i. 300. Katherine Hassok d. and was b. in St Mgt in the same year. CWA i. 298. The joint obit of Robert Hassok and his w., Katherine, was kept in St Mgt 1511. CWA ii, s.a. 1510–11, wk. 29.

HERT, Richard. Gentleman. Chwdn 1486–8. CWA i. 242. R., with w. Margaret, ten. on W. side King St. near Albright Alley 1478–1500 (in 1501/2 the rent was substantially in arrears). WAM 17834; 23095–127; 23580 (attached slip). D. 1503/4; b. at St Mgt. CWA i. 462.

HEYDON, William. Wdn Assmptn guild 1499–1502. Guild accts, s.a.

HOGAN, Thomas. Baker. Wdn (1499–1502) and master (1508–11) Assmptn guild. Guild accts, s.a. 1508; CWA i. 555 (1508/9). C.p. 1495 × 1505–1514–; chief const. 1505. WAM 50770–7. Valet of the bakery of West. Abbey 1511–16. WAM 18922; 23007–12. R. a cott. and close at the W. end of Tothill St. 1511–16. WAM 23283–9. Will made 11 Jan., proved 12 Feb. 1517. PCW Wyks, 242–8. Hogan was b. in the Trinity chapel of St Mgt. CWA ii, s.a. 1516–17, wk. 20. He invited the masters and wdns of his 'occupation' (the bakers' guild of London?), the Austin friars, the grey friars and the brotherhood of the Papey to attend his funeral. The profits of his dwelling-house called 'the bakehouse' (situation uncertain) he bequeathed to Assmptn guild, to purchase ornaments. His widow, Joan, lived until 1530. PCW Bracy, fo. 12^{r-v}.

HOO (*alias* HOUGH), Robert. Tailor. Const. for Charing 1434. WAM 50749. C.p. 1434 × 1445–53 × 1462; chief const. 1450–3. WAM 50753–5. R. tens in King St., principally the Swan inn opposite the Wool Staple, 1423–*c*.1462. WAM 18568–93; 23074–80. D. 1460 × 1462. His widow, Margaret, gave an altar cloth to St Mgt for his remembrance. CWA i. 8, 17. She subsequently m. John Wylkynson. See WAM 23081.

HOREWOOD, Nicholas. C.p. 1422–*ante* 1434. WAM 50745, 50749. Held a mes. in King St. at about this period. PRO, C1/6/73.

HOUGH. See HOO.

HULL (*alias* FOULER), Thomas. C.p. 1386 × 1392–96 × 1402. WAM 50726–34. In 1403, Thomas Hull, *alias* Fouler, quitclaimed the former ten. of his late cousin, William HULL, at the King St. bars. PRO, E40/1557.

HULL, (*alias* FOULER), William. Carpenter. C.p. 1374–80 × 1384. WAM

50705–15. In 1377, he and his w., Helen, acquired a ten. at the bars in King St. PRO, E40/1465; E40/1468. See also Thomas HULL.

HUMFREY, Richard. Gentleman. Wdn (1471–4) and master (1484–7) Assmptn guild. Guild accts. C.p. 1486–7. WAM 50760–1. Kept obits of his parents in St Mgt 1460s. CWA i. 19, 65/66. With his w., Marion, Humfrey acquired 2 tens, a cott. and gdn in Wool Staple Yard 1470. In 1488 he gave a ten. here to Assmptn guild, in exchange for an obit. Guildhall Library, MS 12979; guild accts, s.a. R. the Hart's Horn near the King St. bars 1476–88. WAM 23093–110. In 1480 Humfrey granted a mes. and shops in the parish of St Mary Matfelon, London, to the minoresses without Aldgate. *Cal Pat R 1476–85*, p. 227. Will made 9 Feb., proved 13 May 1488. PRO, PROB11, PCC 9 Milles. Richard Humfrey was b. beside his w. Marion in St Mgt, where their obit was kept. CWA ii, s.a. 1510–11, wk. 37. Left lands in Kentish Town. Thomas BOUGH, William GERARD and William HACHET, executors.

HUNGATE, William. Wdn Assmptn guild 1487–90. Guild accts.

HUNT, John. Gentleman, royal officer. Wdn Assmptn guild 1521–2. Guild accts, s.a. Keeper of West. Palace 1516. *LP* ii, p. 875.

John Hunt, 'gentleman', leased a meadow near West. in 1519. Reg Bk, ii, fos. 134ᵛ–135ʳ. He r. a ten. and gdn in the almonry 1504–5, 1519–22; a forge at the W. end of Tothill St. 1516–22; and 2 cotts near the latter, in Petty France, 1518–22. WAM 19124, 19128–34; 17982; 17991; 23294–8. D. 1522; b. in St Mgt, to which he bequeathed a russet velvet coat, sold for 46s. 8d. CWA ii, s.a. 1521–2, wk. 43.

A Thomas Hunt had been clerk of the royal works 1472–82, and seneschal of the abbot of West. 1465–94. *King's Works*, ii. 1045; WAM 19973–90.

HYLL, Richard. Hosteler. C.p. –1486–1487. WAM 50760–1. Presented for the quality of his ale and horse fodder. Ibid. He and his w. Agnes r. a ten. within the W. gate of the scty 1490–9; and a cott. at Charing –1506–1509. WAM 19739–53; Reg Bk, i, fos. 47ᵛ–48ʳ; WAM 23275*–8.

INGELEY, Hugh. C.p. 1395. WAM 50734.

JACKSON. See CLEMENT.

JAMES, John. Gentleman. Wdn Assmptn guild 1521–4. Guild accts, s.a. Chwdn 1534–6. CWA ii, s.a. Valet of the locutorium of West. Abbey –1530; was made a groom of the abbey cellar 1530. Reg Bk, ii, fos. 264ᵛ, 266ʳ. His goods valued in 1524 at £40. PRO, E179/238/98. R. a ten. and 3 cotts beside the Cock inn in Tothill St. 1493–1531–; and 2 shops in Tothill St. 1520–1532–. WAM 17901; 17974; 23265–311; 23608–22. R. several tens. in scty 1495–1531, including a 'long house' called the Three Tuns, 1526 *et seq.* WAM 19747–807; Reg Bk, ii, fo. 258ʳ. Also leased 'Steynour's Croft' beside the white cross in King St., with its 7 cotts, 1495–1527. WAM 23122–67; 17924; 17965. From 1521, James farmed

the West. Abbey manor of Hampstead. Reg Bk, ii, fo. 174^{r-v}; and see
WAM 30668, 30683. The above refs. give the names of John James's
three successive ws: Elizabeth (1500), Margaret (1511), and Agnes
(1529).

JARDEN, William. Tailor. Wdn Assmptn guild 1455. WAM 17774. C.p.
1464 × 1466–1467–. WAM 50758. Made robes for masons working at
West. Abbey 1455. WAM 23519. Was owed £20 by the monks there
1464. WAM 19070, 19072. With his w., Joan, Jarden r. several tens in
Tothill St. *c*.1447–84. WAM 17775; 23224–57; 23516–59. In 1464 he
acquired the Catherine Wheel, a large hostelry in the same street; in the
same year he was presented for the quality of his ale. WAM 50757; and
see below. A s., John, was b. in the Trinity chapel of St Mgt 1467–8.
CWA i. 70. William Jarden d. 1484; was b. in St Mgt (presumably in the
Trinity chapel). CWA i. 207; WAM 23559. His widow subsequently m.
Hugh MORELAND. Jarden bequeathed the Catherine Wheel to Queen's
College, Oxford. In return, the provost and scholars of the college
undertook to find a university-trained priest who would keep in
perpetuity the obit of Jarden and his w., and who would preach an annual
sermon in St Mgt, West. Oxford, Bodleian Library, MSS D.D. Queen's
Coll. 1759–70. The joint obit of William Jarden, Joan, his w., and their s.,
John, with the addition of Hugh Moreland, was duly kept (presumably
until the Reformation) at the college each year on 10 Dec. *Liber
Obituarius Aulae Reginae in Oxonia*, ed. J. R. Magrath, Oxford
Historical Society, 1st ser., lvi (1910), 46, 105–8.

A 'John Jordayn, taillour,' made a recognizance of debt in London
1460. CLRO, City Journal 7, fo. 8^r (ref. supplied by Miss K. Lacey).
'John Jurdan, tailor', was made a warden of London Bridge 1469. *Cal
Letter-Bk L*, 86.

JENYNGES, William. Royal officer. Chwdn 1540–2. CWA iii, s.a. Wdn
Assmptn guild 1542–5. CWA iii, s.a. 1542–3. Master Rounceval guild
1540–2. CWA iii, s.a. 1540–1; *LP* xvii, no. 283 (54). In Jan. 1555, King
Philip and Queen Mary addressed a letter to the dean and chapter of
West., desiring them to grant to William Jennyns, groom of the royal
chamber, a new lease of his ten. called the Boar's Head in West. WAM
18056.

JOHN, Hervic. Const. 1440. PRO, KB9/232/2/73. C.p. 1450 × 1453–.
WAM 50755. D. *c*.1461; b. at St Mgt; his obit and those of his 2 ws. kept
there by John BRADDING. CWA i. 5, 8, 28, 35, 75.

Another Hervic John, 'brewer', held a ten. in King St. 1467. WAM
50758.

JONESON, Richard. C.p. 1434–. WAM 50749.

JOYNOUR (*alias* VERN), Richard. Esquire; grocer and royal officer. C.p.
1467 × 1486–7. WAM 50760–1. Controller of the mint 1450–2. Vic-

tualler to the crown 1450s. MP Heytesbury 1450–1; Old Sarum 1453–4. Wedgwood and Holt, *History of Parliament 1439–1509*, 504–5.

Active in London 1454–5. *Cal Plea & Mem R 1437–57*, 136, 183. In 1467, the monks of West. pledged to Richard Joynour, citizen and grocer of London, 421 oz. of silver plate, as a partial gauge for a debt of 1,100 marks which they had borrowed of John West, king's coroner, and William Kenyngthorp, gentleman. WAM 9476; 33289, fo. 13^v.

Joynour may have provisioned the Yorkist royal family when it took refuge in the West. scty in 1470–1. The abbot is said (by Wedgwood and Holt, loc. cit.; no ref. given) to have sued Joynour for £133, which the latter had agreed to pay for staying within the scty. (The pattern may be that of Richard Heron, another London merchant who also r. accommodation in the West. scty during the 1470s, and who was later accused of having assisted the Yorkists in 1460. WAM 17822; 23008–102; E. Power and M. M. Postan (eds.), *Studies in English Trade in the Fifteenth Century* (London, 1933), 318–20.)

From 1468 until shortly before his presumed death in 1487, Joynour received from West. Abbey an annuity of 26s. 8d. In the same period he leased, jointly with John West, gentleman (see above), the great West. mes. known as 'Mauduitsgarden' or 'Calais'. WAM 17798; 23093–108; Reg Bk, i, fos. 15^v–16^r. In his last months, Joynour relinquished 'Calais' and retired to a mes. with a gdn in the scty, close to the abbey Lady chapel. WAM 17879. Repeatedly outlawed for debt, he thus remained at his death (c.1487) immune to the claims of his creditors. See Wedgwood and Holt, loc. cit. Richard Joynour kept an obit for his deceased w. in St Mgt as early as 1464, at about which time he gave to that church various hangings and vestments. CWA i. 20, 49/50.

KENTBURY, Robert. Mason. C.p. 1367 × 1374–96 × 1402. WAM 50705–34. Mended the *volta* of a new malthouse in West. Abbey, at the cost of £100, 1383–8. WAM 19876. Was employed on the 'new work' of the abbey 1387–91. *Archaeological Jnl*, cxiii (1957), 98. Held property in West. formerly of Thomas de Sheffield 1379–1391–. WAM 17698, 17701, 17711–12, 17714. See also WAM 17688; LN, fos. 115^v–116^r. With his w., Agnes, Robert Kentbury in 1388 acquired a tavern in King St., without the gateway of West. Palace. Guildhall Library, MS 13002. See also Thomas KENTBURY.

KENTBURY, Thomas. Mason and royal and abbey officer. C.p. 1396 × 1402–*ante* 1407; chief const. –1407. WAM 50735, 50738. Sub-bailiff of West. 1406–7. See app. 1. Was regularly appointed to royal commissions of justice c.1405–10. *Cal Cl R 1405–9*, pp. 91, 117, 152, etc.; *Cal Fine R 1405–13*, p. 48. Worked on the construction of the new malthouse in West. Abbey 1399–1400. WAM 19883. R. a ten. in Long Ditch under the scty wall 1402–8. WAM 18537–42. Also held 2 tens in

King St. See WAM 17746; 19663 *et seq.* Was presumably a relative of Robert KENTBURY.

Simon Kentebury was purveyor of the king's work at the palace of West. 1399. *Cal Pat R 1399–1401*, p. 87.

KINBELL. See KYMBELL.

KNAPPE, Richard. Tailor and royal and abbey officer. Const. for Charing 1398–1410; c.p. 1402 × 1407–10 × 1422. WAM 24748, m. F; 50738–40. Sub-bailiff of West. liberty 1410. See app. 1. In receipt of a corrody in West. Abbey 1399. WAM 5916. Convened regularly with Thomas TOTTESHAM, *et al.*, as mainpernor or witness to West. deeds. e.g. *Cal Cl R 1405–9, apud indicem.* Purveyor of the household to Richard II 1398. *Cal Pat R 1396–9*, p. 456. In Lent 1399, Richard Knappe was said to have conspired, at King Richard's instigation, and with the assistance of men from Richard's stronghold of Cheshire, to ambush at West. Thomas Rydyng, sub-bailiff of the vill. Rydyng was thus captured and held prisoner in St Mgt church until he bought his freedom. PRO, KB9/184/1/9; for Rydyng, see app. 1. At Easter 1400, Richard Knappe and Roger del Eschequer, usher, were accused of abusing royal authority delegated to them in Middx. Knappe was said to have acquired a ten. in West., from which base he oppressed his neighbours; and to be 'radix omnium placitatum infra comitatu praedictu factorum', or in other words, 'imaginator of many fals wyles and of all Middlesex chief caster of gyles'. PRO, KB9/184/1/9. These accusations notwithstanding, in 1401 he was purveyor of the king's works to Henry IV. *Cal Pat R 1399–1401*, p. 486. He r. 3 vacant plots of land opposite St Mary Magdalene's chapel in Tothill St. 1417–c.1430. WAM 17733; 23221; 23213–16.

KNIGHT, John. Chwdn 1522–4. CWA ii, s.a. Wdn Rounceval guild 1516–18. CWA ii, s.a. 1517–18. His goods were valued in 1524 at £30; in 1542 at £40. PRO, E179/238/98; E179/141/127.

KNOWESLEY (*alias* CLOWDESLEY), Thomas. Baker. Const. for Tothill St. 1513–14. WAM 50776. Chwdn 1530–2. CWA iii, s.a. Wdn St Cornelius's guild in St Mgt 1536. PRO, C1/807/41. R. (in succession to Henry Knowesley) 6 tens and a vacant plot on S. side Tothill St. 1519–1536–. W. Elizabeth named. Reg Bk, ii, fos. 150^r–151^r; 19128–52. Knowesley's goods were valued in 1524 at £13. 6s. 8d. PRO, E179/238/98. He was fined in 1523 for overcharging the common with 4 horses. WAM 50778. 'Elizabeth Clowdesley' d. 1523. CWA ii, s.a. 1523–4, wk. 17. 'Thomas Clowdesley' d. 1540; was b. in St Mgt. CWA iii, s.a. 1540–1, wk. 15.

KYMBELL (*alias* KINBELL), John. Tailor. C.p. 1380 × 1384–93. WAM 50716–27. As a trustee of West. Abbey, Kymbell held for the monks certain 'rents of the new purchase' in West., 1381–90. WAM 24263–5; 18520–3; LN, fo. 133^{r-v}. Supplied stone and ironwork for the reconstruction of the cellarium of West. Abbey 1383–8. WAM 19875B. His w., Alice, made albs, amices, etc., for the vestry of West. Abbey 1380s and 1390s. WAM 19643–50. John Kymbell r. 2 shops outside the W. gate of the abbey scty 1363–93. He d. 1393. He was succeeded in the shops by his widow, Alice, 1393–9. WAM 18990–19004.

KYNG, William. Yeoman; brewer. Chwdn 1486–8. CWA i. 242. Chief const. 1510; c.p. 1510–14. PRO, SC2/191/66; WAM 50775–7. Wdn Assmptn guild 1512–14. Guild accts, s.a. Valet of West. Abbey 1495–1514. WAM 19993–9; 23001–10. The abbey sacrist noted each year 1505–12: 'Solut' Willelmo Kyng pro cariagio frondium erga festum Sancti Petri 14*d.* (*or* 16*d.*)'. WAM 19761–8. As 'brewer', Kyng r. a ten. and gdn in Long Ditch 1507–14; and a ten. on N. side Tothill St. 1511–12. WAM 17955; 19115–19; 23594. D. 1514; b. in the Trinity aisle of St Mgt. CWA ii, s.a. 1514–15, wk. 29. Will made 11 Aug., proved 15 Dec. 1514. PCW Wyks, 205–8. Thomas BOUGH was overseer. Kyng bequeathed his dwelling house in West. to his widow, Margery, with the remainder of the lease on her death to his dau., Elizabeth.

William Kyng was evidently related to a London family of leather-sellers. Henry Kyng, citizen and leatherseller of London, was a previous tenant of William's Tothill St. ten. (by right of Henry's w., the widow of Edmund Adam, mason of West.) 1483–1511. WAM 17866; 23560–93. John Kyng, citizen and leatherseller of London, r. the Boar's Head inn in King St. 1486–8. WAM 23108–10.

LAURENCE, John. Yeoman; brewer. Const. 1505, 1508 (for Tothill St.). WAM 50770, 50773. Chwdn 1512–14. CWA ii, s.a. Wdn Rounceval guild 1522–4. Guild accts. R. a brewing ten. in Tothill St., opposite the pillory, 1502/3–1531–. WAM 17930; 17978; 23272–311. R. in addition several cotts and gdns, and barns called 'the timberhawe', all near the W. end of Tothill St., 1513–1531–. WAM 17977; Reg Bk, ii, fos. 92ᵛ–93ʳ; 23285–311. R. meadows nearby called 'Thames Mead' (1504), 'Market Mead' (1517–18), 'Lousmead' (1521–1531–), and 'Long Moor' (1525–). WAM 18913; 18927; 23159–69; Reg Bk, ii, fo. 214ʳ. His goods were valued in 1524 at £66. 13*s.* 4*d.* PRO, E179/238/98. D. 1538; b. in St Mgt. CWA iii, s.a. 1538–9, wk. 12.

The brewer is presumably to be distinguished from the 'John Laurence, brickmaker', who contributed £6. 13*s.* 4*d.* to a loan to the abbot of West. 1522. WAM 12366. It was doubtless the latter who carted sand and gravel and supplied bricks for work at West. Abbey 1501–20. WAM 18909; 18917; 18930; 19764. The brickmaker also worked at Whitehall Palace 1531. PRO, E36/252, p. 300.

LECHE, William. C.p. –1434. WAM 50749.

LEGH, Peter. C.p. 1407 × 1410–. WAM 50740.

LENTALL, Philip. Cutler. Chwdn 1528–30. CWA ii, s.a. C.p. –1555–1556–.

WAM 50782. Wdn Rounceval guild 1536–8; audited Rounceval guild accts 1522. Guild accts. His goods valued in 1524 at £13. 6s. 8d.; in 1544 at £100. PRO, E179/238/98; E179/141/139. Will made 19 Nov. 1558, proved 16 Jan. 1559. PCW Bracy, fo. 144ʳ⁻ᵛ. W. Joan, sole executrix. The will also names a dau., Jane Massy, and son-in-law, Thomas Massy. (Thomas Massy was wdn Rounceval guild 1538–40; chwdn 1544–6; and a headborough or c.p. of West. Guild accts; CWA ii, s.a.; PCW Bracy, fos. 166ʳ–167ᵛ.)

Philip Lentall's cousin, Henry Lentall (d. 1531), was servant to the prior of West. Abbey, and valet of the convent 1515–26. PCW Bracy, fo. 17ᵛ; WAM 23012–25.

LEWYS, John. Wdn Assmptn guild 1490–3. Guild accts. C.p. 1491–1495–; chief const. 1493. WAM 50764–8. Wrote the chwdns' accts of St Mgt 1486. CWA i. 240. D. 1496–7; b. at St Mgt. CWA i. 323.

LIVERMORE, Richard. Gentleman; common lawyer. C.p. 1453 × 1464–1467–. WAM 50757–8. Of Exeter origin. From 1449, represented West. Abbey regularly in the royal courts in local rent cases, etc. WAM 19956–73; 23225–6; 23236; 23241; 19704; 19078–9; 23517. In West., Livermore r. from 1448 the ten. at the S. end of King St., on the W. side, later called the Black Eagle. WAM 19698–728. Belonged to Assmptn guild from *ante* 1477. Guild accts, s.a. 1477 (quarterage arrears). Meanwhile he retained links with Exeter. Was retained by the council of the city of Exeter as its attorney 1453–69; and by the dean and chapter of Exeter likewise 1464, 1471. Exeter City Archives, Exeter Receivers' Accounts, s.a.; Exeter, Dean and Chapter Archives, MS 3778, fos. 1ʳ, 14ᵛ. The dates of his payments indicate that Livermore was based at Westminster during the law terms. (Dr N. Ramsay supplied these Exeter refs.) The Livermores were a prominent Exeter family which in the sixteenth century contributed two mayors to that city. W. T. MacCaffrey, *Exeter, 1540–1640: The Growth of an English County Town* (Cambridge, Mass., 1958), 287–8. Richard Livermore 'of West-minster, gentleman', retained property in Exeter. *Cal Cl R 1447–54*, p. 332. D. 1481–2; b. in St Mgt. CWA i. 181. Was survived by his widow, Margaret. WAM 19741 *et seq.* See also *Jnl of Legal History*, i (1980), 197; ibid. iv (1983), 67.

LOKYNGTON, Walter. Chandler, vintner, and grocer. Const. 1464. WAM 50757. Wdn Assmptn guild 1477(–80). Cambridge, Trinity Coll. MS O.9.1, fos. 230ʳ–231ʳ. Made candles for St Mgt 1460s; and for Assmptn guild 1474. CWA i. 11, 13–15; guild accts, s.a. Received 2d. per diem from the abbey sacrist, possibly for similar services, 1480s. WAM 19729*, 19731. As 'vintner of Westminster', made over his goods in London and elsewhere to trustees (members of the royal household) 1476. *Cal Cl R 1476–85*, p. 10. As 'grocer', witnessed grant of property in West. 1478. PRO, E40/1522. As executor of David SELLY, held the Bell and the Rose in King St. 1473–87, before duly granting them to Assmptn guild, in accordance with Selly's will. WAM 23549–60; 23248–55. A s. of Lokyngton was b. at St Mgt 1466–7; and Joan, w. of 'Watkyn Lokyngton' 1483–4. CWA i. 64, 208, 220. Walter Lokyngton d. *ante* 1492, when his executors were presented in connection with a stable in King St. which had been his. WAM 50765.

LORDE, George. Gentleman; royal officer. Const. for King St. 1509; c.p. 1513–1514–. WAM 50774, 50776. Wdn Assmptn guild 1515–18; 1521–4. Guild accts, s.a. Wdn Rounceval guild 1520–2. Guild accts. Audited chwdns' accts 1528. CWA ii, s.a. Purveyor of the king's works at West. and the Tower of London 1509–33. *King's Works*, iii (1), 407. Usher of the royal exchequer 1522. WAM 12366. His goods were assessed in 1524 at £40. PRO, E179/238/98. Lorde was living at West. by 1503–4, when he reserved a pew in St Mgt for his w. CWA i. 473; see also i. 508. He was accommodated in West. Palace 1508, when he was fined for ale sold by him there. WAM 50773. Later, he r. both the Saracen's Head inn near the palace gate in King St. 1526–33, and the nearby Bell inn, on the opposite side of King St., 1527–33. WAM 23615–25; Reg Bk, ii, fo. 233^{r-v}. He also r. several cotts in Say's Alley, King St., 1521–33, and a house and ten. in Thieving Lane 1528–31 × 1533. WAM 18007; 23298–311; 19802–7. D. 1533; b. in the chapel of the Assumption of the Virgin in St Mgt, 'before my pew there'. CWA iii, s.a. 1533–4, wk. 14. Will made 16 June 1513, proved 3 Oct. 1533. PCW Bracy, fo. 35^{r-v}. Lorde's widow, Alice, executrix. Walter FORSTER and William GOOD-WYN, overseers. In the year of her death, 1539, Alice Lorde was living at the Bell inn. In addition to her West. leases, Alice bequeathed a lease of Sutton in Surrey, held of Chertsey Abbey (Quentin POULET had also held property at Sutton), and another of tens in Mordon (Surrey). These, and extensive household goods, she divided between 7 ss, all born of her marriage with George Lorde: Edmund, James, George, John, Barthole-mew, William, and Henry. PRO, PROB11/27, PCC 32 Dyngeley; PROB 10/8. James Lorde was to act as attorney for the chapter of West. in the exchequer during the 1540s. WAM 37139–40; 37376. Edmund Lorde was a chwdn 1556–8. CWA iv, s.a.

LOTHIAN, Robert. Chwdn 1490–2. CWA i. 267. Joined Assmptn guild 1474 × 1477. Guild accts. Reserved a pew in chapel of St Mary in St Mgt 1495–6. CWA i. 308. D. 1498–9; b. at St Mgt. CWA i. 354.

LOVELL, John. C.p. –1376–1386. WAM 50707–18.

MARBLE, Henry. Gentleman. C.p. and chief const. 1453 × 1464–1467–. WAM 50757–8. Wdn Assmptn guild 1474–7. PRO, E40/1463. Valet of West. Abbey 1451–2. WAM 19957. R. a ten. at the bars of Tothill St. 1455–. WAM 17780; 23227–53. Owned in addition '9 mess called Petty

France in Tothill St.'. Over these his ss, William Marble, clerk, and
James Marble, goldsmith of London, fell out after Henry's death. PRO,
C1/335/64; C1/339/85; C1/148/18. Henry Marble also held 5 mess with
gdns and a close on the W. side of King St., opposite York Place, and land
in Eyemoor and Eyefield, which in 1477 he entrusted to feoffees (John
RANDOLF, William JARDEN, *et al.*); after his death this property was
divided between his children, Richard, Robert, William, and Margaret
(James not being mentioned). PRO, E40/1548; E40/1533; E40/1539.
Henry Marble d. 1479/80; was b. in St Mgt. CWA i. 147.

MARCH, John. ?Royal officer. C.p. 1380 × 1384–1402 × 1407; const.
–1393–. WAM 50715–35. R. a ten. on the W. side of King St. 1399.
WAM 19659. In 1386, John Marche, Noreys king of arms, king's herald-
at-arms, received his wages and lodging in the king's household. *Cal Cl R
1385–9*, p. 166.

MAYBOURNE, John. Draper. Const. for King St. 1493–4. WAM 50766–7.
Chwdn 1500–2. CWA i. 389. Audited Rounceval guild accts 1522. Guild
accts. Reserved his pew in St Mgt 1501–2. CWA i. 417. Attached ribbon
to copes, covered pillows, etc., for the vestry of St Mgt 1500–1. CWA i.
422. Was admitted to the freedom of the London Drapers' Company (by
redemption) 1507–8; in 1518 and 1529, was registered as a member of
that company living at West. A. H. Johnson, *The History of the
Worshipful Company of the Drapers of London*, vol. ii (Oxford, 1915),
260–1. His goods were valued in 1524 at £40. PRO, E179/238/98. D.
1531; b. in St Mgt. CWA iii, s.a. 1530–1, wk. 38. Will made 30 Dec.
1530, proved 17 Mar. 1531. PCW Bracy, fo. 18^r. Requested burial in St
Mgt, 'before oure blessed lady where as I have accustomed to knele'. W.
Margery, executrix; John JAMES, John WRIGHT, and Thomas Bough of
the Temple, overseers. The will names a cousin, Richard Maybourne,
dwelling at Piercebridge, co. Durham.

MAYHEWE, John. C.p. 1396 × 1402–*ante* 1407. WAM 50735, 50738.

MEREDYKE, Richard. Const. for Charing 1422–7; c.p. 1427–53. WAM
50745–55. Bequeathed at his death 5 mess in West. to his widow, Ellen,
for her lifetime. She subsequently m. John Lyon. PRO, C1/31/211.

MERYDEN (*alias* MORE), John. Butcher. Chwdn 1460–2. CWA i, s.a. C.p.
1453–1467–. WAM 50757–8. Wdn Assmptn guild 1466. *Cal Cl R
1461–8*, p. 365. R. a ten. in scty 1458–67 × 1470; and another at Endive
Lane 1468 × 1470–3. WAM 19709–16; 23244–7. Acquired 5 mess in
West. formerly of Richard MEREDYKE, and, in 1477, a further ten. in
King St., on the W. side. PRO, C1/31/211; *Cal Cl R 1476–85*, pp. 35–6.
Trustee of the Swan inn in Tothill St. 1469. *Cal Cl R 1468–76*, pp. 73,
173; ibid. *1476–85*, p. 167; Westminster Public Libraries, Archives
Dept, MS 9/1. R. a croft and meadow at Rosamund's manor
1464 × 1468–9 × 1471, 1472 × 1481–2; and a gdn in Say's Alley, King St.,

1475–7. WAM 18896, 18898; 23250–1. Will (in Latin) made 28 Aug., proved 2 Nov. 1489. PRO, PROB11/8, PCC 20 Milles. Described himself therein as 'John Meryden, *alias* More, senior, of the parish of All Saints, Wing, Bucks.' Left bequests to Dorking parish church, where he had been baptized, and to parish churches and fraternities in Aston Abbots, Aylesbury, ?Crawley, Cublington, Linslade, Mentmore, Stewkeley, and Wing (all in Bucks.), Leighton Buzzard (Beds.) and Sudbury (Middx.). Meryden also left the profits of his ten. called the Ox Head in King St., West., and land at Brent Bridge (Middx.), to endow a hanging lamp, which was to burn perpetually 'coram corpore Christi' in St Mgt, West. His widow, Agnes, when consulted about this endowment, was living at Wing. CWA i. 340–1. Agnes inherited all John's lands and tens in West. and elsewhere in Middx. and Bucks., with remainder at her death or remarriage to his s., John Meryden; with the exception of a ten. at Charing Cross, 'before the door of which is the sign of the bell', which was to maintain the testator's nephew, also named John, 'at the schools'.

MIDDLETON, Thomas. Chwdn 1506–8. CWA i. 545. C.p. 1507–8. WAM 50772–3. Evidently d. 1508; his widow lived in the scty, near the abbey Lady chapel, 1508–12. WAM 23276–302.

A London skinner of the same name r. 5 shops in Tothill St. from 1500 and a ten. in Tothill St. from 1504/5, until his death and burial at St Mgt 1512. WAM 17942; 23270–83; PCW Wyks, 175–6.

A third Thomas Middleton, probably the chandler of this name fined in West. in 1512, inherited the same Tothill St. ten. from the skinner and his w., who were presumably the ?chandler's parents. The ?chandler held from 1519 a life grant of the keepership of the scty gate into King St. He d. 1539. WAM 23284–311; Reg Bk, ii, fos. 139ᵛ–140ʳ; CWA iii, s.a. 1539–40, wk. 8.

MORE, Henry. ?Brewer. Const. for Charing –1445; c.p. 1445–64 × 1467. WAM 50752–7. Henry More, brewer, of the parish of St Mary-le-Strand, was a trustee in 1458. *Cal Cl R 1454–61*, p. 334.

MORELAND, Hugh. Gentleman. C.p. 1491–1495–; supervisor of the ditches of West. 1491. WAM 50764–8. Wdn Assmptn guild 1493–96. PRO, E40/13407 (1494). Earlier, in 1467, Hugh Moreland, 'gentleman', had been a trustee of a London draper. *Cal Cl R 1461–8*, p. 433. Hugh's kinsman, William Moreland (d. *c.*1491), was a chancery clerk and prebendary of St Stephen's chapel. PRO, PROB11/9, PCC 11 Dogett. Hugh Moreland m. in 1485 Joan, widow of William JARDEN. By a posthumous codicil to the latter's covenant with Queen's College, Oxford, the college agreed that the next three scholars to be accepted there should be nominated by Hugh and Joan. Oxford, Bodleian Library, MS D.D. Queen's Coll. 1768. By right of his w., Moreland inherited Jarden's West. leases: a ten. opposite the almonry in Tothill St.; 'Conyngarth', a parcel of

Mauduitsgarden; 3 acres of land towards Eye; a gdn near St Mary
Magdalen's chapel; and several tens at Charing. Moreland also r., in his
last year, a ten. in the scty. WAM 23262–9; 17892; 23114–27; 19749–54;
Reg Bk, i, fos. 89ᵛ–90ʳ, 124ʳ⁻ᵛ. Hugh Moreland d. 1500; was b. in the
Trinity chapel of St Mgt. CWA i. 402, 407; and see the will of his friend
Quentin POULET. Dame Joan Moreland's will was made 31 Mar. 1508,
proved 23 Nov. 1511. PCW Wyks, 141–2. She was b. in St Mgt, before
the vestry door in the Trinity chapel, where her second, and probably
also her first husband lay. CWA ii, s.a. 1511–12, wk. 23. The will of
William Moreland (above) refers to a s. of Hugh, named Henry.

MORLEY, Robert. Citizen and draper of London. Wdn Assmptn guild
1502–5. Guild accts. C.p. 1495 × 1505–6/7. WAM 50770–1. R. 'the
tenement wine tavern in the which I dwell called the Bell' at the S. end of
King St. 1498–1508. WAM 17916; 23576–87; will cited below. Also r. a
small ten. in scty 1504–8. WAM 19760–4. D. 1508; b. in the choir of St
Mgt. CWA i. 548. Will made 10 Oct. 1505, proved 20 May 1508. PCW
Wyks, 84–92. The will refers to w. Elizabeth; bros Christopher Morley
and John Dunstall (*sic*); an aunt, Margaret Lasonby; and other kin
unnamed in Cleveland, N. Yorks, where Robert Morley's father was b.
Left tens and lands in Cambs. Bequeathed £10 or a cup of equal value to
the London Drapers' Company, of which Morley was a member; they to
pray for him in return. This they did. Johnson, *The History of the
Worshipful Company of the Drapers of London*, vol. i (Oxford, 1914), 370.

Robert's widow, Mistress Elizabeth Morley, continued a distinguished resident in West. She kept her own chapel here; her priest is
named in 1521–2. Rounceval guild accts, s.a. She gave substantial sums
towards the rebuilding and decoration of St Mgt. CWA ii, s.a. 1510–11,
1516–17, 1517–18.

MYLLYS, William. Chwdn 1518–20. CWA ii, s.a.

NIGHTINGALE, Thomas. Taverner. C.p. 1402 × 1407–10 × 1422. WAM
50738–40. Was charged with over-pricing his wine 1398–9. PRO, KB9/
183/6; and see WAM 50734–40. R. the Bell inn at the S. end of King St.
1398–1433. WAM 23467–504.

NORANDYN, Geoffrey. C.p. 1374–9. WAM 50705–13. R., with w. Isabel, a
ten. 'in Charing Street in the vill of Westminster', from 1360. WAM
17167.

NOREYS, John. Yeoman. C.p. 1495 × 1505–12. WAM 50770–5. He was the
younger s. of John Noreys, senior (d. *c.*1462), and his w., Alice, who had
held the Swan inn in Tothill St. PRO, C1/38/138. The elder bro.,
Robert, probably d. 1478–9 and was b. in St Mgt. CWA i. 127. As
'yeoman of Eyebury', John Noreys, junior, r. a ten. at Charing opposite
the Rounceval hospital, which ten. he rebuilt as the Rose brewhouse,
1465–1504. In 1513 this passed to his widow, Christina (John having

evidently d. 1512); and she still held it in 1545. Reg Bk, i, fos. 64^v–65^r; WAM 23239–72; 23285–312; Reg Bk, ii, fos. 167^v–168^r; Chicago University, Bacon MS 2444 (last ref. supplied by Dr C. M. Barron).

NORTON, Robert. Gentleman. Chwdn 1476–8. CWA i. 120. Wdn Assmptn guild 1480–3. PRO, C1/66/320; *Cal Cl R 1476–85*, p. 271; PRO, E40/1461 (all dated 1482). Elder s. of William NORTON (2). Robert inherited his father's Antelope inn 1460, and held this until his death in 1485. He was then succeeded by his widow. WAM 23234–60. Robert Norton also r. a ten. at the Clowson bridge in King St. 1473–7. WAM 23090–3; and see 17834.

NORTON, William (1). Royal and abbey officer. C.p. 1377. WAM 50709. Coroner of West. liberty 1379–1410. WAM 50713, 50740; *Cal Pat R 1401–5*, p. 328. Chief servant of the prior of West. Abbey 1373. WAM 23701. Valet of West. Abbey 1380–1405; described in 1387 as 'William Norton of the king's bench'. WAM 19869–90. William Norton was heir to Richard Rooke, junior (*q.v.* s.n. ROOKE). LN, fo. 78^r. Norton held property near the palace gate, and collected a quitrent from the Saracen's Head there. WAM 23460. After he d. *c.*1412 this quitrent was paid to Robert Haxey, bailiff of West., who was therefore probably Norton's executor. WAM 23478; LN, fo. 84^{r-v}; and see app. 1. Later the quitrent came to William NORTON (2), and subsequently to the latter's (probable) dau., Margaret, and so to her husband, Robert FORSTER.

NORTON, William (2). Esquire; royal officer. One of the four re-founders of Assmptn guild 1440. *Cal Pat R 1436–41*, p. 448. C.p. –1445–. WAM 50752. Usher of the receipt of the king's exchequer and keeper of the king's council chamber 1441–. *Cal Pat R 1436–41*, p. 526. Heir (probably a s.) of William NORTON (1). Norton held (with his w., Joan, and children, Robert, Margery, and Nicholas) the Antelope (or White Hart, or Bell), opposite the Staple on the W. side of King St., 1403–48. His widow evidently then m. Richard Aleyn, who held the Antelope 'by the right of his wife' 1454–60. WAM 23227–32. William Norton's other heirs were his ss. Robert (*q.v.*) and Nicholas Norton, gentleman; and his dau., Margaret ('Margery'), who m. (1) Robert FORSTER, and by 1466 (2) Richard Walsh, seneschal of the abbot of West. *Cal Cl R 1461–8*, p. 365; WAM 19955–72.

NYK, John. Brewer. C.p. 1453 × 1464–1467–. WAM 50757–8. Const. 1461. PRO, KB9/297/90. Chwdn 1466–8. CWA i. 59. Valet of West. Abbey 1451–71. WAM 19957–76. Fined by the West. court as a tavern-keeper 1453, etc. WAM 50755 *et seq.* R. a 'cellar ten.' on a corner of King St. near the palace gate 1461–7. WAM 23526–31. Held a ten. in Long Ditch (which had formerly belonged to Robert NYK) *c.*1468. WAM 23243. Also held (with William Broke and William COTMAN) lands in Bucks. *Cal Cl R 1468–76*, pp. 275–6. This ref. shows he was dead by 1472. Obits for

John Nyk and for his w., Alice, were kept by Assmptn guild, with 6 priests and 2 clerks. Guild accts, s.a. 1474–7, 1487–90.

NYK, Robert. Const. in Tothill St. 1422–6; chief const. 1427; c.p. 1422–50 × 1453. WAM 50745–53. One of the four re-founders of Assmptn guild 1440. *Cal Pat R 1436–41*, p. 448. Valet of West. Abbey 1440, 1449–50. WAM 18891, 19955. Held a ten. in Long Ditch and r. (1413–50 × 1453) 3 shops and an old cott. (1429–48) there. WAM 23206–26; 19035–56. He and his w., Alice, leased the great convent gdn N. of the Strand c.1425–47; 2 acres of land in Charing Field 1422 *et seq.*; and 6 acres of pasture on Tothill 1431/2–1440–. WAM 18890–2; 18567; 23219–23. Robert Nyk also r. a ten. within the N. scty gate –1440–50. WAM 19684–99. He d. 1450 × 1453. His executor was John BRADDING. WAM 23227. Nyk's widow m. Richard Heywood of London, and retained the shops in Long Ditch. WAM 23229–38.

OKEHAM, Hugh. Cooper. Const. 1486. WAM 50760. Chwdn 1488–90. CWA i. 243. R. a ten. next to the White Horse on W. side King St. 1502/3–22. WAM 19759–86. 'Hooped' the holy water tub in St Mgt 1502–3. CWA i. 454. His w. b. in St Mgt 1515. CWA ii, s.a. 1515–16, wk. 1.

OLIVER, John. Abbey officer. C.p. 1428 × 1434–50 × 1453. WAM 50749–53. Rent-collector for the abbey in West. 1419, 1427–33; valet of the convent 1422–35. WAM 24622; 19666–76. R. a 'long house' in the scty 1423–46 × 1450; held 2 tens at Charing 1433–50; and in addition a field near Charing Cross late of John VAUNMETH, 1438 *et seq.* WAM 19684–95; 23221–6; 17170B. Presumably d. c.1450.

OSBERN, Thomas. C.p. 1422–. WAM 50745.

PAYABLE, John. Glazier. C.p. 1376–1393 × 1396. WAM 50707–28. Worked for the sacrist of West. Abbey 1364; received both his wages and 11s. rent for 'his house' from the sacrist 1374–5. WAM 19630, 19635. In 1362, Payable reglazed the great rose window in the S. transept of the abbey. W. R. Lethaby, *Westminster Abbey Re-Examined* (London, 1925), 144–5. In 1375–6, he inserted glass into windows in the abbot's house, for Abbot Litlington. J. A. Robinson, *The Abbot's House at Westminster* (Cambridge, 1911), 11.

PERCIVAL, John. Chwdn 1458–60. CWA i, s.a.

PERNE, Thomas. Saddler. C.p. 1396–*ante* 1402. WAM 50734–5. As 'saddler', Perne stood regularly with Thomas TOTTESHAM, Richard KNAPPE, *et al.*, as mainpernor in Middx. e.g. *Cal Cl R 1402–5*, pp. 266, 360.

PHILLIPS, John. Smith. Chwdn 1524–6. CWA ii, s.a. Master Assmptn guild 1536–9. Guildhall Library, MS 12993 (1538). Wdn Rounceval guild 1520–2. Guild accts. Worked for West. Abbey sacrist and 'new work' between 1512 and 1534. WAM 19770; 19775–19775*; 23602; 23625–6. Worked at St Mgt 1514–15, 1538–9. CWA ii, iii, s.a. Worked at

Whitehall Palace 1531. PRO, E36/252, pp. 315 ff. R. the Bell at the S. end of King St., on the W. side, and the ten. adjacent, 1515–21. Assmptn guild accts. R. the Catherine Wheel bakery on the W. side of King St., near the Clowson bridge (formerly of Christopher WODELAND), 1521/2–1550 × 1558. Reg Bk, ii, fo. 189ᵛ; Reg Bk, iii, fo. 161ʳ; 23160–78. Was succeeded here in 1558 by Agnes Phyllips, widow, and her s., John. Reg Bk, iv, fo. 34ʳ.

PHILLIPS, William. ?Tailor. Chwdn 1514–16. CWA ii, s.a. Master Rounceval guild 1524–6. CWA ii, s.a. 1525–6. 'William Phelip, tailour', held a ten. on the E. side of King St. c.1508. WAM 18599. William Phillips's w. mended vestments for the vestry of St Mgt 1515–16. CWA ii, s.a. He d. 1529; was b. in St Mgt. CWA ii, s.a. 1529–30, wk. 19.

PITTER, John. Ale-taster 1428; c.p. 1434. WAM 50748–9.

PITTER (*alias* PETER), Richard. C.p. 1514–. WAM 50777. R., with his w., Rose, the Black Eagle inn in King St. (near the corner of Thieving Lane) 1511–21. WAM 19768–86. D. 1521; b. in St Mgt. CWA ii, s.a. 1520–1, wk. 48.

POMFRETT, John. Gentleman; brewer. Const. for King St. 1509–10. WAM 50774; PRO, SC2/191/66. Chwdn 1516–18. CWA ii, s.a. Wdn Assmptn guild 1522(–4) (in succession to John HUNT, d. 1522). CWA ii, s.a. 1522–3. Audited Rounceval guild accts 1522; and chwdns' accts 1528. Guild accts; CWA ii, s.a. In 1516–18, he returned to St Mgt his wages for the transport of materials required to rebuild the steeple. CWA ii, s.a. 'Mr Pomfrett's' goods were valued in 1524 at £100. PRO, E179/238/98. R. the Lamb brewhouse at Lamb Alley, King St., 1511–31; with (from 1519) additional land and (from 1528) 4 tens adjacent. WAM 19768–807; Reg Bk, ii, fos. 26ʳ⁻ᵛ, 218ᵛ, 245ᵛ–246ʳ. R. the White Lion brewhouse at Charing Cross 1525–31. WAM 23140–69. John Pomfrett d. at another house of his in Long Ditch in 1531, and was b. in the Trinity chapel of St Mgt. CWA iii, s.a. 1530–1, wk. 47. Will made 7 Apr., proved 26 Apr. 1531. PCW Bracy, fos. 18ᵛ–19ᵛ. At his death he held, in addition to the Lamb and the White Lion, further tens, held of his bro., Thomas Pomfrett, in the city and suburb of London. John Pomfrett was survived by his widow, Elizabeth, his dau., also called Elizabeth, and his son-in-law, John Benet, citizen of London.

POULET, Quentin. Royal librarian and clerk of the privy seal. Wdn Assmptn guild 1502. *Cal Pat R 1494–1509*, p. 280. C.p. 1495 × 1505–6. WAM 50770–1. On 30 Mar. 1500 denizen status was granted to Quentin Poulet, keeper of the king's library, a native of 'the castellany of Lille by Flanders'. *Cal Pat R 1494–1509*, p. 208. Poulet r. a close called 'Conyngarth' in Mauduitsgarden 1504–6. WAM 17935; 23131–5. Will made 22 Oct., proved 23 Nov. 1506. PCW Wyks, 65–8. Requested burial either at the Austin Friars' house in London or the the Trinity chapel of St Mgt, West., close to Hugh MORELAND. Bequeathed to his widow,

Margaret, his farm of Sutton and tens in King St., West., until his children should come of age, and 6 tens behind Charing Cross which had been left to Poulet by Hugh Moreland. 'All my books that I have of French and English' Poulet left to his nephew, Baldwin. Robert MORLEY was an overseer of the will. The widow, known as Margaret Quentin, r. 3 tens in Tothill St. and 4 (*sic*), in succession to Joan Moreland, at Charing Cross 1511–22. Reg Bk, ii, fos. 28ᵛ–29ᵛ; 23283–98; 19768–82; 19786; and see also 17951.

PRESTON, John. Tallow-chandler. Const. 1488. WAM 50761. Chwdn 1504–6. CWA i. 497. C.p. 1512–1514–. WAM 50775–7. Goods assessed in 1524 at £20. PRO, E179/238/98. Presented in West. court for the candles he sold 1486–1507. WAM 50760–72. Supplied oil for candles to St Mgt 1500–1512–. CWA i. 382, 425, 570; CWA ii, s.a. 1512–13, etc. R. a ten. in King St. (on the W. side, next to the Wool Sack bakery) 1483–1525. WAM 17934; 23102–63. D. 1525; b. in St Mgt. CWA ii, s.a. 1524–5, wk. 52; 1525–6, wk. 4.

PRUDDE, John. Glazier. C.p. 1445–53; chief const. –1450. WAM 50752–5. Chief glazier to the king 1440–61. *King's Works*, ii. 1052. Prudde's commissions included work at the royal palaces of Sheen (*c*.1440) and Greenwich (*c*.1450); the hall (1445–6) and chapel (1449–50) of Eton College; and the Beauchamp Chapel, Warwick (1447), where windows by him are extant. R. Willis and J. W. Clark, *The Architectural History of the University of Cambridge*, vol. i (Cambridge, 1886), 393–4; H. C. Maxwell-Lyte, *A History of Eton College* (4th edn. London, 1911), 36; *Jnl of the British Society of Master Glass-Painters*, ii (1927–8), 85; *King's Works*, ii. 226 n., 284, 949, 1000–1. In addition, Prudde worked regularly at West. Abbey. WAM 19668 (1426–7); 19694 (1444–5); 23515 (1449–50). From 1443–60 Prudde r. a ten. on the corner of King St. and Endive Lane, with a gdn, 'cloister', dovecote, and stone wall towards the Thames, together with 4 acres of arable land in Eye Field and St James's Field. WAM 17760; 19687–710. His 'glaziers' lodge' at West. was situated in the western part of the royal palace. *Cal Pat R 1436–41*, p. 469. From 1438 he held the ground called 'Scotland' in West., between York Place and the Rounceval hospital. *Cal F R 1437–45*, p. 27. From 1439–50 he also held the adjacent hermitage beside Charing Cross. WAM 23223–6. John Prudde d. *c*.1461. His widow, Elizabeth, gave an altar cloth to St Mgt for prayers for his soul; she subsequently became sub-prioress of Haliwell Priory, Shoreditch. CWA i. 17; WAM 17802. S. and heir of John Prudde was William Prudde. *Cal Cl R 1468–76*, p. 328.

PYKE, Philip. Abbey officer. C.p. 1380 × 1384–92 (d.). WAM 50716–27. Servant of the refectory of West. Abbey 1383–8. WAM 19870–5. With his w., Alice, r. a ten. on the N. side of Tothill St. 1377–92. WAM 23187–94.

RABY, Robert. Abbey officer. Wdn Assmptn guild 1496–9. Guild accts, s.a.

1508. Sub-bailiff of West. 1486–95. See app 1. 'Inhabited' a ten. within the W. gate of the scty 1481–1502/3. WAM 19728–57; Reg Bk, i, fos. 64ᵛ, 84ᵛ. Kept a private chapel, for which he borrowed 'stuff' from St Mgt 1498–9. CWA i. 361. R. another ten. in Tothill St. 1482–1502/3. WAM 23102–30. Held in addition 2 tens in Long Ditch 1489 *et seq.*, and another at the Clowson bridge in King St. 1501 *et seq.* WAM 23262 *et seq.* Raby d. 1503/4; was b. in St Mgt. CWA i. 466. His widow, Agnes Raby, was b. in St Mgt 1525. WAM 23133 *et seq.*; CWA ii, s.a. 1524–5, wk. 41.

RANDOLF, John. Esquire; royal officer. C.p. 1453–90. WAM 50755–64. Wdn (1457) and master (1471–4) Assmptn guild. *Cal Pat R 1452–61,* pp. 362–3; guild accts, s.a. 1474–7. Randolf was described as 'esquire of the king's household' when his dau. was b. at St Mgt *c.*1464; and as 'deputy door-keeper of the king's exchequer' 1478–9. CWA i. 22; PRO, E403/848, m. 3. His presumed father of the same name had been door-keeper of the receipt of the exchequer in 1435, and had then held property in the nearby Wool Staple, as did the younger John Randolf and his w., Margaret, in 1449 and in 1470. Guildhall Library, MSS 12975–6, 12978–9. The later John Randolf was presumably he who also r. a ten. within the N. gate of the abbey scty 1440–1489/90. WAM 19684–737.

In 1451 this John Randolf and his w. Margaret acquired a corrody in West. Abbey for their lifetimes, comprising 10 convent loaves and 10 gallons of convent beer weekly, 10 'wastels' called 'Peter-wastels' on the 10 principal feasts and a furred robe of the livery of the abbey's gentlemen each year. WAM 5904. John Randolf received this annual robe until 1490, when he d. He was survived by 'the widow of John Randolf, late servant of the refectory (of the abbey)'. WAM 19967–99; 23001–23. 'John Randolf, esquire', made his Latin will on 8 Mar. 1488. He requested burial in St Mgt. He left a sapphire ring to Assmptn guild (to which he had also given a standing cup and cover); and his tens and movables in West. and Chertsey to his widow, Margaret. Randolf's widow, John LEWYS and William HUNGATE, executors. PRO, PROB11/17, PCC 25 Fetiplace; Assmptn guild accts, s.a. 1487–90, 1508 (inventory).

A 'John Randolf of London, mercer', presumably a different man, held tens in King St. –1474–1490. Assmptn guild accts (rentals), s.a. The mercer is also recorded in 1466–7. *Cal Plea & Mem R 1458–82,* 40; *Cal Letter-Bk L,* 70.

RAWLYN, John. Skinner. Const. at Temple Bar 1410. WAM 50740. Juror in the abbot's fair court 1417. C.p. 1422. WAM 50743, 50745. Sub-bailiff of the liberty of West. 1434–40. See app. 1. R. houses in King St. 1422–44, with a gdn at Long Ditch 1432–4. WAM 19663–6, 18584–93, 23219–21. His w. Agnes mentioned 1441. *Cal Pat R 1441–6,* p. 265.

RENER, William. Goldsmith. C.p. 1427–8. WAM 50747–8.

ROOKE, Richard. Royal officer. C.p. (affeeror) 1364. WAM 50700. Coroner of Middx. 1368. *Cal Pat R 1367–70*, p. 166. Coroner of the liberty of West. 1376–8. WAM 50707–11.

Two individuals of this name are recorded in the same period, and are sometimes distinguished by the designations 'senior' and 'junior'. Both acted as trustees of West. Abbey, on whose behalf they acquired tens in West. in the mid-fourteenth century. LN, fos. 111ᵛ–112ʳ, 115ᵛ–116ʳ, 132ʳ–133ᵛ; *Cal Pat R 1354–8*, pp. 5–6; ibid. *1361–4*, p. 11; Harvey, *Estates*, 185 and refs.

Richard Rooke, junior, was heir to Gilbert de Claygate, who had given lands to West. Abbey and received a corrody and a sergeanty in the almonry. The dau. of this Richard Rooke, named Joanna, was the mother of William NORTON (1). LN, fo. 78ʳ.

RUSSELL, William. Gentleman; waxchandler. Chwdn 1530–2. CWA iii, s.a. Wdn Assmptn guild 1533–6. PRO, E326/5899 (1536). Master St Christopher's guild in St Mgt 1521–3; wdn St Cornelius's guild 1524/5. CWA ii, s.a. Audited Rounceval guild accts 1524; wdn Rounceval guild 1531. Guild accts; PRO, E36/252, p. 400. The elder s. of Richard Russell, carpenter of West., William Russell was apprenticed to, and remained a friend of, John ATTWELL, waxchandler. PCW Wyks, 249–51; PCW Bracy, fos. 12ᵛ–15ʳ; D. R. Ransome, 'Artisan Dynasties in London and Westminster in the Sixteenth Century', *Guildhall Miscellany*, ii (1964), 236–47, esp. pp. 240–2.

William Russell supplied candles to the Rounceval guild 1522–3; and to St Mgt and to West. Abbey 1530s. Guild accts; CWA ii, s.a. 1530–40; WAM 19826, 19831, 19837* (1543: 'executores Willelmi Russell'). In 1524 his goods were assessed at £10; in 1542 at £50. PRO, E179/238/98; E179/141/127.

R. the Bell inn at the bars in King St. 1522–31. WAM 18012; 18026; *LP* v, no. 408. R. a 'wax house and working house' in the Round Wool Staple –1540–. Guildhall Library, MSS 12986–7. Also leased from the abbey almonry the parsonage of St Mgt 1530 *et seq*. Reg Bk, ii, fo. 265ʳ⁻ᵛ; and see Reg Bk, iii, fo. 267ʳ.

William Russell d. 1543. Will made 19 July 1543. Guildhall Library, Consistory Court of London, Register Thirlby, fo. 31ʳ.

SELLY, David. Gentleman; vintner and merchant. Const. 1438. PRO, KB9/229/2/7. C.p. 1450–1467–. WAM 50753–8. In 1440, Selly was one of the four re-founders of Assmptn guild, of which he was master in 1466. *Cal Pat R 1436–41*, p. 448; *Cal Cl R 1461–8*, p. 365. Of foreign extraction; taxed as an alien householder in West. 1439. PRO, E179/141/69. Acquired exemption for life from holding public office 1437. *Cal Pat R 1436–41*, p. 46. Nevertheless a royal commissioner collecting ships 1450. *Cal Pat R 1446–52*, pp. 437–8. Part-owner of a ship plying from

Bordeaux 1451. *Cal Cl R 1447–54*, p. 275. See also ibid., pp. 159, 405, 420; *Cal F R 1461–71*, p. 213.

R. 3 shops at the end of Tothill St. 1428–63; and a chamber over the inner almonry gate 1447(–72). WAM 19034–89; 17768. Held the Rose at the bars in King St., and r. the Bell at the S. end of King St., 1433–72. WAM 23221–45; 23505–47. Both of these tens Selly bequeathed to Assmptn guild. Guild accts; and see PRO, C1/66/320; C1/61/255. Also held the hermitage at Charing and a meadow opposite to it 1458–72; and the room over the gate into Endive Lane, with 3 cotts in the lane there, 1448–72. WAM 23229–45; 18893–7. Gave 6 silver dishes, marked 'D.S.', to West. Abbey. WAM 19576.

D. *c.*1472. The will of Selly's widow, Cecily Selly, was made 10 Aug. 1472, proved 18 July 1474. PRO, PROB 11/6, PCC 16 Wattys. She requested burial next to her late husband in St Nicholas's chapel in St Mgt. John Selly, clerk, was an executor and apparently the heir of David Selly. PRO, E40/1463. David and Cecily's dau., also named Cecily, m. Nicholas Cleveley, yeoman of the crown. *Cal Cl R 1476–85*, p. 271. Cecily, widow of David Selly, also provided for Isabel, dau. of Thomas Selly. Cecily left, in addition to her interest in the Rose and the Bell, further tens in King St.; a house called Spark's Place in Skinners' Lane, Datchet; properties in Guildford and Windsor; and the Angel in the parish of St Leonard Eastcheap, London. Walter LOKYNGTON an executor both of David and Cecily Selly.

SHARPE, John. C.p. 1386–*ante* 1392. WAM 50718, 50726.

SHELLEY, Richard. Baker and brewer. Chwdn 1532–4. CWA iii, s.a. Master Rounceval guild 1536–8. Guild accts. As 'baker', contributed £2 to a loan to the abbot of West. 1522. WAM 12366. As 'brewer', r. the Hart's Horn brewery on the W. side of King St. 1535 *et seq*. Reg Bk, ii, fo. 308ʳ⁻ᵛ. His goods were assessed in 1524 at £20; in 1544 at £67. PRO, E179/238/98; E179/141/139.

SHORDICH, Thomas. Royal officer. C.p. 1402 × 1407–10 × 1422. WAM 50738, 50740. Commissioner for the carriage of victuals, etc., for the royal household 1402–3. *Cal Pat R 1401–5*, pp. 71, 130, 190.

John Shordich was a valet of West. Abbey 1378–1411. WAM 19868–900.

SHOTER, William. Chwdn 1498–1500. CWA i. 351.

SILVESTER, Thomas. Royal officer. Chwdn 1526–8. Wdn Assmptn guild 1533–6; 1542–5. PRO, E326/5899 (1536); CWA iii, s.a. 1542–3. Held the George inn on the W. side of King St. (near the S. end) 1523. WAM 50778, fo. 4ᵛ. His goods were valued in 1524 and in 1544 at £20. PRO, E179/238/98; E179/141/139. The will of Thomas Silvester of West., groom of the chamber to Queen Mary and King Philip, was made 4 Oct. 1554, proved 17 Mar. 1555. PCW Bracy, fos. 73ᵛ–74ʳ. W. Anne, executrix.

SMALLWOOD, Robert. Beer-brewer. Wdn Rounceval guild 1536–8. Guild accts, s.a. Chwdn 1540–2. CWA iii, s.a. Wdn Assmptn guild 1542/3. CWA iii, s.a. MP Westminster 1545 (the first year in which MPs for Westminster are recorded; John, bro. of William RUSSELL was the other), 1553 (Oct.). S. T. Bindoff, *The House of Commons 1509–1558*, iii (London, 1982), 328. C.p. –1555–1558. WAM 50784. Resident in Long Ditch from *ante* 1530. Bindoff, loc. cit. M. (1) ?Margaret: issue 1 dau.; (2) in 1554 Joan Henbury: issue 2 ss, 1 dau. Ibid. Smallwood made his will 1558; and was b. in St Mgt 1559. Ibid.

SMART, John. C.p. 1393 × 1396–. WAM 50734.

STADOWE, William. C.p. 1453 × 1464–67 × 1486; chief const. –1467–. WAM 50757–8. In 1464 Stadowe kept an obit in St Mgt for his 2 former ws, Agnes Brikchede and Joan Oldebury. CWA i. 21. In 1470 he inherited from Hugh Brikehede, yeoman of West., a lease on a ten. on the W. side of King St., near the Clowson bridge, which he held until 1479. From 1471–86 he held a lease on another ten., opposite the other on the E. side of King St., which he likewise took over from William Oldebury, hosier. WAM 19716–31; see also *Cal Cl R 1461–8*, p. 365.

STAFFORD, William. Chwdn 1464–6. CWA i. 19. His w. was b. in St Mgt 1474–5; as was Stafford himself 1475–6. CWA i. 99, 104. Bequeathed a silver-gilt standing cup to Assmptn guild. Guild accts, s.a. 1475–6 and inventory 1508.

STOKEWOOD, Edward. Gentleman. Chwdn 1518–20. CWA ii, s.a. Wdn Rounceval guild 1520–2. Guild accts. Stokewood and his w. joined Assmptn guild 1515 × 1518. Guild accts. He was presented for failing to maintain a wharf at his house called the Bell in West. c.1540. WAM 50782, fo. 3ʳ. In 1517–18 he gave £2 towards the new steeple of St Mgt in memory of Dr Aynesworth, late of St Stephen's chapel. CWA ii, s.a. In 1523–4 he was repaid c.£60 which he had loaned to the chwdns of St Mgt. CWA ii, s.a. 'Mr Stokewood' in 1521–2 bought 250 lbs of old lead from the Rounceval hospital, and supplied 420 tiles to works there. Guild accts, s.a.

Edward Stokewood was the s. of Bartelina Stokewood. The latter d. a widow in 1528, when she made relatively grandiose arrangements for her burial (she considered the abbey as a possibility, although in the event she was b. in St Mgt). Her will names a dau. of Edward, also called 'Barthelen'. Edward's sister, Jane, m. a wealthy stationer of West., Ellys Snethe. PCW Bracy, fos. 3ʳ–4ᵛ; CWA ii, s.a. 1528–9, wk. 12; PRO, PROB11/2, PCC 29 Porche.

STONE, Richard. Gentleman. Master Assmptn guild 1490–3. Guild accts. C.p. 1495–. WAM 50768. Valet of the locutorium of West. Abbey 1494–. Reg Bk, i. fo. 71ʳ. Held extensive property in West. R. 2 shops by the almonry in Tothill St. 1470–1504; 2 tens on the N. side of Tothill St. 1493–1502/3; and a gdn at Rosamund's Manor nearby 1471–86. Also r. a ten. in King St., at Albright Alley, 1477–1502/3. WAM 19078–114; 23265–71; 18898–901; 19725–57. Built a ten. in the scty near the chapter house 1477 × 1479. Subsequently held a large mes., also in the scty, called 'Delaberes', and r. upwards of 6 tens by the belfry there. WAM 19725–57; 18898; Reg Bk, i, fos. 12ʳ, 20ᵛ, 84ᵛ–85ʳ. Will made 31 Mar., proved 20 May 1504. PRO, PROB11/19, PCC 9 Holgrave. Thomas HOGAN an executor. Stone requested burial in West. Abbey, to 'the old work of the sacristy' of which he bequeathed £30. Founded a chantry for himself in Oxford University. His leases held of West. Abbey and of the Knights of St John, and his tens in Laleham, Littleton and Staines (Middx.), and in Chertsey (Surrey), Stone left to his widow, Emma. Within a year of Richard Stone's death, Emma m. Anthony Leigh, who was to become a gentleman of the household of King Henry VIII. Reg Bk, ii, fos. 34ᵛ–35ᵛ; *LP* i, nos. 20 (p. 17), 82 (p. 39); PCW Wyks, 260–5.

STOWELL, Robert. Gentleman; mason. C.p. 1487/8–1505; chief const. 1489–90. WAM 50761–70. Wdn (1490–3) and master (1499–1502) Assmptn guild. Guild accts. See J. Harvey, *English Mediaeval Architects: A Biographical Dictionary down to 1550* (2nd edn., Gloucester, 1984), 286–8; *Archaeological Jnl*, cxiii (1957), 100; E. Roberts, 'Robert Stowell', *Jnl of the British Archaeological Association*, 3rd ser., xxxv (1972), 24–38; and refs. cited below. Born *c*.1427. Master mason at Windsor 1452–62. Redesigned Broxbourne parish church, Herts., for the Say family, 1476; and may also have designed the Wallingford chantry in St Albans Abbey at this period. Was employed from 1468 on the 'new work' of West. Abbey, becoming master of the abbey masons 1471; which post he held until death in 1505. Stowell brought to virtual completion the buttressing and vaulting of the nave. He lent assistance to the chwdns of St Mgt, West., in 1480 × 1482, and was almost certainly the designer of the new parish church of West., begun *c*.1487 (and standing, in essentials, today); in form this bears close relation to the church at Broxbourne.

From 1472 a 'shed and garden called St Albans'—described in subsequent years, however, as a 'tenement', and after 1505 divided into several 'cottages' and 'tenements'—at the E. end of the abbey scty, was let to William and Joan Stowell; from 1476 the rent payers were Joan and Robert Stowell; and from 1487–97 Robert Stowell alone. After Joan's disappearance from the rental the chwdns note, in 1488–9, the 'burying of Robert Stowell's mother'; Robert was therefore probably the s. of William and Joan. The name of their ten., unrecorded before their tenancy, may strengthen the possibility, noted above, that Robert Stowell had worked at St Albans. WAM 19720–49; CWA i. 243. Robert Stowell, 'gentleman', r. in addition half a dozen tens and cotts within the 'broad' or N. gate of the scty, including one described as his 'mansion', between 1471 and 1505; and from 1470–7 he r. 2 tens on the N. side of

Tothill St. WAM 19718–59; Reg Bk, i, fo. 27^{r-v}; 23535–47. It was a rare distinction for a mason to be accorded the title of 'gentleman' by his neighbours.

Robert Stowell lost a first w. 1474–5; and a second, Joan (whose pew in St Mgt had been reserved 1490–1), in 1500–1, when she was b. in St Mgt. CWA i. 96, 277, 404. Stowell himself d. 1505. Will made 13 Nov., administration instituted 18 Nov. 1505. PCW Wyks, 14b, 43–5. He requested burial in St Mgt, and was duly interred there. CWA i. 528. But in his will he made no committal of his soul, an extremely unusual omission. His s., William Stowell, and son-in-law, Thomas Burgeys (possibly a s. of the elder Thomas BURGEYS), executors. Stowell left money for obits at Brentford and Ealing (Middx.), and for masses at 'scala coeli' (in West. Abbey).

SUDBURY, Roger. C.p. 1364–74 × 1376. WAM 50699, 50705. In 1333, Roger de Sudbury of Westminster, with Lucy, widow of Nicholas de Beck, acquired a ten. on the W. side of King St. and meadow-land nearby (formerly held by Nicholas de Beck). Sudbury held this until 1350. WAM 17610; LN, fos. 131^v–132^r. In 1341, Sudbury acquired a piece of land next to his mes. in Tothill St. He made one grant of a ten., shop and vacant plot in Tothill St. 1346, and another of a vacant plot there 1351. WAM 17630, 17642; Oxford, Bodleian Library, MS D.D. Queen's Coll. 1747. In 1362, Roger Sudbury and his w., Beatrice, acquired a mes. (the later Boar's Head) in King St. LN, fo. 130^v.

SUDBURY, William. ?Tailor. C.p. 1386–96 × 1402. WAM 50718, 50726, 50734. Made a quitclaim of land in Tothill St. to trustees (eminent Londoners) 1381. *Cal Cl R 1377–81*, p. 512. Made, with w. Agnes, a further quitclaim of a piece of arable land in West. called 'Alfhyde' 1382. WAM 17703. A William Sudbury, tailor, represented Walbrook ward in the common council of London 1376, 1384, 1388. *Cal Letter-Bk H*, 42, 238, 334.

SWEET, Thomas. C.p. 1374 – *ante* 1376. WAM 50705–7.

SWYFT, Henry. Cooper. Chwdn 1484–6. CWA i. 221. Henry Swyft, *alias* 'Cowper', mended the pulpit in St Mgt 1467–8, and performed other repairs there regularly. CWA i. 87–8, 116, 160. Made a carved tabernacle of the Virgin for St Mary's guild in St Mgt, 1474 × 1477. Guild accts. R. a ten. on W. side King St., near Lamb Alley, 1482–1500; was succeeded here by his widow, Margery, 1500–6. (This ten. had been occupied by Richard Swyft, *alias* Cowper, 1422–*c*.1455, and by Robert Swyft, cooper, *c*.1455–82.) WAM 19663–761; 17859; Reg Bk, i, fos. 129–30. Henry Swyft d. 1500–1; was b. at St Mgt. CWA i. 400.

TADDELOWE, Geoffrey. C.p. 1392. WAM 50726. Geoffrey Taddelowe of Middx. stood mainpernor (in a £100 bond) of John Wynchecombe 1397. *Cal Pat R 1396–9*, p. 115.

TAILLOUR, Richard. Beer-brewer. Chwdn 1520–2. CWA ii, s.a. Wdn

Assmptn guild 1527. WAM 18035. His goods valued in 1524 at £100. PRO, E179/238/98. R. a beer house in King St. (on the E. side, near the Clowson bridge) 1517–28; and in addition a nearby gdn 1523–8. Reg Bk, ii, fos. 105–6; WAM 23154–68; 19791–800. D. 1528; b. in St Mgt with tapers of St Cornelius's guild (which may, with Taillour's trade, imply *Doche* connections). CWA ii, s.a. 1528–9, wk. 19. Will made 13 Sept., proved 10 Dec. 1528. PRO, PROB11/22, PCC 41 Porche. Taillour bequeathed his brew-house to his bro., Humfrey; £60 to each of his 2 daus, Alice and Margery; and the remainder to his widow, Margaret.

TEBBE, William. Gentleman; royal officer. Wdn (1496–9) and master (1505–8) Assmptn guild. Guild accts, s.a. Sergeant of the vestry in the king's household 1510–14. *LP* i, nos. 352, 707 (p. 382), 930, 1236, 3397. R. (in succession to John Tebbe) the Saracen's Head inn near the palace gate in King St. 1496–1511; and a new ten. adjacent 1499–1520. WAM 17909; 23570–606. John Mane, scrivener of West., was William Tebbe's brother-in-law. PCW Wyks, 180–2.

TETTESWORTH, Andrew. Royal officer, and ?brewer. C.p. 1374–80 × 1384. WAM 50705–15. Purveyor to the royal household 1362; royal sergeant-at-arms 1374. *Cal Pat R 1361–4*, p. 155; ibid. *1370–4*, p. 484. Andrew Tettesworth, 'brewer', was a creditor of a Sussex chaplain 1385. Ibid. *1381–5*, p. 563.

THORNWORK, William (the elder). Mason and abbey officer. Wdn Assmptn guild 1455. WAM 17774. Employed on the 'new work' of West. Abbey 1423–60. *Archaeological Jnl*, cxiii (1957), 100. Collected the rents of the abbey sacristy 1436–7, 1444–5; and of the 'new work' 1445–8, ?1450–1. WAM 19678, 19694; 23511–14, 23517. Received an annual robe from the sacrist 1450–8. WAM 19700–8. R. a ten. in King St., on the W. side, 1427–1429–. WAM 19669–70. R. *c.* 4 tens in the scty 1440–60. WAM 19684–710. R. 5 shops in Tothill St., to the W. of the Cock inn, 1440 × 1443–60; and held a ten. beyond the bars in Tothill St., once called the Catherine Wheel, 1458–9. WAM 23223*–34. D. *c.*1460. Was survived by his widow, Elizabeth, a s., William, and a dau., Isabel. See WAM 19712 *et seq.*; 23259 *et seq.*; PRO, C1/363/8–11.

A Gervase Thornewerke was a monk of West. Abbey *c.*1443–67 (d.). Pearce, *Monks*, 149.

THURLEBY, William. ?Gentleman; royal officer. Master Assmptn guild 1474–7. Guild accts, s.a. C.p. *post* 1467–86. WAM 50760. In 1468, William Thurlby, gentleman, the queen's cook, received (jointly with the yeoman of the pantry) a royal grant of a piece of ground in West Smithfield outside London. *Cal Pat R 1467–77*, p. 125.

TOTTESHAM, Thomas. Tailor. C.p. 1396 × 1402–27; ale-taster 1396; const. 1404, 1410 (for Charing), 1427. WAM 50735–47; and see below. Tottesham's term as const. was marked by a feud over rival jurisdictions

with Robert Sapurton, deputy keeper of West. Palace. PRO, KB9/201/5/
3, 11; KB27/573, rex roll, m. 4 *dors*. Tottesham convened regularly with
John CLYNK, John GEDNEY, John GRENE, Richard KNAPPE, William
NORTON, Thomas PERNE, *et al.*, to act as mainpernor or witness to deeds
in Middx. e.g. *Cal Cl R 1402–5*, pp. 266, 360, 375–6; ibid. *1405–9*,
p. 145; ibid. *1413–19*, pp. 100–1, 355–6.

TOUREFORT, Louis. ?Notary. Wdn Assmptn guild 1515–18. Guild accts,
s.a. His parents were Arthur Tourefort (d. *ante* 1489) and his w.,
Margaret (who subsequently m. Thomas BAROWE). Reg Bk, ii, fos. 8ᵛ–9ʳ,
173; CWA i. 244. From his mother, Louis Tourefort inherited leases on
various tens in West. scty, of which he retained until 1527 1 ten. and 2
shops beside St Mgt church. WAM 19767–96. May have had a legal
training, as he wrote the will of a West. carpenter 1516. PCW Wyks,
238–40. A presumed relative named Arthur Tourefort, 'gentleman of
Westminster', was apparently an attorney, who represented the monks of
West. at the papal court 1474. WAM 19080; *Cal Cl R 1476–85*, p. 165.

TYFFAN, Henry. Const. 1428; c.p. –1434–. WAM 50748–9. A witness to a
deed in St Clement Danes parish 1435. *Cal Cl R 1435–41*, p. 42.

VALENTYNE (*alias* HAREYS), Thomas. Brewer. Chwdn 1524–6. CWA ii, s.a.
Wdn St Cornelius's guild of West, 1536. PRO, C1/807/41. Master
brewer of West. Abbey 1514–28; valet of the convent 1515–32. WAM
18922, 18945; 23012–25; 23028, fo. 5ʳ; 23027, fo. 3ʳ. Shared a pew in St
Mgt with John HENBURY. CWA ii, s.a. 1515–16. Valentyne's goods were
assessed in 1524 at £10. PRO, E179/238/98. R. 'divers tens' in Long
Ditch 1515–1536–. WAM 17976; 19121–52. Will made 8 June, proved
7 Oct. 1537. PCW Bracy, fos. 58ᵛ–59ʳ. The will names a bro., Richard
Valentyne, and a sister, Agnes Owen (to whom Valentyne left his lease of
the house he dwelt in and his 'lease of Honychurch for his garden').
Thomas Owen, executor. William CRYTOFT, a witness to the will.

Hareys was the name of a West. family of brewers recorded in the
fifteenth century. Peter Hareys (or Harry), brewer, r. a brewing ten. in
Tothill St. 1431/2–1440 × 1443. WAM 23219–23. Henry Harrys,
brewer, is documented 1462. *Cal Cl R 1461–8*, p. 150. John Hareys,
brewer, r. 9 cotts near the Rounceval hospital 1487–1504/5. Reg Bk, i,
fo. 17ᵛ; 23262–72.

VAUNMETH, John. Brewer. C.p. 1396 × 1402–10 × 1422; const. for Charing
1407. WAM 50735–40. R. a field near Charing Cross *ante* 1438. WAM
17170B. 'John Vaunmeth of Westminster, brewer', d. *ante* 1432. *Cal Cl
R 1429–35*, p. 229.

VERN. See JOYNOUR.

WALDEN, John. ?Abbey officer. C.p. 1392–6 × 1402. WAM 50726–34. On
23 June 1391, pardon was granted to John Walden of West., for not
rendering account to Richard Greyland, citizen and fishmonger of

London, for the time when he was Greyland's receiver. *Cal Pat R 1388–92*, p. 450. In 1416–17, a ten. in Tothill St. 'nuper Johanne [*recte* Johannis] Walden' was acquired for West. Abbey. WAM 19910; 18562. The monks employed a bailiff named John Walden at Pyrford, Surrey, in 1406–7. WAM 27435.

WALL, John. C.p. 1506; chief const. 1506. WAM 50771.

WALLER, William. Yeoman; brewer. C.p. 1495 × 1505–1514–; const. for King St. 1508. WAM 50770–7. Leased the manor of Knightsbridge and Hyde 1487–1520. Reg Bk, i, fos. 20^{r-v}, 33^v–34^r; WAM 23563–606. R. gdns at Long Ditch 1473–1522 × 1524, and (with his w. Margaret) at Charing 1486–1531–. WAM 17812; 17877; 17998; 23248–311. 'William Waller, brewer', was executor of a barber's widow of West. 1504. PCW Wyks, 24–5.

WEDDISBOROWE, Robert. Chwdn 1532–4. CWA iii, s.a. His goods were assessed in 1524 at £4; in 1544 at £40 (rated in Tothill St.). PRO, E179/238/98; E179/141/139.

WESTON, John. Barber. C.p. 1380–1402. WAM 50715–35. With his w., Margery, Weston acquired 2 shops with solars called 'corner shops', next to 'Colchester's tavern' in West., 1385. WAM 17706. Held the King St. inn later known as the Boar's Head 1376–84. In the latter year Weston sold this to feoffees of West. Abbey. LN, fo. 131^{r-v}; PRO, CP25(1)/151/77/72. Weston and his w. were subsequently accommodated at the abbey's expense in a ten. by the palace gate in King St. John Weston d. 1402. His widow, Margaret, d. *c.*1409. WAM 18525–44; 50735.

WIGMORE, John. Taverner. Const. for King St. 1407; c.p. 1402 × 1407–22 × 1427. WAM 50738–45. John Wigmore, taverner of West., and his w. Agnes, were charged with over-pricing their wares 1398–9. PRO, KB9/183/6. In 1408–9 Wigmore was fined as a 'potcook'. WAM 50737–9. In *c.*1420 he was trustee of the Rose at the bars in King St., which had belonged to the late William HULL, carpenter; in 1433 Wigmore granted this to others, among them David SELLY. PRO, E40/1523; E40/1556; E40/1540.

WILLY, Richard. Gentleman; royal officer. C.p. 1453 × 1464–1467–. WAM 50757–8. Was later said to have been 'one of the founders' of the Assmptn guild of West. CWA i. 555. In 1461 Willy, then yeoman of the king's bed, was promoted to the keepership both of the king's wardrobe and of the prince's palace at West. *Cal Pat R 1461–7*, pp. 16, 18, 111; *Cal Cl R 1461–8*, pp. 29, 298. Collector of customs in Bridgewater from 1465; royal escheator in Middx. and Kent 1467. *Cal Pat R 1461–7*, p. 424; *Cal F R 1461–71*, pp. 178–9, 210, etc. D. *ante* Oct. 1471. *Cal Pat R 1467–77*, p. 281. Was survived by his widow, Maud. His 'place', the Saracen's Head next to the bars in Tothill St., was acquired by Assmptn guild. WAM 23243 *et seq.*; guild accts, s.a. 1474–7.

WITNEY, John. Chwdn 1460–2. CWA i, s.a. Wdn Assmptn guild 1466. *Cal Cl R 1461–8*, p. 365. R. between 2 and 6 tens in scty 1444–79. WAM 19687–727. Also, with John BRADDING, r. 3 shops near the almonry in Tothill St. 1464–73. WAM 19701–9. D. 1478–9; b. in St Mgt. CWA i. 132.

WODELAND, Christopher. Smith. Chwdn 1506–8. CWA i. 545. King's master smith at the Tower of London *c.*1507–1514 (d.). *King's Works* iii (1), 412. Attended Henry VII's funeral 1509 as a royal groom. *LP* i, no. 20 (p. 14). Joined Assmptn guild 1487 × 1490. Guild accts. Repaired a window in St Mgt 1488–9. CWA i. 257. Worked at West. Abbey 1504–10. WAM 19762–5; 23584, 23586–91. R. the Catherine Wheel bakery on W. side King St. 1502–14. W. Margaret named 1502. Reg Bk, i, fo. 143^{r-v}; WAM 23128–46. Margaret Wodeland d. 1504–5; was b. in St Mgt. CWA i. 500. Christopher Wodeland r. a 'storehouse' in Our Lady's Alley on E. side King St. 1505–8. Assmptn guild accts. He d. 1514 (see above). Had by 1504 2 daus, Ellen and Marian. See will of Richard Wodeland, cited below. The Catherine Wheel passed in 1515 to John Scrivener, smith; and in turn in 1521–2 to John PHILLIPS, smith. WAM 23152 *et seq.*

Christopher's bro., Richard Wodeland, smith, who r. a ten. in West. scty and worked at the abbey in the 1480s, was living at his death in 1504 in a house in Tothill St. Richard was survived by a widow, Emma, and 4 children, William, Elizabeth, Elizabeth (*sic*), and Emma. WAM 19730–4; 19731; CWA i. 500; PCW Wyks, 17–18.

WOLLESCROFT, Nicholas. Chwdn 1478–80. CWA i. 123.

WRIGHT, John. Baker. C.p. 1513–1514–; chief const. 1514. WAM 50776–7. Wdn (1518–21) and master (1527–30) Assmptn guild. Guild accts, s.a.; WAM 18035 (Aug. 1527). Master Rounceval guild 1522–4. Guild accts, s.a. Chwdn 1534–6. CWA iii, s.a. R. 3 tens and gdn at Charing Cross 1524–1531–. WAM 18020; Reg Bk, ii, fo. 190^r; 23300–11.

WRYGGER, John. Fishmonger. Chwdn 1502–4. CWA i. 437. C.p. 1506–14; chief const. 1507. WAM 50771–7. Wdn Assmptn guild 1508–11. CWA i. 576 (1510). Supplied rushes to St Mgt and to Assmptn guild. CWA i. 290–1, 421; guild accts, s.a. 1508. Was presented for ale sold from his house in the precinct of West. Palace 1507. WAM 50772. Made over his goods in trust to Robert Lytton (afterwards under-treasurer of England) 1483. *Cal Cl R 1476–85*, p. 334. D. 1515; b. in St Mgt. His widow, Alice, paid for a little stone for his grave. CWA ii, s.a. 1514–15, wk. 43. Will made 1 Jan., proved *ante* 2 Apr. 1515. PCW Wyks, 210–11. 'Lytill Alice', bequeathed household goods by this will, was perhaps a dau.

WYKAM, John. Chwdn 1478–80. CWA i. 123. Reserved his pew in St Mgt 1474–5. CWA i. 102. R. 2 tens opposite the almonry in Tothill St. 1484 × 1486–90. WAM 23560–3. Was succeeded in these tens by

Richard Wykam, baker. WAM 17896; 23565–70. Probate of John Wykam's will 21 July 1507. PCW Wyks, 78.

WYLDE, Thomas. Brewer. Chwdn 1528–30. CWA ii, s.a. Wdn St Cornelius's guild in St Mgt 1521/2–3. CWA ii, s.a. Described as 'brewer' 1522. WAM 12370. His goods valued in 1524 at £13. 6s. 8d. PRO, E179/238/98. R. 1 or 2 tens on N. side Tothill St. 1504–21; 2 successive tens on S. side Tothill St. 1505–11; 2 further tens beside the almonry in the same street 1516–1536–. WAM 23584–608; 19114–16; 19122–52. R. the Hart's Horn brewery on W. side King St. 1520–35; and the nearby Wool Sack bakery 1528–1537–. Reg Bk, ii, fo. 166ʳ⁻ᵛ (and cf. fo. 308ʳ⁻ᵛ), 253; WAM 23158–78.

YONGE, William. C.p. 1467 × 1486–1505. WAM 50760–70. A William Yonge collected the rents of the 'new work' of West. Abbey 1462–3; and was a valet of the convent 1462–7. WAM 23527; 19969–74; 19711–16. It was probably this William Yonge who (as 'yeoman') r. a shop and 3 tens in Long Ditch between 1447 and 1485/6; a meadow at Knightsbridge 1455–6; 2 tens by Lamb Alley in King St. 1465–85; and a ten. with 2 cellars beneath the belfry in West. scty 1465. WAM 19056–93; 23520; 19715–30; 17787. (This man was succeeded in his Long Ditch lease by Thomas Yonge, and later, 1490–5, by the husband of Eve, dau. of William Yonge.) WAM 19095–105. But this William Yonge was probably the one b. at St Mgt 1488–9, and therefore different from the c.p. CWA i. 246.

SELECT BIBLIOGRAPHY

I MANUSCRIPT SOURCES

Westminster Abbey Muniment Room

(i) *Accounts of Conventual Officials*

WAM 18962–19154	Almoner, 1293–1539
WAM 18829–959	Cellarer, 1281–1536
WAM 18519–93; 23074–178; 24562–621; 24622–49	Domestic Treasurer, 1385–1537
WAM 19618–837*	Sacrist, 1317–1540
WAM 19838–999; 23001–29	Treasurers, 1297–1535
WAM 23452–626	Warden of the New Work, 1341–1537
WAM 23627–969	Warden of Queen Eleanor's Manors, 1286–1534
WAM 23179–317	Warden of St Mary's Chapel, 1298–1537

(ii) *Cartularies and Other Registers*

WAM Book 11	'Westminster Domesday', early fourteenth century
WAM Book 1	'Liber Niger Quaternus', late fifteenth century, renewal of an earlier cartulary
WAM Register Books I–IV	Lease-books, 1485–c.1550

(iii) *Court Rolls*

WAM 50699–782	Westminster Manor Court Rolls, 1364–1514

(iv) *Deeds and Leases* — See Index and Calendar in the Muniment Room

(v) *Guild Records*

Accounts of the Westminster guilds of the Virgin's Assumption (1474–7, 1487–90, 1505–8, 1515–21) and of St Mary Rounceval (1520–4, 1538–40), bound in a single volume, unnumbered

(vi) *Miscellanea*

WAM 50684–98	Records of Westminster Fair
WAM 24694–715	Records of the Abbot's Bailiff of West-minster, 1288–1336
WAM 17717–22	Visitation and other records of St James's Hospital, 1317–36
WAM 18048–50, 33308	Lists of properties and tenements in Westminster, early sixteenth century
WAM 33289	Prior's notebook, fifteenth century
WAM 6576	Draft of a petition concerning local government, *c.*1511

Other Repositories

Cambridge, Trinity College Library

MS O.9.1	A manuscript volume (late fifteenth century) containing saints' lives, a chronicle, and an indenture relating to the Westminster guild of the Assumption

Eton, Eton College Collections

ECR 61/RR/A/66	Receiver's Account for St James's Hospital, 1450–1
ECR 61/VR/E/1	Ditto, early sixteenth century
ECR 61/RR/G/9–17	Eton College Receiver's Roll, 1517–18
ECR 62/AB/1–2	Eton College Audit Books, 1506–45

London, British Library

MS Cotton Faustina A.iii	Cartulary, *temp.* Edward I

London, Corporation of London Record Office

Ward Presentments, Portsoken
  Ward, 5–22 Edw. IV, 23
  Hen. VII

London, Guildhall Library

MSS 12805, 12975–13010	Register of Christ's Hospital (1594–1612), and original deeds (fourteenth to sixteenth centuries) relating to properties in Westminster given to the hospital in 1544 by Richard Casteler

London, Public Record Office

C1	*Chancery:* Early Chancery Proceedings
E179	*Exchequer, King's Remembrancer:* Subsidy Rolls, etc.
E40	*Exchequer, Treasury of the Receipt:* Ancient Deeds, Ser. A
KB9	*Court of King's Bench:* Ancient Indictments
CP25	*Court of Common Pleas:* Feet of Fines
PROB 11	*Proceedings Court of Canterbury:* Will Registers (named vols.)

Miscellanea

SC/191/66	Westminster Manor Court Roll, 1510
SC8/78/3889	Petition of the inhabitants of Westminster, 1337

London, Westminster Public Library, Archives Department

MSS E. Deeds, 1, 2	Original letters patent concerning the fairs of Westminster, thirteenth century
MS 10/173	Lease from The Queen's College, Oxford, of the Catherine Wheel, in Tothill Street, 1587

Churchwardens' accounts of St Margaret's, Westminster, 1460–1540
Peculiar Court of Westminster, Will Registers (named vols.), 1504–40

Oxford, Bodleian Library

MSS D.D. Queen's College 1741–70	Westminster Deeds (thirteenth to fifteenth centuries) concerning the Catherine Wheel in Tothill Street

Oxford, The Queen's College Library

MSS 4.N.2, 17, 27, 44, 109, 123	Documents relating to the Catherine Wheel in Tothill Street, 1509 and post-medieval

II PRINTED SOURCES

Beauchamp Cartulary Charters 1100–1268, ed. E. Mason, Pipe Roll Society, new ser., xliii (1980).
Calendar of Charter Rolls (HMSO, London, 1903–).
Calendar of Close Rolls (HMSO, London, 1911–).
Calendar of Entries in the Papal Registers Relating to Great Britain and Ireland, Papal Letters (HMSO, London, 1893–).

Calendar of Fine Rolls (HMSO, London, 1911–).

Calendar of Inquisitions post mortem (HMSO, London, 1904–).

Calendar of Letter-Books Preserved Among the Archives of the Corporation of the City of London, 1275–1498, ed. R. R. Sharpe, 11 vols. (London, 1899–1912).

Calendar of Letters and Papers, Foreign and Domestic, Henry VIII, ed. J. S. Brewer, J. Gairdner, and R. H. Brodie (HMSO, London, 1862–1932).

Calendar of Liberate Rolls (HMSO, London, 1916–).

Calendar of Patent Rolls (HMSO, London, 1901–).

Calendar of Plea and Memoranda Rolls Preserved Among the Archives of the City of London, 6 vols, ed. A. H. Thomas (vols. i–iv) and P. E. Jones (vols. v–vi) (Cambridge, 1926–61).

Curia Regis Rolls (HMSO, London, 1922–).

Customary of the Benedictine Monasteries of Saint Augustine, Canterbury, and Saint Peter, Westminster, ed. E. Maunde Thompson, Henry Bradshaw Society, xxiii, xxviii (1902, 1904).

FLETE, JOHN. *The History of Westminster Abbey by John Flete,* ed. J. A. Robinson (Cambridge, 1909).

HOCCLEVE, THOMAS. *Selections from Hoccleve,* ed. M. C. Seymour (Oxford, 1981).

London and Middlesex Chantry Certificate 1548, ed. C. J. Kitching, London Record Society, xvi (1980).

PARIS, MATTHEW. *Matthaei Parisiensis Chronica Majora,* ed. H. R. Luard, 7 vols., Rolls Series (1872–83).

Rotuli Parliamentorum, 6 vols. (Record Commission, 1783).

SAWYER, P. H., *Anglo-Saxon Charters: An Annotated List and Bibliography,* Royal Historical Society (London, 1968).

SKELTON, JOHN. *John Skelton. The Complete English Poems,* ed. J. Scattergood (Harmondsworth, 1983).

Statutes of the Realm, 11 vols. (London, 1810–24).

STOW, JOHN, *A Survey of London* (1603), ed. C. L. Kingsford, 2 vols. (Oxford, 1908; repr. 1971).

WENLOCK, WALTER DE. *Documents Illustrating the Rule of Walter de Wenlok, Abbot of Westminster, 1283–1307,* ed. B. F. Harvey, Camden, 4th ser., ii (1965).

The Westminster Chronicle 1381–1394, trans. and ed. L. C. Hector and B. F. Harvey (Oxford, 1982).

III SECONDARY WORKS

BARRON, C. M., 'The Quarrel of Richard II with London, 1392–7', in F. R. H. du Boulay and C. M. Barron (eds.), *The Reign of Richard II* (London, 1971), 173–201.

BEAVEN, A. B., *The Aldermen of the City of London*, 2 vols. (London, 1908–13).

BLACK, G., *et al.*, 'Excavations in the Sub-vault of the Misericorde of Westminster Abbey, February to May 1975', *Transactions of the London and Middlesex Archaeological Society*, 2nd ser., xxvii (1976), 135–78.

BLACK, W. H., 'Observations on the Recently Discovered Roman Sepulchre at Westminster Abbey', *Transactions of the London and Middlesex Archaeological Society*, iv (1871), 60–9.

BLAKISTON, N., 'The London and Middlesex estates of Eton College', *Transactions of the London and Middlesex Archaeological Society*, 2nd ser., xx (1959–61), 51–5.

BROWN, R. A., '"The Treasury" of the Late Twelfth Century', in J. Conway Davies (ed.), *Studies Presented to Sir Hilary Jenkinson* (London, 1957), 35–49.

BUTCHER, A. F., 'Rent, Population and Economic Change in Late-Medieval Newcastle', *Northern History*, xiv (1978), 67–77.

—— 'Rent and the Urban Economy: Oxford and Canterbury in the Later Middle Ages', *Southern History*, i (1979), 11–43.

COLVIN, H. M. (ed.), *The History of the King's Works*, 6 vols. (HMSO, London, 1963–82).

DAVIS, N. Z., 'Poor Relief, Humanism and Heresy', in ead., *Society and Culture in Early Modern France* (London, 1975), 17–64.

DOBSON, R. B., *Durham Priory, 1400–1450* (Cambridge, 1973).

—— 'Urban Decline in Late Medieval England', *Transactions of the Royal Historical Society*, 5th ser., xxvii (1977), 1–22.

DOYLE, A. I., 'The Work of a Late Fifteenth-century English Scribe, William Ebesham', *Bulletin of the John Rylands Library*, xxxix (1956–7), 298–325.

DU BOULAY, F. R. H., 'A Rentier Economy in the Later Middle Ages: The Archbishopric of Canterbury', *Economic History Review*, 2nd ser., xvi (1963–4), 427–38.

FINLAY, R. and SHEARER, B., 'Population Growth and Suburban Expansion', in A. L. Beier and R. Finlay (eds.), *London 1500–1700: The Making of the Metropolis* (London, 1986), 37–59.

GALLOWAY, J., *The Hospital and Chapel of Saint Mary Roncevall at Charing Cross* (London, 1913).

—— *Historical Sketches of Old Charing* (London, 1914).

GELLING, M., 'The Boundaries of the Westminster Charters', *Transactions of the London and Middlesex Archaeological Society*, 2nd ser., xi (1953), 101–4.

GEM, R. D. H., 'The Romanesque Rebuilding of Westminster Abbey', in R. A. Brown (ed.), *Proceedings of the Battle Conference of Anglo-Norman Studies III, 1980* (Woodbridge, 1981), 33–60.

GREEN, H. M., 'Evidence of Roman, Saxon and Medieval Westminster

Westminster Revealed During the Current Rebuilding of the Treasury and Downing Street', *Illustrated London News*, ccxlii (1963), 1004–7.

GREEN, H. M. *et al.*, 'Excavations of the Palace Defences and Abbey Precinct Wall at Abingdon Street, Westminster, 1963', *Journal of the British Archaeological Association*, cxxix (1976), 59–76.

——, R. HUGGINS, *et al.*, 'Excavations of the Treasury Site, Whitehall, 1961–1963', *Transactions of the London and Middlesex Archaeological Society*, forthcoming (1989).

HARVEY, B. F., 'Abbot Gervase de Blois and the Fee-farms of Westminster Abbey', *Bulletin of the Institute of Historical Research*, xl (1967), 127–42.

—— 'The Leasing of the Abbot of Westminster's Demesnes in the Later Middle Ages', *Economic History Review*, 2nd ser., xxii (1969), 17–27.

—— *Westminster Abbey and its Estates in the Middle Ages* (Oxford, 1977).

HARVEY, J. H., 'The Masons of Westminster Abbey', *Archaeological Journal*, cxiii (1957), 82–101.

HATCHER, J., *Plague, Population and the English Economy 1348–1530*, Economic History Society (London and Basingstoke, 1977).

—— 'Mortality in the Fifteenth Century: Some New Evidence', *Economic History Review*, 2nd ser., xxxix (1986), 19–38.

HELLINGA, L., *Caxton in Focus. The Beginning of Printing in England* (London, 1982).

HILTON, R. H., 'Some Problems of Urban Real Property in the Middle Ages', in C. H. Feinstein (ed.), *Socialism, Capitalism and Economic Growth* (Cambridge, 1967), 326–37.

—— 'The Small Town as Part of Peasant Society', in id., *The English Peasantry in the Later Middle Ages* (Oxford, 1975), 76–94.

—— 'Towns in Societies—Medieval England', *Urban History Yearbook* (1982), 7–13.

HONEYBOURNE, M. B., 'The Sanctuary Boundaries and Environs of Westminster Abbey and the College of St. Martin-le-Grand', *Journal of the British Archaeological Association*, xxxviii (1932–3), 316–32.

—— 'Charing Cross Riverside', *London Topographical Record*, xxi (1958), 44–78.

—— 'The Leper Hospitals of the London Area', *Transactions of the London and Middlesex Archaeological Society*, 2nd ser., xxi (1963–7), 3–61.

IVES, E. W., 'Coroners, Sanctuary and Royal Authority under Henry VIII', in M. S. Arnold, T. A. Green, S. A. Swilly, and S. D. White (eds.), *On the Laws and Customs of England* (Chapel Hill, 1981), 296–320.

JOHNSTONE, H., 'Poor-relief in the Royal Households of Thirteenth-century England', *Speculum*, iv (1929), 149–67.

KEENE, D. J., *Survey of Medieval Winchester*, 2 vols., Winchester Studies, ii (Oxford, 1985).

—— 'A New Study of London Before the Great Fire', *Urban History Yearbook* (1984), 11–21.

—— and V. Harding, *Cheapside and the Development of London Before the Great Fire* (forthcoming).

KINGSFORD, C. L., 'Historical Notes on Mediaeval London Houses: The Mote, Westminster', *London Topographical Record*, xi (1917), 48–9.

—— 'Historical Notes on Mediaeval London Houses: York Place', *London Topographical Record*, xii (1920), 62–5.

KNIGHTON, C. S., 'Economics and Economies of a Royal Peculiar: Westminster Abbey, 1540–1640', in R. O'Day and F. Heal (eds.), *Princes and Paupers in the English Church, 1500–1800* (Leicester, 1981), 45–64.

KNOWLES, D., *The Monastic Order in England, 940–1216* (2nd edn., Cambridge, 1963).

—— *The Religious Orders in England*, 3 vols. (Cambridge, 1948–59).

LANCASTER, R. K., 'Artisans, Suppliers and Clerks: The Human Factors in the Court Patronage of King Henry III', *Journal of the Warburg and Courtauld Institutes*, xxxv (1972), 81–107.

LETHABY, W. R., *Westminster Abbey and the King's Craftsmen: A Study of Mediaeval Building* (London, 1906).

—— *Westminster Abbey Re-examined* (London, 1925).

—— 'Earliest Westminster', *London Topographical Record*, vii (1912), 21–5.

LOBEL, M. D., *The Borough of Bury St Edmunds* (Oxford, 1935).

MANCHÉE, W. H., *The Westminster City Fathers* (London, 1924).

McCLURE, P., 'Patterns of Migration in the Late Middle Ages: The Evidence of English Surnames', *Economic History Review*, 2nd ser., xxxii (1979), 167–82.

MILLS, P. S., *et al.*, 'Excavations at Broad Sanctuary, Westminster', *Transactions of the London and Middlesex Archaeological Society*, 2nd ser., xxxiii (1982), 345–65.

NEEDHAM, P., *The Printer and the Pardoner: An Unrecorded Indulgence Printed by William Caxton for the Hospital of St. Mary Rounceval, Charing Cross* (Washington, 1986).

NIXON, H. M., 'Caxton, his Contemporaries and Successors in the Book Trade from Westminster Documents', *The Library*, 5th ser., xxxi (1976), 305–26.

NORMAN, P., 'Recent Discoveries of Medieval Remains in London', *Archaeologia*, 2nd ser., xvii (1916), 14–18.

PAINTER, G. D., *William Caxton* (London, 1976).

PEARCE, E. H., *The Monks of Westminster* (Cambridge, 1916).

PHYTHIAN-ADAMS, C. V., *Desolation of a City: Coventry and the Urban Crisis of the Late Middle Ages* (Cambridge, 1979).

POWER, M. J., 'The East and West in Early-Modern London', in E. W.

Ives, R. J. Knecht, and J. J. Scarisbrick (eds.), *Wealth and Power in Tudor England* (London, 1978), 167–85.

RACKHAM, R. B., 'The Nave of Westminster', *Proceedings of the British Academy*, iv (1909), 33–96.

RADFORD, C. A. R., *Westminster Abbey Before King Edward the Confessor*, Westminster Abbey Occasional Papers, xv (1965).

RANSOME, D. R., 'Artisan Dynasties in London and Westminster in the Sixteenth Century', *Guildhall Miscellany*, ii (1964), 236–47.

REYNOLDS, S., *An Introduction to the History of English Medieval Towns* (Oxford, 1977).

—— 'Medieval Urban History and the History of Political Thought', *Urban History Yearbook* (1982), 14–23.

RICHARDSON, H. G., 'William of Ely, the King's Treasurer (?1195–1215)', *Transactions of the Royal Historical Society*, 4th ser., xv (1932), 45–90.

RIGBY, S. H., 'Boston and Grimsby in the Middle Ages: An Administrative Contrast', *Journal of Medieval History*, x (1984), 51–66.

ROBBINS, M., 'A Site in Westminster, or, Whoever was St. Ermin?', *London Topographical Record*, xxiv (1980), 113–30.

ROBINSON, J. A., *Gilbert Crispin Abbot of Westminster* (Cambridge, 1911).

ROSSER, A. G., 'The Essence of Medieval Urban Communities: The Vill of Westminster, 1200–1540', *Transactions of the Royal Historical Society*, 5th ser., xxxiv (1984), 91–112.

—— 'The Town and Guild of Lichfield in the Later Middle Ages', *Transactions of the South Staffordshire Archaeological and Historical Society*, xxvii (1987 for 1985–6), 39–47.

—— 'London and Westminster: The Suburb in the Urban Economy in the Late Middle Ages', in J. A. F. Thomson (ed.), *Towns and Townspeople in the Fifteenth Century* (Gloucester, 1988), 45–61.

Royal Commission on Historical Monuments, *London*, i, *Westminster Abbey* (London, 1924); *London*, ii, *West London* (London, 1925).

RUTTON, W. L., 'The Manor of Eia, or Eye next Westminster', *Archaeologia*, lxii (1910), 31–58.

SABINE, E. L., 'Butchering in Medieval London', *Speculum*, viii (1933), 335–53.

SALZMAN, L. F., *English Industries of the Middle Ages* (London, 1913).

—— *Building in England Down to 1540* (Oxford, 1952).

SAUNDERS, B., 'Results of an Enquiry Concerning the Situation and Extent of Westminster, at Various Periods', *Archaeologia*, xxvi (1836), 223–41.

SCATTERGOOD, V. J. and J. W. SHERBORNE (eds.), *English Court Culture in the Later Middle Ages* (London, 1983).

SEARLE, E., *Lordship and Community: Battle Abbey and its Banlieu, 1066–1538* (Toronto, 1974).

(SMITH, J. E.), *Vestry of the United Parish of St. Margaret and St. John the*

Evangelist, Westminster: Special and Annual Report, with Notes on Local Government in Westminster from Pre-Reformation Times to the Present Day (Westminster, 1889).

SMITH, J. T., *The Antiquities of Westminster, &c.*, 2 vols. (London, 1807; 2nd edn., 1837).

SMITH, R. A. L., *Canterbury Cathedral Priory* (Cambridge, 1943).

—— 'The Central Financial System of Christ Church, Canterbury, 1186–1512', repr. in id., *Collected Papers*, ed. D. Knowles (London, 1947), 23–41.

STANLEY, A. P., *Historical Memorials of Westminster Abbey* (4th edn., London, 1876).

STOREY, R. L., 'Gentlemen-bureaucrats', in *Profession, Vocation and Culture in Later Medieval England*, ed. C. H. Clough (Liverpool, 1982), 90–129.

Survey of London (London County Council, 1900–63; Greater London Council, 1966–83; Royal Commission on Historical Monuments, 1985–).

TANNER, L. E., 'The Nature and Use of the Westminster Abbey Muniments', *Transactions of the Royal Historical Society*, 4th ser., xix (1936), 43–80.

—— 'Westminster Topography', *Transactions of the London and Middlesex Archaeological Society*, 2nd ser., x (1948–51), 234–43; xi (1952–4), 10–15.

THORNLEY, I. D., 'The Destruction of Sanctuary', in R. W. Seton-Watson (ed.), *Tudor Studies Presented to A. F. Pollard* (London, 1924), 182–207.

—— 'Sanctuary in Medieval London', *Journal of the British Archaeological Association*, 2nd ser., xxxviii (1932–3), 293–315.

THRUPP, S. L., *The Merchant Class of Medieval London* (Ann Arbor, 1948).

—— 'Aliens in and around London in the Fifteenth Century', in A. E. J. Hollaender and W. Kellaway (eds.), *Studies in London History Presented to P. E. Jones* (London, 1969), 251–72.

TOUT, T. F., *Chapters in the Administrative History of Medieval England*, 6 vols. (Manchester, 1920–33).

—— 'The Beginnings of a Modern Capital: London and Westminster in the Fourteenth Century', *Proceedings of the British Academy*, x (1921–3), 487–511; repr. in id., *Collected Papers*, iii (Manchester, 1934), 249–75.

TRENHOLME, N. M., *The English Monastic Boroughs*, University of Missouri Studies, ii (3) (Columbia, 1927).

VEALE, E. M., 'Craftsmen and the Economy of London in the Fourteenth Century', in A. E. J. Hollaender and W. Kellaway (eds.), *Studies in London History Presented to P. E. Jones* (London, 1969), 133–51.

Victoria County History of London, i (London, 1909).

WALCOTT, M. E. C., *The History of the Parish Church of St. Margaret, in Westminster* (Westminster, 1847).

—— *The Memorials of Westminster* (Westminster, 1849; 2nd edn., 1851).

WESTLAKE, H. F., *St. Margaret's Westminster. The Church of the House of Commons* (London, 1914).

—— *Westminster: A Historical Sketch* (London, 1919).

—— *The Parish Gilds of Mediaeval England* (London, 1919).

—— *Westminster Abbey: The Last Days of the Monastery* (London, 1921).

—— *Westminster Abbey. The Church, Convent, Cathedral and College of St. Peter, Westminster*, 2 vols. (London, 1923).

WILLIAMS, G. A., *Medieval London: From Commune to Capital* (London, 1963).

IV UNPUBLISHED DISSERTATIONS

BARRON, C. M., 'The Government of London and its Relations with the Crown, 1400–1450', Ph.D. thesis, Univ. of London (1970).

CARLIN, M., 'The Urban Development of Southwark, *c.*1200 to 1550', Ph.D. thesis, Univ. of Toronto (1983).

RIGBY, S. H., 'Boston and Grimsby in the Middle Ages', Ph.D. thesis, Univ. of London (1982).

ROSSER, A. G., 'Medieval Westminster: The Vill and the Urban Community, 1200–1540', Ph.D. thesis, Univ. of London (1984).

SHEAIL, J., 'The Regional Distribution of Wealth in England as Indicated in the 1524/5 Lay Subsidy Returns', Ph.D. thesis, Univ. of London (1968).

INDEX